Also by Chris Ward from Bomber Command Books

Casualty of War: Letters Home from Flight Lieutenant Bill Astell DFC

Dambuster Deering: The Life and Death of an Unsung Hero

Dambusters : The Complete WWII History of 617 Squadron
(with Andy Lee and Andreas Wachtel)

Other RAF Bomber Command Profiles:

10 Squadron (with Ian MacMillan)
35 (Madras Presidency) Squadron
44 (Rhodesia) Squadron
50 Squadron
75(NZ) Squadron (with Chris Newey)
83 Squadron
101 Squadron
103 Squadron (with David Fell)
106 Squadron (with Herman Bijlard)
115 Squadron
138 Squadron (with Piotr Hodyra)
207 Squadron (with Raymond Glynne-Owen)
300 Squadron (with Grzegorz Korcz)
301, 304 and 305 Squadrons (with Grzegorz Korcz)
460 Squadron RAAF
467 Squadron RAAF
514 Squadron (with Simon Hepworth)
617 Squadron
619 Squadron

RAF Bomber Command Profiles

57 Squadron

Chris Ward

www.bombercommandbooks.com

Introduction

RAF Bomber Command Squadron Profiles first appeared in the late nineties and proved to be very popular with enthusiasts of RAF Bomber Command during the Second World War. They became a useful research tool, particularly for those whose family members had served and were no longer around. The original purpose was to provide a point of reference for all of the gallant men and women who had fought the war, either in the air, or on the ground in a support capacity, and for whom no written history of their unit or station existed. I wanted to provide them with something they could hold up, point to and say, "this was my unit, this is what I did in the war". Many veterans were reticent to talk about their time on bombers, partly because of modesty, but perhaps mostly because the majority of those with whom they came into contact had no notion of what it was to be a "Bomber Boy", to face the prospect of death every time they took to the air, whether during training or on operations. Only those who shared the experience really understood what it was to go to war in bombers, which is why reunions were so important. As they approached the end of their lives, many veterans began to speak openly for the first time about their life in wartime Bomber Command, and most were hurt by the callous treatment they received at the hands of successive governments with regard to the lack of recognition of their contribution to victory. It is sad that this recognition in the form of a national memorial and the granting of a campaign medal came too late for the majority. Now this inspirational, noble generation, the like of which will probably never grace this earth again, has all but departed from us, and the world will be a poorer place as a result.

RAF Bomber Command Squadron Profiles are back. The basic format remains, but, where needed, additional information has been provided. Squadron Profiles do not claim to be comprehensive histories, but rather detailed overviews of the activities of the squadron. There is insufficient space to mention as many names as one would like, but all aircraft losses are accompanied by the name of the pilot. Fundamentally, the narrative section is an account of Bomber Command's war from the perspective of the bomber group under which the individual squadron served, and the deeds of the squadron are interwoven into this story. Information has been drawn from official records, such as group, squadron and station ORBs, and from the many, like me, amateur enthusiasts, who dedicate much of their time to researching individual units and become unrivalled authorities on them. I am grateful for their generous contributions, and their names will appear in the appropriate Profiles. The statistics quoted in this series are taken from The Bomber Command War Diaries, that indispensable tome written by Martin Middlebrook and Chris Everitt, and I am indebted to Martin for his kind permission to use them.

Finally, let me apologize in advance for the inevitable errors, for no matter how hard I and other authors try to write "nothing but the truth", there is no such thing as a definitive account of history, and there will always be room for disagreement and debate. Official records are notoriously unreliable tools, and yet we have little choice but to put our faith in them. It is not my intention to misrepresent any person or Bomber Command unit, and I ask my readers to understand the enormity of the task I have undertaken. It is relatively easy to become an authority on single units or even a bomber group, but I chose to write about them all, idiot that I am, which means 128 squadrons serving operationally in Bomber Command at some time between the 3rd of September 1939 and the 8th of May 1945. I am dealing with eight bomber groups, in which some 120,000 airmen served, and I am juggling around 28,000 aircraft serial numbers, code letters and details of provenance and fate. I ask not for your sympathy, it was, after all, my choice, but rather your understanding if you should find something with which you disagree. My thanks to you, my readers, for making the original series of RAF Bomber Command Squadron Profiles so popular, and I hope you receive this new incarnation equally enthusiastically.

While researching 57 Squadron for my original Profile in 1998, I was kindly allowed access to the squadron's wartime diaries, which, at the time, were in the care of F/L Martin Davis of 57(R) Squadron at RAF Lyneham. These were not on the standard RAF Forms 540 and 541 but were hand-written in a ledger and served as an additional record, probably written at the same time, although this is not clear. My thanks are due, as always, to my gang members, Andreas Wachtel, photo editor, Clare Bennett, Steve Smith and Greg Korcz for their unstinting support, without which my Profiles would be the poorer. My gratitude also to Louse Bush and other members of the Panton family at the Lincolnshire Aviation Heritage Centre at 57 Squadron's final wartime home at East Kirkby for assistance with photos and to Pete Sharp and Chris Morffew for allowing use of material from their 57 Squadron website. Finally, my appreciation to my publisher, Simon Hepworth of Mention the War Publications, for his belief in my work, untiring efforts to promote it, and for the stress I put him through to bring my books to publication.

Chris Ward. Skegness, Lincolnshire. April 2022.

Dedication

This WWII history of 57 Squadron is dedicated to the memory of Flight Lieutenant Sydney "Stevie" Stevens DFC, who arrived at Scampton on the 1st of May 1943 as a sergeant pilot and completed his tour at East Kirkby as a pilot officer in October having served with distinction.

Contents

Narrative History

The history of 57 Squadron can be traced back to its original formation, as a flying training unit on the 8th of June 1916. In December of that year it moved to France, and became a fighter squadron, before changing roles yet again in the summer of 1917, and spending the remainder of the war as a bomber and reconnaissance unit, eventually undergoing disbandment on the last day of 1919. The squadron remained on the shelf until its reformation as a light bomber unit in October 1931, and continued in this role, eventually taking delivery of Blenheims at the end of March 1938, and it was with this type that the squadron faced the impending conflict in September 1939.

On the 1st of September, two days before the outbreak of war, in fact, on the day that Germany set the ball rolling towards global conflict with its invasion of Poland, a general inspection of 57 Squadron was ordered at its Upper Heyford station. The purpose of the inspection was to prepare the squadron to join the Advanced Air Striking Force, (AASF), which had been assembling on airfields in France since the 2nd of September. The bulk of the force consisted of Fairey Battle light bomber squadrons formerly of 1 Group RAF Bomber Command, and they were supported by a number of former 2 Group Blenheim squadrons and Hurricane fighter units. It was the 12th of September before the advanced ground party departed Upper Heyford and made its way to Southampton, to be followed by a transport section four days later. The main body set off at 10.30 on the 22nd, led by the squadron commander W/C Harry Day, and travelled by rail to Southampton, before embarking and setting sail at 16.00, initially for Spithead to join a convoy for the night Channel crossing to Cherbourg. Arriving on the 23rd they left by train for Roye, near Montdidier at 16.30, which they reached on the 24th and settled into the billets at Amy, four miles to the south. Food was supplied and cooked by French troops guarding the aerodrome, and consisted of bread and coffee for breakfast, and meat soup, vegetables and wine for lunch and supper. The airmen did not complain about the quantity and quality, but took issue with the method of cooking, whatever that was! The officers and NCOs were accommodated in houses in the village, while the airmen found themselves in barns and sleeping on straw bedding. Initially they were without transport, but ten vehicles arrived on the 26th, and British food supplies were received on the 27th to end reliance upon their hosts. The aircraft and crews flew direct from Upper Heyford on the 30th, and the remaining transport section turned up on the 1st of October after travelling from Brest. 18 Squadron had undergone a similar process, and the two units formed 70 Wing.

The squadron dispatched two Blenheims on the afternoon of the 8th to Metz, from where a strategic reconnaissance of north-western Germany was to be attempted, but unfavourable weather conditions prevented the sorties from taking place and the aircraft returned to Amy on the 10th. W/C Day led six of the squadron's Blenheims to Metz on the 12th, and he took off in L1138 on the following day to reconnoitre roads and railways in the Hamm and Soest area, on the north-eastern rim of the Ruhr, and Hannover, further to the north-east. F/O Norman, meanwhile, steered L1147 in a more north-westerly direction towards Münster and Bremen, with orders to return to England afterwards, and, like his commanding officer, intended to conceal his presence by the use of cloud cover. In that endeavour he was successful, but W/C Day ran out of cloud, and the Blenheim fell victim to an attack by three BF109s, which shot it down in flames near Birkenfeld, some twenty miles east of the frontier with Luxembourg. Although all three crew members escaped by parachute, only W/C Day survived the descent, and he was taken into captivity. Thus, did Sgt Hillier and AC2 Moller become the first to have their names entered into what, by war's end, would be a very long Roll of Honour. The other crew encountered bad weather as they entered English air-space, and ultimately crashed near Harpenden in Hertfordshire, happily, without casualties. Flight commander, S/L Garland, was given the acting rank of wing commander so that he could assume temporary command of the squadron on the 14th, until the appointment of a permanent successor to W/C Day. F/O Casey and crew took L1141 to an alternative forward landing ground at Etain on the morning of the 16th, with orders to carry out a photo-reconnaissance of the railway in the Wesel – Bocholt area north of the Ruhr. They departed Etain at 11.00, and failed to return, it is believed having been forced down by enemy fighters. The crew was unhurt and destroyed the Blenheim by setting it on fire before being taken into captivity.

On the following day, F/L Wyatt and crew took off in L1146 to carry out a reconnaissance of the railway between Münster and Bremen and landed at Honington after almost five hours aloft to report anti-aircraft fire and severe icing conditions. The photographs were developed and found to contain images of a train and an aerodrome. On the 18th the squadron moved further north to Rosieres-en-Santerre and handed Amy back to the French Air Force. Over the ensuing days, sections of three aircraft were sent back to Etain to take over reconnaissance duties, until these were suspended on the 30th. However, the squadron contributed two Blenheims on that day to photograph the Siegfried Line along Germany's frontier with Holland and Belgium. F/O Hird and crew took off in the early afternoon in L1139 but were thwarted by cloud and unable to take photographs. They continued on to reach England, while Sgt Farmer and crew in L1246 found themselves a target for anti-aircraft fire in the border region and encountered ground haze which prevented effective photography. They carried out a visual reconnaissance, during which they were set upon by two BF109s attacking from below and astern. Some rounds struck home, and the fighters then made a second attack, scoring further hits until Sgt Farmer dived for the ground and managed to elude his assailants. The gunner fired off a solitary burst at the enemy but observed no results. The crew escaped injury, for which the armour plate was credited, and the Blenheim was eventually landed safely at Orly, south of Paris, only for one of the oleo legs of the undercarriage to collapse. Bullet holes were visible in the port wing and the tail-plane, but the damage would be repaired within two weeks. Sadly, this episode was not destined to end happily for either the Blenheim or the crew.

Three of the squadron's Blenheims were detailed for reconnaissance duties over the Siegfried Line on the 6th of November, and those bearing the crews of F/L Roncoroni and P/O Stewart completed their sorties before landing at Bircham Newton with six and four photographs respectively. The return of P/O Morton and crew in L1145 was awaited in vain, and news would eventually filter through from the Air Ministry on the last day of the month to confirm that the Blenheim had crashed near Bad Kreuznach, south-west of Mainz, without survivors. The 7th saw P/Os Bewlay and Grant and Sgt Greenleaf take off to continue the surveillance of the border region, but the last-mentioned was forced to turn back after his observer fainted through oxygen starvation. P/O Grant completed his sortie and landed at Hemswell, sadly, without any photographs to back up his report. P/O Bewlay and crew failed to return in L1325, and it would be a further ten days before news came through that they had come down near Mainz and were now in enemy hands. Three replacement Blenheims arrived from England on the 9th, along with news of the fate of W/C Day, and instructions were also received concerning reconnaissance duties in the event of Germany invading Holland and Belgium. Seven aircraft were dispersed to the satellite airfield at Montdidier on the 10th, while, four days later, the recently-acquired replacements had to be flown back to England because they were found to be lacking equipment essential for operational duties. Four replacement pilots, P/Os O'Reilly-Blackwood, Goldie, Herbert and Thomas, were posted in on the morning of the 16th along with an equal number of observers. At 10.50 on that same morning, Sgt Gilmore and crew took off in L1148 to continue the reconnaissance of the region between the Ruhr and the Dutch and Belgian frontiers. They failed to return, but news soon came through that heavy icing conditions had forced them to land in neutral Belgium, where they were being held as internees. The squadron suffered another loss on this day involving L1246, which had been under repair at Orly since the 30th of October. Sgt Farmer lifted the Blenheim off the ground at 16.15 to return to Rosieres, but engine failure shortly afterwards caused it to crash into the River Seine with fatal consequences for those on board. The training of new crews commenced on the 20th at the same time as reconnaissance sorties were scaled back, but tragedy continued to stalk the squadron as another fatality occurred on the 23rd. While carrying out a low pass during training, L1129 struck tented accommodation, causing damage to its control surfaces. P/O Hume managed to maintain control long enough to gain sufficient height for his crew to take to their parachutes but was unable do likewise before the Blenheim stalled and crashed with him still at the controls.

W/C Haworth-Booth arrived on posting from England on the 1st of December as commanding officer elect, and, after a period of settling in, stepped into the role on the 5th, at which point acting W/C Garland reverted to squadron leader rank. W/C Haworth-Booth was already forty years of age and had served in the Royal Naval Air Service and the RAF in the Great War, earning a DFC in 1918. One of the harshest winters on record began to interfere with operational activity, and, apart from a single reconnaissance sortie conducted by F/O Foulsham on the 3rd, during which his camera froze, there were only occasional test and transit flights until the 21st, when F/O Milne took off in L1280 to reconnoitre the Siegfried Line and parts of north-western Germany. He landed at Horsham-St-Faith four hours and twenty-five minutes later to hand over a reel of film containing 120 photographs. On the following day, F/O Nind delivered fifty photographs of the same general area to Honington in Suffolk. Fog, low cloud and snow closed the airfield down over the Christmas period, and, apart from the return of the crews from England, no further flying took place.

It should be understood that in this phase of the war, both sides were reluctant to bomb mainland targets, for fear of hitting private property and encouraging reprisals. This restricted offensive operations from England to "armed reconnaissance" forays in search of the enemy fleet at sea, to avoid bombs landing on docks should they be found and attacked. It should also be remembered that Bomber Command had entered the war as a predominantly daylight force, in the belief that self-defending bombers would be able to fight their way through an enemy fighter screen in sufficient numbers to reach and destroy the target, in accordance with the Douhet theory expounded after the Great War. Only 4 Group had trained its pilots to fly by night, and they had spent the war thus far penetrating deep into Germany to deliver propaganda leaflets in their Whitleys. This had required the crews often to spend ten or more hours aloft in their unheated aircraft, suffering extreme discomfort and demonstrating heroic perseverance. Such sorties would stand them in good stead for what lay ahead and taught them much about flying long distances over a blacked-out, often cloud-covered Europe. It had already been made clear to 57 Squadron that flying over enemy territory in daylight was a hazardous undertaking, and other elements of both the AASF and Bomber Command had likewise sustained heavy and unexpected losses to German fighters. Five 144 Squadron Hampdens had failed to return from Heligoland on the 29th of September, while, on the 30th, three 150 Squadron Battles of the AASF had been shot down either side of the border, another had been abandoned and a fifth destroyed by fire on landing. An armed reconnaissance operation off the Frisian Islands cost 99 Squadron six Wellingtons on the 14th of December, and the final straw came with another reconnaissance of the Schillig Roads and Brunsbüttel areas by elements of 9, 37 and 149 Squadrons on the 18th. Of the twenty-two Wellingtons involved, twelve were lost along with fifty-six lives, and senior figures at Bomber Command, who had initially blamed poor formation flying for the casualties, now had to face the fact that the inviolability of self-defending bombers against determined fighter attack in daylight was a myth. The rest of the Command, with the exception of 2 Group, would now also have to become a largely nocturnal force, and this would be a situation that extended right through to the summer of 1944, by which time air superiority had been wrested from the hands of the enemy.

1940 First Quarter

The severe winter ensured that the air war would remain stagnant during the first quarter of the New Year, and the American press would dub this period the "Phoney War". Whenever the conditions did allow, aircraft took to the air for training if for nothing else, and fighter affiliation exercises were mounted in co-operation with Hurricanes on the 2nd and 3rd. Snow kept them on the ground, thereafter, until the 9th, when F/O Graham-Hogg and crew carried out a reconnaissance of north-western Germany in L1280, before landing in England with 125 photographs. Sgt Richardson and crew were on duty on the 10th, and reconnoitred the same general area in L6597, landing also in England to hand over forty-six photos. On the 17th, P/O O'Reilly-Blackwood and his crew took off for Metz in L1280 to prepare for a reconnaissance sortie and had to wait until the 25th before they could carry it out. They failed to return and were duly posted missing until news came through to confirm that they had come down in Germany, it was believed, in the Duisburg area, and all had been killed.

February brought even worse weather, and just three practice sorties were managed during the first week. W/C Haworth-Booth was posted temporarily to the command of 70 Wing HQ on the 7th, and S/L Garland was again appointed as his successor. The squadron was currently equipped with Mk1 Blenheims, which were due for replacement, and F/L Roncoroni and F/O Grant flew to England on the 10th to pick up the first two Mk IVs. S/L Garland and P/O Saunders flew over to Metz on the 13th to stand-by for operations, and the former carried out a reconnaissance of north-western Germany on the 18th, before landing back at Metz with photographs. P/O Saunders' turn came on the 20th, but he abandoned his sortie after his observer collapsed through oxygen starvation and a forced-landing was carried out south of Reims.

F/L Roncoroni and P/O Grant returned to French soil at Glisy with their Mk IV Blenheims on the 1st of March, and, on the following day, W/C Haworth-Booth also arrived back to resume command of the squadron for what would prove to be a brief spell. F/L Wyatt and P/O Saunders flew to Shawbury on the 3rd to exchange the next pair of Blenheims, and the former was awarded a DFC on the 8th, having learned two days earlier that he had been confirmed in the rank of flight lieutenant. A number of flights took place between Rosieres and Metz during the period, but no reconnaissance sorties resulted. W/C Haworth-Booth was admitted to RAF Hospital Halton on the 10th for treatment for a duodenal ulcer, allowing S/L Garland to step up again, this time with promotion to wing commander rank, initially unpaid, and a lengthy period of tenure in prospect. His elevation allowed F/L

Roncoroni to be handed acting squadron leader rank, while F/O Foulsham, on his return from Shawbury with a Mk IV Blenheim, became an acting flight lieutenant, both, of course, unpaid. F/O Adam and crew were sent to Metz on the 15th to stand-by for a reconnaissance sortie and took off at 23.30 to carry it out. Fifteen minutes later L9249 crashed at Orny, some seven miles to the south-south-east, killing the pilot and one of his crew, after the other had escaped by parachute. The cause of the crash is not specified, but engine failure or icing were most likely responsible. They were buried at Metz on the 18th, the day on which F/L Foulsham carried out a two-hour visual reconnaissance, which was repeated on the following day by P/O Goldie, culminating in a landing at Norwich. There would be no further operational sorties for the squadron during the month, but the re-equipping with Mk IVs continued and training took place when the weather conditions allowed.

At dusk on the 16th, fifteen enemy bombers carried out attacks on elements of the Royal Navy at Scapa Flow in the Orkneys, hitting HMS Norfolk and killing four of her officers. Bombs also fell close to Hatstone aerodrome and Bridge of Wraith on the road between Kirkwall and Stromness on the island of Hoy, and two cottages were damaged, leading to the death of one civilian and injury to seven others. This resulted in the first bombing of German territory by the RAF, which took place on the night of the 19/20th against the seaplane base at Hörnum was attacked first by 4 Group Whitleys and later 5 Group Hampdens in retaliation. The RAF operation made headline news in the British press, announcing large-scale damage to the target, which was not borne out when the first reconnaissance photographs were developed a few days later to reveal no sign of the attack.

1940 Second Quarter

The 9th of April brought with it the German airborne invasion of Norway and the almost unopposed march into Denmark, prompting what for Britain and France would be an ill-fated, ineffective if gallant campaign and the first major activity of the year for the home-based squadrons of Bomber Command. Prevented by the distance from directly supporting British landings at Narvik in the north of Norway, Bomber Command carried out attacks on the southern airfields of Sola and Stavanger, where enemy supplies were being landed. The first mining sorties were also carried out at this time by 5 Group Hampdens, which proved themselves to be eminently suited to the role. Their task was to lay strings of mines in the busy shipping lanes between north German ports and southern Norway, and so successful were they, that mining became a vital part of Bomber Command operations for the remainder of the war. The entire enemy-occupied coast from the Pyrenees in the south-west to Königsberg in the north-east and even the northern coast of Italy was broken up into mining areas known as gardens, and each given a horticultural or marine biological code name. The practice of mining was referred to as gardening, the mines themselves as vegetables and the delivery as planting, and, by war's end, Bomber Command would have sunk and damaged more enemy vessels than the Royal Navy.

The 57 Squadron Operations Record Book (ORB) for April was lost during the evacuation in May, leaving us with little information to go on. A training accident involving L9181 cost the life of the gunner on the 11th, when it crashed at Lihons, a dozen or so miles north-north-west of Roye, but we have no details of the pilot and observer. On the 14th, L9465 fell to the guns of a BF109 over Holland

15

while on a reconnaissance sortie, crashing at 16.00 ten miles south-east of Arnhem, killing F/O Graham-Hogg and his crew.

The Phoney War came to a sudden and dramatic end on the 10th of May, the day upon which Winston Churchill became Prime Minister and the German forces began their advance through the Low Countries. It was on this day also that the wholesale slaughter of the AASF began, as the Battles and Blenheims were pitched into the unequal fight against murderous ground fire and the marauding BF109s and 110s. The French authorities had banned the AASF aircraft from carrying bombs in case it upset the Germans, and the advent of the new Blitzkrieg system of fast-moving armour and infantry overran the defences in Holland and Belgium before any counter-measures could be mounted, allowing the enemy to establish strong anti-aircraft defences at all vital river and canal crossing points. By the time that the AASF was able to launch its first attacks, the skies belonged to the Luftwaffe, and the slow, lumbering Battles had no chance. 57 Squadron sent off three sorties in mid-afternoon, to carry out reconnaissance in a number of locations. F/L Wyatt and crew were sent to reconnoitre the Hertogenbosch area of southern Holland in L9246, which was hit by light anti-aircraft fire near the Dutch-German border, inflicting a wound to F/L Wyatt's arm. He was able to bring the Blenheim back to a forced-landing at base without further casualty, and the aircraft was later abandoned during the withdrawal. P/O Hayter and crew were briefed for Venlo-Wesel-Hamburg-Cologne and landed at Villeneuve after what must have been quite a lengthy sortie. L9245 was shot down over Belgium with no survivors from the crew of P/O Thomas. The Battle squadrons suffered grievous losses during the day amounting to twenty-three, principally while attacking troop columns in Luxembourg, and ten Blenheims were also lost. From this point until the AASF's withdrawal from the continent, 57 Squadron abandoned its photographic reconnaissance role in favour of armed reconnaissance. This required crews to reconnoitre an area in search of targets, and having found and bombed one, return to provide an intelligence report of the situation on the ground. At first light on the 11th, flight commander S/L Roncoroni took off from Lihons to reconnoitre the Dutch/German frontier region of Venlo-Geldern-Wesel, with special attention on the Albert Canal, and completed his sortie without interference before returning safely. P/O Herbert and crew were also in action on this day over the Hasselt region of Belgium, and they, too, made it home in one piece to report what they had seen.

It fell to F/O Grant and crew to conduct the initial reconnaissance sortie of the 12th, the day which would bring the first awards of the Victoria Cross in the present conflict to two members of 12 Squadron. It would also be witness to the further massacre of the Battle and Blenheim squadrons of the AASF. Thrust against the bridges at Maastricht, no amount of gallantry could protect the crews from the accurate barrage from the ground and the attentions of BF109s, and over thirty aircraft were either lost or damaged beyond repair during the course of the day. 12 Squadron alone lost five Battles, while XV and 139 Squadrons each lost seven Blenheims. According to the 57 Squadron ORB, the crews of P/Os Hutchings and Drimmie were sent on reconnaissance sorties over Belgium on the 13th, and the latter failed to return in P6930 after it crashed about fourteen miles south-east of Hasselt. The pilot and gunner were taken into captivity, but the observer lost his life. (According to RAF Bomber Command Losses Vol 1, this occurred on the 12th.) The 13th was a quieter day in comparison to the 12th but was only the lull before the storm broke on the 14th. P/O Spencer and crew took off from the airfield at Poix shortly after 05.30 and encountered a Do17 over Belgium, which they engaged in combat. During the engagement, the Blenheim's gunner was killed, and a shortage of fuel forced P/O Spencer to put L9180 down near Dendermonde, east-south-east of Ghent. While he and the observer were absent from the scene searching for petrol, the aircraft was consumed by fire. In attacks on advancing troop columns and pontoon bridges at Sedan during the course of the day, a further forty aircraft were lost, and, thereafter, the AASF was effectively spent. Some of the squadron's Blenheims were now operating out of the airfield at Lihons, from where P/O Goldie and crew hopped over to Vitry to launch a reconnaissance sortie on the 15th, returning eventually to Lihons via Vitry.

Orders were received at 10.00 on the 17th to pull back the ground element of the squadron, comprising the HQ, messes and billets, from Rosieres-en-Santerre and head for Poix, where they would be joined by the air element. Meanwhile, P/O Ritchie and crew set out from Vitry for an armed reconnaissance sortie, and force-landed at Lequesnil, where their Blenheim was strafed by fifteen BF109s and rendered temporarily unserviceable. At 11.00, F/L Foulsham and P/Os Grant and Hutchings took off from Rosieres to bomb an armoured column, while P/O Goldie and Sgts Greenleaf and Richardson were assigned to targets at Cambrai and Le Cateau. The first few departures from Rosieres left by rail for Poix at 13.00, and the ground party and main stores followed by road at 15.30. S/L Roncoroni, F/L Foulsham, P/Os Goldie, Grant, Hutchings and Saunders, and Sgts Greenleaf and Richardson carried out bombing and reconnaissance sorties after taking off from Lihons, and they all made it safely to land at Poix. Lihons was evacuated at 17.30, P/O Herbert and crew flying out the last serviceable Blenheim, leaving an unserviceable one behind. Personnel spent the night at Poix in the open, while the equipment was dispersed in the woods, but tented accommodation was made available on the following day, while the aircraft were found other dispersals away from the wood. Aircraft and crews were kept on stand-by all day for possible operations on the 18th, but they were not called into action until 19.30, by which time four Blenheims had been received from 139 Squadron, which had been knocked out of the battle and was about to be withdrawn from France. F/Os Blackburn and Nind, P/Os Child-Villiers and Goldie and Sgts Greenleaf and Richardson were dispatched to attack targets at Le Cateau, and, while they were away, orders came through to break camp and proceed to Crecy-en-Ponthieu, the move to be completed by 23.30.

All of the Blenheims had returned to Poix by 20.40, three of them so badly shot-up that they were declared to be unserviceable and were abandoned along with one other. It was actually 23.45 before the main convoy began to move out of Poix, leaving W/C Garland to oversee the departure of most of the serviceable aircraft for Abbeville during the night, he and the rear party finally setting off at 05.30 on the 19th. The motor convoy arrived at Crecy at 06.30, where it was soon joined by the Blenheims flying in from Poix and Abbeville. A camp and field kitchen were established without delay, and the ration and petrol tenders were sent in search of supplies at 14.00. At 17.30, orders were received to pack up the squadron and proceed to Boulogne to arrive not later than 06.00 on the 20th. Part of the road convoy, comprising tractors, water tenders and other heavy equipment, was sent direct to Cherbourg, while the remainder headed for Boulogne. An air raid on Boulogne scattered the convoy, and only a section of it arrived on the quay at 01.30. The remainder could not be located after it had been turned away by the authorities and directed to Cherbourg once the personnel had been allowed to disembark. The ground party arrived at Boulogne on the following morning, when W/C Garland and a total of 298 personnel boarded the SS Mona's Queen at 10.30. Meanwhile, S/L Rogers had led the air element to Lympne in Kent, from where they set off once more for pastures new, this time at Wyton in Cambridgeshire, to await the eventual arrival of the sea party. After landing at Southampton the main party made for Tidworth Camp in Wiltshire, arriving at 18.30 to be divided into two sections and accommodated under canvas. At 14.00 on the following day, the

21st, they set off for Wyton to be reunited with the air element and arrived at 21.30, having been almost constantly on the move since the 17th.

The squadron would be using Hawkinge in Kent as a forward base from which to launch isolated reconnaissance sorties to the Pas-de-Calais area, and the first of these was conducted by P/O Blackburn and crew on the 22nd, the day on which the squadron officially re-joined 2 Group. They landed at Wyton, where the return of P/O Saunders and his crew was awaited in vain. They, too, had been sent to the Pas-de-Calais, where L9148 crashed twenty-five miles inland to the south-east of Dieppe, killing all on board. The ORB recorded P/O Herbert and crew ferrying L9246 from Hawkinge to Rouen on this day and crashing on a small aerodrome without injury to the crew. A similar ferrying incident on the 23rd involved P/O Ritchie and crew, who also crashed on a small aerodrome, causing one broken ankle and a case of concussion. P/O Hayter and crew carried out a reconnaissance sortie on this day and returned safely to Wyton. P/O Goldie and crew took off from Hawkinge at 04.00 on the 24th to reconnoitre the battle area and returned ninety minutes later. F/L Foulsham and F/O Hutchings were also in action on this day, the latter crashing at Lympne in a badly damaged Blenheim after being pursued from Amiens to mid-Channel by eighteen BF110s and barely surviving. The gunner, Cpl Daley, reported shooting one down at the start of the engagement, and claimed the enemy leader over the sea. F/O Hutchings sustained a wound to an arm and was hospitalized, while his crew escaped injury.

At dawn on the 25th, F/O Nind carried out a reconnaissance sortie over Belgium, and, while avoiding a fighter attack near Ypres, his Blenheim was engaged by light flak at low level and the observer hit in the leg by an explosive round, which ultimately resulted in the limb's amputation. Meanwhile, Sgt Richardson and crew completed their reconnaissance sortie without incident. There were just two sorties over Belgium on the 26th, undertaken by the crews of S/L Roncoroni and Sgt Greenleaf. The former returned in a badly shot-up Blenheim, but there were no crew casualties to report. While partial re-equipping took place at Wyton on the 27th, the remaining Blenheims were flown to Gatwick, leaving P/O Grant and crew to conduct the final reconnaissance sortie from Hawkinge on the 28th, after which he landed at Gatwick. Half of the aircrew and a third of the ground crew were granted forty-eight hours leave on the 29th, and thus was concluded a hectic and dispiriting month, not only for the whole of the RAF, but the nation also as the evacuation of an eventual 338,000 men from the beaches of Dunkerque cast a dark shadow over the future prospects for resisting the German tide.

The squadron's time at Gatwick was to be brief, and no operational sorties were conducted before orders came through on the 9th of June to prepare to move back to Wyton. Seven replacement Blenheims had been taken on charge on the 3rd, and they were among those flying to Wyton on the 11th, following in the wake of the ground party, which had undertaken the journey by rail on the previous day. There would be no operations during the month, only bombing practice and the induction of some new crews. By the time that France officially capitulated on the 22nd of June, the AASF had completely evacuated the Continent, and 2 Group operations in support of the country had ceased. It had been a battle that produced heroism of the highest order in the face of impossible odds and cost the lives of many of the finest pre-war airmen.

The threat of invasion now loomed over Britain, and to counter the possibility of it arriving from Norway, 57 and 21 Squadrons were ordered to move to Lossiemouth, located on Scotland's north-eastern coast to the east of Inverness. The rail party, consisting of one officer and seventy-one airmen, left Wyton at 11.30 on the 22nd, to be followed at 15.00 by the road convoy, the former arriving at its destination at 05.00 on the 23rd. We are not told how long it took for the road convoy to complete the 500-mile journey. Fifteen Blenheims were ferried to Lossiemouth on the 24th, landing between 11.45 and 12.30, leaving behind P/O Ryan, who had put his aircraft on its nose while taxying, and he arrived at 17.00 in a different Blenheim. The squadron's brief from the start of July was to target airfields and troop assembly points, and also to assist in attacks on German industrial targets under General Operations Order 11, which would be issued in an Air Ministry directive on the 6th of July. This called for attacks on aluminium plants at four locations, airframe factories at six sites, ten-oil related plants, and shipping in the major ports.

1940 Third Quarter

The squadron was put on stand-by for a raid on Stavanger aerodrome on the 1st and 2nd of July but was not called into action. Six aircraft took part in a navigation exercise on the 3rd, and twelve aircraft undertook a practice shipping sweep on the 4th, during which P/O Ryan crashed at Dyce in R3680, slightly injuring one of the occupants. The squadron continued to practice until the 9th, when the month's only operation was mounted, involving six aircraft targeting Sola aerodrome at Stavanger. F/L Hird led the A Flight section of three aircraft with P/O Hopkinson and Sgt Mills and their crews, while S/L Foulsham, W/C Garland and P/O Grant comprised the B Flight effort, with the first-named specified in the ORB as section leader. They took off at 07.55 to join forces with two similar sections from 21 Squadron, whose commanding officer, W/C Bennett, was in overall control. The target was reached at 09.50 and an attack carried out, following which, the main body of aircraft turned left and ran into fierce ground fire and enemy fighters. S/L Foulsham's section chose a different route away from the target and arrived safely home to land shortly after midday. Thirty minutes later, F/L Hird came back in a badly damaged R3608 and crashed on landing. He reported watching P/O Hopkinson and Sgt Mills, in R3750 and R3847 respectively, being shot down in flames into the sea after a running fight lasting twenty to thirty minutes. 21 Squadron lost five of its number, including its commanding officer, and there was not a single survivor from among the twenty-one crewmen in the seven lost Blenheims.

Operationally, August began slowly, and this gave an opportunity for NCO pilots to be interviewed at the Air Ministry to gauge if they were suitable for a commission. Six aircraft were involved in a North Sea sweep on the 5th, and S/L Foulsham led a similar operation two days later. Berlin Radio announced on the 10th that P/O Drimmie and aircraftman Shuttleworth were prisoners of war, and, on the 11th, six aircraft conducted another sweep over the North Sea in poor weather conditions which prevented any useful observations. Six crews, those of S/L Foulsham, P/Os Ritchie, Holyoke and Denison and Sgts Riley and Whitford were detailed for a special operation on the 12th, and were sent on forty-eight hours leave, on return from which they were to report to Wyton. In the meantime, a detachment was sent to the satellite airfield at Bogs 'O' Mayne near Elgin on the 13th, from where they were to continue conducting sweeps over the North Sea, at a time when the Battle of Britain was entering its most hectic and critical phase. W/C Garland led a sweep by six aircraft on the 14th comprising the crews of F/L Hird, F/O Grant and P/Os Blackburn, Hayter and Taylor. P/O Taylor's Blenheim was attacked by a Dornier, which was beaten off and broke away trailing white vapour. The six crews detached to Wyton returned on the 16th after their special duty was cancelled. Also, on this day, F/L Hird led the North Sea sweep with P/Os Bridger and Taylor, F/Sgt Richardson and Sgts Greenleaf and Onley, while S/L Roncoroni was the senior pilot on duty on the 18th with F/L Nind, F/O Grant, P/O Herbert and Sgts Gillmore and Jordan in support. The sweep on the 19th involved P/Os Bridger, Goldie and Hayter with Sgts Greenleaf, Onley and Riley. Similar operations involving six aircraft at a time were launched on the 22nd, 23rd and 26th, the two last-mentioned led by S/L Roncoroni and S/L Foulsham respectively, and it was from that of the 26th that Sgt Riley and crew failed to return in P6928 and were lost without trace. *(According to Bill Chorley's Bomber Command Losses 1939/40 this operation targeted aerodromes and searchlights, while the 57 Squadron ORB described it as a North Sea sweep).* Further sweeps took place on the 27th, 30th and 31st, by which time most crews had been given the opportunity to operate. During the course of the month the squadron dispatched seventy-eight sorties on thirteen North Sea sweeps for the loss of one Blenheim and crew.

As events turned out, this would be the final operational casualty of the year for 57 Squadron, but two training accidents in early September kept the Grim Reaper busy. On the 2nd, P/O Denison and his crew took off in N8583 at 20.30 for a night-flying cross-country exercise encompassing Cape Wrath–Ronas Isle–Thurso and was last heard from by Kinloss at 23.10. At about that time the Blenheim crashed into the Moray Firth, probably having run out of fuel, and all three occupants lost their lives. Six crews were handed a specific sweep beat on the 3rd, and a further six on the 4th, and, curiously, on the latter occasion, the late P/O Denison is named in the squadron ORB as taking part. Night cross-countries were carried out on both evenings, and it was on return from one of these at 22.10 on the 4th that R3882 crashed as it landed at Bogs O' Mayne, killing P/O Holyoke and his crew. W/C Garland and both flight commanders took their place in the continuing series of North Sea sweeps mounted over the remainder of the month, each involving six Blenheims. They took place on the 7th, 8th, 11th, 12th, 15th, 16th, 19th, 20th, 23rd, 24th, 27th and 28th, resulting in a total for the month of eighty-four sorties from fourteen operations.

1940 Final Quarter

North Sea sweeps by six aircraft at a time continued into October, and with victory secured in the Battle of Britain, the threat of invasion decreased. The squadron was called upon on the 1st, 2nd, 5th, 6th, 13th, 14th, 21st, 25th, 26th and 29th, producing sixty sorties and no major incidents. Sir Charles Portal had departed the helm of Bomber Command on the 5th of October to become Chief of the Air Staff, and he was replaced by AM Sir Richard Peirse, upon whose shoulders would fall the responsibility of implementing future policy. 57 Squadron's time in Scotland came to an end when orders were received on the 29th to return to Wyton. The advanced party headed south on the 31st, to be followed by the remainder of the squadron over the ensuing days, and this signalled the start of a new era for it under the banner of 3 Group, to which it was posted on the 4th of November. P/O Gow was attached from 75(NZ) Squadron on the 10th to instruct crews on the Wellington, by which time, it is believed, on the 7th, a Mk IC, T2804, had arrived on station as the squadron's first example of the type. The first dual instruction flight took place on the 14th in a Mk 1A, the day on which orders came through for yet another change of address, this time to Feltwell, which was already occupied by 75(NZ) Squadron. The main party undertook the move on the 18th, and the aircraft and crews arrived on the 20th to continue training, flying when the weather allowed and ground instruction and lectures when not. There would be no further operational activity for the squadron until the New Year, as it continued to work up on the new type and take on extra crew members.

57 (B) Squadron stationed at Roye, near Montdidier, France. October 1939.

Bristol Blenheim Mk IV L9248 which was lost over France during May 1940. It is pictured as wreckage on an airfield in France with an ME109 about to land.

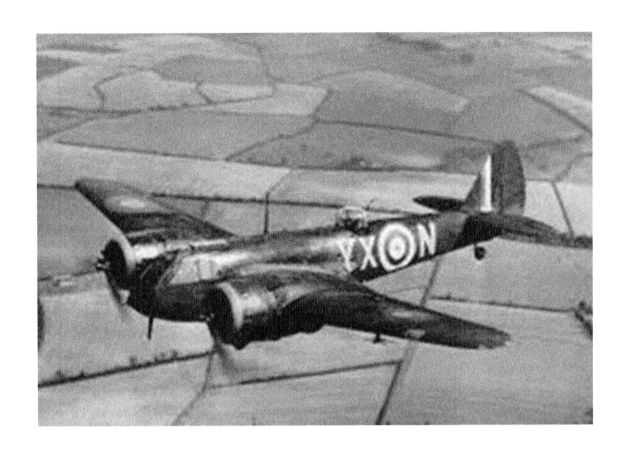

Blenheims Mk Ic. in flight

Blenheim Mk IV

Blenheim Mk IV of 57 Squadron

Bristol Blenheim Mk.IV, Cockpit

Bristol Blenheim Mk1 L1244, having crashed into the woods at Marham on 19th July 1939. The aircraft had been piloted by P/O Ackroyd-Simpson with Cpl Sid Culver as one of the crew. Cpl Culver does not recall the reason for landing at Marham but said that because of heavy rain they flew close to the airfield buildings to judge their height and then they carried straight on and into the trees. It is not known what happened to P/O Ackroyd-Simpson as a result of the crash but both he and Cpl Culver survived the incident without serious injury. Of note is the phoenix within the grenade on the fin.

The demand for aircrew at various stages during the War meant that some groundcrew, flew on operational missions, manning one of the gun positions and undertaking other roles. LAC Sid Culver, a 57 Squadron armourer, is recorded as flying as a wireless operator/gunner on Bristol Blenheim Mk IV's at the outbreak of the War. In March 1940, the Squadron's first gallantry awards were presented, including the Distinguished Flying Medal to Cpl Sid Culver. The citation for the award records that Sid was "... the first member to carry out a second reconnaissance over Germany. Both flights involving fighting in the very cold weather for very long distances. His conduct and ability during these flights had a good effect on the aircraft crews at a time when the Squadron suffered losses."

Sid stayed with 57 Squadron as it re-equipped with Wellingtons and was never far from the action and formally qualified as a wireless operator. Sid managed to escape with his life when his aircraft was forced to crash at East Wretham in March 1941, returning from a raid on Cologne. The following month, his aircraft was forced to ditch off Gibraltar while on a ferry flight from St Eval, after a navigational error led to the aircraft running out of fuel. Sid lost his logbook in the process!
Sid continued to fly throughout the War, following 57 Squadron with a Polish Squadron and also with 7 Squadron Pathfinders. He died, aged 94, in November 2010.

SNCO aircrew of 57 Squadron Elgin 1940.
Rear L-R: Sgts Meikle, Culver, Beagles, Whitby, Armstrong, Lee, Greenleaf.
Middle L-R: Sgts Rudkin, Simpson, Haines, Havard, Park, Gillmore, Brown, Jorden, Onley Simmons.
Front L-R: Sgts Hudspeth, Newman, Daley, Russell, Trickey, Turnidge, Cowen, Patterson, Rock, Slade.

January 1941

Note to readers. The 57 Squadron Operations Record Book Forms 540 and 541 for the first half of 1941 offer almost no detail on operations and the 3 Group record is little better. I apologise for the paucity of detail that I'm able to provide. The New Year began for the Command with the launching of 141 aircraft on New Year's night for a major operation against Bremen, and smaller ones directed at other ports along the occupied coast. Bremen was also the target for smallish forces on the following two nights, before an inconclusive attack on Brest on the 4/5th. Operations did not resume for 57 Squadron until the night of the 13/14th of January, when small-scale raids were launched by the Command against Wilhelmshaven on Germany's north-western coast and French ports. 57 Squadron briefed the crews of S/L Foulsham, F/L Blackburn, P/O Hutchings and Sgts Harvey and Hill, and dispatched them from Feltwell between 04.30 and 04.45 on freshman sorties to Boulogne, but none was able to locate the target hidden beneath ten-tenths cloud. The recently-promoted F/L Blackburn dropped his bombs on Ostend, the only one to find a target, and all returned safely home between 07.05 and 08.55. The splendidly-named S/L Rivett-Carnac arrived on posting on the 15th and would succeed S/L Foulsham as flight commander on the latter's posting to Wyton as Squadron Leader Operations on the 16th.

The 15th was the day on which a new directive was issued by the Air Ministry, whose top brains had decided that an all-out assault against oil related targets would eventually take its toll on the German war effort, and operations from now on would reflect this. A list of seventeen sites was drawn up, the top nine of which represented 80% of Germany's synthetic oil production. They were located in two main areas of Germany, the Scholven-Buer and Nordstern plants in Gelsenkirchen in the Ruhr, while six of the others, Leuna, Politz, Zeitz, Böhlen, Ruhland and Lützkendorf were clustered around Liepzig, and the ninth was at Magdeburg some sixty miles to the north.

It would be February before Peirse was able to comply, and, in the meantime, a force of ninety-six aircraft was assembled on the 15th to target the dock and shipbuilding yards at Wilhelmshaven, while a few predominantly freshman crews cut their teeth at nearby Emden. It should be noted that at this point of the war, "freshman" pilots had usually already flown ten operations as second pilot with an experienced captain before graduating to crew captain status. 57 Squadron made ready four Wellingtons for Emden, one to contain the crew of S/L Foulsham, who would be carrying out his final sortie before the above-mentioned posting. The other crews were those of P/O Hutchins and Sgts Harvey and Hill, and they all departed Feltwell between 18.00 and 18.15 before climbing out into good weather conditions, which held firm for the entire operation. There were largely clear skies over northern Germany and vertical visibility was good as the bombers made their approaches to their respective targets. Those from 57 Squadron returned to Feltwell between 22.00 and 23.00 to report that they had carried out their briefs without major incident. Many squadron ORBs provided scant information at this stage of the war, and the one produced by the designated 57 Squadron scribe was no exception, in fact, the Forms 540 and 541 would remain short on detail until the start of June. It has been necessary, therefore, to supplement the account of 57 Squadron's activities during the first five months of 1941 with reports from other 3 Group squadrons, principally those of 75(NZ) and 115 Squadrons. The 3 Group ORB was no more revealing with regard to the Emden raid but suggested that the attack on Wilhelmshaven had been a major success, which caused fires that left a glow on the horizon for 130 miles into the return flight. The effectiveness of the raid was confirmed by reports from local sources, which described many fires in the town, damage to the head post office, main police station, army barracks, dock offices and seven commercial buildings. This important naval port would be attacked many times in 1941, but not as effectively as on this night.

In fact, Wilhelmshaven was the target again on the following night for a force of eighty-one aircraft, including twenty-four Wellingtons of 3 Group, fewer of which located it than on the previous night, and damage was slight. The harsh winter conditions restricted operations during the remainder of January, and 57 Squadron found itself largely frozen to the ground and managing to launch just one further sortie. A week of inactivity preceded the next operation, and, in the meantime, P/O Hutchings and Sgt Daley of his crew presented themselves at Mildenhall on the 18th to be decorated by His Majesty King George VI. Twenty-eight 3 Group Wellington crews were briefed on the 22nd for a raid that night on Düsseldorf in the southern Ruhr in company with a dozen 2 Group Blenheims. At this stage of the war, there was no concept of the mass attack that would characterise Bomber Command operations in the Harris era from February 1942, and squadrons, having been handed a target, would largely determine the details for themselves. This meant, that while several groups might be involved against a specific target, they would not necessarily be over it at the same time and could be separated by hours. The original plan on this night called for 3 Group to lead the attack and start fires to act as a beacon for the other groups, but poor weather conditions led to a reduction in the size of the force, and, ultimately, it became a 3 Group show of twenty-eight Wellingtons. Five of these were provided by 75(NZ) Squadron, and they took off from Feltwell between 17.35 and 18.00 with no senior pilots on duty and were followed into the air at 18.05 by 57 Squadron's sole representative in the form of Sgt Hill and crew. They all reached the target area, where ten-tenths cloud completely blotted out the ground, and bombs were delivered on estimated positions based on the flashes from flak batteries. It was a wasted effort, but, at least, all returned safely to offer the intelligence section what little information they could. The 3 Group ORB admitted to a poor showing in which just one crew had ventured beneath the cloud cover, while the others had bombed on estimated positions.

Hannover was selected as the target on the night of the 26/27th, and, at briefings, crews were somewhat optimistically told to aim for the main post office and telephone exchange. In the event, a forecast of poor weather reduced the size of the force to just seven Wellingtons from 75(NZ) Squadron, which took off from Feltwell very late, between 01.15 and 01.50, no doubt disturbing the sleep of the 57 Squadron crews in their billets. They had to climb through low cloud to reach the North Sea, but it dispersed gradually until clear skies greeted the arrival of six Wellingtons over the target city. Each was carrying a mixed load of a 1,000 pounder and 500 and 250 pounders, which were dropped in sticks across the city, setting off fires and explosions. All returned safely, confident in the quality of their work, but there was no post-raid reconnaissance or local report to confirm their success.

3 Group sent twenty-six Wellingtons to seek out the battleship Tirpitz at its berth in Wilhelmshaven on the 29th, when only one crew identified it, and the others reaching the target area aimed for the docks generally. 57 Squadron did not take part and ended the month with a tally of three operations, ten sorties and no losses.

February 1941

The weather continued to exert its control over operational activity at the start of the new month, and French ports were to provide the targets for mostly freshman crews. 57 Squadron was not involved in a small-scale 3 Group effort against Boulogne on the night of the 1/2nd, and it was the 4th before the squadron was called into action as part of a 3 Group force of thirty-eight Wellingtons divided 24/14 between the ports of Brest and Le Havre. The crews of S/Ls Rivett-Carnac and Roncoroni, F/L Blackburn and Sgt Hitchcock departed Feltwell at 17.30 bound for the latter, only for S/L Roncoroni to return early and the others to be thwarted by cloud that prevented them from establishing their positions. With an enemy attack on Feltwell in progress, they were diverted to land at Honington, and each brought their bombs home. The Brest force benefitted from favourable weather conditions, and returning crews claimed hits and near misses on the docks area, where a Hipper class cruiser was at berth.

In response to the January directive, AM Sir Richard Peirse had decided upon a policy of one major operation each month, and Hannover was selected to host February's "Big Night". Hannover is an ancient and major city in northern Germany, situated midway between the Dutch coast and Berlin, and was home during the war to many factories contributing to the war effort, including the Accumulatoren-Fabrik A G, manufacturers of lead acid batteries for U-Boots and torpedoes, the Continental tyre and rubber factory at Limmer, the Deurag-Nerag synthetic oil refinery at Misburg, the VLW (Volkswagen) metalworks, and the Maschinenfabrik Niedersachsen Hannover and Hanomag factories, which were producing guns and tracked vehicles. Bomber Command assembled the largest force yet sent to a single target, 222 aircraft, of which 3 Group contributed 103 Wellingtons, while also providing a further fourteen to a freshman raid on the oil storage tanks at Rotterdam. Present in the latter were the first three sorties by Stirlings, three Group's new heavy bomber, which had been brought to operational status by 7 Squadron. This was the first occasion on which any group had put a hundred aircraft into the air on a single night. According to Form 540 in the ORB, 57 Squadron briefed four crews for the main event and three for a freshman operation to Boulogne, while the 3 Group record shows four for Hannover and three for Rotterdam. However, the 57 Squadron Form 541 listed the crews of F/L Hird and Sgt Hitchcock departing Feltwell at 18.30 and 18.40 respectively, and those of S/L Rivett-Carnac, P/O Hutchings and Sgt Hill taking off at 21.15 and 21.20, none with a specific destination. The timings are of no assistance, as the Hannover operation was spread over many hours with aircraft departing their stations throughout the evening between 18.00 and 23.00. The enemy was again active over Feltwell on this night, which may have led to a reduction in the 57 Squadron numbers, but the likelihood is that the record-keeping by the 57 Squadron scribe was inaccurate. The Hannover-bound element flew out over scattered cloud via corridor "B" to enter Fortress Europe by way of the Den Helder peninsula, and those arriving early found the target area to be under clear skies and fires already burning. They carried out their attacks in the face of a heavy, medium and light flak response, and returned to report many fires and explosions, which suggested a successful outcome. Those arriving later found the target area hidden by cloud, and the 3 Group ORB offered a pessimistic assessment of the likely outcome.

57 Squadron was not involved in the following night's operations against Bremen and Hannover, for which 3 Group provided thirty-six and seventeen Wellingtons respectively. The occasion turned into

a disaster, after fog descended upon the bomber counties in time for landing, and twenty-two aircraft crashed, some after being abandoned, and half of the casualties belonged to 3 Group. It was at this point that Peirse turned his attention upon the oil campaign, and an operation was posted on the 14th against the Gelsenkirchener Bergwerke A G coking plant in the Horst district of Gelsenkirchen in the Ruhr. The synthetic oil refinery, referred to by the Germans simply as Gelsenberg A.G., (Aktien Gesellschaft or production company) and Bomber Command as Nordstern, produced high-grade petroleum products such as aviation fuel by the Bergius process, which involved the hydrogenation of highly volatile bituminous coal.

3 Group detailed forty-one Wellingtons, three of them representing 57 Squadron, and the crews of F/L Blackburn and Sgts Harvey and Hill departed Feltwell between 19.10 and 19.30 among a dozen others from 75(NZ) Squadron. A second operation on this night as part of the oil offensive was directed at the Gewerkschaft Rheinpreussen A G synthetic oil plant at Moers/Homberg on the West Bank of the Rhine opposite Duisburg on the western edge of the Ruhr. Forty-four aircraft were detailed, divided equally between Wellingtons and Blenheims, and all of the 3 Group crews reached the primary target, where extreme darkness and industrial haze prevented all but nine from attacking what they believed was the oil plant, leaving others to seek out alternative objectives like nearby Duisburg and Essen. As returning 57 Squadron crews landed at Feltwell at around midnight, a German aircraft touched down, but took off again as soon as the flare path was extinguished. 75(NZ) Squadron's W/C "Cyrus" Kay had seen the aircraft taxy in, turn around and take off immediately, but thought nothing of it, since Feltwell regularly received "strays". A phone call came through shortly afterwards from an unhappy A-O-C 3 Group, AVM Jack Baldwin, asking if he realised that an enemy aircraft had just taken off from Feltwell! As it happened, the lost pilot, low on petrol and realising how far he was from home, landed at another airfield and surrendered.

Twenty-four hours later the target was the Ruhr-Benzin A G plant situated in the Sterkrade-Holten district to the north-west of Oberhausen city centre, for which 3 Group contributed forty-five Wellingtons, while fourteen Wellingtons with freshman crews and two Stirlings targeted the docks and shipping at Boulogne. Homberg was also to be attacked again on this night and was assigned to thirty-seven Blenheims and thirty-three Hampdens of 2 and 5 Groups respectively. The Boulogne-bound 57 Squadron element of six departed Feltwell between 18.15 and 18.45 with W/C Garland the senior pilot on duty but flying as second pilot to S/L Roncoroni. Those operating over the Ruhr found it hidden beneath its blanket of haze, and, on this occasion, extreme darkness, while an unusually high number of searchlights were operating to create a glare that prevented identification of ground detail. All experienced great difficulty in establishing their whereabouts, and it is unlikely that any landed a bomb near the target. The 57 Squadron ORB provided no information concerning the Boulogne raid and 3 Group recorded only that most crews had managed to locate it.

On the 17th, S/L Roncoroni was posted to Bramcote, a training station situated a few miles outside Nuneaton in Warwickshire, where 18 (Polish) O.T.U., was preparing aircrews for service with the two Polish squadrons, 300 and 301, currently operating in Bomber Command's 1 Group, which would be joined by 304 and 305 Squadrons in April. W/C Roncoroni would be appointed commanding officer of 4 Group's 77 Squadron in the autumn of 1943, shortly before the commencement of the five-month-long 1943/44 winter campaign, during which Berlin would be visited by the Command sixteen times and was arguably the most demanding period of the war for bomber crews. He was succeeded at 57 Squadron by S/L Rodney. W/C Garland had also been notified that he was about to be posted to HQ Bomber Command, and he and his wife hosted a farewell party for the squadron officers in their local pub at Northwold on the 19th. W/C Bertram was posted in on the 21st as the new commanding officer elect, and he was introduced to the squadron officers during a farewell dinner that night in the officers' mess. W/C Garland was still officially in command on the 23rd, when five crews were briefed for an operation against the docks and shipping at Boulogne in company with twenty-eight others from 3 Group, including a dozen freshman crews. The crews of F/L Hird, F/O Ritchie, P/O Bridger and Sgts Fletcher and Hitchcock departed Feltwell between 18.20 and 18.35 ahead of eight representing 75(NZ) Squadron and made their way to the French coast over cloud, which was at eight to ten-tenths by the time they arrived at the target. Three Kiwi crews were unable to pinpoint its location, despite the intense searchlight and flak activity, which must have acted as a beacon, but the others carried out their attacks, and returned to report bomb bursts across the docks resulting in small fires and explosions.

W/C Garland left Feltwell on five days leave on the 24th, prior to taking up his new appointment on the 1st of March, and leaving W/C Bertram to stamp his character on the squadron. He presided over his first operation on the 26th, when six 57 Squadron crews were briefed for the main event against Cologne while P/O Hutchings and crew were told that they would be targeting the docks and shipping at Boulogne. 3 Group provided forty-nine of the 126 aircraft assigned to the Rhineland capital city, those from 57 Squadron departing Feltwell between 18.35 and 18.55 with F/L Hird the senior pilot on duty, and they were followed into the air by the 75(NZ) Squadron element of ten Wellingtons. P/O Hutchings and crew got away at 19.25 and all flew out in good weather conditions, but F/O Redford turned back at the coast because of an engine issue. Those bound for Cologne set course via corridor G and ran the gauntlet of searchlights all the way from the Dutch side of the Scheldt estuary to the target area, where haze hampered identification of ground detail. On return, three crews each landed at Marham and Bodney, and P/O Hutchings undershot his landing at one of them, causing damage to R3195 but not to the occupants. Returning crews described explosions and large fires, and all indications pointed to a successful raid, which, as often was the case, was not borne out by local reports. These recorded ten high explosive bombs and ninety incendiaries falling on the western fringes of the city, out of a total of 353 and 15,000 respectively supposedly dropped. This concluded the month's operations for Feltwell, of which there had been eight involving 57 Squadron, and these had generated thirty sorties without loss.

March 1941

Ports would again feature prominently in March, although the first two operations of the new month continued the assault on Cologne. Six Wellingtons were made ready by 57 Squadron on the 1st, five for the main event and one for the freshman crew of P/O Redford to take to Boulogne in company with one other from 311 (Czech) Squadron. The former were to join fifty-two others from the group in an overall mixed force of 131 aircraft and departed Feltwell between 19.00 and 19.35 with F/L Hird the senior pilot on duty. The 75(NZ) Squadron element of six remained on the ground at Feltwell until taking off between 20.50 and 22.00, and this was typical for the period, when an operation could be spread over many hours. They crossed the North Sea in conditions of ten-tenths cloud, which dispersed over enemy territory to leave clear skies at the target, and delivered their loads of 1,000, 500 and 250 pounders in the face of an intense searchlight and heavy and light flak defence and observed bomb bursts in various parts of the city. All returned safely to report many fires, and local authorities confirmed significant damage, particularly in the docks areas on both sides of the Rhine. Meanwhile, one of the freshman crews delivered an attack on Boulogne, while the other was thwarted by cloud and brought their bombs back

Two nights later a reduced force of seventy-one aircraft was made ready for a return to Cologne, among them thirty-two Wellingtons from 3 Group, of which four represented 57 Squadron, while P/O Redford and crew reprised their trip to Boulogne. F/O Ritchie was the senior pilot on duty on this occasion as they departed Feltwell between 19.00 and 19.30 and were followed immediately into the air by the 75(NZ) Squadron element. They headed into fine weather conditions, which produced sufficient cloud over the Rhineland to hamper attempts to locate the primary target. The majority of returning crews claimed to have bombed as briefed, while others reported attacking alternatives in the Ruhr to the north and aerodromes in Holland. Details of the 57 Squadron sorties were not recorded and we know only that four landed at Mildenhall. Local sources reported that no bombs fell in the main city area, and just a few hit the western fringes.

A new Air Ministry directive was issued on the 9th, which would take the Command in a new direction and away from a strictly strategic role. Massive losses of Allied shipping to U-Boots in the north Atlantic demanded an all-out campaign against this menace and its partner-in-crime, the Focke-Wulf Kondor long-range reconnaissance bomber. They were to be pursued where-ever they could be found, at sea, in their bases and at their point of manufacture. Shipyards at Kiel, Hamburg, Bremen and Vegesack (north-west of Bremen) were to be the principal targets, along with a Focke-Wulf factory in the Hemelingen district of Bremen. S/L Peters-Smith was posted in on this day to assume command of B Flight.

Forces of eighty-eight and eighty-six aircraft were assembled on the 12th to send against Hamburg and Bremen respectively, while seventy-two others targeted Berlin. 3 Group contributed fifty-four Wellingtons to the Bremen raid and twenty-seven to Berlin with a further five freshman Wellingtons and a single Stirling assigned to Boulogne. 57 Squadron supported the Bremen and Berlin operations with three Wellingtons each, the crews of P/O Redford and Sgts Harvey and Hitchcock briefed for the former and those of F/L Hird, F/O Ritchie and Sgt Hill to the latter. They took off together between 19.25 and 19.50 and headed for their respective targets in good weather conditions but lost the services of F/L Hird to a fuel issue early on. Once again, details of the conduct of the 57 Squadron sorties were not recorded and we know only that Sgt Hill and crew attacked an alternative target. Post-raid reconnaissance at Bremen revealed that a dozen high explosive bombs had hit the Focke-Wulf aircraft factory, while local sources in Berlin reported a scattered and relatively ineffective raid that damaged sixty buildings in predominantly southern districts. Meanwhile, the attack on Hamburg had caused extensive damage to the Blohm & Voss shipyards, which had built the mighty Bismarck between 1936 and 1940, and other yards had also been hit. Eighteen large fires had to be dealt with among many smaller ones, and the operation was concluded without loss.

On the following night the entire force of 139 aircraft was sent to Hamburg to target the Blohm & Voss shipyards. The 57 Squadron contingent of six Wellingtons departed Feltwell between 19.40 and 20.40 with F/L Hird the senior pilot on duty and made their way across the North Sea in good weather conditions. Searchlights were very much in evidence over enemy territory, and the flak from Bremen to Hamburg was intense and accurate. Returning crews reported bombing within three miles of the aiming-point and observing a number of fires that were visible for up to twenty minutes into the return journey. T2970 fell victim to a night-fighter and was the first 57 Squadron Wellington to be lost on operations. The crew of Sgt Harvey escaped with their lives, both pilots sustaining severe ankle injuries and the rear gunner an eye wound that would result in his repatriation in October 1943. Post-raid reconnaissance confirmed this as another successful operation against Hamburg, adding to the extensive damage caused twenty-four hours earlier, and the Blohm & Voss shipyards sustained further damage to the main office block and two slipways on which U-Boots were under construction.

Just three crews were called to briefing on the 15th, when they learned that they were to participate in a small-scale raid on the newly-begun construction site on the Keroman Peninsula at Lorient, where a massive base was being built to house U-Boots and their crews. The first phase of the massive construction project on the southern extremities of Lorient had begun just weeks earlier, and would continue until January 1942, by which time K1, K2 and K3 would be completed and capable of sheltering thirty vessels and their crews under cover. The complex would boast a revolutionary lift system, which could raise U-Boots from the water and transport them across the facility to repair and servicing bays. The thickness of the concrete would render the structure impervious to the bombs available to Bomber Command at the time, and attacks would be directed predominantly at the town and its approaches to prevent access by road and rail. 3 Group detailed twenty-six Wellingtons and those containing the 57 Squadron crews of F/Os Blackburn and Ritchie and Sgt Hill departed Feltwell in a five-minute slot from 18.40. They reached the target to find clear skies but ground haze, which prevented most crews from being able to assess the outcome, particularly as the burst from semi-armour-piercing (SAP) bombs was not spectacular. Returning crews were met by fog over their stations in northern and eastern England and were diverted to the west country to land either at St Eval in Cornwall or at Boscombe Down in Wiltshire.

Adverse weather conditions interfered with preparations for a planned visit by 3 Group to Berlin on the 18th, and a reduced force of thirty-four Wellingtons was added to a raid on the port of Kiel, situated on the Baltic coast of the Schleswig-Holstein peninsula. This created an overall force of ninety-nine aircraft, of which four belonged to 57 Squadron, and they took off between 19.45 and 19.55 accompanied by the freshman crews of F/O Hayter and P/O Bridger bound for Rotterdam to attack the oil storage tanks. F/L Hird was the senior pilot on duty as they flew out over the Norfolk coast heading north-east across the North Sea. Cloud in the target area forced some to bomb on e.t.a., but most seemed to identify the docks area, and contributed to a very successful attack, which local sources claimed to be the most destructive thus far. Particular damage was inflicted upon the Deutsche Werke U-Boot yards, and the town centre also attracted many bombs.

Three 57 Squadron crews were detailed for operations on the night of the 21/22nd, two to attack the Keroman U-Boot construction site at Lorient and one the docks at Ostend. 3 Group contributed twenty Wellingtons to the overall force of sixty-six aircraft assigned to the former and six freshman crews to the latter, among them F/L Barber and crew, who were undertaking their first operational sortie together and failed to return. X3162 crashed in the sea off Ostend, and only the remains of the pilot were recovered for burial. Tellingly, the squadron ORB recorded the fact that the three commissioned members of the crew had been lost but made no mention of the three

NCOs. The 3 Group ORB recorded that cloud created challenging conditions at both targets, but that most of those at Lorient delivered their loads into the target area without being able to offer an assessment, while the attack on Ostend was thwarted by the conditions and most crews sought out alternative ports.

A force of sixty-three Wellingtons and Whitleys set out for Berlin on the evening of the 23rd, thirty-two of the former provided by 3 Group with the crew of Sgt Hitchcock alone representing 57 Squadron. They departed Feltwell at 20.00 and headed towards a target shrouded in eight to ten-tenths cloud. Attacks were carried out, and some explosions and fires were seen reflected in the clouds, but returning crews were unable to offer an assessment of the results.

Cologne and Düsseldorf were the destinations for forces of thirty-eight and thirty-nine aircraft respectively on the night of the 27/28th, and 57 Squadron contributed six to the raid on the former. They departed Feltwell between 20.05 and 20.20 and, on reaching the target, found their view of it hampered by cloud, haze and searchlight glare and most crews could only bomb on estimated positions. On return, R1441 crashed while Sgt Emmerson was attempting to land at East Wretham in Norfolk and it was written off, happily without crew casualties. At debriefings, crews were unable to offer any assessment of the outcome and the only bombing photographs developed proved to be of Düsseldorf, twenty-five miles to the north.

For the past few days, 3 Group had put aircraft on stand-by for possible action against German surface raiders believed to be heading for Brest. On the 29th, the cruisers Scharnhorst and Gneisenau were reported to be off the port, and, by the following morning, they had taken up residence. This was to be the start of a protracted and distracting ten-month saga, which would cost the Command dearly in crews and effort for precious little return. The first operation of the campaign against Brest and its lodgers, which would sometimes include Prinz Eugen, was carried out by over a hundred aircraft on the night of the 30/31st, for which 3 Group contributed thirty-seven Wellingtons in the absence of any from Feltwell. However, the station did launch five freshman sorties, four by 57 Squadron, among fourteen from 3 Group briefed to attack the docks and shipping at Calais. The Brest operation was conducted in two waves, but cloud prevented many crews from identifying the target and no hits were scored. There was no report from the Calais raid.

A new bomb was about to be introduced to operations, a 4,000lb blockbuster, which, with the advent of four-engine heavy bombers, would become the standard weapon for city-busting and become known as a "cookie". It was a high-capacity device, which meant that the explosive content represented the majority of the weight, and this was contained within a thin, light cylindrical casing with a tail and fin attachment. At the time, the Mk IC Wellington was unable to carry a bomb of this size and 3 Group's 9, 99 and 149 Squadrons were each provided with two Rolls Royce Merlin-powered Mk II Wellingtons, which had a 3,000lb advantage in all-up weight and a modified and strengthened bomb bay. Briefings took place on 3 Group stations on the 31st, when twenty-eight crews learned that they would be targeting shipyards in Bremen, while six, including two Mk II Wellington crews, were assigned to Emden and five freshmen to the oil storage tanks at Rotterdam. The Deutsche Schiff und Maschinenbau Aktien Gesellschaft shipyards in Bremen, abbreviated to Deschimag, had been formed in the mid-twenties as a co-operation of eight shipyards to compete with the Blohm & Voss and Bremer Vulkan yards. The largest was the A G Weser company, which, after six of the others had fallen by the wayside before the outbreak of war, was partnered only by the Seebeckwerft, now as part of the Krupp empire, after that organisation had been handed a controlling interest in 1941. According to the 3 Group ORB, three 57 Squadron Wellingtons departed Feltwell for Rotterdam, but the squadron recorded only two departing Feltwell at 19.40, one captained by S/L Peters-Smith, who was undertaking his first sortie since joining the squadron. Based on the reports from the 75(NZ) Squadron participants, they reached their destination to find cloud, which seriously compromised the raid, and no results were recorded. The 4,000 pounders dropped on Emden apparently sent houses flying into the air and were a great success.

During the course of the month 57 Squadron took part in sixteen operations and dispatched forty-eight sorties for the loss of three Wellingtons and two crews.

April 1941

Brest would open the squadron's April account on the night of the 3/4th, for which a force of ninety aircraft was assembled, fifty-two of them provided by 3 Group with a further five assigned to Rotterdam. The crews of Sgts Fletcher, Fryer and Hitchcock departed Feltwell at five-minute-intervals from 19.00 bound for Brest, leaving S/L Peters-Smith and crew on the ground until 20.15. Those participating in the main event reached the target area to find nine to ten-tenths cloud, which prevented most crews from identifying the aiming-point and forced them to bomb on estimated positions based on dead-reckoning (DR) and e.t.a. The raid was inconclusive, and it is unlikely that the target vessels were damaged.

On the 4th, Gneisenau entered a dry dock, which was to be drained on the following day for an inspection of the vessel. At the same time, a further attempt against the enemy warships was being planned for that night, for which fifty-four aircraft were detailed, forty-one of them belonging to 3 Group, although none from Feltwell. One crew claimed a direct hit on one of the vessels and a number of naval officers were killed when the Continental Hotel in the town was also struck by bombs just as dinner was being served. When Gneisenau's dry dock was drained on the following day, the 5th, a single unexploded 500lb bomb was found nestling at the bottom, and the ship's captain, Kapitän-zur-See Otto Fein, decided to move his vessel out into the harbour while it was dealt with. The dock was refilled to allow Gneisenau to vacate it, and she was spotted by a reconnaissance aircraft at some point, which led to an operation being planned by Coastal Command to be carried out at first light on the 6th. It took place in poor weather conditions, which led to the six Beauforts becoming separated while outbound, and F/O Kenneth Campbell and his crew alone pressed home an attack, which caused damage to Gneisenau that would require six months to repair. In the face of the most concentrated anti-aircraft fire, the Beaufort stood little chance of getting away with it and was shot down without survivors. F/O Campbell was posthumously awarded a Victoria Cross for his actions.

A further raid on the vessels was planned for that night, for which 3 Group detailed forty-four aircraft in an overall force of seventy-one. Feltwell returned to the Order of Battle with eight Wellingtons from 57 Squadron and ten from 75(NZ) Squadron, the former taking off between 20.25 and 20.40 with S/L Peters-Smith the senior pilot on duty and S/L Rodney flying as second pilot to F/L Nind. It is believed that all from 57 Squadron reached the target area to find an impenetrable layer of ten-tenths cloud, which prevented any crews from locating the aiming point. All crews bombed on estimated positions based on e.t.a., DR or the flashes from flak batteries and another inconclusive and probably ineffective operation was chalked up.

In contrast, the weather conditions over north-western Germany on the night of the 7/8th promised to be ideal for bombing operations, with clear skies and bright moonlight to lay bare the port of Kiel. A force of 229 aircraft was dispatched and this represented the largest effort yet against a single target. 57 Squadron contributed eight Wellingtons, which departed Feltwell between 20.25 and 22.45, with S/L Peters-Smith the senior pilot on duty and S/L Rodney again flying as second pilot to F/L Nind. The spread of take-off times reflected the fact that the bombing would be conducted over a five-hour period, which was common practice at this stage of the war for such a large-scale operation. All crews reached the target area and benefitted from the excellent conditions, delivering their bombs and incendiaries into the docks area and the town, and observing explosions and fires. Anti-aircraft fire was fairly intense, and, while searchlights operated mostly in cones, the glare was diffused by the brightness of the moon. Returning crews were confident in the effectiveness of the attack, and this was confirmed by local accounts of widespread damage to buildings in the naval dockyard, civilian housing, industrial units, and to the Germania Werft and Deutsche Werke U-Boot yards, which had to be shut down for several days.

A force of 160 aircraft was assembled for a return to Kiel on the following night, of which fifty-six were provided by 3 Group in the absence of any from Feltwell. Conditions over northern Germany were favourable, and they were greeted at the target by virtually clear skies and excellent visibility. Bombing took place from between 8,500 and 13,000 feet and many explosions and fires were reported, the latter visible for some fifty miles into the return journey. The main weight of the attack fell this time into the town itself, and produced a death toll of 125 people, with a further three hundred injured, and this was almost certainly the highest number of casualties at a German urban target to date.

Preparations were put in hand on the 9th to send eighty aircraft to Berlin, among them thirty-seven Wellingtons and three Stirlings representing 3 Group, which would also target the Bremer Vulkan shipbuilding yards at Vegesack to the north-west of Bremen with eight Wellingtons and the docks at Emden with seven. 57 Squadron made ready seven Wellingtons for the main event plus two for the crews of F/L Way and Sgt Day to take to Vegesack, and they departed Feltwell together between 19.55 and 20.35 with S/L Peters-Smith the senior pilot on duty. They made their way into Germany via northern Holland, where intense searchlight and flak activity greeted the bombers at the frontier, and a number were seen to be shot down. The weather conditions outbound and over the target were excellent, allowing crews to pick out other aircraft up to half a mile away. All from the squadron reached the target to carry out their attacks in the face of an intense and fairly accurate flak defence, and around 60% of returning crews claimed to have bombed within the city, although without any degree of concentration. T2804 failed to return from Berlin, and Sgt Ritchie and crew were almost immediately reported to be alive and in enemy hands, although it is believed that a gunner sustained wounds sufficient to see him repatriated at some time. R1437 was lost from the Vegesack raid after signalling that it was returning early, and Sgt Day died with three of his crew, while the remaining two fell into enemy hands, one of these also to be repatriated eventually because of injuries sustained. This night brought the long-awaited return to operations of 12 Squadron after its conversion from Battles to Wellingtons, which had begun back in November. Four sorties were launched to Emden, no mention of which appeared in the 3 Group ORB and neither did it record the loss of the commanding officer, W/C Blackden, who died with his crew after being shot down over Holland by one of Germany's foremost night-fighter pilots.

Further attacks on Brest involving 3 Group took place on the 10th, 12th and 14th, none of which required participation by 57 Squadron, even though 75(NZ) Squadron did support the last-mentioned. The consensus among crews returning from the first-mentioned was of an effective raid, which was confirmed sometime later when reports were received that four bombs had struck the Gneisenau, killing or wounding over a hundred crew members and German workers. On the 15th, ninety-six aircraft were sent to Kiel, forty-two of them provided by 3 Group from Mildenhall, Stradishall, Honington and Wyton, and 57 Squadron again remained inactive. Orders were received on the 16th to prepare for that night's operation to Bremen, for which 107 aircraft were made ready, fifty-two of them on 3 Group stations including Feltwell. 57 Squadron briefed S/L Peters-Smith and his crew and sent them on their way at 20.15, and we are grateful to the records of other squadrons for informing us that adverse weather conditions greeted them in the target area, and only a quarter of returning crews would claim to have bombed the primary target. The main problem was eight to ten-tenths cloud with a base at around 4,000 feet, which allowed glimpses of the ground but no opportunity to take aim. Bombs were dropped indiscriminately from between 8,500 and 14,000 feet into the general docks area or the town, guided by the flash of explosions, the glow of fires and the evidence of searchlight and flak activity.

Berlin provided the objectives again on the night of the 17/18th, when a force of 118 aircraft was assembled, at least thirty of them provided by 3 Group. 57 Squadron again briefed the crew of S/L Peters-Smith as its only contribution and dispatched them from Feltwell at 21.00 in the wake of the seven 75(NZ) Squadron participants. They made their way out over heavy cloud and were greeted by haze in the target area that presented the usual difficulties of target location. Even though many crews found Berlin, to identify either of the aiming points was a challenge too far and bombing was scattered and largely ineffective. S/L Peters-Smith and crew went on leave on the following day, forcing the squadron to select another one to carry the burden of operations. This turned out to be the freshman crew of Sgt Chapman, who departed Feltwell at 20.40 on the 20th in company with two Kiwi crews bound with eight other 3 Group freshmen for the oil storage tanks at Rotterdam. No report is available from 57 Squadron, but one of the other Feltwell participants reported three dull, red fires, suggesting that at least one bomb had found the mark. The primary target on this night for a force of sixty-one aircraft was Cologne, for which 3 Group put up twenty-nine aircraft. The target was hidden beneath ten-tenths cloud, some of which contained icing conditions and electrical storms, and another inconclusive and unsatisfactory attack ensued.

Further attacks on Brest involved small numbers of 3 Group aircraft on the 22nd and 23rd, none representing 57 Squadron, before Sgt Chapman and crew found themselves on duty again on the 24th, this time attending briefing in the company of Sgt Emmerson and his crew. The destination for them and eight other freshman crews was Ostend, while twenty-seven others from the group took part in a raid on Kiel. The latter took place in favourable conditions and returning crews reported bomb bursts and fires but could offer no detailed assessment. Local reports described a scattered attack and little resultant damage. It was after midnight before the Ostend-bound crews took off, and they were greeted by ten-tenths cloud that prevented a positive identification of the target.

3 Group contributed small numbers of aircraft to raids on Kiel, Emden and Berlin on the 25th, Hamburg and Emden on the 26th and Brest on the 28th, while a few 7 Squadron Stirlings carried out "moling" sorties, which were daylight forays by individual aircraft. The whole concept of sending inadequately armed bombers in daylight to the most heavily defended region of Germany, relying only on cloud for protection, was utter madness, and one wonders who came up with the idea and who sanctioned it. Fortunately, it proved to be a passing phase, but brave and valuable crews would be lost until common sense prevailed. S/L Peters-Smith and crew were back in harness in time for 57 Squadron's next operational activity on the 29th, which involved two crews at Mannheim and one at Rotterdam. The crews of S/L Peters-Smith and Sgt Chapman departed Feltwell for southern Germany at 20.30, leaving Sgt Emmerson and crew on the ground until 23.20. The former were part of an overall force of seventy-one aircraft, which experienced good weather conditions outbound, but encountered ground haze at Mannheim. This, presumably, accounted for the poor bombing performance, which managed to deposit only fifteen bomb loads in the entire area of Mannheim and its neighbour across the Rhine, Ludwigshafen, and destroy a total of four houses. The Rotterdam raid was carried out in the face of searchlights and flak, and a number of incendiaries were observed to burst, but no other results were determined. During the course of the month the squadron operated against twelve targets and dispatched thirty-seven sorties for the loss of two Wellingtons and their crews.

May 1941

Germany's second city, Hamburg, would feature prominently during the first half of the new month, and the Rhineland capital, Cologne, would also receive frequent visits mostly in the second half. Hamburg provided the destination for ninety-five aircraft on the 2nd, thirty-six of them provided by 3 Group, while five and three freshman crews from the group respectively supported small-scale raids on Emden and Rotterdam. 57 Squadron briefed the crews of S/L Peters-Smith and Sgts Chapman and Emmerson for the main event and Sgt Ross for Emden, and it was the last-mentioned who departed Feltwell first at 20.40, twenty-five minutes ahead of their more experienced colleagues. The weather conditions were good for the outward flight, and visibility in the target areas sufficiently good to facilitate accurate bombing. Crews returning from Hamburg claimed to have bombed within the target area, where the searchlights were organised in stationary cones, and reported a successful operation. Local sources reported twenty-six fires, half of them large, but no serious incidents.

The main effort on the night of the 3/4th was directed at Cologne, for which a force of 101 aircraft was made ready, while 3 Group sent a force of twenty-nine Wellingtons and three Stirlings to maintain some pressure on Brest. 57 Squadron remained at home, where, on the following afternoon, the crews of S/L Peters-Smith and Sgts Chapman, Emmerson and Ross attended briefing to learn of their part in another assault on Brest that night. A force of ninety-seven aircraft was made ready, forty-four of them representing 3 Group, and the 57 Squadron quartet departed Feltwell safely between 21.30 and 21.50. No details of the bomb load were provided, but the thirteen 75(NZ) Squadron Wellingtons were each carrying a 2,000 pounder along with 500 and 250 pounders, all of which were delivered within the target area. At debriefings, some crews would claim to have hit the dry dock in which Gneisenau was under repair and two reported straddling one of the ships. One of the Kiwi crews dared to believe that they may have scored a direct hit, as did returning crews from other squadrons, but no damage to the cruisers was confirmed.

Mannheim was posted as the main target on the 5th for what would be a major operation involving 141 aircraft, half of them Wellingtons. 3 Group contributed fifty-five aircraft, mostly Wellingtons, but none from Feltwell. They flew all the way to southern Germany over a blanket of ten-tenths cloud, which hampered navigation, but 120 returning crews claimed to have bombed in the target area. A 115 Squadron crew reported bombing on a north-westerly heading, slightly south-east of the aiming-point, and observing a huge, red, circular explosion emanating from their cookie, with a mushroom of smoke rising out of the centre. Most returning crews claimed to have bombed within the target area, but cloud prevented them from observing results. A local report claimed that around twenty-five bomb loads had hit the city, causing only modest damage, mostly to residential property.

Feltwell, Stradishall and Wyton provided forty-three Wellingtons for Hamburg on the 6th in an overall force of 115 aircraft. 57 Squadron contributed four crews to the main event led by S/L Peters-Smith and those of P/O Cox and Sgt Emmerson for the freshman target of Boulogne. They took off together between 22.30 and 23.00, only to lose the services of Sgt Green and crew to an early return, leaving the others to reach the target and encounter complete cloud cover that persuaded many crews from the force generally to seek alternative objectives. The 57 Squadron ORB recorded only that all six crews operated successfully and those bombing the primary target would have had no idea what happened to them after they disappeared into the cloud. Local sources confirmed this raid as a wasted effort.

On the 7th, 57 Squadron's T2504 was hit by incendiary bombs dropped during a Luftwaffe raid on Feltwell and was consumed on its dispersal pan in the ensuing fire. That night, 3 Group detailed forty-four Wellingtons in an overall force of eighty-nine, the crews of which were briefed for the next round of the campaign against Brest and its lodgers. Feltwell was not involved in the operation, which took place in excellent conditions, and some crews actually claimed to have identified the enemy vessels and scored direct hits. These were not confirmed, but, encouragingly, no aircraft were lost. On the 8th, S/L John Southwell was rewarded for his excellent service as a flight commander with 75(NZ) Squadron with a posting across the tarmac to 57 Squadron as successor to W/C Bertram, who was posted to 1 Group HQ at Hucknall. Southwell's promotion to acting wing commander rank would be confirmed on the 11th. In the meantime, he presided over his first operation on the night of his appointment, when Hamburg was briefed out to 188 crews, 119 assigned to the shipyards lining the banks of the Elbe in the Finkenwerder district to the west of the city centre and sixty-nine to the city itself. 3 Group put up a maximum effort of ninety-eight Wellingtons for the main event, three Wellingtons and two Stirlings for Berlin and two Wellingtons for Emden. Two would fail to take off, but we are not informed from which operation they were withdrawn. A further 133 aircraft were to target Bremen and its shipyards, while support and minor operations also took place, and the combined total of 364 sorties was a new record in a single night. The six 57 Squadron participants departed Feltwell between 22.20 and 22.40 with S/L Peters-Smith the senior pilot on duty, all reaching the target to find good visibility and carry out their attacks under clear skies and based on a visual identification of the aiming-point. Many fires were observed, and all returned safely to Feltwell to report a successful operation. The 57 Squadron ORB again recorded only that all six sorties were successful. Local sources confirmed an effective raid, which caused eighty-three fires, thirty-eight of them classed as large, and resulted in 185 fatalities, the highest death toll to date from a Bomber Command attack.

Twenty-four hours later, attention was shifted to southern Germany and the twin cities of Mannheim and Ludwigshafen, facing each other on the east and west banks respectively of the Rhine. A force of 146 aircraft included forty-seven 3 Group Wellingtons, of which four were made ready by 57 Squadron. The crews of Sgts Chapman, Cox, Green and Ross departed Feltwell between 22.30 and 22.45, and all reached the target area to encounter fine weather conditions and good visibility. This, and the modest searchlight and flak response, enabled the crews to carry out their bombing runs with precision, and all returned safely to report hitting the target and starting fires or adding to those already burning. The catalogue of damage included military, industrial, commercial and residential buildings on both sides of the river, and 3,500 people were bombed out of their homes.

On the 10th, the first anniversary of the German advance into Holland and Belgium and of Churchill's appointment as Prime Minister, orders were received across the Command to prepare 119 aircraft for an operation that night against the shipyards, the city and the Altona power station in Hamburg. 3 Group detailed thirty-nine Wellingtons for the main event along with eight Wellingtons and Stirlings for a small-scale attack on Berlin, but Feltwell was not invited to take part in either. The conditions over Hamburg were ideal with perfect visibility, and the main weight of bombs fell into the city centre where extensive damage resulted. 128 fires had to be dealt with, forty-seven of them classed as large and the success was gained for the loss of three Wellingtons and a Whitley.

3 Group contributed sixty-five Wellingtons and a Stirling for a return to Hamburg twenty-four hours later, the 3 Group contingent representing the main component of a force of ninety-two aircraft, whose crews had been briefed to attack the Blohm & Voss shipyards. 57 Squadron briefed the crews of P/Os Cox and Martin and Sgts Chapman, Emmerson and Ross and sent them on their way from Feltwell between 22.20 and 22.50. Sgt Chapman and crew were airborne for just three hours and twenty minutes, and P/O Martin and crew for twenty minutes longer, suggesting that either could have been the 57 Squadron crew recorded in the 3 Group ORB as being assigned to the oil storage tanks at Rotterdam. The remaining three found Hamburg without difficulty in excellent weather conditions and delivered their bombs into the city, observing many large fires including a blaze in a main oil-storage tank and others in the Holzhafen district on the East Bank of the Elbe, south-east of the city centre. A simultaneous attack on Bremen attracted some of the Hamburg force, partly as a result of mistaking the River Weser for the Elbe. The Hamburg operation was declared a success, and local reports confirmed that the city had taken some

punishment during this series of three raids in four nights, although there was no mention of significant industrial damage.

While the Feltwell squadrons remained at home over the ensuing nights, operations were mounted against Mannheim, Ludwigshafen and Hannover, and the month's other principal target, Cologne, on the nights of the 12/13th, 15/16th and 16/17th respectively, and not one of them was concluded successfully. Nine 57 Squadron crews attended briefing on the 17th, seven in preparation for another attack on Cologne as part of an overall force of ninety-five aircraft, while two freshman crews were assigned to the docks at Boulogne. The two elements departed Feltwell together between 22.15 and 23.00, with S/L Peters-Smith the senior pilot on duty and headed south in order for those bound for Cologne to enter enemy territory via the Belgian coast. Sgt Fryer and crew were back on the ground after eighty minutes because of an engine issue, leaving the others to press on in fair weather conditions to find Cologne covered by ground haze and protected by intense searchlight and flak activity. In the absence of a moon to diffuse the searchlight glare, the crews experienced difficulty in picking out ground detail, but most claimed to have bombed within the city, some observing bursts and others not. The crews of Sgts Green, O'Neill and Stanford returned to Feltwell between 01.20 and 02.30, well ahead of the others, and any two of them could have been those assigned to Boulogne. R1508 was struck by an overshooting 75(NZ) Squadron Wellington and, according to the 57 Squadron ORB, was smashed, when, in fact, it was repaired and eventually found its way to an O.T.U. Local sources in Cologne reported widely scattered bombing with a little concentration in southern districts, but no major incidents.

After almost a week away from the operational scene, the crews of S/L Peters-Smith, P/O Martin and Sgts Chapman, Fryer and Ross were called to briefing on the 23rd to learn of their part in the next assault on Cologne planned for that night. They took-off between 23.30 and 23.55 as part of a force of fifty-one aircraft, twenty-six of them provided by 3 Group and the remainder by 5 Group, and headed for the Belgian coast, where a cone of twenty-two searchlights greeted their arrival over Dunkerque. F/L Way, who had been sent to reinforce the Middle-East detachment and had returned from Gibraltar in mid-May, was flying as second pilot to S/L Peters-Smith. Those reaching Cologne found it concealed beneath ten-tenths relatively thin cloud and only three crews caught a glimpse of the ground through gaps. The conditions led to scattered bombing which damaged some twenty-five houses in what was a disappointing outcome in view of the effort expended.

On the 22nd, a 5 Group element was put on stand-by for a possible operation against German surface raiders, which, although not named, were the battleship Bismarck and heavy cruiser Prinz Eugen. They had put to sea on operation "Rheinübung" (Exercise Rhine), which for Bismarck, would be its first offensive action, and were being shadowed by Coastal Command aircraft as they slipped out of Bergen heading for the Denmark Straits between Greenland and Iceland. In the event, Bomber Command was not called into action and the crews were stood down. On the 24th, the German raiders confronted their Royal Navy pursuers and a salvo from Bismarck penetrated the deck armour of the "unsinkable" HMS Hood, the pride of the navy and a national treasure, and ignited the magazine. The Hood was rent by a violent explosion that tore it apart and killed all but three of its complement of more than fourteen hundred men. Churchill demanded the destruction of Bismarck at any cost and by any means, and as Bismarck raced towards the Biscay coast to gain sanctuary at Brest, elements of the Royal Navy closed in. 5 Group operated alone on the 25th, committing forty-eight Hampdens to mine the approaches to Brest and St-Nazaire, (Jellyfish and Beech gardens), the former, in particular anticipating the arrival of the Bismarck. On the evening of the 26th, Bismarck, which had separated from her consort Prinz Eugen, was attacked by Swordfish torpedo bombers from the aircraft carrier Ark Royal, which crippled Bismarck's rudder, rendering the vessel unable to manoeuvre, and restricted to a top speed of ten knots.

At first light on the 27th, multiple units of the Royal Navy closed in on the helpless ship, and, from 08.47, engaged her with guns and torpedoes until she slipped beneath the waves at 10.39. This left her consort, Prinz Eugen, at large, and the mining at Brest would continue over the succeeding nights in case she put in an appearance. 3 Group had already committed sixty-four aircraft to search for her during daylight on the assumption that she also might make for Brest to join Scharnhorst and Gneisenau. 57 Squadron briefed ten crews and dispatched them from Feltwell between 06.35 and 06.45 with S/L Peters-Smith and the newly arrived S/L Field the senior pilots on duty. It turned out to be a fruitless search in unhelpful weather conditions, during which, crews spent up to two hours in the search area. All would return safely home, some after more than nine hours in the air, and, at debriefing, reported encountering many enemy aircraft sent out to protect the vessel. Sgt Chapman and crew were involved in a brush with an Arado floatplane and R1792 sustained minor damage.

During the course of the month, the squadron took part in twelve operations and dispatched fifty-three sorties for the loss of a single Wellington to a German bomb on the ground.

June 1941

June and July were to be significant months for the Command, as its performance began to be monitored in order to provide an assessment of its effectiveness for the War Cabinet. The project was initiated by Churchill's chief scientific advisor, Lord Cherwell, who handed the responsibility to David M Bensusan-Butt, a civil-servant assistant to Cherwell working in the War Cabinet Secretariat. The new month would be dominated by operations against Cologne, Düsseldorf and Bremen, with Kiel and Brest also receiving their share of attention. During the second half of the month Cologne and Düsseldorf would be attacked simultaneously on no fewer than eight nights by forces of varying sizes, and Bremen, including the shipbuilding yards at Vegesack further downstream of the Weser, would host six raids. On the 1st, the Hipper Class cruiser Prinz Eugen arrived at Brest having evaded detection by the British following the sinking of the Bismarck. She would now join Scharnhorst and Gneisenau to form a powerful battle group that would continue to be a distraction for Bomber Command.

Düsseldorf was posted as the main target on the 2nd, for which a force of 150 aircraft was assembled, fifty-nine of them provided by 3 Group, plus eight Stirlings and three Wellingtons for a 3 Group attack on Berlin. 57 Squadron briefed six crews for the main event, while their Wellingtons were being loaded with six 500 pounders and a single 250 pounder each. Five departed Feltwell between 23.35 and 23.50, leaving S/L Field and crew on the ground until 01.00 and all reached the southern Ruhr at 13,000 feet to encounter cloud and thick industrial haze, which forced many crews to bomb from estimated positions and on e.t.a. The crews of Sgt Green and F/L Way found gaps in the cloud and saw the ground in the light of many illuminator flares before delivering their loads on a west to east heading, while Sgt O'Neill and crew spotted the River Rhine and a fire as they bombed at 02.13. Sgt Stanford and crew were unable to make a positive identification as they searched the target area between 02.00 and 02.13, and let their bombs go over the general target area without observing any results, but they did witness the violent explosion of a cookie with a green flame. Sgt Ward and crew searched for an hour between 01.35 and 02.40 and dropped their bombs on a northerly heading after identifying a bend in the river to the west of a railway line. Six bursts were observed, which appeared to demolish some buildings and start two fires. S/L Field and crew bombed sometime later from 12,000 feet and in keeping with most other returning crews had little to offer at debriefing. Barely two-thirds of the force claimed to have attacked the primary target, and local sources reported a scattered and ineffective raid that caused only minor damage.

Minor operations occupied the ensuing days, and it was the 7th before 3 Group put together a small force of twenty-nine Wellingtons and seven Stirlings to attack Prinz Eugen at berth at Brest. Most found and bombed the docks, but none identified the warship in the face of an effective smoke screen. Feltwell and Marham were alerted to a further attack on Prinz Eugen on the 10th and briefed thirty-eight crews between them in an overall force of 104 aircraft. According to the ORB, 57 Squadron briefed eight crews, but listed only five on the Form 541, those of S/L Peters-Smith, P/O Cox and Sgts Chapman, Emmerson and Ross. The two Feltwell squadrons took off over an extended period, beginning with the dozen 75(NZ) Squadron Wellingtons between midnight and 00.55 with, among them at five-minute intervals between 00.40 and 00.50, the crews of S/L Peters-Smith and Sgts Emmerson and Ross. Finally, the crews of Sgt Chapman and P/O Cox got away at 01.05 and 01.35 respectively and all headed south in fine weather conditions which persisted all the way to the target. Ground haze combined with an effective smoke screen to obscure the aiming point, and, although all from 57 Squadron delivered their bombs into the target area from 12,000 to 14,000 feet between 01.13 and 04.19, no clear results were observed. Returning crews reported bomb bursts, fires and black smoke, and it was established later that many bombs had fallen into the docks and, perhaps, straddled the warships, but had failed to score direct hits on any of the sheltering vessels.

The Ruhr cities of Düsseldorf and Duisburg provided the main targets for the night of the 11/12th, for which, forces of ninety-two and eighty aircraft respectively were made ready. 57 Squadron briefed the crews of Sgts Fryer, Stanford and Ward for the former and the three freshman crews of Sgts Birch, Hill and Rishworth for Boulogne, and sent them on their way from Feltwell between 23.15 and 23.25. The weather conditions were fine at both locations, but a layer of cloud over the Ruhr obscured the ground, and the bombing by the 57 Squadron crews took place on estimated positions from 10,000 to 12,000 feet between 00.53 and 01.35. Inevitably, the raid lacked precision, but no local report emerged to provide details of damage. However, local sources in Cologne, situated some twenty miles to the south, reported extensive damage, particularly on the West Bank of the Rhine, where the main railway station stood in the shadow of the cathedral and was hit by seven bombs. Cologne was frequently bombed either in error or deliberately as an alternative to targets in the Ruhr.

The following night was to be busy as groups were handed marshalling yards to attack, three of them situated north of the Ruhr, at Soest, for ninety-one Hampdens of 5 Group, Hamm for eighty-two Wellingtons of 3 Group, and Osnabrück for sixty-one Wellingtons of 1 Group, while 4 Group was assigned to a similar target at Schwerte, five miles south-east of Dortmund, for which eighty Whitleys and four Wellingtons of 405 Squadron were detailed. In addition to these, eight Halifaxes from 35 Squadron and three from 76 Squadron were to target what Bomber Command referred to as a synthetic rubber factory at Marl/Hüls in company with seven 3 Group Stirlings.

57 Squadron made ready a record fourteen Wellingtons for Hamm, a busy and well-defended railway hub a few miles north of the Möhne reservoir and a vital link in the railway network carrying raw materials into the Ruhr and finished goods out. Six of the squadron's Wellingtons took off from Feltwell among the ten from 75(NZ) Squadron, while eight others began their sorties from Methwold, all getting away safely between 22.55 and 23.59 with W/C Southwell the senior pilot on duty for the first time and supported by S/L Field. They located the target area in conditions of ground haze and found it a challenge to identify the precise location of the marshalling yards. Bombing by the 57 Squadron crews was carried out from 11,500 and 18,000 feet between 01.03 and 02.34, but no assessment was possible. A local report stated that seven bombs fell in the town, six of which exploded with minimal effect, while the seventh, containing a delayed action fuse, killed two bomb-disposal men.

Feltwell was not involved in a return to Brest on the following night for which 3 Group contributed fifty Wellingtons in an overall force of 110 aircraft. The operation proceeded as those before it, with ineffective bombing in the face of a smoke screen that completely concealed the enemy warships. The night of the 15th was to bring with it the first of the simultaneous attacks on Cologne and Düsseldorf, both moderate efforts against railway yards employing forces of ninety and fifty-nine aircraft respectively. The aiming point for the forty-nine 3 Group Wellingtons and forty-two 5 Group Hampdens was Cologne's Gereon marshalling yards, which occupied an area close to the western end of the Hohenzollern railway bridge that spanned the Rhine in the city centre and fed directly into the main station. The crews of Sgts Birch, Stanford and Ward departed Feltwell between 23.15 and 23.25 in the wake of the Dunkerque-bound Sgt Cameron and climbed away into ten-tenths cloud, which would remain in place all the way to the targets. They delivered their six 500 pounders and two small bomb containers (SBCs) of incendiaries each from around 10,000 feet on estimated positions based on e.t.a., and the flashes from flak batteries, and were heading out of the target area by 01.30. They had no idea where their bombs fell, and local sources suggested that only four or five bomb loads had hit the city, causing minor damage. Meanwhile, Sgt Cameron and crew had dropped their similar load on Dunkerque through ten-tenths cloud from 13,000 feet at 00.05 and observed a red glow.

Cologne and Düsseldorf were "on" again twenty-four hours later, when the squadron made ready fifteen Wellingtons, thirteen as part of the all-3 Group force of seventy-two aircraft assigned to the latter, and two for the freshman crews of Sgts Cameron and Osborne to take to the docks at Boulogne. They departed Feltwell between 23.10 and 23.30 with S/Ls Field and Peters-Smith the senior pilots on duty, and all reached Düsseldorf to find poor visibility, although many crews were able to pinpoint on the River Rhine and make a timed run to the target. The 57 Squadron element carried out their attacks from 12,000 to 18,000 feet between 01.25 and 02.35, before returning home to report simply that their bombs had burst in the target area. The exceptions were F/L Way and crew, who observed their bombs to burst among a cluster of buildings and Sgt Birch and crew, who started what they described as a long fire in what appeared to be warehouses. Returning crews reported many fires but less than expected flak activity, which one station commander found to be suspicious, and questioned whether a dummy fire had attracted the bombs. Local reports, suggesting that only two heavy bombs had found their way into a southern suburb, would seem to support this view. Sgt Cameron and crew failed to identify Boulogne and jettisoned their load into the sea, while the Osborne crew delivered six 500 pounders from 12,000 feet at 01.25 and watched them burst across docks 4 and 5.

Feltwell was among the stations not required to operate on the 17th, when 3 Group detailed fifty-seven Wellingtons for Düsseldorf while 4 and 5 Groups attended to Cologne, both without success. S/L Field's brief time with the squadron as B Flight commander ended on the 18th with his posting to 214 Squadron at Stradishall. Thirteen 57 Squadron crews and seventeen from 75(NZ) Squadron were called to briefing that afternoon to be told that they would be operating against Brest that night, for which the former departed Feltwell between 22.05 and 22.30 with W/C Southwell and S/L Peters-Smith the senior pilots on duty. For the second operation running, Feltwell launched thirty Wellingtons without a single take-off failure or early return. They reached the target area to encounter a combination of ground haze and an effective smoke-screen, which prevented most crews from identifying the briefed aiming-point, the Scharnhorst. This led to the general bombing of the docks complex from 1,000 to 14,000 feet between 01.12 and 02.10, the latter time that of P/O Cox and crew, who stooged around for seventy-five minutes waiting for the smoke to clear before delivering their seven 500lb SAP bombs and observing two bursts. 75(NZ) Squadron's P/O Ashworth dropped flares to aid his search and made eight low-level runs across the target during a seventy-five-minute period, establishing in the process that Scharnhorst was not berthed where the raid planners had asserted. None was able to offer any useful information at debriefing having witnessed only flashes through the murk and Sgt O'Neill and crew returned their bombs to store after failing to locate the target.

The Cologne/Düsseldorf operations on the night of the 19/20th were prosecuted by 3 and 4 Groups respectively and were small-scale and ineffective. Sgt Hill was declared tour-expired on the 20th and was posted to the Australian 27 O.T.U., at Lichfield for instructional duties. On the following day, fourteen 57 Squadron crews joined fifteen from their fellow Feltwell residents to learn of that night's return to Cologne and a freshman raid on the docks and shipping at Dunkerque. The 57 Squadron element took off between 22.50 and 23.35 with W/C Southwell and S/L Peters-Smith the senior pilots on duty and the crew of Sgt Rishworth alone heading for the coast of north-eastern France. The weather outbound was fine, but cloud and ground haze over Cologne provided difficult conditions for bombing, and, despite the claims of some crews to have identified ground features, most dropped their loads on estimated positions. Precisely where they fell is uncertain, but local sources would record no bombs falling within the city boundaries, and just a few in villages to the west. Meanwhile, over Dunkerque, Sgt Rishworth and crew dropped six 500 pounders and a single 250 pounder across docks 5 and 6 from 12,000 feet at 00.38 and were perhaps the only ones to be satisfied with their night's work.

Later, on the 22nd, acting S/L Freeman arrived on posting to assume command of B Flight as successor to S/L Field. Following a failed attempt by 4 Group to locate and bomb the battleship

Tirpitz at Kiel on the 20th, 3 Group contributed thirteen Stirlings and three Wellingtons to a second effort on the 23rd in company with six 35 Squadron Halifaxes. Bursts were observed and several small fires broke out, but no detail was gleaned through the searchlight glare, and the Tirpitz was not positively identified. On the 24th, Feltwell provided nineteen Wellingtons for a return to Kiel in company with four from 214 Squadron at Stradishall, while twenty-three others from the two stations continued the rather ineffectual assault on Düsseldorf. 57 Squadron made ready nine Wellingtons for Kiel and five for the southern Ruhr and dispatched the former between 22.15 and 22.55 with S/Ls Freeman and Peters-Smith the senior pilots on duty. They were given a VIP send-off by His Royal Highness the Duke of Kent, who visited the station that evening and met several of the crews, and they enjoyed the rare experience of a Spitfire escort for the first half of the outward flight. The Ruhr-bound quintet departed Feltwell between 23.30 and 23.55, and, except for P/O Cox, all were sergeant pilots. Those heading for Kiel were met at Schleswig-Holstein's North Sea coast by searchlights and heavy, accurate flak, which most negotiated to reach the other side of the peninsula to find fine weather conditions, despite which, few were able to determine the fall of their bombs. The 57 Squadron crews attacked from 11,000 to 15,000 feet between 01.20 and 02.00, some observing bomb bursts, others not and headed home to make their reports. Sgt Ward and crew failed to return in R1608 after it crashed into the Baltic close to the target, and there were no survivors. Five bodies were recovered for burial, while Sgt Ward went down with the Wellington and is commemorated on the Runnymede Memorial.

The assault on Kiel and its illustrious lodger, which had inherited the status of pride of the German fleet since the loss of her sister, Bismarck, continued on the night of the 26/27th, when 3, 4 and 5 Groups committed a force of forty-one of the new bomber types and again failed to find the mark. Fourteen 57 Squadron crews joined sixteen from their fellow residents in the Feltwell briefing room on the 27th to learn that Bremen was to be their target. An attempt to hit the city two nights earlier in the absence of a Feltwell participation had been rendered ineffective by electrical storms on the outward route, which had prevented most aircraft from completing the journey. A force of seventy-three Wellingtons and thirty-five Whitleys prepared for a late take-off, the 57 Squadron element taking off between 23.00 and 23.20 with S/Ls Freeman and Peters-Smith the senior pilots on duty. It would prove to be another night of adverse weather, which included storms and icing conditions, in addition to which, the crews would face, for perhaps the first time, a concerted effort by the Luftwaffe Nachtjagd. Sgt O'Neill and crew had been outbound for forty-five minutes and were at 7,000 feet when they crossed paths with a Ju88 and were persuaded to turn back. Poor visibility in the target area led to many crews finding their way to Hamburg, some fifty miles north-east of Bremen, and seventy-six bombing incidents were recorded there. A few crews caught a glimpse of Bremen through brief gaps in the cloud, and others bombed on the glow of fires, but the majority released their loads from estimated positions on e.t.a. The 57 Squadron crews carried out their attacks from 7,500 to 17,000 feet between 01.20 and 02.00 and had little useful information to impart at debriefing. Absent from that process was the crew of Sgt Ross RAAF, who were last heard from at 01.30 but failed to arrive home in R1794 and presumably disappeared into the North Sea. No report was available from Bremen, but it is unlikely that it sustained more than slight scattered damage in return for a new record loss of fourteen aircraft, eleven of which were Whitleys, 31% of those dispatched.

The squadron operated for the final time in the month on the night of the 30th, when Feltwell was the only 3 Group station called into action and Cologne was the target for twenty-three

Wellingtons, while elements from other groups sent small numbers to Duisburg and Düsseldorf. Eleven 57 Squadron Wellingtons took off between 22.55 and 23.20 with S/Ls Freeman and Peters-Smith the senior pilots on duty and adopted the southerly route to Cologne via Belgium. The weather was fine as they made their way out, and all reached the German frontier after passing through the searchlight belt south-east of Antwerp and skirting Maastricht in southern Holland. The night was very dark, and haze concealed most of the ground detail in the target area as the 57 Squadron crews bombed from 12,000 to 15,000 feet between 01.37 and 02.30. Returning crews reported bursts and fires on both sides of the river and some claimed to have picked out the Rhine and its bridges, but no detail was forthcoming, and no local report emerged.

During the course of the month the squadron took part in sixteen operations and dispatched 116 sorties for the loss of two Wellingtons and their crews.

July 1941

The main focus for operations during July would be on manufacturing centres in the Ruhr, including Cologne, and at other locations in the Münsterland between the Ruhr and northern Germany. The major cities of Bremen, Hamburg and Hannover would continue to attract attention, and it would not be until the final third of the month that targets in southern Germany, principally, Frankfurt and Mannheim, found themselves in the bombsights of moderately sized forces. Brest would continue to be a distraction and an attack there on the night of the 1/2nd resulted in a bomb exploding inside the Prinz Eugen, killing sixty of her crew. Bremen, Cologne and Duisburg were the targets for the night of the 2/3rd, 3 Group providing forty-four Wellingtons and Stirlings for the first-mentioned. Operations began for Feltwell with the call to briefing on the 3rd of fourteen 57 Squadron crews and sixteen from 75(NZ) Squadron, all but one of the former to take part in the main event, a 3 Group show involving sixty-seven Wellingtons against the giant Krupp complex in Essen in the central Ruhr.

The Krupp organisation had been the largest manufacturer of weapons in Europe since before the Great War, had a hand in all aspects of German war production from tanks to artillery and ship and U-Boot construction, and was given a controlling share in all major heavy engineering companies in Germany and the occupied countries. It also built manufacturing sites in other parts of Germany, many situated close to concentration camps, from which it could draw vast numbers of forced workers. Once known as "Die Waffenschmiede des Reichs", the weapons-forge of the realm, its manufacturing sites in Essen included the Friedrich Krupp steelworks, the Friedrich Krupp locomotive and general engineering works, six coal mines and ten coke-oven plants, the Altenberg zinc works, the Presswerk plastics factory, and the Goldschmidt non-ferrous metals smelting plant, all situated either within or close to the four Borbeck districts in a segment radiating out from near the city centre to the Rhine-Herne Canal on the north-western boundary on the banks of the Emscher River. The steel and engineering works alone employed in the region of eighty thousand people, and the company's sites covered an area of more than two thousand acres, of which three hundred acres were occupied by factories and workshops. All of that required massive rail and canal access in the form of marshalling yards and a dedicated harbour, and energy from at least four nearby power stations.

The 57 Squadron Wellingtons for the main event departed Feltwell between 23.05 and 23.20 with S/L Freeman the senior pilot on duty and were followed into the air at 23.30 by Sgt Irwin and crew bound for a freshman raid on the Luftwaffe aerodrome at Gilze-Rijen in southern Holland. Soon afterwards, the pilot reported the failure of his a.s.i., and headed for the landmark beacon close to the airfield to await instructions for his return to base. At 00.08, R1589 crashed at Larman's Fen off Southery Road to the north-west of the Feltwell village, killing all but the rear gunner, who sustained serious injury. The road would have to be closed for several days while unexploded bombs were removed. The others pressed on, probably unaware of the tragedy, and reached the target area to find clear skies but the usual impenetrable ground haze and a hostile and accurate defence from searchlights and flak. Only about half of the force claimed to have bombed in the target area, and among them were all but one of the 57 Squadron crews, who delivered their attacks from 9,500 to 17,000 feet mostly onto existing fires. Sgt Stanford and crew returned their 1,000 pounder and five 500 pounders to store after failing to identify the target and handed T2715 back to the ground crew to repair minor damage sustained in a brush with an enemy night-fighter. Local sources reported minor housing damage in Essen and bombs falling in other Ruhr locations including Duisburg in the west, Hagen in the east and Wuppertal in the south.

While elements of 1 and 5 Groups made a further attempt to incapacitate the enemy "fleet in being" at Brest on the night of the 5/6th, the first of a series of operations against Münster was mounted by elements of 3 and 4 Groups, for which 57 Squadron made ready fourteen Wellingtons as part of a 3 Group contribution of sixty-four. Situated in the agricultural flatlands immediately north of the Ruhr, Münster was a garrison town, home to infantry and armoured units, contained a large marshalling yard south of the town centre and had been left in peace by the Command for five months by the time that this operation was mounted. The 57 Squadron participants departed Feltwell between 22.55 and 23.25 with S/L Freeman the senior pilot on duty and flew out in fine weather conditions, those arriving over the Münsterland region finding it nestling under clear skies. Fires were already taking hold as the majority of the 57 Squadron crews delivered their loads of seven 500 pounders from 8,500 to 15,000 feet between 01.12 and 01.59, while S/L Freeman dived towards the aiming point to release his 1,000 pounder, four 500 pounders and single 250 pounder from 3,500 feet. Many explosions and fires were reported, and the smoke was drifting through 9,000 feet by the end of the raid, which left a glow in the sky visible for sixty miles into the return journey.

Feltwell was among the stations sitting out the ineffective return to Münster by a 3 Group force of forty-seven Wellingtons on the following night but was called into action on the 7th to participate in the next one, for which a force of forty-nine Wellingtons was made ready. 3 Group would also support the main operation taking place on this night, which involved 114 Wellingtons in a raid on Cologne, while 4 Group attended to Münster's near neighbour, Osnabrück, another garrison town. Sgt Cameron and crew took W5616 for an air-test in the late morning and while carrying out a single-engine approach to Methwold, undershot the runway, hit a tree and crashed at 12.15. The rear gunner was killed instantly, but the remainder of the crew scrambled clear before the Wellington was consumed by fire. Later that afternoon, briefing took place for the Münster operation for which the official records are confusing. The 3 Group ORB recorded that thirteen 57 Squadron Wellingtons had been detailed, while the squadron ORB Form 540 stated that eleven crews would be operating against Münster, while one, presumably a freshman, had been assigned to a different target. Form 541, on the other hand, listed fourteen crews for Münster, and all departed Feltwell between 23.00 and 23.20 with S/Ls Freeman and Peters-Smith the senior pilots on duty. They headed for the coast in fine weather and lost the services of Sgt Butt and crew to an unspecified technical problem. The favourable conditions persisted for the duration of the outward flight across the North Sea to the Frisian Islands and provided clear skies over the target area. The lack of a coherent defence from the ground allowed crews to run more-or-less unmolested across the aiming-point to deliver their bombs, those from 57 Squadron from 4,000 to 14,000 feet between 01.06 and 02.02. The aiming-point was claimed to be completely demolished, the marshalling yards were also left in a damaged state, and what was believed to be a gas works erupted, a local report confirming that many bombs had, indeed, fallen within the town. It was during this operation that Sgt James Ward of 75(NZ) Squadron earned a Victoria Cross by climbing out onto the wing of his Wellington to quell a fire.

Münster's ordeal was not yet over, however, and ten 57 Squadron crews joined seven from 75(NZ) Squadron in the briefing room on the 8th to learn the details of that night's return. They were part of an all-3 Group force of forty-nine aircraft, which took off in the late evening in fine weather conditions that would hold all the way to the target. The 57 Squadron element departed Feltwell between 23.05 and 23.40 with S/L Freeman the senior pilot on duty and lost Sgt Stanford and crew to a loose engine cowling that affected control of the Wellington. The others pressed on to the target area to find ground haze and some of the previous night's fires still burning to provide a reference for the bombing run. Seven carried out their attacks from 7,000 to 15,000 feet between 01.28 and 02.28, while the crews of S/L Freeman and Sgt Cleaver dive-bombed from 8,000 to 4,000 feet and 7,000 to 2,000 feet respectively. At debriefing, all reported bombing in the target area and contributing to fires in the town and the marshalling yards that were described as more numerous and more concentrated than those of the previous night.

A new Air Ministry directive issued on the 9th signalled an end to the maritime diversion, which had been in force since March. It was now assessed that the enemy's transportation system and the morale of its civilian population represented the weakest points, and that Peirse should make them his priority. A new list of targets was drawn up, which included all of the main railway centres ringing the industrial Ruhr, destruction of which would inhibit the import of raw materials, and the export of finished products. Railways were relatively precise targets, and were to be attacked during the moon period, while, on moonless nights, the Rhine cities of Cologne, Düsseldorf and Duisburg would be easier to locate for "area" attacks. During periods of less favourable weather conditions, Peirse was to launch operations against more distant objectives in northern, eastern and southern Germany, while still making the occasional concession to the U-Boot campaign and continuing to divert a proportion of the Command's resources to the ongoing situation of the enemy "fleet in being" at Brest.

Cologne was the destination for ninety-eight Wellingtons and thirty-two Hampdens on the night of the 10/11th, and crews were briefed for two aiming-points in the city centre and another, the Klöckner-Humboldt mechanical engineering works situated on the East Bank of the Rhine in the industrial Deutz district, where aero-engines and heavy and tracked vehicles were produced for the Wehrmacht and were served by the nearby Kalk and Gremberg marshalling yards. 3 Group provided sixty-two Wellingtons, of which ten represented 57 Squadron, and they departed Feltwell between 22.55 and 23.10 with S/L Peters-Smith the senior pilot on duty. Adverse weather conditions seriously affected the operation, and fewer than half of those setting out would report reaching and bombing the target. Those arriving over what they believed to be Cologne found the ground obscured by thick haze and had little idea of their true position. Most spent a considerable time stooging around in the hope of catching a break in the cloud and two crews glimpsed an autobahn and a river before bombing on estimated positions. They delivered their bombs over a wide area from 5,000 to 16,000 feet between 01.40 and 02.52, some recognising Bonn and Koblenz as the recipients, and sources in Cologne confirmed the raid as a complete failure.

The ports of Bremen, Vegesack (north-west of Bremen) and Emden were posted as the targets on the night of the 13/14th, 3 Group providing forty-seven Wellingtons for the first-mentioned, each Feltwell squadron making ready eleven Wellingtons. The 57 Squadron element took off between 22.45 and 23.05, with S/L Freeman the senior pilot on duty on a night of adverse weather conditions. Thick, ice and thunder-bearing cloud lay over the entire area from the Dutch coast to the target and would contribute to the early return of ten aircraft. Sgt McGeagh's rear gunner was taken ill, probably as a result of oxygen starvation, and they turned back from north of Amsterdam, leaving the others to press on more in hope than expectation. Six from 57 Squadron released their bombs on e.t.a., or astro-fix from 6,000 to 16,000 feet over the general area of Bremen between 01.34 and 02.30 and observed nothing of the impact, while S/L Freeman and crew bombed the docks at Ijmuiden from 6,000 feet on the way home at 04.10. Sgt Swift and crew were heading home with an empty bomb bay and had begun the North Sea crossing when intercepted by a Ju88, which was seen to crash and burn at 04.45 after a burst of fire from Sgt Polson in the Wellington's rear turret. They were the last to land, at 06.50, after more than eight hours in the air and Sgt Polson would receive the immediate award of a DFM.

Only 3 Group ventured out on the night of the 15/16th, when sending thirty-eight Wellingtons from Feltwell and Marham to the Ruhr city of Duisburg. A dozen 57 Squadron Wellingtons took off between 22.40 and 23.15 with S/L Freeman the senior pilot on duty and headed out in fine weather conditions to encounter a layer of low, thin cloud over the target, which presented the bomb-aimers with a difficult task of establishing their precise position. F/O Martin and crew were still on their way when attacked at 00.44 "von untern hintern", from below and behind by an unidentified enemy aircraft, whose fire killed the rear gunner, Sgt Lane, and caused damage to the port elevator, tailplane, aileron, wing and flaps. A second pass was made from the beam, before the enemy broke off the engagement, and the bombs were dropped on either Düsseldorf or nearby Neuss from 8,000 feet at 00.55. Those reaching the target faced an intense and accurate searchlight and flak response that sent shells to burst at bombing height between 9,000 and 16,000 feet, adding to the difficulties and making it an uncomfortable place over which to be stooging around. The crews of Sgts Green, Durnin, Fryer, Butt and S/L Freeman attacked what they believed was Duisburg from 10,000 to 15,000 feet between 00.48 and 01.20, while P/O Cox and crew carried out a dive attack from 10,000 to release their bombs at 6,000 feet at 01.45. After climbing back up to 11,000 feet they were set upon at 01.59 by a Me110, which attacked from the rear and closed to one hundred yards range before being hit by return fire, stalling and diving for the ground with white smoke pouring from an engine. All on board the Wellington watched it hit the ground and burst into flames to be claimed as a definite kill. Meanwhile, Sgt O'Neill and crew had dropped their bombs on the Hohenbudberg marshalling yards at nearby Krefeld at 01.38, and this may have been the same railway yards attacked by F/L Way and crew some fifty minutes earlier. A garbled W/T message was received from the crew of Sgt Osborne RNZAF in R1624 shortly before the Wellington crashed in Belgium with no survivors. N2784 arrived over Suffolk in a rainstorm and was on approach to Feltwell when it crashed near Brandon some five miles short of the airfield, killing Sgt Rishworth and his crew.

Formation flying practise began for 57 Squadron on the 20th following a stand-down since Duisburg, and it continued on the 21st, almost certainly without its purpose being revealed. Eight crews were summoned to briefing that afternoon to be told that Mannheim was to be their target that night as part of a 3 Group force of thirty-six Wellingtons in company with eight 35 Squadron Halifaxes. They took off between 22.25 and 22.45 with F/L Way the senior pilot on duty and all reached the target area to find clear skies, but extreme darkness in the absence of a moon, and haze to mar the vertical visibility. Nevertheless, the presence of the Rivers Rhine and Neckar provided firm ground features by which to establish their positions, and bombing was carried out in straight and level runs from 9,800 to 16,000 feet between 01.05 and 01.30. The searchlight and flak response was not intense, and this enabled most crews to observe the burst of their 1,000 and 500 pounders in the built-up area, where a number of fires took hold and remained visible for thirty minutes into the return flight. Precisely where the bombs fell is unknown, but a local report claimed that only flares, incendiaries and four high explosive bombs landed in the city, and one of the last-mentioned was a dud.

Formation flying practise continued on the 22nd, followed by a night off and Feltwell was not involved in the return to Mannheim on the night of the 23/24th, which 3 Group supported with thirty-nine Wellingtons plus a handful of freshman crews to bomb the docks and shipping at Ostend and Le Havre. The 57 Squadron crews of Sgts Birch and McGeagh took off for the former at 22.55, and while the latter abandoned their sortie after encountering haze in the target area and brought their five 500 pounders home, the Birch crew delivered theirs from 11,000 feet at 00.10 and observed bursts near the harbour mouth but no detail.

The purpose behind the formation flying training was revealed to the crews at briefings late on the 23rd, the one at Feltwell taken by 57 Squadron's S/L Trevor Freeman, who had served earlier in the war as a junior officer with 75(NZ) Squadron and would shortly take on a training role with 3 Group. He informed the crews that preparations had been ongoing for a number of weeks to carry out an audacious daylight attack on the German warships at Brest under the codename "Operation Sunrise". Scheduled for the 24th, it had been discovered at the last minute that Scharnhorst had slipped away to the La Pallice/La Rochelle region, some two hundred miles further south along the Biscay coast, and this required an adjustment to the original complex plan of attack. The intention had been to send three 90 Squadron Fortress Is in to bomb from 30,000 feet to draw up enemy fighters, while 5 Group Hampdens performed a similar role at a more conventional altitude under an escort of fighters carrying long-range fuel tanks, much in the style of a 2 Group "Circus" operation. Meanwhile, 2 Group Blenheims would create a diversion at Cherbourg, and while this distraction was in progress, it was hoped that Halifaxes and Wellingtons from 1, 3 and 4 Groups could sneak in unopposed to target the ships. Now that Scharnhorst had moved, it was decided to send the Halifax element to deal with her, while the rest of the original plan went ahead at Brest. 4 Group would have a presence at Brest also in the form of eighteen Mk II Wellingtons from 104 and 405 Squadrons, while the Whitley element would act as a cover for the Halifaxes by attacking the town and port of La Pallice.

A force of seventy-nine Wellingtons was assembled, of which thirty-six were provided by 3 Group, among them six each from the Feltwell squadrons. The 57 Squadron element took off in two sections, the first consisting of the crews of S/L Freeman and Sgts O'Neill and Stanford at 10.45 and the second of F/L Way, F/O Martin and Sgt Durnin at 22.50, followed immediately by their Kiwi counterparts. They made their way out over Cornwall in excellent weather conditions to approach the target in vics of three at around 15,000 feet and were able to pick out ground detail as they ran in. Unfortunately, the diversionary measures failed to provide the hoped-for protection, and the Wellingtons were set upon by BF109s and Me110s and were forced to run the gauntlet of intense flak. S/L Freeman's section was first on target, and each watched their four 500lb semi-armour-piercing (SAP) bombs go down from 12,800 feet at 14.55, those of the leader to hit fifty yards to starboard of the aiming point and the others nearby on the dockside. Within seconds, F/L Way's section delivered their attacks from a similar altitude, the leader's and Sgt Durnin's falling two hundred yards short into the water and F/O Martin's unseen but believed to be on land. Ten Wellingtons and two Hampdens were lost to flak and fighters, one of the former belonging to 75(NZ) Squadron, but returning crews claimed six hits on Gneisenau, which were not officially confirmed, and six enemy fighters shot down with a further four damaged.

Operations were not over for the day, and briefings took place at Feltwell, Marham, Oakington, Waterbeach and Wyton for that night's attack on the shipyards at Kiel, to which thirty-one standard Wellingtons were assigned plus four Mk IIs to drop a cookie each on the town. Each Feltwell squadron dispatched five Wellingtons between 22.15 and 22.30, those from 57 Squadron containing all-NCO crews sitting on a variety of high-explosives and incendiary bomb loads. Weather conditions were good, and returning crews reported bombing in the target area and causing a large fire and several smaller ones, which persuaded those at home that a successful operation had taken place. In fact, only a few bombs had hit the town, and the five fatalities occurred in a village. 57 Squadron's R1369 was reported missing over the North Sea and three aircraft were sent in search of survivors on the following morning. It had actually crashed into the sea off the German Frisian Isles and taken with it Sgt Green and three of his crew, leaving the two survivors in enemy hands. The Feltwell squadrons were not involved in 3 Group's contributions to raids on Hamburg and Berlin on the night of the 25/26th or Cologne on the 30/31st, and 57 Squadron ended the month with statistics of eleven operations undertaken, which generated 106 sorties and cost five Wellingtons, four crews and two individual crew members.

During the course of the month the Feltwell station commander, G/C Buckley, was posted to pastures new, and was eventually succeeded by Group Captain John "Speedy" Powell, the gung-ho, high-spirited, uncompromising RAF officer who had relinquished command of 149 Squadron in May. His sometimes-abrasive personality would be in stark contrast to the almost fatherly approach to command of G/C Buckley and 75(NZ) Squadron's W/C Kay and would create a division between him and some of the New Zealanders, which would contribute to a dip in morale. Powell had been very prominent in the propaganda drama film "Target for Tonight", which cast genuine serving Bomber Command personnel in the appropriate roles and starred the legendary W/C Percy "Pick" Pickard as the pilot of F for Freddy, "Speedy" Powell as the squadron commander and G/C "Bull" Staton, the former 10 Squadron commanding officer, as station commander. At his first briefing, to mostly freshman crews, the new station commander's comments implied criticism of the former highly popular and respected New Zealand leadership of 75(NZ) Squadron. After informing his audience that he intended to cut down on petrol and increase bomb loads, a policy which, he may have omitted to explain, came from higher up the chain of command, he reputedly made a callous, and what, for him, was probably a "throw-away" remark intended for impact, the gist of which was, "what are six miserable lives when there's a job to be done". It is said that two crews got up and walked out.

August 1941

The policy of despatching small numbers of aircraft to various targets simultaneously rarely produced effective results, but it would remain the favoured policy throughout the remainder of the year, and, in fact, until a new Commander-in-Chief arrived in 1942 to provide a different direction. Hamburg, Berlin and Kiel were posted as the targets for the first night of operations on the 2nd, the first-two-named supported by 3 Group which detailed respectively fourteen and forty aircraft, all but three of which took off. At 22.05, Feltwell dispatched its only sortie of the night, the 57 Squadron crew of S/L Freeman in W5445, a Mk II Wellington with a cookie in its bomb bay bound for Germany's capital city. They reached their destination to find little cloud but sufficient ground haze to impair the vertical visibility. They had to fly through a forest of searchlight beams as they ran in on the Friedrichstrasse railway station aiming-point located on the East Bank of the Spree, south-east of the city centre, and bombed from 15,000 feet at 02.25 in the face of intense flak. They observed the flash as their 4,000 pounder burst, but no detail, and some fires remained visible for eighty miles into the return journey, which saw them touch down eight hours to the minute after their departure. Flying as second pilot was F/L Warfield, who had arrived recently as a flight commander elect. The impression given by returning crews was of an effective attack, but no post-raid reconnaissance was carried out and there was no report from local sources to provide evidence.

The following night was to bring Hannover into the bomb sights, for which operation the two Feltwell squadrons each made ready ten Wellingtons as part of an all-3 Group force of thirty-four, while Whitleys attacked Frankfurt. The 57 Squadron element took off between 22.05 and 22.50, with S/L Peters-Smith the senior pilot on duty and made their way across the North Sea to a landfall north of Amsterdam. F/O Martin and crew were cruising eastwards about an hour short of their destination when attacked by a night-fighter, the fire from which killed the rear gunner, Sgt Cassells. Evasive action was taken, and the bombs jettisoned from 7,000 feet at 00.28, and the badly damaged T2962 was nursed home to a safe landing. The others reached the target area to find ten-tenths cloud obscuring the ground and bombed on DR, e.t.a., flashes from flak batteries, and the glow of fires from 12,000 to 17,000 feet between 00.57 and 02.10 and returned home with nothing other than bomb bursts and fires to report.

Feltwell was omitted from the Order of Battle on the 5th, when 3 Group detailed sixty-nine Wellingtons for Mannheim and nineteen others for small-scale operations to Karlsruhe and Frankfurt and Boulogne for the freshmen, and all but seven took off. None of the operations resulted in outstanding success, but each achieved a useful degree of damage particularly at Mannheim, where some of the bombing spilled across the Rhine into Ludwigshafen. Acting S/L Foulsham returned to the squadron from 3 Group HQ on the 6th, only to be posted to XV Squadron within days. The same three cities were earmarked for further attention that night, for which Feltwell called both of its squadrons into action, 57 Squadron making ready nine Wellingtons for

Mannheim in an overall 3 Group force of thirty-eight and three for freshman crews to take to Calais. Those bound for the main event took off between 22.20 and 22.35 with S/L Peters-Smith the senior pilot on duty and F/L Warfield flying as his second pilot, leaving the freshman crews of Sgts Birch and Clark and P/O Tong on the ground for a further hour. The weather conditions throughout were unhelpful, and crews had to contend with heavy cloud, thunder, electrical storms and icing. They reached the target area to find it concealed beneath ten-tenths cloud, which precluded any chance of identifying the railway workshops designated as the aiming point but were guided to an extent by the glow of burgeoning fires. The 57 Squadron crews carried out their attacks from 5,000 to 17,000 feet between 01.05 and 01.55, the low height that of P/O Cox and crew who were forced off course by searchlight cones and bombed on the periphery of the fires and bomb flashes. F/L Way and crew witnessed a terrific explosion and blinding flash and somehow observed a bomb burst between the main railway station and the river. Sgt Cleaver and his crew were last heard from at 05.55 reporting that they were about to make a forced-landing. Z8704's position was plotted as still over northern France, and news came through remarkably quickly that they were all now in enemy hands. Meanwhile, Sgt Birch and crew had failed to locate Calais and brought their bombs home, while Sgt Clark and crew dropped four 500 pounders and one SBC of incendiaries from 13,500 feet at 01.16 and P/O Tong and crew a similar load from 10,000 feet at 02.50.

Feltwell sat out 3 Group's involvement in operations against the marshalling yards in Hamm and the Krupp complex in Essen on the night of the 7/8th. The former appeared to be successful and produced a column of smoke rising through 11,000 feet, while the latter was typically scattered and ineffective and produced only minor damage and no casualties. The prospect of poor weather conditions over northern Germany caused a reduction in the numbers of aircraft detailed to attack railway and shipyard aiming-points in Hamburg on the night of the 8/9th, and it was decided to employ only the Feltwell and Marham squadrons. 57 Squadron contributed seven of the twenty-six participating 3 Group Wellingtons, whose crews were briefed to attack the Blohm & Voss shipyards. They took off between 22.05 and 22.15 with F/L Way the senior pilot on duty and carrying either five 500 pounders or a 1,000 pounder, two 500 pounders and one of 250lbs. They crossed the Dutch coast over heavy cloud that accompanied them all the way to the target without once revealing a glimpse of the ground, and all carried out their attacks on e.t.a., from 14,000 to 20,000 feet between 00.56 and 01.48. Sgt O'Neill and crew opted not to waste their bombs and brought them home.

3 Group was handed multiple targets on the 12th, and detailed sixty-five Wellingtons for Hannover, fourteen Wellingtons and three Stirlings for Essen, nine Stirlings and four Wellingtons for Berlin and ten freshman-crewed Wellingtons for Le Havre. According to the Form 540, 57 Squadron prepared eight Mk ICs for Hannover and four for the freshmen and a single Mk II for Berlin, while the Form 541 lists ten for Hannover and just two for Le Havre, which appears to be correct. They all departed Feltwell between 21.00 and 21.30 with S/L Peters-Smith the senior pilot on duty and F/L Warfield undertaking his first sortie as crew captain. The bombing and landing times of S/L Peters-Smith were confused by the squadron scribe with those of the Le Havre duo and have been discounted. They headed for their respective targets in fine weather conditions, which would deteriorate somewhat over enemy territory. Thunderstorms over northern Germany had dissipated by the time the bombers reached the target area, leaving slight cloud and ground haze, which was sufficient to obscure ground detail. The main railway station

aiming-point at Hannover could not be identified and bombs were delivered across the built-up area without precision, the 57 Squadron crews carrying out their attacks from 11,000 to 16,000 feet between 23.45 and 00.35 before setting off for home with little genuine impression of the results. Meanwhile, F/L Way and crew had delivered their cookie at Berlin from 14,500 feet at 00.30 and the freshman crews of Sgts Hutchison and Ravenhill their three 500 pounders and two SBCs each at Le Havre from 9,000 and 10,000 feet at 23.24 and 23.35 respectively.

S/L Freeman's outstanding service had been recognised by higher authority and he was rewarded with a command of his own, 115 Squadron at Marham, where he would succeed W/C Evans-Evans on the 14th. On the evening of the 13th, a farewell party was held in King's Lynn. More than three hundred sorties were planned for the night of the 14/15th, 285 of them divided among the cities of Hannover, Braunschweig (Brunswick) and Magdeburg, which lie in a line from north-west to southeast respectively covered by a little over eighty miles. Railway installations were the objectives at each location for 152 aircraft at Hannover, eighty-one Hampdens at Braunschweig and fifty-two assorted aircraft at Magdeburg. 3 Group contributed sixty-seven Wellingtons to the first-mentioned, for what was to be the final trial of Gee before the device was withdrawn and put into full production for an intended distribution in early 1942. 57 Squadron fuelled and bombed up thirteen Wellingtons, eleven Mk ICs for Hannover, a cookie-carrying Mk II for S/L Peters-Smith to take to Magdeburg and another Mk IC for the freshman crew of Sgt Ravenhill, whose target was the docks and shipping at Boulogne. They departed Feltwell together between 21.15 and 21.40 with S/L Peters-Smith the first off the ground and Sgt Ravenhill last and flew out over heavy cloud, which dispersed to an extent over northern Germany to leave patches that combined with ground haze to partially obscure the railway station aiming-points. Fires were already evident in Hannover as the Feltwell crews arrived, those from 57 Squadron identifying the built-up area through gaps in the cloud and delivering their loads from 10,000 to 16,000 feet between 23.47 and 00.24, some observing them detonate and others not. They left behind them many fires but no detail concerning damage, and no report was forthcoming from local sources to provide clarity. S/L Peters-Smith and crew found Magdeburg completely concealed by cloud, and watched their cookie fall from 12,000 feet at 00.59 and quickly disappear from view, while Sgt Ravenhill and crew failed to locate Boulogne beneath the white stuff and returned their bombs to store.

Feltwell was not required to provide aircraft on the 16th for 3 Group's operation by fifty-four Wellingtons against railway targets in Duisburg, while other forces targeted Cologne and Düsseldorf. Results were poor, but 3 Group was given the opportunity to rectify that in a return to Duisburg twenty-four hours later. They were part of a force of forty-one aircraft, twenty-seven provided by 3 Group, a number that had been reduced late on because of deteriorating weather conditions. 57 Squadron launched thirteen Wellingtons from Feltwell between 23.25 and 00.15 with S/L Peters-Smith the senior pilot on duty and they met with heavy cloud over the target, which precluded any chance of identifying ground detail. Crews were reduced to bombing more in hope than in expectation, and although a number of bursts, flashes and fires were reported, the attack was indiscriminate and ineffective. P/O Cox and crew failed to locate Duisburg and dropped their bombs on aerodromes in Holland on the way home, while Sgt Hutchison and crew retained theirs to return to store.

The 18th was the day on which the Butt Report on the Command's operational effectiveness, was released, and it sent shock waves reverberating around the War Cabinet and the Air Ministry.

Having taken into account around four thousand bombing photos produced during night operations in June and July, it concluded that only a fraction of bombs had fallen within miles of their intended targets, and the poorest performances had been over the Ruhr. It was a massive blow to morale, and demonstrated that thus far, the efforts of the crews had been almost totally ineffective in reducing Germany's capacity to wage war. Exaggerated claims of success born out of enthusiasm on the part of the crews had begun with the very first bombing of German territory in March 1940, but now, incontrovertible proof was to hand, and it would not only unjustly blight the period of the incumbent C-in-C's tenure, but also lead to calls for the dissolution of Bomber Command and the redistribution of its resources to other theatres of operations.

The return of adverse weather conditions allowed limited operational activity over the ensuing week, and the Feltwell squadrons remained at home while others from 3 Group participated in yet another attack on Duisburg railway installations on the night of the 18/19th, Kiel on the 19/20th, Mannheim on the 22/23rd and Karlsruhe on the 25/26th. Not one of them was successful, and the early return of fifteen out of forty-nine from the last-mentioned operation was an indication that all was not well. Feltwell was roused from its inactivity on the 26th, when each of its resident Squadrons made ready fourteen Wellingtons, twenty-two for the main event at Cologne and six for freshman sorties to Boulogne. The Cologne-bound 57 Squadron element of twelve took off between 22.50 and 23.20 with F/L Warfield the senior pilot on duty and were part of a 3 Group contribution of forty aircraft in an overall force of ninety-nine. P/O Tong and crew were back on the ground forty minutes after leaving it having had the pilot's escape hatch blow open on take-off. The others encountered cloud over the target with occasional gaps, through which some crews were able to identify ground detail. Bombs were dropped in the general target area from 10,000 to 16,000 feet between 01.15 and 02.15, but, other than bursts, flashes and a number of fires, one described as large, there was little useful information to pass on to the intelligence section at debriefing. The Boulogne-bound crews of Sgt McGeagh and F/Sgt Purdy departed Feltwell at 01.15 and 01.20 respectively, each carrying four 500 pounders one of 250lbs and two SBCs of incendiaries and encountered ten-tenths cloud over the French coast. They delivered their attacks from 13,000 and 10,000 feet at 02.55 and 03.20, Sgt McGeagh's incendiaries setting off a line of fires.

On the 27th, the squadron bade farewell to S/L Peters-Smith on his posting to 311(Czech) Squadron at East Wretham to act as the British representative and flight commander. It would be a temporary absence from the squadron, to which he would return early in 1942. The main operation on the night of the 28/29th involved a force of 118 aircraft targeting railway installations in Duisburg. 3 Group detailed forty-eight Wellingtons without calling upon the Feltwell brigade to take part and a further ten for freshman crews briefed to attack the docks and shipping at Ostend, and all but six would take off. The 57 Squadron freshman crews of Sgts Esler and Paul departed Feltwell at 21.15 and 21.20 bound for the Belgian coast. Sgt Paul and crew failed to locate Ostend and jettisoned their bombs, while the Esler crew dropped theirs from 11,000 feet at 22.53 and watched them burst across the outer harbour.

Two major operations were planned over southern Germany for the night of the 29/30th, the larger, by 143 aircraft against Frankfurt, and the other, by ninety-four Wellingtons at Mannheim, forty miles to the south. 3 Group contributed seventy Wellingtons, twenty at Feltwell, from where the eleven representing 57 Squadron took off between 20.10 and 20.30 with W/C Southwell the senior pilot on duty. Sgt Durnin and crew turned back after a bolt of lightning temporarily blinded one of the gunners and caused him to collapse, leaving the others to press on and contend with another night of unfavourable weather conditions. The target was concealed beneath ten-tenths cloud, and none was able to positively identify it, the 57 Squadron crews bombing on estimated positions from 6,000 to 17,000 feet between 22.55 and 00.20, aided by the flashes from flak batteries. W/C Southwell descended to 5,000 feet, from where the marshalling yards were identified and attacked, but the bombs fell short at 23.59. Sgt Butt and crew brought their bombs back after failing to identify the primary or suitable alternative target. A local report from Mannheim confirmed a scattered and largely ineffective raid, which caused little damage.

Feltwell was not called into action on the last night of the month when 3 Group contributed forty-nine Wellingtons to a force of 103 to attack Cologne. The region was covered by thick cloud and few bombs found the mark. During the course of the month the squadron operated against sixteen targets and dispatched ninety-six sorties for the loss of a single Wellington and crew.

September 1941

The 1st of the new month brought better weather conditions over western Germany, and Cologne was posted to host its second raid on consecutive nights for which thirty-four Wellingtons were made ready at Marham and Honington. They were to share the airspace over the Rhineland with twenty Hampdens from 5 Group and those reaching the target benefitted from favourable visibility, despite which, few bombs fell in the city and damage was minimal. On the 2nd, 3 Group detailed fifty-three Wellingtons and a Stirling for Frankfurt, thirteen Stirlings for Berlin and seven freshmen for Ostend, all but six of which would take off. 57 Squadron briefed fourteen crews for the first-mentioned as part of an overall force of 126 aircraft and dispatched them from Feltwell between 20.20 and 20.40 with F/L Way the senior pilot on duty and the crews of Sgts O'Neill and Hutchison in cookie-carrying Mk IIs. In contrast to recent experiences, cloudless skies in the target area provided conditions conducive to accurate bombing and enabled many crews to pick out the marshalling yards aiming-point. The 57 Squadron crews mostly arrived early in the proceedings before any fires had broken out and bombed from 10,000 to 15,000 feet between 23.10 and 23.42. Sgt Ravenhill and crew attacked Wiesbaden, some fifteen miles to the west of Frankfurt, from 15,000 feet at 00.20 and were not alone, while Sgt O'Neill and crew bombed at Mannheim from 14,000 feet at 00.26. A number of fires were developing as the bombers retreated to the west, and all from 57 Squadron made it back to home airspace. It was at that point that W5434 struck a house and crashed at Stapleford near Cambridge at 03.20 and burst into flames, killing Sgt Hutchison RAAF and his crew, three of whom were members of the RCAF. Despite the confidence of returning crews, a report from Frankfurt suggested that the raid had failed to make an impact.

Brest had taken something of a back seat since the Operation Sunrise attack in July, but it was time to remind the enemy's resident cruisers that the Admiralty was still pressing for their destruction, and a force of 140 aircraft was assembled on the 3rd for an attack that night. While the Feltwell squadrons remained at home, 3 Group dispatched forty-one Wellingtons and four Stirlings, which, after the 1, 4 and 5 Group elements had been recalled because of worsening weather conditions, continued on alone and delivered an attack on estimated positions through an effective smoke screen.

In the face of continuing adverse weather conditions, and in order to be able to put up a maximum effort on the following night, the number of 3 Group participants for an operation against a "special" target on the 6th was reduced to twenty-seven in an overall force of eighty-six aircraft from 3, 4 and 5 Groups. The target was situated on the north-eastern rim of the Ruhr at Marl-Hüls and was referred to by Bomber Command as a synthetic rubber factory at Hüls. Known locally as the "Buna" works because of the chemicals, butadiene and natrium employed in the manufacturing process, the Chemische Werke-Hüls GmbH had been formed in 1938 after its acquisition by the I G (Interessen Gemeinschaft or common interest group) Farben company in association with the Bergwerkgesellschaft Hibernia A G. Whether or not it was employing slave workers at this time is uncertain but highly probable, and the I G Farben company would become infamous for drawing its labour force from concentration camps and forcing tens of thousands to toil under the harshest conditions at its many manufacturing sites across Germany. The entire 3 Group element was provided by Feltwell, where 57 Squadron made ready fourteen Wellingtons and loaded them with a variety of bombs and incendiaries before sending them on their way between 20.40 and 21.15 with W/C Southwell and the newly promoted S/Ls Warfield and Way the senior pilots on duty. They entered enemy airspace north of Amsterdam and Sgt Durnin and crew had crossed the frontier into Germany when coming under attack by a night-fighter, which damaged an engine and persuaded them to jettison their load ten miles north-west of Münster at 23.10 and head for home. The others reached the target area, where they were greeted by clear skies and, because of its location, many searchlights operating in cones. Despite the favourable conditions, not all crews were able to identify the aiming-point, but many of those from 57 Squadron picked out factory buildings and chimney stacks and released their payloads from 6,000 to 13,000 feet between 23.15 and 00.26. Fires were reported in the built-up area and a large explosion witnessed by Sgt O'Neill and crew sent white smoke several hundred feet into the air. Five Whitleys and two Wellingtons failed to return, one of the latter, Z8794 belonging to 57 Squadron and coming down somewhere in the Ruhr area with no survivors from the crew of Sgt Lake.

Feltwell was invited to play only a minor role in a major night of operations on the 7th, which involved the detailing of seventy-five aircraft for Berlin, twenty-two for Kiel and fifteen freshmen for Boulogne. 57 Squadron dispatched the crews of Sgts Gray and Owens to Boulogne at 20.15 and welcomed them back three-and-a-half hours later to report successful sorties. At debriefing they reported bombing as briefed from 8,000 feet either side of 22.00 and observing their six 500 pounders and two SBCs each detonate across the docks 6 and 7, adding to the fires that were already burning and emitting columns of black smoke. The main events at Berlin and Kiel produced encouraging results by inflicting damage upon war industry factories and shipyards.

Kassel, the industrial city located some eighty miles to the east of the Ruhr, had been an occasional target since the summer of 1940, and was home to the Henschel Company, the presence of whose numerous manufacturing sites dominated the city and employed eight thousand workers in addition to a large number of slaves. Aside from building the Dornier Do17Z bomber under license, Henschel was the main producer of the Panzer III tank and the Tiger I and II, as well as narrow-gauge locomotives. The Fieseler aircraft company also had a manufacturing plant in the city, where it built BF109s and FW190s under licence, but was also responsible for the design of what would become the V-1 flying bomb. A force of ninety-six aircraft was assembled, 3 Group initially detailing forty-six Wellingtons for the main event and eight for freshman crews to take to Cherbourg, and all but six would take off. Eleven 57 Squadron Wellingtons had a variety of ordnance winched into their bomb bays and departed Feltwell between 20.00 and 20.20 with S/L Warfield the senior pilot on duty. Sgt Birch and crew turned back with engine problems after some ninety minutes, leaving the others to press on to reach the target area, where the skies were clear and some ground detail could be identified. The River Fulda provided a strong pinpoint to guide crews to the aiming point, where those from 57 Squadron bombed from 6,000 to 13,000 feet between 23.22 and 00.10. It is remarkable how impressions differed according to crew reports, some observing no fires on their arrival, while others witnessed many, some large, at or close to the same time. There were certainly numerous fires by the end of the raid, which took place with surprisingly little response from the ground, and not a single aircraft was lost. The consensus among returning crews was of a successful operation and local sources confirmed serious damage to a railway-wagon works and an optical instruments factory, while listing the main railway station as one of the public buildings to be hit.

Orders were received on 1, 3 and 4 Group stations on the 10th to prepare for a trip across the Alps that night, some to attack the arsenal at Turin, while others went for the main railway station. The Feltwell squadrons were not represented among the fifty-one 3 Group participants in the seventy-six-strong force, the Wellington element of which was restricted to only 1,750lbs of bombs because of the distance and need to maintain altitude to cross the Alps. There were no early returns on a night of favourable weather conditions, and the only impediments to accurate bombing were haze and drifting smoke as the attack developed. All but one 3 Group Wellington returned safely to enable their crews to report bomb bursts in the city centre and on the Fiat steelworks and many fires, some large, produced a glow in the sky that remained visible for sixty miles into the return flight.

Germany's Baltic coast was the destination for the majority of the aircraft operating on the night of the 11/12th, fifty-six of them assigned to the Heinkel works at Rostock, fifty-five to the shipyards in Kiel, and thirty-two 4 Group Whitleys to the docks at Warnemünde. 3 Group detailed forty-seven Wellingtons for Kiel and five for freshman crews to take to Le Havre, and 57 Squadron supported both endeavours with eleven crews and one respectively. Sgt Gray and crew took off first at 19.50 before heading south for the Channel crossing, leaving those bound for the Baltic coast to depart Feltwell between 20.00 and 20.20 with S/L Warfield the senior pilot on duty. Sgt Durnin and crew turned back early because of an engine issue, while Sgt Gray and crew found Le Havre to be completely cloud-covered and brought their bombs back. The crews of Sgts Birch and Stanford failed to identify Kiel through what they described as eight-tenths cloud, and bombed searchlight concentrations as last resort targets. Other crews reported clear conditions over Kiel with haze obscuring some ground detail, but they were guided by the fires already burning and delivered their bombs from 8,000 to 13,500 feet between 23.33 and 00.50. Bursts were observed across the target area and fires were reported, but it proved difficult to determine the fall of the bombs and it was left to local sources to confirm some damage in the Deutsche Werke U-Boot yards and in the town, although nothing of major significance.

Frankfurt was posted as the target on the 12th for a force of 130 aircraft, for which 3 Group detailed sixty-three plus fifteen for a freshman raid on the docks and shipping at Cherbourg and all but two took off. The Feltwell squadrons were not called into action for what turned out to be a scattered raid through cloud, which caused damage predominantly to housing in the city and nearby Offenbach. All groups called briefings on the 13th for the next round of operations against Brest and its resident Scharnhorst, Gneisenau and Prinz Eugen. A force of 147 aircraft of six different types was assembled, fifty-five of the Wellingtons and four Stirlings provided by 3 Group, of which ten failed to take off. 57 Squadron made ready nine Wellingtons for the main event, and the crews were handed the Prinz Eugen as their specific target, while the 75(NZ) Squadron crews were briefed to attack Scharnhorst and Gneisenau. According to the ORB, P/O Cox and crew had been assigned to Lorient, seventy-five miles further south, and had a Colonel Freemantle on board as a passenger. They departed Feltwell together between 21.45 and 22.15 with S/L Warfield the senior pilot on duty and immediately lost Sgt Gray and crew to a case of pilot error after he throttled back too early. R1792 struggled the mile or two to Methwold before coming to earth with enough force to write it off, happily without crew casualties. The others pressed on to the target, where two aircraft had arrived twenty-minutes early and alerted the defences to the approaching raid. By the time that the main element was ready to run in on the aiming points, they were already concealed beneath an effective smokescreen and crews were forced to bomb on estimated positions, the 57 Squadron crews from 6,000 to 10,000 feet between 00.51 and 01.13. Sgt Stanford and crew saw their cookie detonate on a dock east of Grande Bassin du Nord and in the light of flares a few others plotted the fall of their bombs into the general target area. The 3 Group ORB made no mention of Lorient, where P/O Cox and crew delivered their attack from 10,000 feet at 01.45 and were not alone over this location, where U-Boot slipways existed.

Hamburg was posted as the main target on the 15th and the railway stations and shipyards designated as the aiming-points for a force of 169 aircraft drawn from all groups. It was a night of excellent conditions that would assist navigation and afford unlimited visibility under cloudless skies. The favoured route made landfall on the west coast of the Schleswig-Holstein peninsula. from where they would continue eastwards to the Neumünster area to leave a thirty-mile due-south-run to the target. 3 Group contributed fifty-seven Wellington and four Stirlings to the main event and nineteen other aircraft for freshman crews to employ against the docks and shipping at Le Havre, 57 Squadron providing seven and four Wellingtons respectively. The latter element departed Feltwell first between 19.00 and 19.25, followed by those bound for Germany's second city between 19.40 and 20.10 with P/O Swift the only commissioned pilot on duty. Sgt Durnin and crew had reached a point some twenty miles east of Westerhever when they turned back for an unspecified reason and jettisoned their bombs. The others found searchlights to be plentiful, but the flak strangely quiet, possibly because the majority of the batteries lined both banks of the Elbe, which acted as a main artery into the heart of the city and was avoided if possible. The skies over Hamburg were clear, but this allowed searchlight glare to mask ground detail and have an impact on aiming point identification, which caused the bombing to be scattered over many parts of the city. Five of the 57 Squadron crews carried out their bombing runs from 9,000 to 17,000 feet between 23.15 and 23.45, while Sgt McGeagh and crew attacked Cuxhaven from 10,500 feet at 23.35 after straying off track and leaving themselves insufficient time to reach Hamburg. On return with a flap problem, Sgt Witherington landed X9923 at Marham at 03.15 and collided with R3153 of 218 Squadron, which was parked on its dispersal pan. Both aircraft burst into flames and were consumed by fire, and Sgt Witherington and his wireless operator, Sgt Clark, lost their lives. Returning crews reported fires visible for some distance, and local sources confirmed seven large conflagrations among twenty-six fire incidents, with damage in various parts of the city. The freshman raid on Le Havre had been unusually successful, and at debriefing the 57 Squadron crews reported attacking from 6,750 to 10,000 feet between 21.12 and 21.30 and observing bomb bursts and fires across the docks and much smoke. The Feltwell community had to deal with the sad news that 75(NZ) Squadron's Sgt James Ward VC RNZAF had failed to return, and his death would be confirmed in time.

P/Os Cox and Swift had been declared tour-expired and a farewell dinner was held on the evening of the 16th to bid them "bon voyage" before their departure for instructional duties. S/L Peters-Smith's navigator, P/O Jennings, was also present ahead of his posting overseas. Meanwhile, Marham, Mildenhall and Waterbeach provided thirty-eight Wellingtons in a force of fifty-five assigned to attack Karlsruhe after an intended raid on Berlin had been cancelled because of doubts about the weather. Extreme darkness created difficulties and only thirty-seven crews reported bombing the primary target, the remainder seeking alternatives. Feltwell, Stradishall and Wyton were called into action on the 17th to provide thirty-eight Wellingtons for a return to Karlsruhe, a city located between Saarbrücken to the north-west and Stuttgart to the south-east close to the frontier with France. It was a 3 Group show, for which 57 Squadron made ready ten Wellingtons and another for the freshman crew of Sgt Johnson to take to Le Havre. The latter took off first at 18.50 and would arrive back in the circuit five hours later to report jettisoning their six 500 pounders and two SBCs into the sea. The others took off between 19.20 and 19.40 with S/L Warfield the senior pilot on duty and headed south for the Channel crossing and the flight across France to enter Germany north of Strasbourg. They arrived in the target area to find good visibility and were able to pick out ground features, particularly the railway station, among the fires already burning. All but one carried out their attacks from 5,500 to 9,800 feet and only Sgt Gray and crew allowed themselves the luxury of height at 14,000 feet from where bomb bursts were observed all over the built-up area from north to south. Several fires were burning as they turned away, one in the city centre described as large.

3 Group contributed thirty-eight Wellingtons and Stirlings to a force of seventy-two aircraft for an inconclusive raid on Stettin on the night of the 19/20th, while Feltwell remained inactive. A force of seventy-four aircraft was prepared for Berlin on the 20th, and another of thirty-four for Frankfurt-an-Oder, a city situated some fifty miles east-south-east of the capital on the border with Poland (not to be confused with Frankfurt-am-Main in southern Germany). The number of 3 Group aircraft detailed and dispatched is uncertain as a recall signal was issued to those bound for Germany because of deteriorating weather conditions at home, and the ORB recorded only those failing to respond. These were from the stations of Feltwell, Stradishall and Oakington, which between them sent twenty-eight Wellingtons to Berlin, ten to Frankfurt-an-Oder and seven to Ostend. 57 Squadron had briefed four crews for Berlin, six for Frankfurt, including that of S/L Warfield, and the freshman crew of P/O Walters for Ostend, and they took off together between 19.20 and 19.35 before heading for their respective targets. P/O Walters and crew attacked Ostend docks form 11,000 feet at 22.29 and reported the burst of their 500 pounders and incendiaries among burning buildings.

According to the excellent Bomber Command War Diaries by Martin Middlebrook and Chris Everitt, ten Wellingtons pressed on towards Berlin, but none arrived and all bombed alternative targets. However, the 57 Squadron ORB recorded that the crews of Sgt McGeagh, P/O Tong and F/O Martin attacked Berlin from 5,000 to 13,000 feet between 23.05 and 23.20 and only Sgt Durnin and crew failed to reach it after engine trouble forced them to turn back and bomb an aerodrome at Bergen-Alkmaar close to the Dutch coast. R1271 failed to arrive back after the McGeagh crew had sent a signal, "on fire, losing height", but, fortunately, a fix had been established and the position of the ditched Wellington plotted off the Yorkshire coast, from where all but one member of the crew would be picked up and landed at Grimsby on the 22nd. While the above operation had been taking place at Berlin, the crews of S/L Warfield and P/O Miller and Sgts Backhouse, Johnson and Owens had carried out their attacks on Frankfurt from 6,500 to 11,000 feet between 22.50 and 23.10, while Sgt Ruttledge and crew claimed to have bombed the outskirts of Worms. This could only be possible if they had navigated their way towards Frankfurt-am-Main in southern Germany in error for Frankfurt-an-der-Oder in north-eastern Germany, which seems hardly possible. R1706 returned from Frankfurt at 02.00 in the hands of Sgt Backhouse and was found to be so badly damaged that it was deemed to be beyond economical repair.

On the 24th, acting F/O Martin was granted the acting rank of flight lieutenant, which gave him the status of deputy flight commander. Orders were received on the 26th to prepare for operations against the port of Genoa in northern Italy, the German cities of Mannheim and Cologne, while freshman crews targeted the port of Emden on Germany's north-western coast. Genoa frequently acted as the base for the Italian fleet and was home to the Ansaldo engineering company, which was to Italy what Krupp was to Germany. 3 Group was to support all but the Mannheim undertaking and made ready forty-three Wellingtons and seven Stirlings for Italy, fifteen Wellingtons and eight Stirlings for Cologne and sixteen Wellingtons and two Stirlings for Emden. 57 Squadron dispatched eight Wellingtons for Genoa led by W/C Southwell and three for Cologne, but a recall signal was picked up by all but a single 311 Squadron crew, who reached and bombed Genoa, while the others turned for home and jettisoned their loads.

Genoa was posted again on the 28th for a 3 Group show involving thirty-nine Wellingtons and two Stirlings, the crews of which were given the Ansaldo engineering works, producers of rolling stock and railway control equipment, as their aiming point. A second operation, against the main railway station and marshalling yards at Frankfurt-am-Main was planned as a joint operation by 3 and 5 Groups, 3 Group to provide fourteen Wellingtons, while Emden was again the destination for six Wellingtons and a Stirling crewed by freshmen. The Feltwell station commander, G/C J A "Speedy" Powell, put his name at the top of the Order of Battle for Genoa, and gathered together an experienced crew, which included F/L Watkins from 3 Group HQ as navigator. 57 Squadron's eight Wellingtons departed Feltwell between 18.55 and 20.00 with S/L Warfield the senior pilot on duty, and after climbing out, seven of them headed south, six bound for Italy and Sgt Young and crew for Frankfurt, while Sgt Price and crew set an easterly course to Emden on Germany's north-western coast. P/O Tong and crew dropped out early because of engine problems, but the others crossed the Alps to find eight-tenths cloud over the target, through which they delivered their attacks from 9,000 to 11,000 feet between 23.50 and 01.29, some after making a positive identification based on ground features and fires. Sgt Young and crew identified Frankfurt by the rivers and ran across the city from south-east to north-west under clear skies to deliver their cookie from 7,000 feet at 22.47, observing it to overshoot. By this time, Sgt Price and crew had identified the Binnenhafen (inner harbour) at Emden and had bombed it from 13,000 feet at 22.05 without observing the results. S/L Warfield was given the option to divert on return because of adverse weather at Feltwell, but elected to attempt a landing, which resulted in Z8789 tipping on its nose and catching fire at 05.35. The crew scrambled clear, S/L Warfield and two others with minor facial burns, which were treated in hospital. Absent from debriefing were Sgt Paul and his crew, who are presumed to have come down in the sea in Z8868.

Orders were received across the Command on the 29th for operations against Stettin, now Szczecin in Poland, and the Altona marshalling yards in Hamburg city centre, for which forces of 139 and ninety-three aircraft respectively were assembled. In the absence of a Feltwell involvement, 3 Group detailed forty Wellingtons and ten Stirlings for Stettin, thirteen Wellingtons for Hamburg and six freshmen for Le Havre, all but four of which took off. Good bombing results were claimed by the Stettin force, while searchlight glare hampered efforts at Hamburg and that operation achieved only modest results.

The same two targets were posted on the following day for reduced forces of eighty-two aircraft for Hamburg and forty Wellingtons for Stettin, 3 Group supporting both and detailing thirty-six Wellingtons for Stettin, eleven for Hamburg and six for freshman crews to take to Cherbourg, all but four of which took off. 57 Squadron briefed five crews for Stettin, Sgt Johnson and crew for Hamburg and F/L Donaldson and crew for Cherbourg, the last-mentioned having arrived on posting from 149 Squadron on the 26th. They took off together between 18.50 and 19.15 with F/L Martin the senior pilot on duty and while the Donaldson crew headed for the south coast, the others set an easterly course for the North Sea crossing. As P/O Miller and crew crossed the German coast north of Hamburg, X9874 was hit by flak and damaged further by a night-fighter, which persuaded them to jettison their load north of Hamburg at 21.25 and return home. It was probably at around the same time that Sgt Johnson and crew ran into trouble in the Mk II Wellington, W5445, and confirmation was received eventually via the Red Cross that they were on extended leave in a PoW camp. The others arrived over the Baltic coast to find Stettin under clear skies but shrouded to an extent by ground haze and carried out their attacks from 5,500 to 10,000 feet between 22.55 and 23.20. Bomb bursts were observed close to the marshalling yards and bridgehead aiming points and at least one large red fire had developed along with several smaller ones by the time the bombers turned away to leave a rising pall of black smoke. The impression was of a successful raid, while only modest results were obtained at Hamburg. F/L Donaldson and crew returned safely from Cherbourg to report bombing from 8,500 feet at 21.20 and observing several fires in the docks area.

It had not been a good month for the squadron, which been involved at twenty-three targets and dispatched 123 sorties for the loss of nine Wellingtons, five complete crews, a pilot and one other crew member.

October 1941

There was little activity for 3 Group at the start of the month other than on the night of the 3/4th, when a small-scale attack on Brest had been posted along with freshman raids on Dunkerque, Antwerp and Rotterdam. 7 Squadron put up nine Stirlings for Brest while twenty-eight, twenty-one and twenty-two aircraft respectively were detailed for the freshman operations. 57 Squadron briefed the crews of F/L Donaldson, P/O Watson and Sgts Donnelly and Jeffries for Dunkerque and sent them on their way from Feltwell at 18.50. They all arrived in the target area to find several fires already established and faced a spirited searchlight and flak defence as they delivered their six 500 pounders and two SBCs each from 8,000 to 10,000 feet between 20.00 and 20.10. They returned safely after barely three hours aloft and at debriefing reported bursts across docks 4, 6, 7 and 8, but had been prevented by searchlight dazzle from making a detailed assessment of results.

There were no operations between the 5th and the 10th, as adverse weather conditions kept the entire Command on the ground, and, when they resumed on the night of the 10/11th, Essen and Cologne were the main objectives. Forces of seventy-eight and sixty-nine aircraft respectively were made ready, of which forty-one Wellingtons and six Stirlings were provided by 3 Group for the latter along with twenty-two from Marham assigned to Bordeaux and thirteen freshmen for Rotterdam. 57 Squadron made ready a dozen Wellingtons for Cologne and one for the freshman crew of Sgt Jeffries, who were first away at 23.00 to be followed between 23.40 and 00.10 by the others led by S/L Warfield. All reached the target area to find a few fires already burning and up to nine-tenths low cloud with a number of gaps, and that was sufficient to prevent the crews of P/O Watson and Sgts Donnelly and Ruttledge from making a positive identification. They bombed unidentified built-up areas as last resort targets, leaving their colleagues to attend to the primary objective, which they attacked from 5,000 to 12,000 feet between 02.20 and 02.48 in the face of intense anti-aircraft fire. Not all were able to plot the fall of their bombs, but bursts were observed by some on both sides of the Rhine and fires were reported to be developing. X9756 crashed in the target area killing the crew of Sgt Backhouse and Z8897 came down not far away with no survivors from the crew of Sgt Young. Sgt Jeffries and crew attacked the docks at Rotterdam from a lowly 3,000 feet at 02.37 and were denied sight of the results as they attempted to escape the searchlight beam that ensnared them immediately afterwards.

A busy night of operations was announced across the Command on the 12th, the largest of which, involving 152 aircraft, would bring the first major raid of the war on the southern city of Nuremberg, the scene of massive Nazi rallies during and after Hitler's rise to power in the 1930s and where the Siemens-Schuckert Werke aero-engine factory was among the aiming points. A second force of ninety-nine Wellingtons from 1 and 3 Groups and Hampdens from 5 Group was assigned to Bremen, while 5 Group sent the bulk of its Hampden force, amounting to seventy-nine of the type plus eleven Manchesters to attack the "Buna" synthetic rubber works at Marl-Hüls. 3 Group contributed seventy Wellingtons and ten Stirlings to the Nuremberg force and twenty-six Wellingtons for Bremen plus a dozen Wellingtons for freshman crews to take to Boulogne. 57 Squadron briefed seven crews for southern Germany and two for the north-west and sent them on their way from Feltwell between 19.00 and 20.25 with S/L Warfield the senior pilot on duty. According to the 3 Group ORB, the Nuremberg operation appeared to be very successful and one major explosion was felt by a crew at 6,000 feet. The 57 Squadron crews carried out their attacks from 2,500 to 10,000 feet between 23.40 and 00.10, and those returning home reported the city centre to be ablaze and the glow from the fires to have remained visible for sixty miles into the return flight. R1757 failed to arrive back with the others and the crew of Sgt Jeffries was posted missing, eventually to have the deaths of all but a captured gunner confirmed once the wreckage of the Wellington had been located on the north-eastern edge of the Noord-Oost-Polder in northern Holland. Despite the claims of returning crews, sources in Nuremberg reported only a few bombs falling within the city and causing minor damage, while Schwabach, ten miles to the south suffered the destruction of fifty buildings and the village of Lauingen, sixty-five miles to the south-west, forty-four houses over a four-hour period. Even the town of Lauffen-am-Neckar, situated north of Stuttgart and some one hundred miles from Nuremberg sustained damage to forty-six houses. Meanwhile, at Bremen, the crews of P/O Watson and Sgt Price had encountered nine-tenths cloud, through which glimpses of the River Weser provided a reference, and they had bombed from 10,000 and 12,000 feet at 22.25 and 22.30, observing bursts but no detail.

Bad weather attended the two main operations on the night of the 13/14th, a 1 and 3 Group attack on Düsseldorf and another by 5 Group against Cologne. 3 Group put up forty-five Wellingtons and seven Stirlings for the former, of which seven of the Wellingtons were made ready by 57 Squadron and dispatched from Feltwell between 18.30 and 18.50 with F/L Donaldson the senior pilot on duty. Sgt Donnelly and crew turned back early because of an unserviceable rear turret, and F/L Donaldson and crew reached the western edge of the Ruhr before a port engine issue forced them also to abandon their sortie and drop their bombs from 7,000 feet onto what they believed was Krefeld at 20.40. The others arrived over the southern Ruhr to encounter ten-tenths cloud and thick ground haze, through which no crew was able to locate the aiming-point. Large cones of searchlights were co-operating with flak batteries to the north and west of the target to provide a navigational reference but also a formidable defence, in the face of which, the bombers carried out their attacks on estimated positions, the 57 Squadron crews from 8,000 to 14,000 feet between 20.19 and 20.53.

Feltwell sat out a return to Nuremberg on the night of the 14/15th, for which 3 Group provided fifty-two Wellingtons in an overall force of eighty aircraft. The operation was another abject failure, but among the few high explosive bombs falling within the city was one that hit and destroyed a workshop in the Siemens factory. 3 Group returned to Cologne on the 15th with a force of twenty-seven Wellingtons and seven Stirlings, seven of the former belonging to 57 Squadron. They departed Feltwell between 18.20 and 18.35 with no senior pilots on duty and found the target to be covered by cloud, which forced them to bomb on estimated positions, mostly on the western side of the city, aiming largely at concentrations of searchlights and flak. The 57 Squadron crews delivered their bomb loads from 8,000 to 12,000 feet between 20.40 and 21.20 and all but one returned home to make their reports. There were three empty dispersal pans at Feltwell on the following morning, two of them belonging to 75(NZ) Squadron and the other to 57 Squadron's X9978. It was learned in time that it had been shot down by the night-fighter of Feldwebel Maier of I./NJG1 and had crashed at 21.17 on the East Bank of the Maas at Grevenbicht on the Dutch/Belgian frontier, killing P/O Miller and his crew. Local reports confirmed that very few bombs had fallen within the city, and there were no casualties or any damage, but outlying communities to the east were hit, as was Duisburg, thirty miles away, and a lucky strike on the Wesseling oil refinery seven miles south of Cologne caused eight thousand tons of fuel production to be lost.

Attention turned to Germany's north-western ports of Wilhelmshaven and Emden on the 20th, but it was the shipyards in the port-city of Bremen that were selected to face the night's largest operation, involving 153 aircraft drawn from 1, 3 and 5 Groups, while 4 Group made ready forty-seven Whitleys, Wellingtons and Halifaxes for a special target, probably the battleship Tirpitz, at Wilhelmshaven. 3 Group detailed forty-seven Wellingtons and fifteen Stirlings, among which were five of the former representing 57 Squadron, who were joined at take-off by the Antwerp-bound freshman crew of Sgt Cook. They departed Feltwell between 18.20 and 18.35 on another night of unfavourable weather conditions, the main element to head eastwards and Sgt Cook and crew south, and all reached their destinations only for the Cook crew to fail to identify their target through thick ground haze and return their bombs to store. The others found Bremen to be concealed beneath ten-tenths low cloud, through which a few crews caught a glimpse of the River Weser and followed its course as far as the cloud allowed, before bombing on estimated positions based on searchlight and flak activity. The 57 Squadron crews of P/Os Tong, Walters and Watson and Sgts Donnelly and Ruttledge carried out their attacks from 9,000 and 10,000 feet between 20.42 and 22.15 and, on return, reported bursts and an explosion or two but no detail. It turned into another night of frustration and failure, which added further to the pressure upon AM Peirse to achieve some worthwhile results.

Marham and Stradishall provided twenty-eight Wellingtons between them on the following night for a return to Bremen, while Feltwell put up six of the seven freshman crews assigned to the docks and shipping at Boulogne. The crews of Sgts Cook, Gray, Hudson and Williams took off between 18.20 and 18.30 and all reached the target area, where haze and extreme darkness created challenging conditions that prevented the Gray and Williams crews from identifying the port. The former jettisoned their bombs, while the latter spotted an unidentified flarepath in the target area and bombed it from 9,000 feet at 20.20. Sgt Cook and crew came under attack from a night-fighter, which severely damaged the Wellington and wounded the rear gunner in the legs. The observer and one of two wireless operators were ordered to bale out over enemy territory and Z1087 was then nursed back to a landing at Tangmere on the Sussex coast. Meanwhile, Sgt Hudson and crew had descended to 3,500 feet to obtain a better view of the target and picked up the breakwater and entrance to the docks before delivering their seven 500 pounders and three SBCs at 20.03.

Mannheim was posted as the target for 123 aircraft on the 22nd, of which thirty-two Wellingtons were detailed by 3 Group along with six Stirlings for Brest and five freshmen for Le Havre. Feltwell launched fourteen crews, eight of them representing 57 Squadron between 18.10 and 18.30 with S/L Warfield the senior pilot on duty. They headed into foul weather conditions, which included electrical, thunder and snow storms and icing from the Belgian coast to the target and many crews were persuaded to turn back or seek alternative objectives. Not one of the 57 Squadron crews was able to make a positive identification of Mannheim through the extreme darkness and nine-tenths cloud that topped out at between 10,000 and 17,000 feet and released their bombs instead onto unidentified built-up areas in close proximity to the River Rhine from 7,500 to 13,000 feet between 20.49 and 21.38. On return to home airspace at 00.05, P/O Tong crash-landed Z8792 on the west bank of the River Orwell seven miles south-east of Ipswich. All crew members were able to walk away with a number of minor injuries between them. 75(NZ) Squadron's X9914 failed to return home, and news eventually arrived to confirm that Sgt Taylor RAFVR and his crew had all lost their lives in the crash near Diksmuide, ten miles south of Ostend in Belgium. The second pilot, Sgt Spark RNZAF, had been on the strength of 57 Squadron. An analysis revealed that fewer than half of the force had reached the target area, and local sources confirmed a light and ineffective raid.

The Feltwell squadrons remained at home on the night of the 23/24th when Honington, Marham and Stradishall represented 3 Group in a two-phase operation involving 114 aircraft against the shipyards at Kiel. On another night hampered by adverse weather conditions only sixty-nine aircraft reached their destination, but those in the second wave achieved some success by causing damage in the Deutsche Werke U-Boot yards. On the following night, Feltwell was not required to provide aircraft for Frankfurt and Brest but contributed two crews from each squadron for a freshman operation against the docks and shipping at Emden. The crews of Sgts Gray and Hudson took off at 18.05 and reached Germany's north-western coast to encounter seven to ten-tenths cloud which prevented identification of the target. They dropped their bombs blindly from 8,000 and 9,500 feet at 21.30 and 21.35 and their photos would reveal fields and sea.

Hamburg was posted as the destination for 115 aircraft on the 26th, for which 3 Group detailed eight Wellingtons from each of the Feltwell and Honington squadrons. Those from 57 Squadron took off between 18.05 and 18.20 with S/L Warfield the senior pilot on duty and were followed into the air at 18.30 by the freshman crew of Sgt Edwards bound for Cherbourg. The weather for the outward flight to north-western Germany turned out to be favourable, and all arrived to find clear skies over the target, with moonlight to illuminate ground detail, but a bank of ten-tenths cloud with tops at 8,000 feet was approaching from the east. A fierce searchlight and flak defence awaited the bombers, and those from 57 Squadron picked out fires already burning as they bore down on the target from 6,000 to 12,000 feet, the low height that of S/L Warfield and crew. They carried out their attacks between 21.25 and 22.32 and were largely blinded by searchlight glare, which prevented them from observing the precise impact of their bombs. Many detonations were observed along with fires that suggested an effective raid, which would be confirmed by the mention by local sources of around a dozen fires. Returning with diminishing fuel reserves, R1722 lost height and crash-landed in a railway cutting some two miles from Berners Heath bombing range at 02.20. P/O Watson RCAF was killed, and his front gunner slightly injured, but was able to walk away with the rest of the crew. The crew of P/O Walters were last heard from by W/T at 23.24 in a signal which read "target abandoned", and they failed to return to Feltwell. It was learned later that Z8946 had crashed at 00.20 south of Rømø Island off Denmark's western coast, killing three members of the crew and delivering the pilot and two others into enemy hands. Sgt Edwards and crew overshot their landing with a full bomb bay having been unable to identify Cherbourg, but the Wellington and crew were quickly returned to service.

There was little further operational activity for 3 Group before the month ended, and P/O Watson was buried with full military honours at Feltwell on the 30th. During the course of the month, 57 Squadron took part in thirteen operations, which generated sixty-eight sorties and cost seven Wellingtons, five complete crews and a number of additional airmen.

November 1941

Following the damning disclosures of the Butt Report in August, matters would be brought to a head early in the new month and bring into question the very existence of a strategic bomber force. It all began very badly for the Command, after three operations were posted on the 1st, 3 Group detailing forty-eight Wellingtons as part of an overall force of 134 aircraft for Kiel, seventeen Wellingtons and Stirlings for Brest and nine freshmen for Le Havre. 57 Squadron would support all three with six, three and one aircraft respectively, those bound for Kiel and the freshman crew of P/O Hunter departing Feltwell between 17.25 and 17.50 with S/L Warfield the senior pilot on duty and they were followed into the air between 18.00 and 18.30 by the Brest-bound crews of Sgts Gray and Ruttledge and P/O Tong. They climbed out through ten-tenths cloud before setting course for their respective targets, and P/O Hunter and crew were first to arrive at theirs, where they released seven 500 pounders and three SBCs from 6,000 feet at 19.35, believing them to burst near dock 5, but searchlight glare prevented a detailed assessment of the outcome. Nine to ten-tenths cloud over Brest persuaded the crews of Sgt Gray and P/O Tong to bring their cookies home after spending twenty-five minutes in a vain search for the target, leaving Sgt Ruttledge and crew to deliver theirs from 12,000 feet at 21.10 after pinpointing on the Roscanvel peninsula as they approached. Meanwhile, heavy cloud persisted all the way across the North Sea and the Schleswig-Holstein peninsula and only a little over 50% of the force arrived at Kiel to carry out an attack, Sgt Price and crew having turned back early on because of a port engine problem. So dense was the low cloud that the searchlights were unable to penetrate it, and, although heavy predicted flak reached 14,000 feet, it did not appear to give away the location of the target and the bombers flew past. Those from 57 Squadron reaching the target area released their bombs from 7,000 to 12,000 feet between 21.38 and 22.00, Sgt Williams and crew observing five bursts and a pillar of white smoke, while Sgt Ravenhill and crew reported a terrific flash. According to local sources, no bombs fell within the town and docks area, but the sound of bombs could be heard over to the east.

Twenty-eight crews were called to briefing at Feltwell and Marham on the 4th to be told of their part in a 3 Group attempt to hit the Krupp complex in Essen that night. 57 Squadron made ready six Wellingtons and sent them on their way between 17.30 and 17.55 with S/L Warfield once more the senior pilot on duty. They climbed into ten-tenths cloud, which would blot out the ground for the entire operation and force them to bomb on e.t.a. or seek out alternatives. The 57 Squadron element bombed from 9,000 to 17,000 feet between 20.57 and 21.44 and returned safely after participating in another wasted effort, which, happily, did not cost any crews.

Feltwell operated alone on the 6th when sending nine freshman crews to bomb the docks and shipping at Le Havre. The 57 Squadron crews of P/O Waugh and Sgts Cook, Johnson and Watson took off between 17.45 and 18.00 and reached the target area to find six-tenths cloud, which enabled three of them to make out some ground detail and deliver their seven 500 pounders and two SBCs with a degree of accuracy from 4,500 to 6,500 feet between 20.00 and 20.08. They returned after round-trips of four to four-and-a-half hours, Sgt Watson and crew with their bomb load intact after failing to locate the target and the others to report at least one large explosion and developing fires.

No doubt still frustrated by his inability to deliver a telling blow on Germany during the extended period of unfavourable weather, and almost certainly eager to rescue the besmirched reputation of the Command after the damning Butt Report, Peirse planned a major night of operations on the 7th. The original intention had been to send over two hundred aircraft to Berlin, but continuing doubts about the weather prompted the 5 Group A-O-C, AVM Slessor, to question the wisdom of going ahead with that, and he requested and was allowed to withdraw his force and send it instead to Cologne. A third operation, involving fifty-three Wellingtons and two Stirlings from 1 and 3 Groups was also to take place with the southern city of Mannheim as the target. Ultimately, a force of 169 aircraft was assembled for Berlin, while sixty-one Hampdens and fourteen Manchesters were assigned to the Rhineland capital city of Cologne, in addition to which, other small-scale operations, including "rover" patrols by thirty aircraft over and around the Ruhr, raised the number of sorties for the night to 392. Seventy-three Wellingtons and fifteen Stirlings were detailed by 3 Group for Berlin and eight Wellingtons and two Stirlings for Mannheim, plus eleven Wellingtons for "rover" patrols north of the Ruhr and twenty-two for freshman crews to employ against the docks and shipping at Ostend. 57 Squadron made ready eleven Wellingtons, six for Berlin, four for "rover" patrols in the Münster/Hamm areas and a singleton for Ostend, and it was those bound for Germany's capital that departed Feltwell first between 17.40 and 18.05 with S/L Warfield the senior pilot on duty. The crews of P/O Hunter and Sgts Cook, Gray and Hudson took off for their patrol beats between 19.45 and 20.10, leaving Sgt Pelletier and crew on the ground until their departure for Ostend at 20.45.

The doubts about the weather conditions proved to be well-founded, and crews heading east had to climb through cloud to reach clear air at up to 18,000 feet, although gaps in the Ruhr region would allow some crews a glimpse of the ground and enabled them to establish their position for the bombing run. The Berlin force was accompanied by cloud for the entire outward flight, and many crews turned back, among them those of Sgts Donnelly and Owens because of engine issues. The Stirling element had been assigned to attack the Air Ministry building and the rest of the force the city, but, clearly, this was unrealistic, and bombing took place on estimated positions. The 57 Squadron crews bombed from 10,000 to 14,000 feet between 21.26 and 21.37 and observed either flashes or nothing at all and all made it home after more than eight hours aloft. At Ostend, P/O Pelletier and crew were able to identify the docks and delivered their seven 500 pounders, single 250 pounder and three SBCs from 10,000 feet at 21.55, observing bursts among dock buildings alongside the outer harbour. Sgt Hudson and crew were in cloud when they dropped their cookie on Hamm from 6,500 feet at 22.48 and saw nothing of the impact. Ten minutes later, P/O Hunter and crew let their 4,000 pounder go from 10,000 feet onto the outskirts of a town spotted through a gap in the cloud and illuminated with flares. Z8903 and Z8985 failed to return from Münster, the former disappearing without trace with the crew of Sgt Gray and Z8985 crashing two miles south-south-east of Gouda in southern Holland, killing Sgt Cook RAAF and two others and delivering the three survivors into enemy hands. Once every aircraft from the night's endeavours had landed, it became clear that a record number of thirty-seven were missing, more than twice the previous highest loss in a single night. An analysis revealed that fewer than half of the Berlin force had managed to reach their objective, and twenty-one had failed to return. The Cologne force came through without loss, but left behind them only the slightest damage, and the Mannheim contingent missed its target altogether while losing seven Wellingtons. This was the final straw for the Air Ministry, and Sir Richard Peirse was summoned to an uncomfortable meeting with Churchill at Chequers on the 8th to make his explanations. On the 13th, he would be ordered to restrict future operations while the future of the Command was considered at the highest level.

Feltwell and Mildenhall were alerted to operations on the 8th, the former to provide twenty Wellingtons for an operation against Essen and a freshman crew for Dunkerque, while the latter sent two freshman crews to Dunkerque. 57 Squadron prepared eight Wellingtons for the Ruhr and one for P/O Waugh and crew to take to the French coast, and they took off together between 17.35 and 18.20 with S/L Warfield the senior pilot on duty. The Waugh crew arrived at their destination first and delivered seven 500 pounders and three SBCs onto the docks from 8,000 feet at 18.56, observing them to burst in the vicinity of docks 1 and 4. The Ruhr-bound crews encountered patchy cloud on the way out, and five to nine-tenths in the target area, where they had to run the gauntlet of intense searchlights in cones and heavy flak. S/L Warfield and crew attacked Essen from 8,000 feet at 19.23, Sgt Johnson and crew Cologne from 10,000 feet at 19.30 and Sgt Watson and crew Mülheim-an-der-Ruhr from 14,000 feet at 19.35. The crews of Sgts Williams and Donnelly followed up at Essen from 10,000 and 11,000 feet at 21.39 and 21.45 respectively, while P/O Pelletier and crew attacked Düsseldorf from 9,500 feet at 20.00. Some bursts were observed, but, in truth, it was another example of exposing valuable crews to extreme risk in pinprick attacks causing minimal damage.

Thereafter, most squadrons remained at home as the Command almost withdrew into itself. A number of small-scale operations took place against ports, and others were scheduled, particularly by 3 Group against the enemy warships at Brest but cancelled before they got off the ground. 57 Squadron sat out a modestly effective operation against Hamburg on the night of the 9/10th, and a week elapsed before it was next called into action. Emden provided the objective for a force of forty-nine freshman-crewed aircraft on the 15th, while forty-seven more-experienced crews were briefed for Kiel. 3 Group detailed thirty-six Wellingtons and eleven Stirlings for Kiel and nineteen Wellingtons for Emden, but eleven failed to take off for a variety of reasons. 57 Squadron dispatched the crew of F/L Phipps at 17.25, but they failed to locate the target in the face of ten-tenths cloud and brought their bombs home. The crews of Sgts Watson and Morse departed Feltwell for Boulogne at 17.30 and 17.55 respectively, and both came upon a flarepath running north to south, which the Watson crew bombed from 9,000 feet at 19.00 and the Morse crew from 11,500 feet thirty minutes later.

The Stirling crews called to briefing on the 23rd learned that their target was Brest and its lodgers, while thirty-six Wellington crews and a single Stirling crew were assigned to the docks and shipping at Dunkerque. 57 Squadron made ready four Wellingtons for the freshman crews of Sgts Heald, Morse, Plunkett and Vanexan and dispatched them from Feltwell between 17.25 and 17.35. The Heald and Vanexan crews brought their bombs back after failing to locate the target through ten-tenths cloud, while the Plunkett and Morse crews carried out their attacks from 8,000 and 10,500 feet at 18.40 and 19.02 respectively, the former observing no results and the latter bomb bursts believed to be in the docks area. Z1073 and X9982 both landed heavily in the hands of Sgt Vanexan and Sgt Plunkett respectively and were badly damaged and Sgt Heald and crew handed back a severely flak-damaged X9874 to the ground crew.

Emden was posted as the main target on the 26th and a force of eighty Wellingtons and twenty Hampdens assembled, fifty-one of the former provided by 3 Group, ten of which were made ready by 57 Squadron. Three freshman crews were briefed for a raid on the docks and shipping at Ostend, where they would be joined by eight other Wellington and two Stirling crews. They departed Feltwell together between 17.25 and 18.05 with the recently promoted acting S/L Donaldson the senior pilot on duty and climbed into cloud that persisted all the way to the target area. Many crews failed to locate Emden and either jettisoned their bombs or sought out last resort targets and only fifty-five returning crews would claim to have bombed on estimated positions. P/O Pelletier and crew jettisoned their load into the sea, while the crews of P/O Tong and F/L Phipps returned theirs to store, leaving the others to bomb blindly from 6,800 to 12,000 feet between 19.21 and 20.03. Meanwhile, some 230 miles to the south-west, Sgt Roper and crew dropped nine 500 pounders and two of 250lbs onto Ostend from 12,000 feet at 19.00 and observed them to burst across the docks. It must have been soon afterwards that cloud drifted across to conceal the ground as neither Sgt Vanexan nor Sgt Heald and their crews were able to locate Ostend. The former reported bombing a flarepath somewhere near St-Omer from 800 feet at 19.45, while the latter brought most of their bombs home. The main operation was yet another complete failure, for which stronger than forecast winds were partly to blame after pushing the bombers north of their intended track.

Despite the risks of venturing to the Ruhr with the current restriction in force, on the 27th Peirse decided to send a force of eighty-six aircraft to Düsseldorf, the industrial city perched on the southern edge of the Ruhr to the north of Cologne. 3 Group contributed forty-six Wellingtons from Honington, Marham, Wyton and Waterbeach for what turned into another ineffective operation that caused more damage in Cologne than at the intended target.

The last night of the month brought a major operation against Hamburg involving a force of 180 aircraft, the crews of which were briefed for a number of aiming points including shipyards and railway installations. 3 Group detailed forty-nine Wellingtons and two Stirlings for the main event and a further sixteen Wellingtons and two Stirlings for a return to Emden, and all but five would take off. 57 Squadron briefed a dozen crews for the main event and those of P/O Waugh and Sgt Heald to join the fifty-strong force assigned to the docks at Emden and they departed Feltwell together between 16.50 and 17.15 with F/L Phipps the senior pilot on duty. They headed out over the North Sea intending to make landfall on the western coast of the Schleswig-Holstein peninsula and approach the target from the north. Sgt Morse and crew turned back early because of an engine issue, leaving the others to press on under clear, moonlit skies to be greeted, according to some, by surprisingly little flak at what was usually a hotspot of defensive activity. However, F/L Phipps and crew found themselves constantly ensnared in searchlight cones and bombarded by flak, which caused extensive damage to the Wellington and delayed their approach to the primary target, and they ultimately bombed a searchlight concentration near Stade to the west of the city from 6,000 feet at 20.30. Crews had been warned at briefing that they must vacate the target area by 21.00, but not all complied. Sgt Ruttledge and crew drifted off course and would claim at debriefing that they had been unable to make the deadline, and yet, dropped their bombs on Appen aerodrome, barely a dozen miles north-west of Hamburg, from 12,000 feet at 20.15. P/O Hunter and crew became delayed while evading a BF109 and unloaded the contents of their bomb bay from 10,000 feet onto the little town of Horneburg some five miles west of the River Elbe at

21.05. Another crew to lose their way and arrive late was that of P/O Pelletier, who sought out Bremerhaven as the recipient of their bombs from 9,500 feet at 21.00. The other 57 Squadron crews carried out their attacks from 7,500 to 14,000 feet between 20.05 and 21.10 and observed bursts and a number of fires, one large, but no detail. Local sources confirmed twenty-two fires, two of them large, and 2,500 people bombed out of their homes at a cost to the Command of thirteen aircraft.

During the course of the month, the squadron took part in seventeen operations and dispatched seventy-four sorties for the loss of two Wellingtons and their crews.

December 1941

The dominant theme during December would be the continuing presence at Brest of Scharnhorst, Gneisenau and, sometimes, Prinz Eugen, and no less than fifteen operations of varying sizes would be mounted against the port and its guests during the month, some by daylight. The weather kept the entire Command on the ground for the first six nights of the new month, and it was not until the 7th that a posted operation went ahead. The target for a force of 130 aircraft was Aachen, Germany's most westerly city, perched on the frontiers with both Holland and Belgium. The briefed aiming-point was the Nazi Party HQ, which had no special significance other than the fact that it was situated in the city centre, at a time when it was not yet admitted publicly that population centres were being bombed. 3 Group supported the operation with thirty-two Wellingtons, and also made ready twenty-three Wellingtons and two Stirlings for an attack on the warships at Brest and others for freshman raids on Boulogne and Calais. 57 Squadron began the new month in gentle fashion by sending the freshman crews of Sgts Roper and Watson to Calais, for which they departed Feltwell at 20.50 and 20.55. Sgt Watson and crew returned almost three hours later with a full bomb load after failing to locate the port through ten-tenths cloud, but Sgt Roper and crew enjoyed a more productive sortie despite picking up flak damage and dropped their thirteen 250 pounders and three SBCs in two sticks from 11,000 feet at 22.30, observing them to burst near dock 1. The Aachen raid was largely ineffective in the face of challenging weather conditions and the attack on the warships took place from estimated positions. The 7 and XV Squadron Stirlings were conducting the first trial of the Oboe blind bombing system, but technical malfunctions rendered it a failure on this occasion. It would require a further fifteen months of development work before it was ready for general use against the enemy.

Cologne was posted as the main target on the 11th and a force of sixty aircraft assembled, 3 Group contributing nine Stirlings and eight Wellingtons, while six Stirlings and twenty-four Wellingtons, the latter from Marham only, were made ready to attack the warships at Brest. 57 Squadron was not involved in either endeavour and sent five freshman crews to join twenty-nine others to bomb the docks and shipping at Le Havre. They departed Feltwell between 16.25 and 16.30 and reached the French coast to encounter ten-tenths cloud, which prevented the crews of F/L Phipps and Sgts Watson and Roper from locating the port. As they headed home with their bomb loads intact, the crews of Sgts Johnson and Morse delivered fourteen 250 pounders and three SBCs each from 6,000 and 12,000 feet at 18.40 and 18.44 respectively and watched them burst in the docks area. On return, T2959 crashed at 20.50 at Roudham, some three miles from East Wretham airfield, killing Sgt Watson and his crew.

The weather had improved by the following afternoon, when Feltwell provided all eighteen Wellingtons, nine from each squadron, which were to join forces with six Stirlings for the next assault on the enemy warships at Brest. The 57 Squadron element departed Feltwell over an extended period between 14.40 and 16.10 bound for Brest with S/L Warfield the senior pilot on duty but lost the services of F/L Phipps and crew after they were unable to maintain height and were forced to jettison the bombs and turn for home. The others arrived to find two to four-tenths cloud, a smoke screen and searchlights operating in cones in co-operation with flak batteries that sent an accurate barrage of heavy and light shells to bombing height and beyond. The 57 Squadron crews carried out their attacks from 9,000 to 14,000 feet between 18.55 and 20.52, some observing the bursts of their bombs and others not as they raced to get out of the cauldron of fire as quickly as possible. As a result, no assessment of the raid could be gained. The freshman crew of Sgt Richardson took off for Dunkerque at 04.55 and suffered the frustration of a complete hang-up as they tried to release the thirteen 250 pounders and three SBCs. They carried out three further passes over the aiming point with the same result and set off for home to jettison the bombs over the sea. They were attacked by two Me110s as they crossed the Zuider Zee homebound at around 08.00 and sustained damage while managing to shake off their pursuers. They were escorted over the English coast by friendly fighters and landed at East Wretham with three slightly injured crew members on board. Flying Control reported the dramatic return of a 57 Squadron Wellington with a full bomb load, and the depositing of over a hundred incendiaries in the middle of the flare path, some of which started to burn. The identity of the culprit was not revealed, and the account did not match any crews returning on this night.

Feltwell called five crews from each squadron to briefing on the 15th to inform them of their part in the latest foray against Brest as the sole 3 Group Wellington representatives, while 7 Squadron at Oakington and XV Squadron at Wyton provided six Stirlings and one respectively. The weather conditions had taken a turn for the worse by the time the 57 Squadron element took off between 14.50 and 16.10 with P/O Tong the only commissioned pilot on duty, and they reached the target area to encounter cloud and high winds, the latter having made navigation difficult. They were greeted by the same flak response as before, but much reduced searchlight activity and carried out their attacks from 9,000 to 12,500 feet between 18.55 and 20.00, observing only flashes. All returned safely, but none was able to provide the intelligence section with an assessment of the outcome because of the cloud.

The main operation on the 16th was against Wilhelmshaven, for which a force of eighty-three aircraft was assembled, seventeen of the Wellingtons provided by the 3 Group stations of Honington and Waterbeach. Along with Marham, they also contributed eighteen Wellingtons to Brest in company with five Stirlings, but neither undertaking produced results commensurate with the effort expended, sources in Wilhelmshaven reporting slight damage and, as usual, no news came out of Brest. Brest's 3 Group tormentors on the 17th would be launched from Feltwell, Oakington and Stradishall in the form of thirty-two Wellingtons in an overall force of 121 twin-engine aircraft. 57 Squadron made ready a dozen of its own and dispatched them between 16.40 and 17.00 with S/L Warfield the senior pilot on duty. They arrived over the Finistere region of north-western France to find ten-tenths cloud blotting out the ground and bombing took place on estimated positions from 8,500 to 14,000 feet between 19.00 and 19.45. At debriefing, crews could only report bombing somewhere in the target area and hope for a lucky hit on one of the cruisers.

Brest did not have long to wait for the next attack, which would be delivered in daylight later on the 18th by six aircraft each from the three Halifax squadrons, 10 Squadron now having joined their ranks, in company with eighteen Stirlings and eleven Manchesters under Operation Veracity I. They arrived at the French coast at Lanildut, to the north-west of Brest, under clear skies and with a Spitfire escort, and benefitted from excellent visibility, each squadron initially in a vic formation until the attack began, when those following on behind the Stirling spearhead arranged themselves into line astern to pass singly over the clearly visible aiming-point. They headed to a point some five miles south-east of the target just inside the coastline, before turning for the bombing run with a railway line to the left and the coastline to the right. The flak was intense and accurate and four Stirlings and a Manchester were shot down, while a Halifax ditched on the way home and the crew was rescued. Claims were made of direct hits on Scharnhorst and Gneisenau, and the 4 Group ORB stated that reconnaissance photos confirmed dense smoke pouring from them. It is believed that, in fact, Scharnhorst sustained only slight damage.

Minor operations occupied the ensuing days and, on the 20th, according to the ORB summary of activities for the month of December, acting S/L Donaldson reverted to flight lieutenant rank and was re-posted to Feltwell as non-effective, probably due to illness, paving the way for F/L Phipps to step up a rank to succeed him temporarily as a flight commander. Operations resumed on the 23rd, when sixty-eight aircraft from 1, 4 and 5 Groups were detailed to attack Cologne, while forty Wellingtons and seven Stirlings of 3 Group maintained the pressure on Brest. 57 Squadron dispatched nine Wellingtons between 16.15 and 17.10, although only eight were listed on the Form 541, with F/L Phipps the senior pilot on duty. The weather over the target was good for a change and the reception hostile, as always, and crews bombed in the target area from 7,000 to 12,000 feet between 19.15 and 20.10. Some observed bursts across the docks followed by fires, but searchlight glare was largely responsible for obscuring the results and it was another inconclusive outcome to add to all the others since the end of March.

The third wartime Christmas was observed in traditional RAF fashion on stations across the Command, but there was little cause for cheer other than the fact that Japan had dragged a reluctant America into the war through its treacherous attack on Pearl Harbour. Any festivities ended on the 27th with the call to arms of 132 crews assigned to Düsseldorf and many others for minor operations, including another against Brest. 3 Group detailed twenty-four Wellingtons and five Stirlings for Brest and twenty-six Wellingtons for Düsseldorf, 57 Squadron supporting each operation with six Wellingtons, those bound for Brest departing Feltwell between 16.40 and 16.55 with F/L Phipps the senior pilot on duty and followed immediately into the air by the Ruhr-bound element between 17.00 and 17.05 led by S/L Warfield. Sgt Heald and crew were unable to maintain height after running into severe icing conditions and they turned back to reduce the Düsseldorf element by one. The skies were clear over Düsseldorf, and the bombers were greeted by the usual intense searchlight and flak response, in the face of which, the 57 Squadron crews attacked from 6,500 to 10,000 feet between 18.58 and 19.10 and many bomb bursts were reported in the town and the railway station. The Brest contingent found the target concealed beneath cloud and an effective smoke screen and carried out their attacks from 8,000 to 12,000 feet between 19.05 and 19.40. A number of crews claimed to catch a glimpse of the docks, but the majority bombed on estimated positions before returning home to offer their impressions to the intelligence section. Z1097 failed to return from Düsseldorf after crossing paths on the way home with the night-fighter of Luftwaffe ace, Hptm Werner Streib of I./NJG1, who shot it down to crash some seven miles south-south-east of the Dutch town of Helmond at 20.30. W/O Purdy DFM perished with four of his crew and only the wireless operator survived to be taken into captivity.

Feltwell was not involved in operations against the north-western ports of Wilhelmshaven and Emden on the 28th, but 57 Squadron dispatched the freshman crews of Sgts Knoblock and Richardson to Dunkerque at 17.35, each carrying thirteen 250 pounders and two SBCs for use against the docks and shipping. The Richardson crew actually delivered their first stick of seven 250 pounders from 10,000 feet at Ostend at 19.10, before going on to Dunkerque to drop the rest of the load from the same altitude at 19.50. The Knoblock crew restricted themselves to Dunkerque, where the breakwater and docks stood out clearly in bright moonlight as they dropped their load also in two sticks from 10,000 feet at 19.05, the first falling into the water close to dock 8 and the second near docks 4 and 5.

During the course of the month the squadron operated against nine targets and dispatched fifty-six sorties for the loss of two Wellingtons and crews.

So ended a year of under-achievement and disappointment, which had left the Command languishing in the doldrums and with an uncertain future. There had been few advances on the performance of 1940, and the new bomber types, the Stirling, Halifax and Manchester, had all disappointed and fallen short of their design requirements, and each type had undergone periods of grounding while essential modifications were carried out. 1942 beckoned, a year which would bring changes and eventually the first signs of the emergence of an effective bomber force, but also the stark realisation, that there was a very long and bloody struggle ahead, before any light would appear at the end of the tunnel. In actual fact, a bright light in the form of the Avro Lancaster was already undergoing proving trials in the hands of 5 Group's 44 Squadron and would enter the fray as the "shining sword" in the armoury of a new Commander-in-Chief in the spring.

W/C Stanley Bertram DFC
Commanding Officer 57 Squadron 24th February to 8th May 1941
(photo thanks to the Bertram family for 57 Squadron Assoc.)

57 Squadron at Feltwell 1941. Sgt Norman Hennessey is fourth from right, front row.

Damage in Kiel after March 1941 attack

57 Squadron crew at Wellington OTU Silverstone

Wimpy and crew
(thanks to John Thompson)
(This and several other photographs with kind permission of 57 and 630 Association -
57squadron.wordpress.com and 57-630sqnassoc.org)

January 1942

The New Year began with the continuing pre-occupation with the German cruisers at Brest, and, following the fifteen raids of varying sizes sent against them during December, there would be no fewer than eleven further operations during January, seven during the first ten nights. It would prove to be a low-key month for 57 Squadron, involving just three small-scale operations to keep a few crews active. The first of these took place on the 2nd as part of a 3 Group force of twenty-nine Wellingtons and Stirlings with the warships at Brest as their objective. The squadron briefed six crews and sent them on their way from Feltwell between 16.15 and 16.35 with S/L Warfield the senior pilot on duty. The Stirlings opened the attack and dropped flares for the Wellington element, but ten-tenths cloud obscured the ground and most could bomb only on estimated positions, the 57 Squadron crews delivering their four 500 pounders and two SBCs each from 7,000 to 12,000 feet between 19.15 and 20.02 before returning safely. Feltwell sat out a small-scale return to Brest on the 3rd when adverse weather again left crews with no choice but to bomb on estimated positions.

On the 5th, 57 Squadron's HQ relocated to Methwold, located some five miles to the north-east of Feltwell, leaving the aircraft and flying and ground personnel to continue operations from Feltwell. The main operation that night was to be carried out by 154 aircraft against Brest, eighty-seven of them assigned to the warships and the remainder to the naval docks generally, the 3 Group contingent of forty-three aircraft handed the Brest arsenal power plant. 57 Squadron was not invited to take part but made ready three Wellingtons for the freshman crews of Sgts Knoblock, Richardson and Wilson to employ against the docks and shipping at Cherbourg during the early morning of the 6th. They taxied to the runway for take-off at 05.20, and one minute after leaving the ground, Z1096 crashed at Holmebrink Farm near Methwold and was consumed by fire. The farmer, Mr Thorpe, bravely dragged the badly injured rear gunner, P/O Carter, from his turret and, with the aid of others, lowered him into a water-filled cattle trough, but Sgt Richardson and the rest of the crew could not be saved. *(The Wellington was recorded in the squadron ORB as Z8978 and in Bill Chorley's Bomber Command Losses as Z1096, both of which carried the code DX-S.)* The crews of Sgts Knoblock and Wilson reached the target to deliver thirteen 250 pounders and two SBCs each at 06.52 from 10,500 feet at 07.08 from 8,000 feet respectively, but observed no results before returning home safely.

The squadron was now stood-down from operations to begin a period of training and would conduct only one further operation during the month. AM Sir Richard Peirse left his post as C-in-C Bomber Command on the 8th to be succeeded temporarily by AVM Baldwin, the A-O-C 3 Group. In February, Peirse would take up a new appointment as C-in-C Allied Air Forces in India and South-East Asia, but the sense that he had been "sacked" from Bomber Command would linger, and, perhaps unjustly, tarnish his legacy. In truth, it was his misfortune to head Bomber Command at a time when navigation was an art rather than a science, and the demands and expectations of his superiors were often unrealistic and unachievable with the technology available at the time. It seems that S/L Donaldson had resumed his former role with the squadron, until finally relinquishing his squadron leader rank on the 10th.

The squadron took part in no further operations until the evening of the 15th, by which time 124 aircraft had been sent against Wilhelmshaven on the night of the 10/11th, and ninety-five against Hamburg on the 14/15th. The former raid had been a dismal failure, while the latter resulted in seven large fires but no major incidents. Hamburg was the main target again on the night of the 15/16th for a force of ninety-six aircraft, twenty-two of the Wellingtons provided by 3 Group. Two crews each from the Feltwell squadrons were assigned to intruder duties over aerodromes in Holland, for which the crews of W/C Southwell and Sgt Heald took off at 17.35 bound for Soesterberg near Utrecht, while the Kiwi pair headed for Schiphol. W/C Southwell and crew arrived first at their objective and dropped seventeen 250 pounders in three sticks from 7,000 feet at 19.30, observing the last to start a small fire on the eastern side of the aerodrome, and Sgt Heald and crew followed up fifty-five minutes later from 6,000 feet and watched as all bombs burst.

There were no further operations for 57 Squadron, which concluded the month with a tally of three operations, eleven sorties and the loss of a single Wellington and crew. Modest-scale and minor operations had occupied the rest of the Command during the second half of the month, which ended with another assault on the warships at Brest on the 31st.

February 1942

The new month would bring no increase in operational activity for 57 Squadron, which would find itself required to go to war on just two occasions. In the meantime, it began to acquire Mk III Wellingtons to operate alongside the trusty Mk ICs, which would remain on charge for some time. Although the impending breakout from Brest by the three enemy warships would take the Royal Navy and the RAF by complete surprise in what would be a most humiliating episode for the government and the nation, there was clearly some advance warning, as stations across the Command were put on stand-by from the 4th for daylight operations over Brest in preparation for precisely that event. S/L Warfield was posted to HQ 6 Group on the 6th for Air Staff duties. *(6 Group at the time was devoted to training and should not be confused with the Canadian 6 Group formed in Bomber Command on New Year's Day 1943.)* Several small-scale raids were sent against the port over the ensuing days, the last by eighteen Wellingtons on the evening of the 11th, the crews of which would have been unaware that they were the last to engage in this seemingly endless saga. As the sound of their engines receded into the eastern cloud-filled skies, Vice-Admiral Otto Cilliax, the Brest Group commander, whose flag was on Scharnhorst, put Operation Cerberus into action at 21.14 with Scharnhorst, Gneisenau and Prinz Eugen slipping anchor, before heading into the English Channel under an escort of destroyers and E-Boats. It was an audacious bid for freedom, covered by bad weather, widespread jamming and meticulously planned support by the Kriegsmarine and the Luftwaffe, all of which had been rehearsed extensively during January. The planning, and a little good fortune, allowed the fleet to make undetected progress until spotted off Le Touquet by two Spitfires piloted by G/C Victor Beamish, the commanding officer of Kenley, and W/C Finlay Boyd, both of whom maintained radio silence and did not report their find until landing at 10.42 on the morning of the 12th.

It had always been assumed that the German cruisers would one day break out and make for Germany or the open sea, and in preparation for this eventuality, a plan had been formulated under the code-name, Operation Fuller. 3 Group put twenty-one Wellingtons and three Stirlings on stand-by from

07.00 on that fateful day, and, once the enemy fleet had been spotted in the late morning, frantic efforts were made to get Coastal and Bomber Command aircraft away. At 11.40 the enemy flotilla was reported already to be off Boulogne and Bomber Command ordered all available aircraft to take off at the earliest opportunity. It was 13.30 before the first sorties were launched, and the 3 Group stations worked frantically to get twenty-eight Wellingtons and three Stirlings into the air with the intention of carrying out an interception off The Hague between 16.00 and 16.30. It was hoped to arrange fighter cover, but the idea was abandoned because of lack of endurance. The 57 Squadron crews of P/O Ruttledge and Sgt Heald departed Feltwell at 15.05, but only the latter located a cruiser accompanied by three destroyers. They attacked with nine 500 pounders from 700 feet at 17.05 but were too busy taking evasive action to observe the outcome. A further sixteen Wellingtons and eight Stirlings took off at 16.37 to attack further up the Den Helder peninsula off Haarlem at 18.00, while seventy-three serviceable 3 Group aircraft equipped with the TR1335 "Gee" navigation aid were not allowed to take part. S/L Southwell and crew took off at 17.10 followed closely by S/L Phipps and crew, but neither was unable to locate any targets and jettisoned their bombs into the sea. All crews ran into ten-tenths cloud in the search areas and had to contend with a low base and tops at 9,000 feet and rainstorms and squally conditions, which compounded the difficulties and prevented most crews from locating the enemy fleet. Despite a record daylight commitment of 242 sorties by Bomber Command and others by Coastal Command and the Fleet Air Arm, the heroic actions of the crews were insufficient to prevent the enemy fleet from making good its escape into open sea, although, its own trials and tribulations were not yet over. Scharnhorst struck a mine in the late afternoon and began to fall back, and, at 19.55, a magnetic mine detonated close enough to Gneisenau, when off Teschelling, to open a small hole in the starboard side, and, temporarily, slow her progress also. Later still, at 21.34, when passing through the same stretch of water, Scharnhorst hit another mine which stopped both engines and damaged steering and fire control. The vessel got under way again at 22.23 using its starboard engines and making twelve knots, while carrying an additional one thousand tons of seawater.

Gneisenau and Prinz Eugen reached the Elbe Estuary at 07.00 on the 13th, and tied up at Brunsbüttel North Locks at 09.30, while Scharnhorst arrived at Wilhelmshaven at 10.00 with three months-worth of damage to repair. The mines had been laid almost certainly by 5 Group Hampdens over the preceding nights and demonstrated the remarkable effectiveness of this war-long campaign. The entire episode was a major embarrassment to the government and the nation, but, worse still, cost the Command a further fifteen aircraft and crews on top of all of those sacrificed to this endeavour over the past eleven months. 5 Group alone posted missing nine Hampdens and crews, all lost in the North Sea, six of them without trace. On a positive note, this annoying and distracting itch had been scratched for the last time, and the Command could now concentrate its forces against the strategic targets for which it was best suited. The freshman crews of Sgts Neville and Wilson took off from Feltwell at 18.30 bound for Le Havre, which neither located and the seventeen 250 pounders carried by the Wilson crew ended up on the seabed. Sgt Neville and crew brought theirs home and ran off the end of the runway after hydraulics failure robbed them of flaps and brakes. Z1568 would fly again after repair.

A new Air Ministry directive, issued on the 14th, was to change the emphasis of bomber operations from that point until the end of the war. Lengthy consideration having been given to the Butt

Report and the future of an independent bomber force, the new policy authorized the blatant area bombing of Germany's industrial towns and cities in a direct assault on the morale of the civilian population, particularly its workers. This had, of course, been going on since the summer of 1940, but no longer would there be the pretence of claiming to be attacking industrial and military targets. Waiting in the wings, in fact, at this very moment, four days into his voyage from the United States in the armed merchantman, Alcantara, was a new leader, a man who not only would pursue this policy with a will, but also possessed the self-belief, arrogance and stubbornness to fight his corner against all-comers on behalf of his beleaguered Bomber Command. Also on the 14th, S/L Harvie was posted in from 21.O.T.U to succeed S/L Donaldson as a flight commander.

Air Chief Marshal Sir Arthur Harris took up his post as the new Commander-in-Chief of Bomber Command on the 22nd. He was a man well-known to 5 Group, having served as its A-O-C until November 1940, when he became second deputy to Sir Charles Portal, the Chief-of-the-Air-Staff. Harris arrived at the helm with firm ideas already in place on how to win the war by bombing alone, a pre-war theory, which no commander had yet had an opportunity to put into practice. It was obvious to him, that the small-scale raids on multiple targets favoured by his predecessor served only to dilute the effort, and that such pin-prick attacks could not hurt Germany's war effort. He recognized the need to overwhelm the defences and emergency services, by pushing the maximum number of aircraft across the aiming-point in the shortest possible time, and this would signal the birth of the bomber stream, and an end to the former practice, whereby squadrons or even crews determined for themselves the details of their sorties. He knew also that urban areas are most efficiently destroyed by fire, rather than blast, and it would not be long before the bomb loads carried in his aircraft reflected this thinking.

In the meantime, while he developed his ideas, he would continue with the fairly small-scale attacks on German ports favoured by his predecessor, and later, on the evening of his appointment, he sent thirty-one Wellingtons and nineteen Hampdens to Wilhelmshaven to attack the floating dock likely to be employed during repairs to Scharnhorst. Sadly, the target area was covered by dense cloud and the bombing that took place on estimated positions missed the target altogether. It was Kiel on the nights of the 25/26th and 26/27th, to attack the floating dock at which, it was believed, Gneisenau was moored while undergoing repairs. On the latter occasion, a high explosive bomb struck the bows of Gneisenau, now supposedly in a safe haven after enduring eleven months of constant bombardment at Brest, and not only did it kill 116 of her crew, it also ended her sea-going career for good. Her main armament was removed for use in coastal defence, and she was towed to Gdynia, where she remained unrepaired for the rest of the war. The British authorities were unaware of the success, however, and sent another raid of sixty-eight aircraft on the 27th.

During the course of the month, 57 Squadron was involved in Operation Fuller and one other operation and dispatched six sorties without loss.

March 1942

Bomber Command's evolution to war-winning capability was to be long, arduous and gradual, but the first signs of a new hand on the tiller came early on in Harris's reign with this meticulously planned attack on the Renault lorry factory, which was located in a loop of the Seine in the district of Billancourt to the south-west of the centre of Paris. The plant was capable of producing 18,000 lorries per year, which was a massive boon to the German war effort, and the attempt to destroy it came in response to an Air Ministry request. The operation would be conducted in three waves, led by experienced crews, and would involve extensive use of flares to provide illumination. In time, such operations would be led by Gee-equipped aircraft, but the 3 Group squadrons already employing the device were forbidden from taking part. A force of 235 aircraft was assembled on the 3rd, a new record for a single target, of which thirty-one Stirlings and thirty-nine Wellingtons were provided by 3 Group. A meticulous plan was prepared for the three-wave attack, during which an unprecedented average of 120 aircraft per hour would pass over the aiming point, a 50% increase over the previous highest concentration. The raid was to be led by experienced crews with extensive use of flares to provide illumination, and bombing was to be carried out from as low a level as practicable, both to aid accuracy and to avoid casualties among French civilians in adjacent residential districts. As 57 Squadron was undergoing conversion to Gee-equipped Wellingtons, it was represented in this operation by just two crews, those of W/C Southwell, who had S/L Harvie alongside him as second pilot and S/L Phipps, who took off at 18.45 in the wake of the lone 75(NZ) Squadron participant. They found the target bathed in bright moonlight and W/C Southwell and crew observed large fires already burning in the centre and western end of Seguin Island. They delivered their nine 500 and three 250 pounders in four sticks from 2,000 feet at 21.20 and all were seen to burst on the island. S/L Phipps and crew carried out their attack from the same height at 21.35, dropping three sticks on the main works and one on the power station on the island. The operation was an outstanding success, which destroyed 40% of the factory buildings for the loss of a single Wellington, although sadly, 367 French people lost their lives, and more than nine thousand were rendered homeless. The problem of collateral damage would go unresolved for the remainder of the war.

As an industrial centre of enormous significance and home to the giant Krupp concern, Essen was to feature heavily in Harris's future plans. The first of three raids on its production sites in the Borbeck districts on consecutive nights was posted on the 8th, for which a force of 211 aircraft was assembled, 3 Group initially detailing sixty-eight Wellingtons and twenty-one Stirlings for the main event and thirteen for a freshman raid on the docks and shipping at Le Havre, all but three of which would take off. 3 Group was to lead the attack with twenty Gee-equipped Wellingtons each carrying flares to illuminate the aiming point, and they would be followed by forty-eight Wellingtons and twenty-one Stirlings loaded with incendiaries to start fires as a guide to rest of the force. 57 Squadron briefed the crews of S/L Phipps, F/O Hunter and F/Sgt Donnelly to be part of the flare force and eight other crews, including one captained by the station commander, G/C "Speedy" Powell, with S/L Harvie as second pilot, for the incendiary force, and sent them on their way from Feltwell between 00.20 and 00.50. The crews of Sgts Neville and Webb remained on the ground until their departure for Le Havre at 03.55.

All reached the target area to find favourable weather conditions and the usual industrial haze, and also decoy fires that had been lit in open country south of the target. The crews of F/O Hunter and F/Sgt Donnelly released their twelve bundles of flares, three 500 pounders and single 250 pounder each from 7,000 and 8,000 feet respectively at 02.08, followed two minutes later by those from S/L Phipps from 10,000 feet. The hundreds of flares igniting at 10,000 to 12,000 feet produced a glare, which, together with searchlight dazzle, rendered aiming-point identification something of a challenge. The 57 Squadron crews among the incendiary force dropped nine SBCs each from 10,000 to 14,000 feet between 02.05 and 02.37 but failed to achieve concentration and this would lead to scattered bombing and a disappointing outcome. Local sources reported a light raid with modest damage in southern districts and this was the beginning of Harris's frustrating relationship with Essen until the means were at hand to strike a telling blow twelve months hence. Meanwhile, at Le Havre, Sgt Neville and crew had delivered seventeen 250 pounders across docks 6 and 7 from 10,000 feet at 05.40 and Sgt Webb and crew two sticks on Bassin Bellot from 8,500 feet at 06.00.

The following night brought a return to Essen, for which a force of 187 aircraft was split among three waves as before, 3 Group providing twenty-three Wellingtons for the flare force, eighteen Wellingtons and nine Stirlings for the incendiary force and thirty-one Wellingtons and five Stirlings for the main force. 57 Squadron briefed three crews as illuminators and seven as fire-starters along with the two freshman crews of Sgts Patterson and Webb, who took off first at 19.25 bound for the docks at Boulogne. The main element departed Feltwell between 20.10 and 20.45 with S/L Phipps the senior pilot on duty and adopted the northerly route to the Ruhr, which took the force to a point south of Münster to leave a run of some thirty-five miles to the target. The weather conditions were good, but thick industrial haze created problems and caused the bombing to be widely scattered and spread across twenty-four other towns and cities. On return, the 57 Squadron crews reported establishing their positions by TR-fix and carrying out their assigned tasks from 9,000 to 12,000 feet between 21.45 and 22.20, many claiming that fires remained visible for eighty miles into the return flight, giving the impression of a successful raid. The 3 Group ORB described fires burning in the target area and the attack generally as a 100% improvement on the previous night's effort, while local sources reported just two buildings destroyed in Essen. There was also ground haze at Boulogne, but most crews were able to find something to bomb, Sgt Patterson and crew from 10,000 feet at 21.10, while the Webb crew failed to locate the target and dumped all seventeen 250 pounders into the Channel.

A force of 126 aircraft was assembled for the third attempt on Essen on the night of the 10/11th, for which 3 Group contributed twelve Stirlings and eighteen Wellingtons from Marham, Mildenhall and Wyton. A fine night had been forecast, but unexpected cloud contributed to another dismal display that saw fewer than half of the crews reach the primary target, while thirty-five others bombed alternatives, and the nearest any bombs fell to the Krupp complex was on a railway line serving the area.

Kiel's Deutsche Werke and Germania Werft U-Boot construction yards were posted as the targets for a force of sixty-eight Wellingtons on the 12th, forty-two of them representing 3 Group. 57 Squadron briefed thirteen crews, who were given the Deutsche Werke yards as their aiming point, and they departed Feltwell between 19.25 and 19.45 with W/C Southwell and S/L Phipps the senior pilots on duty. F/Sgt Austin and crew abandoned their sortie at 20.29 after experiencing gun trouble, and they jettisoned four of their 500 pounders over the Berners heath bombing range. Sgt Webb and crew lost their intercom system when a little further out and also turned back early to return their full bomb load to store. The others pressed on and found the conditions on the eastern side of the Schleswig-Holstein peninsula to be sufficiently clear to allow accurate bombing at Kiel, but this had to be carried out in the face of predicted light and heavy flak assisted by cones of searchlights. Sgt Roper and crew suffered a hang-up and had to bring their 1,000 pounder, six 500 pounders and single 250 pounder home, leaving their colleagues to attack from 5,000 to 12,000 feet between 22.15 and 22.58, the low height that of S/L Phipps and crew, who were blinded to the results by searchlight glare. Both the Deutsche Werke and Germania Werft yards sustained damage, as did the naval dockyard and the town, and the success was gained at the fairly modest cost of five Wellingtons.

The main operation on the night of the 13/14th involved a force of 135 aircraft targeting Cologne, for which 3 Group put up thirty-six Stirlings and Wellingtons from Marham and Oakington. It was to be a Gee-led operation, and as usual, there were diverse opinions as to the cloud conditions in the target area. The consensus was that ten-tenths medium cloud hovered to the west and east of the city, while a gap existed right over it in which two to five-tenths cumulus topped out at 11,000 feet. The weather was favourable, and rivers, bridges and autobahns stood out in the partial snow-cover to provide ground features to assist with navigation. Illumination flares were hailed as a great benefit and searchlight beams also provided a reference, and returning crews reported fires to the west and north-west of the city centre. Local sources confirmed that this had been one of the most destructive raids yet against the Rhineland Capital and had caused a loss of production at several war industry factories, while setting off 260 fires and damaging fifteen hundred houses, albeit the majority only lightly.

On the 16th, F/O Hunter RNZAF and his crew took X3599 on a training flight to Aldergrove in Northern Ireland with two passengers on board, acting S/O Blakiston-Houston of the WAAF and Reverend Crawford, a chaplain. In poor weather conditions and low visibility, the Wellington crashed some two miles south of Newcastle, County Down and burst into flames, killing all but the rear gunner, who sustained injuries. There would be no further major operations for most of the Command for almost two weeks, during which period isolated mining and "moling" sorties occupied small numbers of aircraft. "Moling" was a high-risk daylight undertaking by individual aircraft sent over enemy territory with only cloud for protection. To send poorly-armed aircraft to hotspots like the Ruhr for nuisance value was nothing short of madness and must have been thought up by someone who would never have to do it. Sgt Williams and crew drew the short straw on the 17th and were rewarded with a trip to Essen, one of the most heavily defended cities in the Reich. They departed Feltwell at 15.05, and, according to the Form 540, dropped nine 500 pounders on Düsseldorf from 15,000 feet without observing the results through the cloud. The sortie was repeated on the 20th by S/L Phipps and crew, who took off at 11.40 and turned back at the Dutch coast through lack of cloud cover.

W/C Southwell was posted to 311 (Czech) Squadron on the 19th to perform a supernumerary function during its final weeks in Bomber Command before being transferred to Coastal Command. He was succeeded at the helm of 57 Squadron by the familiar personage of W/C Peters-Smith, who came in the opposite direction having served as British advisor to the Czechs. W/C Southwell would return to the front line as commanding officer of 9 Squadron in June and remain in post for nine months, and in August 1943, would be posted to the Middle East to command 150 Squadron, and remain in that post until the middle of October.

In preparation for Harris's next assault on Essen a new record force of 254 aircraft was assembled on the 25th, with crews assigned to the flare, incendiary or main strike force. 3 Group detailed ninety-three Wellingtons and thirty Stirlings, all but three of which would take off. 57 Squadron made ready eight Wellingtons for the main event and four for freshman crews to employ against the docks and shipping at St-Nazaire on the Biscay coast, dispatching them together between 19.55 and 20.10 with S/L Phipps the senior pilot on duty among the Ruhr-bound element and S/L Harvie leading the freshmen. The weather conditions outbound and over Essen were good, and vertical visibility was marred only by the expected industrial haze. Six of the 57 Squadron crews were carrying flares, which they delivered along with their bombs either visually or on TR from 10,000 to 12,000 feet between 21.38 and 21.46, while Sgts Webb and Roper released their incendiaries from 9,000 and 9,500 feet at 21.36 and 21.58. Many crews observed the burst of their bombs, but most were too busy dodging the searchlights and flak to make a detailed assessment. 181 crews returned to report bombing the target, some claiming to have hit the Krupp works, but photographic reconnaissance and local reports revealed this raid to have been another huge failure. A decoy fire-site eighteen miles away at Rheinberg had drawn off the main weight of bombs, and damage in Essen was slight in the extreme in exchange for the loss of nine aircraft. Of the St-Nazaire contingent, Sgt Vanexan and crew turned back with engine failure and landed at Exeter, while S/L Harvie, according to the ORB, bombed Lorient with two sticks of 250 pounders from 10,000 feet at 22.40, the first falling short and the second bursting among buildings at the northern end of the docks. F/Sgt Snook and crew dropped their seventeen 250 pounders from 11,000 feet at 22.50 and Sgt Dickson and crew theirs from 6,000 feet at 23.19 and both observed detonations across the docks.

A much-reduced force of 104 Wellingtons and eleven Stirlings was made ready for a return to Essen on the following night, when, 57 Squadron provided nine Wellingtons for the main event and two for the freshman crews of S/L Harvie and Sgt Dickson to take to Le Havre. The latter took off first at 19.40 and were followed into the air between 20.00 and 20.30 by the Essen-bound element, which arrived in the target area to find excellent weather conditions and smoke and haze less troublesome than expected. The searchlight and flak defence, however, had increased substantially since the previous night, and night fighters were much in evidence throughout the operation. With the exception of S/L Phipps, the 57 Squadron crews carried out their assigned tasks in the flare and incendiary forces from 9,000 to 13,000 feet between 22.03 and 22.20 and observed some bursts, a few developing fires and black smoke rising. S/L Phipps and crew were unable to positively identify Essen and dropped their load on nearby Oberhausen from 13,000 feet at 22.17. X3665 failed to return with the crew of F/Sgt Snook RNZAF, and there were no survivors of the crash, which occurred somewhere in the Ruhr area. Once more the claims of a successful outcome were found to be exaggerated, as only a few bomb loads found their way into the city, and the failure was paid for by the loss of eleven aircraft, more than 10% of those dispatched. Meanwhile, S/L Harvie and crew had successfully bombed the docks at Le Havre from 9,500 feet at 21.26 and Sgt Dickson and crew from 11,000 feet forty-two minutes later.

Harris well understood the difficulties facing his crews in trying to identify a target over a blacked-out and often cloud-covered land in darkness, with only traditional methods of navigation at their disposal to take them to their destination hundreds of miles away. Gee could guide them to an approximate area, but was unable to pinpoint a precise location, and expertly-prepared decoy fire sites could easily be confused with the real thing. Despite this, Harris had faith in the ability of his crews to hit a target, if they were provided with the means to locate it, and coast lines seemed to offer the best prospects. The Hansastadt (ancient free-trade city) Lübeck lies on the River Trave some forty miles south-east of Kiel and was an ideal target because of its close proximity to an easily identifiable coastline, the paucity of its defences and for the fact that it was an old city, with narrow streets and half-timbered buildings, which would aid the spread of fire. The three-wave attack, involving 234 aircraft, was to be conducted along similar lines to those employed against the Renault factory early in the month, and the high proportion of incendiaries carried in the bomb bays reflected Harris's fire-raising intent. 3 Group detailed eighty-eight Wellingtons and twenty-six Stirlings, ten of the former representing 57 Squadron, two loaded with a dozen bundles of flares each plus three 500 pounders and a 250 pounder, five with 810 x 4lb incendiaries and three with a 1,000 pounder and seven of 500lbs. One further Wellington was loaded with 460 bundles of nickels, the code for propaganda leaflets, which F/Sgt Vanexan and crew were to dispense to the citizens of Paris. S/L Harvie was the senior pilot on duty as ten 57 Squadron Wellingtons departed Feltwell between 19.25 and 19.45, leaving S/L Phipps and crew on the ground until 22.00 as one of a number of senior crews scheduled to arrive at the target at the end of the raid to carry out an assessment. Sgt Roper and crew turned back immediately because of an unserviceable a.s.i., and rear turret, while F/Sgt Vanexan and crew headed south to deliver what Harris scathingly called "toilet paper" to litter the streets of Paris from 8,000 feet at 21.42. The others set a course towards the east to make landfall on Denmark's western coast, before crossing the Schleswig-Holstein peninsula and reaching the Baltic.

The target lay beyond the range of Gee, but the device would assist preliminary navigation and help to maintain a coherent bomber stream. At around the same time as the spearhead was closing on the target, S/L Phipps and crew were forced to turn back after the navigator became unwell, probably as a result of oxygen starvation. S/L Harvie and crew ran into searchlights at Kiel and were forced down to 1,500 feet as they struggled to extricate themselves from a cone and opted to aid their escape by dropping the bombs onto the town centre at 22.25. The first wave aircraft arrived in the target area to be greeted by clear skies, bright moonlight and an absence of searchlights, and this anticipated lack of defensive measures would allow crews to carry out their attacks from medium to low level, some descending to 2,000 feet to improve accuracy. The 57 Squadron crews were not among these and performed their respective roles from 8,000 to 12,000 feet between 22.40 and 23.00, contributing to the four hundred tons of bombs, two-thirds of them incendiaries, falling within the city. On return, Sgt Williams and crew reported shooting down an enemy night-fighter. Photo-reconnaissance revealed that approximately 190 acres of the old town had been destroyed, mostly by fire, and this amounted to 30% of the city's built-up area. A total of 1,425 buildings had been destroyed, and almost two thousand others seriously damaged, and this was a triumph for Harris at a time when the very existence of an independent bomber force was still being questioned in high places. Lübeck was the first major success for the area bombing policy, and the principles put into operation on this night would form the basis of all similar operations in the future. There was an outcry following this unexpected attack on Lübeck, which was a vital port for the Red Cross, and an agreement was struck that largely ensured its future protection from bombing.

This was the final operation of a month which had seen the squadron operate against fourteen targets, dispatching seventy-six sorties for the loss of two Wellingtons and crews.

April 1942

April began inauspiciously for the Command in general and for 3 Group in particular, when Operation "Lineshoot", a low-level attack on railway installations at Hanau and Lohr in southern Germany on the night of the 1/2nd went disastrously wrong. 3 Group detailed thirty-five Wellingtons for Hanau, located some five miles east of Frankfurt, while 5 Group targeted Lohr some twenty miles to the east-south-east with fourteen Hampdens. A further ten 3 Group Wellington crews were briefed to attack the docks and shipping at Le Havre. 57 Squadron made ready eleven Wellingtons for the main event and sent them on their way from Feltwell over an extended period between 20.30 and 22.20 with S/L Harvie the senior pilot on duty. G/C "Speedy" Powell had put himself on the Order of Battle and borrowed a 75(NZ) Squadron Wellington for the occasion, inviting W/C Peters-Smith to join him as second pilot. F/Sgt Wilson and crew turned back early because of W/T failure, leaving the others to press on in unfavourable weather conditions, which would make it difficult to identify ground features. F/Sgt Donnelly and crew arrived in the target area only to suffer an electrical malfunction, and they jettisoned their nine 500 pounders "live" from 10,000 feet at 01.15 before turning for home. Sgt Johnson and crew found a stretch of track at Kahl am Main to the south-east of Hanau and dropped their load from 4,500 feet near a bridge and close to marshalling yards and a nickel factory at 23.24. Sgt Williams and crew attacked a moving train between Aschaffenburg and Hanau before aiming the rest of their load at the marshalling yards from 4,500 feet at 23.42 and claiming a very near-miss. F/Sgt Vanexan and crew scored a direct hit from 5,000 feet on railway track between Hanau and Lohr at 00.25 and collected some flak damage, while Sgt Webb and crew could only report bombing in the target area from 7,000 feet at 00.16. These were the only 57 Squadron crews to make it back to England, where F/Sgt Vanexan and crew landed at Manston. Quite how the Kiwis arrived back at Feltwell intact is a mystery, after twelve Wellingtons, five from 57 Squadron and seven from 214 Squadron, were shot down, mostly it appears by night fighters. There was no pattern to their fall, which occurred in Holland, Belgium, Rhineland Germany and the target area. X3410 would appear to have come down somewhere south of the Ruhr and there were no survivors from the crew of S/L Harvie, a native of New Zealand serving in the RAF. X3425 crashed near St-Truiden in eastern Belgium killing Sgt Roper and his crew, while the bodies of F/Sgt Neville and his crew were found in the wreckage of X3607 in a wood near Lorsch some nine miles east-north-east of the city of Worms. X3748 crashed some five miles east-north-east of Bad Kreuznach, south-west of Mainz, killing F/Sgt Knobloch RNZAF and his Canadian second pilot, but at least four of the crew survived to fall into enemy hands. Z1565 was the only victim to fall in the target area where it took the lives of Sgt Patterson RNZAF and all but one of his crew, who was also taken into captivity.

The Command set another new record on the night of the 5/6th, when dispatching 263 aircraft to Cologne. Six 57 Squadron crews had attended briefing to learn that the artillery-producing Klöckner Humboldt A G engineering works in the Deutz district to the east of the Rhine was to be the aiming-point. P/Os Austin and Heald were the only commissioned pilots on duty as they departed Feltwell between 23.20 and 23.35, each carrying a dozen bundles of flares, three 500 pounders and a single 250 pounder on a night of fine weather conditions. They all reached the target area to be greeted by five-tenths cloud and bright moonlight but also an intense searchlight and flak response. The 57 Squadron crews performed their roles according to brief from 10,000 to 17,000 feet between 01.37 and 01.49 but observed little of the results and could only report that they had bombed in the general target area. Opinions as to the effectiveness of the raid were divided, Feltwell, Marham and Oakington crews expressing doubts, while Honington, Mildenhall, Stradishall and Wyton were confident that their bombs had landed in the city. A local report revealed scattered bombing across the city, with one industrial building hit and ninety houses destroyed.

Harris's campaign against Essen continued on the night of the 6/7th, for which a force of 157 aircraft was made ready, including six Wellingtons representing 57 Squadron in a 3 Group contribution of fifty-seven. There was a late take-off on a night of unfavourable weather conditions, into which the 57 Squadron launched themselves between 00.30 and 00.50 with P/Os Austin and Heald once more the only commissioned pilots on duty and each Wellington loaded as for the previous night. They made their way to the Dutch coast in stormy conditions via corridor G to make landfall over the Scheldt estuary, having passed through storms lurking in ten-tenths ice-bearing cloud. A large proportion of the force turned back at this time, among them the crews of Sgts Dickson and Johnson, and Sgt Williams and crew became another victim of icing but pressed on south following the course of the Rhine until reaching Coblenz, which they bombed from 11,000 feet at 02.55. F/Sgt Wilson and crew also turned back early because of the failure of their Gee-box, and this left just the crews of P/Os Heald and Austin to arrive at the target to encounter up to ten-tenths cloud and a hostile searchlight and flak defence. They delivered their flares and bombs on TR references from 12,000 feet at 03.00 and 10,000 feet at 03.23 respectively, and neither observed any results. Local sources confirmed that only a few bombs had found their way into the city and damage was negligible.

Briefings took place on all heavy bomber stations on the 8th, when crews were told that they were to be part of a new record force of 272 aircraft with Hamburg as their destination that night. 3 Group detailed ninety-five Wellingtons and Stirlings for the main event and four each to attack the docks and shipping at Le Havre and conduct mining sorties in the Rosemary garden in the Heligoland Bight. 57 Squadron made ready eight Wellingtons and sent them on their way from Feltwell between 21.20 and 22.05 bound for Germany's second city with P/Os Morse and Austin and the newly promoted W/O Vanexan the senior pilots on duty. Hamburg often enjoyed the benefits of a "gatekeeper" in the form of enormous weather fronts that lay in the path of bombers as they crossed the North Sea to approach the Schleswig-Holstein coast. Giant columns of cumulonimbus cloud towered to 20,000 feet and beyond and contained violent electrical storm and severe icing conditions. Too high to climb over and too wide to circumnavigate, they forced crews to fly through them, and for many it was a terrifying experience that persuaded them to jettison their bombs and head for home. On this night, thirty-one 3 Group aircraft turned back along with some fifty others, and among them were the 57 Squadron crews of F/Sgt Donnelly and P/O Austin, the latter after the front gunner became ill. The others pushed on to reach the target, where they were confronted by ten-tenths cloud permeated by an intense flak barrage, and delivered their nine 500 pounders each from 14,000 and 15,000 feet between 00.11 and 00.50. W/O Vanexan and crew found the bomb release mechanism to be frozen solid and they were unable to let their load go. At debriefing, 188 crews claimed to have bombed in the target area, few with anything of value to report, and absent from the process was the crew of P/O Morse RNZAF, who disappeared without trace in X3757. Local sources estimated some fourteen bomb loads had fallen in the city, causing three large fires but no specific damage, but incendiaries fell in Bremen sixty miles to the south-west and damaged four U-Boots under construction at the Vulkan yards.

The madness of "moling" raised its ugly head again on the 9th, when Feltwell was ordered to send seven Wellingtons to Essen, four of them belonging to 57 Squadron. The crews of S/L Phipps, P/Os Austin and Heald and F/Sgt Donnelly took off at 12.30 and the Heald crew was back on the ground after forty-five minutes because of an issue with the door to the front turret. The others reached the Dutch coast before turning back as the cloud cover thinned and risked leaving them exposed.

Essen was posted as the objective for 254 aircraft on the 10th, an operation supported by 3 Group with 102 Wellingtons and Stirlings, nine of the former provided by 57 Squadron. It was planned as a "shaker" operation, which was the codename given to the dropping of target illuminator flares by 3 Group aircraft employing Gee as a rudimentary form of path finding. The 57 Squadron element became airborne between 21.50 and 22.10 with S/L Phipps the senior pilot on duty and soon lost the services of P/O Heald and crew to TR failure. The others pressed on expecting to find the clear skies forecast at briefing, but, instead, were confronted by a layer of six to ten-tenths cloud across the central Ruhr at between 5,000 and 8,000 feet. The route in was described as "hot", with scores of searchlights from all sides working in conjunction with light and heavy flak. Seven of the 57 Squadron crews were members of the flare force and delivered their bombs and illumination from 9,000 to 12,000 feet between 23.58 and 00.24 based on a TR-fix and saw nothing of the outcome. S/L Phipps and crew failed to identify Essen and dropped their all-incendiary load on the briefed alternative target of Cologne from 9,500 feet at 00.55. Local sources confirmed the operation to have been another dismal failure, which destroyed only twelve houses in Essen and caused no industrial damage.

Orders were received across the Command on the 12th to prepare another large force to return to Essen that night, and 251 aircraft were made ready accordingly, 3 Group responding with ninety-two Wellingtons and thirty-two Stirlings for the main event, Le Havre for the freshmen and gardening, all but five of which would take off. 57 Squadron made ready eight Wellingtons for the Ruhr and one for the crew of Sgt Brown to employ against the docks and shipping at Le Havre, and it was the latter that departed Feltwell first at 21.00. They would fail to identify the target and jettisoned their bombs "safe" into the sea.

The main element took off between 22.10 and 22.45 with W/C Peters-Smith and S/L Phipps the senior pilots on duty, seven of them assigned to the flare force, from which Sgt Johnson and crew dropped out when the wireless operator blacked out, presumably from oxygen starvation. The flare force was depleted further when P/O Austin and crew lost the use of their Gee box and bombed the aerodrome at Schiphol from 10,000 feet at 02.40, and these were among twenty 3 Group crews to return early. Once over enemy territory the others found many night-fighter flares in evidence along with red and green lights, and numerous searchlight cones were accompanied by fairly accurate medium and heavy flak. The weather conditions were good, with visibility estimated by some at a hundred miles, and this may have contributed to the slight improvement in performance. The 57 Squadron crews performed their respective roles from 8,000 to 12,000 feet between 01.17 and 01.38 and observed little of their efforts and just a few scattered fires. Local sources confirmed that five high explosive bombs and two hundred incendiaries had hit the Krupp complex, causing a large fire, and eighty houses were destroyed or seriously damaged, but it was still a poor return for the size of the force. Bombing photographs captured many other Ruhr locations, and, generally, it was another disappointing performance that would provide further ammunition for the detractors. Eight major operations had been mounted against Essen since the night of the 8/9th of March, involving 1,555 sorties, of which 1,006 had claimed to have bombed the city. This huge effort had resulted in very modest residential damage, only two incidents of industrial damage, and had cost sixty-four aircraft and crews. Only twenty-two bombing photos had shown ground detail within five miles of Essen, demonstrating in the eyes of the critics, that there had been no improvement in the effectiveness of operations since the Butt Report.

Acting F/L Forbes arrived from 12 O.T.U., on the 13th to fulfil the role of deputy flight commander and had time to settle in as only Sgt Brown and crew would be operating that night on a freshman trip to attack the docks and shipping at Boulogne. They took off at 21.30 and returned ninety minutes later with a failing starboard engine. Dortmund was posted as the target for a force of 208 aircraft on the 14th, which was by far the largest effort yet against this industrial giant situated at the eastern end of the Ruhr. 3 Group made a contribution to the operation of eighty-six Wellingtons and Stirlings, six of the former representing 57 Squadron, which departed Feltwell as part of the flare force between 22.25 and 22.45 with P/O Austin the only commissioned pilot on duty. The sorties of the crews of Sgts Dickson and Webb were cut short by port engine troubles, leaving the rest to run the gauntlet of intense searchlight and flak activity as they traversed the most heavily defended region of Germany. Clear skies enabled them to map-read their way by river and railway features to the aiming point, where they dropped their flares and bombs from 11,000 to 12,000 feet between 01.56 and 02.00, while attempting to dodge some eighty searchlights in cones. It would be established later that the bombing had been scattered over a forty-mile stretch of the region, with no significant damage to the intended target.

Acting F/L Hicks became another new recruit from 12 O.T.U., on the 15th, and probably sat in on the briefing that afternoon for the return to Dortmund but would not take part, unlike F/L Forbes who would fly to the Ruhr as second pilot to S/L Phipps. 3 Group's contribution to the main event amounted to seventy Wellingtons and Stirlings, 57 Squadron weighing in with six Wellingtons plus one for the freshman crew of Sgt Brown and crew to employ against the docks and shipping at Le Havre. The latter departed Feltwell first at 22.00 and reached their target at the same time as the Ruhr-bound crews were taking off. They carried out a number of runs across the aiming point at 10,000 feet, dispensing a stick of 250 pounders each time until all seventeen had fallen away by 00.10, and were rewarded with the sight of fires. Meanwhile, two hundred miles to the north, the rest of the 57 Squadron Wellingtons took off between 23.30 and 00.20 and lost the services of Sgt Johnson and crew after the pilot became unwell. Sgt Dickson's escape hatch blew open and he opted to bomb the docks at Ostend before turning back, leaving the others to negotiate thick, ice-bearing cloud on the southern approaches to the Ruhr, only then to run into intense searchlight and flak activity over the target, where two-tenths low cloud combined with the industrial haze to muddy the vertical visibility. A little over half of the force reached the target area, where the 57 Squadron members of the flare force carried out their briefed tasks from 11,000 and 12,000 feet between 02.37 and 03.04 and S/L Phipps and crew delivered their cookie from and the same height at 02.55. Some bomb bursts were observed, but the operation was another massive disappointment, which, mercifully, cost a modest four aircraft and crews.

S/L Baron was posted in from 22 O.T.U., on the 16th to fulfil the role of flight commander and had twenty-four hours to settle in before attending his first briefing, which was in preparation for an operation to Hamburg. A force of 173 aircraft was made ready, of which seventy-two Wellingtons and Stirlings were provided by 3 Group, six of the former by 57 Squadron, plus an additional one for the crew of Sgt Brown to employ against the docks and shipping at Le Havre as they continued their apprenticeship. They took off at 21.50 and returned four hours later to report delivering their seventeen 250 pounders onto the docks from 10,000 feet at 23.43, just as the Hamburg-bound element was taxiing to the threshold for take-off. S/L Phipps was the senior pilot as they took to the air between 23.45 and 00.15, and he had S/L Baron alongside him as second pilot. Sgt Webb collapsed at the controls before the target was reached, and second pilot, F/L Forbes, took over to bring the aircraft and crew home. Those arriving at the target found clear skies with ground haze, and a typically fierce response from searchlights and flak. Sgt Williams and crew had a 1,000 pounder and six 500 pounders under their feet, and let them go from 8,000 feet at 03.03, while the crews of Sgts Johnson and Dickson were carrying all-incendiary loads, which they dropped from 12,000 and 11,000 feet at 03.10 and 03.35 respectively. X3542 was outbound at 20,000 feet over the Schleswig-Holstein peninsula and much closer to Kiel than Hamburg when it was attacked and shot down by what was believed to be a FW190 at 03.00. F/Sgt Wilson RNZAF and two of his crew lost their lives leaving their three colleagues, including the recently arrived F/L Hicks, in enemy hands. X3478 was probably homebound and was in sight of the Waddensee in Jade Bay when it came down at Mulsum at 03.18 and delivered S/L Phipps and crew into captivity, thus ending S/L Baron's brief spell with the squadron. At debriefing, only 107 crews claimed to have bombed in the target area, but, according to local sources, they had inflicted upon the city more damage than had been the norm of late, causing seventy-five fires, of which thirty-three were classed as large.

Acting F/L Franks was posted to the squadron from 21 O.T.U., on the 21st to fill the gap for a deputy flight commander left by the failure to return of F/L Hicks. The first attempt to employ Gee as a blind bombing aid took place on the night of the 22/23rd, when Cologne was the target for a 3 Group force of sixty-four Wellingtons and five Stirlings, six of the former provided by 57 Squadron. F/L Forbes was flying as crew captain for the first time since joining the squadron and he would have Le Havre as his destination in company with the crews of P/O Austin and Sgt Abercrombie, who all got away at ten-minute intervals between 21.20 and 21.40. They found good visibility at the Normandy coast, which enabled them to identify ground features before bombing from 9,300 to 12.300 feet between 23.06 and 23.23 and observing bursts. Those bound for Cologne departed Feltwell between 21.55 and 22.05 with P/O Heald the only commissioned pilot on duty and Sgt Brown and crew on their first non-freshman sortie. Sgt Hudson and crew were among nine to turn back early, having lost the use of their intercom, leaving the others to arrive in the target area to find low cloud and haze, which would render the bombing photography ineffective. The 57 Squadron crews carried out their attacks on a TR-fix from 10,000 to 15,000 feet between 00.30 and 00.53 and observed the glow of burning incendiaries but little else. In fact, local sources confirmed that fewer than 20% of the bomb loads had fallen into the city, and some landed up to ten miles away, proving that Gee was capable of guiding a force to a general area, but lacked the precision necessary to deliver a telling blow on an urban target.

Following the series of unsuccessful operations, and, perhaps, recalling the success of the Lübeck raid a month earlier, Harris ordered a series of attacks on Rostock, a town situated some sixty miles further east along the Baltic coast, where the Heinkel Flugzeugwerke HQ and aircraft factory in the Marienehe district on the western bank of the Unterwarnow River on the southern outskirts was an added attraction. A force of 161 aircraft was assembled on the 23rd, 143 to attack the old town with predominantly incendiary bomb loads, while eighteen aircraft from 5 Group carried out a precision attack on the Heinkel works. 3 Group detailed thirty-one Stirlings and thirty-six Wellingtons, six of the latter representing 57 Squadron, and they departed Feltwell between 22.25 and 22.45 with W/C Peters-Smith the senior pilot on duty. They made their way across the North Sea and Schleswig-Holstein peninsula in favourable weather conditions which persisted all the way to the target, where clear skies and good visibility enabled them to identify ground detail. It was at this point that an electrical fault in the bomb-release system caused Sgt Dickson's all-incendiary bomb load to hang up and he would have to bring it home. The others bombed from 8,000 to 10,000 feet between 01.59 and 02.32 and were convinced that they had hit the centre of the town as briefed. In fact, the majority of crews had failed to find the mark at either aiming point, and the bombing had fallen between two and six miles away to provide a disappointing start to what would ultimately be a successful campaign.

On the 24th, 125 aircraft were made ready for round two at Rostock, thirty-four from 5 Group assigned to the Heinkel factory, while ninety-one from the other groups focused on the old town. 3 Group put up twenty-two Stirlings and Wellingtons for the main event and ten freshman crews to target the docks and shipping at Dunkerque, among the latter four Wellingtons representing 57 Squadron. The crews of P/Os Austin, Trant, Sligo and Sgt Abercrombie took off between 20.40 and 20.55 and arrived at the French coast to find clear skies. They delivered their seventeen 250 pounders each from 10,000 to 12,500 feet between 23.43 and 23.55 and watched them detonate across the docks before returning safely. Meanwhile, 460 miles to the north-east, the bulk of those approaching Rostock were drawn on from many miles away by the fires already created by the spearhead. Bright moonlight illuminated the Unterwarnow River running south from the coast to the heart of the town and provided excellent visibility for the low-level attacks. The town seemed to be ablaze as the 5 Group aircraft crossed over it to reach the Heinkel factory, which most attacked on existing fires, while trying to evade the attentions of the many searchlights co-operating with light flak. According to the observations of returning crews, the Heinkel factory and adjacent aerodrome had been hit by many bombs and were left burning, and, while post-raid reconnaissance revealed extensive damage within the town, the factory buildings were revealed to be still intact, demonstrating that the impressions gained by crews in the heat of battle could be somewhat unreliable.

Briefings for the third Rostock raid took place on the afternoon of the 25th, when 110 crews learned that they were to continue the assault on the town, while eighteen from 5 Group targeted the Heinkel factory, led by 106 Squadron's commanding officer, W/C Guy Gibson. 3 Group detailed fifty-seven Stirlings and Wellington for the main event and ten others for freshman crews to take to Dunkerque, 57 Squadron contributing seven and three Wellingtons respectively. The main element departed Feltwell between 22.20 and 22.30 with F/L Forbes the senior pilot on duty, and they were followed closely by the crews of P/Os Sligo and Trant and Sgt Abercrombie bound for the French coast. The latter arrived at their destination a little over an hour later to find eight-tenths cloud with sufficient gaps to allow glimpses of the ground and carried out their attacks from 10,000 to 12,000 feet between 23.38 and 23.48, observing little or nothing of the outcome. Meanwhile, ideal weather conditions again prevailed for the outward flight to the western Baltic and clear skies greeted the arrival of the bomber force over Rostock. A little ground haze was of no consequence and bombing by the 57 Squadron participants was carried out from 7,000 to 10,000 feet between 02.19 and 02.30, most observing numerous bomb bursts and fires in the built-up area. They returned safely, confident of another successful result, and this was confirmed by post-raid reconnaissance, which revealed the factory to have sustained hits, at last, and the town to have suffered severe damage, all without loss to the attackers.

A force of 106 aircraft was detailed for the final raid of the series on the 26th, which included a contribution from 3 Group of nine Stirlings and nineteen Wellingtons from Mildenhall and Wyton, while the Feltwell squadrons remained at home. Those reaching the target area found moonlight, excellent visibility and existing fires to aid target location, and another successful raid ensued. An analysis of the Rostock campaign revealed it to have been highly successful, destroying 1,765 buildings and seriously damaging five hundred more, which represented 60% of the town's built-up area. In his diaries, Propaganda Minister Goebbels used the phrase "Terrorangriff", terror raid, for the first time.

Cologne provided the main target for the night of the 27/28th, for which ninety-seven aircraft were made available, forty-seven provided by 3 Group for the main event and eight for mining duties in the Rosemary garden in the Heligoland Bight. 57 Squadron made ready six Wellingtons for the Rhineland capital and three for the first mining sorties by the freshman crews of P/Os Sligo and Trant and Sgt Abercrombie, and the two elements took off together between 21.50 and 22.05 with P/O Heald the senior pilot on duty. The weather in the Cologne area was favourable with good visibility and just a little ground haze, and the crews took advantage to deliver an unusually effective attack. The 57 Squadron participants carried out their attacks from 8,000 to 10,000 feet between 01.02 and 01.23, a number of crews specifying at debriefing that the industrial East Bank of the Rhine, perhaps, received the main weight of the attack. Many fires, in particular, were seen to develop in the Deutz area where the Klöckner-Humboldt works was located, and local sources would confirm damage to nine industrial premises and more than fifteen hundred houses. The mining element had been depleted by the early return of P/O Sligo and crew for an undisclosed reason, leaving the crews of P/O Trant and Sgt Abercrombie to pinpoint respectively on Westerhever and Utholm on the western coast of the Schleswig-Holstein peninsula before carrying out timed runs to the release point, where they delivered two mines each without opposition from 800 feet at 01.33 and 01.15.

Feltwell was left off the 3 Group Order of Battle on the 28th, when Kiel was the target for a force of eighty-eight aircraft including fifteen Stirlings and twenty-one Wellingtons provided by 3 Group. The attack took place under bright moonlight and in the face of a spirited searchlight and flak defence, and all three shipyards sustained damage to some extent. The final operation of the month to involve the squadron took place on the night of the 29/30th and was directed at the Gnome & Rhone aero engine factory at Gennevilliers, situated in the Port de Paris on the banks of the Seine in north-western Paris. Eighty-eight aircraft were made ready, 3 Group providing six Stirlings and forty-three Wellingtons, nine of the latter representing 57 Squadron, which, according to the ORB, were to target the power station serving the area. They departed Feltwell between 21.15 and 21.25 with W/C Peters-Smith the senior pilot on duty and F/L Franks undertaking his first sortie with the squadron. The good weather continued, and the force arrived in the target area to find perfect conditions and little defensive activity, which enabled crews to identify their respective aiming points and those from 57 Squadron to deliver their attacks from 4,000 to 8,000 feet between 23.40 and 00.18. Returning crews described accurate bombing, with hits on the factory and adjacent power station, and the 3 Group ORB described the operation as an undoubted success. Sadly, the crews were mistaken again, and the factory escaped damage, although other industrial buildings nearby were hit. X3640 failed to arrive back with the others and P/O Heald RNZAF and crew were duly posted missing. The sad news eventually arrived via the Red Cross that the Wellington had crashed some eight miles south-east of Versailles and that all on board had lost their lives. It was remarkable that so many of the missing crews had a Kiwi captain, and their loss would be felt equally keenly by their countrymen across the tarmac in 75(NZ) Squadron.

During the course of the month, the squadron carried out twenty-two operations, four involving single freshman crews, and dispatched 118 sorties for the loss of nine Wellingtons and crews.

May 1942

The first night of the new month passed by without operational activity and the ninety-six crews called to briefings on 3 and 5 Group stations on the 2nd learned that they would be engaging in gardening activities that night in French and German waters. Probably sitting in at Feltwell was S/L Laird, who arrived on this day from 23 O.T.U., to assume a flight commander role with 57 Squadron. 3 Group detailed fifty-five aircraft, of which eight were made ready by 57 Squadron, while their crews were hearing the details of their sorties to the Biscay coast to mine the waters of the Beech garden off St-Nazaire. They departed Feltwell between 20.40 and 21.00 with S/L Franks the senior pilot on duty and headed south under clear skies and bright moonlight only to encounter unhelpful weather conditions in the target area, where thick sea mist afforded poor visibility. Each was carrying two 1,500lb parachute mines and three 500 pounders, the latter for use against targets of opportunity, but the first task was to establish a pinpoint from which to make a timed run to the release point. The regular pinpoints for the Beech garden were Quiberon to the north-west, Belle Isle to the west and Le Calebasse Rocks, which the crews of P/Os Austin and Sligo and Sgts Abercrombie and Brown were unable to locate, and they returned their mines and bombs to store. The crews of S/L Franks, W/O Vanexan and Sgts Dickson and Hudson found suitable references and delivered their vegetables into the briefed locations from 500 to 800 feet between 00.57 and 01.40. The Dickson crew aimed a 500 pounder at a vessel and watched it miss narrowly, and all other bombs were brought home. According to the squadron ORB, Sgt Abercrombie and crew abandoned a fuel-starved X3756 to its fate near Weston-Super-Mare on return, and all landed safely by parachute. Bill Chorley's Bomber Command Losses records this incident as occurring during a night cross-country exercise and Sgt Preston as the pilot, when he was, in fact, the rear gunner.

The main target for what turned out to be a modest force of eighty-one aircraft on the night of the 3/4th was Hamburg, on the one-hundredth anniversary of its great fire, although this was not a motive for the operation. The original intention to send a larger force to north-western Germany had been modified in the face of a forecast of unfavourable weather conditions, and just twenty-seven 3 Group aircraft were involved, none of them from Feltwell. The force was greeted by nine to ten-tenths cloud in the target area and fifty-four crews bombed on a combination of TR and e.t.a., despite which, 113 fires resulted, fifty-seven of them large and the scale of damage was out of all proportion to the numbers attacking and recent performances.

The highly industrialized southern city of Stuttgart had not yet been attacked in numbers and would be the primary target for the next three nights. A force of 121 aircraft was assembled on the 4th and called upon the services of fifty 3 Group Stirlings and Wellingtons, seven of the latter belonging to 57 Squadron. Six 35 (Madras Presidency) Squadron Halifaxes were assigned to a special aiming-point within the city, while the rest of the force targeted the highly important Robert Bosch electrical components factory located in the Feuerbach district to the north-west of the city centre. The 57 Squadron element took off between 22.30 and 22.40 with S/L Franks the senior pilot on duty and S/L Laird flying as second pilot to W/O Vanexan, and climbed away into clear skies and excellent conditions. They made landfall on the French coast, before following the course of the frontier with Belgium to enter Germany near Strasbourg and those reaching the Stuttgart area would find that its location in a series of valleys offered quite a challenge. Even when not covered by cloud, which it frequent was, it could be difficult to pick out, and on this night, ten-tenths cloud led to bombs being scattered over a wide area, and the use of a decoy fire-site at Lauffen, fifteen miles to the north, which was cleverly defended by around thirty-five searchlights, lured away many of the bomb loads. The 57 Squadron crews all returned safely, most to report that they had been unable to identify the target and had bombed on the evidence of a red flare and fires from 4,000 to 12,000 feet between 01.26 and 02.10. Sgt Hudson and crew dropped their 810 x 4lb incendiaries on a location north of Strasbourg at 00.35, while S/L Franks and crew brought theirs home.

The Feltwell squadrons were not invited to take part in the following night's return to Stuttgart by a reduced force of seventy-seven aircraft, thirty of which were provided by 3 Group. Those reaching southern Germany found clear skies but thick haze, which blotted out most ground detail, and this persuaded many crews to bomb the Lauffen decoy site in error for the city, which remained bomb-free. A force of ninety-seven aircraft was assembled for the third operation against Stuttgart on the 6th, 3 Group contributing fifty-five Stirlings and Wellingtons, six of the latter representing 57 Squadron. They departed Feltwell between 21.50 and 22.00 with P/Os Austin and Sligo the only commissioned pilots and set course for the south coast to begin the Channel crossing near Beachy Head. They arrived at the target under clear skies only to find thick haze concealing ground detail, and none was able to positively identify that they were over Stuttgart. P/O Sligo and crew attacked an aerodrome believed to be east of the city, while Sgt Hudson and crew bombed the town of Reutlingen situated some ten miles to the south and set off a few fires. The others carried out their attacks on what they believed was the primary target from 3,000 to 8,000 feet between 01.04 and 01.27 and returned with little of value to pass on at debriefing. The operation was another dismal failure, which, according to local sources, fell partially upon the city of Heilbronn, some twenty miles to the north.

A large mining effort was planned for the 7th involving eighty-one aircraft from 3 and 5 Groups, 3 Group providing thirty-nine Wellingtons and thirteen Stirlings, eight of the former representing 57 Squadron. The crews of S/L Laird and P/O Armin were assigned to the Rosemary garden in the Heligoland Bight, while P/Os Austin and Sligo and Sgt Brown were to operate in the Pumpkin garden at the northern end of the Great Belt in the western Baltic and the crews of Sgts Dickson and Hudson and W/O Vanexan in the Forget-me-not garden in Kiel Harbour. They departed Feltwell between 22.10 and 23.00, each carrying two mines and three 500 pounders, and it is believed that all arrived at their respective destinations to seek out a pinpoint for the start of their timed run to the drop zone. S/L Laird and crew failed to establish their position and returned their ordnance to store, while W/O Vanexan and crew planted their vegetables in the Hawthorn II garden off the west coast of Jutland as an alternative. Five of the others planted as briefed from 600 to 1,000 feet between 01.14 and 02.35, and P/O Sligo and crew, the pilot yet another member of the RNZAF, failed to return after Z1564 came down without survivors somewhere near Esbjerg on the west coast of Jutland.

Having recently dealt a blow upon the town of Rostock and the local Heinkel aircraft factory, it was decided to return to the area on the night of the 8/9th to target the firm's other factory at Warnemünde, situated on the western bank of the Warnow estuary about six miles to the north. The Feltwell squadrons were, perhaps, fortunate in being left off the Order of Battle on this night, as the operation became something of a disaster for little return. Nineteen aircraft failed to return from what was a largely low-level attack, and four of the casualties were 44 (Rhodesia) Squadron Lancasters, one of which contained the newly-appointed commanding officer and his crew.

Twenty aircraft were assigned to gardening duties on the 9th, fourteen of them belonging to 3 Group. 57 Squadron briefed five crews for gardens in the western Baltic, those of Sgts Brown and Hudson for Forget-me-not, P/O Trant and W/O Vanexan for Radish, the Fehmarn Belt, and Sgt Dickson for Carrot, the Little Belt. They departed Feltwell between 22.15 and 22.20 and reached their respective target areas to find a continuation of the favourable weather conditions. The vegetables were planted in the briefed locations from 500 to 800 feet between 01.24 and 02.06 and the crews of Sgts Dickson and Hudson dropped their three 500 pounders each onto a bridge and causeway at Middelfart, which linked Fyn Island with the Danish mainland.

The madness of "moling" saw four Wellingtons dispatched from Feltwell on the 13th to attack Essen by daylight. The 57 Squadron crews of Sgt Hudson, Sgt Brown and F/Sgt Dickson took off at ten-minute intervals from 11.30, only for the Brown crew to be recalled after about an hour. The remaining pair were favoured by sufficient cloud to cloak their presence and managed to penetrate the Ruhr, where they dropped nine 500 pounders each upon a built-up area believed to be Mülheim-an-der Ruhr, located just a few miles short of Essen.

3 Group detailed twenty-six Wellingtons from Feltwell, Honington and Oakington for gardening duties on the 15th, eight of them made ready by 57 Squadron. The crews were briefed to plant their vegetables in the Quince garden, one of a number of mining areas in Kiel Bay, and set off between 22.25 and 23.00 with S/L Franks the senior pilot on duty and S/L Laird flying as second pilot to Sgt Hudson. F/Sgt Anderson and crew turned back early because of a trimming issue, leaving the others to reach the western Baltic in fine weather conditions and carry out their briefs from 500 to 800 feet between 01.49 and 02.49. The Middelfart bridge was targeted again by Sgt

Hudson and crew, while F/Sgt Dickson and crew attacked a bridge at Sønderborg on south Jutland's Baltic coast and P/O Trant and crew oil tanks at nearby Als.

On the 17th, 3 Group briefed thirty-two Stirling and twenty-eight Wellington crews for gardening duties off the Frisians and Heligoland and a further twenty-seven crews to bomb the docks and shipping at Boulogne. 57 Squadron loaded seven of its own with seventeen 250 pounders and sent them on their way from Feltwell between 22.40 and 22.50 with S/L Laird the senior pilot on duty. They encountered seven to ten-tenths cloud at the French coast, and, it is understood, generally adverse weather conditions including severe icing, as a result of which, only two crews, both from 57 Squadron, were able to locate and attack the target. Unable to maintain height outbound, P/O Duffy and crew jettisoned eight 250 pounders and delivered the remainder across dock 4 from 8,000 feet at 00.05. They arrived home with battle damage and a wounded wireless operator, who was admitted to hospital. Five minutes after they attacked, F/O Williams and crew dropped one stick across docks 6 and 7 from 5,000 feet and a second stick to the south, observing bursts. S/L Laird and crew ended up in the Channel two hundred yards off the foreshore at Dungeness on the Kent coast, after DV806's port engine failed suddenly. It is unclear whether this occurred on the way out or when homebound, but all occupants made it safely to dry land none the worse for their experience.

Preparations were put in hand on the 19th for an operation that night against Mannheim, for which 197 aircraft were made ready, around seventy of them on 3 Group stations, six by 57 Squadron plus four more for the use of freshman crews against the docks and shipping at St-Nazaire. The two sections departed Feltwell together between 22.45 and 23.05 with S/L Franks the senior pilot on duty and headed south for the Channel crossing, those bound for the Biscay coast by-passing the Channel Islands to make landfall near St Malo, while the main element crossed into enemy territory further to the east. Nestling on the East Bank of the Rhine, opposite Ludwigshafen, Mannheim was easy to locate by a distinctive bend in the waterway south of the city and was found on this night to be under clear skies, but so cloaked in extreme darkness and ground haze, that most would have to carry out their attacks on DR and TR1335 (Gee). Those heading for southern Germany reached their destination first and dropped their all-incendiary loads from 7,500 to 14,000 feet between 01.13 and 01.48, some observing bursts and others not, but fires appeared to be taking hold. A 115 Squadron crew reported their bombs bursting in a built-up area, and a terrific fire developing which could be seen from a hundred miles into the return journey. This is one of many examples of crews witnessing what they believed to be a successful attack, which was, in fact, absolutely contrary to what actually occurred. The report from Mannheim mentioned a long delay before the bombing began, as aircraft passed to and fro at greater altitude than normal as if searching for the aiming-point, and then, only around ten loads found their way into the city to cause minor damage. The fires were believed to be in wooded areas beyond the city boundaries. Meanwhile, at St-Nazaire, the 57 Squadron crews delivered their seventeen 250 pounders each from 3,000 to 11,000 feet between 02.20 and 02.40, and most were seen to burst in the docks area and close to marshalling yards.

On the 21st, 3 Group detailed twenty-seven Wellingtons and twenty-one Stirlings for mining duties off the Biscay ports of La Pallice (Cinnamon) and Lorient (Artichoke), for which the two Feltwell squadrons provided seven Wellingtons each. The 57 Squadron element took off between 22.20 and 22.50 with S/L Laird taking the lead, but encountered adverse weather conditions in the target area, and only Sgt Hudson and crew were able to establish a pinpoint and deliver their two mines into the briefed location from 400 feet at 02.35. P/O Duffy and crew dropped their 500 pounders on a railway line in the region of Vire as they closed on the Normandy coast homebound, while many of the mines and bombs that left England that night ended up on the seabed.

There now followed another lull in major operations as Harris prepared for his master stroke. At the time of his appointment as C-in-C, the figure of four thousand bombers had been bandied around as the number required to wrap up the war. Whilst there was not the slightest chance of procuring them, Harris, with a dark cloud still hanging over the existence of an independent bomber force, needed to ensure that those earmarked for him were not spirited away to what he considered to be less-deserving causes. The Command had not yet achieved sufficient success to silence the detractors, and the Admiralty was still calling for bomber aircraft to be diverted to the U-Boot campaign, while others demanded support for the North Africa campaign. Harris was in need of a major victory, and, perhaps, a dose of symbolism to make his point, and, out of this was born the Thousand Plan, Operation Millennium, the launching of a thousand aircraft in one night against a major German city, for which Hamburg had been pencilled in. Harris did not have a thousand front-line aircraft and required the support of other Commands to make up the numbers. This was forthcoming from Coastal and Flying Training Commands, and, in the case of the former, a letter to Harris on the 22nd promised 250 aircraft. However, following an intervention from the Admiralty, the offer was withdrawn, and most of the Flying Training Command aircraft were found to be not up to the task, leaving the Millennium force well short of the magic figure. Undaunted, Harris, or more probably his able deputy, AM Sir Robert Saundby, scraped together every airframe capable of controlled flight, or something resembling it, and pulled in the screened crews from their instructional duties. He also pressed into service aircraft and crews from within the Command's own training establishment, 91 and 92 Groups. Come the night, not only would the thousand mark be achieved, but it would also be comfortably surpassed.

During the final week of the month, the arrival on bomber stations from Yorkshire to East Anglia of a motley collection of aircraft from training units gave rise to much speculation among crews and ground staff alike, but, as usual, only the NAAFI staff and the local civilians knew what was really afoot. The most pressing remaining question was the weather, and, as the days ticked by inexorably towards the end of May, this was showing no signs of complying. Harris was aware of the genuine danger, that the giant force might draw attention to itself, and thereby compromise security, and the point was fast approaching when the operation would have to take place or be abandoned for the time being.

Harris released some of the pressure by sanctioning operations on the night of the 29/30th, for which the Gnome & Rhone aero-engine and Goodrich tyre factories at Gennevilliers in Paris were the main targets for a force of seventy-seven aircraft. 3 Group would be out in force on this night, contributing nineteen aircraft to Paris, twenty-nine and fourteen freshmen respectively to Cherbourg and Dieppe and fifteen for gardening duties. 57 Squadron prepared six Wellingtons for Dieppe and sent them on their way from Feltwell between 22.20 and 22.40, only for them to encounter nine to ten-tenths cloud at the French coast and turn back. Sgt Moore and crew were among the few to carry out an attack when dropping their seventeen 250 pounders onto the outer harbour and docks from 700 feet at 00.43. Thirty-two minutes later, F/Sgt Karmylo and crew delivered theirs from 3,000 feet but were prevented by searchlight dazzle from observing their impact. Meanwhile, conditions inland over Paris were almost ideal with bright moonlight shining down from clear skies, and some crews observed vivid bomb bursts and a large red fire in the southern part of the Goodrich factory. Photographic reconnaissance revealed no hits on the Gnome & Rhone factory, but thirty-eight nearby houses had been destroyed and many more had sustained damage.

It was in an atmosphere of frustration and hopeful expectation, that "morning prayers" began at Harris's High Wycombe HQ on the 30th, with all eyes turned upon the civilian chief meteorological adviser, Magnus Spence. After careful deliberation, he was able to give a qualified assurance of clear skies over the Rhineland, while north-western Germany and Hamburg would be concealed under buckets of cloud. Thus, did the fickle fates decree that Cologne would bear the dubious honour of hosting the first one thousand bomber raid in history. At briefings, crews were told that the enormous force was to be pushed across the aiming-point in just ninety minutes. This was unprecedented and gave rise to the question of collisions as hundreds of aircraft funnelled towards the aiming-point. The answer, according to the experts, was to observe timings and flight levels, and they calculated also that just two aircraft would collide over the target. It is said that a wag in every briefing room asked, "do they know which two?"

3 Group had 138 Wellingtons and eighty-eight Stirlings bombed up and ready to go, along with a further thirty-nine Wellingtons from training establishments taking off from its stations, principally from 91 and 92 Groups. The 1 and 3 Group crews were assigned to aiming point A, the Neumarkt, located in the commercial heart of the city on the West Bank of the Rhine, wherein lay the cathedral and main railway station and the western ends of the Hohenzollern and Hindenburg bridges. Late that evening, the first of an eventual 1,047 aircraft took off to deliver the now familiar three-wave-format attack on the Rhineland Capital, the older training hacks struggling somewhat reluctantly into the air, perhaps lifted more by the enthusiasm of their crews than by the power of their engines, and some of these, unable to climb to a respectable height, would fall easy prey to the defences or would simply drop from the sky through mechanical breakdown.

At Feltwell, 57 Squadron's twenty Wellingtons lined up with twenty-three representing 75(NZ) Squadron and four from Flying Training Command and took off between 23.10 and 23.59 with W/C Peters-Smith and S/Ls Franks and Laird the senior pilots on duty. They were carrying either a 1,000 pounder and five 500 pounders or 810 x 4lb incendiaries, and all but one of these loads would find their way to the target. P/O Ravenhill and crew had taken off at 23.15 and were climbing away when the port engine seized through lack of oil pressure. They were forced to jettison the incendiary load to maintain height in a crowded sky until they could safely find somewhere to land, and eventually crash-landed on the Berners Heath bombing range at 00.15, writing off X3387. They were among twenty-two 3 Group aircraft to return early, mostly because of technical issues. The others pressed on in favourable conditions to begin the North-Sea crossing at Southwold and make landfall over the Scheldt estuary on a direct course for the target, with a reciprocal return route a little to the south. Traversing southern Holland, those in the main body of the bomber stream were drawn on for the last seventy miles by the glow emanating from the already burning city and were greeted at the target by precisely the weather conditions of clear skies and a bright, full moon predicted by Magnus Spence. The 57 Squadron crews carried out their attacks from 8,000 to 14,000 feet between 00.49 and 02.35, some delivering their bombs very close to the aiming point and most within a mile of it, and as they turned away, columns of black smoke were drifting up through 10,000 feet, leaving no one in any doubt, that they had taken part in a successful operation. Returning crews described a city on fire from end to end, and never-before-witnessed scenes, 868 of them claiming to have bombed within the target area, while fifteen others attacked alternative targets. Post-raid reconnaissance confirmed that the operation had, by any standards, been an outstanding success, and had destroyed more than 3,300 buildings, while inflicting serious damage on two thousand others. Although the loss of forty-one aircraft represented a new record high, the conditions had favoured both attackers and defenders alike, and, in the context of the scale of success and the numbers dispatched, it could not be considered an inordinately high figure. 3 Group posted missing ten aircraft and a further three crashed at home, but it was the training units that sustained the greatest losses amounting to twenty-one aircraft.

On the following night, Sgt Brown and crew departed Feltwell at 23.20 in the wake of a single 75(NZ) Squadron aircraft and set course for a return to Cologne to carry out a reconnaissance and bombing sortie. They found the city on this occasion to be concealed beneath ten-tenths cloud and established their position by TR before dropping four 500 pounders from 10,000 feet at 00.57. During the course of the month the squadron undertook fourteen separate operations and dispatched ninety-six sorties for the loss of three Wellingtons and two crews.

June 1942

While the Millennium force remained assembled, Harris wanted to exploit its potential again immediately, and was, no doubt, excited about the prospect of visiting upon the old enemy of Essen a similar ordeal to that just experienced by Cologne. Losses and unserviceability meant that 956 aircraft was the best that could be achieved, 3 Group managing to raise 229 aircraft, twenty for the flare force, sixty for the first wave and the remainder for the main force. 57 Squadron was able to put nineteen Wellingtons into the air between 23.05 and 00.30, with W/C Peters-Smith and S/Ls Franks and Laird the senior pilots on duty. Six crews had high-explosives bomb loads beneath their feet and the remainder incendiaries, and they flew out under favourable weather conditions, including a full moon that promised the possibility of actually being able to identify ground detail. Sgt Anderson was taken ill during the outward flight, and in the absence of a second pilot, had no choice but to turn back as one of eight from 3 Group to abandon their sorties. The others pressed on towards the Scheldt estuary, before traversing northern Belgium and southern Holland to reach the target area and find up to ten-tenths low cloud at between 3,000 and 8,000 feet, which combined with the industrial haze and smoke still drifting over from Cologne to prevent any meaningful sight of ground features. Crews had been briefed to employ the sprawl of the Borbeck-located Krupp sector as the aiming-point, and bombing took place largely on TR (Gee) supported by occasional visual references on the River Ruhr and other waterways. Most crews could report only a belief that they had bombed Essen, those from 57 Squadron from 6,000 to 12,500 feet between 00.48 and 02.15 having benefitted from the unusually inactive defences. An accurate assessment of results was not possible, and crews returned with reports of many fires, some identified as dummies, but no detail. They would have to wait for post-raid reconnaissance to assess what had happened on the ground, and, in the meantime, a counting of the cost revealed the loss of thirty-one aircraft, a modest five of which had taken off from 3 Group airfields, two of them from the training establishments. DV816 failed to return with the crew of F/Sgt Kormylo RCAF, and their fate remained uncertain until the Red Cross reported them to be in enemy hands. Sadly, there would be no major success to mitigate the scale of the losses, local reports confirming that only eleven houses had been destroyed in Essen, and fewer than two hundred others damaged, mostly in southern districts, and more bomb loads had fallen on Oberhausen, Duisburg and Mülheim-an-der-Ruhr.

A follow-up raid was planned for twenty-four hours later, and a much-reduced force of 197 aircraft assembled, of which fifty Wellingtons and twenty-one Stirlings were provided by 3 Group. 57 Squadron loaded fourteen Wellingtons with either high-explosives or incendiaries and sent them on their way from Feltwell between 23.15 and 00.20 with S/L Laird the senior pilot on duty. Sgt Barnes and crew were the last to take-off and the first to land with an engine issue after being airborne for just forty-five minutes. Fifteen minutes later, S/L Laird and crew touched down with an ailing wireless operator and they were joined on the ground after a further fifty minutes by Sgt Hunt and crew, whose rear gunner had fallen ill. Both of these indispositions were probably caused by oxygen starvation. The others pressed on through cloudless skies to reach the Ruhr, where the usual industrial haze impaired the vertical visibility, while a low moon provided some illumination. Most crews would describe the visibility as good, and reported being further aided by flares, which highlighted the Rhine over to the west. Those equipped with Gee confirmed their positions over what they believed to be the Krupp complex aiming point and those from 57 Squadron delivered their attacks from 9,000 to 12,000 feet between 01.32 and 02.01. Bomb bursts and fires were observed but no detail, and despite the apparent confidence of the crews that they had attacked Essen, local authorities reported just three high explosive bombs and three hundred incendiaries falling in the city to cause only minor damage. Such was the density of the Ruhr, however, with overlapping town and city boundaries, it was difficult not to hit something urban, but concentration was the key to success, and the scattering of bombs over a wide area was never going to achieve a knock-out blow. Fourteen aircraft failed to return, among them 57 Squadron's X9787, which was shot down by the night-fighter of Oblt Werner Rowlin of III./NJG1. The Wellington crashed at 01.59 in the Münsterland region four miles to the south of Nordhorn on the frontier with Holland and there were no survivors from the crew of F/Sgt Cummock RNZAF.

By the time that preparations were put in hand on the 3rd to send 170 aircraft against it that night, Bremen had been spared the attentions of a large force since the previous October. Among important targets in the city were the previously mentioned Deschimag shipyards and a Focke-Wulf aircraft factory. 3 Group contributed forty-eight aircraft without calling upon the services of the Feltwell squadrons, and those reaching the target found it to be covered by haze, which the employment of flares countered to some extent to enable the River Weser, the docks and built-up area to be identified and bombed. Many returning crews lacked confidence in the effectiveness of their efforts, but the 3 Group ORB recorded a successful operation, which was confirmed by local sources. The latter described the raid as the most destructive to date and catalogued damage to the harbour, industrial premises and housing, while claiming that hits on the shipyards and the Focke-Wulf aircraft factory in the Hemelingen district were of no consequence.

Essen was "on" again on the 5th, for which a force of 180 aircraft was made ready, seventy-five of them provided by 3 Group and ten by 57 Squadron. They departed Feltwell between 23.15 and

23.25 with S/L Franks the senior pilot on duty and adopted the southerly approach to the Ruhr, making landfall over the Scheldt and traversing Belgium before passing between Cologne and Düsseldorf. P/O Trant and crew were no more than an hour out when the rear gunner became unwell, compelling them to turn back and leave the others from the squadron to reach the target area. In conditions of poor vertical visibility caused by the ever-present blanket of industrial haze, they establish their positions through identifying ground detail, like a distinctive bend in the River Ruhr to the south-east of the target, or by TR-fix and flares or evidence of searchlight and flak concentrations. The searchlight and flak activity was intense as they carried out their attacks from 9,000 to 14,000 feet between 01.15 and 01.25, and some were uncertain as to what lay beneath them. HF915 failed to return with the crew of Sgt Barnes RNZAF and no clue to their fate was ever forthcoming. The operation was another failure that scattered bombs over a wide area, with Oberhausen and Bottrop probably receiving the most.

The first of four attacks during the month on the naval port of Emden was posted on the 6th, and a force of 233 aircraft made ready. 3 Group contributed thirty-nine Stirlings and sixty-four Wellingtons, 57 Squadron responsible for nine of the latter, which departed Feltwell between 23.20 and 23.25 with F/L Forbes the senior pilot on duty. P/O Austin and crew were thwarted by engine problems and were among eight from 3 Group to turn back, while those pressing on found the skies over the coast of north-western Germany to be clear of cloud and the visibility to be good. This assisted the flare force crews to illuminate the docks area for the bomb-aimers, and the 57 Squadron crews took advantage to deliver their attacks from 8,000 to 12,000 feet between 01.17 and 01.30. Smoke was rising through 8,000 feet as they retreated, and the glow from the port remained visible for up to eighty miles into the return journey. Photographic reconnaissance and local reports confirmed that the raid had been responsible for the destruction of some three hundred houses, with a further two hundred severely damaged in return for the loss of nine aircraft.

The almost relentless campaign against Essen continued on the 8th, for which a force of 170 aircraft was assembled, 3 Group putting up fifty-five Stirlings and Wellingtons, eight of the latter representing 57 Squadron. They departed Feltwell between 23.30 and 23.35 with no pilots on duty above pilot officer rank, and lost two of their number early on, P/O Austin becoming unwell, while the crew of Sgt Saunders were defeated by the failure of their intercom. The others headed out in favourable conditions, which persisted all the way to the target, where they were greeted by the expected blanket of ground haze, which, together with the glare from the intense searchlight activity, blinded them to ground features and rendered the attack something of a lottery. Bombing by the 57 Squadron crews took place on TR from 9,000 to 12,000 feet between 01.07 and 01.20, and bomb bursts were observed, but those crews returning to base would have no detail to pass on at debriefing.

Feltwell remained operationally inactive during the ensuing week, while 3 Group focused on gardening and "moling", and further attacks on Essen planned for the 13th and 15th were cancelled. When the teleprinters burst into life on the 16th they revealed that Essen would be the destination for a modest force of 106 aircraft that night, thirty-eight provided by 3 Group. 57 Squadron made ready six Wellingtons for crews captained by junior officers and NCOs and dispatched them from Feltwell between 23.20 and 23.25, only for the crews of Sgts Anderson and Brown and P/O Duffy to abandon their sorties because of adverse weather conditions including severe icing, while Sgt Saunders and crew also cited throttle clutch failure. Unfavourable weather had been anticipated and crews had been briefed to employ TR to locate the target, which, under the conditions of up to eight-tenths cloud on a moonless night with visibility down to three miles, was the best that could be expected. Of the two remaining 57 Squadron participants, P/O Trant and crew dropped their 1,000 pounder and seven 500 and three 250 pounders blindly from 11,000 feet at 01.45 and P/O Austin and crew let their all-incendiary load go from 10,000 feet within a searchlight cone believed to be at Bonn at 01.53. The city of Bonn had been briefed out as the alternative target, and forty-five crews took advantage of the fact that it lay close to the southern route to the Ruhr. Sgt Davies and crew returned to Feltwell from a night training flight and crashed on landing at 01.30, writing off X3746 and injuring the pilot and two others.

On the 17th, 3 Group detailed forty-eight aircraft and divided them between gardening duties off the Frisians and a bombing raid on the docks and shipping at St-Nazaire. 57 Squadron prepared seven Wellingtons, six for gardening and one for the freshman crew of Sgt Danahy to take to the Biscay coast. The chain of Frisian Islands off the Dutch and German coasts was divided into three gardens, Nectarine I, II and III, the first covering Texel to Ameland, the second Schiermonnikoog to Borkum, and the third, Juist to Wangerooge. ORBs often failed to specify which Nectarine garden was to be the target area, but the 57 Squadron scribe entered Terschelling as the destination for the Feltwell mining brigade, which identified the target area as Nectarine I. Sgt Danahy and crew took off at 22.55 to head south for the Channel crossing, while the others got away thirty minutes later and set a course slightly north of east, crossing the Norfolk coast south of Sheringham. P/O Duffy and crew were back in the circuit within the hour after suffering complete W/T failure, but the others enjoyed favourable conditions in which four pinpointed on the western end of Terschelling and one on the eastern end. The vegetables were planted according to brief from 600 to 1,000 feet between 00.51 and 01.01, and the 500 pounders returned to store for future use. The Danahy crew lost the use of their TR-box on the way out and were unable to locate their target in cloudy conditions.

The next three operations would be directed at the port of Emden over four nights, with the intention of building on the success of the attack earlier in the month. A force of 194 aircraft was assembled on the 19th, for which 3 Group contributed seventy-eight Stirlings and Wellingtons. At briefings, crews were instructed to switch to Osnabrück, eighty miles to the south, if the weather conditions over the coastal region became troublesome. 57 Squadron loaded four of its own with six 500 pounders and four with 810 x 4lb incendiaries and sent them on their way from Feltwell between 23.30 and 00.05 with F/L Forbes the senior pilot on duty. Sgt Brown became unwell early on and was back on the ground after fifty minutes, leaving the others to reach enemy territory, some to attract the attention of night-fighters. Among those coming under attack were Sgt Saunders and crew, who were already experiencing oxygen supply issues affecting the pilot and they turned for home, taking their incendiaries with them. P/O Trant and crew jettisoned theirs while taking evasive action, and managed to lose their assailant, but only after both gunners had sustained wounds. Part of the flare force initiated an attack on Osnabrück by twenty-nine aircraft, including the one occupied by F/L Forbes and crew, who dropped their high-explosives into the centre of the town from 10,000 feet at 02.07. P/O Duffy and crew failed to locate Emden through ten-tenths cloud and brought their bombs home, and this left just the crew of Sgt Danahy to represent 57 Squadron in attacking the primary target. They released their all-incendiary load from 8,000 feet at 01.45 and were among 131 crews to report bombing the port and town through six to eight-tenths thin cloud. Despite the numbers, the Emden authorities reported only a handful of high-explosive bombs falling and a few hundred incendiaries. It is highly likely that Sgt Ashworth and crew also attacked Emden, but Z1611 was shot down by Oblt Viktor Bauer of III./NJG1 at 02.37 on the way home and crashed three miles north of Hellendoorn in northern Holland without survivors.

Emden remained the objective on the 20th for a force of 185 aircraft, of which fifty Wellingtons and twenty-one Stirlings represented 3 Group. 57 Squadron loaded two Wellingtons with six 500 pounders each for the crews of F/L Forbes and P/O Trant, another with seventeen 250 pounders for Sgt Danahy and crew and two with 810 x 4lbs incendiaries for the crews of W/C Peters-Smith and P/O Duffy. They took of between 23.30 and 23.40 and reached the target area, according to some, to find six to eight-tenths cloud between 4,000 and 8,000 feet, while others reported clear skies with ground haze to impair the vertical visibility. The docks were the briefed aiming-point and the town the alternative, and positions were established by TR-fix and glimpses of the coastline. An intense flak barrage accompanied the bombing runs, but all from 57 Squadron made it through to carry out their attacks from 7,000 to 11,500 feet between 01.19 and 01.42, and, on return, reported bomb bursts and fires visible for sixty miles into the return journey. Local sources confirmed damage to a hundred houses, which was a modest improvement on the previous raid.

The Emden series concluded on the 22nd, when a force of 227 aircraft was put together, of which seventy-six Wellingtons and thirty-eight Stirlings were provided by 3 Group, seventeen of them to form the flare force. Ten 57 Squadron Wellingtons departed Feltwell between 23.20 and 23.30 with S/L Franks the senior pilot on duty, but three were among eleven from 3 Group to return early, P/O Armin and crew because of an unserviceable rear turret, Sgt Brown and crew after the pilot became unwell and Sgt Anderson and crew with an ailing starboard engine. Weather conditions outbound were favourable, with five-tenths cloud at 15,000 feet, but this dispersed to leave clear skies to greet the arrival of the force over the German coast. The flares greatly assisted crews to identify ground detail by illuminating in particular the docks area and bombing by the 57 Squadron crews took place from 9,000 to 11,000 feet between 01.25 and 01.55. At debriefings, 196 crews claimed to have bombed in the target area and several small fires were observed but a local report suggested that only part of the force had correctly identified Emden. Fifty houses were destroyed, a hundred others were damaged, and there was some unspecified damage in the harbour area, but decoy fire sites are believed to have drawn off many bomb loads, and the operation, while the most effective of the three, still fell short of expectations. The freshman crew of Sgt Larkins RNZAF failed to return in X3758, which is presumed to have come down in the North Sea.

For the following night's operations, 3 Group detailed twenty aircraft for mining duties in the Beech garden off St-Nazaire and nine freshman crews to drop seventeen 250 pounders each onto the docks. Feltwell was responsible for fifteen of the Wellingtons, the 57 Squadron armourers loading two mines and three 500 pounders each into six of theirs and the 250 pounders into the one assigned to Sgt Cameron and crew. They began taking off at 23.00 with the Cameron crew last away at 23.15, but they would fail to locate the target through ten-tenths cloud and returned their bombs to store. P/O Duffy and crew were unable to identify a suitable pinpoint off the Biscay coast because of haze, and they brought their load home also. Four of the others planted their vegetables as briefed from 800 feet between 02.04 and 02.35, while S/L Franks and crew selected an unusually high 5,000 feet from which to deliver theirs at 02.55. In time, the low-level mining which had been the norm since its inception in April 1940, would shift to high level, typically from 15,000 feet.

The time had now arrived for the final deployment of the Thousand Force, and, indeed, for 5 Group's ill-fated Avro Manchester in operational service. It was an indication of the failure of the Manchester, that the aircraft it had been intended to replace, the Hampden, would continue to serve 5 Group in small numbers until mid-September. A force of 960 aircraft was assembled, which included seventy-two Stirlings and 124 Wellingtons from 3 Group's front-line squadrons and training units. To the above numbers were added five aircraft from Army Co-operation Command and 102 aircraft from Coastal Command, which had been ordered by Churchill to take part, although, its contribution was to be deemed a separate operation. However, the 1,067 aircraft from all sources would represent a larger combined force than that sent to Cologne at the end of May. Feltwell armourers loaded all incendiary loads into a dozen 57 Squadron Wellingtons and nine 500 pounders into three and sent them on their way between 23.15 and 00.05 with W/C Peters-Smith and S/L Franks the senior pilots on duty. It was not destined to be a memorable night for 57 Squadron, whose Sgt Anderson and crew abandoned their sortie when the wireless operator became unwell. They were among twenty-four 3 Group "boomerangs", while many of those reaching north-western Germany in the light from a full moon and the Northern Lights were defeated by a blanket of ten-tenths cloud and were unable positively to establish their position over Bremen. Gee was employed by those so-equipped, otherwise it was left largely to dead-reckoning (DR), and seven 57 Squadron crews brought their bombs home. Of the remainder, two dropped their loads blindly over what they believed was Wilhelmshaven and two others over Bremerhaven, leaving just the crews of Sgts Croston, Hudson and Saunders to claim to have attacked the primary target from 10,000 and 11,000 feet between 01.45 and 02.13. Returning crews reported the glow of fires as evidence that something had been going on beneath the cloud, but an accurate assessment was out of the question. Local sources confirmed a number of hits on the Focke-Wulf aircraft factory and some shipyards, along with the destruction of 572 houses and damage to more than six thousand others, mostly in southern and eastern districts, but estimated the size of the bomber force to be around eighty aircraft. The level of success fell well short of that achieved at Cologne, but surpassed by far the failure at Essen, albeit at a new record loss of forty-eight aircraft, which represented 5% of those dispatched. The O.T.Us of 91 Group suffered the highest casualty rate of 11.6%, largely because they were employing tired, old Whitleys, Wellingtons and Hampdens, which were not up to the task. 3 Group posted missing a remarkably modest three aircraft from its front-line squadrons and several from its training establishments.

A follow-up operation by 144 aircraft on the 27th included forty-Wellingtons and twenty-six Stirlings from 3 Group but none from Feltwell. Weather conditions over north-western Germany were very much as those of two nights earlier, with ten-tenths cloud up to around 4,000 feet and decreasing amounts thereafter as high as 15,000 feet, with the sky above as bright as day under a large moon, even though the Northern Lights, on this occasion, were masked by high cloud. Most located the target area by TR-fix, and crews could only estimate that they were over the city as they released their mixed high explosive and incendiary loads. Local reports confirmed hits on the previously damaged Atlas Werke shipyard and the Korff refinery, but further details were scant and of little value.

On the following night, 3 Group sent nine Wellingtons and four Stirlings to attack the town of St-Nazaire and its docks, and among them were the 57 Squadron freshman crews of Sgts Croston, Herbert and Hudson and P/O Huggins. They departed Feltwell between 22.55 and 23.00, each carrying seventeen 250 pounders, and all reached the target area to find favourable conditions and an intense searchlight and flak defence. Sgt Herbert and crew made two runs but were held in searchlights and brought their bombs home, while the others were able to carry out an attack from 6,000 to 12,500 feet between 01.05 and 02.00 and observe bursts close to marshalling yards and the docks area.

It was Bremen again on the 29th, for which a force of 253 aircraft was assembled, which included 124 Wellingtons and Stirlings representing 3 Group. 57 Squadron prepared a dozen Wellingtons and dispatched them from Feltwell between 23.20 and 23.45 with S/Ls Franks and Laird the senior pilots on duty. The force flew out over six to ten-tenths cloud at between 3,000 and 5,000 feet with excellent visibility above and encountered around seven to ten-tenths cloud in layers up to 16,000 feet in the target area, with large gaps that afforded some a glimpse of the ground. The 57 Squadron crews delivered their attacks from 7,500 to 11,500 feet between 01.34 and 02.00 and all but two returned to offer only impressions of the raid. F/L Forbes and crew were attacked by a night-fighter and the wireless operator, P/O Bustin, was fatally wounded. Group was notified that Z1618 had ditched off the Dutch coast while homebound and that Sgt Moore and two of his crew had been picked up by an Air-Sea-Rescue launch, but second pilot, Sgt Herbert, and two others were not found. Z1578 disappeared without trace with the crew of S/L Franks, who would be missed by the Feltwell community. Local reports spoke of extensive damage to the Focke-Wulf factory, the A G Weser U-Boot construction yard, three other important war-industry premises and the gas works, and there had been some limited destruction of housing.

On the 30th, F/L Forbes was granted the acting rank of squadron leader to enable him to step into the flight commander role created by the loss of S/L Franks. During the course of the month, the squadron undertook sixteen operations and dispatched 134 sorties for the loss of eight Wellingtons, six crews and four other crew members.

July 1942

The campaign against Bremen continued on the 2nd, with the preparation of a force of 325 aircraft, more than half of which were Wellingtons. 3 Group squadrons contributed 118 Wellingtons and Stirlings, a dozen of the former provided by 57 Squadron, which departed Feltwell between 23.15 and 23.35 with S/L Laird the senior pilot on duty. Sgt Davies and crew were back on the ground at 01.00 complaining that the front bulkhead door would not remain shut, and Sgt Anderson and crew joined them twenty-five minutes later to report the failure of their W/T. It was a further hour before Sgt Saunders and crew touched down with an indisposed rear gunner, probably the victim of oxygen starvation. By this time the others had crossed the Dutch coast near Alkmaar and had reached the target area to find favourable weather conditions, with excellent visibility, no low cloud, high cirrus at around 22,000 feet, a half moon and only a little haze to spoil the view below. Positions were established by TR-fix confirmed by a visual check, but searchlight glare created great difficulty for the bomb-aimers, particularly those assigned to specific aiming-points like the Focke-Wulf aircraft factory and shipyards, and most would settle for estimating the fall of their bombs. The 57 Squadron participants delivered their attacks from 10,000 to 12,500 feet between 01.40 and 02.03 and returned safely to offer their impressions to the intelligence section. A large fire was reported on the aerodrome attached to the Focke-Wulf factory, and another at Delmenhorst to the south-west, and the consensus was of an effective operation. Local reports spoke of a thousand houses damaged, along with four small industrial premises, while three cranes and seven ships were hit in the port, one of the vessels sinking and becoming a danger to navigation. The likelihood is, however, that much of the effort was wasted beyond the city's southern boundary.

Adverse weather conditions kept most of the Command on the ground for the next five nights, 3 Group sending twenty Wellingtons from Mildenhall and Wyton to mine the approaches to Lorient on the night of the 6/7th and detailing sixty-five Wellingtons and Stirlings for similar duties off the Frisians on the 7th. This was the day on which acting F/L Dean arrived from 18 O.T.U., to fill the vacancy for a deputy flight commander following the elevation of F/L Forbes. 57 Squadron made ready eleven Wellingtons and briefed their crews for the Nectarine III garden off the eastern Frisians, although the squadron ORB recorded Nectarine I against the name of Sgt Hudson and crew. They departed Feltwell between 00.05 and 00.35 with S/L Laird the senior pilot on duty and lost the services of Sgt Cameron and crew to gyro compass failure. The others pressed on across the North Sea and encountered low cumulus cloud and extreme darkness, which created challenging conditions for identifying pinpoints. Three crews were defeated by the conditions, while the others established a pinpoint on Norderney and carried out timed runs to release their two mines each from 600 to 900 feet between 01.40 and 02.25.

Orders were received across the Command on the 8th to prepare for that night's operation against Wilhelmshaven, for which a force of 285 aircraft was assembled. 3 Group contributed 113 Wellingtons and Stirlings, eleven of the former belonging to 57 Squadron, and they departed Feltwell between 23.40 and 23.50 with S/L Laird the senior pilot on duty. They lost the services of F/Sgt Plunkett and crew to severe icing conditions, but it seems that they did reach enemy territory and jettison their 1,000 pounder and seven 500 pounders "live", observing two bursts. The others pressed on to the target to find around three-tenths thin cloud at 10,000 feet and haze below, which made it almost impossible for most to identify important ground detail like the docks and shipyard aiming-points. Positions were established on e.t.a., and by TR-fix, some backed up through a brief glimpse of the docks and waterways sparkling in the light of flares, but an unserviceable Gee box prevented Sgt Hudson and crew from finding a pinpoint and they gave up. The first bombs went down before the flare force had provided adequate illumination and appeared to fall to the west of the main town. Thereafter, the attack crept closer to the briefed aiming-point, and the bombing by the remaining 57 Squadron crews took place from 10,000 to 12,000 feet between 01.38 and 02.15. Returning crews reported a few scattered fires and local sources confirmed some damage, but post-raid reconnaissance revealed that much of the bombing had, indeed, missed the town to the west.

A series of five operations over a four-week period against Duisburg would begin on the 13ᵗʰ, but, as a foretaste, four 57 Squadron crews were briefed to conduct a "moling" operation against it on the afternoon of the 10ᵗʰ, while four from 75(NZ) Squadron targeted Düsseldorf, the two cities coded "Cod" and "Perch" respectively. The 57 Squadron element consisting of the crews of P/Os Armin, Duffy and Trant and Sgt Hunt took off between 14.25 and 15.15 and headed for the North Sea relying upon cloud cover to protect them from enemy fighters. P/O Armin and crew signalled insufficient cloud cover at 15.45 and this was backed up by one of the Kiwi crews, which prompted a recall for all aircraft, one of which had penetrated as far inland as Eindhoven. One of the 75(NZ) Wellingtons failed to return, its crew sacrificed for no benefit to the idiocy of unescorted daylight forays. Another at the end of the month would heavily impact 57 Squadron.

A force of 194 aircraft was assembled on the 13ᵗʰ for Duisburg, a number that included seventy-three Wellingtons and Stirlings of 3 Group, ten of the former belonging to 57 Squadron. They departed Feltwell between 00.25 and 00.50 with F/L Dean the senior pilot on duty, and flew out through electrical storms and heavy cloud, which began to thin in places, until a covering of between three and ten-tenths lay over the target with tops at around 10,000 feet. This allowed some crews to glimpse the ground to establish that they were over the built-up area, while others relied entirely on a TR-fix, which all but guaranteed that the bombing would be widely scattered and largely ineffective. The 57 Squadron crews attacked from 10,000 to 14,000 feet between 02.02 and 02.43, some observing bursts and others not, but there was little confidence in the effectiveness of their work as they passed on their impressions at debriefing. A local report stated that eleven houses had been destroyed and some seventy others seriously damaged, and this was a poor return for the effort expended.

Twenty-two 3 Group crews were briefed for mining duties on the 14ᵗʰ to be conducted in the Nectarine I garden off the westerly Frisians. 57 Squadron dispatched the crews of F/L Dean, P/O Duffy, F/Sgt Plunkett and Sgt Saunders between 22.55 and 23.25, and each established their position off Teschelling by TR before carrying out a timed run and delivering two mines each into the briefed locations from 600 to 1,300 feet between 00.16 and 00.39. No major operations were mounted on the ensuing five nights, but 3 Group committed twenty-one Stirlings to a day/night raid on Lübeck on the 16ᵗʰ despite the agreement struck in March to leave the Baltic city-port unmolested. Operation Pandemonium relied on cloud cover during the daylight approach for the dusk attack, which was followed by the return under cover of darkness. In the event, two-thirds of the force turned back, two failed to return and only seven aircraft battled their way through to the target to cause little damage. On the 19ᵗʰ, thirty-one Stirlings were part of a force of ninety-nine four-engine aircraft assigned to the Bremen shipyards at Vegesack to the north of the city. Complete cloud cover forced the bombing to be carried out on Gee, and no bombs fell in the target area.

The madness of daylight operations continued on the 20ᵗʰ, when Feltwell was ordered to send a dozen Wellingtons on cloud cover sorties to Bremen during the afternoon and early evening. Departures were spread over a number of hours, the 57 Squadron pair of Sgts Croston and Cameron taking off at 14.15 to be followed at 16.50 by Sgts Anderson and Hudson and finally at 17.30 by S/L Laird and F/Sgt Plunkett. The first mentioned reached the target and dropped nine 500 pounders each from 4,500 and 5,000 feet at 16.20 and 16.23 respectively without observing the results, and of the others, three abandoned their sorties because of a lack of cloud cover and Sgt Hudson and crew attacked Emden from 3,000 feet at 18.29, again without observing the outcome.

A force of 291 aircraft was assembled on the 21st for the second raid of the series on Duisburg, and this number included a 3 Group contribution of ninety-eight Wellingtons and thirty-six Stirlings, sixteen of the former provided by 57 Squadron. They departed Feltwell between 23.45 and 00.20 with S/Ls Forbes and Laird the senior pilots on duty, and with a variety of bomb loads beneath their feet. Nine were carrying a 1,000 pounder with seven 500 and two 250 pounders, while three each were loaded with 810 x 4lb incendiaries and 72 x 30lb incendiaries and F/Sgt Rowney and crew were sitting on a 4,000lb cookie. Sgt Hudson and crew turned back because of W/T failure, leaving the remainder to reach the target area and find clear skies and the usual industrial haze, but sufficiently good vertical visibility aided by flares to confirm their TR-fixed positions visually. Sgt Anderson and crew were approaching the Rhine when ensnared by searchlights, which forced them to jettison their bombs and descend to 500 feet to make their escape. The others carried out their attacks from 6,800 to 13,500 feet between 01.34 and 01.55 and believed their bombs to have fallen predominantly into the old town, although few saw the results of their efforts and could only report that fires were taking hold as they withdrew westwards into the gloom of a moonless night. Of twelve missing aircraft, five belonged to 3 Group, among them 57 Squadron's X3584, which disappeared without trace with the freshman crew of Sgt Wakefield. The Duisburg authorities confirmed a moderately successful raid, during which ninety-four buildings had been destroyed and 256 seriously damaged, which represented something of a success and this elusive target, and, it is believed, that the Thyssen steelworks was among a number of important war industry factories to sustain some damage.

A reduced force of 215 aircraft was made ready to continue the assault on Duisburg on the 23rd, for which 3 Group detailed 119 Wellingtons and Stirlings, 57 Squadron supporting the operation with a dozen of the former. A very late take-off saw them airborne from Feltwell between 00.40 and 01.15 with S/L Laird the senior pilot on duty, but port engine failure ended his interest in proceedings before reaching the coast. Sgt Anderson became unwell during the sea crossing and also had to abandon his sortie, leaving the others to arrive in the target area over nine-tenths cloud at 8,000 to 12,000 feet, which required them to establish their positions by Gee-fix. Bombing was carried out from 7,000 to 13,000 feet between 02.21 and 02.36, and many crews observed a burst or two and the glow of fires believed to be in the built-up area. A modest seven aircraft failed to return, among them 57 Squadron's BJ673, which was brought down by marine flak and crashed off the Dutch coast with fatal consequences for Sgt Davies and his crew. Local sources confirmed a limited amount of housing damage, and it was another unsatisfactory attempt to hit a major centre of war production.

The fourth raid on Duisburg was posted on the 25th, for which the largest force yet of the series was assembled. Among the 313 aircraft were ninety-one Wellingtons and forty-eight Stirlings belonging to 3 Group, fifteen of the former representing 57 Squadron. They departed Feltwell between 00.25 and 00.45 with S/Ls Forbes and Laird the senior pilots on duty, and all reached the western Ruhr to encounter eight-tenths cloud with thick industrial haze below. They established their positions by TR, before aiming their bombs at existing fires from 6,000 to 12,000 feet between 02.00 and 02.30 and could only assume that they were hitting the built-up area and adding to the damage. Many crews reported one large fire and several smaller ones, but had little of value to offer at debriefing, and local sources described the damage inflicted to be on a smaller scale than that resulting from the previous raids in the series.

A maximum effort was planned on the 26th for the annual last-week-of-July attack on Germany's second city, Hamburg, and 404 aircraft answered the call, among them ninety-eight Wellingtons and thirty-nine Stirlings provided by 3 Group. 57 Squadron made ready fifteen Wellingtons and dispatched them from Feltwell between 22.30 and 23.00 with S/L Forbes the senior pilot on duty. Crews had to negotiate the frequently met conditions on this route of towering cloud, electrical storms and severe icing, and it was probably at this stage of the outward flight that the crews of Sgts Hunt, Cameron and Danahy turned back, the first-mentioned because of an indisposed rear gunner and the others as a result of engine problems. The remainder pressed on through the weather front to reach the target area, drawn on for the last eight minutes by the sight of fires already burning in the docks area and the southern part of the old town. Apart from a little cloud at 15,000 feet, the skies were now clear and the city basking in bright moonlight as the 57 Squadron crews carried out their attacks from 9,000 to 12,000 feet between 01.04 and 01.50. It was impossible to pick out individual bomb bursts among the many detonations, and the hostility of the searchlight and flak defences dissuaded crews from loitering to make an assessment. Smoke was drifting across the city as the bombers retreated into the clutches of the waiting night-fighters, which played their part in bringing down a massive twenty-nine bombers, or 7.2% of those dispatched. 57 Squadron posted missing the experienced RAF, RNZAF and RCAF crew of Sgt Hudson, who all lost their lives when Z1654 came down in the target area.

The full impact of the craziness of "moling" operations was brought home to 57 Squadron on the 27th, when 3 Group ordered eight crews, two each from the Feltwell squadrons and four from 156 Squadron at Wyton, to attack Bremen, Hamburg or Emden by daylight with cloud for protection. Demonstrating good leadership, W/C Peters-Smith DFC put himself up for this dangerous task and took off for Bremen at 15.30, thirty minutes after the crew of Sgt Hunt. He did not return, and there were no survivors after X3653 came down somewhere in north-western Germany. Sgt Hunt and crew dropped nine 500 pounders on Emden from 11,000 feet at 17.12 and returned safely having observed nothing of their impact. One of the 156 Squadron aircraft failed to return, and thus two valuable crews were lost for no gain. W/C Peters-Smith would be sorely missed for his experience and leadership and to risk men, particularly of his calibre, in the prosecution of nuisance raids was unforgiveable.

Another maximum effort was called for on the 28th, and a force well in excess of four hundred aircraft was assembled for the return to Hamburg that night. 165 aircraft were provided by 3 Group and ninety-one by the operational training units, which, in the event, would take off alone, after the deteriorating weather conditions over the 1, 4 and 5 Group stations further north prompted the withdrawal of their contributions. 57 Squadron dispatched fifteen Wellingtons between 22.35 and 23.15 with S/L Forbes the senior pilot on duty, and they headed out into worsening conditions over the North Sea, which resulted in the recall of the O.T.U aircraft. Many of the 3 Group crews turned back also, among them that of Sgt Danahy because of engine issues, but the rest pressed on to the target area. Sgt Cameron and crew were just about to enter the Elbe estuary when they were caught in a searchlight cone and jettisoned their bombs during the successful attempt to extricate themselves. The others found clear skies, which enabled them to identify ground features when not dazzled by searchlights and carried out their attacks from 7,000 to 12,000 feet between 01.02 and 01.45, observing bursts all over the town. Sixty-eight returning crews would claim to have attacked the primary target, where fifteen large fires and forty smaller ones were reported. This modicum of success was gained at the high cost of twenty-five aircraft, 15% of those dispatched, and four O.T.U Wellingtons also failed to return, while a fifth, a Whitley, ditched, and its crew was picked up safely. Z1650 failed to return with the crew of F/L Dean, none of whom had survived the Wellington's demise. Sgt Hunt and crew returned with a fatally wounded observer, P/O Eames, who was presumably a victim of flak.

Saarbrücken was posted as the target on the 29th, and a force of 291 aircraft assembled, which would be the largest force by far to be sent against this major industrial and coal-producing Saarland capital city, situated right on the frontier with France in south-western Germany. 3 Group detailed eighty-three Wellingtons and Stirlings, nine of the former provided by 57 Squadron, and these departed Feltwell between 23.40 and 23.50 with S/L Laird the senior pilot on duty. Sgt Player and crew turned back early because of an engine problem, leaving the others to head for the French coast near Dunkerque and follow a course thereafter parallel to the Franco-Belgian border that would lead them directly to the target south of Luxembourg. They encountered seven-tenths cloud over the target in a band between 2,000 and 9,000 feet, and positions were established by TR and confirmed by visual references on ground features like the River Saar. In the expected absence of a strong searchlight and flak defence, crews had been encouraged to bomb their specific aiming-point from a lower level than customary for the period. Those from 57 Squadron carried out their attacks from 4,000 to 6,000 feet between 01.53 and 02.17 and observed explosions and fires in the northern part of the city around the marshalling yards, some large and emitting black smoke. Returning crews were confident that their bombs had found the mark, and this was confirmed by local reports of severe damage in central and north-western districts, where almost four hundred buildings had been destroyed in return for the loss of nine aircraft.

The month ended with a major assault on the Ruhr city of Düsseldorf, for which a force of 630 aircraft was assembled, the numbers bolstered by a large contribution from the training units. 3 Group contributed seventy-two Wellingtons and sixty-one Stirlings, ten of the former representing 57 Squadron and departing Feltwell between 00.20 and 00.45 with S/Ls Forbes and Laird the senior pilots on duty. Sixteen 3 Group aircraft returned early, Sgt Riddell and crew among them having lost the use of their TR and W/T, but the remainder from 57 Squadron pressed on to the southern Ruhr, where bright moonlight, clear skies and good visibility enabled the crews of the first wave to confirm their TR-fixed positions visually by an S-bend in the River Rhine. They left developing fires for the second wave crews, whose identification of the aiming-point was impeded by the resulting smoke. The 57 Squadron crews carried out their attacks from 9,000 to 11,000 feet between 02.16 and 02.26 in the face of an intense and accurate searchlight and flak defence, observing many explosions and fires and a column of black smoke rising through 10,000 feet as they turned away. At debriefing, they expressed confidence in the quality of their work, having contributed to the delivery of more than nine hundred tons of bombs, some wasted in open country, but the bulk scattered across all parts of the city and the neighbouring city of Neuss on the opposite bank of the Rhine. Local sources confirmed the destruction of 453 buildings, with varying degrees of damage to fifteen thousand more, and 954 separate fire incidents, sixty-seven of them large. Indeed, had it not been for the high casualty rate of twenty-nine aircraft, the operation could have been declared an unqualified success. Five of the missing aircraft were from 3 Group, and the O.T.U.s were again hit disproportionately hard, losing fifteen of their number. F/Sgt Murphy RCAF and crew failed to return to Feltwell in BJ607, which was shot down on the way home by marine flak and crashed into the sea three miles off the island of Walcheren in the Scheldt without survivors.

W/C E J Laine was posted in on the 30th as successor to W/C Peters-Smith. During the course of the month, the squadron took part in fifteen operations and dispatched 151 sorties for the loss of six Wellingtons and their crews and one other crew member.

August 1942

A gentle start to the new month saw the heavy brigade remain at home because of unfavourable weather and it was the 4th before 3 Group ventured forth in modest numbers dispatched from Feltwell to raid Essen. 57 Squadron loaded four Wellingtons with nine 500 pounders each and sent them on their way between 22.45 and 23.00 bearing aloft the crews of F/L Huggins, P/O Duffy, W/O Walsh and Sgt Croston. They ran into severe icing conditions and not one would reach the target, but straggled back to Feltwell between 01.45 and 03.30, two with TR failure, one with engine trouble and the last because of the conditions. Just two of the 75(NZ) Squadron Wellingtons made it all the way to bomb on e.t.a., as TR faded out. It was a similar story of failure on the following day when a further nine "moling" Wellingtons from other 3 Group stations were sent to Essen and seven abandoned their sorties because of a lack of cloud cover.

3 Group's contribution to the fifth and final operation of the three-week campaign against the Ruhr industrial giant of Duisburg amounted to eighty-three Wellingtons and Stirlings, nine of the former provided by 57 Squadron in an overall force of 216 aircraft. Enemy intruders were active over East Anglia as the Feltwell elements prepared to take-off and there was a slight delay before they got away between 01.50 and 02.00 with F/L Huggins the senior pilot on duty. P/O Duffy and crew returned after ninety minutes claiming that they would not have been able to reach the target within the allotted time, but the others continued on to the target, where cloud was reported at between zero and ten-tenths with tops at 10,000 feet and barrage balloons tethered as high as 12,000 feet. Positions had to be established by TR, which was not working well on this night, and confirmed by visual reference aided by fires, flak and flares. The bombs were delivered blindly by the 57 Squadron crews from 8,500 to 13,300 feet between 03.19 and 03.43 in the hope and belief that they were over the target and a scattering of fires was the impression they brought home to debriefing. Local sources confirmed the failure of the operation, which destroyed eighteen buildings and seriously damaged a further sixty-six, while wasting most of the effort on open country to the west. An analysis of the five-raid series made sorry reading and revealed that 212 houses had been destroyed, 741 seriously damaged, and significant industrial damage had resulted from just one raid. In return for this modest gain, Bomber Command had lost forty-three aircraft and crews from 1,229 sorties.

The garrison town of Osnabrück was posted as the target on the 9th, and a force of 192 aircraft assembled accordingly. 3 Group contributed forty-eight Wellingtons and forty-two Stirlings, eight of the former representing 57 Squadron, and they departed Feltwell between 00.05 and 00.25 with F/L Huggins the senior pilot on duty. They flew out over Lowestoft on their way to the Den Helder peninsula on a direct course to the target, situated north of the Ruhr and south of Bremen, but lost the services of Sgt Riddell and crew to an unserviceable rear turret. There were clear skies over the flatlands of the Münster region as the bombers closed on the target, but haze contributed to the poor visibility, and all found that they were unable to establish their positions by TR after it was jammed by the enemy on crossing the Dutch coast. Flares were dropped by the lead aircraft to illuminate the area, and some crews picked out railway lines, a canal and the River Hase, but it was mainly the fires, searchlights and flak that pointed the way to the aiming-point. Bombing was carried out by the 57 Squadron crews from 8,500 to 12,000 feet between 02.09 and 02.22, and their all-incendiary loads appeared to fall into the built-up area. The resulting fires remained visible for eighty to a hundred miles into the return flight, and TR functioned again once the Dutch coast had been crossed homebound. P/O Armin and crew brought their bombs home after failing to locate the target. Local sources confirmed an effective raid, which destroyed 206 houses and a military building, and damaged a number of industrial premises along with four thousand other buildings, mostly lightly.

On the 11th, in a rare training accident involving a 57 Squadron aircraft, BJ593 crashed on approach to Methwold at 12.00, and the three occupants, among which F/Sgt Lewis was the pilot, sustained injuries. The main operation that night was to be the first of two on consecutive nights against the city of Mainz, situated to the south-west of Frankfurt-am-Main in southern Germany, for which 154 aircraft were made ready. The number included a contribution from 3 Group of forty-two Stirlings and thirty-seven Wellingtons, eight of the latter representing 57 Squadron, for what would be the first large-scale raid on this target. In addition, the freshman crews of P/O Bowles and F/Sgt McLaren were to target the port of Le Havre with seventeen 250 pounders each. The main element departed Feltwell first between 22.40 and 22.55 with S/L Laird the senior pilot on duty, leaving the freshmen on the ground until their take-off at 01.15, just as the attack was taking place at Mainz some four hundred miles to the south-east. The Mainz-bound crews had made their way south to the French coast to adopt the well-worn route for this part of Germany, and all reached the target area after flying out in favourable weather conditions to be greeted by up to eight-tenths cloud with tops at 11,500 feet and a base at 4,500 feet. The 57 Squadron crews carried out their attacks from 7,000 to 11,500 feet between 01.07 and 01.14, Sgt Player and crew dropping a cookie and the others all-incendiary loads, and nothing was seen of the impact. S/L Laird and crew returned their bombs to store after failing to locate the target. Returning crews were encouraged by the fires to believe that an effective operation had taken place, and this was confirmed by local sources, which reported major destruction in the central districts, where many historic and cultural buildings were damaged or destroyed. In the excellent tome, Bomber Command War Diaries by Martin Middlebrook and Chris Everitt, the losses from this operation are put at six aircraft, but the actual number failing to return was fourteen, while four others were lost in crashes at home. 57 Squadron posted missing the crews of P/O Dawson and Sgt Riddell RNZAF in Z1656 and BJ830 respectively, the former disappearing into the sea and the latter falling in Germany, neither with a survivor. Meanwhile, P/O Bowles and crew had bombed the docks at Le Havre from 11,500 feet at 03.20 without observing the results, but F/Sgt McLaren and crew had failed to locate the target and brought their load home.

The details of the return to Mainz were briefed out to 138 crews on the afternoon of the 12th, sixty-one of them on 3 Group stations including Feltwell, where five crews from each squadron listened intently. This would be the final operation for 75(NZ) Squadron from Feltwell before its move on the 15th to Mildenhall to join 149 Squadron, which had been in residence there since 1937. The 57 Squadron quintet took off between 22.30 and 23.15 with S/L Forbes the senior pilot on duty and were accompanied into the air by the freshman crews of P/O Bowles and Sgt Brooks, who were bound for the Nectarine I garden off the southern Frisians. Sgt Saunders and crew were deep into enemy territory when they were attacked by a night-fighter, which they evaded, but the encounter had delayed them sufficiently to put them too far behind schedule to reach the target in the allotted time. The crews of S/L Forbes and Sgts Cameron and Player, having flown out over ten-tenths cloud, were unable to locate the target and turned for home bringing their loads with them. This left just F/L Huggins and crew to represent the squadron at the target, where they dropped 810 x 4lb incendiaries from 6,500 feet at 01.00 and observed an explosion with a brilliant blue flash. There was some stray bombing by the rest of the force, but much further destruction was inflicted on the city's central districts and also in industrial areas, and the main railway station was severely damaged. The gardeners, meanwhile, had delivered their two mines each into the briefed locations from 800 and 1,000 feet at 00.33 and 00.53 before returning safely.

The 15th brought the start of a new era for Bomber Command with the formation of the Path Finder Force as the four founder heavy squadrons arrived on their stations in Huntingdonshire and Cambridgeshire. 83 Squadron moved into Wyton, the Path Finder HQ, as the 5 Group representative operating Lancasters, while 156 Squadron retained its Wellingtons for the time-being at Warboys, drawing fresh crews though, not from its parent 3 Group, but from 1 Group, while 3 Group would be represented by the Stirling-equipped 7 Squadron at Oakington and 4 Group by 35 (Madras Presidency) Squadron with its Halifaxes at Graveley. In addition to the above, 109 Squadron was posted in to Wyton, where it would spend the next six months developing the Oboe blind-bombing device and marrying it to the Mosquito under the command of W/C Hal Bufton. The new force would occupy 3 Group stations, falling nominally under 3 Group administrative control and receiving its orders through that group, which was commanded by AVM Baldwin, whose tenure, which had lasted since just before the outbreak of war, was shortly to come to an end.

A "Path Finder" force was the brainchild of the former 10 Squadron commanding officer, G/C Sid Bufton, Hal's brother, and now Director of Bomber Operations at the Air Ministry. He had used his best crews at 10 Squadron to find targets by the light of flares and attract other crews by firing off a coloured Verey light, and, it could be said, that the concept of target-finding and marking had been born at 10 Squadron. Once at the Air Ministry, Bufton promoted his ideas with vigour, and gained support among the other staff officers, culminating with the idea being put to Harris soon after his enthronement as Bomber Command C-in-C. Harris rejected the principle of establishing an elite target-finding and marking force, a view shared by the other group commanders with the exception of 4 Group's AVM Roddy Carr. However, once overruled by higher authority, Harris gave it his unstinting support, and his choice of the former 10 Squadron commanding officer, and still somewhat junior, G/C Don Bennett, as its commander, was both controversial and inspired, and ruffled more than a few feathers among more senior officers. Australian, Bennett, was among the most experienced aviators in the RAF, a pilot and a Master Navigator of unparalleled experience, with many thousands of hours to his credit. He was blessed with a brilliant mind, which made him prone to set standards that few others could achieve, and this created a demanding, exacting, but fair leader. It had been he who had been entrusted with setting up the Atlantic Ferry Service earlier in the war, to bring much needed aircraft over from America. He also had the recent and relevant experience as a bomber pilot through his commands of 77 and 10 Squadrons and had demonstrated his strong character when evading capture and returning from Norway after being shot down while attacking the Tirpitz in April. Despite his reserve, total lack of humour and his impatience with those whose brains operated on a lower plane than his, he would inspire in his men great affection and loyalty, along with an enormous pride in being a "Path Finder". He would forge the new force into a highly effective weapon, although this would not immediately be apparent.

Düsseldorf was posted as the target for 131 aircraft on the 15th, an operation supported by 3 Group with forty-three Wellingtons and Stirlings, nine of the former provided by 57 Squadron. The details of the operation were recorded by the squadron scribe on Form 540 rather than Form 541 and lacked take-off and landing times, leaving us only with the information that Sgt Player and crew turned back early because of an unserviceable rear turret and Sgt Saunders and crew abandoned their sortie after failing to locate the target through complete cloud cover. The others navigated to the target by DR and bombed on e.t.a., from 9,000 to 12,000 feet between 02.16 and 02.42 before returning safely. A single 4,000 pounder caused extensive blast damage to buildings in Neuss city centre, but that apart, the operation was a total failure that had no effect on industrial production.

It had been intended to send the fledgling Path Finder Force into battle for the first time at Osnabrück on the 17th, but the commanding officers declared their squadrons to be unready, and the raid went ahead without them at the hands of a force of 139 aircraft. 3 Group detailed fifty-five Wellingtons and Stirlings, eleven of the former made ready by 57 Squadron, which departed Feltwell between 22.05 and 22.20 with S/L Forbes the senior pilot on duty. F/Sgt McLaren and crew abandoned their sortie because of an unserviceable rear turret, but the others from the squadron pressed on to reach the target area and find three to five-tenths cloud at between 11,000 and 14,000 feet. 5 Group had been developing a "time-and-distance" method of final approach to bomb and practiced it on this night from the Dümmer Sea, a large lake situated some twenty miles to the north-east. The vertical visibility was further compromised by haze, but some were able to identify the river and railway lines, and bombing was carried out by the Feltwell crews on the built-up area generally from 9,000 to 11,000 feet between 00.16 and 00.45, with little regard for where it fell. Local reports confirmed a moderately destructive raid, which hit mainly northern and north-western districts, and, thereby, built on the damage inflicted eight nights earlier.

The Path Finder Force took to the air in anger for the first time on the 18th, when contributing thirty-one aircraft to an overall force of 118 bound for the naval and shipbuilding port of Flensburg, situated on the eastern coast of the Schleswig-Holstein peninsula close to the border with Denmark, where the U-Boot pens were the briefed aiming-point. It had been selected as a worthwhile and easy-to-locate coastal target, for which the five participating 57 Squadron Wellingtons took off between 20.40 and 20.50 with S/L Laird the senior pilot on duty. P/O Duffy and crew became victims of the recent spate of rear turret malfunctions and turned back, leaving the others to press on across the Schleswig-Holstein peninsula, unaware that the wind forecast guiding the Path Finder navigators was incorrect. The ground was largely concealed by haze and extreme darkness, and unknown to the crews, the entire force was being pushed to the north of the intended track and over southern Denmark. Over time, Path Finder equipment and tactics would evolve to highly sophisticated levels, but, in the early stages, its role was simply to lead the main force crews to a target and establish its position with incendiaries and illumination. The lead crews identified what appeared to be Flensburg Fjord and the inlet at its head and dropped their incendiaries onto what they believed was the aiming point, observing nothing of the impact, and the main force crews simply followed suit with their high explosives and incendiaries, those from 57 Squadron from 8,000 to 11,000 feet between 23.22 and 23.45. In fact, they had strayed over a similar-shaped coastal inlet across the Danish frontier, and this led to a scattering of bombs across territory up to twenty-five miles north of the frontier, and into the towns of Abenra and Sønderborg. Flensburg was untouched by this inauspicious operational debut of a force, which, in time, would become a highly efficient, successful and vital component in Bomber Command's armoury. Sgt McLaren RCAF and crew, three of whom were members of the RNZAF, failed to return in X3371 after coming down without survivors into the sea.

Mining and minor operations occupied the ensuing five nights until Frankfurt was posted as the target for the second Path Finder-led operation on the 24th, for which a force of 226 aircraft was made ready, 3 Group providing the thirty-seven Path Finders along with forty-five Stirlings and fifty-nine Wellingtons as part of the main force. 57 Squadron put up fourteen Wellington for the main event and another containing the crew of Sgt Langley for mining duties in the Nectarine I garden off the southern Frisians. Those bound for the main event departed Feltwell between 21.15 and 21.30 with S/Ls Forbes and Laird the senior pilots on duty, and they were well on their way to the target when the Langley crew took off at 22.00. The last-mentioned arrived off Teschelling a little over an hour later and carried out a timed run to the release point, where they let two mines go with a five-second interval from 1,000 feet at 23.22. Meanwhile, those participating in the main event had headed out across The Wash on course for the Belgian coast and entered Germany via the heavily wooded Eifel region. Not among them were the crews of Sgt Cameron, F/Sgts Moore and Rowney and Sgt Brooks, who were defeated respectively by stability problems, the rear turret malaise and generator failure. Those reaching the target were greeted by five to ten-tenths cloud at between 7,000 and 9,000 feet, with ground haze adding to the difficulties of locating the aiming-point. It was the flak that guided many to the approximate location of the target, where the remaining 57 Squadron crews delivered their high-explosive or incendiary bomb loads on estimated positions from 7,500 to 11,500 feet between 23.22 and 00.03, observing two large fires as they turned away. Local sources confirmed seventeen large and fifty-three small fires and moderate property damage, but most of the bombing had been wasted on open country to the north and west.

Kassel was posted as the target for the night of the 27th, for which 3 Group detailed thirty-three Path Finder and ninety-eight main force aircraft in an overall bomber fleet of 306 aircraft. 57 Squadron bombed and fuelled up a dozen Wellingtons, which departed Feltwell between 20.50

and 21.20 with F/L Huggins the senior pilot on duty. They set out for the Dutch coast in fine conditions, each carrying an all-incendiary bomb load, unaware that a major night fighter response awaited them. The crews of Sgt Croston and F/Sgt Danahy abandoned their sorties after they were unable to gain height, while the crews of F/L Huggins and Sgt Player turned back with engine issues and were among twenty-one "boomerangs" from 3 Group. Meanwhile, the Path Finders had managed to locate the target under largely clear skies and illuminate it for the main force, which exploited the opportunity to deliver an effective attack. The main weight of bombs fell mainly in the south-western districts and destroyed 144 buildings, while seriously damaging more than three hundred others. All three Henschel factories were among the industrial concerns hit, but it was not a one-sided affair, and thirty-one bombers, 10% of the force, failed to return home, a third of them belonging to 3 Group squadrons. 57 Squadron was represented among the missing by X3331, which came down somewhere north of the Ruhr killing three of the occupants and delivering Sgt Saunders, his second pilot and rear gunner into enemy hands.

Nuremberg was posted as the main target on the 28th, for which a force of 159 aircraft was assembled, 3 Group contributing thirty-one Path Finders and sixty-two Wellingtons and Stirlings for the main force. A simultaneous operation by 113 aircraft was to target Saarbrücken and would involve eight 3 Group Wellingtons and a single Stirling in what was an experimental raid. There were no Path Finders and the force consisted of oddments, including the few remaining Hampdens in front-line service and 4 Group Halifaxes, which had been withdrawn temporarily from operations while investigations were carried out into a spate of unexplained crashes that had damaged crew confidence in the type. The eight 57 Squadron crews departing Feltwell on this night would be the last to do so in anger from what had been the squadron's home since November 1940. Seven of them were bound for the main event and one for Saarbrücken, and sadly, not all lifting into the air between 20.45 and 21.00 would return. S/L Laird was the senior pilot on duty on a night when the Path Finders were to employ target indicators (TIs) for the first time in adapted 250lb bomb casings. Seventeen 3 Group aircraft, including six Path Finders, turned back early, but 57 Squadron was not represented among them and all completed the six-hundred-mile outward leg across France to southern Germany. They found the target city under clear skies, which combined with a four-fifths moon to enable crews to pinpoint on ground features like the lakes some fifteen miles to the north-west of the city, the River Pegnitz to the north of the city centre and canals to the south. The Path Finders exploited the opportunity to deliver their TIs with great accuracy, and the Feltwell crews followed up as part of the main force to deliver their high-explosives and incendiaries from around 8,000 to 10,500 feet shortly after midnight. The squadron scribe had again substituted Form 540 for Form 541 and consequently, details were lacking. Local reports suggested that about a third of the force had landed bombs within the city, causing damage to the Altstadt, but that others had wasted their effort on communities up to ten miles to the north. Twenty-three aircraft failed to return, 14.5% of those dispatched, and the Wellingtons sustained a loss rate of 34%. 57 Squadron posted missing BJ619, which, it was learned in time, had crash-landed in Germany near Wahlenau, some thirty miles east of the frontier with Luxembourg and delivered the crew of Sgt Brooks into captivity. BJ701 crashed in southern Germany without survivors from the crew of F/Sgt Rowney RCAF, three of whom were members of the RNZAF. Meanwhile, Sgt Langley and crew had dropped their cookie onto Saarbrücken from 8,000 feet at 23.10 and observed nothing of the impact. When F/Sgt Moore and crew touched down at Feltwell at 04.35 on the 29th, they brought to an end 57 Squadron's twenty-two-month-long 3 Group and Wellington service, of which it could be proud.

During the course of the month the squadron took part in fourteen operations and dispatched ninety-six sorties for the loss of six Wellingtons and crews.

September 1942

The advent of the Path Finder Force had a massive impact on 57 Squadron and entirely changed the course of its war. When 83 Squadron, one of 5 Group's most prestigious units, was transferred out as a founder member of the PFF, it left a void in 5 Group ranks which needed to be filled. 5 Group had now fully converted to the Lancaster after its unhappy experience with the Manchester and its last remaining Hampden unit was about to join 4 Group to convert to the Halifax. A decision had just been taken which would rescue 1 Group from the brink of exchanging its Wellingtons for Halifaxes, although not in time to save 103 Squadron from the nasty experience of operating the type for three months, during which its crews became deeply concerned by the loss rate. 101 and 460 Squadrons were shortly to begin conversion training but dodged a bullet when it was decided that 1 Group would operate Lancasters. Harris had a poor opinion of the Stirling, an aircraft with design flaws that restricted its service ceiling, limited the type of bombs it could carry and caused its undercarriage to collapse at the drop of a hat. It had no development potential but was in full production and 3 Group was committed to retaining it until Lancasters became available, which would not be until 1 Group and elements of the PFF had converted. Had 57 Squadron remained in 3 Group, it would have become a Stirling unit faced with the challenges of operating the type, particularly during the major campaigns of 1943. Fortunately, in seeking to expand 5 Group and secure a replacement for 83 Squadron, it made good sense to raid 3 Group, and 9 Squadron, which had been a 3 Group front-line squadron since before the war, had made the move from Honington to Waddington in August. 57 Squadron was plucked out of the Norfolk fens and deposited on the 4th in the equally rural countryside at Scampton, a pre-war station situated six miles north of the city of Lincoln. It had been home to 49 and 83 Squadrons since March 1938 and 57 Squadron would occupy the accommodation left vacant by 83 Squadron.

Lancaster W4132 arrived on the following day, and 57 Squadron thus became the eleventh operational unit in the Command to receive the type. All available aircrew reported to 49 Squadron Conversion Flight on the 6th to begin training and the working up period would occupy the whole of September and the first third of October. This would be a busy time for 5 Group, which 57 Squadron could only watch from the side-lines.

The first half of the new month would distinguish itself through an unprecedented series of effective operations, although, it would begin ignominiously for the Path Finder Force, when posting a "black" on the night of the 1/2nd by marking the wrong town. The city of Saarbrücken had been briefed out to 231 crews, of which sixty-nine represented 5 Group, sixty-two to fly Lancasters and seven in Hampdens, a type with just two more weeks of front-line service ahead of it. South-western Germany was found to be under clear skies with good visibility, and crews established their positions by TR, confirmed by visual identification of the River Saar and Path Finder flares. There was no question in the minds of the crews as they retreated to the west, that this had been an outstandingly accurate attack, and some claimed to be able to see the glow of fires from up to 140 miles into the return flight. It was only later that the truth emerged, that the Path Finders had not marked Saarbrücken, but the non-industrial town of Saarlouis, situated thirteen miles to the north-west. Much to the chagrin of its inhabitants and those in surrounding communities, the main force bombing had been particularly accurate and concentrated and heavy damage had been inflicted.

This could have been an ill-omen for the month's efforts, but, in fact, the Command now embarked on the unprecedented run of effective operations mentioned above. It began at Karlsruhe on the night of the 2/3rd, for which a force of two hundred aircraft was made ready, the 4 Group Halifax brigade having now returned to operations following intensive training to restore confidence in the type after a period of above average losses and a series of design-flaw accidents. 5 Group put up sixty Lancasters and five Hampdens, which flew out over Belgium and France to reach the target area under clear skies and in bright moonlight. Karlsruhe was naked to the eyes of the bomb-aimers high above, the autobahn and the Rhine and its docks standing out clearly as a guide to the aiming point, which appeared to be swallowed by a sea of flames before becoming obscured by smoke. Returning crews reported as many as two hundred fires, the glow from which remained visible for a hundred miles into the homeward journey. Post-raid reconnaissance confirmed much residential and some industrial damage, and local reports mentioned seventy-three fatalities.

When Bremen was posted as the target on the 4th, 5 Group responded with a contribution of forty-six Lancasters in an overall force of 251 aircraft. Crews were told at briefing that the Path Finders would be rolling out a new three-phase technique of illumination, visual marking and backing-up, which, if successful, would form the basis of Path Finder operations for the remainder of the war. Some 5 Group crews were assigned to the Focke-Wulf aircraft factory in the Hemelingen district, while others were to aim for the general built-up area, and those reaching the target found cloudless skies and good visibility, although ground haze and smoke created challenging conditions for target identification. Twelve aircraft failed to return from this successful operation, and debriefing reports of fires in the central districts were confirmed by a local assessment, which listed 460 dwelling houses, six large/medium industrial premises and fifteen small ones destroyed, and a further fourteen hundred buildings seriously damaged.

The next operation was to be directed at the Ruhr city of Duisburg on the night of the 6/7th, for which a force of 207 aircraft was assembled that included fifty-four Lancasters and four Hampdens representing 5 Group. The target area was partially concealed by cloud, below which, the usual industrial haze rendered ground detail indistinct, and positions had to be established by TR and confirmed as far as possible by visual reference. The attack took place in the face of a searchlight and flak defence operating to its usual high standard, despite which, the Duisburg authorities reported the heaviest raid to date, the destruction of 114 buildings and serious damage to more than three hundred others. While this was a relatively modest achievement, it still represented something of a victory at this notoriously elusive target.

There was no pattern to the choice of targets thus far in the month, southern and north-western Germany and the Ruhr all featuring during the busy first week, and Frankfurt in south-central Germany was posted as the latest target on the 8th, for which a force of 249 aircraft was assembled.

5 Group contributed sixty-two Lancasters and nine Hampdens, and those reaching the target area encountered either clear skies and good visibility or up to eight-tenths cloud at 2,000 feet and poor to moderate visibility, depending upon which report one believes. Another factor was the intensity of the searchlight and flak activity, which should, perhaps, have helped to guide the Path Finders to the aiming point, but, surprisingly, they failed to locate the city. Path Finder flares were in evidence, but scattered over a wide area, and it was clear that they were by no means certain of their position in relation to Frankfurt. According to local reports, only a handful of bomb loads hit the intended target, and this halted the run of successes thus far in the month. The majority of bombs appeared to have fallen to the south-west of Frankfurt as far as Rüsselsheim, fifteen miles away. The Rüsselsheim authorities confirmed damage to the Opel tank works and a Michelin tyre factory, which compensated in small measure for the failure to hit the primary target.

The Path Finder Force was constantly evolving in tactics and equipment and had a new weapon in its armoury for the next operation, which was to be against the Ruhr city of Düsseldorf on the 10th. "The Pink Pansy", which weighed in at 2,800lbs, was the latest attempt to produce a genuine target indicator, and used converted 4,000lb cookie casings. A force of 479 aircraft included a contribution from the training units of 91, 92 and 93 Groups, and eighty-one Lancasters and eight Hampdens from 5 Group. Clear skies prevailed over the target with the usual industrial haze muddying the vertical visibility, but fires were already burning to help bomb-aimers to identify the target visually and pick out major features like a bend in the Rhine and the docks complex. The red flares were reported by some to be a little north of the main city area, and the greens to the west, while the white illuminators highlighted the more central districts. Returning crews made complimentary comments about the performance of the Path Finders and reported the glow of the fires to be visible from the Scheldt. Post-raid reconnaissance and local reports confirmed this operation to have been probably the most successful since Operation Millennium at the end of May. Other than the northern districts, all parts of the city and its neighbour, Neuss, had been hit, and 911 houses had been destroyed with a further fifteen hundred seriously damaged. In addition to the destruction also of eight public buildings, fifty-two industrial firms in the two cities sustained damage sufficient to cause a total shut down of production for varying periods. It had been an expensive victory for the Command, however, with thirty-three aircraft failing to return, of which sixteen were from the training units.

For the second time in the month, Bremen was posted as the target on the 13th, and a force of 446 aircraft assembled, the numbers again bolstered by aircraft and crews from the training groups, and there was a contribution from 5 Group of ninety-eight Lancasters and seven Hampdens. Those reaching the target were greeted by clear skies but considerable ground haze, which made pinpointing something of a challenge, but some major ground features, like the docks, could be identified visually, otherwise it was down to flares and fires to point the way. A number of crews were convinced that some early arrivals had bombed at Delmenhorst, a few miles to the south-west of Bremen, and the 5 Group ORB described the Path Finder performance on this occasion as unhelpful. However, the successes of the operation suggested otherwise, and by far exceeded the destruction resulting from June's Thousand Bomber raid. A total of 848 houses was destroyed, and much damage was inflicted on the city's industry, including to the Lloyd Dynamo works, where two weeks production was lost, and parts of the Focke-Wulf factory were put out of action for between two and eight days. Of the twenty-one aircraft lost, fifteen belonged to the training units and only one to 5 Group.

The end of the Hampden era arrived on the following night when the naval port of Wilhelmshaven was posted as the target for 202 aircraft. Sixty-two Lancasters and four Hampdens were made ready as the 5 Group contribution, the latter from Syerston's 408 (Goose) Squadron RCAF. There were clear skies over the coastal region of Jade Bay, with extreme darkness and ground haze to impede vertical visibility, but the waterline and the docks had provided an adequate pinpoint for the Path Finders to establish their position and mark accurately. It was difficult to distinguish individual bomb bursts, but the consensus was of a successful outcome, and quite a number of crews reported an enormous explosion, believed to be from an ammunition dump. It lit up the ground for five seconds and emitted flames a hundred feet into the air along with a cloud of smoke that rose to several thousand feet. Local sources confirmed that this had been the port's most destructive raid to date.

After such a run of successes, Harris had to have another go at Essen, and a force of 369 aircraft was assembled on the 16th, which again called upon the training units to supply aircraft and crews. Ninety-three Lancasters represented 5 Group, and those arriving in the target area encountered between three and eight-tenths cloud, but generally good visibility despite the industrial haze, which could be penetrated sufficiently for some ground detail to be identified visually by the light of Path Finder flares. Even so, the overlapping boundaries of the Ruhr towns and cities made it difficult to establish positions with absolute certainty, and some of the crews dropping their bombs on e.t.a., would find, from the evidence of their bombing photos, that they had been over Bochum, Oberhausen or some other built-up expanse. Some of the Path Finder flares were estimated to be falling some twenty miles to the east of Essen, which would have put them over Dortmund and Hagen. Returning crews reported an intense searchlight and flak response and the glow of fires visible for a hundred miles into the return journey, and local sources would confirm this to be Essen's worst night of the war to date. In addition to much housing damage and more than a hundred medium and large fires, fifteen high-explosive bombs had found their way into the Krupp complex, as did a crashing bomber loaded with incendiaries. A post-raid analysis revealed that bombs had been scattered across a large part of the Ruhr, with Bochum, Wuppertal and Herne among the hardest hit, and, until the advent of Oboe in the coming spring, such inaccuracies remained a fact of life. It was far from a one-sided affair, and cost the Command a massive thirty-nine aircraft, 10.6% of those dispatched, nineteen of them from the training units.

If any period in the Command's gradual evolution to war-winning capability could be seen as a turning point, then, perhaps, the first half of September 1942 qualified. It can be no coincidence, that the Path Finder Force was emerging from its hesitant start, as the crews got to grips with the complexities of their demanding role, and new tactics and aids were being brought to bear against the enemy. It would be no overnight transformation, and failures would still outnumber victories for some time to come, but the encouraging signs were there, that all of the elements of technical and tactical advance were coming together, and, with other technological wizardry in the pipeline, it boded ill for Germany's industrial towns and cities.

Extensive mining operations occupied 115 aircraft on the night of the 18/19th, 5 Group supporting the effort with forty-nine Lancasters assigned to six separate gardens, five in the western Baltic and one located off south-western France. Munich was posted as one of two targets on the 19th, and would involve sixty-one 5 Group Lancasters, seven Lancasters and seven Stirlings from 83 and 7 Squadrons of the Path Finders and twenty-one Stirlings from 3 Group, while a simultaneous operation by 118 aircraft of 1, 3 and 4 Groups would target Saarbrücken, also with Path Finder support. The two forces would follow a common route as far as Saarbrücken, leaving the 5 Group element a further 220 miles to travel to reach the Bavarian capital, the birthplace of Nazism and a city of cultural and industrial significance. They flew out across France, entering southern Germany near Strasbourg to be greeted by clear skies and good visibility, which enabled them to identify the lakes to the south-west of the city. Most crews adopted a time-and-distance run from Lake Constance to bring them to the aiming point, which had been well-illuminated by Path Finder flares, and bomb bursts were observed in the city centre, along with a large explosion to the north and numerous fires, including a large one to the south-west. 40% of returning crews would claim to have bombed within three miles of the city centre but reports rarely emerged from this city to confirm or deny. Saarbrücken was reported to be well-alight by crews passing by on the way home, and the Path Finders were complimented on their performance at debriefings. Bombing photos revealed that the main weight of the attack had fallen into western, southern and eastern suburbs of Munich, while Saarbrücken had largely escaped damage after the bombing became widely scattered.

The target for an all-5 Group force of eighty-three Lancasters on the 23rd was the Baltic coastal town of Wismar and the nearby Dornier aircraft factory. Two-thirds of the force were assigned to the town, situated some thirty miles east of Lübeck, and a third to the factory, but first they had to negotiate a violent electrical storm when around a hundred miles short of Denmark's western coast, which caused many to turn back and added to a total of twenty-one early returns from all causes. Those reaching the target found ten-tenths cloud with tops at 8,000 feet and a base at 800 feet, with intense and accurate searchlight and flak activity awaiting any crews brave enough to venture so low. Those attacking the town did so in a rainstorm from 1,500 to 4,000 feet and on return reported fires in the town and at the Dornier factory, while local reports listed thirty-two houses and eight industrial buildings seriously damaged.

5 Group went mining on the night of the 24/25th, and again in small numbers on the 29/30th to bring the month's activities to a close. It was a busy month for postings to and from 57 Squadron during the month, and the Lancaster's standard crew of seven demanded an influx of new recruits. Among the movements of senior officers, S/L Forbes was posted to 20 O.T.U., on the 2nd and S/L Carter and crew arrived on the same day from 11 O.T.U. S/L Long was posted in from 23 O.T.U on the 9th and S/L Laird went in the opposite direction having completed his tour. On the 21st, W/C Laine relinquished command of 57 Squadron to become station commander at Watton in Norfolk, and he was succeeded by W/C Hopcroft DFC on his arrival from 1654 Conversion Unit on the 23rd.

October 1942

5 Group's October account opened on the 1st with news of a return to Wismar that night, for which a force of seventy-eight Lancasters was prepared, the plan calling for three-quarters of the force to attack the town, with the main square as the aiming point, while the remainder targeted the Dornier aircraft factory. The bomber stream crossed Jutland seemingly without incident and arrived in the target area to encounter three to ten-tenths cloud with a base at between 1,500 and 7,000 feet. Poor visibility over the town was caused by heavy ground haze and an effective smoke

screen, which combined with intense searchlight glare to blot out identifying features. Brief glimpses of the coastline provided a scant reference by which some established position, but bombing runs had to be carried out largely on DR, and no crew was able to establish a firm pinpoint. This led to the bombing of a number of locations along a 150-mile stretch of coastline from Wismar eastwards, and the entire undertaking proved to be a wasted effort.

The Ruhr city of Krefeld was posted as the target for a force of 188 aircraft on the 2nd, for which 5 Group contributed twenty-four Lancasters from Waddington, Coningsby and Syerston, while the rest of the group stood down. Those reaching the western edge of the Ruhr encountered dense industrial haze, which thwarted the Path Finders' best efforts to provide a reference for those following behind. Returning crews reported some scattered fires, and local sources confirmed that three streets in the northern part of the city had sustained damage, but nothing commensurate with the size of the force and the effort expended.

Although no longer in the front line, Manchesters were still employed for multi-engine training and P/O Walsh DFC & Bar and crew were flying in L7386 on the 5th, when an engine fire broke out. P/O Walsh crash-landed the aircraft at Scampton at 14.45 without damage to the crew, and this was probably the last Manchester to be written off by an operational squadron. All heavy groups were alerted on this day to an operation that night against the city of Aachen, for which a force of 257 aircraft was put together, 5 Group detailing sixty-nine Lancasters. At least part of the bomber stream passed through a violent thunderstorm eighty miles south of Waddington, and having crossed the Channel, the stormy weather extended inland, which encouraged some of the force to descend for the rest of the journey to the target, Germany's most westerly city, nestling just inside the German borders with southern Holland and Belgium. On arrival in the target area, flares were visible, but up to nine-tenths cloud and poor visibility created challenging conditions, and much of the bombing missed the mark. Local sources reported that Aachen's southern district of Burtscheid had suffered quite extensive damage to housing and industry, and five large fires had required attention, but even so, they estimated the attack to have involved only around ten aircraft. Some bombs fell seventeen miles away onto the small Dutch town of Lutterade, and this would have minor consequences for the trials of the Oboe blind-bombing device in late December.

Osnabrück was posted as the target on the 6th, for which 237 aircraft were made ready, including fifty-nine Lancasters of 5 Group. The Path Finders dropped flares over Makkum in Holland and the Dümmer See to the north-east of the target as route markers, and these proved to be very effective in guiding the main force in, although, inevitably, some bomb loads were released early during the twenty-mile leg between the Dümmer See and the town. Four to eight-tenths cloud lay over the town at 8,000 feet, and provided challenging conditions for accurate bombing, although opinions varied as to the quality of the visibility. Returning crew described many fires and a glow visible by some from the Dutch coast homebound, and most had confidence in the effectiveness of the raid. According to local reports, 149 houses and six industrial buildings were destroyed, 530 houses seriously damaged and more than 2,700 others slightly damaged.

Most of the following week was devoted exclusively to mining operations, and there would be little activity for 5 Group squadrons other than daylight formation-flying exercises for some in preparation for an audacious operation in mid-month. 5 Group announced another shot at Wismar and the Dornier aircraft factory on the 12th and put together a force of fifty-nine Lancasters, which included for the first time an element from 57 Squadron. While the crews of W/C Hopcroft, S/L Long, F/L Curry, P/O Miles, F/Sgts Croston, Lancaster and Moore and Sgt Singer were undergoing briefing during the afternoon, their Lancasters were being loaded with either all-incendiary loads or three 1,000 pounders topped up with eight SBCs of 4lb incendiaries. During his stewardship of 57 Squadron, W/C Hopcroft named his Lancasters "Frederick", his own first name, and in regal style, added a number to signify the sequence of their accession. We know that ED707 was Frederick II and ED989 Frederick III, and it is believed that W4201, his mount for this maiden operation, was Frederick I.

They departed Scampton for their Lancaster operational debut between 17.57 and 18.34 on what turned out to be a night of challenging weather conditions, particularly over the North Sea, which prevented many crews from establishing a pinpoint on the Danish coast at Mandø Island and forced them to navigate across southern Jutland by DR. Some may have identified the briefed navigation pinpoint at Nakskov on Denmark's Lolland Island before arriving at Wismar to find it under six to ten-tenths cloud in a band between 1,000 and 7,000 feet. The lack of pinpoints forced some crews to search for up to thirty minutes before bombing eventually on estimated positions. Those from 57 Squadron mostly found a ground reference on the Baltic coast for their timed runs, while P/O Miles and crew picked out three lakes to the south and south-east of the town. The 57 Squadron crews carried out their attacks from 7,000 to 11,000 feet between 20.45 and 21.25 and contributed to a scattered and probably ineffective raid, despite which, some returning crews reported that the factory had been left burning furiously and the flames had remained visible for seventy miles into the homeward journey. F/L Curry and crew were attacked by an unidentified aircraft while homebound near Funen (Fyn), Denmark's third largest island and W4232 sustained extensive damage (Cat C), while the bomb-aimer and rear gunner picked up non-life-threatening wounds that were treated in hospital.

The naval and shipbuilding port of Kiel was posted as the target for a force of 288 aircraft on the 13th, for which 5 Group weighed in with sixty-nine Lancasters, ten of them provided by 57 Squadron and loaded with a cookie each and either eight SBCs of 30lb incendiaries or nine of 4lbs. They took off between 18.50 and 19.10 with S/L Carter the senior pilot on duty and lost the services of F/L Huggins and crew after fifty minutes when the pilot became unwell, probably through lack of oxygen. The route was similar to that employed for Wismar with landfall over Mandø Island and a race across southern Jutland to the target, where almost clear skies and good visibility prevailed and red and white flares marked out the Selenter Lake, some ten miles to the east. Illuminator flares were also deployed over the town, revealing a built-up area, which the 57 Squadron crews bombed from 8,500 to 12,000 feet between 21.25 and 21.45, most without plotting the fall. Probably half of the crews were deceived by a decoy fire site, but the rest hit the town and caused an appropriate amount of damage. Returning crews reported a much-reduced searchlight and flak defence, and, conscious that defensive measures attracted attention, this was a tactic employed occasionally and effectively by the Luftwaffe.

A force of 289 aircraft was assembled on the 15th to send against Cologne, which had been left in peace for a considerable time, and the operation was supported by sixty-two Lancasters of 5 Group from Coningsby, Scampton, Syerston and Waddington. 57 Squadron made ready ten Lancasters and sent them on their way from Scampton between 19.00 and 19.16 with S/L Long the senior pilot on duty. F/Sgt Player and crew were closing on the enemy coast at Ouddorp on Goeree Island in the Scheldt estuary, when a hydraulics pipe burst and rendered the rear turret inoperable, forcing them to turn back. The others pressed on through icing conditions and across northern Belgium to be eased off track by inaccurately forecast winds and found the Rhineland capital to be concealed beneath a layer of ten-tenths cloud. The Path Finder flares were scattered, and a large, effective decoy fire site combined with that to attract the main force away from the target. The 57 Squadron crews carried out their attacks mostly on estimated positions from 8,000 to 13,000 feet between 20.36 and 21.06, observing bursts and explosions but no detail, and it was left to local sources to report damage within the city to be slight and superficial. P/O Wallis and crew had the sad distinction of being the first from 57 Squadron to be posted missing in a Lancaster, and no trace of W4130 or its crew was ever found.

On the 17th, the purpose behind the formation-flying training that had been causing speculation for more than a week, was revealed to crews in 5 Group briefing rooms. They learned that Operation Robinson was a daylight attack on the Schneider armaments works at Le Creusot, deep in eastern France, and the nearby Montchanin transformer station, which provided its power. Often referred to as the French "Krupp", the company belonged to the Schneider family, which had donated the famous aviation trophy bearing its name. The Schneider Trophy was initially a prize to encourage technical advances in civil aviation, but, eventually, became a speed contest for float and seaplanes competed for biannually by Britain, France, Italy and the USA. It was a massively prestigious and popular spectator event that drew crowds of up to 200,000 people. Britain claimed it outright after three consecutive wins culminating in 1931, when the revolutionary Supermarine S6B triumphed in the hands of 44 Squadron's first wartime commanding officer, W/C Boothman. Ninety-four Lancasters were to take part in the operation, which required an outward flight at low level by daylight, the attack at dusk, and a return under the cover of darkness. It was a bold plan to commit such a large force, which would be difficult to conceal, and it was only six months since six Lancasters each from 44 and 97 Squadrons had carried out a similar day/night operation against the M.A.N diesel engine works at Augsburg in Bavaria and lost seven Lancasters between them.

The plan called for eighty-eight aircraft to bomb the factory complex from as low as practicable, led by W/C Len Slee of 49 Squadron, while six others, two each from 106, 61 and 97 Squadrons, led by W/C Gibson, went for the power station in a line-astern attack. The 57 Squadron contribution amounted to ten Lancasters, which departed Scampton between 12.12 and 12.15 with W/C Hopcroft and S/L Long the senior pilots on duty. They would join up with the rest of the force over Upper Heyford, before heading for Land's End at under 1,000 feet, and, once over the sea, aim for a point just south of the Ile d'Yeu to cross the French coast midway between St Nazaire and La Rochelle at around 100 feet. Shortly before the sea crossing began, Coastal Command Whitleys had carried out a sweep to force enemy U-Boots beneath the surface and prevent them from spotting the force and transmitting a warning. There were two pilots bearing the surname Singer, and it was Sgt A Singer and crew who turned back from a position some twenty miles south of Exeter after the rear turret had been rendered unserviceable by a fractured hydraulics pipe, while F/Sgt Danahy and crew lost contact with the formation in a fog bank near the Isles of Scilly and lost the use of their mid-upper turret to another hydraulics failure. This left the remainder to complete the Channel crossing and skirt the Finistere region to reach the Biscay coast, after which, for most, the three-hundred-mile low-level dash across France would be relatively uneventful. Bird strikes became a constant threat, and Sgt King, the flight engineer in the crew of Sgt P Singer, sustained severe cuts to his eyes when his Perspex screen was shattered, leaving him in need of hospital treatment on return. The Lancaster also suffered damage to the port leading edge and the radiator shutter, while a number of other aircraft ingested body parts into their engines. An extreme physical strain was placed upon the pilots as they wrestled with slipstream turbulence, and at times, sections bunch-up to cause congested pockets of airspace, despite which, the middle leg terminated successfully at the predetermined point some forty-five miles from the target.

It was at this juncture that the main force broke up to form into a fan and climb to a bombing height of between 4,500 and 7,000 feet. The target was reached at dusk under clear skies and in good visibility, and crews were able to follow a railway line directly to the heart of the factory complex, where the 57 Squadron crews bombed as briefed from 5,000 to 8,000 feet between 18.13 and 18.15. Not all were able to plot the fall of their bombs, but Sgt P Singer and crew watched their four 1,000 pounders and two SBCs of 30lb incendiaries explode on a large shed with tall chimneys. The impression was of a highly successful operation that landed bombs in the steelworks and rolling mill, and a large volume of smoke was observed to ascend through 3,000 feet and obscure the entire target area. There were complimentary comments concerning the 49 Squadron leadership during the outward flight, and 44 Squadron's S/L Burnett claimed that it was the most successful operation that he had participated in. All from Scampton returned safely home after a round-trip of ten hours, and, at debriefing on all stations, it was unanimous that the target had been utterly devastated in return for the loss of a single 61 Squadron Lancaster from the Montchanin element. The success prompted a message from the A-O-C 5 Group, AVM Coryton, who added to his own congratulations with similar sentiments from the Secretary of State for Air, Sir Archibald Sinclair. Unfortunately, it would be discovered later, that the damage had been less severe than first thought, and production had soon returned to normal. Another raid would be mounted by other groups against the plant eight months hence.

A new campaign against Italian cities began on the night of the 22/23rd in support of land operations in North Africa under Operation Torch. It was the eve of the opening of the Battle of El Alamein, which, after twelve days' fighting, would see Montgomery push Rommel's forces all the way back to Tunisia and out of the war. The target for this first operation was the port-city of Genoa and its naval dockyard, where part of the Italian fleet was sheltering. It was also home to the Ansaldo engineering works, which was to Italy what Krupp was to Germany. Ten 5 Group squadrons mustered between them 101 Lancasters, while 83 Squadron of the Path Finders contributed eleven more to take care of target marking. 57 Squadron made ready thirteen Lancasters and dispatched them from Scampton between 17.23 and 17.38 with W/C Hopcroft and S/Ls Carter and Long the senior pilots on duty. They began the Channel crossing at Selsey Bill, and not long afterwards, F/Sgt Lancaster and crew turned back with engine issues and Sgt P Singer and crew suffered electrical failure at around the same time to end their interest in proceedings. The others crossed the Normandy coast over Isigny-sur-Mer and flew on towards the wall of rock that was the Alps, which formed the frontier between France and Italy and glistened under clear skies and an almost full moon. On the other side the perfect visibility over Italy was a joy to behold after contending with the industrial haze at German targets, and the Path Finder flares could be seen by approaching main force crews from sixty miles away. On their arrival over the city, they found the flak defence to be wildly inaccurate, while a smoke screen proved ineffective as the wind blew it straight out to sea. The crews were able to establish their positions visually on the layout of the docks and the city, and the 57 Squadron crews carried out their attacks from 5,500 (Sgt A Singer) to 15,000 feet between 21.18 and 21.40. Some returning crews described the raid as a "miniature-Cologne", in reference to the first thousand bomber raid at the end of May, and local sources confirmed heavy damage in central and eastern districts, which, because of the need for fuel over bombs, had been achieved with just 180 tons of high-explosives and incendiaries, and, remarkably, without loss.

Twenty-four hours later, a force made up of elements from 3 and 4 Groups and the Path Finders attempted to follow up at Genoa, but, in cloudy conditions, attacked in error the town of Savona, thirty miles to the west. Eighty-eight 5 Group crews attended briefings on the morning of the 24th to learn that they would be undertaking the first daylight crossing of the Alps to attack the northern city of Milan. The city was home to many war industry factories, including the Isotta Fraschini luxury car works, which had been converted to military vehicle and aero engine manufacture, the Pirelli rubber works, Alfa Romeo, the Caproni aircraft plant, the Breda locomotive, armaments and aircraft works and the Innocenti machinery and vehicle factory. The operation would require an even longer flight over fighter-defended territory than the Le Creusot operation a week earlier, but it was forecast that cloud would protect them for most of the way. 57 Squadron made ready ten Lancasters, which departed Scampton between 12.24 and 12.34 with S/L Carter the senior pilot on duty and headed for Selsey Bill, from where they would cross the Channel at very low level with the rest of the loose formation under a Spitfire escort. F/Sgt Langley and crew turned back with engine trouble, leaving the others to press on in the expectation of running into the cloud of a warm front at the Normandy coast. However, to their discomfort, they saw that it had formed further inland, and they had to run the gauntlet of anti-aircraft fire as they raced over the clifftops with three hours to go before even reaching the Alps. A bank of cloud could be seen in the distance, to which the force climbed as rapidly as possible, and once reached, the crews had to plot their own individual course via Saumur and Montluçon until rendezvousing over Lake Annecy, sixty miles short of the target. From there they formed a loose formation and lost height, until reaching the target to find eight to nine-tenths cloud with a base at 3,000 feet, but sufficient gaps through which to establish their positions visually. The marshalling yards, a seaplane base and an aerodrome were among ground features identified as the 57 Squadron crews delivered their high-explosive and incendiary payloads from a courageously low 3,000 to 6,000 feet between 17.03 and 17.11. Some squadrons had loaded their Lancasters with a cookie, which required a minimum clearance of 4,000 feet, demonstrating the disregard for their safety of those attacking from such a low level, and even down to a few hundred feet to strafe factories and other targets of opportunity. The sun was setting ahead of them as they crossed the Alps homebound, and France passed beneath them unseen in darkness, with enemy night-fighters waiting over the coastal region as the returning bombers passed through. At debriefing, crews were enthusiastic about the effectiveness of the raid, which had cost three Lancasters, each of them shot down into the Channel. Among them was 57 Squadron's W4251 with the crew of P/O Miles, and his remains were eventually recovered for burial along with two others. Post-raid reconnaissance revealed that the 135 tons of bombs had caused extensive damage to housing, public buildings and a number of war-industry factories, including the Caproni aircraft works, and had also seriously affected railway communications between Italy and Germany. Local reports confirmed a figure of 441 houses destroyed or seriously damaged along with nine public buildings.

During the course of the month the squadron took part in six operations and dispatched sixty-one sorties for the loss of two Lancasters and crews.

November 1942

There would be no operations for the majority of the Command during the first week of the new month as those posted were cancelled as a result of adverse weather conditions. The first operation to take place was posted on the 6th and turned out to be a "moling" operation, to which 5 Group contributed five Lancasters. The target for 57 Squadron's P/O Walsh and F/Sgt Moore was the garrison town of Osnabrück, for which they departed Scampton at 11.38 and 11.50 respectively, each loaded with a dozen 1,000 pounders. The intention was to employ Gee (TR) as a blind bombing aid, but the signal faded out at 4.30°E and they pressed on in the hope of finding a gap in the ten-tenths cloud. When one did not materialise, the Walsh crew abandoned their sortie and turned for home, while F/Sgt Moore and crew turned north for the port of Emden. Conditions were no better there, and they bombed on DR from 16,000 feet at 13.04.

By the time they landed, Genoa had been posted as the target for that night and the seven 57 Squadron crews attending briefing learned that they were to be part of a force of fifty-seven 5 Group Lancasters and fifteen belonging to 83 Squadron of the Path Finders. As the 57 Squadron element taxied towards take-off, the Lancasters of F/L Huggins (Q) and S/L Avis (V) came together and their participation had to be scrubbed, and, as the reserve aircraft were not ready, just five departed Scampton between 21.16 and 21.32 with W/C Hopcroft and S/L Long the senior pilots on duty. F/Sgt Boyd and crew were approaching the French coast when they lost one of their port engines and W/C Hopcroft had just entered French airspace when he lost one of his starboard power plants. It had not been a productive day for the commanding officer, who had intended to take part in the earlier daylight operation but had been thwarted by a hydraulics issue. The three remaining 57 Squadron crews reached the target after an uneventful outward flight of four hours in favourable weather conditions. The excellent visibility, along with accurate Path Finder flares, enabled them to locate the aiming point visually after identifying ground features like the breakwater, harbour and town, and they carried out their attacks from 8,000 to 10,000 feet between 01.35 and 02.05. Fires of increasing intensity were concentrated in the docks area, and several ships appeared to be burning in the harbour, in addition to which, F/O Biggane of 44 (Rhodesia) Squadron counted a total of 116 fires across the city. Crews at the tail end of the bomber stream found the effectiveness of the attack laid out before them and described a colossal fire on a hill near the city centre. The glow from the burning city remained visible from the Alps and Nice, some eighty miles away, but, as no local report emerged, the full extent of the damage could not be assessed. Returning crews were confronted with rain and a cloud base at 200 feet as they crossed the south coast, persuading F/Sgt Croston and crew to abandon the fuel-starved W4246 to its fate over Kent at 07.00. A number of crew members sustained injuries in awkward landings, while the Lancaster ended its days on farmland sixteen miles south-west of Sevenoaks. At debriefing, S/L Long reported that one of his engines had run rough from the French coast to Genoa and another had caught fire over the target area and had to be feathered.

Another operation against Genoa was posted on 3, 4 and 5 Group stations on the 7th, and a force of 175 aircraft assembled, which included Halifaxes, Stirlings and a handful of Wellingtons to join eighty-one Lancasters of 5 Group. The eight 57 Squadron participants departed Scampton between 17.33 and 17.40 with W/C Hopcroft and S/Ls Avis and Carter the senior pilots on duty. S/L Avis had just arrived from 1654 Conversion Unit after learning to fly the Lancaster and had served, among other units, with 44 Squadron during the Hampden era in 1941/42. S/L Carter and crew returned early because of excessive fuel consumption, and P/O Bowles and crew after their immersion pump failed. The bomber stream traversed France without incident and climbed to 17,000 feet in the Dijon area as it approached the foothills of the Alps. It was here that crews ran into extreme icing conditions, but most negotiated them successfully, ultimately to experience the same ideal conditions as on the previous night, particularly on the far side of the Alps, where they were able to make a visual identification of the coastline, harbour and aiming point in the light of the punctual and accurately delivered Path Finder flares. A smoke screen failed to shield the city, and the flak defence seemed to give up once the bombing began, although light flak from rooftops continued to fire, even if inaccurately. The 57 Squadron crews bombed from 7,000 to 11,500 feet between 21.40 and 21.48, and, on return, reported bombs exploding in the built-up area causing numerous fires. Many crews brought home an aiming point photograph to add to those from reconnaissance flights, which confirmed the operation to have been highly successful.

The campaigns against Italy and Germany would have to run side-by-side for the time being, and, in a break from Italy, Hamburg was posted as the target on the 9th. No mention was made by the "met boys" during briefing of strong winds and ice-bearing cloud of the type that often lay in wait across the bombers' path to Germany's second city. The four heavy groups put together a force of 213 aircraft, of which, sixty-seven Lancasters were provided by 5 Group, seven of them made ready by 57 Squadron. They were loaded with a cookie and incendiaries each before departing Scampton between 17.55 and 18.10 with W/C Hopcroft the senior pilot on duty, and supported, somewhat unusually, by all three flight commanders. F/L Huggins and crew lost all three turrets to a hydraulics issue and had no choice but to turn back, leaving the others to press on through the troublesome cumulonimbus cloud over the North Sea, which they negotiated successfully to reach the target area. However, on arrival they found it to be completely hidden by ten-tenths cloud with a base at 2,500 feet and tops at 16,000 feet, which forced them to bomb on e.t.a., in the absence of Path Finder flares, but in the presence of heavy flak, particularly from naval guns, the shells from which were detonating above the bombing height. The 57 Squadron crews of W/C Hopcroft, S/L Long and S/L Avis attacked from 5,500, 13,000 and 14,000 feet respectively between 20.29 and 21.05, but found it impossible to assess what was happening beneath the cloud. A strong wind from the north almost certainly pushed the bombing south of the intended aiming point, and this seemed to be confirmed by local reports, that many bombs had fallen into the River Elbe or into open country, and only three large fires had required attention. Fifteen aircraft failed to return, five of them belonging to 5 Group, which also registered nine early returns. There was shock at Scampton when only three 57 Squadron Lancasters returned, and it soon became clear that the others were not coming home. It is believed that W4165 crashed in the Brackeswalde district of Cuxhaven, W4247 somewhere near Hamburg and W4307 also near Hamburg, perhaps a little to the south, and there were no survivors from the crews of S/L Carter, P/O Walsh DFC & Bar and F/Sgt Boyd. Such losses were keenly felt by the squadron and station communities but were not allowed to impact operational efficiency. Within hours, members of the Committee of Adjustment would have removed all personal belongings from the billets to leave no trace of their former occupants and the accommodation would welcome new arrivals later in the day.

Mine-laying would occupy the ensuing two nights, and 5 Group detailed a dozen Lancasters on the 10th to send that night to the Biscay coast to the Elderberry and Furze gardens, located respectively off Bayonne and a dozen miles further south at St-Jean-de-Luz, right down on the border between France and Spain. The 57 Squadron crews of F/Sgt Abercrombie and Sgt Haye departed Scampton at 17.21 and 17.26 respectively bound, according to the squadron ORB, for the Gironde estuary, which was the Deodar garden located to the north of the Elderberry and Furze gardens. The Gironde River leads to the port of Bordeaux, which was highly important to the Germans as the gateway to the Atlantic for U-Boots and merchant shipping, while the banks of the river were home to a number of oil production and storage sites at Pauillac and Bec d'Ambes. As such, it became a frequent destination for mining, and in 1944, bombing operations. Sgt Haye and crew delivered their five mines into the briefed location from 500 feet at 20.57, before returning safely to land at Honeybourne in Worcestershire after being diverted. W4772 was also diverted on return and crashed atop a 400-foot hill at Burgh-on-Bain in Lincolnshire at around 22.23, killing F/Sgt Abercrombie and his crew.

Orders were received on several 5 Group stations on the 13th to prepare for a return to Genoa as part of a 5 Group effort involving sixty-one Lancasters acting as the main force with a Path Finder element comprising six Lancasters of 83 Squadron and nine Stirlings of 7 Squadron at Oakington to carry out the illumination and marking. Nineteen of the 5 Group element were to attack the Ansaldo engineering works, while the remainder had their own aiming point in the town. The sole representatives of 57 Squadron were P/O Bowles and his crew, who departed Scampton at 18.22 carrying a cookie and two SBCs of 4lb incendiaries. They joined up with the bomber stream as it made its way south and crossed the Alps in good weather conditions that allowed the target to be identified visually from cloudless skies. They had been assigned to aiming point A, which is believed to be the docks, and delivered the contents of their bomb bay from 9,000 feet at 22.33 in the face of a "beefed-up" searchlight and flak defence. They observed their own bombs to impact among buildings close to the docks, and many others were seen to detonate right across the target area, but there would be no attempt to assess the outcome through aerial reconnaissance. Some returning crews reported the glow of fires to be visible for 130 miles into the return flight, and confidence was high that the loss-free raid had been successful. The bombing photo provided by the Bowles crew was plotted at eight hundred yards east of the aiming point.

Two days later, a force of seventy-eight aircraft was made ready to continue the assault on Genoa, and twenty-one of twenty-seven Lancasters were provided by 5 Group and just two by 57 Squadron. The crews of S/L Avis and F/Sgt Langley took off a fraction before 18.00 and enjoyed an uneventful outward flight across France, and the ten-tenths cloud to the south of the Alps stopped just short of the target to provide clear skies and moonlight. The Path Finders performed well to illuminate the aiming point, allowing it to be identified visually for a force largely untroubled by the defences and a smoke screen that drifted away towards the sea. The 57 Squadron duo carried out their attacks within two minutes of each other at 22.22 from 10,000 and 6,500 feet and observed bursts but no detail. Six large fires were reported in the built-up area, and the glow was still visible from up to a hundred miles into the return journey.

On the 18th, attention shifted from Genoa to Turin, the major city in northern Italy located some eighty miles west-south-west of Milan, which was home to Fiat's Lingotto and Mirafiori car plants, the Lancia motor works, the Arsenale army munitions factory, the Nebioli foundry and plants belonging to the American Westinghouse company. A force of seventy-seven aircraft was made ready, which had been reduced considerably by the withdrawal of forty-two 5 Group Lancasters because of doubts about the weather over their stations. This left a twenty-five-strong 5 Group element, the crews of which had learned at briefing that the Fiat works was to be the aiming point. They arrived at the target some three-and-a-half hours later to find clear skies that left the city at the mercy of the bomb-aimers, who benefitted from another excellent performance by the Path Finders to ensure that the aiming point was squarely in their bomb-sights as they ran in. Many fires broke out in the city centre, and the Fiat works sustained an unspecified degree of damage, which was confirmed by bombing photos.

Following the recent run of moderate-scale operations to Italy, the 20th brought a return to Turin in greater numbers, amounting this time to 232 aircraft, of which seventy-eight Lancasters were provided by 5 Group. 57 Squadron made ready eleven of its own and dispatched them from Scampton between 18.21 and 18.44 with W/C Hopcroft and S/L Long the senior pilots on duty. It would take almost four hours to reach the target, but all from the squadron negotiated the seven-hundred-mile outward leg without incident, and those arriving at the front end of the attack were able to establish their position by following the autostrada and identifying ground features in the light of flares. However, by the time that the majority of the Scampton crews arrived over the city, smoke was already drifting across it, and ground features appeared fleetingly, creating challenging conditions for target identification. Ground haze added to the difficulties, but, even so, by running in at low to medium level, some crews were able to identify the factory visually and deliver the bombs with some degree of accuracy. The 57 Squadron participants attacked from 4,000 to 8,500 feet between 22.10 and 22.46, and most believed their bombs to have fallen close to the factory. They left behind them massive fires raging in the city centre, with smoke rising already through 6,000 feet as they turned away, and returning crews were confident in the effectiveness of their work.

Sixty-four 5 Group crews attended briefings on the 22nd to learn that their destination that night was to be Stuttgart as part of an overall force of 222 aircraft. 57 Squadron made ready eight Lancasters, some to carry all-incendiary loads and others a mix of high-explosives and incendiaries and sent them on their way from Scampton between 18.21 and 18.41 with F/L Curry the only commissioned pilot on duty. Located in a series of valleys, Stuttgart was always a difficult city to identify, but three hours and fifteen minutes later the first of the main force crews had Path Finder flares in their sights, illuminating the target area to apparently enable a visual identification of the aiming point. Bombing by the 57 Squadron crews took place from 6,500 to 11,000 feet between 22.04 and 22.23, and bursts were observed in the built-up area, where a large fire was seen to develop. Returning crews described a quiet trip with a satisfactory result, but it was soon discovered that a thin layer of cloud and ground haze had prevented the Path Finders from identifying the centre of the city, and much of the bombing had fallen onto south-western and southern districts and outlying communities up to five miles from the city centre. Local reports confirmed that a modest eighty-eight houses had been destroyed and described two bombers attacking the city centre at low level and causing extensive damage to the main railway station. 57 Squadron was represented among ten missing aircraft by W4360, which was shot down by the night-fighter of Oblt Ludwig Meister of I./NJG4 and crashed at 23.48 on farmland some fifteen miles south-east of Brussels, killing Sgt Ashton and his crew.

F/Sgt Danahy and crew departed Scampton at 17.06 on the 23rd bound for the Furze garden off St-Jean-de-Luz near the Franco-Spanish frontier. They arrived more than four hours later to deliver four mines from 750 feet at 21.32 and returned safely from an uneventful sortie.

Instructions were received by all heavy groups on the 28th to prepare their aircraft and crews for operations that night against Turin, and a force of 228 aircraft was made ready, ninety-one of the Lancasters on 5 Group stations. *(1 Group was in the process of converting from Wellingtons to Lancasters, and 101, 103 and 460 Squadrons had begun to operate the type in the past week).* 57 Squadron made ready ten aircraft, their bomb bays containing either a cookie and three SBCs of 4lb incendiaries or thirteen SBCs and launched them from Scampton between 18.52 and 19.07 with F/Ls Curry and Huggins the senior pilots on duty. F/Sgt Lemon and crew turned back early with a fuel feed problem that caused two engines to cut, leaving the others to continue on across France without incident to reach the target area under clear skies, with just a little haze to mar the vertical visibility. This was of no consequence to those arriving in the early stages and they were able to establish their positions by visual reference of the River Po assisted by Path Finder flares. The 57 Squadron crews bombed from 6,000 to 10,000 feet between 22.20 and 22.54, observing bursts in the town and on the Fiat works, and F/Sgt Player and crew counted forty-six as they began their homeward journey. Others confirmed that the city was a mass of flames and commented on a particularly large blaze in the centre and some others around the Royal Arsenal, which, together, produced a heavy pall of smoke. During the course of the attack, W/C Gibson and F/L Whamond of 106 Squadron dropped the first two 8,000 pounders to fall on Italy, and all indications were that the operation had been entirely successful.

November had been the first full month of Lancaster operations for 57 Squadron, which took part in eleven and dispatched fifty-seven sorties for the loss of six Lancasters and five crews.

December 1942

The weather at the start of the new month restricted operations, and an unsuccessful raid on Frankfurt involving 112 aircraft on the 2nd did not include a contribution from 5 Group. Squadrons were warned of operations daily between the 2nd and 5th, but each was cancelled, and it was the 6th before an operation was posted at Scampton that would actually go ahead. Three 57 Squadron crews attended briefing to learn that Mannheim was to be their target in company with seventy-one other Lancasters of 5 Group in an overall force of 272 aircraft. The freshman crews of Sgts Hawkings and Warlow and F/Sgt Ramey attended a separate briefing for a small-scale mining operation in the Nectarine II garden off the central Frisians and departed Scampton between 17.12 and 17.25. The bombing trio, consisting of the crews of F/L Huggins and both Sgts Singer, took off between 17.46 and 17.54 and were just starting the Channel crossing as the gardeners reached their target area to seek pinpoints off the eastern end of the island of Schiermonnikoog. Each delivered five mines into the briefed locations from 700 to 900 feet between 18.37 and 19.14 and returned home safely, two after being diverted to Docking. Meanwhile, the Mannheim force had reached the target, where they encountered eight to ten-tenths cloud between 4,000 and 12,000 feet, which rendered ineffective the Path Finders' efforts to mark the city with flares. A decoy site was also operating some twenty miles to the south, and this, inevitably, attracted a proportion of the bombing. Crews could bomb only on DR and e.t.a., in the case of those from 57 Squadron from 8,500 to 10,500 feet between 20.18 and 20.27. Several crews from other squadrons descended to 5,000 feet, from where the Rhine and a built-up area were visible, and they observed scattered fires and square factory buildings ablaze. Other returning crews had little of interest to report to the Intelligence section at debriefing and local sources mentioned only five hundred incendiaries falling within the city along with propaganda leaflets (nickels).

On the following night, 5 Group called for nine crews to carry out gardening duties in the Elderberry and Furze gardens off the south-western coast of France. The 57 Squadron crews of F/Sgt Ramey and Sgt Haye departed Scampton at 16.33 and 17.02 respectively and began the Channel crossing at Bolt Head on the Devon coast. They found up to three-tenths cloud and visibility of four miles in the Elderberry garden off Bayonne, and lights from the notoriously poor blackout at Biarritz to provide a solid reference. Lights were blazing in Spain also, and a steel works at Bilboa appeared to be in full production as they planted their vegetables from 700 and 500 feet at 21.54 and 22.19.

Notification was received on 5 Group stations on the 8th that Turin was to be the target for that night, in an operation to be conducted by a 5 Group main force of ninety-eight Lancasters supported by thirty-five Path Finder aircraft of all types. The 57 Squadron element of eleven departed Scampton between 17.38 and 17.48 with S/Ls Avis and Long the senior pilots on duty, and, after climbing out, headed for Debden to exit the English coast over Dungeness. The final pinpoint before the Alps was Lake Annecy, and once over the peaks they had a gentle descent to the target, where a thirty-minute bombing window had been set between 21.15 and 21.45. Reaching the Italian side of the Alps they encountered clear skies and good visibility, with the city visible to the south as they approached the final turning point. Swinging towards the start of their bombing run, over to port to the east of the city, a large bend in the River Po provided a strong reference, which enabled the Path Finders to identify the aiming point and deliver their flares right on the mark. The main force crews followed in their wake and registered that the aiming point was well-defined by two arcs of Path Finder flares, and one massive explosion a mile-and-a-half to the south-west. The bombing was carried out by the 57 Squadron crews from 6,000 to 10,000 feet between 21.14 and 21.33, and the city could be seen to be well-alight. Those arriving when the attack was already well underway reported smoke drifting across the aiming point and counted thirty to forty sizeable fires burning across the city. A huge pall of smoke was rising through 8,000 feet as the force retreated towards the Alps, and the fires would still be burning when the next bomber force arrived twenty-four hours later.

Orders came through on the 9th to prepare for another assault on Turin that night, and a dozen 57 Squadron crews attended the briefing at Scampton to learn that they would be part of a 5 Group effort of eighty-two Lancasters in an overall force of 227 aircraft. Two 57 Squadron Lancasters became bogged down as they taxied from their dispersal pans and another dropped out because of an overheating engine, leaving nine to take-off between 17.32 and 17.56 with S/L Long the senior pilot on duty. Sgt Haye and crew had penetrated a hundred miles into France when their port-inner engine caught fire and put an end to their sortie, but the others enjoyed an uneventful outward flight, guided for the final few miles to the target by the fires still burning from the previous night. This, however, proved to be a double-edged sword, as the smoke hanging over the city created challenging conditions for the Path Finders, who failed to deliver as strong a performance this time. The raid was spread out over more than thirty minutes, during which the 57 Squadron crews attacked from 7,500 to 9,000 feet between 21.35 and 21.52, helping to create many more fires that produced even larger volumes of smoke to obscure much of the ground from those arriving at the tail end of proceedings. Returning crews reported explosions and fires, but the consensus was of a less effective raid than that of the previous night. On return, W4250 stalled while approaching Woodhall Spa and crashed one mile north of the airfield, killing F/Sgt Ramey RCAF and three of his crew. Three others sustained serious injuries and were taken to Rauceby hospital, where two lost their fight for life a few days later.

For the third night in succession the torment of Turin continued, although at the hands of a reduced force of eighty-two aircraft drawn from 1 and 4 Groups and the Path Finders. They had to fight their way through severe icing conditions over France, and more than half of the force turned back before reaching the Alps. Those completing their sorties failed to inflict more than the slightest damage on the city, in what proved to be the final raid of this first Italian campaign. The 57 Squadron crews of Sgts Leach and Warlow and F/Sgt Lovell were among sixty-eight aircraft sent mining off the Frisians and in the Heligoland Bight on the night of the 14/15th. They took off between 17.14 and 17.21, but they and the other twenty from 5 Group were recalled after an hour because of concerns about the weather for their return. Sgt Manson RNZAF and crew were engaged in a training exercise on the night of the 16/17th, when they crashed at 03.00 five miles north-east of Predannack airfield in Cornwall, it is believed, after W4359 was struck by lightning, and there were no survivors.

5 Group detailed twenty-seven Lancasters to target eight small German towns on the night of the 17/18th, seventeen for what was referred to in the 5 Group ORB as a "Batter" operation, against Soltau, some forty miles east of Bremen, and Neustadt-am-Rübenberge and Nienburg, located between Bremen to the north-west and Hannover to the south-east. A further ten Lancasters were assigned to "moling" sorties over five other towns in north-western Germany including, Cloppenburg, Diepholz and Quakenbrück, and one wonders if, in the cold light of dawn, anyone in raid planning recalled the disaster that had afflicted 57 and 214 Squadrons of 3 Group as a result of similar operations on the first night of April. 57 Squadron was fortunate to stay at home on this night as nine Lancasters failed to return from these foolhardy nuisance raids, and six Stirlings and two Wellingtons were lost raiding the Opel works at Fallersleben, further to the east. Thus, a total of seventeen aircraft and crews had been sacrificed for little or no return.

Apart from isolated "moling" daylight operations, the Ruhr had been left in peace since Krefeld at the start of October, while attention had been focussed on Italian targets. Now, on the 20th, Duisburg was posted as the target, and this would mask another operation of great significance for the Command that was taking place at the same time over Holland, and although, in the event, not all would proceed according to plan, it would be a mere blip in the development of the Oboe blind-bombing device. A force of 232 aircraft was assembled for the main event, of which seventy-five were Lancasters of 5 Group, six of them representing 57 Squadron. They departed Scampton between 18.13 and 18.22 with S/L Avis the senior pilot on duty, and, as they climbed out, may have observed the tragic consequences of a collision over Lincoln between two Lancasters from Waddington, from which none survived. Collision was an ever-present risk at take-off as large numbers of aircraft took to the skies from overlapping circuits, and the dangers were, perhaps, even greater as tired crews funnelled towards their stations on return. The route on this night took the bomber stream across the North Sea on a heading for Enkhuizen on the shore of the Ijsselmeer, where it turned towards the south-south-east on a direct course for the target. Favourable weather conditions prevailed, and condensation trails formed in the cold, clear air at 15,000 feet, attracting the attention of night-fighters. The ground was bathed in bright moonlight, which allowed the River Rhine and the Ruhrort docks to stand out through the haze to provide a strong visual reference for marking and bombing. The 57 Squadron crews carried out their attacks from 8,000 to 14,000 feet between 19.55 and 20.02, and at least fifteen fires were observed, many of them large.

Meanwhile, six 109 Squadron Oboe-equipped Mosquitos had targeted a power station at Lutterade in Holland, in a test to gauge the device's margin of error, believing the target to be free of bomb craters so as not to impair the data. Unfortunately, three of the Mosquitos suffered Oboe failure, and went on to bomb Duisburg instead, leaving W/C Hal Bufton and two other crews to deliver the bombs. What they hadn't bargained for was a whole carpet of bomb craters left over from the attack on Aachen, seventeen miles away, in October, and it proved impossible to identify those aimed by Oboe. The calibration tests would continue, however, and, come the spring, Oboe would be ready to unleash to devastating effect against the Ruhr.

Munich, the Bavarian capital city and birthplace of Nazism, was posted as the target on the 21st, and a force of 137 aircraft made ready, which included eighty-two 5 Group Lancasters and a further thirty-seven of the type provided by 1 Group and the Path Finders, the latter also contributing nine Stirlings and nine Wellingtons. 57 Squadron briefed nine crews, but the two most senior, those of S/L Long and F/L Curry, dropped out with technical problems before take-off. The remaining seven departed Scampton between 17.32 and 17.44 and made their way south to exit the English coast at Dungeness, before pushing on across France on the long trek to the target area. They arrived after a three-and-a-half-hour outward journey, only to find it concealed beneath ten-tenths cloud with tops at a lowly 2,000 feet. The Path Finders illuminated the Ammersee to the south-west of the city, and crews carried out a time-and-distance run from there to the aiming point, the 57 Squadron crews bombing from 6,500 and 11,000 feet between 21.16 and 21.40. There were plenty of flashes below the cloud, together with the glow of fires to convince the crews that they had found the mark, but it is likely, that these came from a decoy site, as most bombing photos would reveal open country. Twelve aircraft failed to return, six of them belonging to 5 Group, and among them was 57 Squadron's W4234, which was shot down by a night-fighter on the way home and crashed at Oudenaarde, some twenty miles from the Belgian coast, killing P/O Bowles and all but his Kiwi mid-upper gunner, who landed by parachute unconscious within sight of the burning wreckage and was taken into captivity.

The fourth wartime Christmas was celebrated in traditional style across the Command, and operational activity ceased until the 29th, when fourteen 5 Group Lancasters took part in mining operations off France's Biscay coast. 57 Squadron was not involved but detailed six freshman crews for similar activity on the 31st as part of a force of twenty-nine aircraft. They departed Scampton between 21.45 and 22.07 bound for the Deodar garden in the Gironde estuary with P/Os Ritch and Roberts the only commissioned pilots on duty. They all reached the target area to find ten-tenths low cloud and pinpointed on Cordouan lighthouse in the mouth of the estuary or

Graves Point, before releasing their mines into the briefed locations from 500 to 900 feet between 00.30 and 00.53. P/O Roberts and crew were attacked by four enemy night-fighters near Nantes, but evaded them without damage, and arrived home with a dead port-outer engine. A rapid thaw had created treacherous conditions at Scampton, and Sgts Rice and Ritch skidded off the grass runway causing minor damage to their Lancasters. Elsewhere on this night, the first of a series of "live" trials of the Oboe blind bombing system was carried out at Düsseldorf and involved two Oboe Mosquitos marking for eight Lancasters. Later in the night, three Oboe Mosquitos attacked a night-fighter control centre at Florennes aerodrome in Belgium. The Oboe equipment broke down in two aircraft, but this was very much early days, and the trials would continue on a greater scale in the New Year. During the course of the month, 57 Squadron took part in nine operations and dispatched fifty sorties for the loss of three Lancasters and their crews.

As the New Year beckoned, a great responsibility lay on the nine operational Lancaster squadrons of 5 Group to carry the war to the enemy. There was no question that the Stirling and Mk II and V Halifaxes were inferior aircraft, and their limited availability and restricted bomb-carrying capacity meant that the Command still had to rely very much on the trusty but aging Wellington to make up the numbers if the defences were to be overwhelmed. That said, the advent of Oboe and the ground-mapping radar, H2S, would greatly enhance the Command's ability to deliver a telling blow, and 1943 would see the balance of power shift massively in the Command's favour.

S/L Henry Melvin Young DFC & Bar *F/L William (Bill) Astell D.F.C.*
Both later killed with 617 Squadron on Dams Raid.

P/O Geoff Rice DFC
Later served with 617 Squadron and took part in the Dams Raid

P/O William George Divall
Later killed with 617 Squadron while attacking Dortmund-Ems Canal.

The Focke-Wolf works after the Bremen raid on the 27ᵗʰ July 1942.

W/C Murrey Vernon Peters-Smith DFC
KIA 27ᵗʰ July 1942

Wellington Mk.II

Wellington Mk.III

Sgt Frederick Jones pictured with his wife.

Lancaster I W4360 of 57 Squadron took off from RAF Scampton on the 22nd November 1942. It was shot down on its way home by a night fighter The aircraft crashed at 2348 in Brabant, Belgium. All crew members died and are buried at the cemetery of Heverlee.

Sgt Jack Ashton	*Pilot*
Sgt Alfred Stansfield	*Flight Engineer*
Sgt Alan Mckinlay	*Navigator*
Sgt Leonard Webber	*Bomb Aimer*
Sgt Frederick Jones	*Wireless Operator*
Sgt Clyde Neilson	*Upper Gunner*
Sgt Gordon Chisholm	*Rear Gunner*

F/Sgt James Edward Linehan
(Linehan family photo for 57 Assoc.)

P/O Noel "Bill" Morse

57 Squadron Wellington X3757 took off from RAF Scampton for an operation to Hamburg on the 9th April 1942. Homeward-bound, the aircraft was shot down by a night fighter. The six crew members were all missing in action:
P/O Noel Percy Morse RNZAF Pilot, 2nd Pilot: F/Sgt James Edward Linehan, Observer F/Sgt George Vogan RNZAF, (W.Op/AG), Sgt Graham Lakeman, (W.Op/AG), Sgt Norman Joseph Naylor AG), Sgt Roland Richards.(AG).

Sgt Graham Lakeman

Sgt Norman Naylor

P/O George Hillary Vogan

Sgt Roland Geoffrey Richards

Wellingtons under construction, showing the geodetic airframe

A wartime poster using a cutaway of a Vickers Wellington to illustrate how scrap and salvage was recycled for use in the production of war material. The poster expands on how different materials were used to make specific components of the bomber.

*A crew member inside rear of Wellington fuselage. Probably **not** 57 Squadron*

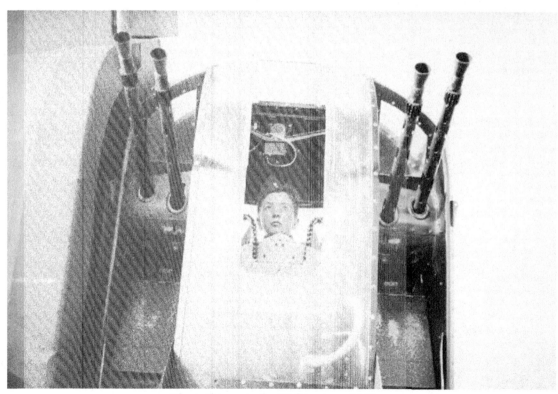

The tail turret of a Wellington, 1942

January 1943

The year began with the official formation on New Year's Day of the Canadian 6 Group, and the handing over to it of the former 4 Group stations in North Yorkshire on which its squadrons had been lodging. Eventually, all Canadian squadrons would find a home in the group, which was financed by Canada and controlled by Harris, but, initially, there were eight founder members, including 408 and 420 Squadron, which had left 5 Group during the autumn. Further south, a continuation of the Oboe trials would occupy the first two weeks, during which 109 Squadron marked for small forces of 1 and 5 Group Lancasters at Essen on seven occasions and Duisburg once. For the first time, the cloud cover and ever-present blanket of industrial haze would have no bearing on the outcome of the raid as reliance on e.t.a., DR and Gee was cast aside in favour of Oboe, at least, that is, at targets within the device's range. Until the advent of mobile transmitter stations late in the war, Oboe would be restricted by the curvature of the earth and the altitude at which Mosquitos could fly, but this meant that the entire Ruhr lay within range of Harris's bombers. That said, the success of a raid would still rely on the ability of the Path Finders to back up the initial Oboe markers and maintain a supply of target indicators (TIs) on the aiming point.

57 Squadron found itself alone at Scampton after 49 Squadron moved out on the 2nd to take up residence at Fiskerton. It was for the first of the forays against Essen on the 3rd, that 5 Group detailed nineteen Lancasters, the crews benefitting from Path Finder warning flares dropped at various points short of the target, and red and green flares to identify the aiming point over the Krupp complex in the Borbeck district. The high-level attack was carried out from 20,000 to 22,000 feet and bursts were observed but not their precise location. Much valuable information was gleaned from this second "live" trial of Oboe, and more would be gleaned over the ensuing nights. The next two forays against Essen were mounted on the 4th and 7th and involved twenty-nine 1 Group Lancasters and nineteen from 5 Group respectively, before a switch to Duisburg on the 8th employed three Mosquitos and thirty-eight Lancasters. It was on this night that 57 Squadron returned to the offensive after a week without operations, briefing five crews for the main event and five for mining duties in the Little Belt region of the western Baltic. There were two gardens in the Little Belt, Carrot to the north and Endive to the south and it is believed that the former was the target area for 57 Squadron on this night, while other 5 Group elements operated further east and south in The Sound (Oresund) between Denmark and Sweden, and Kiel Bay. The gardeners departed Scampton between 16.45 and 17.08 with F/L Huggins the senior pilot on duty, and they were followed into the air between 17.33 and 17.39 led by the bombing quintet led by S/L Avis.

It was destined to be a testing night over the western Baltic, where a thick wedge of ice-bearing cloud topped out at 8,000 feet and extended to below 1,000 feet, creating challenging conditions for target location. The crews of F/Sgt Lovell and Sgt P Singer identified Halskov from which to carry out a timed run and delivered their three mines each from 600 and 800 feet at 19.38 and 19.41 respectively. The others were unable to establish a pinpoint despite square searches and two returned their mines to store, while F/L Huggins and crew jettisoned theirs as their Lancaster began to accumulate ice. Meanwhile, some three hundred miles to the south at Duisburg, the five 57 Squadron crews approached the aiming point in clear skies at 20,000 above a layer of ten-tenths cloud ten thousand feet below them, which completely obscured the ground. They focused purely on the Path Finders' red and green parachute flares to establish the position of the target and let their cookie and twelve SBCs of 4lb incendiaries go between 19.25 and 19.31 in the face of intense and accurate flak. No assessment of the results was possible, and flashes beneath the cloud might have been from bombs or flak batteries.

A return to Essen was posted on some 1 and 5 Group stations on the 9th and fifty Lancasters detailed to take part in the night's activities, of which five belonged to 57 Squadron. They departed Scampton between 17.18 and 17.22 with F/L Curry the senior pilot on duty, and all reached the target area to encounter favourable weather conditions in which the city could be identified visually without the aid of flares. However, it was the Path Finder flares that guided them to the aiming point, where they delivered their standard city-busting loads from 18,000 and 20,000 feet between 19.20 and 19.25, observing bursts and fires. P/O Danahy and crew reported being "shot up by cannon shells" on the way home, and this was the fate of Sgt Warlow RNZAF and crew in ED319, which was shot down by a night-fighter and crashed some eight miles north-west of Utrecht in Holland with no survivors.

The squadron sat out the next two Essen raids on the nights of the 11/12th and 12/13th, involving seventy-two and fifty-five Lancasters from 1 and 5 Groups respectively, but was invited to join in on the final raid of the current series on the 13th. Three of the sixty-six Lancasters were provided by 57 Squadron and took off from Scampton between 17.02 and 17.07 with no commissioned pilots on duty, only to lose the services of Sgt Haye and F/Sgt Lancaster and their crews to engine issues. Sgt Hawkins and crew pressed on to the central Ruhr, which lay beneath seven to ten-tenths cloud with tops at 7,000 to 10,000 feet. Some crews arrived about fifteen minutes early, in the light of a moon that had waxed to half-size, and all was eerily quiet until others started to bomb on DR seven or eight minutes before H-Hour, bringing the flak batteries to life. As had happened on previous operations, the Oboe Mosquito element experienced technical difficulties, two returning without marking, while the flares of the third failed to ignite. The Path Finder Lancaster crews took over responsibility, and those in the main force were guided to the aiming point, the Krupp district, by red warning flares, while greens and whites marked the release-point. The Hawkins crew bombed from 19,800 feet at 19.38, all the time under fire from a box-barrage and returned safely with nothing of interest to report at debriefing. Bombing photos showed only cloud, and it was left to local sources to report that more than a hundred buildings had been either destroyed or seriously damaged.

A new Air Ministry directive was issued on the 14th, which authorized the area bombing of the French ports providing a home for U-Boots with concrete bunkers and support facilities. A list was drawn up accordingly, headed by Lorient, and included St-Nazaire, Brest and La Pallice. The concrete roofs of the K1, K2 and K3 constructions at Lorient remained impregnable to the bombs available to Bomber Command and the purpose of this new campaign was to render the town and port uninhabitable, and block or sever all road and rail communications to them. The first of the series of nine attacks on Lorient over the ensuing four weeks took place that very night at the hands of a force of 122 aircraft in the absence of 5 Group, and, despite accurate marking by the Path Finder element, the main force bombing was scattered and destroyed a modest 120 buildings. An attack on the following night by a force of 157 aircraft from the other groups was more successful and destroyed eight hundred buildings.

5 Group's involvement with Lorient would come in February, and, in the meantime, Harris planned two operations against the "Big City", Berlin, beginning on the 16th, for which a force of

201 aircraft was made ready. This would be the first raid on Germany's capital for fourteen months and would bring with it the first use of custom-designed target indicators (TIs). The main force would be made up predominantly of 5 Group Lancasters, with others from 1 Group, while eleven Halifaxes would be included in the Path Finder element. A number of war correspondents were allowed to fly on this night, and those crews reaching the target would be sharing the airspace over it with the broadcaster, Richard Dimbleby, who was in a 106 Squadron Lancaster captained by W/C Guy Gibson of 106 Squadron. *(Most commentators mistakenly record the Dimbleby flight as taking place during the following night's Berlin raid, and I have perpetuated the error in many of my books. However, official records show that Gibson participated only in the first Berlin operation.)* 57 Squadron prepared ten Lancasters, which departed Scampton between 16.21 and 16.35 with S/Ls Avis and Long the senior pilots on duty and war correspondents flying with the crews of F/Sgt Croston and Sgt Hawkins. The bomber stream headed for Mandø Island off the west coast of Denmark, before traversing southern Jutland to reach the western Baltic over a blanket of ten-tenths cloud. The route then followed the coastline eastwards until reaching the final turning point at Swinemünde, where it headed south for the final moonlit run-in on the target. Good vertical visibility allowed the built-up area of Berlin to stand out clearly through the six-tenths cloud at 10,000 feet, and the initial red warning flares appeared to be over the south-eastern corner, where they highlighted the lakes and autobahns. The Path Finders edged nearer to the centre as the raid progressed, and it was then that red and green TIs were seen to burst on what was assumed to be the aiming point. The 57 Squadron crews dropped their cookies and incendiaries from 16,000 to 23,000 feet between 20.17 and 20.40, recognising that they were over the southern outskirts of the city, where the Tempelhof district could be identified. All returned safely to Scampton to report bomb bursts and fires, while crews from other squadrons observed black smoke rising through 5,000 feet as they turned away. Many returning crews were unconvinced of the effectiveness of the raid, and this was borne out by local sources. One notable scalp was the ten-thousand-seater Deutschlandhalle, the largest covered venue in Europe, which was hosting the annual circus as the bombers approached and was efficiently emptied of people and animals with only minor injuries to a few people. Shortly afterwards, incendiaries set fire to the building and reduced it to ruins. Remarkably, only a single Lancaster failed to return from this operation, but the balance would be redressed somewhat twenty-four hours later.

170 Lancasters and seventeen Halifaxes were made ready on 1, 4, 5 and 8 Group stations for the return to Berlin that night, 57 Squadron loading six of its own with a cookie and incendiaries after cancelling the participation of five others because of a concerning raft of serviceability issues. They departed Scampton between 16.37 and 17.02 with F/L Curry the senior pilot on duty and would follow the same route as twenty-four hours earlier with a three-and-a-half-hour outward flight ahead of them. F/Sgt Croston was unable to coax sufficient height out of R5865 to enable him and his crew to continue, and the bomb-aimer dropped the cookie towards a vessel off the Danish coast but missed. P/O Roberts and crew had possibly made landfall before their oxygen system failed and this ended their interest in proceedings. The bomber stream was stalked constantly by night-fighters once it reached western Denmark but arrived in the target area to be greeted by eight to ten-tenths cloud with tops at between 10,000 and 14,000 feet. It was possible for most to pick out the Müggelsee to the south-east of the Capital, from where a timed run was carried out to the target. Some crews failed to see any flares, which was understandable as the Path Finders turned up thirty-seven minutes late, and so bombed on e.t.a., or DR. Some did benefit from target marking, which, sadly, was once more concentrated over the southern fringes of the

city rather than over the centre. The 57 Squadron crews carried out their attacks from 17,000 to 19,000 feet between 20.33 and 20.45, and, by the latter time, some Path Finder flares were evident. Little was seen of the results of the bombing, and local reports confirmed that the operation had not been successful, and no significant damage had occurred. The disappointment was compounded by the loss of twenty-two bombers, 11.8% of those dispatched, and many of these disappeared without trace in the Baltic or North Sea.

A force of seventy-nine Lancasters and three Mosquitos was detailed to resume the Oboe trials programme against the Krupp complex at Essen on the 21st, for which 57 Squadron briefed six crews and dispatched them from Scampton between 17.30 and 17.34 with S/L Avis the senior pilot on duty. Following in their wake at 17.36 and 17.40 were the freshman crews of Sgt Fisher and P/O Greenan, who were bound for the Nectarine I garden off the southern Frisians. The record of poor serviceability continued with a 50% fall-out from the main element affecting the crews of Sgt Hawkins, F/Sgt Langley and F/Sgt Lovell, the last-mentioned turning back when within fifty miles of the target because of oxygen system failure. Those reaching the target area noted that condensation trails were forming at 18,000 feet to advertise their presence to the German defences. There was a question as to the cloud conditions, some reporting clear skies and others ten-tenths cloud, neither of which would have mattered if the Oboe marking had worked and been visible to all. In the event, the entire Ruhr was concealed beneath thick industrial haze, which proved to be impenetrable. As far as the crews of P/O Ritch and S/L Avis were concerned, there were no Path Finder flares to point the way as they bombed from 18,000 and 22,400 feet at 19.46 and 19.58 respectively, and Sgt Singer and crew only saw release point flares as they bombed on e.t.a., from 18,000 feet at 19.48 in the face of an intense flak barrage. Four Lancasters failed to return, and the outcome of the raid remained undetermined. Meanwhile, the gardeners had successfully delivered their mines into the briefed locations off Ameland from 600 feet at 19.05 and 500 feet at 19.15.

The crews of F/L Huggins and F/Sgt Croston were declared tour-expired on the 21st, and it was always a cause for celebration when anyone reached that milestone with the prospect of six months away from operations before being called back for a second tour. They would be posted from the squadron early in the coming month. The Oboe trials programme moved to Düsseldorf on the 23rd, the huge industrial city situated some fifteen miles south-south-east of Essen. 1, 5 and 8 Groups assembled a force of eighty Lancasters and three Mosquitos, of which six Lancasters belonging to 57 Squadron were loaded at Scampton with a cookie each and a dozen SBCs of 4lb incendiaries. They took off between 17.31 and 18.00 with S/L Long the senior pilot on duty, but he lost his port-inner engine, while Sgt P Singer's port undercarriage could not be retracted, and both had to abandon their sorties. Those reaching the target area found ten-tenths cloud at 12,000 feet, heavy, accurate flak and Path Finder flares drifting towards the cloud tops. The 57 Squadron crews bombed on these from 18,000 to 23,000 feet between 19.53 and 19.57 but saw nothing of the outcome through the cloud. Lorient had faced another assault on this night with a token Lancaster presence in a force of 121 aircraft, which inflicted further heavy damage. The fourth raid took place on the night of the 26/27th at the hands of an initial force of 157 aircraft, which attacked in poor weather conditions.

Sgt Wood and his crew were engaged in a training exercise in W4267 on the 27th, when it crashed two miles north-east of Caistor killing all but the rear gunner, who managed to escape by parachute in time. This was the day on which F/O "Bill" Astell joined the squadron from 1654 Conversion Unit after serving thus far on Wellingtons in the Middle-East. On return from Egypt via Canada in September, Bill found himself posted to 5 Group, his arrival coinciding with the campaign against Italian cities, although Bill would have to learn the ways of the Lancaster before he could resume his operational career. On the 4th of October he was posted to 1654 Heavy Conversion Unit at Wigsley in Nottinghamshire, where 5 Group trained its new crews on Manchesters and Lancasters, and it was also where airmen assembled in a kind of meat market to form themselves into new crews. Bill was promoted to flight lieutenant rank on the 3rd of November, and, shortly afterwards, was sent to Hullavington in Wiltshire for a short course, before being posted again on the 3rd of December, this time to 1485 Bombing and Gunnery School at Fulbeck in Nottinghamshire. Men of his experience were at a premium to pass on their skills as instructors, but it was not a job relished by most seasoned operational types and Bill sought an opportunity to get back to a squadron. On his arrival at Scampton, he was teamed up with a "headless" crew, whose original pilot had failed to return from an operation on which he had been gaining experience as a second pilot.

Düsseldorf was selected again as the primary target on the 27th, when the Path Finders were to use ground marking for the first time, rather than skymarking. Ground markers, which were TIs fused to burst and cascade just above the ground, could be seen through thin or partial cloud and industrial haze, and were much more reliable than the previously-employed parachute flares, that had a tendency to drift at the behest of the wind. However, skymarkers would remain an indispensable part of target marking techniques on nights of heavy cloud or to use in combination with ground markers. From this night onwards, Path Finder heavy aircraft would back-up the Mosquito-laid Oboe markers, to ensure that the aiming point remained marked throughout the operation. A heavy force of 124 Lancasters and thirty-three Halifaxes was made ready on 1, 4, 5 and 8 Group stations, 57 Squadron providing six of the Lancasters, which, with Scampton waterlogged, took off from Fiskerton between 17.14 and 17.29 with P/O Greenan the only commissioned pilot on duty. The poor rate of serviceability continued with the early returns of Sgt Fisher and F/Sgt Lemon and their crews, both because of engine issues. The remaining 57 Squadron crews pressed on to reach the target and find a thin layer of five to ten-tenths cloud at 10,000 feet, through which the red and green TIs could be seen burning on the aiming point. They carried out their part in the proceedings from 14,500 and 18,000 feet between 20.05 and 20.12, and returned safely to Fiskerton, impressed by the potential of ground marking and confident that they had hit the aiming point. This was confirmed by local reports, which spoke of widespread destruction in southern districts, amounting to 456 houses, ten industrial premises and nine public buildings destroyed or seriously damaged, with many others affected to a lesser extent.

Seventy-five aircraft of 1, 4 and 6 Groups carried out the fifth attack of the series on Lorient on the night of the 29/30th, but, in the absence of a Path Finder element and in the face of adverse weather conditions, bombing was scattered and largely ineffective.

Another new blind-bombing device, the ground-mapping H2S radar, was to be employed operationally for the first time at Hamburg on the 30th, for which a force of 135 Lancasters of 1, 5 and 8 Groups would be joined by thirteen H2S-equipped Path Finder Stirlings and Halifaxes of 7 and 35 Squadrons respectively. The H2S equipment was housed in a cupola aft of the bomb bay and projected an image of the terrain onto a cathode-ray tube in the navigator's compartment. It was the job of the operator to interpret what he was seeing, and guide the pilot to the aiming point, but this was no easy task, particularly with the Mk I set, and it proved difficult to distinguish particular ground features in the jumble of images presented to him. It would take much practice and experience to master the device, but, in time, and once the Mk III set became available, it would become an indispensable tool, which, ultimately, would become standard equipment for main force as well as Path Finder aircraft.

57 Squadron made ready eleven Lancasters, loading each with a cookie and incendiaries, and sent them on their way from Scampton between 00.08 and 00.32 with S/L Long the senior squadron pilot on duty and W/C Penman guesting to gain experience before assuming command of 61 Squadron two weeks hence. Sadly, the oxygen supply to the rear turret failed and he had to turn back, as did the crews of F/O Greenan and Sgt P Singer because of hydraulics and rear turret failure respectively. As previously mentioned, north-western Germany had a "gatekeeper" in the form of weather fronts, which, on this night, contained severe icing conditions and electrical storms for the bombers to negotiate as they made their way across the North Sea. Sgt Haye and crew fell victim to the icing conditions at the mid-point of the North Sea crossing and were unable continue. This left just seven crews to fly the 57 Squadron flag over Germany's second city, where they encountered between zero and ten-tenths cloud, according to which crew report one reads, with tops at between 6,000 and 15,000 feet. They bombed onto flares or TIs from 17,000 to 19,500 feet between 03.04 and 03.21, and observed the reflections of explosions in the cloud, which led to a consensus that the operation had been effective. This was partially confirmed by local reports that mentioned seventy-one large fires, but much of the bombing fell either into the Elbe or into marshland outside of the city. This would have been disappointing to the raid planners, as Hamburg, with the nearby coastline and wide River Elbe, was an ideal target for H2S and should have been easy to identify on the cathode-ray tubes. Five Lancasters failed to return, among them 57 Squadron's W4189, which crashed at Lüneburg, some twenty miles south-east of Hamburg, killing S/L Long DFC AFC and his crew.

During the course of the month, the squadron participated in eleven operations and dispatched sixty-five sorties, fifteen of which returned early on top of the eight that had been cancelled late on because of servicing issues. Two Lancasters and their crews were lost on operations and one while training, producing a single survivor.

February 1943

It was a time of honing and refining for Bomber Command in preparation for the launching of a major campaign a month hence. W/C Hopcroft was called upon to step in as temporary station commander on the 1st, and S/L Avis was recalled from leave to stand in as squadron commander. February opened with the posting of Cologne as the target for an experimental operation on the 2nd, in which two marking methods were to be employed. Situated just to the south of the Ruhr, the Rhineland's capital city was within range of Oboe Mosquitos, and these were to be supplemented by Path Finder heavy aircraft relying on H2S. A force of 159 heavies included seventy-four 5 Group Lancasters, while two Path Finder Mosquitos of 109 Squadron carried the Oboe markers. The eight 57 Squadron Lancasters departed Scampton between 18.36 and 18.43 with F/O Greenan the only commissioned pilot on duty but lost the services of F/Sgt Langley and crew after the heating to the rear turret failed. The others pressed on through severe cold, which caused almost all of the guns to freeze solid but reached the target to find a layer of two to five tenths thin cloud up to 8,000 feet and patches above. This afforded good vertical visibility and a clear sight of the red and green skymarkers, even from some distance on approach to the bombing run. There was some debate as to the accuracy and concentration of the markers, which a few crews from other squadrons would report as five to ten miles to the north-west of the city, while others described them as scattered. Most of the 57 Squadron crews picked up the red and green TIs burning on the ground and had them in the bomb sight as they delivered their cookie and incendiaries from 17,000 to 20,000 feet between 21.05 and 21.10. Although few were able to observe their own bombs burst, many scattered fires were evident, the glow from which could be seen from a hundred miles into the return journey. Local reports confirmed bombs falling all over the city, but nowhere with concentration, and damage was, consequently, not commensurate with the size of the force and the effort expended. Five aircraft failed to return, three of them belonging to 5 Group.

Hamburg was posted as the target on the 3rd, for which a force of 263 aircraft was made ready, unusually, with Halifaxes representing the most populous type followed by Stirlings. 5 Group contributed forty of the sixty-two Lancasters but did not call upon the services of 57 Squadron. Fifteen of the 5 Group crews turned back on encountering the towering cloud and severe icing conditions common to this route over the North Sea, and most of them cited frozen guns. The bomber stream arrived in the target area to find nine to ten-tenths cloud, which some crews estimated as topping out at between 7,000 and 8,000 feet, while others reported it to be at 17,000 to 20,000 feet. Scattered red and green Path Finder H2S-laid skymarker flares were in the bomb sights as the main force crews attacked, but no results were observed, and the impression was of an ineffective attack. This was confirmed by local reports, which mentioned forty-five large fires but no concentration or significant damage, and this disappointing outcome cost the Command sixteen aircraft. The losses by type made interesting reading and would reflect the trend for the remainder of the year, with the Stirlings suffering the highest numerical and percentage casualties, followed by the Halifaxes and Wellingtons, with the Lancasters clearly at the top of the food chain.

A return to Italy was posted on the 4th with Turin the target for a force of 188 aircraft, while 128 others, mostly Wellingtons, were prepared to continue the assault on Lorient. 5 Group contributed forty-eight Lancasters to the former and eight with freshman crews to the latter, 57 Squadron putting up nine Lancasters for Italy. They departed Scampton between 18.00 and 18.08 with P/O Ritch the only commissioned pilot on duty after W/C Penman's aircraft blew an exhaust stub at start-up. They followed the usual route across France, and Sgt Dutton and crew had reached a point some eighty miles south of Paris when the oxygen supply to the flight engineer and mid-upper gunner failed, compelling them to turn back. After crossing the Alps in cloud at 21,000 feet, the others found conditions on the Italian side much improved with clear skies and excellent visibility, which facilitated a visual confirmation of the accuracy of the Path Finder TIs. An estimated one hundred searchlights were active, and the flak defence had also been "beefed-up" but was still inaccurate and in keeping with expectations at an Italian target. *(Following a raid on a German target, a bomb symbol would be painted on the forward fuselage of a bomber, but after a raid on an Italian target, the symbol would be an ice-cream cone.)* Red TIs were much in evidence in the city centre as the 57 Squadron crews carried out their attacks from 9,000 to 16,000 feet between 21.42 and 21.59, and returning crews were enthusiastic about the effectiveness of their work. Three 5 Group Lancasters failed to return, among them 57 Squadron's ED352, which crashed in a mountainous region six miles north-east of Bourg-Saint-Maurice, killing P/O Ritch RCAF and his crew. The likelihood is that they flew into a mountain while in cloud. Local sources in Turin confirmed later that serious and widespread damage had been inflicted upon the city.

On the 6th, W/C Hopcroft resumed command of the squadron on the return of G/C Whitworth as station commander. The seventh raid in the series on Lorient was posted on the 7th, and would be by far the largest to date, employing 323 aircraft, of which forty-three of eighty Lancasters were provided by 5 Group. The operation was to be conducted in two waves, an hour apart, and it was for the second wave that 57 Squadron made ready four Lancasters for freshman crews and sent them on their way between 19.21 and 19.29. They arrived in the target area to find good visibility in spite of the volume of smoke ascending from a town already engulfed in a sea of flames and carried out their attacks from 12,000 and 13,000 feet between 21.35 and 21.57. Returning crews reported an outstandingly destructive raid, which left a glow in the sky visible from the English coast.

Before the penultimate raid on Lorient took place, attention was switched to the important naval port of Wilhelmshaven, situated on the north-western coast of Jade Bay, some sixty miles to the west of Hamburg. A force of 177 aircraft was put together on the 11th, of which 129 were Lancasters, sixty-eight of them representing 5 Group. Eight Lancasters were made ready by 57 Squadron at Scampton, and they took off between 17.40 and 17.47 with F/O Greenan the senior pilot on duty. The crews of Sgts Fisher and Haye turned back early after running into severe icing conditions over the North Sea, leaving the others to reach the target area to find ten-tenths cloud with tops at around 10,000 feet and the least reliable marking method, H2S skymarking, in progress. On the credit side, at a smaller, more compact urban target, like Wilhelmshaven, it was easier to interpret the images on the cathode-ray screens, and, on this night, great accuracy was achieved. The red and green flares were right over the aiming point as the 57 Squadron crews delivered their cookies and incendiaries from 15,000 to 19,000 feet between 20.04 and 20.20, but it was impossible to assess what was happening beneath the cloud, until an enormous explosion took place, the glow from which lingered for ten minutes. Many crews commented on this at debriefings across the Command, and there must have been much speculation about the source, which turned out to be the naval ammunition depot at Mariensiel, situated to the south of the town. It blew itself into oblivion, devastating 120 acres and causing widespread damage in the dockyard and town. Just three Lancasters failed to return, including W4384 with the crew of Sgt Dutton on board, and no clue as to its fate ever emerged.

Crews attending briefings on the 13th learned that they were to be part of the largest force yet sent to the port of Lorient of 466 aircraft, 103 of them 5 Group Lancasters, of which thirteen were made ready by 57 Squadron at Scampton. Among the crews taking off between 18.50 and 19.03 as part of the second wave was that of F/O Astell for his maiden operation in the western theatre. S/L Avis was the senior pilot on duty as they climbed out and set course for the south coast, losing the services along the way of Sgt McCrea and crew to rear turret failure and Sgt Rice and crew to a fire in the port-outer engine. The others began the Channel crossing in the Exmouth area and F/Sgt Lemon and crew reported being able to see flares over the target and the glow from the fires from 125 miles away as they headed south. With such a beacon to draw them on, navigation was a simple task and under clear skies affording excellent visibility, bomb-aimers were able to make a visual identification of both aiming points, the U-Boot pens on the Keroman peninsula and the town before smoke began to drift across the area. The 57 Squadron crews bombed from 9,000 to 13,000 feet between 21.30 and 21.42 and returned safely to report massive fires right across the town and the port area.

Orders came through from 5 Group on the 14th to make ready for a return to Italy that night for a crack this time at Milan. A force of 142 Lancasters of 1, 5 and 8 Groups was assembled to carry out the attack, while 243 Halifaxes, Stirlings and Wellingtons were made ready to try their hand at Cologne. Among the eighty-nine 5 Group Lancasters were eleven representing 57 Squadron, which took off from Scampton between 18.30 and 18.49 with S/L Avis the senior pilot on duty. F/Sgt Lemon and crew turned back early with an engine issue, while Sgt Hawkins and crew reached the Alps, but were prevented by engine failure from gaining sufficient altitude to cross them and had to abandon their sortie. The others continued on to reach the target area after a trouble-free outward flight and were guided to the aiming point by green and red Path Finder route-marker flares. They were able to identify the aiming point visually after carrying out a timed run from Lake Maggiore and delivered their payloads from 10,000 to 16,000 feet between 22.37 and 22.59, observing them to hit the city. Many fires were reported, the glow from which remained visible for at least a hundred miles into the return journey. The operation was hailed as a success, although no local report was forthcoming to confirm or deny.

The final raid of the series on Lorient was posted on the 16th, for which another large force was made ready, this time of 377 aircraft. Of seventy-five Lancasters offered by 5 Group, six were made ready by 57 Squadron at Scampton and took off between 18.55 and 19.00 with W/C Hopcroft the senior pilot on duty. For once, the 57 Squadron effort was not depleted by early returns, and its crews were among the earlier arrivals at the target, where they encountered clear conditions aided by an almost full moon. This enabled them to deliver their cookies and SBCs of incendiaries on red TIs onto the Keroman peninsula from 11,000 to 20,000 feet between 20.49 and 20.54. The majority of the force dropped incendiaries into the town, which, after nine attacks, 1,926 sorties and four thousand tons of bombs, was now a desolate and deserted ruin.

Preparations were put in hand on the 18th to make ready 195 aircraft for the second of four raids on Wilhelmshaven during the month. 5 Group contributed seventy-nine Lancasters, including five belonging to 57 Squadron, which departed Scampton between 18.25 and 18.29 with W/C Hopcroft the senior pilot on duty. All reached the target area, which was identified visually in excellent conditions, and red TIs were in the bomb sights as the 57 Squadron bomb bays were emptied from 18,000 to 20,000 feet between 20.34 and 20.38. Bombs were observed to burst and fires to spring up, and returning crews were confident that an accurate and concentrated attack had taken place. However, bombing photos revealed that the operation had been a failure, after the main weight of bombs had fallen into open country to the west of the town, and this demonstrated how easy it was to be misled by what the eye saw. Local reports admitted to a number of bombs hitting the town but causing no serious damage or casualties. 57 Squadron's W4375 was absent from its dispersal pan, and no trace of it and its crew of F/Sgt Langley was ever found.

Twenty-four hours later, a force of 338 aircraft set off to return to Wilhelmshaven, with Wellingtons and Halifaxes accounting for 230 of the number and Stirlings and Lancasters the rest. 5 Group dispatched thirty-three Lancasters, with only those of Sgts Hawkins, Haye and Leach representing 57 Squadron. They departed Scampton between 17.48 and 17.50 and, once again, found the conditions to be excellent, with visibility that enabled crews to identify the coastline and line themselves up on the target, which was being marked by green TIs. Bombing took place from 12,000 to 19,000 feet between 20.03 and 20.07, and the bursts and fires observed in the docks area and the town left the crews with the impression that another successful raid had taken place. However, bombing photos told a different story, and revealed that the Path Finder marking had fallen to the north of the built-up area, partly through reliance upon outdated maps, which would now be replaced. Of the twelve missing aircraft five were Stirlings and represented 8.9% of those dispatched, thus confirming the type's vulnerability compared with the Lancaster and Halifax. The four missing Lancasters represented a 7.7% loss rate, while no Halifaxes failed to return, but this would prove to be a blip. During the course of the year, the food chain would become established with Lancasters firmly at the top, Halifaxes in the middle and Stirlings at the bottom, when all types operated together.

An all-Lancaster main force from 1 and 5 Groups was made ready to attack the U-Boot construction yards at Vegesack to the north-west of Bremen on the 21st, with Path Finder Lancasters, Halifaxes and Stirlings to provide the marking in an overall force of 143 aircraft. Seventy-four of the Lancasters were put up by 5 Group, and the six representing 57 Squadron departed Scampton between 18.23 and 18.28 with F/Os Astell and Greenan the senior pilots on duty. F/Sgt Lemon and crew turned back early because of an overheating starboard-inner engine, but the others reached the target area after attempting to follow scattered route-marker flares. They were greeted by ten-tenths cloud at 3,000 feet, above which, red and green skymarker flares drifted down, also in a somewhat scattered manner and up to nine minutes late to join the TIs dimly visible burning on the ground. The 57 Squadron crews carried out their attacks from 15,000 to 16,500 feet between 20.50 and 20.55, and a considerable glow from beneath the clouds suggested a successful outcome. Bombing photos depicted only cloud, and no local report was available to provide details of damage.

The current series of raids on Wilhelmshaven was concluded on the night of the 24/25th by 115 aircraft of 6 and 8 Groups with indeterminate results, and the port would now be left in peace until October 1944. A major operation against Nuremberg was posted on stations across the Command on the 25th, and 5 Group responded with a maximum effort of 101 Lancasters, ten of them made ready by 57 Squadron at Scampton. They took off between 19.15 and 19.38 with W/C Hopcroft the senior pilot on duty and Bill Astell now wearing the insignia of a flight lieutenant. Eight of the 57 Squadron Lancasters were carrying a cookie and twelve SBCs of 4lb incendiaries and the remaining two four SBCs of 30lb incendiaries to supplement the cookie. Not all of this ordnance made it all the way as the crews of Sgt Hawkins and F/Sgt Lemon dumped their cookies as they turned back with engine issues. The others made it to the target area, which they found to be under cloudless skies, and had to wait for the Path Finder element to turn up, some sixteen to twenty minutes after the raid was due to begin. They dropped marker flares on the approach, and the 5 Group crews carried out a time-and-distance run to the aiming point, which was marked by red and green TIs. The 57 Squadron element bombed from 11,000 to 15,000 feet between 23.22 and 23.28 and all of the indications, including what looked like an oil-depot exploding, suggested a concentrated attack falling predominantly in northern and western districts. This was confirmed by local reports, which mentioned damage to three hundred buildings, but also revealed that bombs had fallen onto other communities and open country up to seven miles to the north.

When Cologne was posted as the target on the 26th, 5 Group responded with ninety Lancasters, seven of which were made ready by 57 Squadron at Scampton as part of an overall force of 427 aircraft. They took off between 18.53 and 18.58 with F/Ls Astell and Wareing the senior pilots on duty, the latter undertaking his first sortie since joining the squadron, and there were no early returns. In fact, it was a night of almost perfect serviceability for 5 Group, its crews reaching the Cologne area to be greeted by good vertical visibility to aid the bomb-aimers, some of whom were able to identify the bridges over the Rhine. It seems from some comments from other squadrons that a proportion of the force bombed before the Path Finders had a chance to mark, but, once the red and green TIs were seen on the ground, the 57 Squadron crews aimed their cookies and incendiaries at them from 15,000 to 18,500 feet between 21.18 and 21.26. As F/Sgt Lancaster and crew were heading out of the target area, a heavy flak shell burst under the tail and sent the aircraft into what appeared to be an uncontrollable dive. Passing through 4,000 feet he ordered the crew to prepare to bale out but managed to arrest the descent at 1,500 feet only to find that both gunners and the wireless operator had gone. Fires were reported in the city centre, as were decoys to the west of the city, and bombing photos showed fire tracks and smoke that suggested an effective raid. In fact, a large proportion of the effort had fallen to the south-west of the city, and perhaps, only a quarter had landed in the built-up area, causing much damage to housing, minor industry and public buildings.

5 Group underwent a change of leadership on the 27th, when AVM Coryton relinquished the post of Air-officer-Commanding and was succeeded by AVM Sir Ralph Cochrane, formerly A-O-C 3 Group. Cochrane enjoyed close ties with Harris, having served under him as a flight commander in Mesopotamia during the 1920s alongside Harris's Deputy Commander -in-Chief, AM Sir Robert Saundby. Later that day, the crew of Sgt McCrea was one of thirteen freshmen to be detailed by 5 Group to conduct mining sorties off the Frisians in company with seventy-eight other aircraft. They departed Scampton at 18.52 bound for Nectarine III, where they encountered poor visibility and extreme darkness, but managed to pinpoint on Juist and carry out a timed run to the drop zone to release six mines from 1,500 feet as briefed at 20.56.

Having dealt with Lorient under the January Directive, attention now turned upon St-Nazaire, situated further south along the Biscay coast. The force of 437 aircraft assembled on the 28th included a contribution from 5 Group of eighty-nine Lancasters, of which five represented 57 Squadron, each containing a freshman crew. They departed Scampton between 18.35 and 18.39 with F/O Jenks the senior pilot on duty after F/L Wareing's participation had been scrubbed at the last minute because of a brake-pressure problem. The number was further reduced when P/O Jeavons and crew experienced an issue with their port-inner engine, leaving the others, including recent arrivals, Sgt Divall and crew, to continue on to the target area where clear skies prevailed and only a little ground haze impaired the vertical visibility. They bombed on red TIs from 13,000 and 14,000 feet between 21.16 and 21.27, and it was clear from the many explosions and at least forty fires burning in the docks that the port was undergoing an ordeal of destruction. Post-raid reconnaissance revealed that the marking had been concentrated and the bombing accurate, and local reports confirmed that 60% of the town had been destroyed. This concluded the month's activity, during which, the squadron had taken part in fourteen operations and had dispatched ninety-six sorties for the loss of three Lancasters and their crews plus three airmen who had baled out over enemy territory.

March 1943

March would bring with it the opening rounds of the Ruhr campaign, the first for which the Command was adequately equipped and genuinely prepared, with a predominantly four-engine bomber force to carry an increasing weight of bombs and Oboe to provide accuracy. First, however, the crews would have to negotiate operations to Germany's capital and second cities, and it was the "Big City" itself, Berlin, that opened the month's account on the 1st. A force of 302 aircraft was assembled, made up of 156 Lancasters, eighty-six Halifaxes and sixty Stirlings, 5 Group putting up a maximum effort of ninety-eight Lancasters, of which nine represented 57 Squadron. They departed Scampton between 19.01 and 19.09 with S/L Avis the senior pilot on duty and lost the services of the crews of F/L Astell and P/O Roberts at the Danish coast, the former because of an inability to climb and the latter through engine failure, and they were among eleven from 5 Group to abandon their sorties. The target was found to be under clear skies with only haze to impair the vertical visibility, however, reliant upon H2S, the Path Finder navigators experienced great difficulty in establishing their positions based on the images on their cathode-ray tubes over such a massive urban sprawl. This led to scattered marking, and the main weight of the attack falling into south-western districts, where the 57 Squadron crews bombed from 15,000 to 20,000 feet on red and green TIs between 22.08 and 22.21. Many fires were reported, the glow from which, according to some, could be seen from two hundred miles away on the return flight. Seventeen aircraft failed to return, but all from Scampton arrived back in home airspace, only for 57 Squadron's R5894 to crash at 02.00 at Riseholme, three miles south-south-east of the airfield, after hitting high tension cables. There were no survivors from the crew of F/O Greenan RCAF, two others of which were members of the RCAF. The squadron ORB speculated that a collision may have occurred with a 9 Squadron Lancaster from Waddington, which crashed some four miles away at Heighington at around the same time, but we will never know for certain. A post-raid analysis based on bombing photos revealed the attack to have been spread over an area of a hundred square miles, but, because of the increasing bomb tonnage now being carried, more damage was inflicted on the city than on any previous raid. 875 buildings, mostly houses, were destroyed, and twenty factories seriously damaged, along with railway workshops in the Tempelhof district.

On the following night, 5 Group detailed eight Lancasters for mining duties in the Deodar garden in the Gironde estuary. 57 Squadron dispatched the recently arrived crews of F/L Leland and P/O Jeavons shortly before 18.30 and both reached the target area after outward flights of four hours. Visibility was not ideal, but the Leland crew pinpointed on Cordouan lighthouse and then Pointe-de-Graves before delivering four mines into the briefed location at 22.49. The Jeavons crew experienced greater difficulty in locating the drop zone and searched for fifty minutes, before planting their vegetables in an estimated position in the mouth of the Estuary.

A force of 417 aircraft was assembled to send against Hamburg on the 3rd, and eighty-nine of 149 Lancasters were provided by 5 Group, seven of them by 57 Squadron at Scampton, where each had a cookie and SBCs of 4lb or 30lb incendiaries winched into its cavernous thirty-three-foot-long bomb bay. They took off between 19.10 and 19.16 with F/Ls Astell and Wareing the senior pilots on duty, but Astell was forced to abandon his sortie because of an unserviceable rear turret and an oil leak in the starboard-outer engine. The others continued on to find the target basking under clear skies and in good visibility and carried out their attacks from 19,000 to 20,500 feet between 21.31 and 21.36, aided by the H2S-laid Path Finder TIs. Numerous fires were observed in the docks area along with black smoke rising to meet the bombers as they turned away. What was not appreciated, was the fact that some markers had fallen onto the town of Wedel, situated some thirteen miles downstream of the Elbe, and they had attracted perhaps the bulk of the bombs, while those hitting the primary target had caused a hundred fires that needed to be dealt with before the fire services could go to the aid of their neighbour. Ten aircraft failed to return, but there were no empty dispersal pans at Scampton.

On the following night, 5 Group sent six Lancasters to mine the waters of Danzig Bay and two others for similar duties in the Kattegat. The 57 Squadron crews of F/L Leland and Sgt Hawkins departed Scampton at 17.15 for what was among the most distant mining destinations visited by the Command, but the ORB does not specify whether their target area was the Spinach garden off the port of Gdynia or the Privet garden, a dozen or so miles further south off Danzig (Gdansk). In any event, they had a ten-hour round trip ahead of them, except for the fact that F/L Leland and crew lost their intercom system over the North Sea and turned back, leaving Sgt Hawkins and crew to press on across southern Jutland and the western Baltic into Swedish airspace. The Swedes were accustomed to such incursions and sent two fighters with navigation lights burning to shepherd the Lancaster until it had passed through. Favourable weather conditions in the target area enabled them to plant their vegetables into the allotted location at 22.03, before returning safely to land at Downham Market.

The decks were now cleared for the opening of the Ruhr offensive, which, over the ensuing months, would change the face of bombing and provide for the enemy an indication of the burgeoning power of the Command. This was a momentous occasion, a culmination of all that had gone before during three and a half years of Bomber Command operations. The backs-to-the-wall desperation of 1940, the tentative almost token offensives of 1941, the treading water and gradual metamorphosis under Harris in 1942, when failures still far outnumbered successes, had all been leading to this night, from which point would begin the calculated and systematic dismantling of Germany's industrial and population centres. The only shining light during these dark years had been the quality and spirit of the aircrew, and this had never faltered. It would begin on the 5th at Essen, Harris's nemesis thus far and the home of the giant armaments-producing Krupp complex occupying the Borbeck district, and, for the first time since the war began, the Command would have at its disposal a device which would negate the industrial haze protecting this city and its neighbours. The magnificent pioneering work on Oboe by W/C Hal Bufton and his crews at 109 Squadron was about to bear fruit in spectacular fashion, and the towns and cities of Germany's arsenal would suffer destruction on an unprecedented scale.

A force of 442 aircraft included ninety-seven Lancasters representing 5 Group, 57 Squadron contributing six of them containing the crews of F/Ls Astell, Leland and Wareing, P/O Reid, F/Sgt Lovell and Sgt Haye, who departed Scampton between 18.54 and 19.21. For once, the squadron was not involved in the unusually high number of early returns, although, only seven from 5

Group, and, together with those bombing alternative targets, this would reduce the size of the force reaching Essen and bombing as briefed to 362 aircraft. 5 Group favoured a time-and-distance approach to the aiming point, and the 57 Squadron crews used the Path Finders' yellow route markers as the initial reference point, before exploiting the good visibility to bomb through the industrial haze onto red and green TIs from 16,500 to 22,000 feet between 21.17 and 21.38. The overwhelming impression was of a concentrated attack, which left many fires burning, and a glow in the sky reported by some to be visible from the North Sea homebound. At debriefings, crews reported terrific explosions among fires, which lit up the sky, and a pall of smoke hanging above the dull, red centre of the conflagration. Post-raid reconnaissance revealed 160 acres of devastation and damage to fifty-three buildings within the Krupp district, and the success of the operation was confirmed by local reports of 3,018 houses destroyed and more than two thousand others seriously damaged. The operation cost the Command an acceptable fourteen aircraft, and it was a most encouraging start to what would become a five-month-long offensive.

It would be a further week before round two of the Ruhr offensive was mounted, and, in the meantime, Harris turned his attention upon southern Germany, beginning with Nuremberg on the 8th. A force of 338 aircraft included 105 Lancasters of 5 Group, of which eight represented 57 Squadron, and they departed Scampton between 19.34 and 20.14, Sgt Rice and crew last away after having to transfer to the spare Lancaster. Rice hailed from Burbage on the outskirts of the Leicestershire town of Hinckley and was a keen cricketer, who had been about to trial for the county when the war intervened. He was sent to America for training and was there in December 1941 when the Japanese bombing of Pearl Harbour brought America into the war. The recently promoted S/L Curry had just returned to the squadron following a flight commander's course at 5 Group HQ, and he was the senior pilot on duty as they climbed away and headed south, each carrying a cookie and assorted incendiaries. Again, there were no 57 Squadron early returns among the eight from 5 Group, and they reached the target by following yellow route markers to find clear skies but ground haze and extreme darkness. The conditions seemed to impede the Path Finders' ability to locate the city centre blind by H2S, and the main force crews experienced the same difficulty in identifying ground detail, allowing themselves to be guided to the aiming point by a few red and green TIs, which appeared to lack concentration and soon burned out. The 57 Squadron crews had predominantly red TIs in the bombsights, but also a few scattered greens, and carried out their attacks from 13,000 to 14,400 feet between 23.32 and 23.53. The initial impression was of a scattered raid, but a greater concentration of fires developed, and the glow from these was reported by some to be visible for two hundred miles into the return journey. Local reports confirmed the marking and bombing of Nuremberg to have been spread along a ten-mile stretch, half of it falling short of the city boundaries, while the rest destroyed six hundred buildings and damaged fourteen hundred others, including a number of important war-industry factories.

On the following day, preparations were put in hand to return to southern Germany to attack the Bavarian capital city of Munich, situated deep in the mountains of south-eastern Germany, a round-trip of more than 1,200 miles. A force of 264 aircraft included eighty-one Lancasters of 5 Group, of which seven belonging to 57 Squadron were loaded with a cookie each and SBCs of incendiaries. They departed Scampton between 20.43 and 20.51 with F/L Leland the senior pilot on duty on a night when the servicing gremlins returned to the squadron. S/L Avis had been due to take part, but a brake-pressure issue forced him to drop out at the last minute, and Sgt Hawkins and crew turned back with starboard-inner engine failure and P/O P Singer also with an engine issue and excessive fuel consumption. The others reached the target area, where clear skies and good visibility prevailed, and the Path Finder green and white TIs could be seen to have fallen within the built-up area. P/O Greig and crew were among many to witness an enormous orange explosion in a south-western district at 00.17 as the first Scampton arrivals began their timed runs to the aiming point from the Ammersee, and these had the TIs in the bomb sights as they released their loads from 14,000 to 17,000 feet between 00.25 and 00.50. Another huge explosion at 00.25 lit up the sky for twenty seconds and illuminated an area of ground with a ten-mile radius, described by some as the largest they had experienced, and another particularly large one occurred at 00.43. Fires were taking hold and sending a large pall of smoke rising above the city as the bomber force withdrew to the west, and eighteen blazes were counted in or close to the city centre. A relatively modest eight aircraft failed to return, and only two of these were from 5 Group. A post-raid analysis concluded that a strong wind had pushed the attack into the western half of the city, where 291 buildings had been destroyed and 660 severely damaged. The aero-engine assembly shop at the B.M.W factory was put out of action for six weeks, and many other industrial concerns also lost vital production.

While the above operation was in progress, four 5 Group Lancasters took part in mining operations in the Kattegat off north-eastern Denmark. 57 Squadron's Sgt Russell and crew took off at 17.30 bound for either the Silverthorn 4 or 6 garden off Anholt Island and successfully deposited six mines into the briefed location at 21.25. P/O Jeavons and crew departed Scampton at 17.44 for the Yewtree garden located further north between the Danish mainland and Laeso Island, and also fulfilled their brief at 21.02. Later, on the 10th, the squadron was informed that it was to form a third, or C Flight, and increase its complement of Lancasters to twenty-four and to expect the arrival of an additional seventy-four airmen.

The trio of operations to destinations in southern Germany concluded with the highly industrial city of Stuttgart, for which a force of 314 aircraft was assembled on the 11th, 5 Group contributing ninety-six of 152 Lancasters. Thirteen of these were made ready by 57 Squadron at Scampton, where take-off was accomplished safely between 19.39 and 19.49 with W/C Hopcroft and S/Ls Avis and Curry the senior pilots on duty. Sgt Divall and crew turned back when the navigator became unwell, leaving the others to press on across France to the target, where visibility was found to be excellent as the main force element arrived late to observe Path Finder TIs already burning out on the ground and leaving the way clear for dummy TIs to lure the bombing away from the city centre. In this endeavour they were largely successful, although, to the bomb-aimers high above, the green TIs appeared to be legitimate, and were bombed by the 57 Squadron crews from 11,000 to 16,000 feet between 23.21 and 23.38. Most of the effort was wasted in open country, but the south-western suburbs of Vaihingen and Kaltental were hit and 118 buildings, mostly houses, were destroyed. It was a disappointing outcome, which cost eleven aircraft, only one of which was from 5 Group.

Round two of the Ruhr campaign was posted on the 12th, when 457 crews learned at briefing that Essen was once more to be their destination. 5 Group detailed ninety-five Lancasters, of which eleven were made ready by 57 Squadron at Scampton and took off between 19.10 and 19.33 with W/C Hopcroft and S/L Avis the senior pilots on duty. F/O Jeavons and crew were thwarted by a broken oxygen pipe and had to abandon their sortie, while the others reached the target to find it well marked by red and green Path Finder TIs, and only smoke to mar the visibility. They carried out their attacks from 15,000 to 20,000 feet between 21.33 and 21.47 and it was clear that the bombing was accurate and mostly concentrated around the Oboe-laid TIs. This time, the Krupp complex found itself in the centre of the area of destruction and although substantially fewer buildings were destroyed, post-raid reconnaissance confirmed that greater concentration had been achieved, and 30% more damage inflicted upon Krupp than during the raid of a week earlier. The defences fought back to claim twenty-three bombers, and, on the way home, S/L Avis and crew had a brief encounter with an Me210 night-fighter, which they claimed as damaged. A crash-landing was carried out at Wittering as a result of hydraulics failure, but there were no crew casualties and W4358 would be returned to flying condition.

On the following day, S/L Henry Melvin Young arrived on posting to assume command of C Flight, having returned in the previous year from serving in the Middle East. He had been born in Belgravia in London in 1915 to an English father and an American mother, and between 1928 and 1933 lived in California. On his return to England, he attended Westminster School before following in his father's footsteps by going up to Oxford. He joined the rowing club and was a member of the Oxford crew that won the 1938 Boat Race. He joined the RAF Volunteer Reserve shortly before the outbreak of war, and, after training was posted in June 1940 to 4 Group's 102 Squadron, which, in September of that year, was loaned to Coastal Command. Returning from a patrol, Young was forced to ditch in the Atlantic, where he and his crew spent twenty-two hours afloat before being rescued. In November, he ran out of fuel while returning from Turin, and had to paddle ashore, from which point the name "Dinghy" became a permanent attachment. In October 1941 he went with 104 Squadron to Malta, before moving to Egypt, in January 1942, where he served until August. On his way back to the UK, he stopped off in America to marry his fiancée, and then re-joined Bomber Command to continue his operational career.

On the afternoon of the 13th, 5 Group briefed seventeen crews for mining duties in the waters of the Baltic, for which 57 Squadron made ready four Lancasters for the crews of F/Os Jeavons and Jenks and Sgts Divall and Russell. They took off from Scampton between 19.55 and 19.58 bound, it is believed, for the Tangerine garden off Pillau at the eastern end of Danzig Bay and the most distant of the Command's mining locations. They arrived in their target areas some four hours later to be confronted by a wall of fog, which prevented them from locating their briefed target areas, and Sgts Russell and Divall backtracked to the Silverthorn II garden off Anholt Island in the Kattegat, where they delivered their four mines each at 02.11 and 02.24. P/O Jenks and crew carried out a DR run from the Swedish coast to Danzig Bay, a distance not far short of two hundred miles, and delivered their mines in poor visibility at 00.57. F/O Jeavons and crew also established an initial pinpoint on the south-eastern coast of Sweden, before crossing a large expanse of sea to reach the Pillau area. They identified it through a gap in the cloud and released their mines at the end of a timed run, before heading home to be intercepted by a night-fighter some thirty miles out from Denmark's western coast. W4201, the commanding officer's personal Lancaster, sustained extensive damage from cannon shells, which created handling difficulties, and was crash-landed just short of the airfield on return at 06.10. The rear gunner had been wounded during the engagement, and the pilot and flight engineer injured during the landing, but all would recover, which was more than could be said for Frederick I, which was written off.

On the morning of the 15th, a cookie fell accidentally out of W4834 on its dispersal pan and detonated with such force that six nearby Lancasters, three of them belonging to 50 Squadron, were wrecked and three others severely damaged. 57 Squadron's ED306 and ED594 were the others to be destroyed in what was the worst accident of its kind during the year. Thereafter, the weather caused a lull in operations, and it was the 22nd before orders came through to prepare for the next assault on St-Nazaire. A force of 357 aircraft was assembled, including a contribution from 5 Group of 120 Lancasters, of which ten were provided by 57 Squadron. They departed Scampton between 19.05 and 19.39 with S/L Curry the senior pilot on duty but lost the services of P/O P Singer to starboard-inner engine failure before reaching the French coast. A recall signal was sent by 3 Group to its Stirlings, and fifty-five responded, leaving eight to carry on to the target, which they reached with the rest of the force to find good visibility impeded only by ground haze, which did not prevent a visual identification of ground features. Red and green Path Finder TIs confirmed the location of the aiming point, and the 57 Squadron crews released their eleven 1,000 pounders each from 13,000 to 14,000 feet between 21.30 and 22.00. Fires were taking hold as they turned away, and the town and its port facilities sustained massive damage. F/Sgt Lemon attempted to land ED348 on an 800-yard runway at Chedworth in Gloucestershire and ran off the end, causing Cat. B damage to the Lancaster but no crew casualties.

On the 25th, the C Flight crews of S/L Young, F/L Astell, P/O Rice and F/Sgts Lancaster and Lovell were posted across the tarmac with nineteen members of ground crew to join Squadron X, a top-secret unit being formed under W/C Guy Gibson DSO, DFC and soon to be given the number 617 Squadron. It is said, that P/O Rice, a man who in today's parlance would be described as having "attitude", was unhappy with the move. The purpose behind 617 Squadron's formation would remain classified right up until the morning after its epic attack on the Ruhr dams, when its fame would spread immediately across the world. S/L Wallage was posted to 57 Squadron on the same day to succeed S/L Young as C Flight commander

A force of 455 aircraft was assembled on the 26th for the third operation of the Ruhr offensive, this one to be directed against Duisburg, for which ninety-four Lancasters were provided by 5 Group. 57 Squadron made ready nine at Scampton and they took off between 18.46 and 18.54 with F/Ls Leland and Roberts the senior pilots on duty, having learned at briefing that marking would be by "Musical Wanganui", the code for Oboe skymarking to be carried out by nine Mosquitos of 109 Squadron. The crews of Sgt Hawkins and F/Sgt Leach turned back early because of instrument and intercom failures respectively, while Sgt Grimwood and crew were defeated by navigational difficulties, possibly resulting from their inexperience. The remaining six pressed on to the target area, where they found ten-tenths cloud with tops at 10,000 feet and good visibility above. They were greeted by the Oboe release-point parachute flares, which were in the bomb sights as they dropped their cookies and incendiaries from 18,000 to 19,500 feet between 21.45 and 22.01, and a large explosion was witnessed at 21.53. What the crews could not know, was that five of the Oboe Mosquitos had returned early with equipment failure and a sixth had been shot down, leaving just three to deliver what could only be sparse marking. This was insufficient, and led to a scattered and ineffective attack, which, according to local reports, caused only minor damage. Fortunately, the failure cost a modest six aircraft, none of them belonging to 5 Group.

Orders were received on stations across the Command on the 27th to prepare for a trip to the "Big City" that night, and a force of 396 aircraft was duly assembled, which included 111 Lancasters from 5 Group. Thirteen of these were made ready by 57 Squadron at Scampton, and they took off between 20.07 and 20.19 with F/Ls Jenks, Leland and Wareing the senior pilots on duty. F/L Jenks and crew turned back because of an unserviceable rear turret, and they were followed home an hour later by F/Sgt Haye and crew with both inner engines overheating. The remainder continued on to approach the city from the south-west, each carrying a cookie and SBCs of incendiaries and advancing in the wake of the Path Finder element, who were again reliant upon H2S to locate the city-centre aiming point. However, the sheer size of Berlin thwarted the attempts of the H2S operators to establish their positions accurately, and this resulted in the marking of two areas at least five miles short of the centre. Crews reported three-tenths cloud at 13,000 feet and five tenths stratus at 19,000 feet with moderate to good visibility, and those from 57 Squadron bombed on red and green TIs from 17,500 to 20,000 feet between 23.06 and 23.22. From bombing altitude, the attack appeared to be effective but local reports confirmed that the main weight of bombs had fallen between seven and seventeen miles short of the target and 25% of those hitting the city had failed to detonate. Nine aircraft failed to return, three of them Lancasters, but only one belonged to 5 Group.

There would be an opportunity to rectify the failure two nights hence, but, in the meantime, St-Nazaire would face its third heavy assault under the January Directive, for which a force of 323 aircraft was made ready on the 28th. 5 Group detailed twenty-one freshman crews, five of them from 57 Squadron, which departed Scampton between 20.00 and 20.04 with S/L Wallage the senior pilot on duty. Sgt Divall and crew abandoned their sortie when the navigator became indisposed, leaving the others to reach the target area and encounter good visibility in which the red and green Oboe-laid TIs could be seen clearly marking out the aiming point. The cookies and incendiaries were delivered by the Scampton crews from 13,000 to 14,000 feet between 22.21 and 22.29 and on their return they reported concentrated fires and a successful outcome, which post-raid reconnaissance confirmed.

On the following day, the 29th, a force of 329 aircraft was assembled for the return to Berlin that night, 5 Group contributing 106 of the Lancasters and 57 Squadron a dozen, which departed Scampton between 21.45 and 22.03 with S/L Curry the senior pilot on duty. An alarming eighteen 5 Group crews abandoned their sorties for a variety of causes, many as a result of severe icing conditions over the north-west German and Danish coastal regions. Among those falling foul of the icing and electrical storms were the 57 Squadron crews of F/O Reid and P/O P Singer, who found themselves unable to climb to the briefed operational altitude. The remainder arrived at Berlin with the rest of the main force but behind schedule because of inaccurately forecast winds. They mostly carried out a timed run from a lake and found the visibility to be sufficiently good to enable bomb-aimers to visually identify the River Spree and other landmarks. The aiming point was marked by red TIs and bombing was carried out by the 57 Squadron crews from 17,000 to 21,000 feet between 01.00 and 01.26. They returned with the impression that the attack had lacked concentration, and this was confirmed later, when bombing photos revealed that most of the effort had fallen into open country south of the city, a disappointment compounded by the loss of twenty-one aircraft. 57 Squadron's ED761 was homebound over Holland with the crew of Sgt Fisher and only minutes from the safety of the North Sea when crossing paths with the night-fighter of Lt Werner Rapp of III./NJG1, who shot the Lancaster down to crash without survivors at Waverveen, some ten miles north-west of Utrecht.

During the course of the month, the squadron took part in sixteen operations and dispatched 127 sorties for the loss of three Lancasters and two crews and three further Lancasters on the ground.

April 1943

April would be the least rewarding month during the Ruhr offensive, principally, because of the number of operations directed at targets in regions of Germany beyond the range of Oboe. It began for three 5 Group squadrons with the preparation of eight Lancasters on the 2nd, to join forty-seven others to carry out the final raid on St-Nazaire, while forty-seven aircraft from other groups dealt with Lorient to bring down the curtain on the January Directive. The freshman crews of Sgts Broadbent and Pickup took off from Scampton at 20.05 and 20.07 respectively bound for the former, Sgt Pickup having attended a commissioning interview at 5 Group HQ earlier in the day. The Broadbent crew found good visibility and released their eleven 1,000 pounders over a concentration of markers from 14,000 feet at 22.22 in the face of heavy and accurate flak and observed fires but no detail because of a smoke screen. W4257 crashed in the target area without survivors from the all-NCO crew of Sgt Pickup.

The Lancaster and Halifax stations received orders on the 3rd to prepare for an operation that night against Essen, for which the Krupp complex was designated as the aiming point. They responded with forces of 225 and 113 aircraft respectively, 5 Group contributing 123 of the Lancasters, and this would be the first time that more than two hundred of the type had operated together. 57 Squadron loaded its thirteen aircraft with a cookie and SBCs of 4lb or 30lb incendiaries and dispatched them from Scampton between 19.14 and 19.42 with W/C Hopcroft and S/L Wallage the senior pilots on duty, the former in Frederick II, ED707. Sgt Broadbent and crew experienced navigational problems and abandoned their sortie, leaving their colleagues to cross the Dutch coast near Haarlem, uncomfortably close to the Amsterdam defences. Almost clear skies prevailed over the central Ruhr, and, because of uncertainty by the Command's meteorological section of the likely weather conditions, the Path Finders had prepared both sky and ground marking plans, which led to a degree of confusion among the main force crews as towards which they should aim their bombs. Most picked up red and green release-point flares when a dozen miles north of the target over Dorsten before observing the TIs on the ground, and the bombing by the Scampton crews was carried out from 15,500 to 20,000 feet between 22.11 and 22.21. F/L Leland and crew suffered the frustration of a complete hang-up and following several unsuccessful attempts to dislodge the contents of the bomb bay, set course for home, managing eventually to dump the cookie in the North Sea. Returning crews reported many explosions with fires emitting large volumes of smoke and the glow from the burning city was still visible to some from the Dutch coast homebound. The consensus was of a successful raid, matching those in March, and this was confirmed by bombing photographs and local reports, which spoke of widespread destruction in central and western districts, where 635 buildings had been reduced to rubble and many more seriously damaged. The searchlight and flak defence had been intense, and it became an expensive night for the Command, which registered the loss of a dozen Halifaxes and nine Lancasters. This represented 6% of those dispatched, but it was the respective loss rates of the types that was most telling, with the Halifaxes suffering 10.62% compared with 4% for the Lancasters.

The largest non-1,000 force to date of 577 aircraft was made ready on the 4th for an attack that night on the shipbuilding and naval port of Kiel, for which 5 Group put up 112 Lancasters, fifteen of them representing 57 Squadron. They departed Scampton between 21.03 and 21.20 with S/L Wallage the senior squadron pilot on duty, and W/C McGhie guesting to gain experience before assuming command of the newly-forming 619 Squadron later in the month. Also gaining operational experience as second pilot to P/O A Singer was W/C Johnson, who was about to take command of 49 Squadron. Sgt Russell and crew suffered port-outer engine failure and turned back, while the others reached the target area to be guided towards the aiming point by yellow route marker flares, released by the Path Finder heavy brigade either side of 23.00. On arrival, Kiel was found to be concealed beneath ten-tenths cloud with good visibility above, and the cookies and incendiaries were released from estimated positions onto the glow of fires below the cloud from 16,000 to 19,000 feet between 23.26 and 23.40. It was not possible to assess the outcome, and, as bombing photos revealed only cloud, it was left to a post-raid analysis to conclude that decoy fires were operating, and probably lured away a proportion of the effort, while the strong wind caused the markers to drift, leading the remainder astray and resulting in most of the bombs missing the target altogether. According to local reports, only eleven houses were destroyed, and this was a major disappointment in view of the size of the force involved. A message was received from the crew of S/L Wallage at 00.40 to the effect that the bomb-aimer had been wounded and an engine had failed. A fourth and final fix was obtained at 01.43, which placed W4252 at the mid-point of the North Sea between the Danish and Yorkshire coasts, but, despite an extensive air and sea search, no trace of the Lancaster and its crew was found. On the 7th, F/L Leland was granted the acting rank of squadron leader to enable him to succeed S/L Wallage as a flight commander.

On the 8th, Sgt Lovell and crew returned to 57 Squadron from 617 Squadron having apparently failed to attain the standard required by Gibson. That night, the Ruhr offensive continued at Duisburg, for which a mixed force of 379 Lancasters, Wellingtons, Halifaxes and Stirlings was assembled as the heavy element, while ten Oboe Mosquitos would provide the initial marking. 5 Group was responsible for eighty-four of the Lancasters, eleven of them belonging to 57 Squadron, which departed Scampton between 21.00 and 21.29 with S/L Leland the senior squadron pilot on duty and W/C McGhie guesting once more. Each was carrying the standard Ruhr payload of a cookie and either 4lb or 30lb incendiaries as they climbed away and set course, but not all would reach their intended destination. F/Sgt Haye and crew were back on the ground after three hours having been compromised by severe icing conditions and F/L Greig was forced to turn back when oxygen starvation left his rear gunner temporarily unconscious. The remainder reached the western Ruhr to encounter ten-tenths cloud with tops in places as high as 20,000 feet, which completely nullified the Path Finders' attempts to mark either the route or the target, and the bombing had to be carried out on e.t.a., some crews embarking on a time-and-distance run from as far away as the Dutch coast as the last visual reference. The 57 Squadron crews attacked from 17,000 to 21,500 feet between 23.35 and 23.46 and had nothing of value to pass on to the intelligence section at debriefing. Local reports confirmed a widely scattered raid, which hit at least fifteen other Ruhr locations and destroyed just forty buildings in Duisburg. Nineteen aircraft failed to return, but there was no empty dispersal pan at Scampton.

Not content with the outcome, Harris ordered another raid twenty-four hours later, only this time, employing a much-reduced force of 104 Lancasters and five Mosquitos. 5 Group detailed seventy

Lancasters, of which ten represented 57 Squadron and departed Scampton between 20.31 and 20.38 with four pilots of flight lieutenant rank leading the squadron contingent and W/C McGhie operating for the third time as a guest. Sgt McCrea and crew lost their port-inner engine to an oil leak and turned back, while their colleagues were guided to the target by red route-marker flares, and then red and green skymarkers over the aiming point, which was hidden by ten-tenths cloud with tops at 5,000 to 15,000 feet. They delivered their cookies and SBCs from 17,000 to 22,300 feet between 23.09 and 23.14, some observing a large red glow reflected in the clouds. Local reports confirmed that this was another highly scattered raid, which spread bombs over a wide area of the Ruhr and destroyed only fifty houses in Duisburg. Sgt Broadbent and crew were attacked by a night-fighter on the way home and the pilot and rear gunner sustained wounds. ED308 was extensively damaged and both main tyres burst, but despite suffering from shock and blood loss, Sgt Broadbent brought the Lancaster and crew home to a good landing.

P/O Divall and his crew were posted across the tarmac to 617 Squadron on the 10th as replacements for the Lovell crew but would have a lot of catching up to do to attain the required standard. Later in the day, Frankfurt was posted as the destination for 502 aircraft, on a night when Wellingtons would represent the most populous type, demonstrating that this trusty old warhorse still had an important part to play in Bomber Command operations. 5 Group provided sixty-six of 136 Lancasters, ten of them provided by 57 Squadron at Scampton, and they took off between 00.10 and 00.25 with no senior pilots on duty. They adopted the usual route for south-central Germany across France with, on this night, ten-tenths cloud beneath them at around 11,000 feet and carried out time-and-distance runs from green route marker flares to deliver their loads from 10,800 to 17,000 feet between 02.53 and 03.20. No one saw anything other than an apparent glow of fires beneath the cloud, and bombing photos would reveal nothing, while local reports suggested that most of the bombing had missed the city altogether. On return, Sgt McCrea reported the loss of his starboard-outer engine at 02.10 when some twenty miles inland from the French coast, but had continued on to the target to carry out an attack. Absent from debriefing was the experienced predominantly Canadian crew of F/Sgt Lemon RCAF, who all lost their lives when ED766 crashed at Darmstadt.

A force of 208 Lancasters was assembled on the 13th as their crews were being briefed of a change of scenery for their next operation. This was to be against the docks at La Spezia on Italy's northern coast some forty miles south-east of Genoa, where elements of the Italian fleet were believed to be at berth. 5 Group detailed 124 of the Lancasters, with the remainder provided by 1 and 8 Groups, the latter also sending three Halifaxes as part of the marker force. 57 Squadron loaded thirteen of its aircraft with four 1,000 pounders each supplemented with either 4lb or 30lb incendiaries and made ready three other Lancasters for the crews of Sgt Grimwood and F/Sgts Haye and Leach to employ on mining duties outside the port in the Mullet garden. They took off together between 20.29 and 21.07 with W/C Hopcroft and S/L Avis the senior squadron pilots on duty and W/C McGhie continuing his operational apprenticeship. All sixteen from Scampton arrived on the Italian side of the Alps to find almost cloudless skies and only haze and smoke to mar the vertical visibility, although the moonlight bounced off it to produce a glare. Sgt Gifford's starboard-outer engine caught fire over the Bay of Genoa, and he ordered the bombs to be jettisoned as he turned for home. The others established their positions by visual reference of ground detail, such as rivers and the docks, confirmed by Path Finder flares, but few were able initially to pick out warships. The 57 Squadron crews carried out their attacks from 7,800 to

12,000 feet between 01.40 and 02.25 and observed many explosions and fires, F/L Greig and crew reporting six vessels to be on fire, while reports from other squadrons claimed that three large vessels tied together east of the outer harbour were ablaze. The naval oil stores and the arsenal were also said to be on fire and by the later stages of the raid, the smoke had effectively obscured the town. The bomber force headed home confident that a successful operation had taken place, for which confirmation would eventually be forthcoming. Much of the action had been observed by the gardeners, who laid four mines each from 4,000 to 6,000 feet between 01.39 and 02.06 and returned safely after around ten hours aloft. Three aircraft landed on recently captured airfields in North Africa, and it is believed that the one containing 57 Squadron's F/O Wilson and crew was among them and put down at Maison-Blanche. These crews were the first to take advantage of such landing grounds in the face of dwindling fuel or battle damage that might have prevented them from reaching England. It would not be long, however, before so before so-called "shuttle-raids" became a feature of operations to the Mediterranean region.

The busy round of non-Ruhr operations would continue at Stuttgart, for which a force of 462 aircraft was made ready on the 14th, 5 Group detailing fifty-seven Lancasters, four of which were made ready by 57 Squadron. The crews of P/O Haye, W/O Mapp and F/Sgts Lovell and Leach took off from Scampton between 21.57 and 22.00 and lost the services of P/O Haye within an hour when the navigator became unwell. The others approached the target city from the north-east to find an absence of cloud, but haze was aggravated by smoke rising through 8,000 feet to make ground detail indistinct. The aiming point was established by the green and red Path Finder TIs, and bombing was carried out by the three 57 Squadron crews from 13,500 to 15,000 feet between 01.24 and 01.35. Few crews were able to make out the impact of their own bombs and noted only a concentration of fires and considerable amounts of smoke. Post-raid reconnaissance revealed that the Path Finders had marked the centre of the city, but that a "creep-back" had developed, which had spread back along the line of approach. Creep-back was a feature of many large raids and was caused by crews bombing the first fires they came upon, rather than pushing through to the planned aiming point. It could work for or against the effectiveness of the attack, and, on this night, worked in the Command's favour by falling across the industrial district of Bad-Canstatt, before spreading further back onto the residential suburbs of Münster and Mühlhausen. It was here that the majority of the 393 buildings were destroyed and more than nine hundred others severely damaged.

S/L Curry was declared tour-expired on the 15th and was posted to 1660 Conversion Unit for instructional duties and S/L Smith arrived at 57 Squadron as his replacement.

Two major operations were planned for the 16th, the main one employing 327 Lancasters and Halifaxes to target the Skoda armaments factory at distant Pilsen in Czechoslovakia, while a force of 271 aircraft, consisting predominantly of Wellingtons and Stirlings, created a large-scale diversion at Mannheim some 240 miles to the west. 197 Lancasters and 130 Halifaxes were detailed for Pilsen, of which 102 of the former were provided by 5 Group. The plan of attack called for the Path Finders to drop route markers at the final turning point, seven miles from the target, which the crews were to then locate visually in the anticipated bright moonlight, and bomb from as low a level as practicable. It was a complicated plan that invited confusion and failure, and the outcome would question the quality of some of the briefings. 57 Squadron made ready thirteen Lancasters, seven to carry a cookie and two 1,000 pounders and six with all-incendiary loads and dispatched them from Scampton between 21.01 and 21.18 with S/L Avis the senior pilot on duty. Ahead of them lay a round-trip of some 1,500 miles, the outbound route for which would take them across France to enter Germany near Strasbourg before passing between Nuremberg to the north and Munich to the south on a course slightly north of east. F/L Roberts and crew were north of Munich when their starboard-inner engine failed, and they unloaded the contents of their bomb bay on a crossroads south-east of the Bavarian capital as they headed home at 02.05. P/O Collins and crew were experiencing navigational problems and had reached the Regensburg area, some seventy miles from the target, when they abandoned their sortie and brought their all-incendiary load home to a landing at Beaulieu.

The remaining 57 Squadron participants arrived in the target area to find the forecast favourable weather conditions, with a layer of eight-tenths cloud at between 8,000 and 15,000 feet, below which, visibility was good and ground features could be made out clearly. F/O Wilson and crew were unconvinced that they had identified the target and set course for Mannheim, which they found to be already on fire from the attack by the dedicated force and added their incendiaries from 12,000 feet at 02.35. Meanwhile, at Pilsen, matters were not proceeding according to brief, which should have made clear that the bombing was to be carried out visually from below the cloud base after making a timed run from the turning-point marked by TIs. Many 5 Group crews reported bombing from 7,000 to 10,000 feet visually and on TIs between 01.42 and 01.55, proving that they had failed to understand and comply with the instructions at briefing, and had bombed the turning point. Some of the 57 Squadron crews described a factory and chimneys in their bomb sights and made reference to yellow and green TIs and white illuminator flares, but all described difficulty in locating and identifying the aiming point, some after spending time searching, while having to dodge searchlights and flak. They bombed from 5,000 to 8,000 feet between 01.44 and 01.59, and reported many cookies bursting in open country, and intense night-fighter activity in the Mannheim area on the way home. The details of the crew reports across the group demonstrated that they could not have related to the Skoda works. Post-raid reconnaissance revealed the truth, that, despite the claims of returning crews, no bombs had fallen within miles of the factory, and had been concentrated instead around an asylum at Dobrany, some seven miles to the south-west. This failure was compounded by the loss of thirty-six aircraft, split equally between the two types, and eighteen aircraft were also missing from the Mannheim contingent, which had, at least, achieved the destruction of 130 buildings and damage to some degree to three thousand others. The combined casualty figure of fifty-four aircraft, represented a new record for a single night. F/L Jenks and crew almost became casualties but survived flak hits both on the way out and on the way in. Sadly, this was a precursor of events a few days hence.

Over at 617 Squadron, training for Operation Chastise was intense with low-level bombing practice the overriding priority. The best results were achieved by F/Sgt Clifford, F/Sgt Lancaster's bomb-aimer, who managed an amazing average error of four yards, compared with thirty to forty yards by the others. Despite this, Gibson considered the crew's navigator to be unreliable, and offered F/Sgt Lancaster the choice of replacing him or returning to 57 Squadron. Loyalty was the glue that bonded crews together, and, to his credit, Lancaster refused to ditch his colleague and the crew apparently returned to 57 Squadron on the 17th, although no further mention is made of them in the ORB.

A return to the docks at La Spezia was notified to the Lancaster squadrons of 1, 5 and 8 Groups on the 18th, and 8 Group would also contribute five Halifaxes to the overall force of 178 aircraft. The eighty-nine 5 Group Lancasters included fourteen representing 57 Squadron, which made ready two further aircraft for the crews of F/Sgts Leach and Lovell to take mining in the Mullet garden in the approaches to the port. They departed Scampton together between 20.43 and 20.56 with S/Ls Avis, Leland and Smith the senior pilots on duty, seven sitting on a cookie and a single 2,000 pounder and the others on all-incendiary loads. S/L Leland and crew were close to the French coast when they lost an engine and turned back, and they were joined on the ground soon afterwards by F/L Jenks and crew for the same reason. S/L Avis jettisoned his load into Lake Bourget in the foothills of the Alps after also suffering engine failure, while Sgt Allwright and crew, who were behind schedule as they reached the Alps, abandoned their sortie in the knowledge that they would not reach the target within the allotted time. F/L Roberts dumped his 2,000 pounder to enable him to scale the Alps, on the other side of which the weather was found to be ideal and visibility good. An effective smoke screen partially obscured the town and docks until it drifted to the south to hang over the gulf, leaving the aiming point to be identified visually after a timed run from Palmaria Island to the south. The aiming point was confirmed by red Path Finder TIs, on which the 57 Squadron crews bombed from 7,000 to 9,500 feet between 01.48 and 02.07. The fires were becoming concentrated as they turned away and set course for home, most completely satisfied with their night's work.

While the above was in progress, the crews of F/Sgts Leach and Lovell delivered four mines each into the briefed locations from 4,000 and 5,000 feet at 01.53 and 01.58 respectively. Photographic reconnaissance revealed that the marking and bombing had missed the dockyards to the north-west but had caused extensive damage to the railway station and public buildings in the town centre. F/O Crocker and crew were not at debriefing, having been persuaded by two dead engines to head towards North Africa, where they landed safely at Maison Blanche in Algeria. Malcolm Crocker was an American who had been rejected by his own Army Air Force and had joined the RCAF instead. He had arrived at 57 Squadron on the 8th and would prove himself to be popular and an outstanding crew captain.

Orders were received on the 20th to prepare for another long-range operation that night, this one against the port city of Stettin, situated 640 miles away as the crow flies at the midpoint of Germany's wartime Baltic coast. 5 Group contributed ninety-one Lancasters to the force of 339 aircraft, eleven of them belonging to 57 Squadron, whose crews learned at briefing that the route would take the bomber stream across the North Sea to a point north of Esbjerg on the Danish coast, before traversing Jutland to then head south-east towards the target. A cookie was loaded into each Lancaster and supplemented by either 1,080 x 4lb or 96 x 30lb incendiaries, and these were lifted into the air at Scampton between 21.42 and 21.54 with S/Ls Leland and Smith the senior pilots on duty. The attention of the serviceability gremlins must have been elsewhere on this night as no 57 Squadron aircraft returned early. There were targets, like Duisburg, that seemed to enjoy something of a charmed life, and managed to dodge the worst ravages of a Bomber Command attack, but Stettin was not among them, perhaps because of its location near an easily identifiable coastline. On this night, clear skies and good visibility paved the way for the Path Finders to deliver a perfect marking performance, which was exploited by the main force crews to devastating effect. The Scampton crews arrived to find the city laid out before them with the river, built-up area and the docks clearly defined, and the aiming point marked by green TIs. They carried out their attacks from 7,200 to 14,000 feet between 01.10 and 01.41, and, on return, reported fires raging across the built-up area and the glow from the burning city visible for ninety miles into the return journey. As the homebound crews of P/O P Singer and S/L Smith flew westwards across Denmark, they came under machine gun fire from the ground and the Lancasters sustained extensive damage. There were no casualties among the Singer crew in ED308, but the bomb-aimer and flight engineer in ED411, Sgts Bagley and Bigg respectively, were fatally wounded. ED770 failed to return with the crew of F/L Jenks after it crashed in the target area without survivors and W4254 went missing without trace with the crew of P/O Collins. It was thirty-six hours before a reconnaissance aircraft captured photographs of the still-burning city, and these revealed an area of one hundred acres of devastation across the centre. Local reports confirmed that thirteen industrial premises and 380 houses had been destroyed, and the cost to the Command of this success was twenty-one aircraft, four of them 5 Group Lancasters.

Orders on the 26th signalled a return to the Ruhr and Duisburg, for which a large force of 561 aircraft was assembled, the numbers bolstered by the inclusion of 135 Wellingtons, while 215 Lancasters represented the largest contribution by type. 5 Group was responsible for 105 of them, and 57 Squadron thirteen, which departed Scampton between 23.27 and 00.02 with S/Ls Avis and Smith the senior pilots on duty. They set course for the Dutch coast for the northern approach to the Ruhr, but F/O Wilson and crew had to turn back when the oxygen feed to the rear turret failed. They were the squadron's only "boomerang", leaving the others to reach the target area after approaching from the north-east to find largely clear skies and good visibility. They were guided to the aiming point by red and green TIs and carried out their attacks from 17,000 to 21,800 feet between 02.19 and 02.52 and opinions were divided as to the degree of concentration achieved. A large orange explosion was witnessed to the east of the aiming point at 02.34, but fires had not gained a hold by the time they withdrew, although black smoke was rising through 7,000 feet. Seventeen aircraft failed to return, but only one of these was from 5 Group. Post-raid reconnaissance revealed that the attack had fallen short of the city centre and had been focused around the north-eastern districts under the line of approach, thus sparing Duisburg yet again from the full weight of a Bomber Command heavy raid. Even so, local reports confirmed the destruction of more than three hundred buildings, which represented something of a telling blow upon this target.

Having received back from 617 Squadron the standard Lancasters of the departed C Flight, 57 Squadron now reputedly had on charge a massive thirty-six aircraft. This was possibly as the result of hoarding those out of service with minor repairs while claiming replacements.

The 27th was devoted to the largest mining operation of the war to date, which involved 160 aircraft targeting the waters off the Brittany and Biscay coasts and the Frisian Islands over many hours. Twenty-eight 5 Group Lancasters were detailed, just three of them representing 57 Squadron and containing the crews of P/O P Singer and Sgts Farmer and Glotham, who departed Scampton between 01.54 and 02.10 bound for the Nectarine I garden off the southern Frisians. The visibility was poor, and positions were fixed by Gee, although the Glotham crew managed to secure a visual pinpoint on Ameland before carrying out a timed run. Only the Singer crew provided the details of their run at 2,000 feet at 03.33, and a total of eighteen mines found their way from 57 Squadron bomb bays into the briefed locations. The following night brought an even larger gardening effort involving 207 aircraft, of which forty-one Lancasters were provided by 5

Group, five of them by 57 Squadron. The crews of P/Os Singer and Singer and Sgt Parker were assigned to the Pumpkin garden situated between Denmark's Sams and Serejø Islands in the Kattegat, while the destinations for the crews of F/Sgt Leach and Sgt McCrea were the Hollyhock and Jasmine gardens off Lübeck and Rostock/Warnemünde respectively. They departed Scampton together between 20.48 and 20.58 and all reached the western Baltic, where clear skies and good visibility prevailed as the first three-mentioned pinpointed on either Kullen point or Serejø Island before releasing their mines from 1,500 to 2,000 feet between 23.52 and 00.08. The low height was that of the Parker crew, who shot it out with a flak ship and managed to silence it. F/Sgt Leach and crew delivered their six mines from 3,500 feet at 00.32, while Sgt McCrea and crew brought theirs home after running into adverse weather conditions. Elsewhere, low cloud had been encountered, and the flak had proved to be troublesome, contributing to the loss of twenty-two aircraft, just one of them from 5 Group. This would be the largest-ever loss to result in a single night from mining, but, on the credit side, the 593 vegetables planted represented a new record for one night and would not be surpassed.

F/O Crocker and crew returned from their sojourn in Algeria on the 29th. Essen was posted as the target on the 30th, as attention swung once more towards the Ruhr, and would remain upon it almost exclusively now until well into July. A force of 305 aircraft included 101 Lancasters of 5 Group, of which a dozen were loaded with a cookie and twelve SBCs of 4lb incendiaries at Scampton and dispatched between 23.52 and 00.09 with W/C Hopcroft and S/L Avis the senior pilots on duty. A layer of ice-bearing cloud lay across the bomber stream's path over the North Sea, which most crews negotiated to reach the target, where they were greeted by ten-tenths cloud with tops in places as high as 21,000 feet and red and green Oboe-laid Wanganui flares (skymarkers) identifying the aiming point. Some crews carried out a time-and-distance run from green tracking markers, and all had some kind of flare in the bomb sight, or, at least the glow of one, as they released their loads from 18,000 to 22,500 feet between 02.47 and 03.07. Returning crews reported the glow of fires beneath the cloud and a number of large explosions, but it was impossible to determine whether or not concentration had been achieved, particularly as bombing photos showed only cloud. Post-raid reconnaissance and local reports confirmed a lack of concentration and the liberal distribution of bombs onto ten other Ruhr locations, particularly Bottrop to the north, but 189 buildings were destroyed and 237 severely damaged in Essen, and, importantly, Krupp sites sustained further damage. Among six missing Lancasters was 57 Squadron's ED706, which crashed into the Ijsselmeer some nine miles east-south-east of Amsterdam with no survivors from the crew of Sgt Glotham. As a freshman crew, they were at their most vulnerable during the first six or so sorties and did not have time to gain the experience that might have extended their lives.

May 1943

May would bring a return to winning ways, with a number of outstanding successes and new records as the Ruhr offensive expanded its horizons to include targets other than Essen and Duisburg. The first of these "new" targets was Dortmund, which had been attacked many times before, but not on the scale that it was about to face on the 4th, when the largest non-1,000 effort to date of 596 aircraft was assembled. 5 Group made available 125 Lancasters, of which fourteen were prepared at Scampton and loaded with a cookie and SBCs of 4lb or 30lb incendiaries, before taking off between 21.26 and 21.36 with W/C Hopcroft and S/Ls Avis and Leland the senior pilots on duty. W/C Hopcroft's port-outer engine caught fire as he climbed away and that ended his interest in proceedings. The others pushed on across Holland to enter Germany to the north of the Ruhr and make their way to the eastern end, where they found clear skies, good visibility and only industrial and smoke haze to spoil the vertical view. Yellow Path Finder tracking skymarkers were used as the starting point for a timed run to the aiming point, while the defences responded with many searchlight cones and intense heavy flak, and much evasive action would be required after bombing to vacate the target area intact. The initial Path Finder marking was accurately placed around the city centre, but some of the backing-up fell short, and a decoy site was also successful in luring away a proportion of the bombing. The 57 Squadron crews bombed on red or green TIs from 18,000 to 22,000 feet between 01.02 and 01.39, many leaving a gap of up to ten seconds between the release of the high explosives and incendiaries. On return, Sgt McCrea and crew reported bombing an aerodrome after sustaining damage in an engagement with a night-fighter, during which the rear gunner was wounded, and a challenging return flight had ensued. Others reported many sizeable explosions, including a particularly large on at 01.12, which may have been the one reported by a 50 Squadron crew that threw flame to a height of 2,000 feet and burned for ten seconds. They also described developing fires, the glow from which could be seen, according to some, from 150 miles into the return flight. Post-raid reconnaissance revealed that approximately half of the force had bombed within three miles of the aiming point and had destroyed 1,218 buildings and seriously damaged more than two thousand. Local reports confirmed a death toll of 693 people, which was a record from a Bomber Command attack, but it was not a one-sided affair and the loss of thirty-one aircraft was a foretaste of what was in store for the bomber crews operating over "Happy Valley". Sgt Farmer and crew failed to return in ED390, which crashed without survivors at Brandlecht, south-east of the Münsterland town of Nordhorn on the frontier with Holland, and they were another "sprog" crew to be lost at the start of their tour.

A week-long break from major operations took the Command through to the 12th, when Duisburg was posted as the target for a heavy force of 562 aircraft with ten Oboe Mosquitos to take care of the initial marking. 5 Group was responsible for 119 of the 238 Lancasters, and they would be accompanied by 142 Halifaxes, 112 Wellingtons and seventy Stirlings. 57 Squadron managed to dispatch a record twenty Lancasters from Scampton between 23.45 and 00.08, and the ORB trumpeted this as the largest effort yet by any squadron operating four-engine aircraft. W/C Hopcroft and S/Ls Avis, Leland and Smith were the senior pilots on duty as they climbed away, five crews sitting on ten 1,000 pounders and the remainder on the usual cookie and incendiary combination. Sgt Parker's navigator became unwell during the sea crossing, and when there had been no improvement in his condition as the Dutch close drew near, it was decided to turn back. The others reached the target area guided by yellow tracking flares and found ideal bombing conditions with no cloud and good visibility, which helped the Path Finders to mark with great accuracy and focus. The main force crews were able to identify ground features and exploited the opportunity by producing a display of unusually concentrated bombing. Many of the 57 Squadron crews carried out a timed run from the yellow markers and released their loads onto red and green TIs from 18,000 to 21,000 feet between 02.02 and 02.38, and, at last, the attack proceeded according to plan at this elusive target, which finally succumbed to a devastating assault. Returning crews described a large explosion at 02.30, streets outlined by fire and a highly successful outcome, the best yet witnessed by some, and their impressions were confirmed by photo-reconnaissance, which revealed extensive damage in the city centre and the Ruhrort Rhine docks, the largest inland port in Germany. 1,596 buildings were totally destroyed and the Thyssen steelworks was hit, while dozens of barges and ships were sunk or damaged. Such was the level of destruction inflicted, that Duisburg would now be left in peace for a year. Many crews were absent from debriefing at stations across the Command, and it soon became clear that the success had been gained at the high cost of thirty-four aircraft. The loss rates by type again made interesting reading and confirmed the established food chain, the Lancasters sustaining a 4.2% loss, compared with 8.9% for Wellingtons, 7.1% for Stirlings and 6.3% for Halifaxes.

57 Squadron's ED329 was shot down by a night-fighter on the way home and crashed at Maasniel in southern Holland at 03.05, killing F/O Wilson and all but his bomb-aimer, who was taken into captivity. By this time, ED778 had crashed at Netterden on the outskirts of Emmerich at 02.13, killing five members of the predominantly Canadian crew of F/Sgt Leach RCAF. Four nights hence, while returning from Operation Chastise, 617 Squadron's S/L Henry Maudslay and crew would lose their lives in a crash at Klein Netterden, just half a mile to the south-west. After the war, on his return from a French PoW camp, former soldier, Rolf Feldmann, filed the following report: "The aircraft returned from the Ruhr in the early morning, and was fired upon first by the anti-aircraft battery in the keep. Along the Nierenbergerstrasse and near the harbour there were 2cm anti-aircraft batteries belonging to home flak units, each battery consisting of three guns. The plane turned away, and its rear gunner fired at the battery near the lock. Then all twelve guns were shooting at the plane, and the engines caught fire, after which it crashed and exploded. People said there were seven crew members on board. Our battery was situated on the harbour breakwater, and our fire shaved the poplar trees standing on the harbour. The aircraft was flying at such low level, that we had to aim the guns at a very shallow angle. Reported by Rolf Feldmann." He was referring to the 57 Squadron aircraft, but, over the years, local historians have confused this incident with the Maudslay crash four nights later. Comparing the above report with that filed by Johannes Doerwald, who was decorated for bring down Maudslay's Lancaster, reveals the two incidents to be so at variance that they could not be the same one. Arising out of this was the persistent rumour of a war crime committed against the Maudslay crew by local civilians, who, it is said, arrived on the scene ahead of the police and murdered five members of the crew. The pilot and flight engineer apparently hid and gave themselves up when the police and Luftwaffe arrived to protect them. We know that none from Maudslay's crew could have survived the crash, which leaves us with the possibility, on the basis of "no smoke without fire", that the rumour, which has never been substantiated, relates to 57 Squadron's F/Sgt Leach and Sgt Rees, who alone survived. Remarkably, these were the first survivors from a shot down 57 Squadron Lancaster since the 20/21st of December, and that one was the only previous instance of a survivor since the squadron had operated the type. In other words, from twenty-two missing Lancasters since the middle of October 1942, carrying together a total of 154 crewmen, only four had lived to tell the tale, and one wonders just how many selfless acts of courage had been enacted, never to be related.

On the following night, the squadron contributed a dozen aircraft to a 5 Group force of 124 Lancasters, which, with thirty-two other Lancasters and twelve Halifaxes of 8 Group, would attempt to rectify the recent failure at the Skoda armaments works at Pilsen. A simultaneous raid on the Ruhr city of Bochum was planned, and would involve 442 aircraft from the other groups, and, perhaps, split the defences. The Scampton element took off between 21.29 and 21.39 with

S/Ls Leland and Smith the senior pilots on duty, and lost S/L Smith and crew to an inability to gain height during the North Sea crossing. The others completed the 650-mile outward leg across France and southern Germany to reach the target and find clear skies and good visibility, but with ground haze and a smokescreen to impair the vertical view. The Path Finders dropped yellow and white track markers and red TIs with a fairly good concentration that would have been perfectly adequate over a built-up area, but at a precision target like the Skoda works, they were too scattered to be effective. Bombing by the 57 Squadron crews was carried out from 8,300 to 10,000 feet between 01.20 and 01.28, and the impression was that most of it fell among the TIs. The opinion of returning crews was that, if the TIs had been on the target, the operation had been successful. Sadly, they were found to have missed the factory complex, and most of the bombs had fallen into open country to the north. Some compensation was gained at Bochum, where almost four hundred buildings were destroyed and seven hundred seriously damaged at a cost of twenty-four aircraft, and these were added to the nine Lancasters missing from Pilsen. 57 Squadron posted missing the crews of P/O Haye and Sgt Barker RCAF in ED667 and W4944 respectively, the former falling to the night-fighter of Hptm Herbert Lütje of III./NJG1 and crashing at Albergen in east-central Holland at 00.15. The time suggests that they had abandoned their sortie and were on their way home when the end came. P/O Haye evaded capture, four crew members were taken into captivity and both gunners lost their lives. This was Lütje's second victim of the night, having shot down a 44 (Rhodesia) Squadron Lancaster just sixteen minutes earlier. W4944 was also homebound when accounted for by another night-fighter from III./NJG1, this one flown by Oblt Dietrich Schmidt, who claimed it at 03.44 ten miles south-west of Meppen in sight of the Dutch frontier. The navigator alone survived, and he was taken into captivity.

The above operations proved to be the last major outings for the Path Finders and main force squadrons for nine days, during which period a major expansion would take place within Bomber Command. 57 Squadron carried out both day and night high-level bombing practise on the 15th, during which, W/C Hopcroft managed to attain a staggering 30,000 feet. Since the first crews arrived at 617 Squadron on the 25th of March, they had endured gentle ribbing by their 57 Squadron counterparts for being an "armchair unit", which trained incessantly but did not go to war. Sunday the 16th dawned bright over Scampton and developed into a warm and fine early summer's day with an electric tension that hinted that the armchair days might be over. During the night, lorries had delivered huge oil-drum-shaped bombs hidden beneath tarpaulins and some servicemen and women going about their work during the morning noticed the presence of a tall, white-haired civilian. In the early afternoon, tannoys called various groups to briefing sessions and ground crews swarmed over the strangely-modified Lancasters out on the dispersal pans. The call for the main briefing went out shortly before 16.00 when more than 130 airmen funnelled through the doors of the main block and climbed the stairs to the briefing room to await the arrival of W/C Gibson, G/C Whitworth, AVM Cochrane and the white-haired gentleman, engineer, designer and inventor, Barnes Wallis.

Two of the Type 464 Provisioning Lancasters could not be made ready in time, leaving nineteen to take part in Operation Chastise and one of the crews to miss out was that of P/O Divall, formerly of 57 Squadron. Shortly before 21.30, the five Lancasters of the second wave began taking off, to be followed immediately by nine of the first wave, leaving the five in the third wave on the ground until their departure after midnight. On the following morning, the BBC announced that, during the night, a force of RAF Lancasters had attacked with mines the Möhne, Eder and Sorpe Dams to the south and east of the Ruhr, breaching the first two and damaging the third and that eight Lancasters had failed to return. Two of those missing were the former 57 Squadron crews of F/L "Bill" Astell and S/L "Dinghy" Young, none of whom survived. Astell and crew were outbound and approaching the small towns of Raesfeld and Marbeck when they flew full tilt into an electricity pylon, burst into flames and crashed, while Young and crew were the last to be shot down, almost three hours later, as they crossed the Dutch coast homebound. P/O Geoff Rice and crew had flown so low on approach to the Dutch coast that they bounced off the water, lost their Upkeep weapon, and had to abandon their sortie, lucky, indeed, to have escaped with their lives.

By the time that the next major operation was launched on the 23rd, many main force squadrons had added a third or C Flight, which, in most cases, would eventually be hived off to form the nucleus of a brand-new squadron, as had been the case with 57 and 617 Squadrons. The giant force of 826 aircraft was the largest non-1,000 force to date and surpassed the previous record set three weeks earlier by a clear 230 aircraft. The number of available Lancasters had leapt by eighty-eight, Halifaxes by forty-eight, Stirlings by forty, and Wellingtons by forty-one, and their destination for the second time in the month was to be Dortmund. The entire Command was rested and replenished, and ready to resume the Ruhr offensive, and activity on all participating stations was hectic. 5 Group detailed a record 154 Lancasters, and twenty-four of them were made ready by 57 Squadron at Scampton, where they were loaded with the standard Ruhr load of a cookie and SBCs of 4lb and 30lb incendiaries. They took off between 22.02 and 23.04 with W/C Hopcroft and S/Ls Avis, Leland and Smith the senior pilots on duty and lost the services of F/O Crocker and crew to intercom failure after around an hour. F/L Roberts and crew were within six miles of the target at 00.58, when ED779 went into a steep dive to starboard and lost seven thousand feet before control was regained, by which time the bombs had been jettisoned. The others reached the target area to find clear skies but considerable industrial haze, which, before the advent of Oboe, would have rendered the attack a lottery, but now, the thirteen Path Finder Mosquitos marked the centre of the city accurately, and the Path Finder heavy brigade backed-up to maintain the aiming point with red and green TIs. These could be seen from twenty miles away on approach, as could the yellow track markers assisting the early 5 Group arrivals for their time-and-distance runs. The 57 Squadron crews bombed largely on the clusters of red and green TIs from 18,600 to 22,500 feet between 01.00 and 01.50, observing many explosions and fires, which were merging into a large area of conflagration with thick columns of black smoke rising up through 18,000 feet as they turned away.

Returning crews reported fierce night-fighter activity over the target and on the way home, and this was reflected in the high casualty rate of thirty-eight aircraft, the largest loss of the campaign to date. Almost half of these were Halifaxes and eight were Lancasters, 5 Group posting missing just four crews, among which were those of 57 Squadron's F/O Chivers RAAF and Sgt Leslie in ED707, Frederick II, and ED970 respectively. The former was shot down by the night-fighter of Lt Heinz Grimm of IV./NJG1 at 02.47 and crashed into the Marsdiep, the tidal channel between Den Helder and Texel, and the latter fell to the ace, Major Helmut Lent from the same Luftwaffe unit, and went into the North Sea some twenty-five miles off the Dutch coast at Egmond. Neither crew produced a survivor, but a few bodies eventually came ashore for burial. Post-raid reconnaissance revealed the operation to have been an outstanding success, which had hit mainly central, northern and eastern districts, where almost two thousand buildings had been destroyed, and some important war industry factories had suffered severe damage and loss of production.

The scale of the success was such, that, like Duisburg, this city would remain unmolested by the heavy brigade for a year.

The Ruhr offensive continued with the posting of Düsseldorf as the target on the 25th, for which a force of 759 aircraft was assembled. 5 Group contributed 139 Lancasters, nineteen of them representing 57 Squadron, and they departed Scampton between 22.55 and 23.28 with W/C Hopcroft and S/Ls Leland and Smith the senior pilots on duty. On a night of poor serviceability for the squadron, four crews dropped out because of mechanical problems, a rear turret issue for F/L Reid, cockpit instrument failure for P/O Hodgkinson and engine failure for Sgt Gifford and S/L Smith. S/L Smith jettisoned his load "live" over Haamstede aerodrome on Schouwen Island in the Scheldt before turning back. On arrival at the Dutch coast, some crews were able to observe feverish activity at the target some one hundred miles and thirty minutes flying time away. It lay beneath two layers of thin cloud, and the generally poor visibility impacted the Path Finders' ability to back up the Mosquito-laid TIs to the extent that two red TIs were seen to be thirty miles apart. There were also decoy markers and dummy fire sites operating, which succeeded in causing confusion and prevented a concentration of bombing. The 5 Group crews carried out time-and-distant runs from yellow track markers, before identifying the target visually and by red and green TIs, the 57 Squadron participants bombing from 14,500 to 24,000 feet between 01.44 and 02.26. Post-raid reconnaissance and local reports confirmed that the raid had failed to achieve concentration and had developed into an "old-style" scattering of bombs across a wide area, leading to the destruction in Düsseldorf of fewer than a hundred buildings. Twenty-seven aircraft failed to return, five of them from 5 Group, but all from Scampton returned safely.

During the course of Thursday, the 27th, the King and Queen visited a number of RAF stations, beginning at North Coates before moving on to Binbrook. At 13.00 hours the royal party arrived at Scampton and proceeded to the Officers' Mess for lunch. The seating plan had G/C Whitworth at the centre, flanked on his right by the King and on his left by the Queen. AVM Cochrane sat on the King's right, while to the Queen's left sat G/C Leonard Slee, who had recently completed a tour as 49 Squadron's commanding officer, and in August would move on to lead the Path Finder's 139 Squadron. Gibson sat opposite the King, W/C Hopcroft of 57 Squadron opposite the Queen, and, between them, facing Whitworth, was Wallis. After lunch the party moved outside to the tarmac, where an inspection of the aircrew from 617 and 57 Squadrons began at 14.05. This was followed by an inspection of one aircraft from each squadron complete with air and ground crew, before adjourning to the No 2 hangar crew room, where the models of the dams were on display along with a collection of reconnaissance photographs. Gibson gave a full description of Operation Chastise assisted by the participating crew captains. Wallis was on hand as the royal couple inspected a modified Lancaster with Upkeep, and then the inspection moved on to other sections. At 15.30 the royal party departed Scampton and headed to their final appointment of the day at Digby.

Harris was not yet done with Essen, and the fifth visitation by the bomber force during the campaign had been notified to stations before the royal visits began. A force of 518 aircraft was assembled, of which 133 Lancasters were provided by 5 Group, sixteen of them from Scampton, which took to the air between 21.58 and 22.36 with S/L Smith the senior pilot on duty. They all reached the target to be greeted by six to eight-tenths cloud with tops at 12,000 feet, with tracking flares to guide them in and Wanganui skymarkers gently descending into the cloud tops over the aiming point. The 5 Group crews carried out time-and-distance runs and bombed on white flares and red parachute markers with green stars, those from 57 Squadron from 19,000 to 22,000 feet between 00.45 and 01.30. S/L Smith was the first from the squadron to bomb before release point flares were visible, and the likelihood is that his bomb-aimer was misled by decoy flares. F/L Roberts and crew were on their timed run when, for the second time, ED779 went into a dive to starboard, which was arrested once the bombs had been jettisoned. Returning crews spoke of several large explosions and concentrated fires, and while post-raid reconnaissance revealed that much of the bombing had fallen short, 488 buildings had been destroyed, mostly in central and northern districts, and ten nearby towns reported themselves to be victims of collateral damage. Twenty-three aircraft failed to return, and the Halifaxes again represented almost half of the casualties.

A force of 719 aircraft, including a 5 Group contribution of 129 Lancasters, was assembled on the 29th, to pitch against a new Ruhr target, the conurbation known as Wuppertal, perched on the southern rim of the Ruhr Valley east of Düsseldorf. It consisted of the towns of Barmen and Elberfeld, which were built on the proceeds of the rich coal deposits in the region. The aiming point for this night's attack was the Barmen half at the eastern end, for which the 57 Squadron element of sixteen Lancasters departed Scampton between 22.10 and 22.40 with W/C Hopcroft and S/Ls Leland and Smith the senior pilots on duty. There were three early returns to deplete the squadron's impact, the crews of P/O Hawkins and S/L Smith because of engine failure and F/Sgt Lovell with an unserviceable mid-upper turret. The others negotiated the southern approach to the Ruhr, running the gauntlet of searchlights and flak in the Cologne and Düsseldorf corridor, and were greeted by clear skies over the target with the usual industrial haze extending up to 10,000 feet. The yellow tracking flares clearly identified the final turning-point, and first, concentrated green and then red TIs marked out the aiming point. The 57 Squadron crews carried out their attacks with cookies and incendiaries from 19,000 to 22,000 feet between 00.59 and 01.37, and it was clear to all that something extraordinary was taking place as the built-up area beneath them became a sea of explosions and flames with smoke rising very quickly through 15,000 feet. Post-raid reconnaissance revealed this to be the most awesomely destructive raid of the campaign thus far, which devastated by fire a thousand acres, or around 80% of the built-up area and destroyed almost four thousand houses, five of the six largest factories and more than two hundred other industrial buildings. It would be some time before the human cost could be established, but it is now accepted that 3,400 people lost their lives during this savage Saturday night. The defenders had their say also, and fought back to claim thirty-three bombers, seven of which were Lancasters, three belonging to 5 Group.

During the course of the month, the squadron conducted seven operations and dispatched 121 sorties for the loss of seven Lancasters and crews.

June 1943

June began with rain and mist, and there were no major operations, despite the fact that 5 Group stations were alerted on most of the first ten days, only to be stood down. This kept the Path Finder and main force crews kicking their heels on the ground until the 11th, when Düsseldorf was briefed out to 783 crews. 5 Group was responsible for 162 of the 326 Lancasters, twenty-three of which were loaded with a cookie, four 500 pounders and SBCs of 4lb or 30lb incendiaries each at Scampton and dispatched between 22.07 and 22.48 with W/C Hopcroft and S/Ls Avis, Leland and Smith the senior pilots on duty. P/O Hawkins turned back early because of an unserviceable rear turret and F/Sgt Irwin with engine failure, leaving the others to negotiate static and lightning conditions in towering cloud with tops as high as 23,500 feet as they made their way across the North Sea. The ten-tenths cloud gradually dissipated to leave just small amounts at 2,000, 5,000 and 10,000 feet, dependent upon their time of arrival on final approach to the target. Those in the vanguard of the main force were drawn on by yellow tracking flares from 01.05, and red skymarkers with green stars at 01.16, while those a little further back in the bomber stream were guided on by red and green skymarkers. They carried out time-and-distance runs to the aiming point five minutes away, noting that fires were beginning to build and join together. The Paramatta marking (ground-marking TIs) did not seem to appear until these crews were turning away, but they were clearly visible to the crews in the rear-guard, who described a sea of flames covering a massive area and columns of smoke rising through 21,000 feet. The 57 Squadron ORB provided scant detail, but, as a rough guide, the 44 (Rhodesia) Squadron effort was spread throughout the duration of the raid and attacks were carried out from 18,000 to 22,500 feet between 01.25 and 02.15. The Scampton crews returned home to pass on their impressions to the intelligence section at debriefing, but not all squadrons had fared so well, and, when all aircraft had been accounted for, thirty-eight were found to be missing, a figure that equalled the heaviest loss of the offensive to date. Post-raid reconnaissance revealed an area of fire across central districts measuring eight by five kilometres, and local reports confirmed 8,882 individual fire incidents. More than seventy war-industry factories suffered a complete or partial loss of production, 140,000 people were bombed out of their homes and 1,292 lost their lives. Had it not been for an errant Oboe marker attracting a proportion of the bombing onto open country some fourteen miles to the north-east, the destruction would have been greater.

Beginning with the above operation and for the rest of 1943 and part of 1944, the squadron scribe reverted to the style of record keeping of early 1941, which meant that all details of bombing heights and timings and crew observations were omitted from the Form 541, restricting the information to take-off and landing times, "sortie completed" or "sortie not completed" and the bomb load. The rationale for such paucity of information was probably the amount of time it took the adjutant or designated scribe to compile each operation's details now that the squadron was able as a matter of course to put high numbers of aircraft into the air. That said, other high-volume squadron's managed to hand down a more detailed record.

Bochum would face its second heavy visitation of the campaign on the 12th, and a force of 503 aircraft was made ready for the purpose. 5 Group contributed 165 Lancasters, of which twenty-two were provided by 57 Squadron. They departed Scampton between 22.22 and 22.59 with W/C Hopcroft and S/Ls Avis and Leland the senior pilots on duty but were depleted by four early returns. The crews of W/C Hopcroft, S/L Leland and Sgts Parker and Josling dropped out respectively because of oxygen system, intercom, rear turret and oxygen failure. The remainder carried on to the target, passing over central Holland and entering Germany to the west of Münster, before turning south for a direct run on Bochum, situated between Essen to the west and Dortmund to the east. It is believed that night-fighters were waiting over Dutch airspace and the frontier region, and a number of bombers fell victim at this stage of the operation. According to the superb book, the Bomber Command War Diaries, by Martin Middlebrook and Chris Everitt,

Bochum was completely covered by ten-tenths cloud, but, according to many 5 Group crew reports, they encountered three to six-tenths patchy cloud, and many described almost clear skies and good visibility. The 57 Squadron record is incomplete, but 5 Group crews carried out time-and-distance runs from yellow tracking markers and had green or red TIs in the bombsights as they let their loads go from an average of 20,000 feet between 01.20 and 02.00. Returning crews reported concentrated fires, the glow from which was visible for up to a hundred miles into the return flight. Photo-reconnaissance revealed 130 acres of devastation, backed up by local reports that 449 buildings had been destroyed and more than nine hundred severely damaged at a cost to the Command of twenty-four aircraft, at least nine of which had fallen victim to night-fighters. 57 Squadron posted missing the crew of Sgt Dowding, who were lost without trace in ED668.

Following a night's rest, the Ruhr offensive continued at Oberhausen, a major centre of oil production situated between Duisburg to the west and Essen to the east for which a 197-strong all-Lancaster heavy force was made ready. 5 Group was responsible for 108 of the Lancasters, and 57 Squadron eleven, which departed Scampton between 22.25 and 22.36 with F/L Roberts the senior pilot on duty, and each bomb bay containing a cookie, four 500 pounders and thirteen and a third SBCs of 4lb incendiaries. After climbing out they set course for the Scheldt estuary to bypass Antwerp on their way to the Belgian/German frontier, and on the way, lost the crews of Sgt Piggin to oxygen failure, F/O Wilson to starboard-inner engine failure and F/L Roberts to engine and brake issues, leaving the others to press on to the target area in very bright moonlight over three to ten-tenths cloud with tops in places at 18,000 feet. Tracking flares were drifting above from which to make time-and-distance runs, and the bomb-aimers focused on red skymarkers with green stars and white skymarkers dropped by the six Oboe Mosquitos and the backing-up Path Finder heavy brigade. The attack was carried out from either side of 20,000 feet in the face of intense heavy flak, which continued to chase the bombers out of the target area into the guns of night-fighters, and between them, the defences accounted for seventeen Lancasters, 8.4% of the force. Local reports confirmed that the Wanganui flares had been right over the city centre, where 267 buildings had been destroyed and 584 seriously damaged. ED413 was attacked by four Ju88s, the fire from which killed Sgt Moores' rear gunner, Sgt Haynes.

On the 16th, 1, 5 and 8 Group stations were notified that Cologne was to be the target for that night, for which a force of 202 Lancasters and ten Halifaxes was made ready. They learned at briefings that there would be no Oboe Mosquitos on hand to mark the target, as that role was to be undertaken by the Path Finder Halifax element and six Lancasters employing H2S. 5 Group detailed eighty Lancasters, nine of them at Scampton, which would carry the same bomb load as for the previous operation and took off between 22.14 and 22.26 with S/L Smith the senior pilot on duty. S/L Smith turned back very early because of electrical failure and F/L Roberts dropped out later because of an oxygen system issue, on top of which, the crews of Sgt Parker, P/O Hodgkinson and F/O Whittam were defeated by severe icing conditions over the North Sea, which frosted over the glazing and left them struggling to see their way ahead. This meant that five of 5 Group's early returns involved 57 Squadron crews. The others arrived in the target area to find seven to ten-tenths cloud with tops at 10,000 to 15,000 feet, and green tracking flares from which to make a time-and-distance run to the aiming-point. The Path Finders were late on target, and problems with some of the H2S sets led to sparse and scattered skymarking with solid white flares and reds with green stars. Bombing took place from either side of 20,000 feet and a number of crews witnessed a large orange explosion at 01.08, although, generally, it was not possible to assess the outcome. The impression was that a proportion of the bombing had been concentrated where intended, but that some crews had been lured away by dummy markers, and local reports, which suggested that only around a hundred aircraft had been involved, tended to support this view. Residential districts bore the brunt of the raid, in which 401 houses were destroyed, 13,000 others damaged to some extent, mostly lightly, and sixteen industrial premises and nine railway stations were hit, along with public and utility buildings.

The recent successes in the Ruhr had been aided by the sheer size of the urban areas below, which all but guaranteed that the bombs would hit something useful, even after smoke had obscured the aiming-point TIs. It was a different matter at a small or precision target, however, which would rapidly be enveloped in smoke from the first bombs before the rest of the attacking force had a chance to draw a bead on the aiming-point. When, therefore, an attack was scheduled for the 20th under the codename, Operation Bellicose, against the production site of the Würzburg radar sets, which the enemy was employing very successfully to warn of and intercept Bomber Command raids, a plan was already in place to combat the problem by adopting the oft-used and still-under-development 5 Group time-and-distance method. Briefings actually took place on the day before, when crews learned that the factory was housed in the old Zeppelin sheds at Friedrichshafen, situated on the shore of Lake Constance (Bodensee) on the frontier with Switzerland, and represented a very small target. The plan was to use a designated "Master of Ceremonies" to direct the bombing, much in the manner of Gibson at the Dams, and the officer chosen was the highly experienced G/C Len Slee, the former 49 Squadron commanding officer, with W/C Gomm of 467 Squadron as his deputy. 5 Group was to provide the main force element of fifty-six Lancasters, seven of them from 57 Squadron, with four others from 8 Group's 97 Squadron to provide the marking for the selected crews at the head of the stream. The plan called for the Channel to be crossed at a standard altitude, before descending gradually to 10,000 feet by the time that Orleans was reached, and, thereafter, to fly at between 2,500 and 3,000 feet all the way to the Rhine. After crossing the Rhine, they were to climb to their briefed bombing height of between 5,000 and 10,000 feet for the rendezvous over the north-western shore of Lake Constance, and then circle until receiving the start signal.

The Scampton element took off between 21.42 and 21.50 with S/L Leland the senior pilot on duty, and, in contrast to the previous operation, all would make it to the target on a rare night when not a single aircraft from the entire force turned back, despite encountering electrical storms and having to adjust the briefed course. That said, G/C Slee lost an engine over France, and was forced to drop back into the formation and, at 02.25, hand over the lead to W/C Gomm, who, on arrival at the target under clear skies and in bright moonlight, became concerned about the hostility of the searchlight and light flak defences. In order to reduce the very real risk of heavy casualties, he decided to add five thousand feet to the bombing height, where, unknown to him, the wind was stronger and would push the bombing towards the north-east. The Path Finder element also had little time to climb to the new height, and this caused a slight delay in the opening of the attack. The first TI fell wide of the aiming-point, but the second one was assessed by W/C Gomm to be accurate, upon which he called in the first crews, whose high explosives and incendiaries created the expected smoke and obscured the target. He decided that another TI on the aiming-point might still provide a reference for some crews, but the Path Finders were driven off by the searchlights and light flak and abandoned the attempt. They were then ordered to drop flares along the shore of Lake Constance, to enable the remaining crews to begin their runs from a pre-determined landmark, fly across the lake to the opposite shore, pick up another landmark 2,000 yards from the target, and continue at a constant speed for the requisite number of seconds to cover the distance to bomb release. Employing the Mk XIV bombsight on which 5 Group crews had been training intensively, the bombs were aimed at cascading green TIs and were delivered from medium level. The attack ended at 03.02, and rather than turn for home, the bombers outwitted the waiting night-fighters by continuing on to landing grounds liberated from the Germans in Algeria in North Africa, with the glow from the burning target visible behind them for eighty miles. They landed at Maison Blanche and Blida in what was the first official shuttle operation of the war. Post-raid reconnaissance revealed that a proportion of the bombs had hit the target, causing extensive damage, and there had been no losses among the attacking force.

While these crews were absent from England, a hectic round of four major operations to the Ruhr in the space of five nights began at Krefeld on the 21st, for which a force of 705 aircraft was assembled. 5 Group contributed ninety-two Lancasters, of which thirteen represented 57 Squadron, and they departed Scampton in two sections, the first between 22.50 and 22.53 and the second between 23.16 and 23.26 and F/L Roberts was the senior pilot on duty. Each 57 Squadron Lancaster was carrying the standard Ruhr load of a cookie, four 500 pounders and thirteen and a third SBCs of 4lb incendiaries, almost all of which reached the target area, situated a short distance to the south-west of Duisburg and on the opposite side of the Rhine. Sgt Piggin and crew were attacked close to the target by a night-fighter, which knocked out the rear turret and persuaded them to drop the bombs on a flak position as they headed for home. The others found conditions in the target area to be ideal, with small amounts of thin cloud between 6,000 and 10,000 feet and bright moonlight, which would benefit attacker and defender alike. The Path Finders delivered a near-perfect marking performance, dropping red TIs to cascade and fall in concentrated fashion to clearly identify the city centre aiming-point for the main force crews. Attacks were carried out from an average of 19,000 to 20,000 feet, the first phase either side of 01.40, and the second some thirty minutes later, and crews described a sea of red fire giving off masses of smoke, with one particular jet-black column rising through 18,000 feet as they turned away. All were convinced of the success of the operation, and one crew likened it to the Wuppertal-Barmen raid. There was no hint of troublesome flak or night-fighters, and yet, forty-four aircraft failed to return, the heaviest casualties of the campaign to date, and many of these were lost to the Nachtjagd. Remarkably, only three 5 Group Lancasters were among the missing, including 57 Squadron's W4377, which was homebound when crashing at 02.50 just north of Boxtel in southern Holland with no survivors from the crew of Sgt Kitson. In contrast to the 5 Group casualties, 35 (Madras Presidency) Squadron of the Path Finders lost six of its nineteen Halifaxes. Three-quarters of the bombing photos were plotted within three miles of the aiming-point, and the 2,306 tons of bombs wiped out by fire and blast an estimated 47% of the built-up area. 5,517 houses were destroyed, the largest number to date at a single target, and more than a thousand people lost their lives.

The medium-sized town of Mülheim-an-der-Ruhr, a close neighbour of Duisburg, Oberhausen and Essen, lies around a dozen miles to the north-east of Krefeld, and it was here that the red ribbon terminated on the target maps at briefings across the Command on the 22nd. A force of 557 aircraft was prepared, of which ninety of the Lancasters were provided by 5 Group, a dozen of them representing 57 Squadron. They departed Scampton again in two elements, the first between 22.35 and 22.41 and the second between 23.00 and 23.09 with S/L Smith the senior pilot on duty. F/Sgt Pickett and crew returned early because of an engine problem, leaving the others to make their way via the Scheldt estuary on the southerly route to the Ruhr through the Cologne corridor. They arrived at the target to find small amounts of cumulostratus cloud at between 5,000 and 10,000 feet and red and green TIs clearly defining the aiming-point. The bombing took place from an average 19,000 to 20,000 feet and was delivered in two phases thirty minutes apart roughly between 01.15 and 02.00. The development of a concentrated area of fire ensued, the glow from which was visible from the Dutch coast homebound. Returning crews commented on the intense searchlight and flak response and the number of night-fighters, and reported that Krefeld was still burning from the night before. Local reports confirmed that the town had suffered severe damage, particularly in the northern districts, where 1,135 houses had been destroyed and more than 12,000 others damaged to some extent. The road and telephone communications to Oberhausen had been cut, preventing any passage out of the town other than on foot, and, in fact, some of the bombing had spilled into the eastern districts of Oberhausen, which was linked to Mülheim for air-raid purposes. It was another expensive night for the Command, however, which registered the loss of thirty-five aircraft, with the Halifaxes and Stirlings representing two-thirds of them and suffering a respective loss rate of 7.7% and 11.8%.

While the Path Finder and main force units were enjoying a night off on the 23rd and girding their loins for the next round of the Ruhr offensive, fifty of the 5 Group Lancasters that had landed in North Africa following the Friedrichshafen raid took off with two 97 Squadron Path Finder aircraft to bomb the docks at La Spezia on the way home to England. The 57 Squadron crews took off between 19.43 and 19.50 and arrived in the target area to find clear skies but hazy conditions made worse by a smoke-screen. There appeared to be a degree of confusion in getting the raid started, but a lucky hit on an oil storage facility at Marola resulted in a large explosion at 23.41 just as the main force was running-in, and most crews were able to identify the target visually, thereafter, by red, green and white Path Finder flares. Bombing was carried out in accordance with the instructions of a Master Bomber from an average 10,000 feet either side of midnight, and most returned home to moan about the length of time it had taken for the raid to develop and the poor communications with the raid controller. The authorities seemed happy to claim the destruction of the oil depot and an armaments store and declared the operation to be a success. The crews of P/O Grimwood and P/O Hawkins returned to North Africa, the former having turned back because of engine trouble, while the latter completed the operation but clearly had a reason not to undertake the journey to England. Both would return safely within a few days.

Having destroyed the Barmen half of Wuppertal at the end of May in one of the most devastating attacks to date, it was time to visit the same catastrophe on the western half, Elberfeld, for which a force of 630 aircraft was made ready on the 24th. 5 Group managed to support the operation with 103 Lancasters, thirteen of which were provided by 57 Squadron, and they departed Scampton in two elements between 22.18 and 22.23 and 22.52 and 22.59 with S/L Smith the senior pilot on duty. They adopted the southerly route to the Ruhr via the Scheldt estuary and passed south of Mönchengladbach before running the usual gauntlet of searchlights and flak from the Cologne and Düsseldorf defence zones. The defenders were assisted in this regard by the formation of condensation trails at between 18,000 and 21,000 feet to advertise the presence of the bomber stream. There seemed to be fewer guns firing at them over the target, where small amounts of cloud with tops at 17,000 feet were insufficient to obscure the ground. The 5 Group crews carried out time-and-distant runs from yellow tracking flares until they observed cascading red and green TIs at which to aim their cookies, 500 pounders and assorted incendiaries from an average 19,000 feet. Those arriving at the tail end of the attack, when the built-up area was well-alight, described thick columns of smoke already passing through 19,000 feet and the glow of fires visible from the Dutch coast. Post-raid reconnaissance revealed another massively concentrated and accurate attack, which had reduced to rubble an estimated 90% of Elberfeld's built-up area, including three thousand houses and 171 industrial premises. It had also severely damaged 2,500 houses and dozens of important factory buildings, and the fact that more buildings were destroyed than damaged provided a telling commentary on the conditions on the ground. The number of fatalities stood at around eighteen hundred, and some of the survivors might have been cheered to know that thirty-four bombers, containing 240 of their tormentors, would not be returning to England that night. Remarkably, only two of these belonged to 5 Group. 57 Squadron's ED781 fell victim to the night-fighter of Oblt Wilhelm Telge of Stab II./NJG1 and crashed some five miles north-west of the centre of Liege in Belgium, killing Sgt Fallows and all but his bomb-aimer, who was taken into captivity.

Instructions were received across the Command on the 25th to prepare for the first major attack on the Ruhr city of Gelsenkirchen since 1941, when it had been a regular destination under the Oil Directive. It was home to a number of synthetic oil refineries, including the Nordstern (Gelsenberg A G) plant, which employed the Bergius process, involving the hydrogenation of highly volatile bituminous coal to produce high-grade petroleum products, particularly aviation fuel. 114 Lancasters were made ready on 5 Group stations as part of an overall force of 473 aircraft, and at Scampton, fourteen Lancasters were loaded with standard war load for the Ruhr and dispatched between 22.46 and 23.09 with F/Ls Crocker, Reid and Roberts the senior pilots on duty. There were no early returns as they crossed the North Sea to make landfall on the Dutch coast, before reaching the target area to find ten-tenths stratus lying over the region with tops at 10,000 to 15,000 feet. This would not have been a problem for Oboe, had five of the twelve participating Mosquitos not suffered equipment failures, but their absence caused tracking flares to be late and to drop in the wrong sequence in a somewhat scattered manner, at a time when the crews were contending with an intense flak barrage. Searchlights illuminated the cloud as the 5 Group crews bombed on red flares with green stars from an average 19,500 feet either side of 01.30. A large explosion was witnessed at 01.43, and the glow from the target was visible from the Dutch coast, to which the returning bombers were chased by a large deployment of enemy night-fighters. Post-raid reconnaissance and local reports confirmed that the operation had failed to achieve accuracy and concentration, and, in an echo of the past, bombs had been sprayed all over the Ruhr, leaving Gelsenkirchen largely untouched. Thirty aircraft were missing, and, this time, eight of them were from 5 Group, four alone from 106 Squadron.

57 Squadron posted missing the hugely experienced crew of F/L Reid DFC in ED943, which was shot down by the BF110-G4 night-fighter of Oblt Martin Drewes while homebound and crashed at 02.40 onto the Frisian Island of Texel, killing all eight occupants. Twenty-five-year-old Drewes was actually a member of VII./NJG3 based at Kastrup near Copenhagen but had been loaned to II./NJG1 to operate out of Leeuwarden, the famed "Wespennest" or "wasps' nest" in northern Holland to help relieve the pressure created by the Ruhr offensive. He was operating on this night in tandem with his Staffel Kapitän, Hauptmann Hans-Joachim Jabs, who was vectored by the controller to a 102 Squadron Halifax, which he shot down south of Den Helder. Drewes was given a contact a little further north over Texel and latched onto ED943 before opening fire at sixty yards range from from behind and below. He aimed at the fuel tank between the port engines and

the Lancaster immediately caught fire and descended in a large spiral out to sea before turning back towards Den Hoorn at the southern end of the island. F/L Reid attempted a forced-landing on the beach at De Hors, but the Lancaster was wrecked and consumed by fire and all eight occupants lost their lives. This incident occurred early in the career of Martin Drewes and was his fifth kill in a total that would reach forty-nine by war's end.

A series of three operations against Cologne would span the turn of the month and began on the 28th, when a force of 608 aircraft was assembled, 131 of the Lancasters provided by 5 Group and eighteen by 57 Squadron. They departed Scampton between 22.35 and 23.11 with S/L Smith the senior pilot on duty and began what could be a lengthy climb-out over the station lasting an hour, before setting course and rendezvousing with the rest of the bomber stream. Between 01.32 and 01.55 the crews of P/O Hawkins, F/O Gobbie and F/O Levy returned to Scampton, respectively because of an indisposed pilot, engine trouble and intercom failure, leaving the others to press on to the target area, where they encountered ten-tenths cloud below them at 8,000 to 10,000 feet with good visibility above. The main force crews were unaware that five of the Oboe Mosquitos had turned back and a sixth was unable to drop its skymarkers, and that the six still heading for the target were behind schedule by seven minutes and would be able to provide only intermittent flares. The omens for a successful attack were not good, particularly as drift rendered skymarking the least reliable target marking method, but the main force crews arrived to be greeted by red and white flares and began their bombing runs with green tracking flares ahead. They carried out their attacks from an average of 19,000 feet either side of 02.00 and deduced from the glow beneath the clouds and the presence of smoke rising through them to 15,000 feet that they had contributed to a successful operation. This was confirmed by post-raid reconnaissance and local reports, which provided details of forty-three industrial buildings and 6,374 others completely destroyed, and a further fifteen thousand damaged to some extent. The death toll was put at 4,377, the greatest by far from a Bomber Command attack, and 230,000 others had lost their homes for varying periods. By recent standards, the figure of twenty-five missing aircraft could be considered moderate, but that was no consolation to the individual stations with an empty dispersal pan.

During the course of the month the squadron participated in eleven operations and dispatched 149 sorties for the loss of four Lancasters and their crews.

July 1943

5 Group began the new month by sending a dozen Lancasters to mine the waters around the Frisians on the 1st. The services of 57 Squadron were not called upon until the 3rd, when twenty Lancasters were detailed as part of 5 Group's contribution of 141 to the 653-strong force assembled for the second of the raids on Cologne. They departed Scampton between 22.20 and 23.12 with S/Ls Avis and Smith the senior pilots on duty and headed for the East Anglian coast to begin the North Sea crossing. P/O Hodgkinson and crew were off Lowestoft in ED941 when they hit another aircraft and turned back, and they were joined on the ground at Scampton eight minutes later by Sgt Howe and crew, whose compass had let them down. The others benefitted from the night's favourable conditions to reach the target, which they found clearly visible under two to three-tenths cloud at 8,000 feet and protected by many searchlight cones and a moderate flak defence. Green tracking flares guided the first wave crews to the aiming-point, which the

Path Finders marked with red skymarkers with green stars and red and green ground markers, achieving great accuracy and concentration, while later crews were drawn on for the final one hundred miles by the sight of the city already burning fiercely. The bombing took place on the TIs from an average of 20,000 feet roughly between 01.15 and 02.00 and crews reported the city to be a mass of flames, the glow from which remained visible for 170 miles into the return journey. Some commented on the presence of day fighters over the target, and this was clear evidence of a new tactic being employed by the Luftwaffe.

The newly formed JG300 was operating for the first time, employing the Wilde Sau (Wild Boar) tactics, which was the brainchild of former bomber pilot, Major Hans-Joachim (Hajo) Herrmann. The unit had been formed in June with borrowed standard BF109 and FW190 single-engine day fighters to operate directly over a target, seeking out bombers silhouetted against the fires and TIs. On this night, the unit would claim twelve victories, but would have to share them with the flak batteries, which claimed them also. Unaccustomed to being pursued by fighters over a target, it would take time for the bomber crews to work out what was happening, and, until they did, friendly fire would often be blamed for damage incurred by unseen causes. Post-raid reconnaissance and local reports confirmed another stunningly accurate and concentrated attack, in which twenty industrial premises and 2,200 houses had been destroyed, and 72,000 people bombed out of their homes at a cost to the Command of thirty aircraft, mostly to night-fighters.

The third and final raid of the current series against Cologne was posted on the 8th and would involve an all-Lancaster heavy force of 282 aircraft drawn from 1, 5 and 8 Groups, with six Oboe Mosquitos to carry out the initial marking. 5 Group provided 151 Lancasters, of which nineteen were made ready at Scampton and took off between 22.10 and 22.30 with W/C Hopcroft and S/Ls Avis and Leland the senior pilots on duty. The bomber stream flew through the tops of towering cumulonimbus as they made their way across the North Sea, while over the target, the ten-tenths cloud topped out at around 15,000 feet and concealed the ground from view. However, tracking flares were on hand to guide the main force crews to the aiming-point, where the release-point flares were late, and some crews bombed on e.t.a., before they were deployed. The bombing was carried out from an average of 20,000 feet between in the face of an intense flak barrage, and a number of Lancasters were handed back to their ground crews bearing the scars of battle. A very large orange explosion was witnessed at 01.23, but, otherwise, the cloud prevented a detailed assessment of the outcome. F/L Greig and crew survived several night-fighter attacks over the target, during which the mid-upper gunner, F/Sgt Nutt, sustained severe facial wounds. Greig landed at the earliest opportunity, which turned out to be at Manston in Kent, and the wounded man was rushed to hospital, where he lost his fight for life on the following day.

Post-raid reconnaissance and local reports revealed another highly successful operation, which had caused extensive damage in north-western and south-western districts, where nineteen industrial premises and 2,381 houses had been destroyed. The success cost a modest seven Lancasters, five of them from 5 Group, and among these was 57 Squadron's ED947. The Lancaster crashed on the way to the target, coming down at Evergem, some four miles north-north-west of the centre of Ghent in Belgium, and there were no survivors from the crew of Sgt Lewis. When the dust had settled over Cologne, the local authorities catalogued the destruction over the three raids of more than eleven thousand buildings, and a death toll of almost 5,500 people, with a further 350,000 rendered homeless.

The Ruhr campaign was winding down by the time that Gelsenkirchen was posted across Lancaster and Halifax stations as the target on the 9th, for which a heavy force of 408 aircraft was made ready supported by ten Oboe Mosquitos. Eleven 57 Squadron Lancasters were among the 112 representing 5 Group, and they departed Scampton between 22.01 and 22.27 with no senior pilots on duty. F/O McCrea and crew were not long into the outward flight when engine failure ended their interest in proceedings. The others flew out over ten-tenths cloud, which stretched across the Ruhr at around 16,000 feet and topped out in places at 20,000 feet. The Path Finder skymarkers were several minutes late, partly as a result of a 50% failure rate of the Oboe equipment, while a sixth Mosquito dropped its markers ten miles to the north. The 5 Group crews timed their runs from red and green tracking flares and were over the aiming-point during a thirty-minute period either side of 01.30. They delivered their bombs from an average 20,500 feet onto the Wanganui markers as they drifted into the cloud tops, and the scene was punctuated by the flash of explosions, one particularly large one at 01.40 lighting up the area like day. However, the impression gained by those taking part was that the raid had fallen short of the recent outstanding successes, and this was confirmed by local reports. To those on the ground, it appeared that the attack had been meant for Bochum and Wattenscheid, which received more bombs than Gelsenkirchen, where limited damage occurred in southern districts.

Although two more operations to the region would be launched late in the month, Harris was already planning his next attempt to shorten the war by bombing and was buoyed by the success of the spring offensive. He could look back on the past four and a half months with genuine satisfaction at the performance of his squadrons, and, as a champion of technological innovation, take particular pride in the performance of Oboe, which had been the decisive factor. Although losses had been grievously high, and the Ruhr's reputation as "Happy Valley" well earned, its most important towns and cities had suffered catastrophic destruction. In Britain, the aircraft factories had more than kept pace with the rate of attrition, while the training units both at home and overseas were pouring eager new crews into the fray to fill the gaps. With confidence high in the ability of his Command to destroy almost any target at will, Harris prepared for his next major campaign, the erasure from the map of a prominent German city in a short, sharp series of maximum effort raids to be launched during the final week of the month.

In the meantime, 1, 5 and 8 Groups were alerted to a trip to Italy to attack the city of Turin, for which a force of 295 Lancasters was made ready on the 12th. 5 Group contributed 130 of them, fifteen representing 57 Squadron and departing Scampton between 21.59 and 22.11 with S/L Leland the senior pilot on duty. F/Sgt Heazlewood and crew turned back after their port-inner engine failed, leaving the others to continue on and negotiate icing conditions in a weather front at Amiens in northern France. The remainder of the three-and-a-half-hour outward flight to the foothills of the Alps was undertaken in generally poor weather conditions, but, once over the mountains, matters improved, and the crews were greeted at the target by clear skies and good visibility. The defences performed to their usual poor standard, characterised by ineffective searchlights and inaccurate light flak rising to 15,000 feet. The marking was punctual, accurate and concentrated, inviting the bombing to be carried out from an average 17,000 feet in a thirty-minute window either side of 02.00, and a column of black smoke was observed rising through 12,000 feet as they withdrew. The homeward route had involved a low-level circumnavigation of the Brest peninsula, and many of the thirteen missing Lancasters disappeared without trace into the sea after running into enemy night-fighters in this area. This was the fate of the crew of 44 (Rhodesia) Squadron's famous commanding officer, W/C Nettleton VC, and probably that of 57 Squadron's F/Sgt Pickett RNZAF, who also disappeared without trace in ED861. The crews of Sgt Scott and F/O Levy proceeded on to landing grounds in North Africa rather than risk a return to England in aircraft compromised by technical issues.

Orders were received at Scampton and a number of other 5 Group stations on the 16th to prepare a total of eighteen Lancasters for a "shuttle" operation against two transformer stations in northern Italy and within sight of the Swiss frontier. These raids would follow on the heels of similar ones twenty-four hours earlier against targets near Bologna and Genoa, which had involved Lancasters from 617 Squadron operating for the first time since Operation Chastise. The target for the 57 Squadron crews of W/C Hopcroft, Lt Russell and P/O Grimwood was at Brugherio, situated in the north-eastern suburbs of Milan, and the plan was to land afterwards in North Africa. As each Lancaster was being loaded with a dozen 500 pounders and two SBCs of 30lb incendiaries, the crews were being briefed on the details of the route and the target. The ORB did not record the time of departure, but it would have been some time around 22.30, and ahead of them lay a four-hour outward flight. There were no early returns, and all reached the target area to find clear skies, moonlight and moderate visibility with just some ground haze to spoil the view. W/C Hopcroft attacked the primary target, while the Russell and Grimwood crews were diverted to the secondary objective at Reggio Emilia, believed to be nearer the centre of the city. They all made it safely to Blida and awaited instructions for the return journey.

The above crews apart, the squadron would spend ten nights away from the operational scene after Turin, and such long periods of inactivity had to be filled with training, lectures, sporting activities and performances by Entertainments National Service Association or ENSA, which visited bomber stations to present the most prominent names of stage and screen, including the likes of Gracie Fields, Vera Lynn and George Formby, to hordes of star-struck young men and women who were serving their country. W/C Hopcroft and crew returned from North Africa on the 21st, leaving two crews to follow on in three days' time.

Hamburg had been a regular target for the Command throughout the war to date, and had been attacked, amongst other occasions, during the final week of July in 1940, 1941 and 1942. It had been spared by the weather from hosting the first "One Thousand" bomber raid at the end of May 1942, but Harris, buoyed by his success at the Ruhr, now identified it as the ideal candidate for destruction under Operation Gomorrah, the intention of which was to cause the maximum impact to the enemy's morale in a short, sharp campaign, employing ten thousand tons of bombs. Hamburg's political status was second only to Berlin, and its value to the war effort in terms of ship and U-Boot construction and other war production undeniable, but it suited Harris's criteria also in other respects. Its location close to a coastline aided navigation and made it accessible from the North Sea without the need to spend time over hostile territory, and its relatively short distance from the bomber stations enabled a force to approach and retreat during the few hours of darkness afforded by mid-summer. Finally, lying beyond the range of Oboe, which had proved so decisive at the Ruhr, Hamburg had the wide River Elbe to provide a solid H2S signature for the navigators high above.

The campaign would begin on the night of the 24/25th, for which a force of 791 aircraft was assembled, 143 of the Lancasters provided by 5 Group, and seventeen of these by 57 Squadron. The crews would be aided by the first operational use of "Window", tinfoil-backed strips of paper of precise length, which, when released in bundles into the airstream at a predetermined point, would drift down slowly in vast clouds to swamp the enemy night-fighter, searchlight and gun-laying radar system with false returns and render it blind. The device had actually been available for a year, but its use had been vetoed in case the enemy copied it for use against Britain. It was not realized that Germany had, in fact, already developed its own version called Düppel, which it had withheld for the same reason. The first nine Scampton crews took off between 22.32 and 22.41 led by S/L Smith, and they were followed into the air by the others between 23.05 and 23.19, while 1,150 miles away in North Africa, the crews of 2Lt Russell and P/O Grimwood were on their way to bomb the docks at Leghorn on Italy's Tuscan coast before heading home. They found the aiming-point clearly visible in the light of parachute flares and carried out their attacks from around 15,000 feet shortly before 01.00. It was not possible to determine the precise fall of bombs because of partial cloud cover or, perhaps, smoke, but a number of explosions were observed, and both crews would return safely to Scampton at dawn.

Meanwhile, at a predetermined point over the North Sea, the Hamburg force began to dispense Window, normally a job for the wireless operator, beginning shortly after 00.30, and the effects appeared to be immediate as few fighters rose to meet the approaching bombers. A number of aircraft were shot down over the sea during the outward flight, two of them 103 Squadron Lancasters, but these were off course, and outside of the protection of the bomber stream, and may well have been returning early with technical difficulties. The efficacy of Window was made more apparent in the target area, where the crews noticed an absence of the usually efficient co-ordination between the searchlights and flak batteries, and defence appeared random and sporadic. This offered the Path Finders the opportunity to mark the target by visual reference and H2S virtually unmolested, and, although the red and green TIs were a little misplaced and scattered, they landed in sufficient numbers close to the city centre aiming-point to provide the main force crews with ample opportunity to deliver a massive blow. The 5 Group crews were guided in by yellow tracking flares and red and green skymarkers, and the 57 Squadron participants delivered their loads of a cookie, four 500 pounders and thirteen and a third SBCs of incendiaries onto red TIs from an average height of 19,000 feet either side of 01.30 At debriefing, they reported a successful operation that had left part of the city ablaze with a column of smoke rising through 20,000 feet. Post-raid reconnaissance revealed that a six-mile-long creep-back had developed, which cut a swathe of destruction from the city centre along the line of approach, out across the north-western districts and into open country, where a proportion of the bombing had been wasted. In fact, less than half of the force had bombed within three miles of the city centre during the fifty-minute-long raid, in which 2,284 tons of bombs had been delivered, but, despite that, the city had suffered a telling blow, and fifteen hundred of its inhabitants lay dead. For the Command it was an encouraging start to the campaign, particularly in the light of just twelve missing aircraft, for which "window" was largely responsible.

On the following night, and in the expectation that Hamburg would be covered by smoke, Harris switched his force to Essen, where he could take advantage of the body blow dealt to the enemy defensive system by "window". A force of 705 aircraft included 136 Lancasters of 5 Group, the sixteen at Scampton taking to the air in two sections between 21.45 and 22.28 with S/L Smith the senior pilot on duty. There were seventeen early returns from the 5 Group contingent, and among them were the 57 Squadron crews of F/Sgt McCrea and Sgts Bourdon and Ryrie, who were thwarted respectively by engine trouble, an unserviceable rear turret and a break in the bomb-release electrical circuitry. The others arrived in the target area to be greeted by clear skies, with just the usual ground haze to spoil the vertical visibility and were guided to the aiming-point by yellow tracking flares. The aiming-point itself was marked by red and green TIs, at which the main force crews aimed their bombs from 17,000 to 21,000 feet between 00.33 and 01.15, reporting concentrated fires in a one-and-a-half-square-mile area of the city. LM336 was turning on finals when the port-outer engine caught fire, and the undercarriage collapsed when F/O Gobbie put it onto the runway, but there were no crew casualties. Other returning crews reported two large, red explosions at 00.36 and 00.39, and a column of smoke rising through 20,000 feet as they withdrew to the west. Post-raid reconnaissance confirmed the raid to be another outstanding success against this important war materials producing city, with more than 2,800 houses destroyed, while the complex of Krupp manufacturing sites suffered its heaviest damage of the war to date. Twenty-six aircraft failed to return, and just two of them were from 5 Group.

After a night's rest, a force of 787 aircraft was made ready for round two of Operation Gomorrah, for which 57 Squadron bombed-up and fuelled seventeen Lancasters as part of 5 Group's contribution of 155. They departed Scampton in sections of seven and nine between 22.20 and 22.26 and 22.47 and 23.05 with S/L Smith the senior pilot on duty and lost the services of Sgt Josling and crew to an undisclosed cause. The others pushed on towards Hansastadt Hamburg, crossing the enemy coast over the Schleswig-Holstein peninsula to the north, and finding the target under three-tenths cloud topping out at 4,000 feet. At this stage of the operation, none of those involved had any concept of the events that were to follow their arrival. A previously unknown and terrible phenomenon was about to present itself to the world and introduce a new word "firestorm" into the English language. A number of factors would conspire on this night to seal the fate of this great city and its hapless inhabitants in an orgy of destruction quite unprecedented in air warfare. An uncharacteristically hot and dry spell of weather had left the city a tinderbox, and the spark to ignite it came with the Path Finders' H2S-laid red and green TIs, which fell with almost total concentration some two miles to the east of the intended city-centre aiming-point, and into the densely populated working-class residential districts of Hamm, Hammerbrook and Borgfeld. To compound this, the main force, which had been drawn on to the target by yellow release-point flares, bombed with rare precision and almost no creep-back, and deposited much of its 2,300 tons of bombs into this relatively compact area. The 5 Group squadrons carried out their attacks from an average of 18,000 feet and crews observed many explosions emanating from the sea of flames developing below. Those bombing towards the later stages of the raid observed a pall of smoke rising through 20,000 feet, and the glow of fires was reported to remain visible for up to two hundred miles into the return journey.

On the ground, individual fires began to join together to form one giant conflagration, which sucked in oxygen from surrounding areas at hurricane speeds to feed its voracious appetite. Trees were uprooted and flung bodily into the inferno, along with debris and people, and temperatures at the seat of the flames exceeded one thousand degrees Celcius. The defences were overwhelmed, and the fire service unable to pass through the rubble-strewn streets to gain access to the worst-affected areas. Even had they done so, they could not have entered the firestorm area, and, only after all of the combustible material had been consumed did the flames subside. By this time, there was no-one alive to rescue, and an estimated forty thousand people died on this one night alone. A mass exodus from the city, which would ultimately exceed one million people, began on the following morning, and this undoubtedly saved many from the ravages of the next raid, which would come two nights later. Seventeen aircraft failed to return, reflecting the enemy's developing response to the advantage gained by the Command through "window" and demonstrating that no gain was ever permanent as the balance of power continued to shift from one side to the other for the next year. On landing, EE193's undercarriage collapsed but there were no casualties among the crew of F/Sgt Heazlewood. For a change, it was the Lancaster brigade that sustained the highest numerical casualties on this night of eleven, six of them belonging to 5 Group.

W/C Hopcroft DFC relinquished command of the squadron on the 28th after a highly successful ten-month tenure. He handed the reins to W/C Haskell DFC, who, in contrast, would remain at the helm for just three weeks. Bomber Command's heavy brigade stayed at home that night, while four Mosquitos carried out a nuisance raid on Hamburg, to ensure that the residents' sleep was disturbed. A force of 777 aircraft was put together to continue Hamburg's torment on the 29th, and, this time, 5 Group contributed 148 Lancasters, of which eighteen represented 57 Squadron. They departed Scampton in two sections of nine between 22.20 and 22.28 and 23.20 and 23.28 with W/C Haskell demonstrating good leadership skills by putting himself immediately on the Order of Battle flying as second pilot to the recently promoted S/L Crocker. This suggests that W/C Haskell had no recent operational experience. All from the squadron reached the target, which they found under clear skies and protected only by slight ground haze. The plan was to approach from due north to hit the northern and north-eastern districts, which, thus far, had escaped serious damage, but the Path Finders strayed two miles to the east of the intended track, and dropped their markers just to the south of the already devastated firestorm area. A four-mile creep-back rescued the situation for the Command, by spreading along the line of approach into the residential districts of Wandsbek and Barmbek, and parts of Uhlenhorst and Winterhude. The 5 Group squadrons bombed on yellow, red and green TIs from an average height of 18,000 feet and reported rising smoke at that level and fires visible for two hundred miles into the return journey. It was another massive blow against this proud city, but, as the defenders began to recover from the effects of "window", so the bomber losses began to creep up, and twenty-eight aircraft failed to return home on this night, five of them from 5 Group. 57 Squadron had to post missing two crews, those of P/O Parker and F/Sgt Allwright in ED616 and ED931 respectively, the former brought down by the Hamburg flak to crash at Fuhlsbüttel to the north of the city, suggesting that they were on their bombing run when their lives were snuffed out. The latter was homebound when it fell victim to a night-fighter and exploded, before crashing at Tostedt, a dozen miles south-west of the centre of Hamburg. The navigator alone survived, and he was taken into captivity.

Before the final round of Operation Gomorrah took place, the curtain on the Ruhr offensive was brought down with a raid on the town of Remscheid, situated on the southern edge of the region, about six miles south of Wuppertal, where the main industries were mechanical engineering and tool-making. Up until this point, only twenty-six people had lost their lives in this town as a result of stray bombs, but it was now to face a modest force of 273 aircraft consisting of roughly equal numbers of Lancasters, Halifaxes and Stirlings with nine Oboe Mosquitos to mark out the aiming-point. 5 Group put up thirty-nine Lancasters, four of which were loaded with a cookie and assorted incendiaries at Scampton and took off between 21.59 and 22.02 bearing aloft the crews of W/C

Haskell, F/O Whittam, F/Sgt Gifford and Sgt Moores. They all reached the target area to find clear skies and good visibility and bombed on red TIs from around 18,000 feet, observing the burst of many cookies and a pall of smoke rising through 5,000 feet. They returned home with a lingering red glow in the sky behind them that remained visible as they crossed the enemy coast homebound. It gave promise of another devastated Ruhr town, and it would be left to a post-war bombing survey to establish that a mere 871 tons of bombs had laid waste to around 83% of Remscheid's built-up area, destroying 107 industrial buildings and 3,117 houses. Three months war production was lost, and the town's industry never recovered fully. Fifteen aircraft failed to return, and the Stirling brigade suffered 10% casualties.

During the course of the month, the squadron participated in ten operations and dispatched 138 sorties for the loss of four Lancasters and their crews and an individual crew member.

August 1943

Briefings for the final act of Operation Gomorrah took place on the 2nd, and a force of 740 aircraft was made ready, 128 of the Lancasters provided by 5 Group. 57 Squadron detailed seventeen, the first five of which took off between 23.30 and 23.35 with S/L Smith the senior pilot on duty and a further five got away between 00.01 and 00.10, before LM322 ground-looped in the hands of F/O Hodgkinson, crashed and caught fire, preventing the final six from departing. The crews of S/L Smith and F/L Wilson turned back with engine and rear turret failure respectively, and it appears that P/O McCrea and crew also failed to complete their sortie for an undisclosed reason. The weather conditions were good initially, until 7 degrees East, where a towering bank of ice-bearing cumulonimbus cloud was encountered, which could not be circumnavigated and stretched upwards to 20,000 feet and beyond. Upon entering it, aircraft were thrown around by violent electrical storms, and it was a hugely terrifying experience beyond anything that most crews had ever experienced, with enormous flashes of lightning, thunder, electrical discharges and instruments going haywire. Many crews simply abandoned their sorties and jettisoned their bombs over Germany or into the sea, leaving the remainder to battle through the conditions to reach the target area, which was concealed beneath seven to ten-tenths cloud. While some crews caught a glimpse of the Elbe and isolated yellow and green Path Finder flares, the majority bombed on e.t.a., and on the glow of fires beneath the cloud and the smoke rising through it. Returning crews across the Command were unanimous in reporting an unsuccessful operation, described by some as "pure hell". At debriefing, 44 (Rhodesia) Squadron's S/L Lewis and crew reported bombing an area of incendiary fires and green TIs, with additional red flares with green stars, and this was plotted to be some twenty-five miles due west of Hamburg city centre. Little fresh damage occurred in Hamburg as bombs were sprayed over an area of a hundred miles, but that was of little consequence in view of what had gone before. The Command suffered the relatively heavy loss of thirty aircraft, and some of these had fallen victim to the weather conditions. JA696 failed to return to Scampton, having been brought down on the final leg to the target at Nindorf, some forty miles north of Hamburg, and there were no survivors from the freshman crew of Sgt Browning, who were undertaking their first operation. During the course of the four raids of Operation Gomorrah, the squadron despatched sixty-three sorties, of which fifty-five bombed as briefed and lost three Lancasters.

Italy was now teetering on the brink of capitulation, and Bomber Command was invited to help nudge it over the edge with a short offensive against its major cities. It began with elements of 1, 5 and 8 Groups making ready to attack Genoa, Milan and Turin on the 7th, and, with preparations already in hand for, perhaps, the most important operation of the war to date to be launched in ten days' time, the Turin raid was to be used to test the merits of employing a raid controller, or Master of Ceremonies, in the manner of W/C Gibson during Operation Chastise. The man selected for the job was Group Captain John Searby, currently serving as commanding officer of 83 Squadron of the Path Finder Force, and, before that, Gibson's successor as commanding officer of 106 Squadron. Scampton was not to be involved as 5 Group detailed seventy-eight Lancasters divided between Genoa and Milan, and it is believed that all 197 aircraft reached their respective targets after flying out in excellent weather conditions. At Genoa, the visibility was good enough for the crews to pick out ground features like the docks and seaplane base, before bombing on green TIs, and a large orange explosion was observed by some at around 01.40. The glow of fires remained visible for a hundred miles into the return flight and many crews returned with an aiming-point photograph. Just two aircraft were missing, and, although the Master Bomber experiment at Turin was not entirely successful, experience was gained which would prove useful for the forthcoming Operation Hydra.

The rest of the heavy brigade remained inactive until the 9th, when a force of 457 Lancasters and Halifaxes was made ready for an operation that night against Mannheim. 57 Squadron prepared sixteen Lancasters as part of a 5 Group contribution of 143, and they departed Scampton between 22.57 and 23.29 with W/C Haskell and S/L Crocker the senior pilots on duty. After climbing out, they headed for the rendezvous point over Reading, before exiting England via Beachy Head on course for the French coast at Boulogne. W/C Haskell and crew turned back early because of an unserviceable rear turret, leaving the others to make their way across Belgium on a direct track to the target to be greeted by a five-tenths layer of broken cloud at 4,000 feet and eight-tenths at 10,000 feet. Despite this, the visibility was fair, and the yellow skymarkers and green TIs were sufficient to provide a reference for the bomb-aimers. The 5 Group Squadrons carried out their attacks from an average 18,000 feet either side of 02.00 and all but two returned home to report a number of very large fires but a generally scattered raid. In fact, according to local reports, 1,316 buildings had been destroyed, forty-two industrial concerns had lost production, and more than fifteen hundred fires of varying sizes had required attention.

Nuremberg was posted as the target on the 10th, for which a force of 653 aircraft was assembled, 128 of the Lancasters provided by 5 Group. 57 Squadron briefed sixteen crews while their Lancasters were being loaded with a cookie and mix of 4lb and 30lb incendiaries and sufficient fuel and reserves for the 1,300-mile round-trip. Take-off was safely accomplished between 21.40 and 22.17 with W/C Haskell and S/L Smith the senior pilots on duty, and, after climbing out and forming up, they set course for Beachy Head on the Sussex coast to follow a route similar to that of the previous night. For the second operation running, ED827 DX-Z returned early, this time with the crew of S/L Smith and for an undisclosed reason. The others arrived in the target area to find conditions also reflecting those of twenty-four hours earlier with eight to ten-tenths cloud at 12,000 feet. The Path Finders had prepared a ground-marking plan, and there were no release-point flares to draw the head of the main force on, but the green TIs on the ground were visible to most, as were the fires for those arriving later. Returning crews reported a good concentration of fires, the glow from which remained visible for 150 miles into the return journey. Post-raid reconnaissance and local reports confirmed that the city had sustained much housing and industrial damage in mostly central and southern districts, and a death toll of 577 people was evidence of the intensity of the bombing. 57 Squadron's ED992 crashed at Rummelsberg to the south of Munich and there were no survivors from the eight-man crew of F/L Wilson.

During the course of the 12th, two forces were prepared for a return to Italy that night, one of 504 Lancasters and Halifaxes to attack Milan, and the other of 152 Stirlings, Halifaxes and Lancasters to target Turin. 5 Group contributed 130 Lancasters to the former, of which eighteen represented 57 Squadron and departed Scampton between 21.20 and 21.47 with W/C Haskell and S/Ls Crocker and Smith the senior pilots on duty. The route would take the bomber stream via Selsey Bill to Cabourg on the Normandy coast, and then south-east in a straight leg across central France to the northern tip of Lake Bourget, to cross the Alps and skirt southern Switzerland before the final run-in on the target. This represented a round-trip of some sixteen hundred miles, which all but F/Sgt Gifford and crew would complete after they suffered a starboard-outer engine fire. They arrived at the target under clear skies with just ground mist to spoil the view and bombed visually or on yellow flares and green TIs from an average 18,000 feet either side of 01.30. Large fires were observed surrounding the aiming-point in the city centre, and a thick column of black smoke rising through 20,000 feet as they turned away, and, with the glow in the sky remaining visible for 150 miles into the return flight, crews were confident of success. Local reports, though short on detail, confirmed that four important war-industry factories had sustained serious damage during August, and most of it probably occurred on this night, as did the majority of the 1,174 fatalities in the city in 1943.

Milan would face two further attacks before the Command's interest in Italy ceased for good, and the first of these was posted on the 14th, for which 1, 5 and 8 Groups put together a force of 140 Lancasters. Fifty-nine of them represented 5 Group, with 57 Squadron providing just six, which departed Scampton between 21.25 and 21.29 with the recently posted-in F/L Dunn the senior pilot on duty. They all reached the target under clear skies and in good visibility aided by a brilliant moon and Path Finder route markers and found the marking with green TIs to be accurate and concentrated. This was exploited by the main force crews, who delivered their loads from an average of 15,000 feet and observed many fires to take hold as they turned away. The glow from the burning city remained visible on the horizon for a considerable distance into the return flight.

There was to be no respite for Milan as a force of 199 Lancasters was made ready later, on the 15th, for a return that night that would be the last for main force Lancasters over Italy. 57 Squadron provided ten of the eighty-five 5 Group Lancasters, and they took off from Scampton between 20.20 and 20.29 with S/Ls Crocker and Smith the senior pilots on duty. Each was accompanied by a second pilot, S/L Crocker having the Scampton station commander, G/C Davies, alongside him and S/L Smith the recently arrived F/L Paterson. As the bomber stream entered northern France, night-fighters were waiting to pounce and succeeded in bringing down five Lancasters, three from 61 Squadron and two belonging to 467 Squadron. Among the latter was the highly popular squadron commander, W/C Gomm, who was on the twenty-fourth sortie of his second tour. His loss would be the bitterest possible blow to the squadron and the entire Bottesford community. The main force crews reached the target to find clear skies and were guided to the aiming-point by green Path Finder flares over lake Bourget. Haze and smoke hung over the city from the previous night to spoil to an extent the vertical visibility, but the Path Finders marked the city-centre aiming-point with green TIs, and these were bombed to good effect from an average of 16,000 feet. On return to Scampton at 04.47, JA896 overshot the runway and crashed, killing P/O Smithers RAAF and the other three crew members in the front section and injuring the wireless operator and both gunners. The rear gunner, F/Sgt Haskins RAAF, lost his fight for life a few hours later. Returning crews were confident that they had been part of an effective raid, but no report came out of the chaotic city to confirm or deny.

The final raid of the war on an Italian city was carried out by 154 aircraft of 3 and 8 Groups against Turin that night. A successful raid was claimed at the modest cost of four aircraft, but many of the participating Stirlings were diverted on return and did not reach their home stations in time to be made ready for the night's highly important operation, for which a maximum effort had been planned. This would deplete the available number of Stirlings by sixty and heap an even greater responsibility upon the rest of the force to complete the job at the first attempt.

Since the very beginning of the war, intelligence had suggested that Germany was researching into and developing rocket technology, and, although scant regard was given to the reports, photographic reconnaissance had confirmed the existence of an establishment at Peenemünde at the northern tip of the island of Usedom on the Baltic coast. The activities there were monitored through Ultra intercepts and surreptitious reconnaissance flights, and the V-1, known to the photographic interpreters at Medmenham because of its wingspan as the "Peenemünde 20", was captured on a photograph. The brilliant scientist, Dr R V Jones, had been able to gain vital information concerning the V-1's range, which would ultimately be used to feed disinformation to the enemy, largely through the double agent "Zigzag", otherwise known as Eddie Chapman. Unfortunately, Churchill's chief scientific adviser, Professor Lindemann, or Lord Cherwell as he became, steadfastly refused to give credence to the existence and feasibility of rocket weapons and held stubbornly to his viewpoint even when presented with a photograph of a V-2 on a trailer, taken by a PRU Mosquito in June 1943. It required the combined urgings of Duncan Sandys and Dr Jones to persuade Churchill of the urgency to act, and Operation Hydra was planned for the first available opportunity, which occurred on the night of the 17/18th.

Earlier in the day, the USAAF 8th Air Force had carried out its first deep-penetration raids into Germany to attack ball-bearing production at Schweinfurt and the Messerschmidt aircraft plant at Regensburg, and, to the shock of its leaders, had learned the harsh lesson that unescorted daylight raids in 1943 were not viable. The folks at home would not be told that sixty B17s had failed to return. It was vital that the Peenemünde installation be destroyed, ideally, at the first attempt, and a force of 596 aircraft and crews answered the call. 5 Group contributed 117 of the 324 Lancasters, with Scampton making ready sixteen, and the rest of the force was comprised of 218 Halifaxes and fifty-four Stirlings.

The operation had been meticulously planned to account for the three vital components of Peenemünde, the housing estate, where the scientific and technical staff lived, the factory buildings and the experimental site. Each was assigned to a specific wave of aircraft, which would attack from medium level, with the Path Finders bearing the huge responsibility of shifting the point of aim accordingly. After last minute alterations, 3 and 4 Groups were given the first mentioned, 1 Group the second, and 5 and 6 Groups the third. The whole operation was to be overseen by a Master of Ceremonies (referred to hereafter as Master Bomber), and the officer selected for this hazardous and demanding role was G/C Searby of 83 Squadron, who, as already mentioned, had stepped into Gibson's shoes at 106 Squadron after Gibson was posted out to form 617 Squadron. Searby's role was to direct the marking and bombing by VHF, and to encourage the crews to press on to the aiming-point, a task requiring him to remain in the target area and within range of the defences throughout the attack. In an attempt to protect the bombers from the attentions of enemy night-fighters for as long as possible, eight Mosquitos of 139 Squadron were to carry out a spoof raid on Berlin, led by the previously mentioned highly experienced G/C Slee. In the expectation of encountering drifting smoke as the last wave on target, the 5 Group crews were instructed to employ their time-and-distance approach to the aiming-point and had practiced this over a stretch of coast near the Wainfleet bombing range at the mouth of the Wash in Lincolnshire, progressively cutting the margin of error from one thousand to three hundred yards.

The 57 Squadron element took off between 21.40 and 22.04 with W/C Haskell and S/Ls Crocker and Smith the senior pilots on a night when many squadron commanders elected to put themselves on the Order of Battle. S/L Crocker and P/O Heazlewood returned early for undisclosed reasons, but the overall early-return rate was lower than normal, suggesting that crews had taken to heart the importance of the operation. The various groups made their way individually to a rendezvous point some ninety minutes flying time or three hundred miles from the English coast and sixty miles from Denmark's western coast, where they became a stream. Darkness had fallen as they crossed the North Sea, and twenty miles short of landfall over the southern tip of Fanø island, south of Esbjerg, windowing began in order to simulate a standard raid on a northern or north-eastern city. Southern Denmark was traversed by the Lancaster brigade at 18,000 feet, twice the altitude required for the attack, but, worryingly, in a band of cloudless sky under a bright moon. They adopted an east-south-easterly course and began to shed altitude gradually during the 240-mile run to the target a little over an hour away, and, at the rear of the stream, the 5 Group crews focused on the island of Rügen, the ideal starting point for their time-and-distance run to Peenemünde, which lay some fifteen miles beyond to the south-east.

The initial marking of the housing estate went awry, and some target indicators fell onto the forced workers camp at Trassenheide, more than a mile south of the intended aiming-point. Many of the 3 and 4 Group bombs fell here, inflicting grievous casualties on friendly foreign nationals, who were trapped inside their wooden barracks. Once rectified, however, the attack proceeded according to plan, and several important members of the technical staff were killed. The 1 Group second-wave crews encountered strong crosswinds over the narrow section of the island where the construction sheds were located, but this phase of the operation largely achieved its aims, and they were on their way home before the night-fighters arrived from Berlin, having been attracted by the glow of fires well to the north. On arrival at Rügen, the 5 Group crews began their timed run to the experimental site, where they encountered the expected smoke, before delivering their mix of high explosive bombs onto green TIs from around 6,000 to 8,000 feet either side of 01.00. They and the 6 Group Halifaxes and Lancasters then ran into the night-fighters, which proceeded to take a heavy toll of bombers both in the skies over the target, and on the route home towards Denmark. Twenty-nine of the forty missing aircraft came from this third wave, seventeen of them belonging to 5 Group and twelve to 6 Group, which represented a loss rate for the Canadians of 19.7%. Among the missing was the eight-man crew of W/C Haskell DFC, who disappeared without trace in ED989, Frederick III. 619 Squadron also lost its commanding officer, W/C

McGhie, and 467 Squadron its stand-in commander, S/L Raphael, while 426 Squadron RCAF posted missing W/C Crooks, all from the final wave. Many returning crews brought home aiming-point photographs, even though the time-and-distance method was found to have been not entirely effective. They praised the work of the Path Finders and the Master Bomber and post-raid reconnaissance revealed the raid to have been sufficiently effective to delay the V-2 development programme by a number of weeks, and, ultimately, to force the manufacture of secret weapons underground. The flight testing of the V-2 was eventually withdrawn eastwards into Poland, beyond the range of Harris's bombers, and thus, the attempt to nullify Peenemünde as a threat had been achieved.

On the 19th, acting W/C Fisher was posted in from 5 Group HQ to assume command of the squadron. Born in western Australia in March 1917, Hurtle "Bill" Fisher had joined the RAF in 1939 and was still under training when war broke out. Initially posted to 185 Squadron, a training unit, he joined 49 Squadron at Scampton in November 1940 and immediately demonstrated outstanding qualities as a Hampden pilot. He was awarded the DFC in November 1941 after completing twenty-seven sorties and the citation stressed his press-on spirit and determination to hit the target. He rose quickly through the ranks and arrived at 5 Group HQ as a squadron leader to work in Air Operations, during which period he authored an operational handbook for 5 Group.

The Ruhr city of Leverkusen was posted on the 22nd as the target for a heavy force of 449 Lancasters and Halifaxes with 8 Group Oboe-Mosquito to provide the initial marking. The aiming-point was to be a factory belonging to the infamous I G Farben chemicals company, which was engaged in the development and production of synthetic oil and employed slave labour at all of its factories across Germany, including 30,000 from the Auschwitz concentration camp, where it had built a plant. One of the company's subsidiaries manufactured the Zyklon B gas used during the Holocaust to murder millions of Jewish victims. 57 Squadron made ready fourteen Lancasters in a 5 Group contribution of 108, and they departed Scampton between 21.10 and 21.37 with F/L Paterson the senior pilot on duty. After climbing out, they headed for the Belgian coast at Knokke, to follow a well-worn route to the southern Ruhr, which would require them to pass through the searchlight and flak belt near Cologne that was guaranteed to provide a hot welcome. The crews of F/Sgt Parker and F/O Levy returned early through undisclosed causes, while the remainder made it safely through the narrow searchlight and flak corridor to reach the target, situated on the eastern bank of the Rhine between Düsseldorf to the north and Cologne to the south. Ten-tenths cloud topped out as high as 18,000 feet and blanketed the area and Oboe-equipment failures forced most crews to bomb on e.t.a., in the absence of markers. Eventually, the glow of fires came to their aid to provide a reference as the raid developed, although a small number of crews spotted green TIs on the ground and aimed for them. Bombing was carried out by the 5 Group Squadrons in the face of intense flak from an average of 18,000 feet from midnight onwards for at least forty minutes. The glow of fires and the flash of explosions was initially the only confirmation of something happening under the cloud, until a column of smoke was observed to be rising through 12,000 feet. Local reports would reveal that up to a dozen neighbouring towns had been hit, Düsseldorf suffering the destruction of 132 buildings. F/L Paterson and crew survived a brush with a FW190 and claimed it as damaged.

Harris had long believed that the key to ultimate victory lay in the destruction of Berlin, the seat of the Nazi government and the symbol of its power. On the 23rd, orders were received on stations across the Command to prepare for a maximum effort that night against Germany's capital city, which had not been visited by the heavy brigade since the end of March. The crews, of course, could not know that this was to be the first of an eventual nineteen raids on the "Big City" in a campaign which, with an autumn break, would drag on until the following spring. It was a campaign that would test the resolve of the crews to the absolute limit, whilst also sealing the fate of the Stirlings and the Mk II and V Halifaxes as front-line bombers. There are varying opinions concerning the true start date of what became known as the Berlin offensive or the Battle of Berlin, some commentators believing these first three operations in August and September to be the start, while others point to the sixteen raids from mid-November. However, there was little doubt in Bomber Command circles that this was it, a fact demonstrated by the comments in numerous squadron ORBs, which speak of the "long-awaiting Berlin campaign" and similar sentiments.

There would be a Master Bomber on hand for this operation, and the officer chosen was Canadian W/C "Johnny" Fauquier, the tough, grizzled and popular onetime bush pilot and frequent brawler, who was enjoying his second spell as the commanding officer of 405 (Vancouver) Squadron, now of the Path Finder Force, and formerly of 4 Group. The route had been planned to take the bomber stream to a rendezvous point over the North Sea, before crossing the Dutch coast near Haarlem on course to enter Germany between Meppen to the north and Osnabrück to the south. After passing to the south of Hannover, they were to head to a turning point south-east of Berlin, where they were to turn sharply to port to adopt a north-westerly course across the city centre, and, after bombing, to pass out over the Baltic coast and make for the Schleswig-Holstein peninsula. Finally, seventeen Mosquitos were to precede the Path Finder and main force elements to drop route markers at key points in an attempt to keep the bomber stream on track.

A force of 727 aircraft was assembled, of which 124 Lancasters represented 5 Group, eighteen of them belonging to 57 Squadron, which departed Scampton between 20.00 and 20.26 with S/L Crocker the senior pilot on duty. After climbing out, they joined the bomber stream over the North Sea, losing the services of F/O Pratt and F/Sgt Parker and their crews to undisclosed causes on the way. Those of the main force that reached the target area found clear skies and moonlight, but the Path Finders had been unable to identify the aiming-point in the centre of the city, a result of the inherent difficulties of interpreting the H2S images over such a massive urban sprawl. They released their TIs over the southern outskirts instead, prompting many main force crews to cut the corner and approach the city from the south-west rather than south-east, which would result in the wastage of many bomb loads in open country and on outlying communities. The 57 Squadron crews each delivered their cookie and incendiaries visually and on red and green TIs from an average of 19,000 feet either side of midnight in the face of intense searchlight activity and moderate flak. Returning crews reported large explosions and many fires, the glow from which remained visible for at least 140 miles, and a pall of smoke had already risen to meet them as they turned towards the north-west. Curiously, only a few crews commented on hearing the Master Bomber and finding his instructions helpful. A new record of fifty-six aircraft failed to return, twenty-three Halifaxes, seventeen Lancasters and sixteen Stirlings, representing a percentage loss rate respectively of 9.1, 5.1 and 12.9, which perfectly reflected the food chain when all three types operated together. Berlin experienced a scattered raid, but, because of the numbers attacking, extensive damage was caused, a little in or near the centre, but mostly in south-western residential districts and industrialized areas a little further east. 2,611 buildings were reported to have been destroyed or seriously damaged, and the death toll of 854 people was surprisingly high, caused largely, perhaps, by a failure to heed the alarms and go to the assigned shelters.

Orders were received on the 27th to prepare for an operation that night against Nuremberg, for which a force of 674 aircraft ultimately lined up for take-off in mid-evening. 5 Group contributed 140 Lancasters, the nineteen at Scampton taking to the air between 21.00 and 21.36 with F/Ls Gobbie and Paterson the senior pilots on duty. After climbing out, they headed for the French coast, and, once there, followed the line of the frontier with Belgium until crossing into Germany south of Luxembourg on course for the target, where clear skies and intense darkness prevailed. The Path Finders had been briefed to check their H2S equipment by dropping a 1,000 pounder on Heilbronn, and some crews complied, while others, it seems, experienced technical difficulties. The initial marking was accurate, but a creep-back developed, which the backers-up and the Master Bomber could not correct, and this resulted in many bomb loads falling into open country, while others hit Nuremberg's south-eastern and eastern districts. The 57 Squadron crews aimed at green TIs from an average of 19,000 feet from around 00.30 and gained an impression of a fairly concentrated and accurate attack, which produced many fires. ED827 crashed on landing at Scampton at 04.17 and was damaged beyond repair but P/O Heazlewood and crew walked away apparently unscathed. The incident blocked the landing strip and eleven crews had to be diverted. At debriefing, crews described searchlights and night-fighters as numerous, and this was confirmed by the failure to return of thirty-three aircraft, eleven of each type, which again confirmed the vulnerability of the Stirlings and Halifaxes when operating alongside Lancasters. The loss rate on this night was 3.1% for the Lancaster, 5% for the Halifax and 10.6% for the Stirlings. 57 Squadron's W5008 failed to return with the crew of F/O Levy, from which only the bomb-aimer survived in enemy hands after coming down in southern Germany.

Remarkably, Scampton was still a grass airfield, but the increasing tonnage of bombs demanded the laying of concrete runways and 57 Squadron bade farewell on the 28th to move twenty-six miles to the south-east to a brand-new station hewn out of the farmland in the Lincolnshire Fens at East Kirkby. 617 Squadron moved to Coningsby two days later, and when Scampton reopened in October 1944, it would be under the banner of 1 Group. Later, on the day of the move, ED946 took off from Swinderby at 12.58 on a training flight in the hands of Sgt Josling and crew, apparently without being fuelled up. Both inboard engines cut, and the Lancaster crash-landed a mile from the airfield at 13.01, without injury to the occupants. Navigator, S/L Vivian DFC, was posted to the squadron from Scampton on this day and would assume the role of navigation leader.

The twin towns of Mönchengladbach and Rheydt were posted as the targets for a two-phase operation on the 30th, and it would be the first major attack for both of them. Situated some ten miles west of the centre of Düsseldorf in the south-western Ruhr, they would face an initial force of 660 aircraft of four types, in what, for the crews, was a short-penetration trip across the Dutch frontier and a welcome change from the recent long slogs to eastern and southern Germany. The plan called for the first wave to hit Mönchengladbach, before a two-minute pause in the bombing allowed the Path Finders to head south to mark Rheydt. 57 Squadron made ready fourteen Lancasters as part of a 5 Group contribution of 138, and divided them between the two waves, the first departing Scampton between 23.32 and 23.38 and the second between 23.45 and 00.11 with S/L Crocker the senior pilot on duty. F/O Duff and crew returned early because of engine failure, leaving the others to reach the target, where they encountered good visibility above the seven to ten-tenths cloud at 8,000 feet. A near-perfect display of target-marking by Oboe Mosquitos delivered red and green flares, which the main force crews focused on to bomb with scarcely any creep-back. The 57 Squadron element carried out their bombing runs from an average 18,500 feet from around 02.00 onwards, and on return reported many fires, the glow from which could be seen from the Dutch coast homebound. Photo-reconnaissance confirmed a highly accurate and concentrated attack, which destroyed more than 2,300 buildings in the two towns, 171 of them of an industrial nature, along with 869 residential properties. Twenty-five aircraft failed to return, and Halifaxes narrowly sustained the highest numerical casualties.

The month ended with preparations for the second of the Berlin operations on the night of the 31st, for which 622 aircraft were made ready, more than half of them Lancasters, 129 of them provided by 5 Group. 57 Squadron loaded fourteen of its own with a cookie and incendiaries each and dispatched them between 20.01 and 20.44 with F/Ls Dunn, Gobbie and Paterson the senior pilots on duty. The route on this night took the bomber stream on an east-south-easterly heading across Texel to a position between Hannover and Leipzig, before turning to pass to the south-east of Berlin and approach the city-centre aiming-point on a north-westerly track. The return leg would involve a south-westerly course to a position south of Cologne for an exit over the French coast, but despite the attempts to outwit the enemy night-fighter controller, he would be able to predict to some extent where to concentrate his fighters. The crews of F/L Gobbie, F/O Munday and P/O Stevens abandoned their sorties for undisclosed reasons, leaving the remainder to press on, and, for the first time, report the use by the Germans of "fighter flares" to mark out the path of the bombers to and from the target. The Path Finders encountered five to six-tenths cloud in the target area, and this combined with H2S equipment failure and a spirited night-fighter response to cause the markers to be dropped well to the south of the planned aiming-point. The main force crews became involved in an extensive creep-back, which would stretch some thirty miles into open country and outlying communities. The 5 Group crews reported up to eight-tenths thin cloud and bombed on red and green TIs from an average of 18,500 in a thirty-minute slot to around midnight, observing many fires over a wide area. It was noted by some that two groups of green TIs were ten miles apart, and both attracted attention from the main force. The outcome of the raid was a major disappointment, brought about by woefully short marking and a pronounced creep-back, and resulted in the destruction of just eighty-five houses, a figure in no way commensurate with the effort expended and the loss of forty-seven heavy bombers. The percentage loss rates made alarming reading at Bomber Command HQ, the Lancasters with an acceptable and sustainable 3%, the Halifaxes with 11.3% and the Stirlings with 16%.

While the above operation was taking place, ENSA presented a concert starring Gracie Fields, the Rochdale "lass" who was one of the most popular singers and actresses in Britain. The performance was held in a hangar at Bottesford and was attended by guests from neighbouring stations, with senior officers present including the 5 Group Air-Officer-Commanding, AVM Cochrane. Despite the absence of so many on operational duties, an estimated 1,500 people attended and enjoyed a wonderful evening with excellent catering, which continued for the more distinguished guests in the mess.

During the course of the month the squadron participated in twelve operations and dispatched 170 sorties for the loss of six Lancasters, four crews and five crew members.

September 1943

Probably as a result of the heavy losses recently incurred by the Halifaxes and Stirlings, an all-Lancaster force of 316 aircraft would conclude the current series of operations against the "Big City" on the 3rd. 5 Group detailed 121, of which fourteen were provided by 57 Squadron and departed East Kirkby between 19.29 and 19.46 with no senior pilots on duty. P/O Stevens and crew returned early because of engine and turret heating issues, while the others rendezvoused with the bomber stream over the North Sea and crossed the Dutch coast over the Den Helder peninsula, before adopting a direct course of 350 miles, which took them north of Hannover to Brandenburg, some thirty-five miles short of the target. Long, straight legs were rarely employed because of the risk of interception by the Luftwaffe, but the forecast heavy cloud with tops at up to 22,000 feet accompanied the stream all the way from the Dutch coast to the target area and helped to keep the enemy at bay. The Path Finders had been briefed to use H2S to navigate their way via the region's lakes to the city centre aiming-point, but the cloud miraculously dispersed in time to leave clear skies and allow the Path Finders to drop ground-marking TIs rather than the less reliable skymarkers. The first TIs fell right over the aiming-point, before others crept back for between two and five miles along the line of approach from the west. Fortunately, the backers up maintained the marking as the main force Lancasters came in in a single wave, and, although much of the bombing fell short of the city centre, most of it landed within the city boundaries, principally into the largely residential districts of Tiergarten, Wedding, Moabit and Charlottenburg and the industrial Siemensstadt, where much useful damage occurred and caused loss of war production. The 5 Group Squadrons carried out a time-and-distance run from yellow track markers and bombed on red and green TIs from an average 20,000 feet from around 23.15 onwards. Many fires were observed, which appeared to be merging as the bombers turned towards the north for a return route that would intentionally violate Swedish airspace. Four Mosquitos laid spoof route marker flares well away from the actual track to mislead the night-fighters, but, in the absence of the poorer performing Halifaxes and Stirlings, twenty-two Lancasters failed to return, almost 7% of those dispatched. 57 Squadron's JA914 crashed on the northern side of the Grosser Wünsdorfer See, a lake some twenty miles south of Berlin, and there were no survivors from the crew of P/O Grindley RAAF, who had been commissioned on the previous day.

Whether by design, or as a result of the losses sustained, Berlin was now shelved for the next ten weeks, while Harris sought other suitable targets, of which there were many. He would shortly begin a four-raid series against Hannover stretching over a four-week period, but, first, he focussed on southern Germany, beginning on the 5th with the twin cities of Mannheim and Ludwigshafen, which face each other from the East and West Banks respectively of the Rhine. The plan was to exploit the creep-back phenomenon that attended most large operations, by approaching the target from the west, and marking the eastern half of Mannheim, with the expectation that the bombing would spread back along the line of approach across central and western Mannheim and into Ludwigshafen. A force of 605 aircraft was assembled, which included 108 Lancasters of 5 Group, eleven of them at East Kirkby loaded with a cookie each and a mix of 4lb and 30lb incendiaries. They took off between 19.38 and 20.09 with F/Ls Dunn and Paterson the senior pilots on duty, and, after climbing out, set course for Beachy Head and the Channel crossing. It was not an outstandingly good night for serviceability as ten 5 Group crews returned early, those of F/Sgt Evans, P/O Piggin and F/O Perrers to East Kirkby because of oxygen supply and engine failures. The others made it all the way in favourable weather conditions to find clear skies over the target, where the Path Finders performed at their absolute best. After first observing red and yellow markers, the 5 Group crews had green TIs in their bomb sights as they let their loads go from an average 18,000 feet from 23.00 onwards and all reported hitting them. Those arriving towards the later stages of the raid were drawn on by the burgeoning fires fifty miles ahead, and a number of large, red explosions were observed at 23.12, 23.23 and 23.27, the last of which was followed by a purplish-red mushroom of fire. Searchlights were numerous, but the flak negligible, and it was the abundance of night-fighters that posed the greatest risk to life and limb, although most of the East Kirkby crews appeared to avoid any contact. Black smoke was rising through 15,000 feet as the bombers withdrew to the west, and the glow from the burning cities was visible for 150 miles into the return journey, which thirty-four aircraft would fail to complete. Thirteen Lancasters, an equal number of Halifaxes and eight Stirlings were missing, and the percentage loss rates continued to tell the same story. Local reports confirmed that both Mannheim and Ludwigshafen had suffered catastrophic destruction, with almost two thousand fires in the latter alone, 986 of them classed as large. Mannheim's reporting system broke down completely, and little detail emerged of this raid, although it would recover in time for the next assault in fewer than three weeks' time.

Munich was posted as the target on the 6th, for which 57 Squadron made ready nine Lancasters as part of the ninety-two-strong 5 Group element in an overall force of 257 Lancasters and 147 Halifaxes, the Stirling brigade made conspicuous by its absence. The East Kirkby crews were airborne between 19.52 and 20.12 with F/L Dunn the senior pilot on duty and S/L Vivian flying with the crew of F/O Josling. Each Lancaster carried a similar bomb load and adopted the same initial route as for the previous night and there were no 57 Squadron early returns. Conditions over the Bavarian capital city were not ideal, with cloud varying between three and nine-tenths with tops at 16,000 feet, although some ground features, like the river Isar, could be identified and the red, yellow and green TIs observed. The 57 Squadron crews were among those carrying out a timed run from the Ammersee, located twenty-one miles away to the south-west, and bombed the northern aiming point from an average 19,500 feet shortly after 23.30. A large number of fires was observed to be grouped around the markers, but an accurate assessment was not possible, and local reports would suggest that the attack had been scattered across southern and western districts. The searchlights were ineffective because of the cloud, but large numbers of night-fighters were again evident, and sixteen aircraft failed to return, thirteen of them Halifaxes, a percentage loss rate of 8.8, compared with 1.2 for the Lancasters.

5 Group largely left the war to the other groups for the ensuing two weeks, during which period, Italy's unconditional surrender was announced on the 8th, while, that night, attacks were carried out against coastal batteries at Le Portel near Boulogne under Operation Starkey, a kind of rehearsal for the invasion. On the 9th, W/C Fisher and his crew were sent to 1664 Conversion Unit to begin Lancaster training and would return a week later fully qualified to add their names to the Order of Battle. Industrial and railway installations in France were targeted in mid-month, when only 617 and 619 Squadrons were in action on behalf of 5 Group, first on the night of the 15/16th, when the former sent eight Lancasters to attack the raised earthen banks of the Dortmund-Ems Canal at a point south of the twin aqueduct section near Ladbergen. Five of them failed to return, including the one containing the crew of P/O George Divall, who had departed 57 Squadron in April and had trained for Operation Chastise but not taken part. They all lost their lives when their

Lancaster crashed in flames on the banks of the Mittelland Canal after sustaining flak damage. On the following night, small elements from the two squadrons combined to attack the Antheor viaduct in southern France. What had been known as RAF Base Scampton since the "Base" system had been adopted in May, was redesignated 52 Base on the 16th, and, with Scampton out of commission for a year, included the stations at Fiskerton and Dunholme Lodge.

It was not until the commencement of the series of raids on Hannover that 5 Group, as a whole, was roused from its slumber. The irony of such long layoffs was, that despite occupying the most dangerous jobs in the fighting services, aircrew personnel grew listless and bored when left to kick their heels, attend lectures and take part in PT, and, no doubt, cheered when the tannoys called them to briefing on the 22nd. They learned that they were to be part of a force of 711 aircraft to attack the ancient city of Hannover, situated in northern Germany midway between the Dutch frontier and Berlin. As highlighted before, the city was a major centre of war production and was also the location of seven Nazi concentration camps, although, this was not known to the Allies at the time. According to Martin Middlebrook and Chris Everitt in Bomber Command War Diaries, the first two operations produced concentrated bombing, but mostly outside of the target, while only the third one succeeded in causing extensive damage, which, if the figures are to be believed, seem to be massively out of proportion. The author contends that the reports of the crews after the first two operations suggest strongly that the damage to Hannover was accumulative over the first three raids and did not result from just one, as will be explained in the following narrative. The telling feature is, perhaps, that no reports came out of Hannover to corroborate the testimony of the crews on the first two raids, although post-raid reconnaissance by the RAF after the second one did show that some of the bombing had fallen into open country, and the Path Finders did admit to at least one poor performance.

57 Squadron prepared a twenty-one Lancasters, which took off between 18.40 and 19.22 with S/L Smith the senior pilot on duty, and beside him in the cockpit as second pilot S/L Heward. Having climbed out over East Kirkby, they joined up with the other 135 participants from 5 Group for the 430-mile outward leg and none turned back early, all reaching the target area, where good visibility prevailed but stronger-than-forecast winds played their part in pushing the marking and bombing towards the south-east. S/L Smith and crew bombed a last resort target, but we are not told where and why. The other 57 Squadron crews carried out their bombing runs from an average of 19,000 feet from around 21.30 onwards, aiming at red and green TIs and dodging the intense searchlights and heavy flak, which was bursting at 18,000 feet. W4948 was heading towards East Kirkby on return when it was intercepted south-south-east of Louth by an enemy intruder at 00.43 and shot down. The flight engineer and bomb-aimer alone had time to take to their parachutes, while P/O Duff RAAF and the other occupants, including both RAAF gunners, perished in the crash and subsequent fire. Some returning crews reported a line of fires developing from west of Hannover to east, with smoke rising through 14,000 feet, while others claimed that fires ran from the aiming-point in a north-north-westerly direction across the city, but all were unanimous, that the raid had been highly successful, and that the glow of fires was still visible from the Dutch coast, a distance of two hundred miles. Twenty-six aircraft failed to return, twelve of them Halifaxes, which, again, sustained the highest numerical losses, and, this time, at 5.3%, even exceeded the loss rate of the Stirling.

Let us now examine the claim that the main weight of bombs fell two to five miles south-south-east from the city centre, and that the operation largely failed. Firstly, two to five miles in any city means that the bombing fell within the boundaries, and, therefore, within the built-up area. Secondly, the majority of crews, if not all, reported a highly successful raid with fires right across the city, smoke rising to 14,000 feet as they left the scene and the glow visible from the Dutch coast. It is true that crews were very frequently mistaken in their belief that an attack had been successful, but the evidence on this occasion would seem to confirm their testimony. Decoy fire-sites do not produce a glow visible from a distance of two hundred miles, or sufficient volumes of smoke to reach bombing height during the short duration of a raid and be dense enough to be visible at night.

On the 23rd, and for the second time in the month, Mannheim was posted as the target for that night, and would face a force, which, at take-off, numbered 628 aircraft, 139 of them 5 Group Lancasters. Twenty of these were made ready at East Kirkby and took off between 18.56 and 19.16 with S/Ls Heward and Smith the senior pilots on duty. F/Sgt Evans noticed early on that he lacked full aileron and rudder control and had no choice but to abandon his sortie, leaving the others to join the bomber stream and push on across France and into southern Germany, where they encountered largely clear skies and good visibility. At the head of the stream, the Path Finders had marked out the northern districts, which had not been hit so severely during the previous operation. The marking was accurate and concentrated, allowing the 5 Group crews to attack on red, green and yellow TIs from an average of 18,000 feet either side of 22.00. Later bombing spilled over into the northern fringe of Ludwigshafen and out into the nearby towns of Oppau and Frankenthal, where much damage resulted. Returning crews reported that smoke had reached around 6,000 feet as they turned away, and that the glow of fires remained visible for 150 miles into the return journey. Thirty-two crews were absent from debriefing, and, this time, eighteen of them were in Lancasters, compared with seven each for the Halifaxes and Stirlings. This provided a somewhat topsy-turvy and unusual loss-rate of 5.7%, 3.6% and 6% respectively. Ten 5 Group Lancasters failed to return and three empty dispersal pans at East Kirkby told their own stories, although news of the fate of the missing crews would take time to filter through from the Red Cross. DV201 had come down in the general area of the Ruhr killing F/Sgt Austen and all but the bomb-aimer, who was taken into captivity. JA875 crashed on the south-western extremities of the city of Worms, some ten miles north-west of Mannheim, killing P/O Bourdon RCAF and two others and delivering the survivors into enemy hands. LM336 had the misfortune to be hit by flak as it flew at low-level over the north-eastern suburbs of Paris at 01.00 and crashed on fire into the city with fatal consequences for P/O Hogan RCAF and his crew. It was an unhappy night for the Dominion members of the squadron in particular, which lost six Canadians and two Australians from their number. Post-raid reconnaissance and local reports revealed that 927 houses and twenty industrial premises had been destroyed in Mannheim, and that the I G Farben factory in Ludwigshafen had sustained serious damage.

A force of 678 aircraft was assembled for Hannover on the 27th, 5 Group contributing 141 Lancasters, of which eighteen were made ready by 57 Squadron at East Kirkby. They took off between 19.23 and 19.48 with F/Ls Eggins and Whittam the senior pilots on duty and climbed out over the station before setting course through ice-bearing cloud for the North Sea. 5 Group registered eleven early returns and among them was F/Sgt Evans and his crew, who were defeated by the failure of their oxygen system, while others in the bomber stream found instruments freezing up in the continuing poor weather conditions over the North Sea. The remainder pressed on in the wake of the Path Finders, who were unaware that the weather forecasts on which their performance would be based, were incorrect. The result of that would be to push the marking some five miles from the city centre towards the north of the city, but, at least, the weather improved markedly over Germany to present the crews with clear skies at the target. The 5 Group squadrons delivered their cookies and 4lb and 30lb incendiaries mostly on green TIs from an average of 20,000 feet from around 22.00 onwards, and crews observed many fires with smoke rising to 15,000 feet. At debriefing they again reported the glow of fires visible from the Dutch coast, and confidence in the success of the operation was unanimous across the Command, giving lie to the claim that little damage resulted. Post-raid photos did reveal many bomb craters in open country, but the fire and smoke evidence did not support decoy fire-sites, and no local report was forthcoming to shed further light. The loss of thirty-eight aircraft was probably something of a shock, but, at least, common sense returned to the statistics to re-establish the status-quo after the topsy-turvy outcome of the Mannheim raid. Seventeen Halifaxes, ten Lancasters, ten Stirlings and one Wellington failed to return, giving loss-rates for the four-engine types of 9% for the Stirling, 7.3% for the Halifax and 3.2% for the Lancaster. P/O Hargrave and crew landed at Waterbeach and set off to return to East Kirkby during the following afternoon. Eyewitnesses at East Kirkby were watching ED941 approach to land and saw both port engines cut, before the Lancaster crashed on the north side of the airfield, killing the pilot, flight engineer and navigator. The four survivors were apparently unhurt.

The month ended with an operation against Bochum in the central Ruhr on the 29th, for which a heavy force of 343 aircraft was assembled made up of 213 Lancasters and 130 Halifaxes with nine Oboe Mosquitos to provide the initial marking. 5 Group contributed 111 of the Lancasters and 57 Squadron fourteen, which departed East Kirkby between 18.09 and 18.35 with F/L Paterson the senior pilot on duty. P/O Stevens turned back when his navigator became unwell and P/O Tansley and crew bombed an aerodrome on Texel as a last resort target before also curtailing their sortie. The others arrived at the Dutch coast guided by two route-marker flares at 20,000 feet, and after a two-and-a-half-hour outward flight, up to an hour of which was consumed by the climbing-out process, they established their positions visually in good visibility. The aiming-point was marked by the Path Finders with green TIs and the bombing was carried out by the 5 Group squadrons from an average 19,500 feet either side of 21.00 in the face of a strong searchlight and moderate flak defence. Some returning crews described the target as a mass of flames, with smoke rising rapidly to meet them, while local reports confirmed the destruction of 527 houses, with 742 others seriously damaged. Among nine missing aircraft was 57 Squadron's JA910, which was outbound at 19,000 feet when shot down by Oblt Fritz Lau of III./NJG1 and crashed at 21.37 near Raalte in central Holland. The entire crew of P/O Wangler took to their parachutes and were soon in enemy hands.

During the course of the month, the squadron carried out seven operations and dispatched 107 sorties for the loss of seven Lancasters, five complete crews and eight other crew members.

October 1943

The start of October was a busy time for the Lancaster squadrons, which would be called upon to participate in six major operations in the first eight nights. The month's account was opened at Hagen, a town at the eastern end of the Ruhr on the 1st, for which a moderately sized heavy force of 243 Lancasters was drawn from 1, 5 and 8 Groups. 5 Group contributed 125 aircraft, fourteen of them representing 57 Squadron, and they were each loaded with a cookie and mix of incendiaries before departing East Kirkby between 18.24 and 18.50 with F/L Eggins, Hodgkinson and Whittam the senior pilots on duty. They flew out over Skegness aiming for Egmond on the Dutch coast, to then skirt the northern edge of the Ruhr as far as Werl, to the north of the now famous Möhne reservoir, from where they would turn sharply to the south-west to run in on the target. They arrived to find ten-tenths cloud with tops up to 12,000 feet in places and red and green Oboe-laid skymarkers to aim at and carried out their attacks from an average 18,500 feet from around 21.00 onwards. Returning crews reported a column of black smoke rising through the clouds and described a large bluish-green explosion at 21.03, the glow of fires beneath the cloud and an effective Path Finder performance. Only two Lancasters failed to return in exchange for the usual housing damage, and, according to local sources, the destruction of forty-six industrial firms, among them a manufacturer of accumulator batteries for U-Boots, and this would have an impact on U-Boot production.

Munich was posted as the target for 294 Lancasters from 1, 5 and 8 Groups on the 2nd, 5 Group briefing its 113 crews to adopt the time-and-distance method of bombing. 57 Squadron made ready fifteen Lancasters at East Kirkby and sent them on their way between 18.38 and 19.02 with S/L Crocker the senior pilot on duty. The plan was to make landfall in the Dunkerque region, before traversing France to enter Germany south of Strasbourg, and all from 57 Squadron reached the target area after an outward flight of some three-and-a-half hours. They encountered cloud over the Wörthsee, situated some fifteen miles west-south-west of the centre of Munich, which was the starting point for the time-and-distance run. The skies over the city were clear of cloud, but the marking was scattered and led to most of the early bombing falling into southern and south-eastern districts. The 5 Group crews were unable to establish a firm fix on the Wörthsee, and this would lead to a creep-back of up to fifteen miles along the line of approach. They bombed on red and green TIs from an average of 18,500 feet and intense, concentrated fires were reported along with fierce night-fighter activity. 57 Squadrons DV235 failed to return with the crew of P/O Clements RCAF after crashing in southern Germany without survivors and was one of six missing from 5 Group's ranks. Returning crews suggested that the raid appeared to be concentrated on the eastern side of the city, and local authorities reported that 339 buildings had been destroyed.

Kassel, the industrial city located some eighty miles to the east of the Ruhr, had been an occasional target since the summer of 1940, and would receive two visits from the Command during the month. The first was posted on the 3rd, for which a force of 547 aircraft was assembled consisting of 223 Halifaxes, 204 Lancasters and 113 Stirlings. 5 Group supported the operation with ninety-two Lancasters, of which nine were made ready at East Kirkby and took off between 18.44 and 18.58 with F/Ls Dunn and Paterson the senior pilots on duty. F/O Munday's mid-upper gunner became unwell forcing an early return, but the others reached the target area to find largely clear skies with thick ground haze. The Path Finder H2S "blind" markers overshot the planned aiming-point, and, because of the haze and, possibly, decoy markers, the backers-up, whose job was to confirm their accuracy by visual means, were unable to correct the error. The 5 Group crews identified the target visually and by green TIs and bombed from an average 19,000 feet either side of 21.30, reporting on their return what appeared to be a good concentration of fires and a pall of smoke rising to meet them. In fact, the main weight of the attack had fallen onto the western suburbs, where the Henschel aircraft and tank factories and the Fieseler aircraft plant were hit, but a stray bomb load had also detonated an ammunition dump at Ihringshausen, situated close to the north-eastern suburb of Wolfsanger, which was left devastated by the blast witnessed by many crews at 22.06. Twenty-four aircraft failed to return, fourteen Halifaxes, six Stirlings and four Lancasters, which gave a loss-rate of 6.3%, 3.2% and 2.9% respectively.

The busy schedule of operations was to continue at Frankfurt on the 4th, for which a force of 406 aircraft was made ready. The American confidence in the ability of its forces to deliver daylight attacks on military and war production targets in Germany had been shaken by the high loss rates, which were not sustainable. Since the first Hannover raid, a small number of 8th Air Force B17s had been flirting with night raids alongside their RAF colleagues, and this night would bring their final involvement. 5 Group detailed ninety-five Lancasters, of which a dozen would represent 57 Squadron, and they departed East Kirkby between 17.53 and 18.13 with S/L Heward the senior pilot on duty. They had to follow a somewhat circuitous route, which departed England over the Sussex coast and tracked across Belgium as if heading for southern Germany, before swinging to the north-east and passing to the west of Frankfurt for the final run-in of around eighty miles. This added significantly to the mileage but avoided the flak hotspots from the Dutch coast and north of the Ruhr. F/L Gobbie and crew returned early because of an unserviceable supercharger, leaving the others to reach the target after a four-hour outward flight. Frankfurt was found to be clear of cloud, and the Path Finders produced a masterful marking performance to leave the city at the mercy of the main force element. The 5 Group crews bombed on red and green TIs from an average 18,500 feet and witnessed a highly-concentrated attack that left the eastern half of the city and the docks area a sea of flames. A large red explosion was observed at 21.37, which threw flames up to 3,000 feet, and smoke was rising through 8,000 feet as the bombers turned away, some crews reporting the glow from the burning city to be visible for 120 miles into the homeward leg. The success was gained at the modest cost of ten aircraft, half of which were Halifaxes.

The hectic first week of the month concluded with an operation against Stuttgart, for which a force of 343 Lancasters was drawn from 1, 3, 5, 6 and 8 Groups on the 7th. A new weapon in the Command's armoury was introduced for the first time in numbers on this night with the participation of a night-fighter-communications-jamming device called "Jostle". It required a specialist operator in addition to the standard crew of seven, who, though not necessarily a German speaker, could recognise the language, and, on hearing it, jam the signals on up to three frequencies by broadcasting engine noise over them. At 101 Squadron, where the device was being pioneered, it was referred to as ABC or Airborne Cigar, and, once proved to be effective, ABC Lancasters would be spread throughout the bomber stream for all major operations, whether or not 1 Group was otherwise involved. The Lancaster would also carry a full bomb load reduced by 1,000lbs to compensate for the weight of the equipment and its operator. 5 Group put up 128 Lancasters, of which twenty were made ready at East Kirkby and took off between 20.10 and 20.29 with W/C Fisher and S/L Heward the senior pilots on duty, with S/L Crocker acting as second pilot to the commanding officer on his first Lancaster sortie. It was a night to forget for 57 Squadron as the crews of P/Os Howe, Stevens and Walton, F/O Munday, F/L Dunn and Sgt

Fearn failed to complete the outward leg for a variety of reasons from engine trouble to icing, and only P/O Stevens and crew found a suitable last-resort target for their bombs at Amiens-Glisy aerodrome. They remainder flew out over France and reached the target area to find ten-tenths cloud at 10,000 feet, which concealed the ground from view and led to the Path Finders employing H2S. They established two areas of marking, which resulted in bombs falling in many parts of the city from the centre to the south-west, the 5 Group squadrons bombing from an average 19,500 feet from around midnight onwards. The 57 Squadron crews returned safely to report their impressions of a scattered attack, which cost a remarkably modest four aircraft. Whether or not the presence of the radio-countermeasures Lancasters was responsible could not be certain, but it was a promising start, and would lead, ultimately, to the formation of the RCM-dedicated 100 Group in November.

The third raid of the series on Hannover was posted on the 8th, for which a force of 504 aircraft was duly assembled, eighty-four of them belonging to 5 Group. 57 Squadron made ready fourteen Lancasters, which took off between 22.36 and 22.53 led by four pilots of flight lieutenant rank, and, after climbing out, set course for the northern tip of Texel, to cross northern Holland and pass south of Bremen on their way to the target area. P/O Smith and crew turned back with engine trouble, leaving the rest to arrive in the target area under largely clear skies and observe red and green TIs marking out the city-centre aiming-point. They bombed from an average 19,000 feet, watching as fires began to take hold, and it soon became clear as they retreated westwards, that the fires were developing into a serious conflagration. Curiously, despite the claim by some commentators that this was the one successful raid of the series, there was no mention of the glow being visible from a considerable distance, as had been the case with the first two operations. This time a local report did emerge, which described heavy damage in all districts except for those in the west, with a large area of fire engulfing the central districts. A total of 3,932 buildings was destroyed, and thirty thousand others damaged to some extent, with a death toll of 1,200 people. These statistics seem somewhat excessive for a single operation by fewer than five hundred aircraft, particularly in the absence of the kind of crew reports common to the first two raids, and this adds weight to the author's contention, that the damage was accumulative over the three operations. Twenty-seven aircraft failed to return, but there were no unaccounted-for empty dispersal pans at East Kirkby.

The Path Finder and main force heavy squadrons would effectively stand down now for a period of ten days, while 8 Group Mosquitos took the war to Germany. Lectures, training and sporting activities filled the time, and all-ranks dances were very popular. The crews were, no doubt, relieved, when the lull in operations came to an end on the 18th with a call on Lancaster stations to attend briefings. The wall map revealed Hannover as the target for the fourth and last time in this series, and the crews learned that this was to be an all-Lancaster affair involving 360 aircraft. 5 Group provided 143 of them, twenty-one made ready by 57 Squadron, two of which would contain crews from 207 Squadron. They departed East Kirkby between 17.12 and 17.47 with S/Ls Crocker and Heward the senior pilots on duty, the former flying as second pilot to mentor the crew of F/Sgt Homewood. There were no early returns to East Kirkby during the North Sea crossing, which terminated with landfall over Texel, after which the bomber stream continued on an easterly track across Holland aiming for Cloppenburg, and thence Nienburg and Celle, before turning to the south-west to run in on the target close to the Misburg oil refinery. They remained unmolested by the defences until encountering a nest of night-fighters on crossing the frontier into

Germany, and at least thirteen aircraft were brought down during the ensuing forty-five minutes that encompassed the approach and withdrawal phases. A layer of eight to ten-tenths cloud hung over Hannover with tops at 12,000 to 15,000 feet, and these conditions made it difficult for the Path Finders to establish the aiming-point. It resulted in them dropping both sky and ground markers, which lacked concentration, and led to a scattering of the effort. The 5 Group crews bombed mostly on red and green TIs or on release-point flares from an average of 20,000 feet, and a colossal explosion was observed at around 20.19. The strong night-fighter presence dissuaded crews from hanging around to assess the outcome further, and the impression of those returning was of a scattered attack. F/Sgt Grimbley and crew were on their maiden operation and were attacked by a BF109 as they left the target. EE197 sustained extensive damage from cannon and machine-gun fire, which left both gunners wounded, and the rear turret wrecked, despite which, its occupant, Sgt Cowham, refused to leave his station and drove off two subsequent fighter attacks aided by the mid-upper gunner. It was established later that most of the bombs had fallen into open country, a disappointment compounded by the loss of eighteen Lancasters. The four raids on Hannover had cost the Command 110 aircraft from 2,253 sorties, a loss rate of 4.9%, but much of the city now lay in ruins and would receive no further attention for a year, until a new oil offensive brought it back into the firing line.

The first major attack of the war on the eastern city of Leipzig was planned for the 20th, and an all-Lancaster force of 358 aircraft representing 1, 5, 6 and 8 Groups assembled. 5 Group was responsible for 140 Lancasters, and 57 Squadron nineteen, which took off from East Kirkby between 17.22 and 17.36 with S/L Heward the senior pilot on duty. Atrocious weather conditions were encountered outbound, with a towering front of ice-bearing cumulonimbus east of Hannover extending beyond 20,000 feet, and this persuaded many crews to turn back as engines began to falter and ice-accretion destroyed lift. The crews of P/O Shewan and F/Sgt Edwards were among sixteen from 5 Group to turn back early, both with unserviceable rear turrets, while the rest pushed on in the face of almost insurmountable weather conditions to reach the target after a three-and-a-half-hour outward flight. Having arrived, they then encountered seven to ten-tenths cloud with tops at between 14,000 and 20,000 feet, which prevented the Path Finders from establishing and marking the aiming-point, and condemned the crews to bomb on e.t.a., on fires glimpsed through the cloud or on scattered skymarkers. The 5 Group crews carried out their attacks from an average of 21,000 feet from around 21.00 onwards, and all but one from East Kirkby made it home, relieved to have come through such a demanding and frightening experience. Sixteen Lancasters failed to return, four of them belonging to 5 Group, and the 57 Squadron representative was JB234, which crashed somewhere between Berlin and the target with no survivors from the crew of P/O Parker.

The final major operation of the month was the second one against Kassel, for which preparations were put in hand on the 22nd. A force of 569 aircraft stood ready to take off in the early evening, 133 of them 5 Group Lancasters, nineteen of which were provided by 57 Squadron. They departed East Kirkby between 17.57 and 18.16 with S/L Crocker the senior pilot on duty, and there were no early returns to blunt the squadron's impact. They traversed Belgium in continuing unfavourable weather conditions, which miraculously improved in the target area to leave clear skies between the bombers and the target, but ten-tenths cloud above them at 24,000 feet. At the opening of the raid, the H2S "blind" markers overshot the city-centre aiming-point, leaving the success of the operation reliant upon the visual marker crews backing up, and they did not disappoint. The red and green TIs were concentrated right on the aiming-point, and the main force followed up with accurate and concentrated bombing with scarcely any creep-back. The 57 Squadron crews carried out their attacks from an average of 20,000 feet either side of 21.00 and observed the fires just beginning to take hold as they turned away. It was after the sound of their engines had receded that the fires joined together to engulf the city in what, in some areas, developed into a firestorm, though not one as fierce as that experienced in Hamburg. The shell-shocked inhabitants emerged from their shelters to find their city devastated and unrecognizable, and, after 3,600 fires had been dealt with, it would be established eventually that more than 4,300 apartment blocks containing 53,000 dwelling units had been destroyed or damaged, leaving up to 120,000 people without homes and more than six thousand others killed. 155 industrial buildings had also been destroyed or severely damaged, along with numerous schools, hospitals, churches and public buildings. This massively successful operation was achieved at a high cost of forty-three bombers, twenty-five of them Halifaxes, and among the missing Lancasters were two belonging to 57 Squadron. Based on the time and location of JB320's demise, it is possible that it was approaching the target at the tail end of the raid when crashing at 21.40 at Dransfeld, some fifteen miles north-east of Kassel, with fatal consequences for P/O Miller and his crew. JB237 was on the way home when coming down at 22.15 at Polle on the west bank of the Weser some thirty miles south-west of Hannover. F/L Novick RCAF and both gunners lost their lives, and the four survivors were taken into captivity.

During the course of the month, the squadron participated in nine operations and dispatched 143 sorties for the loss of four Lancasters and their crews.

November 1943

November brought with it the long, dark, cloudy nights which enabled Harris to return to his main theme, the destruction of Germany's capital city. The next four months would bring the bloodiest, hardest fought air battles between Bomber Command and the Luftwaffe Nachtjagd and test the hard-pressed crews to the limit of their endurance. On the 2nd, for his outstanding conduct during the final Hannover operation, rear gunner, Sgt Cowham, was awarded the Conspicuous Gallantry Medal, CGM, which in status came only slightly below the Victoria Cross. In a minute to Churchill on the 3rd, Harris stated, that with the participation of the American 8th Air Force, he could "wreck Berlin from end to end". He estimated that the campaign would cost the two forces between four and five hundred aircraft, but that it would cost Germany the war. This would remove the need for the kind of bloody, expensive and protracted land campaign, which he had personally witnessed during the Great War, and had prompted him to "get into the air" at the earliest opportunity. It should be remembered that this was the first time in the history of air warfare, that the means had existed to prove the theory, that an enemy could be defeated by bombing alone. It is only in the light of more recent experiences, that we have learned of the need, in a conventional conflict at least, to occupy the enemy's territory to secure submission. The Americans, however, were committed to victory on land, where film cameras could capture the glory, and would not accompany Harris to Berlin.

Düsseldorf was selected to open the month's operational account that very night, and, no doubt, while the Prime Minister was digesting Harris's epistle, a force of 589 Lancasters and Halifaxes was being prepared for action. 5 Group's contribution amounted to 147 Lancasters, of which twenty represented 57 Squadron, and they departed East Kirkby between 16.59 and 17.28 with S/L Crocker, the senior pilot on duty. The crews of P/Os Piggin and Smith turned back early, each because of an indisposed crew member, while the others joined the bomber stream over the North Sea and set course to approach the south-western Ruhr after flying out over Belgium and passing through the concentration of fifty to sixty searchlights in the Mönchengladbach-Cologne corridor, some fifteen miles from the target. It was at this point that W4822 was attacked by a night-fighter and sustained damage sufficient to persuade 1Lt West to turn back and attempt to make it home. Sadly, the Lancaster crashed at Hechtel in Belgium, killing the pilot and four others and delivering the navigator into enemy hands. The second pilot, F/O Clements RCAF, and bomb-aimer, F/O Elliott, managed to retain their freedom and were spirited away by local civilians. Meanwhile, the others encountered small patches of cloud and smoke from the early fires drifting across the target at 12,000 feet, despite which, the visibility remained generally good, and the Path Finders employed both sky and ground markers to good effect to identify the aiming-point in the city centre. Bombing by the 57 Squadron crews took place on red and green TIs and skymarkers from an average of 20,000 feet either side of 20.00, and fires were observed to develop on both sides of the Rhine with black smoke rising through 6,000 feet as they turned away. Eighteen aircraft failed to return, and, unusually, eleven were Lancasters and only seven Halifaxes. It was on this night, that 61 Squadron's F/L Bill Reid earned the award of a Victoria Cross for pressing on to bomb the target after his Lancaster had been severely damaged and a number of his crew either killed or wounded. Post-raid reconnaissance revealed that central and southern districts had sustained widespread damage to industry and housing, but no report came out of Düsseldorf to provide detail.

The only serious activity for 57 Squadron, thereafter, until the resumption of the Berlin campaign, came on the 10th as part of a 5 and 8 Group force of 313 Lancasters sent to destroy railway yards at Modane, situated in the foothills of the Alps in south-eastern France. 5 Group supported the operation with 136 Lancasters, of which the fourteen representing 57 Squadron departed East Kirkby between 20.55 and 21.22 with S/L Crocker the senior pilot on duty. Ahead of them lay an outward flight of more than 650 miles, which all from 57 Squadron would negotiate, arriving at their destination after around four-and-a-quarter hours to be rewarded by the presence of a full moon shining brightly from a cloudless sky. They pinpointed on Lake Bissorte, from where they carried out a time-and-distance run to the target, which they identified visually and by red and green TIs, before bombing from around 15,000 feet either side of 01.00. The attack seemed to be concentrated around the markers, and fires appeared to be taking hold, while a large explosion was observed at 01.13. No aircraft were lost and returning crews had the confidence in the quality of their night's efforts confirmed by two hundred bombing photos, which revealed extensive damage to track and installations within one mile of the aiming-point.

Undaunted by the American response to his invitation to join the Berlin party, Harris would return there alone, and the rocky road to the Capital was re-joined by an all-Lancaster heavy force on the night of the 18/19th, while a predominantly Halifax and Stirling contingent of 395 aircraft acted as a diversion by raiding Mannheim and Ludwigshafen three hundred miles to the south-west. The Berlin-bound crews would benefit from four Mosquitos dropping dummy fighter flares, while other Mosquitos carried out a spoof raid on Frankfurt to protect the Mannheim force. The two forces would cross the enemy coast simultaneously some 250 miles apart to confuse the enemy night-fighter controllers, and the route chosen for the Berlin brigade was via the Frisian Island of Texel to a point north of Hannover, and thence to the target to pass over its centre on an east-north-easterly heading. After bombing they would return south of Berlin and Cologne, before crossing central Belgium to gain the English Channel via the French coast. An innovation for this operation was a shortening of the bomber stream to reduce the time over the target to sixteen minutes. When the first Thousand Bomber raid had taken place in May 1942, with an unprecedented twelve aircraft per minute crossing the aiming-point, there was considered to be a high risk of collisions. The number had since been increased to sixteen per minute, with large raids lasting up to forty-five minutes, but, on this night, twenty-seven aircraft per minute were to pass over the aiming-point.

57 Squadron made ready sixteen Lancasters as part of a 5 Group force of 182 and dispatched them from East Kirkby between 17.00 and 17.29 with S/L Heward the senior pilot on duty. After climbing out, they set course for the North Sea, and undertook the journey to Germany's capital over a blanket of cloud covering the whole of northern Germany. They were grateful for the red spotfire route marker dropped by the Path Finders north-east of Hannover, which confirmed that they were on track, and described the horizontal visibility as good, despite the absence of a moon. The cloud persisted all the way to the target with tops at 6,000 feet and was illuminated by searchlights as the Path Finder red and green skymarkers were delivered by H2S to drift down over the aiming-point. The 57 Squadron participants delivered their loads from an average of 20,000 feet either side of 21.00 before returning home with nothing useful to pass on to the intelligence section at debriefing. In fact, most considered the bombing to have been scattered and probably ineffective, and local sources confirmed that there had been no concentration and that a modest 169 houses and a number of industrial units had been destroyed, with many more damaged to some extent. The diversion at Mannheim was deemed to have been successful in its purpose, and caused some useful industrial damage, most seriously to the Daimler-Benz motor factory, which suffered a 90% loss of production for an unknown period. In addition to this, more than three hundred buildings were destroyed at a cost of twenty-three aircraft, while the losses from Berlin were encouragingly low at just nine. F/L Gobbie and crew failed to return to East Kirkby in JB418, which is believed to have come down seven miles north-north-west of the centre of Dresden, killing the navigator and bomb-aimer and delivering the rest of the crew into enemy hands. F/L Gobbie had been awarded the DFC eleven days earlier.

In the early afternoon of the 14th, the crews of P/Os Tansley and Ryrie took off for a dinghy search over the North Sea and returned later with nothing to report. The plan to equip main force aircraft with H2S was under way, and S/L Heward was among 57 Squadron crews undertaking what was referred to as "Y" training during the lull in operations. On the 15th, the whole of B Flight comprising nine crews and 106 ground crew was posted across the tarmac as the nucleus of a new squadron to be numbered 630. In recognition of his outstanding service to date and leadership qualities, S/L Crocker was handed the acting rank of wing commander and put in command. This was part of a general increase in the number of Lancaster squadrons during the Autumn and most of those newly forming would remain on the station of their parent unit, as in the case of 57 and 630 Squadrons, which would share East Kirkby for the remainder of the war. The Lancasters stayed at home on the 19th, while 3, 4, 6 and 8 Groups combined to put 170 Halifaxes, eighty-six Stirlings and ten Mosquitos into the air for a raid on the Ruhr city of Leverkusen. They were greeted in the target area by ten-tenths cloud and an absence of marking, which was caused by equipment failure among the Oboe Mosquitos. A few green TIs were spotted some five to ten miles to the north-west of the target during the approach, but the crews were left to establish their positions on the basis of their own H2S, which, over a region as densely built-up as the Ruhr, was a challenge. As a result, the operation was a complete failure, which sprayed bombs over twenty-seven towns in the region, mostly to the north of Leverkusen.

Harris called for a maximum effort on Berlin on the 22nd, and 764 aircraft were made available, of which 166 Lancasters were provided by 5 Group. Fourteen 57 Squadron Lancasters were made ready and two of them would be taken into battle by 630 Squadron crews. They departed East Kirkby between 16.40 and 17.00 with F/L Hodgkinson the senior pilot on duty, and, after climbing out, they rendezvoused with the rest of the bomber stream to adopt an outward route similar to that employed by the all-Lancaster force four nights earlier. This took them from Texel to a point north-west of Hannover, where a slight dogleg to port put them on a due-easterly heading directly to the target. Unlike the previous raid, however, rather than the circuitous return south of Cologne and out over the French coast, they would come home via a reciprocal route. This was based on a forecast of low cloud and fog over Germany, which would inhibit the night-fighter effort, while broken, medium-level cloud over Berlin would facilitate ground marking. An additional bonus was the availability to the Path Finders of five new H2S Mk III sets, while a new record of thirty-four aircraft per minute passing over the aiming-point would be achieved by abandoning the long-standing practice of allocating aircraft types to specific waves. On this night, aircraft of all types would be spread through the bomber stream, and this was bad news for the Stirlings, which, by the very nature of their design, would be below the Lancaster and Halifax elements and in danger of being hit by friendly bombs.

F/Sgt Atcheson and crew returned early because of instrument failure, leaving the others to arrive at the target and discover that the meteorological forecast had been inaccurate, and that the city was hidden under a blanket of ten-tenths cloud with tops at around 12,000 feet. This meant that the planned ground marking would be largely ineffective, and that the least reliable Wanganui (skymarking) method would have to be employed. Crews ran into intense predicted flak and a mass of searchlights as they began their bombing runs, and those from 57 Squadron aimed at red and green TIs and release-point flares from an average of 19,000 feet from around 20.00. The glow of fires was observed beneath the clouds, and a very large explosion lit up the sky at 20.10. The impression was of a successful operation, but an assessment through the clouds was impossible, and it required post-raid reconnaissance and local reports to confirm that this attack on Berlin had been the most effective of the war to date and had caused a swathe of destruction from the city centre through the western residential districts of Tiergarten and Charlottenburg as far as the suburb town of Spandau. A number of firestorm areas were reported, and the catalogue of destruction included three thousand houses and twenty-three industrial premises. Many thousands more sustained varying degrees of damage, costing 175,000 people their homes and an estimated two thousand their lives, and, by daylight on the 23rd, the smoke had risen to almost 19,000 feet.

Twenty-six aircraft failed to return, eleven Lancasters, ten Halifaxes, and five Stirlings, which amounted to a loss-rate among the types respectively of 2.3%, 4.2% and 10.0%. This proved to be the final straw for Harris as far as the Stirling was concerned, which, because of its short wing design, was restricted to a low service ceiling, and by the configuration of its bomb bay to small calibre bombs. Unlike the Lancaster and Halifax, it lacked development potential, and was immediately withdrawn from future operations over Germany. It would still have an important role to play on secondary duties, however, bombing over occupied territory, mining, and, in 1944, it would replace the Halifax to become the aircraft of choice for the two SOE squadrons, 138 and 161, at Tempsford. Many of those released from Bomber Command service would find their way also to 38 Group, where they would give valuable service as transports and glider-tugs for airborne landings.

A heavy force of 365 Lancasters and ten Halifaxes was made ready with some difficulty on the 23rd for a return to Berlin. Back-to-back long-range operations put a strain on those charged with the responsibility of getting the aircraft off the ground, and the Ludford Magna armourers were unable to load all nineteen 101 Squadron Lancasters with the intended weight of bombs, sending them off 2,000lb short. 5 Group detailed 141 Lancasters, of which the dozen belonging to 57 Squadron were each loaded with a cookie and mix of 4lb and 30lb incendiaries. They took off between 16.51 and 17.11 with no senior pilots on duty and soon lost the services of the crews of P/Os Grimbley and Ryrie to mid-upper turret and intercom failure respectively, the latter bombing Texel as a last resort target. These were among eighteen "boomerangs" from 5 Group and forty-six from the force as a whole, many of whom might have pressed on in other circumstances. Another sign of malcontent was the dumping of bombs over the North Sea by crews intending to push on to the target but wanting to gain more height. It involved largely those from 1 Group, who were shedding their cookies in protest at their A-O-C's policy of loading each Lancaster to its maximum all-up weight at the expense of altitude. The slogan "H-E-I-G-H-T spells safety" could be found on the walls of most bomber station briefing rooms at the time. The target was reached by way of the same route adopted on the previous night and was found to be covered by ten-tenths cloud with tops at between 10,000 and 15,000 feet. Guided by the glow of fires still burning beneath the clouds from the night before, and the presence of red and green TIs, the 57 Squadron crews bombed from an average of 20,000 feet and contributed to another stunning blow. Returning crews described a column of smoke reaching 20,000 feet, and the glow of fires visible again from the Hannover area some 150 miles from the target. It was on this night that fake broadcasts from England caused annoyance to the night-fighter force by ordering them to land because of fog over their bases, despite which, they still had a major hand in the bringing-down of twenty Lancasters, five of them from 5 Group. Post-raid reconnaissance and local reports confirmed that this operation had destroyed a further two thousand buildings and killed around fifteen hundred people.

A force of 262 aircraft, mostly Halifaxes, from 4, 6 and 8 Groups was assembled on the 25th to target Frankfurt and produced a scattered attack that destroyed a moderate amount of housing at a cost of eleven Halifaxes and a single Lancaster.

After a three-night rest for most of the Lancaster crews, 443 of them were briefed on the 26th for a return to the "Big City" for the fourth attack on it since the resumption of the campaign. 5 Group detailed 161 Lancasters, fourteen of them made ready by 57 Squadron, and they departed East Kirkby between 17.10 and 17.30 with F/L Eggins the senior pilot on duty. A diversionary raid on Stuttgart by a predominantly Halifax force followed the same route as those bound for Berlin, which involved an outward leg across the French coast and Belgium to a point north of Frankfurt, where they separated. An indication of the beneficial effects of the three-day lay-off was a 44%

reduction in early returns by 5 Group crews compared with the previous Berlin raid, and all from 57 Squadron pressed on to find Berlin under clear skies. Despite such favourable conditions, the Path Finders overshot the city centre aiming-point by six or seven miles, and marked an area well to the north-west, which happened to contain many war-industry factories. The 5 Group squadrons bombed on red and green TIs from an average 22,000 feet and returning crews spoke of a mass of fires and thick smoke rising to 15,000 feet. At debriefing, a number of crews commented on a chaotic situation over Beachy Head on the way out, where some sections of the bomber stream were orbiting to shed time, while others were arriving to begin the next leg, all at the same altitude. It was learned later that thirty-eight war-industry factories had been destroyed in Berlin and many others damaged, in return for the loss of twenty-eight Lancasters, many of which had fallen victim to night-fighters on the return flight. 57 Squadron's JB485 was shot down by a night-fighter and crashed five miles north-west of Delmenhorst, near Bremen, killing Sgt Beane and four of his crew and delivering the navigator and bomb-aimer into enemy hands.

These last three operations against Berlin undoubtedly represented the best phase of the entire campaign, and, according to local reports, the total death toll on the ground resulting from them amounted to 4,330 people, while the destruction of 8,700 apartment buildings containing more than 104,500 flats and damage to several times that number robbed 450,000 residents of their homes for varying lengths of time. However, Berlin was not Hamburg, where narrow streets had aided the spread of fire. Berlin was a modern city of concrete and steel with wide thoroughfares and open spaces to create natural firebreaks, and each building destroyed added to these, so that the campaign would become a bitter struggle of ever decreasing returns. During the course of the month, the squadron took part in six operations and dispatched ninety sorties for the loss of three Lancasters and crews.

December 1943

Berlin would continue to be the dominant theme during December, and, as November had ended, so December would begin. A heavy force of 443 aircraft stood ready to take off in the late afternoon of the 2nd, all but fifteen of them Lancasters, after the main Halifax element had been withdrawn because of fog over their Yorkshire stations. 5 Group contributed 145 Lancasters, of which fourteen represented 57 Squadron, and they departed East Kirkby between 16.19 and 16.43 with F/L Eggins the senior pilot on duty. After climbing out, they headed for the Lincolnshire coast to rendezvous over the North Sea with the rest of the force for a straight-out-straight-in route across Holland and northern Germany with no feints or diversions. First, however, the crews had to negotiate a towering front of ice-bearing cloud over the North Sea, which would contribute to a 10% rate of early returns. Nine 5 Group crews turned back for a variety of reasons, leaving the others to push through the challenging conditions to then contend with large numbers of enemy night-fighters that would harass sections of the bomber stream all the way to the target, after the controller had been able correctly to predict it. When the Path Finder spearhead arrived, the blind markers realised that they were mostly south of track after variable winds had thrown them off course and dispersed the bomber stream. They were employing H2S to establish their position at Stendal, but had strayed some fifteen miles south of track and mistakenly used the town of Genthin as their reference for the run-in. The 57 Squadron crews found good visibility and were drawn by release-point flares to the aiming-point, where they encountered a thin layer of two to three-tenths cloud at around 5,000 feet, but up to nine-tenths between 10,000 and 12,000 feet, which the searchlights were unable to pierce. They bombed on skymarkers and red and green TIs, and, where possible, ground detail like burning streets from 19,500 feet either side of 20.30. They reported light flak hosing up to 14,000 feet and observed scattered fires and a number of large explosions, some claiming the glow from the burning city to be visible from 120 miles into the homeward leg. The Bombing photographs suggested that the raid had been only partially successful, causing useful damage in industrial districts in the west and east, but scattering the main weight of bombs over the southern districts and outlying communities to the south. It was a bad night for the bomber force, which lost forty aircraft, mostly in the target area and on the way home. 57 Squadron's JB372 disappeared without trace with the crew of F/O Williams and JB529 is thought to have crashed near Trebbin, some fifteen miles south-west of Berlin taking the lives of P/O Tansley and crew and second pilot, Sgt Dalton. East Kirkby also had the loss of a 630 Squadron crew to mourn.

Having been spared by the weather from experiencing an effective visitation from the Command in October and exploiting the enemy expectation that Berlin would be the target again, Leipzig found itself at the end of the red tape on briefing-room wall-maps from County Durham to Cambridgeshire on the 3rd. A force of 527 aircraft was made ready, which included 103 Lancasters of 5 Group, eight of them belonging to 57 Squadron and they departed East Kirkby between 00.04 and 00.33 with no senior pilots on duty. P/O Grimbley and crew lost the use of their rear turret and bombed Texel after turning for home, while the rest of the bomber stream headed for Berlin as a feint, passing north of Hannover and Braunschweig with ten-tenths cloud beneath them and an hour's journey to Leipzig still ahead of them. Then, as they turned towards the south-east, the Mosquito element continued on to carry out a diversion at the Capital. Night-fighters had already infiltrated the stream at the Dutch coast, but the feint had the desired effect, and few enemy aircraft were encountered in the target area, where two layers of ten-tenths cloud topped out at around 7,000 and 15,000 feet. The Path Finders marked by H2S with green skymarkers, and the 57 Squadron crews bombed on these from an average 20,000 feet, some two thousand feet above the barrage of bursting heavy flak shells and observed explosions and a strong glow beneath the clouds. The emergence through the cloud tops of black smoke suggested that an accurate and concentrated attack had taken place, and the smoke and glow remained visible for 150 miles into the return journey south-east towards the French frontier. Had many aircraft not then strayed into the Frankfurt defence zone, the losses may have been fewer, but twenty-four aircraft failed to return, fifteen of them Halifaxes. At debriefing, P/O Smith and crew reported that they had counted forty bombs splashing into the North Sea on the way out. Local reports confirmed this as a highly successful operation, which had hit residential and industrial areas, and was the most destructive raid visited upon this eastern city during the war. Sadly, for the Command, it would take its revenge in time.

W/C Fisher had been working up to operational qualification with training flights whenever he could fit them in to his schedule, and he became attached to 5 Lancaster Finishing School on the 4th to complete the process. Fog and frost impacted the flying programme for almost the next two weeks, during which period minor operations by 8 Group Mosquitos held sway, but the news of an operation on the 16th was greeted enthusiastically by crews of the heavy brigade, particularly when Berlin was posted as the target. The crews learned at briefing that it was to be an all-Lancaster affair involving 483 of the type and ten Mosquitos for what would be the sixth attack on the city since the resumption of the campaign. 5 Group put up 165 aircraft, fifteen of them representing 57 Squadron, which departed East Kirkby between 16.20 and 17.02 with S/L Heward the senior pilot on duty. They were to cross the Dutch coast in the region of Castricum-aan-Zee, and then head due east all the way to the target with no deviations. A three-quarter moon would rise during the long return leg over the Baltic and Denmark, but it was hoped that the very early take-off and the expectation of fog over Luftwaffe aerodromes would reduce the risk of interception. F/Sgt McGillivray and crew lost the use of their H2S and DR compass and had to turn back, while the remainder continued on to the Dutch coast, where the bomber stream encountered the first night-fighters. The 57 Squadron crews appeared to avoid contact and pressed on to find Berlin obscured by ten-tenths cloud with tops at around 5,000 feet. However, its location was established by red and green skymarkers, which were bombed from an average 19,500 feet from around 20.00. The return over Denmark passed largely without major incident leaving the long final leg over the North Sea to negotiate. A W/T signal from Sgt Hinde and crew stated that they were ditching, and when rescue arrived, only the wireless operator, Sgt Hurley, was found in the dinghy and brought ashore, and it must be assumed that the remainder of the crew went down with JB373. The greatest difficulties awaited the 1, 6 and 8 Group crews as they arrived home to find their airfields covered by a blanket of dense fog. With little reserves of fuel, the tired crews began a frantic search to find somewhere to land, stumbling blindly through the murk to catch a glimpse of the ground. For many, this proved fatal, while others gave up any hope of landing, and abandoned their aircraft. Twenty-nine Lancasters and a mine-laying Stirling were thus lost, and more than 150 airmen killed in these most tragic of circumstances. To this number were added the twenty-five Lancasters failing to return from the raid, many of which were accounted for by night-fighters over Holland and Germany while outbound. At debriefing, some crews reported the glow of fires, while others saw nothing through the cloud, and it was a local report that confirmed a moderately effective raid, which had fallen predominantly onto central and eastern residential districts.

This was not the only operation to take place during the evening, and one of those of a more minor nature was to have great significance for the future of the Command, 5 Group and the Path Finder Force. Two flying bomb sites in the Pas-de-Calais, at Tilley-le-Haut and Flixecourt, were attacked by small forces, the former by 3 Group Stirlings, and the latter by nine Lancasters of 617 Squadron under the command of W/C Leonard Cheshire. The marking was carried out by Oboe Mosquitos at both locations, although it was by just a single aircraft at the latter. Neither operation was a success, after the markers missed the aiming points by a few hundred yards, and this demonstrated the shortcomings of the Oboe system. Whilst it was ideal for marking an urban target, where there was a large margin for error, it was too imprecise for use against a small target like a flying bomb site or an individual building. This was precisely the kind of target to which 617 Squadron was to be assigned for the remainder of the war, and it was frustrating for Cheshire and his crews to have plastered the markers, only for the target to escape damage. A similar disappointment would take place at the end of the month at the same flying bomb site, and this set minds working at 617 Squadron.

A three-day stand-down allowed the crews to recover from the Berlin operation, and it was during this period that P/O Josling was declared tour-expired and posted on the 18th to 1660 Conversion Unit. His navigator, S/L Vivian, was awarded an immediate DSO three days later. On the 20th, all stations were notified of an operation that night against Frankfurt, for which a force of 390 Lancasters and 257 Halifaxes was assembled. 5 Group made ready 168 Lancasters, sixteen of them belonging to 57 Squadron, which departed East Kirkby between 16.56 and 17.23 with W/C Fisher and S/L Heward the senior pilots on duty, the former conducting his first sortie as crew captain since taking command. While the main operation was in progress, forty-four Lancasters and ten Mosquitos of 1 and 8 Groups were to carry out a diversion at Mannheim, some forty miles to the south of the primary target. After climbing out, the crews set course for Southwold and the North Sea-crossing to the Scheldt estuary, before passing north of Antwerp and flying the length of Belgium to the German frontier north of Luxembourg. The German night-fighter controller had picked up transmissions from the bomber stream as soon as it left the English coast and was able to track it all the way to the target and vector his fighters into position. Many combats took place during the outward flight, and the diversion failed to draw fighters away from the main action. The problems continued at the primary target, where the forecast clear skies failed to materialize, and the crews were greeted by four to nine-tenths cloud at between 5,000 and 10,000 feet. This allowed some of them to pick out ground features, while others fixed their positions by H2S, if so equipped, and the main force Lancaster crews simply waited for TIs on e.t.a. The Path Finders had prepared a ground-marking plan in expectation of good vertical visibility, and dropped red, green and yellow TIs, while the Germans lit a decoy fire site five miles to the south-east of the city. Some crews described the marking as late and erratic, and bombing took place on red and green TIs from an average of 20,000 feet either side of 19.30. Most thought the attack to be scattered in the early stages, becoming more concentrated as it progressed, and many commented on the new cookies detonating with a brighter flash than the old ones. All of the 57 Squadron Lancasters returned to East Kirkby having contributed to a moderately successful raid, and at least one crew reported the glow of fires remaining visible for 150 miles into the return journey. Any success was achieved largely as the result of the creep-back from the decoy site, which fell across the suburbs of Offenbach and Sachsenhausen, situated on the southern bank of the River Main, where 466 houses were destroyed and more than nineteen hundred seriously damaged. Despite the scale of destruction, the operation fell well short of its aims, and the loss of forty-one aircraft was a high price to pay. The Halifaxes suffered heavily, losing twenty-seven of their number, a loss-rate of 10.5%, compared with the Lancasters' 3.6%. While the above operation was in progress, eight 617 Squadron Lancasters had attempted to bomb the Browning armaments works neat Liege in Belgium. In the event, the cloud prevented sight of the Oboe marking and the operation was abandoned. On the way home, the Lancaster containing the former 57 Squadron crew of F/L Geoff Rice was intercepted by a night-fighter and broke up as it plunged to earth, according to eyewitnesses, with rear gunner, "Sandy" Burns still firing at the assailant. Only Rice survived and came to hanging from a tree having lost hours of memory. He would remain at large for six months before being betrayed and handed over to the enemy and would spend the rest of the war as a PoW.

Just two more operations remained before the year ended, and both were to be directed at Germany's capital city. The first was posted on the 23rd and would involve an all-Lancaster heavy force with seven 35 (Madras Presidency) Squadron Halifaxes among the Path Finder element and eight Mosquitos to provide a diversion. The 130 Lancasters of 5 Group included a dozen from 57 Squadron, which were loaded with the usual cookie and mix of incendiaries and launched into the cold night air between 23.48 and 00.17 with F/Ls Eggins, Laing and Spriggs the senior pilots on duty. The crews of F/O Thomas and Sgt Beaumont were afflicted by the illness of a crew member and had to turn back, leaving the others to adopt the somewhat circuitous route to the target, which took the bomber stream in a south-easterly direction to the Scheldt estuary, before hugging the Belgian/Dutch frontier to cross into Germany south of Aachen, as if threatening Frankfurt. When a point was reached south of Leipzig, the route turned sharply towards the north and Berlin, while the Mosquito feint threatened Leipzig as the target. The vanguard of the bomber stream reached the target to find it enveloped in up to eight-tenths cloud at between 5,000 and 10,000 feet, which might not have been critical had the Path Finders not suffered an unusually high failure rate of their H2S equipment, which resulted in scattered and sparse sky-marking. The 57 Squadron crews found red and green skymarker flares at which to aim their bombs from an average of 19,000 feet and observed well-concentrated fires and at least four large explosions, one described as being orange and red and lasting for thirty seconds. A relatively modest sixteen Lancasters failed to return, six of them from 5 Group, and East Kirkby's single failure to return was from 57 Squadron. JB233 crashed at Meppen, close to Germany's frontier with northern Holland, and P/O Knights RCAF survived with two other members of his mixed RCAF, RAAF and RAF crew to fall into enemy hands. A local report named the south-eastern suburbs of Köpenick and Treptow as sustaining the most damage, with 287 houses and other buildings suffering complete destruction.

The fifth wartime Christmas was observed like all of the others, and the break from operations continued until the "Big City" was posted as the target again on the 29th, for what, for the Lancaster operators, would be the first of three raids on it in five nights spanning the turn of the year. A force of 712 aircraft included 163 Lancasters of 5 Group, of which fifteen represented 57 Squadron and departed East Kirkby between 16.55 and 17.18 with W/C Fisher the senior pilot on duty. It was from this juncture that the intolerable strain on the crews of successive long-range flights in difficult weather conditions would begin to become manifest in some squadrons through the rate of early returns, which on this night reached forty-five or 6.3%. The bomber stream was routed out over the Dutch Frisian islands pointing directly for Leipzig, and, having reached a point just to the north of that city, was to turn to the north towards Berlin, while Mosquitos carried out spoof raids on Leipzig and Magdeburg. 57 Squadron was exempt from early returns, and its crews reached the target area to find ten-tenths cloud with tops at anywhere between 7,000 and 18,000 feet. Red and green Path Finder release-point flares could be seen hanging over the city, upon which they aimed their bombs from an average of 20,000 feet sometime after 20.00. At debriefing, crews reported a considerable red glow beneath the clouds, which remained visible for a hundred miles, and gave the impression of a concentrated and successful assault. This was not entirely borne out by local reports, which revealed that the main weight of the raid had fallen onto southern and south-eastern districts, and, also, into outlying communities to the east. 388 buildings were destroyed, although none of significance, and ten thousand people were bombed out of their homes. Eleven Lancasters and nine Halifaxes failed to return, a loss-rate of 2.4% for the former and 3.5% for the latter.

During the course of the month, the squadron participated in six operations and dispatched eighty sorties for the loss of four Lancasters and crews. It had been a testing end to a year which had brought major successes and advances in tactics, but it had also been a year of high losses, particularly among the Stirling and Halifax squadrons. While "window" had been an instant success, it had also caused the Luftwaffe to rethink and reorganise, and the night-fighter force that emerged from the ruins of the old system was a leaner, more efficient and altogether more lethal beast than that of before. As far as the crews of Bomber Command were concerned, the New Year offered the same fare as the old one, and few would view that with relish.

57 Squadron Lancaster ED781 DX-J took off from RAF Scampton on 24th June 1943 for Wuppertal in the heart of Germany's Ruhr industrial region but the aircraft was intercepted and shot down by a German night fighter and crashed near Lantin, near Liege in Belgium. Only Sgt Lambdin, managed to bale out and was taken PoW; the rest of the crew are buried at the cemetery of Heverlee.. Crew:
Sgt Stanley Fallows Pilot, Sgt John Sykes (FE), Sgt Harry Naiman (Nav), Sgt I.H. Lambdin, (BA), Sgt William Day (W.Op), Sgt Francis Steer (MUG), Sgt Raymond Simpson (RG).

Pilot Sgt Stanley Fallows

220

57 Squadron Lancaster mid-upper-gunner in his turret. February 1943.

F/O Jimmy Elliot and F/O Robert Clements, crew of Lancaster W4822.
On the night of 3/4th November 1943, 57 Squadron LancasterW4822 DX-P piloted by 1st Lt.Don West took off from RAF East Kirkby bound for Düsseldorf. It was attacked by an unknown German fighter while outbound to the target near Monchengladbach and subsequently crashed at Hechtel-Eksel, Belgium. Crew: 1st Lt D. West USSAF pilot, Sgt William F. Neill, (FE) ; Sgt Harry McKernin, (W/Op); Sgt Francis Heaton and Sgt John Edmunds, the two gunners were all killed while P/O N.F. Buggey the navigator became a PoW, Jimmy Elliott and Robert Clements evaded.

W/C F C Hopcroft with crew and Lancaster "Frederick II"

Crew of Lancaster ED547 which crashed 9ᵗʰ June 1943. All crew were taken prisoner. Back row: Sgts Hodgson, Walker. Front row: Sgts Bailey, Lewis and Twigg.

F/L A. J. A. Day RAAF observer (left), with W/C F C Hopcroft, who is captain of the Lancaster, May 1943.

King George VI inspecting ground crewmen during his visit to 617 Squadron (Dambusters) and 57 Squadron at RAF Scampton, Lincolnshire, England, United Kingdom, 27th May 1943; note Lancaster B Mk I bomber 'Frederick III', the aircraft of W/C Campbell Hopcroft, commanding officer of 57 Squadron

57 Squadron Lancaster W5008 DX-B in North Africa (on loan to 617 Squadron)

57 Squadron Lancaster with "Usual" area bombing load of 4000lbs "blockbuster" bomb and incendiary bombs.

57 Squadron Lancaster JA914 DX-O lost 4th September1943. Remains in Deutches Teck Museum, Berlin.

57 Squadron Lancaster JB529 DX-F crash site 2nd December 1943.

F/O R.W. Stewart, a wireless operator on a Lancaster of 57 Squadron based at RAF Scampton speaking to the pilot from his position in front of the Marconi T1154/R1155 transmitter/receiver set.

57 Squadron Lancaster

57 Squadron Lancasters

57 Squadron Lancaster LL940 DX-S

57 Squadron Lancaster JB370 DX-O Owen crew

57 Squadron Lancaster JB485 DX-L. Don Peterson and crew.

57 Squadron Lancaster W4201 DX-F

Crew of 57 Squadron Q for Queenie, end of first tour 19th September 1943. L-R Smith, R Green, R C Lowe, Spencer, Upton, Edwards, Brown.

Ronald Charles Lowe RAAF 57 Squadron rear gunner.

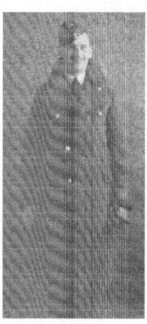

Sgt Charles Luke Flight Engineer

Jimmy Scoggie and Johnny Johnson

Laden with flight equipment and parachutes, F/O J F Greenham RCAF and crew board the crew bus that will take them to Lancaster W4201.

Canadian skipper F/O Greenham (third from left) and crew photographed in front of Lancaster W 4201 prior to an operation. The Lancaster was the usual mount of the Squadron CO W/C Campbell Hopcroft DFC. Note the Wing Commander's pennant painted below the cockpit. This aircraft was damaged by a night fighter during a mining sortie 14th March 1943 and crashed on return to Scampton.

W/O A A Garshowitz and F/Sgt F A Garbas of 57 Squadron. Killed while on F/L Astell's crew during Dams Raid.

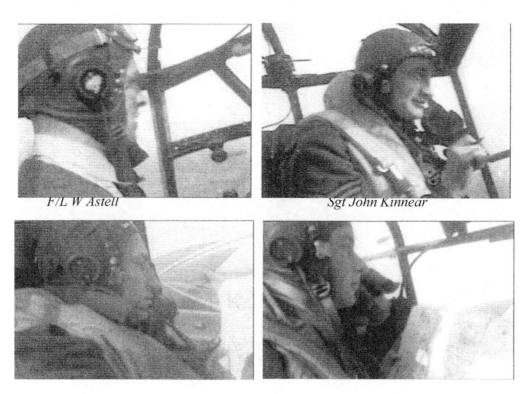

F/L W Astell   *Sgt John Kinnear*

W/O Albert Garshowitz   *P/O Floyd Wile*

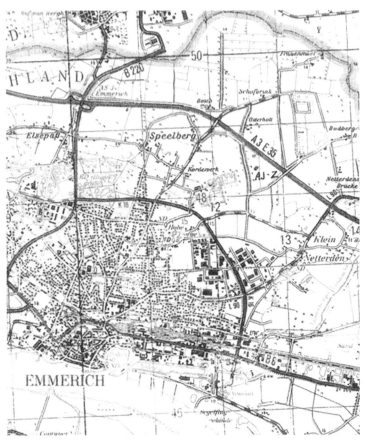

*Rolf Feldmann, whose account of
the shooting down of a 57 Squadron
Lancaster was confused with that
of AJ-Z four nights later.*

Maudslay's crash site at Klein Netterden

*57 Squadron LancasterED655 DX-X
at Scampton July 1943.*

Sgt George Hull. KIA 22nd June 1943

57 Squadron East Kirkby
P/O Sandy Duff   F/Sgt Bill Pride   P/O Phil Rolfe   Sgt Bob Brown
Lancaster W4849 took off 22nd Sept 1943 from East Kirkby. Intercepted by an intruder on the return to base and shot down 0043 23rd September 1943 over Driby 9 miles SSE of Louth Lincolnshire. Sgt R C Brown also baled out and survived and. (Photo courtesy of David Nunn)

Bert Cherrington survivor of crash of Lancaster W4948. He went onto join 617 Squadron and took part in all three Tirpitz raids.(David Nunn).

Sgt J B Mallett, Sgt H H Turkentine and Sgt R H P Roberts, flight engineer, bomb aimer and rear gunner, respectively, of a Lancaster B Mark I of No. 57 Squadron RAF, eat breakfast in the Sergeants' Mess at Scampton, Lincolnshire, following their return from a night raid. All three were killed with the rest of the crew of Lancaster R5894 'DX-T' ("T for Tommy") when it collided with high tension cables near Scampton upon returning from a raid on Berlin in the early morning of 2nd March 1943.

Hamburg docks after the 1943 raids.

January 1944

The change of year was not destined to effect a shift in the emphasis of operations, and this was, no doubt, a disappointment, not only to the har-pressed crews of Bomber Command, but also to the beleaguered residents of Germany's Capital City. Proud of their status as Berliners first and Germans second, they were a hardy breed, and just like their counterparts in London during the Blitz of 1940, they would bear their trials with fortitude and humour, and would not buckle under the constant assault from above. "You may break our walls", proclaimed banners in the streets, "but not out hearts", and the most popular song of the day, "Nach jedem Dezember kommt immer ein Mai", "After every December there's always a May", was played endlessly over the airwaves, its sentiments hinting at a change in fortunes with the onset of spring. This was, to an extent, prophetic, as both camps would, indeed, have to endure throughout the remainder of the winter, before Berlin ceased to be the main focus of attention. Harris allowed the Berliners little time to enjoy New Year, and, as New Year's Day dawned, plans were already in hand to continue the onslaught. Before it ended, the first of 421 Lancasters, 161 representing 5 Group, would be taking off and heading eastwards to arrive over the city as the clock showed 03.00 hours on the 2nd.

Take-off had actually been delayed because of doubts over the weather, and this meant that insufficient hours of daylight remained to allow the planned outward route over Denmark and the Baltic. Instead, the bomber stream would adopt the previously used almost direct route across Holland and northern Germany, but return, as originally planned, more circuitously, passing east of Leipzig, before racing across Germany between the Ruhr and Frankfurt and traversing Belgium to reach the Channel near the French port of Boulogne. 57 Squadron's fourteen participants took off between 23.52 and 00.18 with F/Ls Eggins, Laing, Munday and Spriggs the senior pilots on duty, each Lancaster carrying a cookie and mix of 4lb and 30lb incendiaries. They climbed away to rendezvous with the rest of the force, which was gradually depleted by twenty-nine early returns, although none from 57 Squadron. The bomber stream covered the four-hundred-mile leg from the Dutch coast to Berlin in under two hours without once catching a glimpse of the ground through the dense cloud, and it was no different at the target, which was completely obscured by a layer of ten-tenths cloud with tops in places as high as 19,000 feet. The Path Finders had to employ skymarking (Wanganui), which was somewhat scattered, and the 57 Squadron crews aimed for these parachute flares from around 20,000 feet sometime after 03.00. They observed the glow of fires and smoke rising through the cloud tops, and some crews witnessed a huge explosion at 03.07, which lit up the clouds for three seconds, but it was impossible to assess what was happening on the ground. It was established, ultimately, that the operation had been a failure, which had scattered bombs across the southern fringes of the city, causing only minor damage, while the main weight of the attack had fallen beyond the city boundaries into wooded and open country. The disappointment was compounded by the loss of twenty-eight Lancasters, and there was one empty dispersal on the 57 Squadron side of East Kirkby, which should have been occupied by JB548. Information of its fate would take time to filter through the channels, but the happy news was eventually received from the Red Cross that the entire crew of P/O Grimbley RAAF had survived and were now in captivity.

During the course of the 2nd, F/L Boyle was posted to the squadron and immediately granted the acting rank of squadron leader to enable him to assume command of B Flight as successor to S/L Heward, who was posted out on this day to take command of 50 Squadron at Skellingthorpe. S/L

Heward had been an exacting flight commander and would take his stern attitudes to 50 Squadron and in June to 97 (Straits Settlement) Squadron. During the afternoon a heavy force of 362 Lancasters and nine of the new Mk III Hercules-powered Halifaxes was made ready for a return to Berlin that night. There was snow on the ground, and many of the crews called to briefing were still tired from being late to bed following the almost-eight-hour round trip the night before, some in a mutinous frame of mind at being on the Order of Battle again so soon. 5 Group cancelled twenty-five of its intended contribution, leaving 119 to take part, thirteen of which belonged to 57 Squadron. The outward route crossed the Dutch coast near Castricum and took the bomber stream to a point south-east of Bremen, followed by a dogleg to the north-west and, finally, a ninety degree change of course to the south-east in the Parchim area to leave a ninety-mile run to the target. The 57 Squadron element departed East Kirkby between 23.09 and 23.40 with F/L Laing the senior pilot on duty and headed for the rendezvous point over the North Sea, from where F/O Thomas and crew were among nineteen 5 Group crews to turn back early. It may be that they had been defeated by the severe icing conditions that persuaded many crews to abandon their sorties, while others dropped out because of minor problems that might have seen them carry on had they been fully rested.

The route changes worked well to throw off the night-fighters, but they would congregate in the target area after the controller correctly identified the "Big City" as the target forty minutes before zero-hour. Ten-tenths cloud with tops at 16,000 feet forced the bombing to take place on the red skymarkers with green stars or on the glow of fires, the 5 Group squadrons carrying out their attacks from around 19,000 to 20,000 feet before 03.00. They reported smoke rising to 20,000 feet as they turned away, but it was not possible to make an accurate assessment of the outcome, and the impression was of an effective attack, when, in fact, it had been another failure. Bombs had been scattered across the city and destroyed just eighty-two houses for the loss of twenty-seven Lancasters, most of which had fallen victim to night-fighters in the target area. Among these was 57 Squadron's JB364, which was shot down either on its bombing run or immediately afterwards and only the rear gunner survived from the crew of F/O Shewan RCAF. It emerged later that JB681 had come down near Rheinsberg in a lake-dominated region north-north-west of Berlin with no survivors from the crew of the recently commissioned P/O Ely RAAF.

After three trips there in five nights, Berlin would now be left to the Mosquitos of 8 Group until the final third of the month, allowing Harris to turn his attention on the 5th upon the Baltic port-city of Stettin, which had not been attacked in numbers since the previous April. It was to be another predominantly Lancaster affair, involving 348 of the type accompanied by ten Halifaxes, with a 5 Group contribution of 120 aircraft, nine of them provided by 57 Squadron. They took off from East Kirkby between 23.46 and 00.03 with W/C Fisher and S/L Boyle the senior pilots on duty, and, in contrast to the high number of early returns by 5 Group crews during the last Berlin operation, only one came home early on this night. As they made their way eastwards, crews found themselves in thick cloud at cruising altitude, some struggling to find a clear lane even when as high as 23,000 feet. On the plus side, they all benefitted from a Mosquito diversion at Berlin, which kept the night-fighters off the scent. Stettin was found to be partially visible through five-tenths thin cloud with tops at around 10,000 feet, and the main force crews were able to identify some ground features before focusing on the Path Finder H2S-laid flares and green TIs, which those from 5 Group bombed from around 20,000 to 22,500 feet either side of 04.00. At debriefing, the intelligence section was provided with accounts of a highly accurate and concentrated attack, which seemed to leave the entire city on fire and smoke rising through 20,000 feet. Fourteen Lancasters and two Halifaxes failed to return, and among them was 57 Squadron's JB541, which crashed in the target area with no survivors from the crew of P/O Douglas. Post-raid reconnaissance and local reports confirmed heavy damage in central and western districts, where 504 houses and twenty industrial buildings had been destroyed, while a further 1,148 houses and twenty-nine industrial buildings had been seriously damaged, and eight ships had been sunk in the harbour.

Following this operation, the crews of the heavy squadrons were rested until mid-month, and when briefings finally took place on the 14th, there was, doubtless, some relief to see the red tape on the wall maps terminate some way short of Berlin. It led, in fact, to Braunschweig (Brunswick), the historic and culturally significant city situated some thirty-five miles to the east of Hannover. It had not been attacked by the Command in numbers before, and, on this night, would face a force, which, at take-off, numbered 496 Lancasters and two Halifaxes. 5 Group supported the operation with 153 Lancasters, of which eleven represented 57 Squadron, and they departed East Kirkby between 16.39 and 16.57 with S/L Boyle the senior pilot on duty. After climbing out, they headed towards Germany's north-western coast, where they would be met by part of the enemy night-fighter response and face harassment all the way to the target and back. P/O Smith's rear gunner collapsed through lack of oxygen, and the bombs were dropped on Texel on the way home. Complete cloud cover at the target, at around 15,000 feet in places, dictated the use of red skymarkers with green stars, at which the 5 Group squadrons aimed their cookies and incendiaries from an average of 20,500 feet. The enemy fighters scored consistently and accounted for the majority of the thirty-eight missing Lancasters, many of which came down around Hannover. The attack almost entirely missed the city, falling mostly onto outlying communities to the south, and was reported locally as a light raid. This would be a continuing theme in future attacks up to the autumn, as Braunschweig enjoyed something of a charmed life, leading to a belief among the populace that the surrounding villages were being targeted intentionally in an attempt to drive the residents into the city, before a major operation destroyed it with them in it! One concern to emerge was the number of aircraft narrowly escaping destruction by cookies from above or actually being hit by incendiaries.

The Path Finders, in particular, had been taking a beating since the turn of the year, with 156 Squadron alone losing fourteen Lancasters and crews in just three operations, four and five on Berlin, and five again on Braunschweig. This was creating something of a crisis in Path Finder manpower, particularly with regard to experienced crews, and a number of sideways postings took place between the squadrons to ensure a leavening of experience in each one. One of the solutions was to take the cream from among the crews emerging from the training units, rather than wait for them to gain experience at a main force squadron.

Another lull in operations kept the crews on the ground until the 20th, when orders were received to assemble a maximum effort force for the next round of the Berlin offensive. The Halifax squadrons, which had appeared to be in hibernation since late December, were roused from their slumber, and 264 of them joined 495 Lancasters to constitute the Path Finder and main force elements, while two small Mosquito sections carried out spoof raids on Kiel and Hannover. 5 Group weighed in with 155 Lancasters, of which ten were made ready by 57 Squadron, and they took off between 16.25 and 16.53 with S/L Boyle the senior pilot on duty. Flying as second pilot with F/L Laing was Malta's P/O "Jimmy" Castagnola, who would be recruited by 617 Squadron later in the year. It was a rare pleasure for crews to be taking off while some daylight remained, and they circled as they climbed out before setting course, while observing the dozens of Lancasters rising up into the dusk to join them from the neighbouring stations. They turned their snouts towards the west coast of the Schleswig-Holstein peninsula at a point opposite Kiel, rendezvousing with the other groups over the North Sea and all the time shedding individual aircraft as a hefty seventy-five crews abandoned their sorties and turned back. The head of the bomber stream made landfall over the Nordfriesland coast, before turning to the south-east on a more-or-less direct course for Berlin, and the main force crews soon found themselves being hounded by night-fighters. The enemy controller had fed a proportion of his resources into the bomber stream east of Hamburg, and they would remain in contact until a point between Leipzig and Hannover on the way home, although, curiously, the 5 Group brigade saw nothing of this and would complete the operation for the loss of a single Lancaster. The two Mosquito diversions had been completely ignored by the Luftwaffe controller, who knew well in advance that Berlin was to be the target. The Path Finders arrived over the Müritzsee to the north of Berlin with a sixty-mile run-in to the aiming-point, and they found this to be concealed beneath the same ten-tenths cloud that had accompanied them for the entire outward leg. The tops of the cloud lay beneath the bombers at up to 15,000 feet as the main force crews carried out their attacks on red skymarkers with green stars, running in at an average of 20,500 feet between 19.30 and 20.00. On return, the crews commented on the lack of flak activity over Berlin and reported the glow of large fires under the cloud and smoke rising through the tops. Thirty-five aircraft failed to return, twenty-two of them Halifaxes, which represented an 8.3% casualty rate compared with 2.6% for the Lancasters. The only missing 5 Group Lancaster was 57 Squadron's JB419 containing the crew of P/O MacGillivray RCAF, from which only the bomb-aimer survived to fall into enemy hands. It took a little time for an assessment of the operation to be made because of continuing cloud over north-eastern Germany, by which time four further raids had been carried out. It seems from local reports that the eastern districts had received the heaviest weight of bombs in an eight-mile stretch from Weissesee in the north to Neukölln in the south, although no details of destruction emerged.

On the following day, the city of Magdeburg was posted to host its first major attack of the war. Situated some fifty miles from Braunschweig and slightly to the south of east, it was on an increasingly familiar route as far as the enemy night-fighter controllers were concerned, and within easy striking distance of the night-fighter assembly beacons. As the home of a ship lift at the eastern end of the Mittelland Canal at its junction with the Elbe, and a Bergius-process synthetic oil refinery (hydrogenation plant), both located in the same Rothensee district to the north of Magdeburg city centre, it had been a target for small-scale Bomber Command attacks from time to time since the summer of 1940. Also, on the target list at that time had been a second ship lift at Hohenwarthe, close by to the north-east, which, in reality, had not been built, and, as a result of the war, would not be. In an attempt to deceive the enemy, a small-scale diversion was planned at Berlin involving twenty-two Lancasters of 5 Group and twelve Mosquitos of 8 Group. 5 Group contributed 122 Lancasters to the main event, ten of them made ready by 57 Squadron, while the crews of S/L Boyle and F/L Laing would take part in the diversion. They departed East Kirkby together between 19.38 and 20.24 with F/Ls Munday and Spriggs the senior pilots on duty for the main event and flew out over the North Sea to a point some one hundred miles off the west coast of the Schleswig-Holstein peninsula, before turning to the south-east to pass between

Hamburg and Hannover. F/O Waugh and crew turned back with engine failure when still over the North Sea. Enemy radar was able to detect H2S transmissions during night-flying tests and equipment checks, and the night-fighter controller was, thereby, always aware of an imminent heavy raid. On this night, the night-fighters were able to infiltrate the bomber stream even before the German coast was crossed, and the recently introduced "Tame Boar" night-fighter system provided a running commentary on the bomber stream's progress, enabling the fighters to latch onto it and remain in contact. The final turning-point was twenty-five miles north-east of the target, and this was identified by Path Finder route markers, while, ahead, the target was brought into focus by the bombs from twenty-seven main force aircraft. These had been driven by stronger-than-forecast winds to arrive ahead of schedule and contained crews anxious to get the job done and get out of the target area as soon as possible. They bombed using their own H2S without waiting for the TIs to go down, and, together with dummy fires, were blamed by the Path Finders as the reason for their failure to produce concentrated marking.

The conditions over Magdeburg varied according to the time of arrival, the early birds encountering seven to nine-tenths thin cloud at around 6,000 feet, while those turning up towards the end of the raid found the northern half of the city completely clear with cloud over the southern half only. The 57 Squadron crews experienced between three and seven-tenths thin and broken cloud with tops at up to 8,000 feet, and, in the face of fairly modest opposition, bombed on green TIs from an average of 20,000 feet either side of 23.00, gaining the impression that the attack was concentrated around the markers. Returning crews reported explosions and fires or their glow, and smoke beginning to rise as they turned away. A number reported a flash some twelve minutes after bombing, that lit up the clouds for seven seconds, and two large explosions at 23.15. Fires that initially seemed to be scattered, became more concentrated as the crews headed for home, and the impression was of a successful operation. However, some crews were of the opinion that they had attacked a dummy target between Magdeburg and Berlin, while a few overshot the aiming-point and let their bombs go randomly rather than go round again. While all of this was in progress, the diversionary force arrived at Berlin, some eighty miles away to the north-east, where they found a layer of eight to ten-tenths cloud at 10,000 feet. They had been told at briefing that there would be no Path Finder presence, and crews bombed on e.t.a., mostly from above 20,000 feet at around 23.00, observing the activity over Magdeburg as they turned for home. The 5 Group ORB expressed the opinion that the diversion had succeeded in the early stages in reducing the impact of the Nachtjagd, although this was not borne out by the figures. In the absence of post-raid reconnaissance and a local report, the outcome at Magdeburg was not confirmed, and it is generally believed now that most of the bombing fell outside of the city boundaries. A record fifty-seven aircraft failed to return, thirty-five of them Halifaxes, and this provided another alarming statistic of a 15.6% loss-rate compared with 5.2% for the Lancasters.

The final concerted effort to destroy Berlin began on the 27th with the first of three operations in the space of an unprecedented four nights. This hectic round came after five nights of rest since the bruising experience of Magdeburg and involved an all-Lancaster heavy force of 515 aircraft. 5 Group put up a record 172, sixteen of them belonging to 57 Squadron, which departed East Kirkby between 17.31 and 17.58 with S/L Boyle the senior pilot on duty. After climbing out and rendezvousing with the rest of the group, they set course on a complex route that would take the bomber stream towards the north German coast, before swinging to the south-east to enter enemy territory over the Frisians and northern Holland. Having then feinted towards central Germany, suggesting Leipzig as the target, the force was to turn north-east to a point west of Berlin, from where the final run-in would commence. The long return route passed to the west of Leipzig before turning due east to skirt Frankfurt on its northern side and traverse Belgium to gain the Channel south of Boulogne. The crews of F/L Laing and F/O Briggs were back in the circuit within two and three-and-a-half hours respectively for undisclosed reasons, leaving the others to press on towards the target, while a mining diversion off Heligoland and the dispensing of dummy fighter flares and route-markers partially succeeded in reducing the numbers of enemy night-fighters making contact. It was, therefore, a relatively intact bomber force that approached the target over ten-tenths cloud with tops at 15,000 feet, which required the Path Finders to use sky-marking. Red Wanganui flares with green stars led the main force crews to the aiming-point, where bombing took place from either side of 20,000 feet and produced a glow of fires and the appearance of a successful raid. Of course, not all would make it back to tell their stories at debriefing, and thirty-three Lancaster dispersal pans stood empty in dawn's early light, one of them at East Kirkby. JB366 was brought down over the target, killing P/O Wright and both gunners, while the four survivors soon found themselves in enemy hands. Reports from Berlin described bombs falling over a wide area, more so in the south than the north, and damage to fifty industrial premises, a number of them engaged in important war work, while twenty thousand people were bombed out of their homes. A feature of the campaign was the number of outlying communities suffering collateral damage, and on this night, sixty-one such hamlets recorded bombs falling.

The early time-on-target had allowed crews to get a full night in bed, and they were, hopefully, fully rested, when news came through on the 28th that many of them would be returning to the "Big City" that night. A heavy force of 673 aircraft was assembled, of which 432 were Lancasters and 241 Halifaxes, 155 of the former provided by 5 Group. 57 Squadron made ready sixteen Lancasters, which departed East Kirkby between 23.42 and 00.34 with S/L Boyle the senior pilot on duty. They were routed out over southern Denmark before turning south-east on a direct course for the target, with an almost reciprocal return, and various diversionary measures to distract the night-fighter controller. Sixty-six crews turned back early, suggesting some adverse reaction to the back-to-back operations, but those from 57 Squadron all reached the target area to encounter ten-tenths cloud and a mixture of sky and ground-marking to aim at. They delivered their bombs on red and green release-point flares from an average of 20,000 feet sometime after 03.00 and some crews reporting two huge explosions at 03.18 and 03.25, the earlier one described by a 10 Squadron crew as lighting up the sky over a radius of fifty miles. Forty-six aircraft failed to return, twenty-six of them Halifaxes as the defenders fought back to exact another heavy toll of bombers, and 57 Squadron was represented again among the missing by one of its more senior crews. The crew of F/O McPhie DFC, RAAF all lost their lives when JB311 was brought down in the target area, and among them were two other members of the RAAF, both holders of a DFC. Two other empty dispersal pans at East Kirkby belonged to 630 Squadron aircraft, one of which had contained the commanding officer, W/C Rollinson, who had succeeded W/C Crocker. The impression gained from returning crews at debriefing was of a concentrated and effective attack, and this was partly borne-out by local reports of heavy damage in western and southern districts, where 180,000 people were bombed out of their homes. However, as had been the pattern throughout the campaign against Berlin, seventy-seven outlying communities had also been afflicted.

After a night's rest a force of 534 aircraft was made ready on the 30th for the final operation of this concerted effort against Berlin. 5 Group offered 156 Lancasters, of which fourteen were made ready by 57 Squadron, and they took off between 17.10 and 17.32 with F/Ls Munday and Spriggs the senior pilots on duty. After climbing out, they joined with the rest of the group to follow a route similar to that adopted two nights earlier, losing the 57 Squadron crews of P/Os Fearn, Oberg and Ross along the way, the first-mentioned bombing Heligoland as they headed home. The bomber stream remained relatively free of harassment until approaching the target, where it was greeted by ten-tenths cloud at around 8,000 feet and the sight of Path Finder skymarking in progress. Above the cloud the bomber stream basked in bright moonlight under a canopy of stars, and the 57 Squadron crews bombed on the red-with-green-stars skymarkers from around 20,000 feet either side of 20.30. On return, all commented on the smoke rising through 12,000 feet and the glow of fires beneath the cloud, which, according to some, was still visible from a hundred miles into the return flight. Thirty-two Lancasters and a single Halifax failed to make it home, but all who had set out from East Kirkby more than six hours earlier arrived back. In return for these significant losses, and according to local reports, central and south-western districts of Berlin suffered heavy damage and serious areas of fire. Other parts of the city were also hit and at least a thousand people lost their lives, while many bomb loads were again scattered liberally onto outlying communities. 112 heavy bombers and their crews had been lost to the Command as a result of these three operations, and, with the introduction of the enemy's highly efficient Tame Boar night-fighter system based on running commentaries, the advantage had swung back in the defenders' favour.

Two further heavy raids would be directed at Berlin before the end of the winter offensive, one in February and the other in March, but they would be almost in isolation. There is no question that Germany's capital had been sorely afflicted by the three latest operations, but it remained a functioning city, and showed no signs of imminent collapse. During the course of the month, the squadron participated in ten operations, six of them to Berlin, and dispatched 115 sorties for the loss of seven Lancasters and their crews.

February 1944

Bad weather during the first two weeks of February allowed the crews to draw breath and the squadrons to replenish. Harris had intended to maintain the pressure on Berlin, and would have launched a further attack, had he not been thwarted by the conditions, and as a result, the time was filled with training, lectures and mining operations. S/L Wigg and crew were posted to the squadron on the 3rd, and he would take over as A Flight commander. The newly promoted acting F/L Arthur Fearn was posted with his crew to 617 Squadron at Woodhall Spa on the 15th, where they would enjoy a successful tour operating against special targets. When the Path Finder and main force squadrons next took to the air, it would be for a record-breaking effort to Berlin later, on the 15th, and it would also be the penultimate operation of the campaign, and, indeed, of the war by Bomber Command's heavy brigade, against Germany's capital city. The force of 891 aircraft represented the largest non-1,000 force to date, and, therefore, the greatest-ever to be sent against the Capital, and it would be the first time that more than five hundred Lancasters and three hundred Halifaxes had operated together. 5 Group would surpass its previous best effort by fifty Lancasters when putting 226 of them into the air, nineteen of them representing 57 Squadron. The bomb bays of this huge armada would convey to Berlin the greatest-ever tonnage of bombs to any target to date. The 57 Squadron element departed East Kirkby between 17.06 and 17.35 with S/L Boyle the senior pilot on duty, and, after joining up with the rest of the 5 Group squadrons, they set course for the western coast of Denmark, before crossing Jutland and entering Germany via the Baltic coast between Rostock and Stralsund, with a direct heading, thereafter, for the target. The return route would require the bombers to pass south of Hannover and Bremen, and cross Holland to the North Sea via Castricum. Extensive diversionary measures included a mining operation in Kiel Bay ahead of the arrival of the bombers, a raid on Frankfurt-an-Oder to the east of Berlin by a small force of 8 Group Lancasters, and Oboe Mosquitos attacking five night-fighter airfields in Holland. The force had been depleted by seventy-five early returns by the time the remainder homed in on the target, and among these were the crews of F/L Smith, P/O Carr and F/Sgt Marland, the two because of the failure of the mid-upper gunner's electrically heated suits and the other as a result of generator failure.

Those reaching the target found it concealed beneath ten-tenths cloud at around 10,000 feet, which was not a problem for the H2S-equipped aircraft, while the others relied on the Path Finders' red release-point flares with green stars and red and green TIs on the ground. The 5 Group Squadrons bombed on these from around 20,000 to 24,000 feet either side of 21.30 and on return, reported the markers to be highly effective and well-concentrated, while the burgeoning glow beneath the clouds convinced them that they had taken part in a successful operation. This was borne out by local reports, which confirmed that the 2,642 tons of bombs had caused extensive damage in central and south-western districts but had also spilled out into surrounding communities. A thousand houses and more than five hundred temporary wooden barracks were destroyed, and important war-industry factories in the Siemensstadt district were damaged in return for the loss to the Command of forty-three aircraft, twenty-six of them Lancasters (4.6%) and seventeen Halifaxes (5.4%). Perhaps slightly disturbing was the fact that eight of the missing Halifaxes were Mk IIIs, only one fewer than the nine Mk II/Vs. 57 Squadron's JB420 was homebound and within sight of the Ijsselmeer when shot down to crash some eight miles south-west of Steenwijk, killing F/O Briggs and crew.

Despite the recent heavy losses, when orders were received on the 19th to prepare for another major assault that night, this time on Leipzig, the heavy squadrons were able to offer 816 aircraft, 561 Lancasters and 255 Halifaxes. 5 Group managed 209 Lancasters and 57 Squadron twenty, which departed East Kirkby between 23.32 and 00.13 with W/C Fisher and S/Ls Boyle and Wigg the senior pilots on duty. After climbing out over the station, they joined up with the others heading for the Dutch coast, where a proportion of the Luftwaffe Nachtjagd was waiting for them, while others had been drawn away by a mining diversion off Kiel. The crews of P/Os Cliburn and Ross returned early, each because of an indisposed crew member, and as the others continued on their way, many became embroiled in a running battle with night-fighters all the way into eastern Germany. Inaccurately forecast winds caused some aircraft to arrive at the target early, forcing them to orbit, while they waited for the Path Finders to arrive to mark the aiming point. The local flak batteries accounted for around twenty of these, while four others were lost through collisions. The 5 Group crews encountered ten-tenths cloud with tops at around 10,000 feet and bombed on green Wanganui flares and red and green TIs from around 20,000 to 23,000 feet either side of 04.00. It seems that there was a brief period during the attack when skymarking stopped and led to some scattering of bombs, but the marker-flares were soon replenished with the arrival of more backers-up, and a considerable glow beneath the cloud remained visible for some fifty minutes into the return journey, giving the impression of a successful assault. When all of those aircraft returning home had been accounted for, there was a massive shortfall of seventy-eight, a record loss by a clear twenty-one aircraft. Forty-four Lancasters and thirty-four Halifaxes had failed to return, a loss-rate of 7.8% and 13.3% respectively, and a dozen of the former were from the ranks of 5 Group. 57 Squadron's ND503 was damaged by flak and finished off by a night-fighter and crashed eight miles south-west of Gifhorn, some thirty miles east of Hannover, and only the flight engineer survived in enemy hands from the crew of P/O Davies. The Halifax casualty figure prompted Harris to immediately withdraw the Mk II and V variants from further operations over Germany, which, at a stroke, removed a proportion of 4 and 6 Groups' fire-power from the front line until they could be re-equipped with the Mk III. In the meantime, the Mk II and V operators would focus their energies for the remainder of the month on gardening duties.

Despite this depletion of available numbers, a force of 598 aircraft was made ready on the 20th for a two-phase operation that night against Stuttgart, which would be the first of three against the city over a three-week period. 5 Group contributed 176 Lancasters, fifteen of them belonging to 57 Squadron and they were each loaded with a cookie and SBCs of incendiaries, before being dispatched as part of the first wave between 23.14 and 00.23 with S/Ls Boyle and Wigg the senior pilots on duty. There would be no early returns to blunt the squadron's impact as they headed south over Cambridgeshire to begin the Channel crossing on their way to the French coast, from where the cloud remained at ten-tenths with tops at 8,000 feet all the way into southern Germany. A North Sea sweep and a diversionary raid on Munich two hours ahead of the main activity had caused the Luftwaffe to deploy its forces early, and this allowed the bomber stream to push on unmolested to the target. By the time it hove into view, the cloud had thinned to five to eight-tenths at up to 12,000 feet, and the excellent visibility enabled the crews to draw a bead on the Path Finder red and green sky-markers and similar-coloured TIs on the ground. The 57 Squadron crews bombed from around 20,000 feet after 04.00, observing many large fires, and, on return, there were reports that the glow from the burning city had remained visible from 250 miles into the return flight. Despite some scattering of bombs, local reports described central districts and those in a quadrant from north-west to north-east suffering extensive damage, and a Bosch factory was one of the important war industry concerns to be hard-hit. In contrast to twenty-four hours earlier, a modest nine aircraft failed to return.

In an attempt to reduce the prohibitive losses of recent weeks, a new tactic was introduced for the next two operations. A force of 734 aircraft was assembled on the 24th for an operation to Schweinfurt, the centre of Germany's ball-bearing production, situated some sixty miles to the east of Frankfurt in south-central Germany. The plan called for 392 aircraft to depart their stations between 18.00 and 19.00 and to be followed into the air two hours later by 342 others in the hope of catching the night-fighters on the ground refuelling and re-arming as the second wave passed through. While this operation was in progress, extensive diversionary measures would be put in hand that involved more than three hundred other aircraft, including 179 from the training units conducting a North Sea sweep, and 110 Halifaxes and Stirlings mining in northern waters. 5 Group contributed 204 Lancasters, of which eighteen were made ready by 57 Squadron, all assigned to the first phase and departing East Kirkby between 18.02 and 18.41 with W/C Fisher and S/L Wigg the senior pilots on duty. They reached the target area to find, according to some, up to three-tenths cloud at 3,000 to 4,000 feet and haze, which spoiled the vertical visibility to an extent, while other crews over the target at this time saw no cloud, and described the visibility as excellent, enabling them to pick out the River Main as they ran in to bomb. The aiming-point was identified by red and green TIs and already established fires towards the south-western edge of the town, which the 57 Squadron participants bombed from around 21,000 feet shortly after 23.00. Two columns of black smoke were observed to be rising through 5,000 feet as they turned away, and the consensus was of an effective, if, somewhat scattered attack.

Meanwhile, the second phase crews were well on their way, and picked up the glow of fires from the earlier raid at a distance of two hundred miles. The visibility in the target area remained good, despite the rising smoke, and bombing took place out of almost cloudless skies onto red and green TIs from around 01.00. All indications suggested an effective raid, but, unfortunately, both phases of the operation had suffered from undershooting after some Path Finder backers-up had failed to press on to the aiming-point and much of the effort was wasted on open and wooded country. In that regard, it was a disappointing night, but an interesting feature was the loss of 50% fewer aircraft from the second wave in comparison with the first, in an overall casualty figure of thirty-three, and this suggested some merit in the tactic. 57 Squadron's JB565 had been outbound at 21,000 feet when shot down in flames by a night-fighter to crash at Reutenbourg, some fifteen miles from the German frontier north-west of Strasbourg. P/O Harland and three of his crew parachuted into the arms of their captors, while the bomb-aimer retained his freedom after being spirited away by local civilians.

Since the turn of the year a wind-finder system had been in use, in which selected crews monitored wind speed and direction, and passed their findings back to HQ, where the figures were collated, and any changes from the briefed conditions re-broadcast to the bomber stream. This had been found to be extremely useful, but, as would be discovered in the ensuing weeks, the system had its limitations.

The main operation on the following night was directed at the beautiful and culturally significant Bavarian city of Augsburg, situated around thirty miles north-west of Munich. It was home to a major Maschinenfabrik Augsburg Nuremberg (M.A.N) diesel engine factory, which had been the target for the epic low-level daylight raid by 44 and 97 Squadrons in April 1942. On this night, 594 aircraft were divided into two waves, and among them were 164 Lancasters of 5 Group, including fourteen representing 57 Squadron. Thirteen of these were assigned to the first phase and were to act as Path Finder supporters, a new role designed to "beef up" the numbers passing over the aiming point in the vanguard of the attack and prevent the flak batteries from latching on to individual Path Finder aircraft. They were then to orbit and make a second pass to deliver their bombs. They took off between 18.09 and 18.36 with S/Ls Boyle and Wigg the senior pilots on duty, while F/L Walton and crew were assigned to the second phase and would depart East Kirkby at 21.58. S/L Wigg and F/L Spriggs turned back early because of turret failures, while the others of the first wave continued on over Belgium with ten-tenths cloud beneath them, that had dissipated by the time the target drew near. On arrival, it was possible for crews to gain a visual reference confirmed by the Path Finders' red and green TIs, and these were in the bomb sights as the 57 Squadron crews carried out their attacks from an average of 21,000 feet shortly before 23.00. Fires were beginning to take hold as they turned away and the second wave crews were drawn on by the glow in the sky from a hundred miles out, arriving to find visibility still good despite copious amounts of smoke rising through 10,000 feet. They bombed on existing fires and red and green Wanganui flares and TIs from 20,000 feet and above from around 01.15. The loss of twenty-one aircraft seemed to confirm the benefits of splitting the forces, and this tactic would remain an important part of Bomber Command planning for the remainder of the war. It had been a devastatingly destructive operation, in which all facets of the plan had come together in near perfect harmony, spelling disaster for this lightly defended treasure trove of culture. Its heart was torn out by blast and fire that destroyed almost three thousand houses along with buildings of outstanding historical significance, and centuries of irreplaceable culture was lost forever. There was also some industrial damage, and around ninety-thousand people were bombed out of their homes.

During the course of the month, the squadron carried out five operations and dispatched eighty-six sorties for the loss of three Lancasters and their crews.

March 1944

March would bring an end to the winter campaign, but a long and bitter month would have to be endured first before any respite came from long-range forays into Germany. The crews had benefitted from a few nights off when the second raid of the series on Stuttgart was posted on the 1st, for which a force of 557 aircraft was made ready. This number included 178 Lancasters representing 5 Group, sixteen of which were provided by 57 Squadron and loaded with a cookie and mix of 4lb and 30lb incendiaries before setting off from East Kirkby between 22.51 and 23.20 with W/C Fisher and S/Ls Boyle and Wigg the senior pilots on duty. They set course for the French coast and must have been quite deep into enemy territory when F/L Munday and crew turned back because of an oil leak in the port-inner engine. The others pressed on over ten-tenths cloud with tops at between 12,000 and 17,000 feet, and encountered similar conditions in the target area, where the Path Finders employed a combination of sky and ground-marking techniques. This, unfortunately, became scattered, and the bombing was directed between two main concentrations, the 57 Squadron crews carrying out their attacks on Wanganui red skymarkers with green stars from an average of 20,500 feet shortly after 03.00. It was not possible to assess the accuracy of the attack, although a column of smoke had reached 25,000 feet by the end of the raid, and large fires were evident from the glow in the sky visible from up to 150 miles away. The presence of thick cloud all the way there and back made conditions difficult for enemy night-fighters, and a remarkably modest four aircraft failed to return. It was eventually established that the raid had been an outstanding success, which had caused extensive damage in central, western and northern districts, where a number of important war-industry factories, including those belonging to Bosch and Daimler-Benz, had sustained damage.

At the end of the first week, the Halifax brigade, particularly those withdrawn from operations over Germany, fired the opening salvoes of the Transportation Plan, the pre-invasion campaign to dismantle by bombing thirty-seven railway centres in France, Belgium and western Germany. It began on the night of the 6/7th at Trappes marshalling yards, situated some ten miles west-south-west of Paris, and continued at Le Mans in north-western France on the following night. For most of the heavy crews, however, there was no employment following Stuttgart, until a return there in mid-month, but, in the meantime, matters were afoot at 5 Group, and had been ever since the frustrating series of operations against flying bomb launching sites by 617 Squadron since December had produced disappointing results. The problem had been an inability to achieve pinpoint accuracy, which was vital to destroy small, precision targets, and Oboe was just not precise enough. Accurate though Oboe undoubtedly was at an urban target, where a margin of error of 400 to 600 yards was considered pinpoint, precision targets required more. W/C Cheshire and S/L Martin experimented with a dive-bombing technique, which had proved to be successful, but impracticable in a Lancaster, and Cheshire had borrowed a Mosquito for further trials. These were so promising, that the 5 Group A-O-C, AVM Cochrane, authorized a number of operations by the squadron against factory targets in France, before taking the idea to Harris. Harris approved, paving the way for 5 Group to take on its own target marking force and become effectively independent of the main bomber force.

To this end, orders were received at the 53 Base stations of Bardney, Skellingthorpe and Waddington on the 9th to prepare eleven Lancasters each for a 5 Group operation against the Lioré et Olivier aircraft factory at Marignane, situated a few miles to the north of Marseilles in southern France. The area had been the main pre-war hub for commercial flying boat operations, particularly for the Pan American Clipper Class flights, and the factory had been engaged in the manufacture of the LeO 45 twin-engine medium bomber for the French Air Force. The crews faced a round-trip of some 1,350 miles if they flew direct and arrived in the target area under clear skies and bright moonlight, which facilitated an easy identification of the factory buildings. They circled for more than thirty minutes while it was marked with red spotfires, after which the bombing was carried out in accordance with the instructions of the Master Bomber, W/C "Ted" Porter, the commanding officer of 9 Squadron. The bombing was carried out from medium level and the high-explosive content was seen to fall among the buildings, while the incendiaries appeared to be a little scattered, but a large explosion was witnessed at 01.24 and a huge pall of smoke was rising through 6,000 feet as the force turned away. This operation set a pattern which would be employed by 5 Group for the remainder of the war.

5 Group's 54 Base, consisting of the stations at Coningsby, Woodhall Spa and Metheringham, and Base East Kirkby, which on the 15th of April would add Spilsby and Strubby to become 55 Base, received orders on the 10th to prepare 102 Lancasters to form four small forces, each to attack a specific factory in France that night. The targets were the Michelin tyre factory at Clermont-Ferrand, the Bloch aircraft factory at Châteauroux, which was the first to be set up by the famed designer, Marcel Dassault in 1935, the Morane Saulnier aircraft plant at Ossun, just north of the Pyrenese and the Ricamerie needle-bearing works at St-Etienne, the last-mentioned the objective for sixteen Lancasters from 617 Squadron. 57 Squadron briefed eleven crews for the attack on the Michelin factory and dispatched them from East Kirkby between 19.37 and 20.14 with W/C Fisher and S/L Boyle the senior pilots on duty. P/O Carr and crew were soon back on the ground after being let down by their a.s.i. The others arrived along with eleven Lancasters each from 630 and 207 Squadrons to find bright moonlight and a Master Bomber on hand to direct the bombing, and he issued appropriate instructions to compensate for the inaccurate delivery of red spotfires a hundred yards to the south and four hundred yards to the south-west of the aiming point. Despite that, the bombs appeared to fall around the markers, and when S/L Boyle went in to attack at the end, he gained a clear sight of the buildings but saw no evidence of damage. In the absence of opposition at all four targets, the operations were concluded for the loss of a single Lancaster belonging to 207 Squadron.

Now that the Mk III Halifax was becoming available in larger numbers, the Command was quickly returning to full strength, and it was a force of 863 aircraft that set out for Stuttgart in the early-evening of the 15th. This number included 206 Lancasters provided by 5 Group, twenty-one of them containing 57 Squadron crews, which departed East Kirkby between 18.53 and 19.31 with no fewer than five pilots of flight lieutenant rank leading the way. They rendezvoused with the rest of the force as they passed over Reading on their way to the south coast and it was an elongated bomber stream that entered France at 20,000 feet over broken cloud with clear conditions above. It was about this time that F/O Bayley and crew turned back with an unserviceable rear turret, while the others maintained a course parallel with the frontiers of Belgium, Luxembourg and Germany as if heading for Switzerland, before turning towards the north-east for the run-in to the target. It was during this final leg that the night-fighters managed to infiltrate a section of the stream and score heavily. 57 Squadron's JB474 was still about an hour from the target when all four engines were found to be on fire and P/O Atcheson DFC set a new course for Switzerland. Once he was certain that the frontier had been crossed, he ordered the crew to bale out, and it must have been at that moment that the Lancaster fell out of control and crashed at Saignelégier killing all but the mid-upper gunner, who was interned. Adverse winds were responsible for the Path Finders' arrival up to six minutes late to open the attack with both sky and ground-markers in the face of seven to ten-tenths cloud at between 8,000 and 15,000 feet. The Wanganui flares drifted in the wind, marking an area to the north-east of the river Neckar, while the TIs landed far apart in the north and south of the city. The 57 Squadron crews bombed on whatever markers presented themselves, mostly red TIs, from around 21,000 feet between either side of 23.30, observing a spread of fires, including two large ones ten miles apart, and smoke rising to bombing altitude. It would be established later that some of the early bombing had been accurate, but, that most of it had undershot and fallen into open country, a disappointment compounded by the loss, mostly to night-fighters, of thirty-seven aircraft.

Many operations had been mounted against Frankfurt during the preceding two years, only a small number of which had been really effective. This situation was about to be rectified, however, and the first of two raids against this south-central powerhouse of industry was posted on the 18th, and a force of 846 aircraft made ready. 5 Group supported the operation with 212 Lancasters, nineteen of which were made ready by 57 Squadron and loaded at East Kirkby with a cookie each and a mix of 4lb and 30lb incendiaries. They took off between 19.00 and 19.37 with S/L Boyle the senior pilot on duty and adopted the familiar route to the region via France. P/O Carr and crew lost their starboard-outer engine and bombed an aerodrome at Swevezele in Belgium after turning for home. The others benefitted from good weather conditions as they crossed into Germany, where they encountered a layer of haze 20,000 feet thick over the target, and, according to most, no more than three-tenths cloud. This allowed the Path Finders to employ the Newhaven ground marking technique (blind marking by H2S, followed by visual backing-up), which the 57 Squadron crews exploited when carrying out their attacks on red and green TIs from an average of 20,000 feet from around 22.00. A large explosion was witnessed at 22.05, and the participants in the raid flew home confident that their efforts had been worthwhile. They had, indeed, contributed to an outstandingly successful raid, during which, 5 Group alone dropped more than one thousand tons of bombs for the first time at a single target. Local reports calculated that six thousand buildings had been destroyed or seriously damaged in predominantly eastern, central and western districts, and this was in return for the loss of twenty-two aircraft, five of which were from 5 Group.

Frankfurt was named again on the 22nd as the target for that night, and 217 crews of 5 Group learned that they were to be part of another huge force of 816 aircraft. The nineteen participants from 57 Squadron took off from East Kirkby between 18.37 and 19.12 with S/L Wigg the senior pilot on duty. After climbing out above their stations and forming up, they adopted an unusual route for a target south of the Ruhr, crossing the enemy coast over Vlieland and Teschelling, before passing to the east of Osnabrück on a direct course due south for the target. F/L Smith and crew lost their port-outer engine somewhere near the junction of the Dortmund-Ems and Mittelland Canals and bombed the aerodrome at Rheine before recrossing the Dutch frontier, while P/O Cliburn's mid-upper gunner's electrically heated suit failed, forcing them to turn back also. The others arrived at the target to find five to six-tenths thin, low cloud at around 4,000 feet, and Paramatta marking (blind marking by H2S) in progress. They focused their attention on the release-point flares and red and green TIs marking out the aiming-point, before bombing from an average of 21,500 feet either side of 22.00. A massive rectangular area of unbroken fire was observed across the centre of the city, the glow from which could be seen for at least a hundred miles into the return flight. Crews reported numerous searchlights lighting up the cloud, and moderate to intense flak that reached up to the bombers' flight level, while local sources confirmed the enormity of the devastation, which was particularly severe in western districts and left this half of the city without electricity, gas and water for an extended period. More than nine hundred people lost their lives and a further 120,000 were bombed out of their homes, at a cost to the Command of twenty-six Lancasters and seven Halifaxes, a loss-rate of 4.2% and 3.8% respectively. It was a bad night for senior officers, 207 and 7 Squadrons losing their commanding officers, while Bardney's station commander, G/C Norman Pleasance, failed to return in a 9 Squadron Lancaster. What was about to happen over the next week and a half, however, would overshadow anything that had gone before, and would certainly not fall within what might be considered acceptable.

It was more than five weeks since the main force had last visited the Capital, and 811 aircraft were made ready on the 24th for what would be the final raid of the war by RAF heavy bombers on the "Big City". 5 Group put up 193 Lancasters, of which seventeen were made ready by 57 Squadron, and they departed East Kirkby between 18.35 and 19.03 with S/L Boyle the senior pilot on duty. They had a long flight ahead of them, which would take them across the North Sea to the Danish coast near Ringkøbing and then to a point on the German Baltic coast near Rostock. When north-east of Berlin they were to adopt a south-westerly course for the bombing run, and, once clear of the defence zone homebound, dogleg to the west and then north-west to pass around Hannover on its southern and western sides, before heading for Holland and an exit via the Castricum coast. The extended outward leg provided a time-on-target of around 22.30, but an unexpected difficulty would be encountered, which would render void all of the meticulous planning. The existence of what we now refer to as "Jetstream" winds was unknown at the time, and the one blowing from the north with unprecedented strength on this night pushed the bomber stream south of its intended track. Navigators, who were expecting to see the northern tip of Sylt on their H2S screens, were horrified to find the southern end, which meant that they were thirty miles south of track, and about to fly over Germany rather than Denmark. The previously mentioned "wind finder" system had been set up for precisely this eventuality, but the problem on this night was that the wind finders refused to believe what their instruments were telling them. Winds in excess of one hundred m.p.h had never been encountered before, and, fearing that they would be disbelieved, many modified the figures downward. The same thing happened at raid control, where the figures were modified again, so that the information rebroadcast to the bomber stream bore no resemblance to the reality of the situation.

The crews of P/O Carr and crew returned early with a frozen rear gunner after his heated suit failed, while the others pressed on across the North Sea, and by the time that they had reached Westerhever on the west coast of the Schleswig-Holstein peninsula, most realized that they were some distance south of track. A new course was worked out to try to regain the planned route and avoid the defences that would be met if they turned east while still over Germany. Many commented on the inaccurate wind information received during the outward journey, and having arrived in the target area, some were convinced that the Path Finders were up to ten minutes late in opening the raid. This was confirmed to some by the voice of the Master Bomber exhorting them to hurry up. Crews reported a variety of cloud conditions, from three to ten-tenths at between 6,000 and 15,000 feet, but most were able to pick out the red and green TIs on the ground, and, if not, found red Wanganui flares with green stars to guide them to the aiming-point. The 57 Squadron crews confirmed their positions by H2S before bombing from an average of 20,000 feet and observed what appeared to be a scattered attack in the early stages, until fires began to become more concentrated in three distinct areas, and large explosions were witnessed at 22.42 and 22.54. The defences were very active with moderate flak bursting at up to 24,000 feet, and light flak attempting to shoot out the skymarkers, but night-fighter activity was described by the 5 Group ORB as unusually quiet. There was a shock awaiting the Command as the returning aircraft landed to leave a shortfall of seventy-two, and it would be established later that two-thirds of them had fallen victim to the Ruhr flak batteries after being driven into that region's defence zone by the wind on the way home. 57 Squadron's JB539 was homebound when shot down by a night-fighter to crash fifteen miles east of Münster and burst into flames, killing F/O Cliburn and his crew. ND671 was also on the way home at 21,000 feet when falling victim to flak and crashing at Geseke on the south-eastern approaches to Lippstadt. P/O Hampton RAAF and four others lost their lives while the navigator and wireless operator survived in enemy hands. Post-raid analysis revealed that the wind had also played havoc with the marking and bombing and had pushed the attack towards the south-western districts of the capital, where most of the damage occurred, while 126 outlying communities also received bombs. 57 Squadron had been present on each of the nineteen main raids to Berlin and the diversion there on the night of the Magdeburg debacle in January and had despatched 282 sorties for the loss of sixteen of its Lancasters, with eighty-seven men killed and twenty-five surviving as PoWs. This meant that the squadron flew the most sorties to Berlin in 5 Group and shared the highest losses with 44 (Rhodesia) Squadron. (The Berlin Raids. Martin Middlebrook).

Twenty 5 Group Lancasters from 53 Base were invited to take part in an attack on the extensive railway yards at Aulnoye in north-eastern France to be carried out on the evening of the 25th, while twenty-two 617 Squadron Lancasters returned to the Sigma aero-engine factory at Lyons. They found clear skies at the target and ground haze, through which a bend in the river Sambre provided a useful pinpoint, although the aiming-point had been clearly marked by concentrated red and green TIs. They bombed from 7,000 to 8,400 feet between 22.01 and 22.23 and observed fires and a large explosion at 22.03.

Although Berlin had now been consigned to the past, the winter campaign still had a week to run and two more major operations for the crews to negotiate. The first of these was posted on the 26th and would bring a return to the old enemy of Essen that night, for which a force of 705 aircraft was made ready. 5 Group contributed 172 of the 476 Lancasters, a dozen of them provided by 57 Squadron, which took off from East Kirkby between 19.17 and 19.44 with S/L Wigg the senior pilot on duty. They climbed out over the flat fenlands and set course for the Dutch coast to pass north of Haarlem and Amsterdam, before swinging to the south-east on a direct run to the target. There were no early returns, and all reached the target area to find it under eight to ten-tenths cloud with tops in places as high as 14,000 feet. Oboe performed well and enabled the Path Finders to mark the city with red and green TIs and Wanganui flares, which the 57 Squadron crews bombed from an average of 20,500 feet, before returning safely, having been unable to assess the results of their efforts. The impression was of a successful raid, and this was based on a considerable glow beneath the clouds as they withdrew. Post-raid reconnaissance soon confirmed another outstandingly destructive operation against this once elusive target, thus continuing the remarkable run of successes here since the introduction of Oboe to main force operations a year earlier. Over seventeen hundred houses were destroyed in the attack, with dozens of war industry factories sustaining serious damage, and, on a night when the night-fighter controllers were caught off guard by the switch to the Ruhr, the success was gained for the modest loss of nine aircraft.

The period known as the Battle of Berlin, but which was better referred to as the winter campaign, was to be brought to an end on the night of the 30/31st, with a standard maximum-effort raid on Nuremberg. The plan of operation departed from normal practice in only one important respect, and this was to prove critical. It had become standard routine over the winter for 8 Group to plan operations and to employ diversions and feints to confuse the enemy night-fighter controllers. Sometimes they were successful and sometimes not, but with the night-fighter force having clearly gained the upper hand with its "Tame Boar" running commentary system, all possible means had to be adopted to protect the bomber stream. During a conference held early on the 30th, the Lancaster Group A-O-Cs expressed a preference for a 5 Group-inspired route, which would require the bomber stream to fly a long straight leg across Belgium and Germany, to a point about fifty miles north of Nuremberg, from where the final run-in would commence. The Halifax A-O-Cs were less convinced of the benefits, and AVM Bennett, the Path Finder chief, was positively overcome by the potential dangers and predicted a disaster, only to be overruled. A force of 795 aircraft was made ready, of which 201 Lancasters were to be provided by 5 Group, eighteen of them representing 57 Squadron, and the crews attended briefings to be told of the route, wind conditions and the belief that a layer of cloud would conceal them from enemy night-fighters. Before take-off, a 1409 Meteorological Flight Mosquito crew radioed in to cast doubts upon the weather conditions, which they could see differed markedly from those that had been forecast. This also went unheeded, and, from around 21.45 for the next hour or so, the crews took off for the rendezvous area, and headed into a conspiracy of circumstances that would inflict upon Bomber Command its heaviest defeat of the war.

At East Kirkby, the 57 Squadron Lancasters took off between 21.54 and 22.24 with S/Ls Boyle and Wiggs the senior pilots on duty, and it was not long into the flight before they and the other crews began to notice some unusual features in the conditions, which included uncommonly bright moonlight, and a crystal clarity of visibility that allowed them the rare sight of other aircraft in the stream. On most nights, crews would feel themselves to be completely alone in the sky all the way to the target, until bang on schedule, TIs would be seen to fall, and other aircraft would make their presence felt by the turbulence of their slipstreams as they funnelled towards the aiming-point. Once at cruising altitude on this night, however, they were alarmed to note that the forecast cloud was conspicuous by its absence, and instead, lay beneath them as a white tablecloth, against which they were silhouetted like flies. Condensation trails began to form in the cold, clear air to further advertise their presence to the enemy, and the "Jetstream" winds, which had so adversely affected the Berlin raid a week earlier, were also present, only this time blowing from the south. As then, the wind finder system would be unable to cope, and this would have a serious impact on the outcome of the operation. The final insult on this sad night was, that the route into Germany passed close to two night-fighter beacons, which the enemy aircraft were orbiting while they awaited their instructions, unaware initially that they were about to have the cream of Bomber Command handed to them on a plate.

The carnage began over Charleroi in Belgium, and from there to the target, the route was sign-posted by the burning wreckage on the ground of eighty Bomber Command aircraft. 57 Squadron's ND622 was the seventieth victim and fell to the guns of Oblt Helmut Schulte of II./NJG5, crashing at Bischwind, some fourteen miles south-west of Coburg and still fifty miles north of the target. F/L Tickler CGM survived with the American bomb-aimer and the mid-upper gunner to be taken into captivity, but the remaining four crew members lost their lives. The wind finder system broke down again, and those crews who either failed to detect the strength of the wind, or simply refused to believe the evidence, were driven up to fifty miles north of their intended track, and consequently, turned towards Nuremberg from a false position. This led to more than a hundred aircraft bombing at Schweinfurt in error, which combined with the massive losses sustained before the target was reached to reduce considerably the numbers reaching the primary target. The remaining 57 Squadron crews arrived over Nuremberg to encounter eight to nine-tenths cloud with tops as high as 16,000 feet and bombed from an average of 20,000 feet either side of 01.30, aiming at red and green TIs and sky-markers. Many fires were observed, the glow from which, according to some reports, remained visible for 120 miles into the return journey. Ninety-five aircraft failed to return home, twenty-one of them from 5 Group, and many others were written off in landing crashes or with battle damage too severe to repair. The shock and disappointment were compounded by the fact that the strong wind had driven the marking beyond the city to the east, and Nuremberg had, consequently, escaped serious damage. P/O Castagnola and crew claimed the destruction of a Ju88.

During the course of the month, the squadron participated in eight operations and dispatched 133 sorties for the loss of four Lancasters and their crews.

April 1944

The winter campaign had brought the Command to its low point of the war and was the only time when the morale of the crews was in question. What now lay before the hard-pressed men of Bomber Command was in marked contrast to that which had been endured over the seemingly interminable winter months. In place of the long slog to Germany on dark, often dirty nights, shorter range hops to France and Belgium in improving weather conditions would become the order of the day. However, these operations would be equally demanding in their way, and would require of the crews a greater commitment to accuracy to avoid casualties among friendly civilians. Despite this, a decree from on high insisted that such operations were worthy of counting as just one third of a sortie towards the completion of a tour, and, until this flawed policy was rescinded, the hint of a mutinous air would pervade the crew rooms. In fact, the number of sorties to complete a tour would fluctuate between this point and the end of hostilities. Despite the horrendous losses of the winter campaign, the Command was in remarkably fine fettle to face its new challenge, with 3 Group gradually changing to Lancasters, and the much-improved Hercules powered Halifaxes equipping 4 Group and most of 6 Group. Harris was now in the enviable position of being able to achieve what had eluded his predecessor, namely, to attack multiple targets simultaneously with enough strength to be effective. Such was the hitting-power now at his disposal, he could assign targets to individual groups, to groups in tandem, or to the Command as a whole, as dictated by operational requirements. Although invasion considerations would come first, while Harris was at the helm, his favoured policy of city-busting would never be entirely shelved.

5 Group returned to operations on the 5th, for which a force of 144 Lancasters was assembled plus a Mosquito flown by W/C Cheshire of 617 Squadron. The target was the former Dewoitine aircraft factory located on the Montaudran aerodrome south-east of Toulouse city centre deep in south-western France, which, under a nationalization plan in 1936 involving six aircraft companies, including Lioré et Olivier and Potez, was now operating under the name SNCASE, or Sud Est for short. Cheshire was to mark it with spotfires from low level, using the system that he was instrumental in developing, and one which would become an integral part of 5 Group operations, with refinements, from this point on. This would be Cheshire's first operational flight in a Mosquito, and the first time that he marked a target for 5 Group, rather than just for 617 Squadron. Much depended upon its success if Harris were to become sold on the idea of the low-level visual marking technique and give it his backing. The Master Bomber for the occasion was Wing Commander Operations, W/C James "Willie" Tait, a veteran of operations with 4 Group, former commanding officer of 51 and 10 Squadrons, future commanding officer of 617 Squadron and now a member of the 5 Group Master Bomber fraternity based at Coningsby. He would be flying from Waddington in a 467 Squadron Lancaster with a borrowed crew. W/C Fisher and S/L Wigg were the senior 57 Squadron pilots on duty as they departed East Kirkby between 19.46 and 20.14 with an outward flight ahead of them of more than four hours, which all of the 57 Squadron crews negotiated. They arrived at a datum point, which they orbited until called in to attack and watched Cheshire lob two red spotfires onto the roof of the factory at 00.17 during his third pass. So accurate were they, that the two 617 Squadron Lancaster backers-up were not required before the main force element was called in to bomb in bright moonlight from 8,000 to 17,000 feet either side of 00.30 in the face of a hostile and accurate flak defence. Explosions were observed among buildings, large fires sending smoke rising through 7,000 feet, and the only 5 Group casualty from this outstandingly successful operation was a 207 Squadron Lancaster, which was hit by flak over the target at 00.30 and exploded, killing all on board. Within hours of receiving a report of the raid, Harris gave the go ahead for 5 Group to take on its own marking force, and become, in effect, an independent entity.

It would be almost two weeks before the necessary moves took place, and, in the meantime, the pre-invasion campaign got into full swing with the posting of two operations on the 9th.

Responsibility for the destruction of the Lille-Delivrance goods station in north-eastern France was handed to 239 aircraft from 3, 4, 6 and 8 Groups, while the marshalling yards at Villeneuve-St-Georges, on the southern outskirts of Paris, were to be targeted by 225 aircraft drawn from all groups. The weather conditions were excellent, and clear skies greeted the latter force as it crossed the French coast at around 14,000 feet. The target could be identified visually, but crews aimed for the red and green TIs that had been accurately placed by the Path Finders, delivering their hardware from between 13,000 and 14,500 feet in the face of little opposition. Many bomb bursts were observed along with orange explosions, and, to those high above, the raid appeared to be highly successful. In fact, many bomb loads had fallen into adjacent residential districts, where four hundred houses had been destroyed or seriously damaged, and ninety-three people killed. This was far fewer than had died in the simultaneous operation at Lille, many miles to the north-east, where over two thousand items of rolling stock had been destroyed, and buildings and installations seriously damaged, but at a collateral cost of 456 French civilian lives. Civilian casualties would prove to be an unavoidable by-product of the campaign.

57 Squadron did not take part in the above operation but was called into action anyway to provide a dozen of 103 Lancasters from 1 and 5 Groups to mine the waters in the Gulf of Danzig, specifically in the Spinach, Privet and Tangerine gardens respectively off the ports of Gdynia, Danzig (Gdansk) and Pillau. The 57 Squadron element was divided between Privet and Tangerine and departed East Kirkby between 21.11 and 21.37 with W/C Fisher the senior pilot on duty. P/O Finch RAAF and crew were outbound over Denmark in JB725 when intercepted and shot down by a night-fighter to crash at 00.25 near Jelling in central Jutland with no survivors. The others arrived in the target area to be greeted by ideal conditions in which they easily identified pinpoints from which to make timed runs, and all returned safely after round trips of roughly nine hours.

Monday the 10th brought five further railway yards into the spotlight, four in France and one in Belgium, each of which was assigned to an individual group. 5 Group was handed those at Tours in the Loire region of western France, for which 180 Lancasters were made ready, fourteen of them on the 57 Squadron dispersals at East Kirkby. The first wave trio took off between 22.06 and 22.15 with S/L Boyle the senior pilot on duty and they were followed into the air between 22.30 and 22.45 by the others led by S/L Wigg. They set course for England's south coast to begin the Channel crossing, and all arrived at the target to find bright moonlight and red spotfires marking the aiming-points. Master Bombers, including W/C Tait, were on hand to direct the two phases of the attack, the first against the western side of the yards and the second its eastern counterpart. The attack on the western aiming-point took place from 8,000 to 10,000 feet either side of 02.00, and crews described the yards as an avenue of fire. The scene soon became confused as smoke began to spread across the site and billow into the air, rising through 8,000 feet in the later stages. This affected to an extent the second phase bombing, which was carried out from around 5,500 to 10,000 feet either side of 22.30. The main force had been called upon to approach the aiming-point in a left-hand orbit from the east, during which the Master Bomber called a temporary halt as he reassessed the changing visibility, before reinstating the bombing order, until the smoke forced him to end the attack at 02.48 and send home any crews with bombs still on board. There were mixed opinions as to the effectiveness of the operation, some gaining the impression that the eastern half of the yards had not been touched, but others claimed the attack to have been accurate and concentrated within the yards, and two large fires were observed. Post-raid reconnaissance confirmed the success of the operation, but the Germans would round up local civilians and force them into repairing the damage to get the yards working again before long.

Aachen was a major railway centre with marshalling yards at both the western and eastern ends, but the size of the force assembled for the attack planned for the night of the 11/12th was clearly designed to cause as much damage as possible within what was Germany's most westerly city. The force of 341 heavy aircraft was drawn from 1, 3, 5 and 8 Groups with eleven of the Lancasters provided by 57 Squadron, their bomb bays loaded with a dozen 1,000 pounders each and 300 x 4lb incendiaries. They departed East Kirkby between 20.18 and 20.32 with S/Ls Boyle and Wigg the senior pilots on duty and lost the services of F/L Laing and crew early because of the failure of their starboard-inner engine. The others joined the bomber stream as it climbed to between 18,000 and 20,000 feet by the time it reached the Belgian coast at 3 degrees east, an altitude maintained all the way to the target, where six to ten-tenths thin cloud was encountered at between 7,000 and 8,000 feet, through which the red and green TIs could be seen identifying the aiming point. The 5 Group bombing was carried out from an average of 18,000 feet and many bomb bursts and fires were observed, which suggested that the attack had been accurate. The crews maintained height on the way home until fifty miles from the coast, at which position they began a gentle descent to exit enemy territory at 15,000 feet or above. Reports coming out of Aachen revealed this to be the city's worst experience of the war to date, with extensive damage in central and southern districts, disruption of its transport infrastructure and a death toll of 1,525 people, in return for which, Bomber Command registered the loss of nine Lancasters. However, post-raid reconnaissance revealed that the railway yards had not been destroyed and would require further attention.

On the 14th, the Command became officially subject to the orders coming from the Supreme Headquarters of the Allied Expeditionary Force (SHAEF), under General Dwight D Eisenhower, and would remain thus shackled until the Allied armies were sweeping towards the German frontier at the end of the summer. On the 15th, W/C Fisher was posted to HQ 21 Group, and he was succeeded as commanding officer of 57 Squadron by W/C Humphreys who arrived from 51 Base, the 5 Group training establishment with HQ at Swinderby.

On the 18th, 83 and 97 Squadrons were loaned to 5 Group from the Path Finder Force, on what amounted to a permanent detachment, along with the Mosquito unit, 627 Squadron. The Lancaster units were to become the 5 Group heavy markers, while the Mosquitos would eventually take over the low-level marking role currently performed by 617 Squadron. This was a major coup for AVM Cochrane and 5 Group and a bitter blow to AVM Bennett, the Path Finder chief, whose relationship had never been cordial, but this plunged it to new depths. Both were brilliant men, Bennett, an Australian, a man of the greatest intellect, who, despite his total lack of humour, commanded the deepest respect and loyalty from his men, while Cochrane enjoyed a closer relationship with Harris, having served as a flight commander under him in Mesopotamia between the wars. Each had a strong opinion on the subject of target marking, Bennett believing that a low-level method exposed the crews to unnecessary danger, while Cochrane insisted that the risks in a fast-flying Mosquito were negligible and would produce greater accuracy. Though 83 and 97 Squadrons were formerly of the elitist 5 Group, and relied on it to supply new crews, once part of 8 Group, their members had come to see that as the pinnacle, and were upset at being removed from what they considered to be an elevated status. Once entitled, they were fiercely proud to wear the Path Finder badge and enjoyed the enhanced promotion opportunities, but, happily for them, as the squadrons were only officially on loan to 5 Group, these were privileges that they would retain.

Any resentment might have been smoothed over had their reception at Coningsby been handled better, but, as the newly arrived crews tumbled out of their transports, they were summoned immediately to the briefing room, to be lectured by the 54 Base commander, Air Commodore "Bobby" Sharp, a pompous and self-important link in the chain of command. Rather than welcoming them as brothers-in-arms, he harangued them over their bad 8 Group habits and ordered them to buckle down to learning 5 Group ways. This was an insult to experienced airmen, for whom the task of illuminating targets for 5 Group would be a piece of cake in comparison with the complexities of their 8 Group duties. The fact that the insult was being delivered by a man with no relevant operational experience, made it doubly unpalatable. From this point on, 5 Group would be known in 8 Group circles somewhat disparagingly as the "Independent Air Force", or "The Lincolnshire Poachers".

The 5 Group target on the 18th was the marshalling yards at Juvisy, situated on the West Bank of the Seine south of Paris, which was one of four similar targets for the night. The intention had been for the new arrivals to participate, but the disgruntled commanding officers, G/C Laurence Deane of 83 Squadron and W/C Jimmy Carter of 97 Squadron, announced that they were not yet ready, and the operation would have to go ahead without them. 202 Lancasters and four Mosquitos were made ready, the latter belonging to 617 Squadron, and 8 Group would provide three Oboe Mosquitos to deliver the initial marking. 57 Squadron made ready eighteen Lancasters and dispatched them from East Kirkby between 20.37 and 21.06 with W/C Humphreys and S/L Wigg the senior pilots on duty. All reached the target to find clear skies and ideal bombing conditions, in which they observed W/C Cheshire release red spotfires, which were backed up by green TIs. Despite black smoke drifting across the aiming-point and upwards from the destruction of a fuel dump at 23.32, the crews were able to hit the markers from an average of 10,000 feet and were enthusiastic about the success of the operation. This was confirmed by post-raid reconnaissance and prompted the crews to make the valid comment that, to count this operation as just one-third of a sortie was undervaluing it, and this was a sentiment shared by all whose job involved putting their lives on the line. The crews of F/Os Grubb and Thomas brought their bombs home as instructed after failing to observe the spotfires and it seems possible that the experienced and mature crew of P/O Oberg RAAF may also have been sitting on a full bomb load when ND475 crashed near Whittlesey in Cambridgeshire at 01.00 and spread itself over a wide area of fenland. Such was the violence of the explosion, that the remains of only one of the eight occupants were recovered for burial. Rear gunner, P/O Adams, was forty years old and the pilot and navigator were in their thirties, which made them ancient in the eyes of the average crew member.

Briefings on 5 Group stations on the 20th informed crews of their part in the first operation to include the three newly transferred squadrons, a two-phase attack on railway yards at La Chapelle, situated just to the north of Paris. Meanwhile, the night's main event was to be conducted by a force of 357 Lancasters and twenty-two Mosquitos drawn from 1, 3, 6 and 8 Groups against Cologne. A meticulous plan had been prepared for 5 Group, in which the phases were to be separated by an hour, each with its own specific aiming-point, and 83 Squadron's W/C Deane was to be the Master Bomber with S/L Sparks his deputy. The plan called for 8 Group Mosquitos to drop cascading flares by Oboe to provide an initial reference, and for a Mosquito element from 627 Squadron to lay a Window screen ahead of the main force Lancasters. Once the target had been identified, the first members of the 83 Squadron flare force were to provide illumination for the low-level marker Mosquitos of 617 Squadron, which would mark the first aiming-point with red spot fires for the main force element to aim at. The whole procedure would then be repeated at the second aiming point. At Coningsby, W/C Deane conducted the briefing, and, at its conclusion, wished the assembled throng good luck, before dismissing them, whereupon a voice from the back declared that the briefing wasn't over, and that the base and station commanders wanted their say. This had not been standard practice in 8 Group, and left Deane mystified and a little humiliated. The senior officers had only waffle to offer, but it made them feel important, while confirming the first impressions of A/C Sharp.

57 Squadron made ready sixteen Lancasters in an overall force of 247 Lancasters of 5 Group and twenty-two Mosquitos of 5 and 8 Groups, and W/C Tait would again be performing the role of Master Bomber in a Lancaster borrowed from 463 Squadron. The 57 Squadron element departed East Kirkby between 21.33 and 21.51 as part of the first wave with W/C Humphreys and S/L Wigg the senior pilot on duty. Each Lancaster was carrying thirteen 1,000 pounders, and it is believed that all arrived at the target to find largely clear skies, good visibility and only some ground haze to mar the view. Zero hour for the opening phase had been set for 00.05, but the Oboe Mosquitos were two minutes late, and some communications problems had to be ironed out before matters began to run smoothly. A large orange explosion at 00.28 sent a column of black smoke skyward, which impaired visibility to some extent, but those attacking afterwards were able to identify a red spotfire and bomb it, observing large explosions and fires that were visible to the second phase crews as they approached. LL893 was most likely on the way home when it crashed at St-Omer, killing S/L Wigg and his experienced crew, and their loss would be keenly felt by the squadron and the East Kirkby community. F/O Young RCAF was attempting to land at Croydon airport but overshot the runway at 02.20 and crashed into three houses bordering the airfield in the village of Wallington. The pilot, flight engineer and navigator died in the wreckage and the wireless operator succumbed to his injuries while being treated in Croydon hospital.

The second phase attack took place either side of 01.30, and crews had the glow of the burning target visible behind them for a hundred miles into the return flight. At debriefing, confidence was expressed in the effectiveness of the operation, and post-raid reconnaissance confirmed the success of both phases, which had left the yards severely damaged for the loss of six Lancasters. A congratulatory message from A-O-C Cochrane was received on all participating stations.

The real test for the 5 Group low-level marking system would come at a heavily defended German target, for which Braunschweig was selected on the 22nd, while the rest of the Command targeted the Ruhr city of Düsseldorf. 5 Group put together a force of 238 Lancasters and seventeen Mosquitos, with ten ABC Lancasters of 1 Group's 101 Squadron to provide radio countermeasures (RCM). 57 Squadron contributed sixteen Lancasters, which departed East Kirkby between 23.07 and 23.38 with W/C Humphreys the senior pilot on duty. There were no early returns among the 57 Squadron element, and all reached the target area after being guided by Path Finder route-markers. They encountered six to eight-tenths thin cloud at between 8,000 and 10,000 feet and benefitted from accurate marking by the 617 Squadron Mosquito element. The first clear bombing directions were heard from the Master Bomber at 01.56 to aim for the red spotfires and at 02.04 to bomb a second spotfire indicated by green TIs. Despite the guidance, the main force crews were unable to properly identify the target, a situation again compounded by communications problems between various controllers caused by the failure of VHF and the consequent need to pass on instructions instead by W/T. This led to confusion, and many crews were forced to orbit for up to fifteen minutes before bombing. The 57 Squadron crews carried out their attacks on green TIs and red spotfires from an average of 17,000 feet at around 02.00, before returning safely to report what appeared to be a successful operation, while also complaining about the dangers of orbiting a target with aircraft heading in a variety of directions. Although some bombs did fall in the city centre, most were directed at reserve H2S-laid TIs to the south of the city, and damage was less severe than might otherwise have been.

On the following night, 114 aircraft, mostly Halifaxes and Stirlings, were sent mining in five gardens in the Baltic. 57 Squadron's S/L Boyle and crew took off at 21.05 bound for the Geranium garden off the port of Swinemünde and returned seven hours later to report planting six mines in the briefed location during an entirely uneventful sortie.

When Munich was posted across 5 Group as the target on the 24th for another live test of the low-level visual marking method, it might have been seen as somewhat ambitious to select such a major city, that was protected by two hundred flak guns. The main operation on this night was to be conducted by a force of 637 aircraft against Karlsruhe, 150 miles to the north-west, which, it was hoped, would help to distract the night-fighters. 234 Lancasters were made ready by 5 Group and supplemented by ten of the ABC variety from 101 Squadron, while four Mosquitos of 617 Squadron were loaded with spotfires to carry out the marking and twelve of 627 Squadron with "window" to dispense during the final approach to the target. 57 Squadron's sixteen Lancasters took to the air between 20.41 and 21.15 with W/C Humphreys the senior pilot on duty and headed for the south coast before setting course across France towards the south-east and feinting towards Italy. The 617 and 627 Squadron Mosquitos took off three hours after the heavy brigade and adopted a direct route, the latter laying a "window" screen from high level six minutes from the target, masking the arrival of the flare force that was to provide seven minutes of illumination for the 617 Squadron marker Mosquitos. 57 Squadron's recent excellent record of serviceability continued as all reached the target area to encounter clear skies and good visibility, in which W/C Cheshire dived onto the aiming-point in the face of murderous light flak, before racing away across the rooftops to safety. The main force followed hard on his heels, the 57 Squadron crews bombing on the red spotfires and green TIs from an average of 18,000 feet either side of 02.00 in the face of intense searchlight and flak activity. Many fires were seen to take hold, and, as the bombers pointed their snouts back towards France to eventually pass to the north of Paris, Karlsruhe could be seen burning over to starboard. Post-raid reconnaissance and local sources confirmed the success of the raid, which left 1,104 buildings in ruins and a further thirteen hundred severely damaged. Some among the experienced crews described the attack as the best they had seen, and it was probably this operation that sealed the award to Cheshire of the Victoria Cross at the conclusion of his operational career in July, after completing one hundred sorties.

At briefing on the 26th, fourteen 57 Squadron crews were told that Schweinfurt was to be their target that night, after the failure of the RAF to destroy it in February and the American 8th Air Force just two weeks ago. The tone was very much, "leave it to RAF Bomber Command", and, with the satisfaction of Munich still fresh in the mind, and the natural rivalry existing between the two forces, such attitudes were to be expected. They learned that, for this operation, 627 Squadron would act as the low-level marker force for the first time and for a main force of 215 Lancasters, including nine from 101 Squadron to provide RCM protection. This was just one of three major operations taking place, with the main event at Essen, while the railway yards at Villeneuve-St-Georges were being attended to by a predominantly Halifax main force. The 57 Squadron element departed East Kirkby between 21.14 and 21.37 with F/Ls Beaumont and Ludford the senior pilots on duty and set course for the French coast. Stronger-than-forecast head winds delayed the arrival in the target area of the heavy brigade, which found generally clear skies and good visibility that the 627 Squadron crews failed to exploit, as their debut marking effort proved to be inaccurate. The 83 Squadron crews remarked on the lack of illumination, and those carrying hooded flares were called in a number of times to back-up, while bombing instructions generally were transmitted by W/T. The 57 Squadron crews bombed from an average of 19,000 feet, aiming at red spotfires and green TIs, some following the instructions of the Master Bomber to overshoot by a thousand yards. A large white explosion was witnessed at 02.29, and many fires were reported, but, once again at this target, most of the hardware fell outside of the target area, leaving ball-bearing production more or less unaffected. Night-fighters had got amongst the outbound heavy force from the French coast all the way to the target, and twenty-one Lancasters were shot down, a hefty 9.3%. 57 Squadron's ME679 collided in the air with 44 (Rhodesia) Squadron's LL920 and both Lancasters came down near Oberkirchen, south-east of the Ruhr, killing all but one of the fifteen occupants. The sole survivor was the Canadian bomb-aimer in the crew of S/L Boyle DFC, who was taken into captivity. Also failing to return was the crew of P/O Mee RNZAF in ND786, which was shot down by a night-fighter to crash at Miltenberg in northern Bavaria, killing the pilot and four others and delivering the two survivors into enemy hands. 57 Squadron had now lost both of its well-established flight commanders in a matter of a week.

5 Group made preparations on the 28th to send a force of eighty-eight Lancasters and four Mosquitos to attack the Alfred Nobel Dynamit A G explosives works at St-Médard-en-Jalles, situated in a wood on the north-western outskirts of Bordeaux in south-western France. A further fifty-one Lancasters and four Mosquitos would head in the opposite direction to target an aircraft maintenance facility at the Kjeller Flyfabrikk, some ten miles north-east of Oslo, which had been occupied by the Germans since April 1940 and was used by Junkers, Daimler-Benz and BMW. Clear skies prevailed over south-western France, but some flares had landed in a nearby wood, causing volumes of smoke to drift across the factory and obscure it from view. A few bomb loads went down before a signal was picked up from the Master Bomber instructing crews to withhold their bombs and orbit while he assessed the situation, and he eventually called a halt to proceedings at 03.30 and sent the rest of the force home with their bombs. Meanwhile, more than eleven hundred miles to the north, the crews had found clear skies and excellent visibility, and had identified the target by H2S, confirmed by yellow TIs at the start of the bombing run and flares and red spotfires supposedly on the aiming-point. In the event, a two-thousand-yard correction was broadcast to compensate for a poor marking performance, which resulted in explosions on the airfield and runway and among barrack buildings and some of the sheds, and an ammunition dump went up at 01.40.

55 Base sat out the above and was called into action on the following night when the operation against the dynamite works was rescheduled and the Michelin tyre factory at Clermont-Ferrand was added to the target list. Sixty-eight Lancasters were assigned to the explosives works and

fifty-four, including the 57 Squadron element of thirteen, to the tyre factory, with five 627 Squadron Mosquitos at each to provide the low-level marking. The 57 Squadron crews were sent on their way from East Kirkby between 21.54 and 22.08 with W/C Humphreys the senior pilot on duty and S/L Fairbairn, who had been posted in on the 25th as the new A Flight commander, flying as second pilot to F/L Smith. All reached the target area, where they identified the aiming-point both visually and by red spotfires and red and green TIs, which could be seen burning between factory buildings. They attacked from around 6,000 feet, before returning home filled with enthusiasm at the explosions that had ripped the site apart, some from other squadrons commenting that it was the most destructive attack they had taken part in. Post-raid reconnaissance confirmed that both targets had been severely damaged with a massive loss of production.

During the course of the month the squadron participated in eleven operations and dispatched 143 sorties for the loss of four Lancasters and their crews.

May 1944

Twelve 57 Squadron crews were called to briefing at East Kirkby on the 1st, to learn that they would be going to western France to attack an aircraft repair workshop at Tours as part of a 5 Group force of forty-six Lancasters from 55 Base and four Mosquitos. This was one of three 5 Group operations for the night, the others involving a total of 131 Lancasters and eight Mosquitos against a SNCASE aircraft assembly factory at Saint-Martin-du-Touch, a western suburb of Toulouse, and the Poudrerie explosives works in the same city. The 57 Squadron element took off between 22.13 and 22.33 with S/L Fairbairn the senior pilot on duty for the first time and each Lancaster carrying thirteen 1,000 pounders. They all reached the target to find moonlight, mostly clear skies and excellent visibility, and were able to identify the factory buildings visually, confirmed by yellow TIs on a datum point and red spotfires on the aiming-point. They carried out their attacks from 6,000 to 9,000 feet between 00.38 and 01.13 in accordance with the instructions of the Master Bomber and the detonations appeared to be concentrated around the spotfires. Meanwhile, at Toulouse, the attacks were clearly focused on the aiming-points, and the main assembly shop and boiler house at the SNCASE site were observed to be hit, although there was a degree of disappointment that fire was less extensive than anticipated as they withdrew to the north. All crews returned to their respective stations confident of a successful outcome, and post-raid reconnaissance revealed all three factories to have been heavily damaged.

On the 2nd, S/L Drew Wyness was posted in to succeed S/L Boyle as B Flight commander, having completed a tour of operations with 50 Squadron in 1942. Briefings took place on 1 and 5 Group stations on the 3rd, for what would become a highly contentious operation that night against a Panzer training camp and transport depot at Mailly-le-Camp, situated some seventy-five miles east of Paris in north-eastern France. The units based there posed a potential threat to Allied forces as the invasion unfolded and needed to be eliminated. The events of the operation proved to be so controversial, that recriminations abound to this day concerning the 5 Group leadership provided by W/Cs Cheshire and Deane. Although the grudges by 1 Group aircrew against them can be understood in the light of what happened, they are unjust, and based on emotion and incorrect information, and it is worthwhile to examine the conduct of the operation in some detail. W/C

Cheshire was appointed as marker leader, and was piloting one of four 617 Squadron Mosquitos, while 83 Squadron's commanding officer, W/C Deane, was overall raid controller, with S/L Sparks as Deputy. Deane and Cheshire attended separate briefings, and neither seemed aware of the complete plan, particularly the role of the 1 Group Special Duties Flight from Binbrook, which was assigned to mark its own specific aiming point for an element of the 1 Group force.

The twelve 57 Squadron participants became airborne between 21.39 and 21.49 with S/L Fairbairn the senior pilot on duty, and each Lancaster loaded with a cookie and fifteen 500 pounders. All reached the target area to find clear skies, moonlight and excellent bombing conditions, but confusion already beginning to influence events. 617 Squadron's W/C Cheshire and S/L Shannon were in position before midnight, and, as the first flares from the 83 and 97 Squadron Lancasters illuminated the target below, Cheshire released his two red spot fires onto the first aiming-point at 00.00½ from 1,500 feet. Shannon backed them up from 400 feet five and a half minutes later, and, as far as Cheshire was concerned, the operation was bang on schedule at this stage. A 97 Squadron Lancaster also laid markers accurately, to ensure a constant focal point, and Cheshire passed instructions to Deane to call the bombers in. It was at this stage of the operation that matters began to go awry. A communications problem arose, when a commercial radio station, believed to be an American forces network, jammed the VHF frequencies in use. Deane called in the 5 Group element, elated that everything was proceeding according to plan, but nothing happened. He checked with his wireless operator that the instructions had been transmitted, and called up S/L Sparks, who was also mystified by the lack of bombing. A few crews from 9, 207 and 467 Squadrons had heard the call to bomb, and did so, but, for most, the instructions were swamped by the interference.

Post raid reports are contradictory, and it is impossible to establish an accurate course of events, particularly when Deane and Cheshire's understanding of the exact time of zero hour differed by five minutes. Remarkably, it also seems, that Deane was unaware that there were two marking points, or three, if one includes 1 Group's Special Duties Flight. Cheshire, initially at least, appeared happy with the early stages of the attack, and described the bombing as concentrated and accurate. It seems certain, however, that many minutes had passed between the dropping of Cheshire's markers and the first main force bombs falling, during which period, Deane was coming to terms with the fact that his instructions were not getting through. A plausible scenario is, that in the absence of instructions, and with red spot fires clearly visible in the target, some crews opted to bomb, and others followed suit. These would have been predominantly from 5 Group, but as the 1 Group crews became increasingly agitated at having to wait in bright moonlight, with evidence of enemy night fighters all around, some of them inevitably joined in.

Now a new problem was arising. Smoke from these first salvoes was obliterating the entire camp, and Cheshire had to decide whether or not to send in Fawke and Kearns to mark the second aiming-point. His feeling, and that of Deane, as it later transpired, was, that it was unnecessary, as the volume of bombs still to fall into the relatively compact area of the target would ensure destruction of the entire site. By 00.16, the first phase of bombing should have been completed, leaving a clear run for Fawke and Kearns across the target. In the event, the majority of 5 Group crews were still on their bombing run, a fact unknown to Cheshire, who asked Deane for a pause in the bombing, while the two Mosquitos went in. As far as Cheshire was concerned, there was no response from Deane, who would, anyway, have been confused by mention of a second aiming point. In the event, Deane's deputy, S/L Sparks, eventually found a channel free of interference, and did, in fact, transmit an instruction to halt the bombing, both by W/T and R/T, and some crews reported hearing something. While utter chaos reigned, Kearns and Fawke dived in among the falling cookies at 00.23 and 00.25 respectively to mark the second aiming-point on the western edge of the camp. At 2,000 feet, they were lucky to survive the turbulence created by the exploding 4,000 pounders, when 4,000 feet was considered to be a minimum safe height. They were not entirely happy with their work, but F/O Edwards of 97 Squadron dropped a stick of markers precisely on the mark, and S/L Sparks was then able to call the 1 Group main force crews in along with any from 5 Group with bombs still on board. Because of the absence of information in the 57 Squadron ORB, it is not possible to place the squadron's bombing within a time frame, but the few details provided include the comment that the marking was prompt and accurate and the bombing concentrated around the markers, and that smoke obscured the target as the attack developed. There was no hint of communications difficulties or delays, but it was stated that fighter activity was intense and that the ground defences were aided by the brightness of the moon. The night-fighters continued to create havoc among the Lancasters as they milled around in the target area, and, as burning aircraft were seen to fall all around, some 1 Group crews succumbed to their anxiety and frustration. In a rare breakdown of R/T discipline, the Australian contingent from 460 Squadron in particular, let fly with comments of an uncomplimentary nature, many of which were intended for, and, indeed, heard by Deane.

Despite the problems, the operation was a major success, which destroyed 80% of the camp's buildings, and 102 vehicles, of which thirty-seven were tanks, while over two hundred men were killed. Forty-two Lancasters failed to return, however, two thirds of them from 1 Group, and 50 Squadron was 5 Group's most afflicted unit with four Lancasters and crews unaccounted for. 57 Squadron posted missing the crew of F/O Scrivener, a Rhodesian, who all lost their lives when ND468 was shot down by a night-fighter homebound and crashed at le Vaudoué, some thirty miles south of Paris. At debriefing, S/L Blome-Jones of 207 Squadron described the situation as a complete shambles and chaos, the controller as inefficient and the discipline of some crews as bad. Others voiced the opinion that this was a trip worthy of counting as more than one-third of a sortie. On the following day, an inquest into the conduct of the raid revealed that the wireless transmitter in Deane's Lancaster had been sufficiently off frequency to allow the interference from the American network to mask the transmission of instructions and prevent the call to bomb from reaching the main force crews. The 1 Group A-O-C, AVM Rice, decided he would not participate in further operations organized by 5 Group, which was probably not a blow to Cochrane, who was confident that his group did not need back-up.

Five small-scale operations were mounted on the night of the 7/8th, against airfields, ammunition dumps and a coastal battery, all in support of the coming invasion. 5 Group was involved in two raids, the airfield at Tours in north-western France and an ammunition dump at Salbris, some sixty miles to the east. A force of fifty-three Lancasters was assigned to the former, fifteen of them provided by 57 Squadron, and eight Mosquitos would be on hand to carry out the low-level marking. They departed East Kirkby between 00.32 and 00.47 with W/C Humphreys and S/Ls Fairbairn and Wyness the senior pilots on duty and each crew sitting on a cookie and sixteen 500 pounders. Eleven crews had been briefed to attack the main buildings, while four others went for the hangars on the south side of the aerodrome. W/C Tait would be acting as overall raid controller from the pilot's seat of a 467 Squadron Lancaster with two photographers also on board, although an electrical fault in the bomb-aimer's compartment would cause a fire that rendered the nose camera inoperable. All reached the target area after an outward flight of two-and-a-quarter hours and encountered clear skies and good visibility. The target was identified initially by red spotfires, but the runways and surrounding road network could be seen clearly as the bombing runs began. The Master Bomber controlled the attack by R/T backed up by W/T and announced the markers to be "bang-on" before giving the order to proceed. W/C Tait bombed in the middle of the attack from 6,000 at 02.59 and observed cookies and 500 pounders detonating across the airfield, hitting the runways, hangars and other buildings. Thick smoke was drifting over the area as they turned away, which made it difficult to assess the outcome, but post-raid reconnaissance would reveal heavy damage. Photographically, it was a disappointing raid captured by just the one camera. P/O Walker and crew barely survived a brush with a Ju88, which left their Lancaster badly shot-up and the rear gunner wounded, and they landed at Tarrant Rushton shortly after crossing the Dorset coast.

Another small-scale operation was mounted by the group on the 8th against the airfield and seaplane base at Lanveoc-Poulmic, located on the northern side of the peninsula forming the southern boundary of the L'Elorn estuary opposite Brest. A force of fifty-eight Lancasters from 53 Base and six Mosquitos easily identified the target after pinpointing on the coastline, and bombing was carried out from low to medium level either side of midnight. Hangars and other buildings were seen to be on fire and enveloped in smoke at the conclusion of the attack, from which all but one Lancaster returned safely.

55 Base was called into action on the 9th to participate in an attack by thirty-nine Lancasters and four Mosquitos on a small ball-bearing factory at Annecy, situated in south-eastern France close to the frontiers with Switzerland and Italy. While this was in progress, more than four hundred aircraft were to target seven coastal batteries in the Pas-de-Calais to confirm in the mind of the enemy the false belief that the Allied invasion forces would land at Calais. Right up to D-Day itself, the coastal region between Gravelines to the east of the port and Berck-sur-Mer to the south-west, would be subjected to frequent bombardments. A second 5 Group operation on this night involving fifty-six Lancasters and eight Mosquitos was to be directed at two factories, the Gnome & Rhône aero-engine works and the Goodrich tyre factory at Gennevilliers in northern Paris. 57 Squadron briefed eleven crews for Annecy and dispatched them from East Kirkby between 21.06 and 21.36 with S/Ls Fairbairn and Wyness the senior pilots on duty. Ahead of them was an outward flight of four-and-a-half hours, which all of them completed without incident, while two of the Mosquitos had to turn back. On arrival in the target area, they found a green TI on the datum point and generally clear conditions with some haze to contend with. The aiming-point was identified by red spotfires, but it was not long before the early bombing caused smoke to obscure ground detail, and there appeared to be a degree of overshooting. A very large yellowy-orange explosion occurred at 02.02, from which point, smoke became a problem, and some crews reported the bombing falling to starboard of the spotfires. Concentration was achieved later, and many explosions and fires were observed, although the large clouds of smoke rendered an accurate assessment difficult. It was this that caused problems for F/Sgt Lumsden and crew, who were preparing for their bombing run, when they received instructions from the Master Bomber to cease bombing and take their bombs home. It would require post-raid reconnaissance to confirm that a successful operation had taken place.

Meanwhile, moonlight and clear skies had enabled the Paris-bound crews to map read after Gee was jammed at the French coast, and H2S proved useful as they closed on the target. Yellow TIs and red spotfires identified the aiming-point, and detonations appeared to be focused, as intended, in the centre of the marked area. Local sources confirmed damage to the target, but, also, collateral damage that killed twenty-seven French civilians and injured more than a hundred.

Five railway targets were selected for attention on the night of the 10/11th, among them the marshalling yards at Lille, situated close to the Belgian frontier in north-eastern France, which would be the target for a 5 Group main force of 53 Base squadrons with 97 Squadron from 54 Base providing the illumination and back-up marking. W/C Tait was guesting again in a 467 Squadron Lancaster with two photographers on board to record the outcome and they found the target area to be under clear skies with the aiming-point slightly obscured by ground haze, a situation easily negated by red spotfires and green TIs. The attacks were delivered in the light of flares from 7,000 to 10,000 feet and bomb bursts were observed across the tracks and resulted in two large explosions that confirmed a successful assault on this important hub linking north-eastern France with Belgium. There was shock at Waddington when six of its crews failed to return, and deep sadness at the loss, in particular, of a highly popular flight commander on the last sortie of his tour.

5 Group put together a force of 190 Lancasters and eight Mosquitos on the 11th, to target a military camp at Bourg-Leopold in north-eastern Belgium, for which 57 Squadron made ready fourteen Lancasters. They departed East Kirkby between 22.36 and 22.49 with S/Ls Fairbairn and Wyness the senior pilots on duty, each Lancaster carrying a cookie and sixteen 500 pounders. They made landfall over the Scheldt and reached the target to find hazy conditions and a little thin cloud at around 10,000 feet, despite which, they would be able to identify ground detail in the form of buildings and huts in the light of illuminating flares. Three Oboe Mosquitos were on hand to deliver the initial marking, but inaccurately forecast winds caused the 83 Squadron heavy element to arrive late, by which time the main force crews had begun to orbit to await instructions. A communications problem prevented some crews from hearing the Master Bomber's broadcasts, but the aiming-point could be seen to be marked by red spotfires and green TIs. From the Master Bomber's perspective, the initial Oboe marker had been visible only to a few crews, and quickly burned out, and so he called for another Mosquito to drop a red spot fire onto the aiming-point. Before this was accomplished, however, the main force crews began to bomb and among them were four of those from 57 Squadron. As smoke began to obscure the ground, the Master Bomber, S/L Mitchell, quickly became uncomfortable about the close proximity of civilian residential property and called a halt to the bombing at 00.35, before sending the rest of the force home, some of them after circling for more than twenty minutes. A few crews failed to hear the signal and continued to bomb, and two 57 Squadron crews found last resort targets while the others jettisoned part of their loads and brought the rest home.

On the 19th, after a week of minor operations, the station teleprinters worked overtime dispensing the details of five operations that night targeting marshalling yards, two on coastal batteries and one against a radar station. 5 Group detailed 225 Lancasters for railway targets, 112 from 52 and 55 Bases to be sent to Amiens with eight Mosquitos, and 113 from 53 and 54 Bases for Tours with four Mosquitos. Sixteen 57 Squadron Lancasters departed East Kirkby for the former between 22.54 and 23.10 with W/C Humphreys and S/L Wyness the senior pilots on duty and set course for north-eastern France, where they found the target shrouded in a layer of eight to ten-tenths cloud at between 6,000 and 11,000 feet. The target was identified by red spotfires, but when checked on H2S, these appeared to be up to five miles from the planned aiming-point. Thirty-seven aircraft had bombed when instructions came through by W/T at 01.25 to terminate the attack and return home. Four of the 57 Squadron crews were among those carrying out their attacks, while the majority of the others returned their ordnance to store.

Meanwhile, at Tours, where a previous attack by 5 Group had targeted the railway installations on the outskirts of the town, this night's effort was directed at those in the central district between the rivers Loire to the north and La Cher to the south. The crews found largely clear skies over north-western France and visibility good enough through the four-tenths cloud to identify ground detail. The aiming-point was marked by red spotfires, and, in view of the close proximity of civilian housing, the Master Bomber took great care and much time before issuing the order to bomb. This would extend the time on target, but, fortunately, the Luftwaffe was absent, and the accuracy of the bombing was sufficient to cause massive damage to the target with only a little collateral damage and no losses.

For the first time in a year, Duisburg was posted as the target for a heavy raid on the 21st, for which a force of 510 Lancasters was drawn from 1, 3, 5 and 8 Groups. They would be supported by twenty-two Mosquitos, and, while this operation was in progress, seventy Lancasters, including some from 5 Group, and thirty-seven Halifaxes would undertake gardening duties in the Nectarines and Rosemary gardens around the Frisians and off Heligoland, and in the Forget-me-not, Silverthorn and Quince gardens in the Kattegat and Kiel Bay regions of the Baltic. 57 Squadron briefed a dozen crews for mining duties in the Forget-me-not garden in Kiel harbour and three for the main event, dispatching the former from East Kirkby between 21.53 and 22.12 with S/L Wyness the senior pilot on duty. They encountered night-fighters over Denmark and F/Sgt Lumsden and crew were attacked by three off the coast, one of which they claimed as destroyed in return for themselves being badly shot up and having to jettison the mines. The others faced searchlights and flak as they began their timed runs to the release point, but all delivered their six mines each into the allotted locations before turning for home. ND960 was shot down by a night-fighter and crashed near Gelsted on Denmark's Fyn Island, and there were no survivors from the crew of F/L Richards.

The crews of P/Os Anderson, Smith and Winneke took off for the Ruhr between 22.54 and 22.56 having been instructed at briefing to adhere to the plan for the outward route, which involved a few aircraft from 3 Group gaining height as they adopted a north-westerly course as far as Sleaford, so as not to cross into enemy radar cover earlier than necessary. The groups would rendezvous at 18,000 feet over the North Sea at 3 degrees east to cross the enemy coast via the western Frisians at 20,000 feet and climb to 22,000 or 23,000 feet, before increasing speed for the run across the target. The 57 Squadron trio reached the western edge of the Ruhr to find it concealed beneath ten-tenths cloud with tops at between 11,000 and 20,000 feet, into which the red Wanganui markers with-yellow-stars fell almost before they could be seen. A number of crews commented on the data provided by the wind-finder system to be inaccurate, and this made it a challenge to establish positions. The main force crews used the explosion of cookies, the glow of fires and the evidence of intense flak as references and bombed from 15,000 to 22,000 feet either side of 01.30, before returning home with little useful information to report. The loss of twenty-nine Lancasters was a reminder to the Command that the Ruhr remained a dangerous destination, although most of the missing aircraft had come down onto Dutch and Belgian soil or into the sea homebound after falling victim to night-fighters. Martin Drewes of III./NJG1 alone accounted for at least three Lancasters. Returning crews were not enthusiastic about the outcome, and post-raid reconnaissance confirmed that a modest 350 buildings had been destroyed in the southern half of Duisburg, and 665 others had been seriously damaged.

Just like Duisburg, Dortmund was posted on the 22nd to host its first large-scale visit from the Command for a year and would face an all-Lancaster heavy force of 361 aircraft drawn from 1, 3, 6 and 8 Groups. While this operation was in progress, 220 Lancasters of 5 Group and five from 101 Squadron were to target Braunschweig, which, thus far, had evaded severe damage at the hands of Bomber Command. 57 Squadron made ready sixteen Lancasters, which departed East Kirkby between 21.58 and 22.24 with W/C Humphreys and S/L Wyness the senior pilots on duty. Each Lancaster was carrying a single 2,000 pounder and a dozen 500lb J-Cluster bombs, and it was the big one and five small ones that F/L Beaumont and crew jettisoned into the North Sea after their starboard-outer engine let them down. The others pressed on through the clearly-evident night-fighter activity from the Dutch coast all the way to the target, having to negotiate the patches of ten-tenths cloud over northern Germany and intense searchlight activity as they passed between Bremen and Osnabrück. The forecast at briefings had suggested clear skies over Braunschweig, but, in fact, the marker force encountered four to seven-tenths drifting cloud with tops up to 7,000 feet. Although highly effective in the right weather conditions, the 5 Group low-level visual marking method could easily be rendered ineffective by cloud cover. The blind heavy markers dropped skymarkers by H2S, while the 627 Squadron Mosquito element went in at low level to release red spotfires. Some crews described "hopeless confusion" with flares and incendiaries spread over a distance, and many had to rely on their own H2S to establish their position. Some found a complete absence of marking and orbited for up to fifteen minutes until a few green TIs appeared and bombing took place on these or on incendiary fires from an average of 19,000 feet either side of 01.30. Considerable interference over R/T communications added to the problems, and, although the Master Bomber could be heard in discussions with his Deputies, no instructions were received from him, and the attack lacked cohesion. Thirteen Lancasters failed to return, five of them having taken off from East Kirkby, three of them belonging to 57 Squadron. NE127 was shot down by a night-fighter over Holland while outbound and crashed north-west of Groningen at 23.45 killing F/Sgt Henley and all but the gunners, who survived in enemy hands. ND879 produced no survivors from the crew of P/O Marland, and none either from the crew of P/O Winneke RAAF in ND878, which exploded at 02.15 over Ottersberg, east of Bremen, after being intercepted by a night-fighter. LL967 joined the circuit for landing, and collided with 97 Squadron Lancaster ND415, which crashed at Revesby, some two miles west of East Kirkby killing all on board. F/L Bayley crash-landed on the runway and all occupants walked away to contemplate their lucky deliverance. At debriefing, crews reported heavy predicted flak bursting at 18,500 feet and intense searchlight activity co-operating with night-fighters, and a number of Lancasters were handed back to their ground crews with flak holes to patch. Post-raid reconnaissance confirmed that most of the bombing had fallen onto outlying communities, confirming in the minds of the residents that this was an intentional ploy by the Command.

The main operation on the 24th would involve 442 aircraft in an attack on two marshalling yards at Aachen, Aachen-West and Rothe-Erde in the east. As the most westerly city in Germany, sitting on the frontiers of both Holland and Belgium, it was a major link in the railway network that would be a route for reinforcements to the Normandy battle front. Other operations on this night would be directed at coastal batteries in the Pas-de-Calais and war-industry factories in Holland and Belgium. 5 Group detailed forty-four Lancasters, mostly from 55 Base to attack the Ford and General Motors works in Antwerp, and fifty-nine from 53 and 54 Bases for the Philips electronics factory at Eindhoven in southern Holland, and it was for the former that 57 Squadron made ready a dozen of its own. They departed East Kirkby between 22.52 and 23.11 with W/C Humphreys the senior pilot on duty and each Lancaster carrying eleven 1,000 and four 500 pounders, some with a long delay fuse. They headed for the Norfolk coast, running into a bullseye (cross-country) exercise, and having to avoid weaving Lancasters and intense searchlight activity. Matters settled down as they crossed the North Sea towards the Scheldt Estuary, where they found slight ground haze but generally good visibility. The target was identified by illuminating flares and marked by a yellow TI and red spotfires, and was bombed from between 6,000 to 8,000 feet at around 00.45. On return, crews reported a good concentration of bomb bursts around the markers, and were, no doubt, disappointed to discover later that the factory had escaped damage. Meanwhile, those bound for Eindhoven were more than an hour into the outward journey and some eight minutes from the target when the Master Bomber sent them home by W/T, presumably after a Met Flight Mosquito crew had found poor visibility in the target area. As a result, and because the long-delay fuses had been activated, hundreds of perfectly serviceable 1,000 pounders ended up on the seabed.

The night of the 27/28th was to be one of feverish activity, which would generate more than eleven hundred sorties, reflecting the close proximity of the invasion, now just ten days away. The largest operation would bring a return to the military camp at Bourg Leopold in Belgium, the previous attack on which, two weeks earlier, had been abandoned part-way through. There was also a repeat of the Aachen attack of the 24th, which had failed to destroy the Rothe-Erde marshalling yards at the eastern end of the city and needed further attention. 5 Group was not involved in either of the above, and, instead, prepared forces of one hundred Lancasters and four Mosquitos and seventy-eight Lancasters and five Mosquitos respectively to target marshalling yards and workshops at Nantes and the aerodrome at Rennes, situated some fifty miles apart in north-western France. The group would also support operations against coastal batteries, of which there were five on this night, including one at Saint-Valery-en-Caux, situated a dozen or so miles west of Dieppe for which 57 Squadron made ready twelve Lancasters. They departed East Kirkby between 23.21 and 23.35 with F/Ls Beaumont and Twiggs the senior pilots on duty and each carrying eleven 1,000 pounders and four 500 pounders. They all reached the target area to find clear skies and good visibility, but the initial flares fell over the sea to the north-west of the town and crews were ordered to orbit for up to twenty-five minutes until further flares and the red spotfires were released over the aiming-point. The Master Bomber ordered the main force in at 01.53 and bombing was carried out from an average of 7,000 feet until the order to go home was issued at 02.09. The consensus among returning crews was of an accurate attack.

On the 28th, 181 Lancasters and twenty Mosquitos were made ready to attack three coastal batteries overlooking the Normandy beaches, which, a week hence, would be the scene of Operation Overlord. The target for the 53 Base force was at Sainte-Martin-de-Varrevilles, situated close to what would be Utah Beach, the landing ground for the American 1st Division. On the 31st, 5 Group detailed eighty-two Lancasters and four Mosquitos to attack a railway junction at Saumur in the Loire Valley, and another sixty-eight Lancasters to deal with a coastal battery at Maisy, overlooking Omaha Beach. 57 Squadron did not take part in these operations, but on the last occasion, sent four Lancasters for mining duties in the Kraut garden in Lim Fjord, a narrow waterway in northern Jutland linking Ålborg with the coast at Hals. The crews of P/Os Nicklin, Spencer, Walker and Wardle departed East Kirkby between 21.37 and 21.44 and returned between seven and eight hours later to report delivering a total of twenty-four mines into the briefed locations.

During the course of the month, the squadron took part in twelve operations and dispatched 139 sorties for the loss of five Lancasters and crews.

June 1944

June was to be a hectic month which would make great demands on the crews. The bombing of coastal batteries was to be the priority during the first few days of the month leading up to D-Day, but 5 Group would open its account by returning to Saumur to attack a second railway junction on the 1st. The day dawned cloudy and cold, and these conditions would persist throughout the first week, causing concern among the invasion planners. 55 and 54 Base squadrons briefed fifty-eight crews, fifteen representing 57 Squadron, while their Lancasters were having ten 1,000 and four 500 pounders winched into their bomb bays. They departed East Kirkby between 22.15 and 22.28 with S/Ls Fairbairn and Wyness the senior pilots on duty and climbed out through cloud before losing the services of F/L Grubb and crew to an unserviceable rear turret. The others flew south over a blanket of ten-tenths cloud that persisted to within twenty miles of the town of Saumur, where it dispersed completely to leave clear skies and good visibility under a three-quarter moon. The flare force was almost superfluous in the conditions, but the first wave was called in by the Master Bomber, W/C Jeudwine in a 54 Base Mosquito, to release from 15,000 feet at 01.08, and the first red spot fire from an Oboe Mosquito fell bang on the aiming-point two minutes later. Smoke became a problem as it drifted across the area to obscure the spotfire that was still burning, and a green TI was dropped to maintain the aiming-point. Apart from a few scattered sticks to the north, and on an island in the Loire to the south, the attack seemed to be accurate. S/L Wyness arrived after the "cease bombing" order had been issued at 01.39 and brought his bombs home. Returning crews reported little opposition, fires in the yards and a large explosion at 01.35, and the success of the raid was confirmed by photo-reconnaissance, which showed severe damage to the track.

53, 54 and 55 Bases joined forces on the 3rd for an attack on a listening station at Ferme-d'Urville, situated on the Cherbourg peninsula to the west of the port, which had escaped damage when attacked by Halifaxes two nights earlier. 101 Lancasters were made ready, ten of them by 57 Squadron, into each of which the East Kirkby armourers loaded a cookie and sixteen 500 pounders. They took off between 22.56 and 23.05 with F/Ls Grubb and Twiggs the senior pilots on duty and all reached the target area to find clear skies and good visibility apart from ground haze. The first of three Oboe Mosquitos dropped a red TI at 00.50, and this was followed by a second one seven minutes later, supplemented shortly afterwards by green TIs from the heavy marker aircraft. The main force bombs were delivered from 6,000 to 10,000 feet from at around

01.00 and a large explosion was witnessed at 01.02. Returning crews reported a successful attack that had been focused in a five-hundred-yard radius of the aiming-point, and photographic reconnaissance confirmed that the listening station had ceased to exist.

Orders came through on the 4th to prepare for attacks that night on coastal batteries, three in the Pas-de-Calais to maintain the deception, and the one at Maisy, overlooking what would be the American landing grounds of Utah and Omaha beaches. 259 aircraft of 1, 4, 5, 6 and 8 Groups were made ready, the majority for the deception targets, while fifty-two of the Lancasters from 54 and 55 Bases were assigned to Maisy. 57 Squadron made ready fifteen Lancasters for these pre-dawn attacks, loading each with eighteen 500 pounders and dispatching them from East Kirkby between 01.04 and 01.22 with F/Ls Beaumont and Twiggs the senior pilots on duty. They all reached the target area to encounter ten-tenths cloud with a base at around 4,000 feet, which necessitated the use of Oboe skymarkers. Positions were confirmed by Gee-fix and a faint red or green glow, before the bombing was carried out from just above the cloud tops. It was impossible to assess the outcome, and similar cloudy conditions had thwarted two of the three attempts in the Pas-de-Calais, although the outcome there was secondary to the deception aspect.

The night of the 5/6th was D-Day Eve, and, during its course, a record number of 1,211 sorties would be flown against coastal defences and in support and diversionary operations. Sixteen 57 Squadron crews attended the briefing at East Kirkby, where no direct reference was made to the invasion, but, unusually, strict instructions were issued with regard to altitudes and there was a complete ban on dumping bombs into the Channel. They learned also that they would be among more than a thousand aircraft targeting ten heavy gun batteries along the Normandy coast, and that their specific objective was at La Pernelle, the most north-westerly, and, although not disclosed to them, the closest to Utah Beach. The plan called for 52, 54 and 55 Bases to provide 122 Lancasters and four Mosquitos, among which would be a six-strong flare force provided by 83 Squadron led by W/C Northrop as Deputy Master Bomber to W/C Jeudwine. At the same time, 115 Lancasters and four Mosquitos from 53 and 54 Bases would be targeting a battery at Sainte-Pierre-du-Mont, which was the closest to Omaha Beach, and among the number were seventeen Lancasters of 97 Squadron to provide the illumination and marking. The 57 Squadron Lancasters were loaded with eleven 1,000 and four 500 pounders each and departed East Kirkby between 01.27 and 01.43 with S/L Fairbairn the senior pilot on duty. They all arrived in the target area to find two layers of thin cloud at 7,000 and 10,000 feet, through which the Oboe markers went down at 03.32, to be followed by the first flares thirty seconds later. The low-level Mosquitos backed-up at 03.36, only for the first bombs to be dropped before W/C Jeudwine gave the order. He described the bombing as appalling and called for a halt at 03.45 to allow re-marking to take place, but the main force, as usual, took no notice. Another red spot fire was delivered within thirty yards of the aiming point at 03.51, and the order was given to continue bombing at 03.57. Six minutes later, after additional cloud had rolled in, W/C Jeudwine called a halt to proceedings, but some elements of the main force again took no notice. The bombing was carried out from 5,000 to 12,000 feet and returning crews would have little to report other than bomb bursts and a mushroom of black smoke. Any homeward-bound crews looking down through the occasional gaps in the clouds were rewarded by the incredible sight of the greatest armada in history, ploughing its way sedately southwards towards the French coast. A total of five thousand tons of bombs was dropped during the night, and this was a new record. Only seven aircraft failed to return from these operations, three of them from Sainte-Pierre-du-Mont, two from 97 Squadron, including the one containing W/C "Jimmy" Carter and seven highly experienced others, all but one of whom held either a DFC or DFM.

As the beachheads were being established during the course of the 6th, preparations were put in hand to support the ground forces by attacking nine road and railway communications centres through which the enemy could bring reinforcements. 5 Group was assigned to two targets, Argentan railway centre located some thirty miles south-east of Caen, and a road bridge in Caen itself, for which forces of 112 Lancasters and six Mosquitos and 120 Lancasters and four Mosquitos respectively were assembled. 54 and 55 Bases were assigned to the latter, for which 57 Squadron made ready fourteen Lancasters, while their crews attended briefing to learn that 83 Squadron's S/L Mitchell was to act as Deputy Master Bomber to W/C James Tait. They departed East Kirkby between 00.05 and 00.30 with W/C Humphreys and S/L Fairbairn the senior pilots on duty, and all reached the target area to find ten-tenths cloud with a base at 5,000 feet. Whether or not that was responsible, W/C Tait did not see any Oboe markers and suspected that none had been delivered. However, the 83 Squadron illumination was good, and the low-level marking of the road bridge with red spotfires backed up with green TIs was accomplished punctually and largely accurately, despite smoke drifting across from a fire to the north of the town. The bombing was carried out from below the cloud base at 3,000 to 5,000 feet in accordance with the Master Bomber's instructions, and bomb bursts were observed along with a large fire to port of the aiming-point. W/O Findley's bomb sight failed at the last minute and most of the eighteen 500 pounders were returned to store. P/O Walker and crew were attacked by a Ju88, and the mid-upper gunner, F/O Quayle, was killed. Six Lancasters failed to return, and this was largely as a result of the need to orbit while the markers were assessed, followed by bombing-runs at just a few thousand feet over masses of enemy armour. There were also some light flak batteries on an airfield to the west, which may have come into play.

Four railway targets were earmarked for attention by a force of 337 aircraft on the 7th, while elements of 5 Group were being prepared to join forces with 1 and 8 Groups to attack a six-way road junction at Balleroy, situated fifteen miles west of Caen on the approach to the Foret-de-Cerisy, where it was believed the enemy was concealing a fuel dump and tank units. 57 Squadron put up eleven of the thirty-eight Lancasters provided by 55 Base in an overall force of 112 Lancasters and ten Mosquitos, and they departed East Kirkby between 23.27 and 23.37 with no senior pilots on duty. P/O Owen and crew lost their starboard-outer engine and turned back, leaving the others to arrive in the target area and encounter ten-tenths cloud with a base at 8,000 to 10,000 feet with haze below. The initial Oboe markers appeared to be accurate and on time, but another marker fell simultaneously some five miles to the south-west and attracted some bomb loads. The Master Bomber quickly gained control of the situation and redirected the focus upon the correct marker, which was pounded by concentrated bombing. The attack was carried out from 5,000 to 7,000 feet and set off a large explosion at 01.44 among many smaller ones, and they were accompanied by dense clouds of black smoke.

The 55 Base squadrons sat out 5 Group operations on the 8th, which included the first dropping of the Barnes Wallis-designed 12,000lb Tallboy deep-penetration bomb by 617 Squadron on the Saumur tunnel. The group also attacked railway installations at Pontabault, a town situated at the mouth of the Selune River in the Gulf of St Malo, south-west of the beachhead, and at Rennes further west. 401 aircraft from 1, 4, 6 and 8 Groups were detailed on the 9th to target airfields in the battle area, while 5 Group concentrated on a railway junction at Etampes, south of Paris. 108 Lancasters and four Mosquitos were made ready, fifteen of the former representing 57 Squadron, which took off between 21.33 and 21.46 with S/L Fairbairn the senior pilot on duty and each carrying eighteen 500 pounders, two of which had delay fuses of between twelve and thirty-six hours. Those reaching the target found eight to ten-tenths cloud with a base at 8,000 feet and patches of two to three-tenths lower down at 4,000 feet. The yellow TIs and red spotfires went down on time but the first spotfire fell some four hundred yards north-east of the aiming point at 23.59 and immediately attracted bombs. The Master Bomber called for crews to stand-by and stop bombing while the aiming point was re-marked with red spotfires backed up with green TIs, and bombing resumed at 00.13. Crews confirmed their positions by Gee-fix before bombing from 5,000 to 7,000 feet between 00.09 and 00.20, some after the Master Bomber had called a halt to proceedings at 00.17. Photo-reconnaissance confirmed that all tracks had been cut for a distance of four hundred yards to the north-east of the junction, but it revealed also that the town had sustained collateral damage, which caused many civilian casualties. The operation cost six Lancasters.

The squadron was not involved in the 5 Group attack by 108 Lancasters on a railway junction at Orleans on the 10th, one of four similar targets for the night, and the group enjoyed the next night off altogether. The campaign against communications targets continued on the 12th at six locations, including Caen and Poitiers, for which 5 Group detailed forces of 109 Lancasters and four Mosquitos and 112 Lancasters and four Mosquitos respectively. 57 Squadron made ready eighteen Lancasters to take part in the former, and they departed East Kirkby between 23.52 and 00.10 with W/C Humphreys and S/L Fairbairn the senior pilots on duty. P/O Guy and crew turned back early because of the failure of their starboard-inner engine, but the others all reached the target area with thirteen 1,000 pounders each and encountered six to ten-tenths cloud with tops at between 4,000 and 6,000 feet. This made it difficult to see the red spotfire and green TIs, despite which, those arriving in the early stages of the attack bombed from above cloud from up to 10,000 feet, before the Master Bomber issued an order at 02.18 to cease bombing and orbit, presumably while he assessed the situation. At 02.20 he ordered crews to bomb visually, which left them confused as to whether that meant coming beneath the cloud base to bomb TIs or the bridge itself or to wait for further illumination. In the event, there was insufficient time for all to break cloud and complete a run before the order to cease bombing was issued at around 02.30. Eight of the 57 Squadron crews were able to get their loads away from 5,000 feet or a little higher, but the others failed to beat the deadline, and either brought their bombs home or jettisoned them. Photo-reconnaissance revealed this to have been the night's most scattered operation.

A new oil campaign began on this night, prosecuted by 286 Lancasters and seventeen Mosquitos of 1, 3 and 8 Groups, whose target was the Nordstern (Gelsenberg A G) plant at Gelsenkirchen. Such was the accuracy of the attack, that all production of vital aviation fuel was halted for a number of weeks at a cost to the Germans of a thousand tons per day.

The 14th brought the Command's first daylight operation since the departure of 2 Group twelve months earlier. The target was Le Havre, from where the enemy's E-Boats and other fast, light marine craft were posing a threat to Allied shipping supplying the Normandy beaches. The two-phase operation was conducted by predominantly 1 and 3 Groups with 617 Squadron representing 5 Group and took place in the evening under the umbrella of a fighter escort. The attack was highly successful, and few craft survived the onslaught. Other operations on this night targeted railway installations at three locations in France, while elements of 4, 5 and 8 Groups attended to enemy troop and vehicle concentrations at Aunay-sur-Odon and Évrecy near Caen. 5 Group assembled a force of 214 Lancasters and five Mosquitos for the former, of which seventeen representing 57 Squadron departed East Kirkby between 22.06 and 22.26 with S/L Wyness the senior pilot on duty. The weather was generally clear with some low cloud, but this did not hamper the marking process, which proceeded punctually and accurately. W/C Jeudwine was the Master Bomber, with 83 Squadron's W/C Northrop as Deputy, and the latter made four passes over the target, at 00.30 at 8,000 feet, 00.41 at 10,000 feet, and at 00.54 and 01.00 at 11,000 feet, dropping clusters of flares on the first two, green TIs on the third and red TIs on the fourth. The bombing was carried out on the above-mentioned TIs from 6,000 to 10,000 feet until shortly after 01.00 and appeared to be accurate and concentrated and produced fires and much smoke.

A force of 297 aircraft from 1, 4, 5, 6 and 8 Groups was assembled on the 15th to try to do to Boulogne what had been done to Le Havre twenty-four hours earlier. It was again left to 617 Squadron to represent 5 Group, and the operation was concluded with equal success. While this was in progress, 5 Group dispatched 110 Lancasters and four Mosquitos to deal with a fuel dump at Châtellerault, situated between Tours and Poitiers in western France. Clear skies and good visibility greeted their arrival in the target area, and red spotfires and green TIs marked out the aiming-point for the attack from 7,000 to 10,000 feet either side of 01.00. Post-raid reconnaissance confirmed that eight out of thirty-five individual fuel storage sites within the target had been destroyed. Returning crews complained that the greatest danger to life and limb on French targets came from London flak and that fired by the Royal Navy.

55 Base squadrons had remained at home on this night, and, on the 16th, awaited orders for the coming night's activities. Just three days earlier, the first V-1 flying bombs had landed on London, and this prompted a response in the form of a second new campaign to open during the month, this one against the revolutionary weapon's launching and storage sites in the Pas-de-Calais. Four targets were earmarked for attention, 5 Group handed a storage site at Beauvoir, located some twenty miles inland from Berck-sur-Mer. Such sites were referred to in Bomber Command parlance as "constructional works", and many were, indeed, large concrete structures in various stages of completion. 112 Lancasters were detailed, of which the nineteen representing 57 Squadron were loaded with eighteen 500 pounders before departing East Kirkby between 23.00 and 23.24 with W/C Humphreys and S/L Fairbairn the senior pilots on duty. There was only one early return from the entire force, and all of the 57 Squadron participants reached the target area to find nine to ten-tenths cloud with tops at 6,000 to 8,000 feet. The Oboe markers went down on time, but few crews were able to see them through the cloud and resorted to bombing on the reflected glow. The bombing, that took place from 10,000 to 13,000 feet, was concluded by 01.00 and on return, crews could only report observing bomb bursts.

The oil campaign continued on this night in the hands of 1, 4, 6 and 8 Groups at the Ruhr-Chemie synthetic oil plant at Sterkrade-Holten, a district of Oberhausen in the Ruhr, but cloudy conditions caused the bombing to be scattered, and there was little impact on production. 617 Squadron went alone to attack constructional works at Watten and Wizernes with Tallboys in daylight on the 19th and 20th, but cloudy conditions affected accuracy at the former and caused the latter to be aborted.

5 Group had to wait until Mid-Summer's Night, the 21st, before becoming involved in the oil offensive, and was handed two targets to attack simultaneously. A force of 120 Lancasters and six Mosquitos was assembled from 52, 54 and 55 Bases for the refinery at Wesseling, or to give it its full name, the Union Rheinische Braunkohlen-Kraftstoff Aktien Gesellschaft, situated on the East Bank of the Rhine south of Cologne. A second force of 120 Lancasters and four Mosquitos drawn from the squadrons of 53 and 54 Bases was assigned to the Hydrierwerke-Scholven plant in the Buer district of Gelsenkirchen. Included in the numbers of both elements was a sprinkling of ABC Lancasters of 101 Squadron for RCM duties, and the latter including a number of Oboe Mosquitos to carry out the initial marking. 57 Squadron made ready eighteen Lancasters for Wesseling, and they departed East Kirkby between 22.59 and 23.31 with S/L Wyness the senior pilot on duty, before heading into the greatest disaster to afflict the squadron thus far in the war. Enemy night-fighters pounced as soon as the enemy coast was crossed at the Scheldt Estuary, and many combats took place between there and the target. The expectation provided at briefing was of clear skies and conditions ideal for the 5 Group low-level marking method, but crews were greeted instead by ten-tenths low cloud and accurate predicted heavy flak. This meant, that low-level marking was not an option, and, faced with this situation, the Master Bomber, W/C Tait, ordered a blind attack that forced the Lancaster crews to bomb on H2S alone. They attacked on the glow of red TIs from approximately 17,000 to 20,000 feet but were unable to assess the outcome. After the war, a secret German report would suggest a 40% loss of production at the site, but this was probably of very short duration as the limited number of casualties on the ground pointed to a scattered and largely ineffective raid.

Whatever success was gained came at the high cost of thirty-seven Lancasters, a massive 28%, and all but two of them belonged to 5 Group Squadrons. 44, 49, 57 and 619 Squadrons each lost six Lancasters, while 207 and 630 Squadrons each had five empty dispersals to contemplate in the cold light of dawn. There must have been a sense of disbelief at East Kirkby when eleven of its Lancasters containing seventy-seven crew members failed to return, and the shock was only tempered slightly with the news that one 630 Squadron crew had abandoned their Lancaster over Bedfordshire and all were safe. Some time later, the news was received that 57 Squadron's ND471 had ditched off the Norfolk coast at 02.10 and the crew of P/O Nicklin RNZAF had been rescued later in the day by an ASR launch sent out from Yarmouth. On their return to the squadron two days later they reported having been attacked on a number of occasions by rocket-firing night-fighters, which shattered the fuel lines and resulted in three engines cutting out through petrol starvation. As far as the others were concerned, LM115 crashed two miles east of Turnhout in northern Belgium, killing P/O Bayley, his wireless operator and rear gunner, while delivering the flight engineer and mid-upper gunner into enemy hands. The navigator and bomb-aimer managed to retain their freedom, helped in no small measure by the courage of Belgian civilians. There were three evaders also from LM580, which was shot down by a night-fighter while outbound over Belgium and crashed five miles north-east of Genk with just P/O Guy still on board. His sacrifice saved six lives, even though survival for three of them meant enduring the remainder of the war in a PoW camp. Unusually, and probably as a result of their Lancasters being rent by an explosion, pilots, P/O Weightman and P/O Carr RAAF, were the sole survivors from JB526 and LM573 respectively after they were brought down, the former while outbound some ten miles inside Germany near Koslar and the latter on the way home four miles west of the Dutch town of s'Hertogenbosch. NN696 apparently crashed west of Gelsenkirchen with no survivors from the crew of F/L Beaumont DFC, and it is difficult to understand how it had come to be in the central Ruhr unless the crew had intentionally joined the Scholven-Buer operation.

Meanwhile, the Scholven-Buer force arrived in the target area also expecting to find clear skies, instead of which, they encountered ten-tenths cloud. This was the only flaw in the highly-effective 5 Group low-level marking method, which required the Mosquito element to go in beneath the cloud base and drop spotfires on the aiming point in the light of illuminating flares. However, when the cloud base was almost at ground level, nothing could be done. The preliminary Oboe markers were backed up by red and green TIs, the glow from which could be observed only dimly through the cloud, and the attack was carried out on them confirmed by Gee and H2S. It was impossible to assess the outcome, and to compound any sense of disappointment, eight Lancasters from the group failed to return. A secret German report surfaced post-war for this operation also and suggested a 20% loss of production at the plant, but this was probably for a limited period only.

While more than four hundred aircraft of 3, 4, 6 and 8 Groups targeted four flying-bomb sites on the 23rd, 1 and 5 Groups were sent respectively against railway yards at Saintes and Limoges in western France. Ninety-seven Lancasters and four Mosquitos were detailed from 53 and 54 Base squadrons, and they found clear skies and good visibility, in which ground features like the River Vienne and the railway sidings stood out prominently. Red spotfires and green TIs marked out the aiming-point, which was bombed from 5,000 to 8,000 feet between either side of 02.00 and several large explosions created clouds of smoke. 617 Squadron had attempted to continue the Tallboy assault on the constructional works at Wizernes in daylight on the 22nd, but the attack had been abandoned in the face of ten-tenths low cloud. The squadron returned the bombs to store and brought them back to France on the 24th to score a number of direct hits.

Nine 57 Squadron crews were called to briefing on the 24th to learn of their part in a busy night of operations that involved more than seven hundred aircraft targeting seven flying-bomb sites. Wesseling was still and open wound, but all trace of the missing had been removed and their billets repopulated with fresh faces, most of whom would ask the same question, "how long does it take to complete a tour?" In truth, crews joining Bomber Command at this stage of the war could finish within two months rather than the twelve to eighteen months it might have taken their predecessors. It is unlikely that any new faces attended briefing on this afternoon, when it was learned that "the targets for tonight" were at Pommeréval and Prouville, situated respectively some fifteen miles south-east of Dieppe, and east of Abbeville, for each of which 103 Lancasters and four Mosquitos were made ready. The 57 Squadron element took off for the former between 22.12 and 22.27 with W/C Humphreys the senior pilot on duty, and all reached the target area, where W/C Tait was again on hand in the role of Master Bomber. The weather conditions were favourable as he arrived and watched the Oboe marker going down on time at 23.50, only to assess that it was five hundred yards south of the aiming point. He directed the flare force to illuminate another Oboe marker that was much closer, and then sent in the low-level Mosquitos to mark the aiming point with red spotfires. This delayed the opening of the attack by two minutes, before the main force Lancasters delivered concentrated bombing from 6,000 to 9,000 feet shortly after midnight, and all of the bomb bursts were observed to be within a few hundred yards of the aiming point.

More than seven hundred aircraft were detailed for operations against six flying-bomb sites on the 27th, while two railway yards would occupy the attention of other elements. There were two targets for 5 Group, a flying-bomb site at what the 5 Group ORB identified as Marquise/Mimoyecques, situated some five miles inland from Cap Gris-Nez, and railway yards at Vitry-le-Francois south-east of Reims. Mimoyecques is actually five miles north-east of Marquise and the 57 Squadron ORB identified the former rather than Marquise as the target for thirteen of its Lancasters in a force of eighty-six provided by 52 and 55 Bases. Mimoyecques had been targeted earlier in the day by 4 Group Halifaxes with Path Finder support and would continue to attract attention over the ensuing days. Originally planned as one of two V-3 super-gun sites, each containing twenty-five barrels angled at 50 degrees and aimed at London, test failures and delays meant that a single three-barrel shaft stretching a hundred metres into the limestone hill, five miles from the coast and 103 miles from its target, was all that existed at the time. Each fifteen-metre-long smooth-bore barrel, which was designed on the multiple-charge principle to progressively boost the acceleration of the one-ton projectile as it travelled towards the muzzle, was to be capable of pounding London at the rate of hundreds per day without let-up. It was protected by a concrete slab thirty metres wide and five-and-a-half metres thick, which was correctly believed by the designers to be impregnable to conventional bombs. The 57 Squadron element departed East Kirkby between 23.14 and 23.24 with S/Ls Fairbairn and Wyness the senior pilots on duty and completed the outward flight within seventy-five minutes under clear skies and in good visibility. The attack began at 00.48½ with punctual and accurate marking and the East Kirkby crews delivered their eleven 1,000 and four 500 pounders each onto red TIs until the Master Bomber called a halt at 01.01. It was clear that the bombing had been concentrated on the markers, but it was impossible to assess if any damage had occurred.

While this operation was in progress, the second 5 Group force of 103 Lancasters and four Mosquitos from 53 and 54 Bases carried out an attack on the railway yards at Vitry-le-Francois. They were greeted by varying amounts of cloud reported at between zero and seven-tenths at around 7,000 feet, but the visibility was good, and the aiming-point was clearly marked by red spot fires and green TIs. Bombing took place from 4,500 to 8,000 feet between 01.44 and 01.54, at which point the Master Bomber called a halt and ordered crews with bombs still aboard to take them home. 50 Squadron's commanding officer, W/C Frogley, was critical of the decision to abandon the attack, suggesting that, if the first spotfire had not been accurate, the bombing should never even have started. In fact, it had been smoke obscuring the aiming-point that prompted the Master Bomber to send the final wave home with their bombs.

During the course of the month , the squadron undertook thirteen operations and dispatched 190 sorties for the loss of six Lancasters, five crews and a single airman.

July 1944

Sadly, July would bring further traumas for 5 Group, the first occurring early on, while the disaster of Wesseling remained an open wound. The month began as June had ended, with flying-bomb sites providing employment for over three hundred aircraft on both the 1st and 2nd. It was the 4th before the "Independent Air Force" was invited to re-enter the fray, when it was called upon to attack a V-Weapon storage site in caves at St-Leu-d'Esserent, some thirty miles north of Paris. The caves had originally been used for growing mushrooms, and they were protected by some twenty-five feet of clay and soft limestone, to say nothing of the anti-aircraft defences brought in by the Germans. The operation involved not only seventeen Lancasters, a Mustang and a Mosquito from 617 Squadron, but also 211 other Lancasters and eleven Mosquitos from the group, with three ABC Lancasters to provide RCM cover and three Path Finder Oboe Mosquitos to carry out the marking of an initial reference-point. There were actually two aiming-points, the road and railway communications to the area dump for the main force, and the tunnel complex at Creil, a settlement located three miles north-east of St Leu, for 617 Squadron.

57 Squadron supported the operation with seventeen Lancasters, which departed East Kirkby between 23.20 and 23.43 with S/L Fairbairn the senior pilot on duty. P/O Simson and crew turned back after responding to a message in plain language at 01.12, repeated at 01.15, which seemed to indicate a "return to base" order. This was not the only crew to respond to what may have been a spoof message sent by the Luftwaffe in a tactic employed successfully in the past by the RAF. The others pressed on to reach the target area under clear skies and in good visibility, which would prove to be of equal benefit to the night-fighters. There were no searchlights, but the expected volume of flak was thrown up at the main force element as it ran across the aiming-point to deliver loads mostly of eleven 1,000 and four 500 pounders from an average of 16,000 feet onto green TIs between 01.33 and 01.45. Night-fighters pounced on the bombers over the target and on the route home, and thirteen Lancasters failed to return, two of them belonging to 57 Squadron. JB486 was homebound when set upon by a night-fighter, which shot id down at around 02.00 to crash near Breteuil, a dozen or so miles south of Amiens. It contained the experienced crew of F/L Grubb, none of whom survived. JB723 was within fifteen miles of the coast at Le Treport when it crashed near Foucarmont before the crew of P/O Smith RAAF could save themselves. Post-raid reconnaissance revealed that a large area of subsidence had blocked the side entrance to the caves and that the road and railway links had been cut over a distance of four hundred yards.

On the 6th, more than five hundred aircraft were engaged on operations against V-Weapons targets, and 617 Squadron was assigned to the V-3 super-gun site at Mimoyecques. Direct hits were scored with the 12,000lb Tallboy earthquake bomb, which was designed to penetrate deep into the ground and destroy concrete structures by the effect of shock waves. An unexpected bonus of the weapon was its ability to drill though many feet of reinforced concrete and detonate inside a building, which would prove to be useful against U-Boot bunkers. A provisional reconnaissance revealed four deep craters in the immediate target area, one causing a large corner of the concrete slab to collapse. The extent of the damage underground would not be apparent to the planners at Bomber Command, but the shafts and tunnels had been rendered unusable and would remain so. Although W/C Cheshire did not know it, this was to be his final operation, not only with 617 Squadron, but also of the war in Europe. His one hundred-operation career would see him awarded a Victoria Cross, and his successor as commanding officer of 617 Squadron would need to be someone of immense stature, which was found in the person of W/C James "Willie" Tait.

The authorities were not convinced that the site at St-Leu-d'Esserent had received terminal damage and scheduled another attack on it for the late evening of the 7th. Before they took off, more than 450 aircraft from 1, 4, 6 and 8 Groups had carried out the first major operation in support of the Canadian 1st and British 2nd Armies, which were trying to break out of Caen. The target had been changed from German-fortified villages to an area of open ground north of Caen, where almost 2,300 tons of bombs were dropped somewhat ineffectively, and, ultimately, the decision to shift the point of aim proved to be counter-productive by causing damage to the northern suburbs of the city rather than to German forces. 5 Group detailed 208 Lancasters and fifteen Mosquitos for St-Leu, the 57 Squadron element of fifteen departing East Kirkby between 22.10 and 22.28 with W/C Humphreys and S/L Wyness the senior pilots on duty. It is believed that P/O Shamback and crew returned early because of engine failure, leaving the others to arrive in the target area and find medium-level cloud, which prevented the moonlight from providing illumination, although, below the cloud level, the visibility was good. The Master Bomber was W/C Ed Porter, and he oversaw the delivery of the Oboe yellow TI at 01.06, which was followed by the first stick of flares four minutes later. The first red spotfire went down at 01.08, a hundred yards south of the aiming-point, but in line with the direction of the bombing run and backing-up by red and green TIs continued until 01.13. The marking was assessed as sufficiently accurate to call in the main force crews at 01.15, and those from 57 Squadron dropped their loads of eleven 1,000 and four 500 pounders each from an average of 13,000 feet between 01.15 and 01.25, the time at which the Deputy Master Bomber, 83 Squadron's S/L Eggins, formerly of 57 Squadron, assumed control and sent the force home after the Master Bomber's VHF was found to be indistinct. On return, F/O Wardle and crew claimed the destruction of an unidentified twin-engine enemy aircraft. Twenty-nine Lancasters and two Mosquitos failed to return after night-fighters got amongst them, and this represented 14% of the force. It was another sombre dawn for East Kirkby, which had four empty dispersal pans to contemplate, three belonging to 57 Squadron Lancasters and the one that should have been occupied by the 630 Squadron aircraft in which the commanding officer, W/C Deas, had set off with his crew on the previous evening. 57 Squadron's ME868 was closing on the French coast near Dieppe when crashing near Fresnay-le-Long, killing P/O Rose RAAF and both gunners. The navigator and wireless operator were captured, the latter succumbing to his injuries soon afterwards, but the flight engineer and bomb-aimer managed to retain their freedom with the assistance of local civilians. JB370 came down in open country some six miles from Montdidier at 01.45, and all survived, three in captivity, while P/O Owen and three others evaded a similar fate. LM522 crashed some seven miles south-east of Dieppe and there were no survivors from the crew of P/O Findley.

The crews of S/L Wyness, F/L Walker and F/O Wardle took off from East Kirkby between 22.21 and 22.23 on the 10th bound for mining sorties in the Kattegat but returned within five hours because of adverse weather conditions.

Operations were posted and then cancelled on each of the four days after St-Leu until the 12th, when eleven 57 Squadron crews were called to briefing to be given the details for that night's operation against railway installations at Culmont-Chalindrey in eastern France. Two aiming-points were planned, at the western and eastern ends, for which a force of 157 Lancasters and four Mosquitos was made ready. While this operation was in progress, another by elements of 1 Group further south at Revigny would, hopefully, help to dilute the night-fighter response. The 57 Squadron crews departed East Kirkby between 21.46 and 22.01 with S/Ls Fairbairn and Wyness the senior pilots on duty and flew south for the Channel crossing. On arrival at the French coast, ND977 was attacked by a Ju88, which wrecked the bomb sight, but F/L Walker and crew had the satisfaction of shooting down their assailant before turning for home. The others continued on over eight-tenths low cloud until shortly before reaching the target area, where the conditions improved to provide clear skies, and, promisingly, no sign of defensive activity from the ground.

The controller at the eastern aiming-point experienced VHF communications problems, which delayed that part of the attack, and eventually, the entire force was directed to the western aiming-point. A pause in the bombing from 01.52 allowed the aiming-point to be re-marked, after which, bombing continued from 5,000 to 8,000 feet until around 02.16. Explosions were observed, followed by fires that remained visible for fifty miles into the return flight, but the high proportion of delayed action fuses in use prevented an immediate assessment of results, and post-raid reconnaissance would ultimately confirm an effective operation. Cloud interfered with the 1 Group operation at Revigny and only half of the force had bombed by the time the Master Bomber called a halt. It was an expensive failure that cost ten Lancasters.

A new policy was introduced on the 14th that raised most pilot officers to flying officer rank, which meant that a flight sergeant, on commission, would progress directly to flying officer. This certainly applied in 5 Group, but to what extent it was universal in Bomber Command is uncertain. Nine 57 Squadron crews were informed at briefing that day, that their target was to be the huge marshalling yards at Villeneuve-St-Georges situated on the southern rim of Paris. They would be part of a force of 111 Lancasters, six Mosquitos and an American twin-engine P38 Lightning containing the Master Bomber, W/C Jeudwine. The 57 Squadron crews departed East Kirkby between 21.49 and 21.55 with F/Ls Spencer and Thomas the senior pilots on duty and each Lancaster loaded with eighteen 500 pounders. All reached the target area to find a large amount of cloud with a base at 5,000 feet, but clear conditions below. W/C Jeudwine was having compass trouble, and would arrive on target twelve minutes late, so contacted his Deputy, 83 Squadron's W/C Joe Northrop, to take matters in hand. Joe could clearly see the target and judged the Oboe marker to be within fifty yards of the planned aiming-point. He called in the 5 Group marker force, which lobbed the TIs within the confines of the yards, and the operation appeared to be proceeding smoothly and precisely according to plan. Bombing took place on red and green TIs from 6,000 to 9,000 feet between 01.36 and 02.00 and most of the hardware hit the yards, while a proportion also fell outside to the east. Meanwhile, 1 Group had returned to Revigny, but had been thwarted by ground haze, which forced the Master Bomber to abandon the attack before any bombing could take place. Seven Lancasters were lost for no gain, and it would fall to 5 Group to finish the job a few nights hence at great expense.

Flying-bomb sites and railways dominated the target list on the 15th, and 5 Group was handed a railway junction at Nevers, a city on the North Bank of the Loire in central France. 57 Squadron contributed eight of its own to the force of 104 Lancasters with four Mosquitos to carry out the low-level marking, and they departed East Kirkby between 22.01 and 22.10 with S/L Fairbairn the senior pilot on duty. They bypassed the Channel Islands on their way to the French coast and reached the target after an outward flight of more than three-and-a-half hours. They were greeted by clear skies and a little haze and, initially, inaccurate marking, which led to inaccurate bombing. However, once corrected, the red spotfires and green TIs attracted the bomb loads and the 57 Squadron crews delivered their nine 1,000 and four 500 pounders each from around 5,000 feet between 01.59 and 02.18. A very large explosion occurred at 02.09, which might have been from an ammunition train or dump, but the use of largely delayed-action ordnance prevented an immediate assessment of results. Photographic reconnaissance later in the day revealed that the site had been all but obliterated, and there was much damage to rolling stock.

Seventeen 57 Squadron crews were called to briefing at midnight on the 17/18th to learn of their part in a tactical support operation to be carried out at dawn by a force of 942 aircraft, of which 201 of the Lancasters were to be provided by 5 Group. It was the start of the ground forces' Operation Goodwood, which, General Montgomery hoped, would be a decisive breakout into wider France as a prelude to the march towards the German frontier. The aiming-points were five enemy-held villages to the east of Caen, Colombelles, Mondeville, Sannerville, Cagny and Manneville, all of which stood in the path of the advancing British 2nd Army. The 57 Squadron element departed East Kirkby between 03.28 and 04.03 with S/Ls Fairbairn and Wyness the senior pilots on duty and all reached the target area to find their aiming-point, the Mondeville steel works, already marked by red and yellow TIs, but about to be swallowed up and obscured by drifting smoke. The target, which the Germans had converted into a strongly defended fortress, was actually situated south of the River L'Orne in an industrial suburb of the city itself, to the east of the marshalling yards. The 57 Squadron crews delivered their eleven 1,000 and four 500 pounders from 6,000 to 10,000 feet between 05.44 and 06.13 in accordance with instructions from the Master Bomber, and, as far as could be determined, they fell accurately onto the markers. The RAF dropped five thousand tons of bombs to good effect onto the two German divisions in just half an hour, and the Americans followed up with a further two thousand tons.

Crews returning from the above operation took to their beds after breakfast to get as much sleep as possible before many were called into action again that night. Following two failed attempts by 1 Group to cut the railway junction at Revigny in France's Marne region, at a cost of seventeen Lancasters, the job was handed to 5 Group, which assembled a force of 109 Lancasters, four Mosquitos and a P38 Lightning containing the Master Bomber, W/C Jeudwine. It was to be a busy night of operations, which included another railway and two oil targets, along with support and diversionary activities involving a total of 972 sorties. Ten 57 Squadron crews attended briefing at teatime to learn of their part in what promised to be an unspectacular and routine operation, all but one of them about to undertake their second sortie of the day. They departed East Kirkby between 22.51 and 23.10 with F/Ls Bulcraig and Scutt the senior pilots on duty and lost the services of F/O Southfield and crew to an oil leak in the front turret. The others crossed the French coast near Dieppe, before passing through an intense searchlight belt some twenty miles inland. JB318 was ensnared in a cone and although F/L Bulcraig DFM (earned as an NCO navigator with 50 Squadron) managed to break free, he and his crew were now off course, outside of the protection of the bomber stream and easy prey for a night-fighter. Soon afterwards, an explosion in the port wing signalled the end and only the navigator and two gunners managed to take to their parachutes before the Lancaster crashed with a full bomb load at Bassevelle, some forty-five miles east-north-east of Paris city centre, the sixth victim of the raid thus far. The navigator fell into enemy hands, while the two gunners were spirited away by local civilians and were still under their care when the region was liberated by American forces on the 3rd of September.

The bomber stream continued to be harried all the way into eastern France by night-fighters, which had been fed into the stream shortly after it entered enemy airspace, and it was at this stage of the outward flight that matters began to go awry. In just forty-five minutes, sixteen Lancasters fell victim to night-fighters and one to flak, leaving the survivors to reach the target and find clear skies but haze obscuring ground detail. This elusive target continued to present problems, beginning with the first wave of flares delivered at about 01.30, which were too far to the east.

More flares were ordered, and the bombing was put back by five minutes, while Wanganui markers were dropped by Mosquito and the situation was assessed. The whole attack seemed chaotic, and the use of many delayed-action bombs meant that it was difficult to see what was happening on the ground. The 57 Squadron crews were over the target at 7,000 to 10,000 feet between 01.43 and 01.57 and released their ten 1,000 and four 500 pounders each onto a red spotfire in accordance with instructions from the Master Bomber. On return, F/O Beard and crew claimed the destruction of a Ju88. Photo-reconnaissance revealed, that the operation had been successful in cutting the railway link to the battle front, but had cost twenty-four Lancasters, almost 22% of those dispatched. *(For a full and highly detailed account of the three Revigny raids, read the amazing book, Massacre over the Marne, by Oliver Clutton-Brock.)*

5 Group crews stood-by on the 19th for a possible daylight operation, and it was evening before orders came through to prepare for an attack on a flying-bomb storage site at Thiverny, situated just to the north of St-Leu-d'Esserent and separated from the recently attacked site at Creil by the river Oise. A force of 103 Lancasters and two Mosquitos was detailed, ten of the former provided by 57 Squadron, which departed East Kirkby between 19.07 and 19.28 with S/Ls Fairbairn and Wyness the senior pilots on duty. The attack was to take place in daylight under the protection of a Spitfire escort, which was picked up at the south coast. All from the squadron reached the target in fine weather conditions, but ground haze created challenging conditions in which to identify the aiming-point. Late preliminary marking by the Path Finder element and communications problems between the Master Bomber and his Deputy added to the frustrations and led to most crews having to bomb visually in the face of moderate to intense heavy flak bursting as high as 18,000 feet. The 57 Squadron crews were over the target between 21.30 and 21.39 at altitudes ranging from 13,000 to 18,000 feet, and, although there was moderate to intense heavy flak, the absence of enemy fighters contributed to a loss-free operation. Reconnaissance revealed some loose bombing, but sufficient aiming-point photographs were brought back to suggest that the railway tracks to the storage caves had been cut, while the caves themselves were undamaged.

On a busy night on the 20th, when three of the four campaigns were to be prosecuted, oil at Bottrop and Homberg and V-Weapons sites at Ardouval and Wizernes, elements of 1, 5 and 8 Groups were detailed to attack railway yards and a triangle junction at Courtrai (Kortrijk) in Belgium. 57 Squadron contributed fourteen Lancasters to the 5 Group force of 190 Lancasters and five Mosquitos, and they departed East Kirkby between 23.09 and 23.23 with F/Ls Scutt, Spencer and Thomas the senior pilots on duty. They all reached the target area to find it free of cloud, if slightly obscured by ground haze, but the Oboe marking was well-placed in the marshalling yards and backed up by green TIs, onto which the squadron's participants delivered their eleven 1,000 and four 500 pounders each from 10,000 to 14,000 feet between 00.56 and 01.03. They returned home safely to report a large, orange explosion at 00.57 and a successful outcome, which was confirmed by post-raid reconnaissance that revealed both aiming-points had been obliterated and locomotive and repair shops partially destroyed along with a large amount of rolling stock. The success was achieved for the loss of nine Lancasters, most of them belonging to 1 Group.

Following two nights at home for 5 Group and a two-month break from city-busting, Harris sanctioned a major raid on the naval port of Kiel on the 23rd, for which a force of 629 aircraft was made ready. 5 Group contributed ninety-nine of the Lancasters, six of them representing 57 Squadron and an additional three for the crews of F/Os Thomas and Wardle and F/L Spencer to take to the Forget-me-not garden in Kiel harbour. They departed East Kirkby together between 22.35 and 22.42 with each of the bombers captained by a pilot of flying officer rank and, unusually for an urban target, carrying eleven 1,000 and four 500 pounders. They headed for the rendezvous point, where they formed up behind an elaborate "Mandrel" jamming screen laid on by 100 Group, before setting course for Denmark's western coast. *(In November 1943, 100 Group had been formed to take over the Radio Countermeasures (RCM) role, which had been the preserve of 101 Squadron since its introduction a number of months earlier. 101 Squadron, however, would remain in 1 Group and continue to provide RCM for the remainder of the war.)* F/O Wardle and crew turned back before reaching the enemy coast after their a.s.i., failed. When the head of the bomber stream arrived unexpectedly and with complete surprise in Kiel airspace, its presence rendered the enemy night-fighter controller confused and unable to bring his resources to bear. Kiel was covered by a nine to ten-tenths veil of thin cloud with tops at 4,000 feet, and a skymarking plan was put into action, which enabled the main force crews to bomb on the glow, first of the flares, and then of fires. The 57 Squadron crews bombed from 14,000 to 20,000 feet between 01.27 and 01.32, aiming at the glow of red and green Wanganui markers as they disappeared into cloud. Flak was mostly in barrage form and exploding at 15,000 to 22,000 feet, without being overly troublesome. It was not possible to determine the outcome of the raid, but the glow of fires remained visible for a hundred miles into the return journey, which suggested that it had been effective. This was confirmed by local reports, which conceded that this had been the town's most destructive raid of the war and had inflicted heavy damage on the port and shipyards and cut off water supplies for three days and gas for three weeks. Many delayed-action bombs had been dropped, and these continued to cause problems for some time. While the above was in progress, the gardeners sneaked in to deliver six mines each by H2S into the briefed locations.

5 Group divided its forces on the 24th to enable it to support the first of a three-raid series in five nights on the city of Stuttgart, and an oil refinery and fuel dump at Donges. Situated on the North Bank of the Loire to the east of St Nazaire, the latter target had been attacked successfully by elements of 6 and 8 Groups on the previous night, but clearly required further attention. The group detailed ninety-nine Lancasters for southern Germany in an overall force of 614, while 104 Lancasters and four Mosquitos were made ready for western France, with five 8 Group Mosquitos in attendance. 57 Squadron would support both operations with eight Lancasters for each, and those bound for Stuttgart took off between 21.40 and 21.54 with F/Ls Spencer and Thomas the senior pilots on duty and were followed into the air between 22.03 and 22.35 by the second element led by F/Ls Scutt and Weber. The crews of F/Os Kelton and Wardle turned back early from the Stuttgart force, leaving the others from the squadron to reach their respective destinations at around the same time. They were greeted at Stuttgart by nine to ten-tenths cloud with tops at 4,000 to 7,000 feet, which required the employment of Wanganui flares to mark the aiming-point. The bombing was carried out on the red glow on the cloud base from 18,000 to 22,000 feet from around 01.50 in accordance with the instructions of the Master Bomber, and crews set course for home fairly satisfied with the outcome, although it was impossible to make an accurate assessment. At debriefings across the Command, crews reported a glow of fires covering an area of perhaps five square miles, which remained visible for eighty miles into the return journey. No local report came out of Stuttgart for this night, but it had been a successful and destructive raid, although gained at a cost of seventeen Lancasters and four Halifaxes. 57 Squadron's ND560 crashed near Orleans and there were no survivors from the crew of F/O Simson.

Meanwhile, 290 miles to the west of Stuttgart, clear skies and good visibility greeted the 5 Group crews, who were able to pick out ground detail in the light of the illuminator flares. Bombing by the 57 Squadron element took place on concentrated red and green TIs from 8,000 to 11,000 feet between 01.43 and 01.51 in accordance with the Master Bomber's instructions, and the glow of fires through thick smoke, along with a large explosion at 01.49, indicated a successful outcome. Post-raid photo-reconnaissance confirmed the success of the operation, revealing the site to have been devastated at a cost of three Lancasters.

5 Group split its forces again on the 25th to support the second of the raids on Stuttgart with eighty-three Lancasters from 52, 54 and 55 Bases and a daylight attack on an aerodrome and signals depot at Saint-Cyr involving ninety-four Lancasters and six Mosquitos from 53 and 54 Bases. *(There are at least four locations called Saint-Cyr, and it is believed that the one targeted on this night was in the Ile-de-France to the west of Paris.)* 57 Squadron briefed twelve crews for the former operation, while loading its Lancasters with a 2,000 pounder and a dozen 500lb J-cluster bombs each. They departed East Kirkby between 21.15 and 21.29 with S/L Wyness the senior pilot on duty and rendezvoused with the rest of the 550-strong force as they made their way via Reading to the south coast. They crossed the Channel and France and entered Germany near Strasbourg accompanied by layers of cloud, which, over the target, was at five to ten-tenths with tops in places as high as 20,000 feet. There was haze below the cloud level to create further challenges for the marker force, and the red and green TIs appeared to the main force crews to be somewhat scattered. The 57 Squadron crews bombed from 17,000 to 21,000 feet between 01.53 and 02.20, and the glow from the resulting fires remained visible for a hundred miles into the return flight. Despite that, there appeared to be little optimism at debriefings, and no report came out of Stuttgart to provide a clue concerning the outcome. In fact, this was probably the most destructive of the three raids in this current series, but it would be only after the third one that cumulative reports came out of the city to confirm much destruction and heavy casualties.

The hectic round of operations continued for 5 Group on the 26th with preparations for an attack on two aiming-points in the marshalling yards at Givors, situated on the West Bank of the River Rhône in south-eastern France. 178 Lancasters and nine Mosquitos were made ready, ten of the former by 57 Squadron, and they departed East Kirkby between 21.12 and 21.25 with S/L Fairbairn the senior pilot on duty and a round-trip of eleven hundred miles ahead of them. Bad weather had been anticipated, but the conditions during the outward leg over France were even worse than forecast, with icing and electrical storms contributing to the early return of fourteen aircraft. 57 Squadron was not affected by the conditions and covered the almost five-hour outward flight to reach the target to be greeted by a continuation of the severe weather in the form of rain, thunderstorms and lightning. The cloud was down to around 7,000 feet with poor visibility below, and the flare force made a number of runs across the target, orbiting in between awaiting instructions. There were occasional glimpses of the ground, but the Master Bomber was experiencing great difficulty in getting Mosquito TIs onto the two aiming points. Eventually, one of the Deputies managed to put a green TI onto the southern aiming-point, and the main force crews began to bomb at around 02.00. The 57 Squadron crews carried out their attacks from 4,700 to 7,500 feet between 02.07 and 02.29, using the light from flares and aiming at green TIs, all in accordance with instructions. They could offer little to the intelligence section at debriefing, but post-raid reconnaissance revealed that the tracks to the north of the junction were closed, and the locomotive depot in the yards had been damaged.

The night of the 28/29th would prove to be busy, eventful and expensive as the Command prepared for major operations against Stuttgart and Hamburg and a number of smaller undertakings involving a total of 1,126 aircraft. The final raid of the series on Stuttgart was to be an all-Lancaster affair of 494 aircraft drawn from 1, 3, 5 and 8 Groups, while 307 Lancasters and Halifaxes of 1, 6 and 8 Groups carried out the annual last-week-of-July attack on Hamburg, a year and a day after the devastating firestorm of Operation Gomorrah. 5 Group put up 176 Lancasters, fifteen of them made ready by 57 Squadron, and they were each loaded with a 2,000 pounder and a dozen 500lb J-cluster bombs. They departed East Kirkby between 21.37 and 21.52 with W/C Humphreys the senior pilot on duty and were represented among the five early returns of 5 Group aircraft by the crew of F/O Kelton, whose mid-upper gunner became indisposed. The others flew across France in bright moonlight above the cloud layer and exposed themselves to the night-fighter hordes that had infiltrated the bomber stream as it closed on the target. It was the Luftwaffe's Nachtjagd that would gain the upper hand on this night and claimed 57 Squadron's PD212 at around 00.30 somewhere near Romilly in the Loire Valley. F/O Nicholls and crew were on the fourth sortie of their tour and all survived, the pilot and three others to evade capture, while their three crew colleagues were apprehended. The outward flight of ME864 lasted a further fifty minutes before it was brought down in southern Germany, killing F/O Wardle DFC, his flight engineer and rear gunner and delivering the four survivors into enemy hands. They had been undertaking their thirty-first sortie and were in sight of the end of their first tour. Those arriving in the target area found a layer of up to ten-tenths thin cloud over the city, with tops in places at around 10,000 feet, and the Path Finders initially employed skymarker flares (Wanganui), at which the 57 Squadron crews aimed their bombs either side of 02.00. F/O Watt and crew landed at Woodbridge with a severely damaged Lancaster after surviving three attacks by enemy night-fighters. The rear gunner, Sgt West, sustained severe wounds, to which he succumbed later on the 29th. Thirty-nine Lancasters failed to return, fourteen of them from 5 Group, and night-fighters also caught the Hamburg force on its way home, and an additional twenty-two aircraft were shot down, bringing the night's casualty figure to sixty-one aircraft. Although it was difficult to make an accurate assessment of this night's attack on Stuttgart, the series had severely damaged the city, leaving its central districts devastated, with most of its public and cultural buildings in ruins, while 1,171 of its inhabitants had lost their lives.

Thirteen 57 Squadron crews were briefed and put on stand-by at East Kirkby late on the 29th in anticipation of an early-morning tactical support operation in the Villers Bocage-Caumont region of the Normandy battle area south-west of Caen. They were to be part of an overall force of 692 aircraft to attack six enemy positions facing predominantly American forces, and they took off for their aiming-point at Cahagnes between 05.39 and 05.55 with W/C Humphreys and S/L Fairbairn the senior pilots on duty. They approached the target over ten-tenths cloud with tops at 5,000 feet and a base at 3,500 feet with haze below and were five minutes from the bombing run at 07.59, when the Master Bomber sent them home. Later, on the 30th, 57 Squadron Lancaster LM284 was taken for an air-test by a predominantly 207 Squadron crew and failed to return. A single body came ashore on a Norfolk beach, suggesting that the Lancaster had gone down in the Wash.

5 Group prepared for two daylight operations on the 31st, one of them an evening attack on a flying bomb storage tunnel at Rilly-la-Montagne, some five miles south of Reims. A 5 Group force of ninety-seven Lancasters and three Mosquitos included sixteen Lancasters of 617 Squadron, led by its recently appointed successor to Cheshire, W/C Tait, and three 57 Squadron Lancasters. A second operation was to be directed at locomotive facilities and marshalling yards at Joigny-la-Roche, situated north of Auxerre and some ninety miles south-east of Paris, and would involve 127 Lancasters and four Mosquitos of 1 and 5 Groups including seven of the former provided by 57 Squadron. They departed East Kirkby together between 17.29 and 17.59 with S/L Fairbairn the senior pilot on duty and made their way south to rendezvous with the rest of the two forces. 83 Squadron formed into two vics, one at 15,000 and the other at 18,000 feet, to lead the Rilly force to the target under a fighter escort. Weather conditions at the target were clear, and it could be identified visually, but once the Tallboys went down, dust and smoke made it difficult to assess the outcome, and the use of delayed fuses added to that problem. The ORB provides scant detail, but it seems that the 57 Squadron element identified the target visually and delivered ten 1,000 and four 500 pounders each through four-tenths cloud from around 17,000 feet at 20.20 and reported a successful outcome. Meanwhile, the Joigny-la-Roche force had arrived in the target area to find no more than three-tenths cloud with tops at 7,000 feet, and good enough visibility to enable a visual identification of the aiming-point. The marking was concentrated, as was the bombing onto the red TIs, and the squadron crews delivered their standard bomb loads from 12,000 to 14,000 feet almost as one shortly before 20.30, doing so under the umbrella of a fighter escort. ND954 was unable to maintain formation on the way home and crashed at 21.45 near Caen, killing F/L Spencer and four of his crew and delivering the two survivors into enemy hands. This was a particularly sad loss involving a crew on their thirty-first sortie and was the only failure to return from what post-raid reconnaissance confirmed as a successful operation.

This was the final operation of one of the Command's and the squadron's busiest months of the war to date, during which 57 Squadron launched twenty operations that generated two hundred sorties and cost eleven Lancasters, ten crews and an individual airman.

August 1944

August would bring an end to the flying bomb offensive and also see a return to major night operations against industrial Germany. Flying bomb sites were to dominate the first half of the month and would be targeted in daylight on each of the first six days. It began with the commitment of 777 aircraft to operations against numerous flying bomb-related sites on the afternoon of the 1st, although there were serious doubts about the weather conditions, which were poor over England. 5 Group's targets were at La Breteque, situated in Normandy, some ten miles east-south-east of Rouen, Mont Candon, a mile or two south-west of Dieppe, and Siracourt, located some thirty miles east of the coastal town of Berck-sur-Mer. Forces of fifty-three Lancasters, fifty-nine Lancasters and a Lightning and Mosquito and sixty-seven Lancasters and four Mosquitos respectively were made ready, the first and last mentioned supported by 57 Squadron with two and six Lancasters respectively. Those bound for Siracourt departed East Kirkby between 14.55 and 15.08 with F/Ls Anderson, Nicklin and Weber the senior pilots, and they joined forces with the others as they made their way towards the south. The formation was led by a vic of Lancasters from 83 Squadron, which included the Deputy Master Bomber, F/L

Meggeson. Conditions became clear over the Channel, but the cloud built again to nine-tenths stratocumulus with tops at 4,000 feet over the target, and F/L Meggeson took the decision upon himself to abandon the operation. At almost at the same time, 18.33, he received a confirmatory call by VHF from the Master Bomber, by which time one crew had spotted the target through a gap and had taken the opportunity to bomb it. The crews of S/L Fairbairn and F/O Blank, meanwhile, had taken off at 16.36 and met with similar conditions over the Pas-de-Calais region. One Lancaster bombed at La Breteque before the Master Bomber called a halt to proceedings, and it was a similar story for the other groups at their targets, and, in total, only seventy-nine aircraft bombed. Crews were eager to operate against the enemy and were scathing in their condemnation if the meteorological people got the weather wrong and wasted the efforts of all of those involved in launching a raid. Sadly, weather forecasting in the 1940s was an art, not the science it is today.

On the following afternoon, 5 Group contributed 194 Lancasters, two Mosquitos and a P38 Lightning to operations by 394 aircraft against one flying bomb launching and three supply sites. Eleven Lancasters were made ready by 57 Squadron to participate in a 5 Group attack on a storage site at Trossy-St-Maximin, situated north of Paris and close to St-Leu d'Esserent. They were part of a heavy force of ninety-four Lancasters and two Mosquitos and took off between 14.17 and 14.30 with W/C Humphreys the senior pilot on duty, and each carrying eleven 1,000 and three 500 pounders, some with a delay fuse of up to thirty-six hours. There were complaints that the formation leaders flew too fast, and there were comments also about excessive weaving, but all from 57 Squadron reached the target to find three to seven-tenths patchy cloud. The Oboe proximity markers went down on time, and were backed up with TIs, and, once the bombing started, the defences opened up with accurate flak that caused damage to twenty-seven aircraft. Despite that, most of the formation passed over the aiming-point and plastered it from 15,000 to 18,000 feet between 17.01 and 17.05. Post-raid reconnaissance revealed many new craters, a large rectangular building stripped of its roof and sides, and the southern end of two road-over-rail bridges demolished.

Despite the effectiveness of the operation, the same site was included among targets for more than eleven hundred aircraft on the following day. The reason given to the 1 and 5 Group crews at briefing was, that the importance of the site to the Third Reich demanded that no building be left intact, and one or two may have escaped damage during the previous day's attack. 187 Lancasters, one Mosquito and the P38 Lightning were made ready as 5 Group's contribution to the operation, the eight 57 Squadron participants departing East Kirkby between 11.43 and 12.02 with F/Ls Nicklin and Weber the senior pilots on duty. They were to attack about fifteen minutes after 1 Group, and, as they reached the target, smoke could be seen rising to 8,000 feet, and this combined with a fierce flak defence to present the crews with challenging conditions. The 57 Squadron element bombed from 16,000 to 17,000 feet between 14.31 and 14.33 by visual reference, having been prevented by the smoke from seeing the markers. The bombing was not as concentrated as on the previous day, and much of it fell short. Many aircraft returned to their respective stations bearing flak damage, and at some debriefings, complaints were aired that there had been too much chat on VHF between the Master Bomber and his Deputy. Photo-reconnaissance was unable to confirm that the site had been obliterated, and it would need to be attacked again on the following day, a job that would be handed to 6 Group, while most of 5 Group stayed at home.

The 5th dawned bright and clear and brilliant sunshine glinted off the Perspex of thirteen 57 Squadron Lancasters as they took off from East Kirkby between 10.39 and 10.51 bound for familiar airspace over St-Leu-d'Esserent. They were part of a 5 Group force of 189 Lancasters and one Mosquito, which, in turn, represented about 25% of the effort by 4, 5, 6 and 8 Groups against two flying-bomb sites, the other in the Forét-de-Nieppe, close to the Belgian frontier. Among those waving them off was the crew of F/O "Jimmy" Castagnola, who were about to embark on well-earned end of tour leave. On their return they would join 617 Squadron to continue their outstanding operational career and live to see the end of hostilities. The lead formation remained well to starboard of track for most of the outward flight, and only adjusted its course when some thirty seconds from the target, which created difficulties for those following and attempting to set up their bombing run. It was, at least, an almost intact force that homed in on the target to find it partly protected by up to six-tenths patchy cloud with tops at about 12,000 feet. This prevented the Master Bomber from picking up the aiming-point until thirty seconds from it, and smoke added to the challenges, hiding the yellow TIs from the view of the main force bomb-aimers, and most picked up the aiming point by means of ground features. The 57 Squadron crews ran through a spirited flak defence and bombed from 16,100 to 17,500 feet between 13.32 and 13.35, before returning home to report what they assessed as a somewhat chaotic and scattered attack. Others thought it to have been reasonably concentrated and PRU photos seemed to confirm that view with images of fresh damage and heavily cratered approaches.

Seven 57 Squadron crews were in their Lancasters before 09.00 on the 6th to carry out the checks before departing for a flying-bomb launching site at Bois-de-Cassan in the L'Isle-Adam, a few miles to the south-west of St-Leu. They were part of a 5 Group force of ninety-nine Lancasters and the P38 Lightning and departed East Kirkby between 09.21 and 09.29 with W/C Humphreys the senior pilot on duty. They joined up with the rest of the formation as they made their way south, the heavy element led by 83 Squadron's G/C Deane with F/L Drinkell acting as his deputy. Deane began to experience problems with his navigation homing equipment as he crossed the English coast outbound and decided to hand over to F/L Drinkall. When about forty miles inland of the French coast, a large cumulus cloud extended up to 30,000 feet to bar the way, and F/L Drinkall communicated his intention to take the force below it, descending to 16,000 feet. G/C Deane warned him not to go below 15,000, and advised him not to enter the cloud, but to turn to starboard. However, they were immediately enveloped in cloud, and G/C Deane did his best to hang on to F/L Drinkall's tail, as he continued to descend, and the two eventually became separated. Emerging on the other side of the cloud, Deane saw a large formation in the distance, and followed it. Passing through the cloud had caused the formation to become widely scattered, and it could not be reformed. Thirty-eight aircraft bombed after picking up the aiming point visually, those from 57 Squadron from 12,500 to 17,000 feet between 12.14 and 12.21, but fifty-eight others did not, and all had to contend with a fierce flak and fighter defence. W/C Humphreys and crew endured a forty-minute combat with a BF109, during which the mid-upper gunner, F/O Porter, sustained serious wounds and the Lancaster extensive damage. Perfect crew co-operation, the result of many hours of fighter affiliation practice, enabled them to survive the encounter and ultimately break free to land at Ford, while the rest of the squadron made it back to base. Three Lancasters failed to return, and among them was that of F/L Drinkall and crew, who all lost their lives. Photo-reconnaissance revealed some fresh damage to the eastern side of the target, but two large buildings on the main roadway immediately south of the aiming point remained intact, and further operations would be required.

Other than night flying tests (NFTs), there was little activity during the day on the 7th, the first time during the month that no daylight operations had been mounted. It was from teatime onwards that the feverish activity began, to prepare 1,019 aircraft for attacks on five enemy positions facing Allied ground forces in the Normandy battle area. The aiming-point for 179 Lancasters and one Mosquito from 5 Group was the fortified village of Secqueville, situated some fifteen miles east of Le Havre. Thirteen 57 Squadron Lancasters departed East Kirkby between 21.18 and 21.44 with S/L Wyness the senior pilot on duty and joined up with the others as they travelled south. The target could be seen by the approaching bombers to be under clear skies, although haze shrouded ground detail to an extent, and star shells were fired from the ground to illuminate the aiming-point. This enabled the Path Finder aircraft to drop red TIs onto it for the main force crews to aim at, those from 57 Squadron delivering their eleven 1,000 and four 500 pounders from 8,000 to 8,500 feet at around 23.21. The first phase of bombing was concentrated and lasted fifteen minutes, after which, smoke began to obscure the markers, persuading the Master Bomber to call a halt to proceedings and send everyone home.

A rare day off for 5 Group crews on the 8th led to another for them on the 9th until late afternoon, when briefings took place for that night's operation against an oil storage dump in the Forét-de-Châtellerault, situated south of Tours in western France. It was to be predominantly a 5 Group show involving 171 Lancasters and fourteen Mosquitos, but with five 101 Squadron Lancasters to provide RCM cover. 57 Squadron dispatched twelve Lancasters between 20.28 and 20.45 with S/L Wyness the senior pilot on duty and lost the services of F/O Waugh and crew to an unserviceable rear turret and bomb sight. The others arrived in the target area to find no cloud, but the presence of considerable ground haze created poor visibility for the marker crews attempting to identify the two aiming-points. The flares dropped by the first two waves of the marker force were scattered, and this prompted the Mosquito marker leader to drop a Wanganui flare as a guide to the third flare-force crews. This meant that some crews had to orbit for up to twenty minutes before the Master Bomber was satisfied that the green TIs were in the right spot and called in the main force. They produced accurate bombing, resulting in three large explosions and volumes of black smoke, which, within five minutes, completely obscured the aiming-point. A pause in the bombing was called, before it recommenced, until the lack of a verifiable marker compelled the Master Bomber to call a halt. All but one of the 57 Squadron crews carried out an attack from 4,800 to 8,000 feet between 00.02 and 00.27, while F/O Shamback and crew misinterpreted the signal to temporarily stop bombing as an order to abandon the attack altogether.

The Gironde Estuary, situated on France's Biscay coast, narrows as it leads inland towards the south-east, before dividing to become the Garonne River to the west and the Dordogne to the east. Its banks and islands were home to a number of important oil production and storage sites at Pauillac, Blaye, Bec-d'Ambe and Bordeaux, and the region was a frequent destination for gardening activities. Bordeaux itself was a vitally important port to the enemy as a gateway to the Atlantic for its U-Boots and was heavily defended along the entire length of the waterway. Orders were received on 54 and 55 Base stations at teatime on the 10th to prepare sixty-two Lancasters and five Mosquitos to bomb oil storage facilities at Bordeaux. 57 Squadron loaded each of five Lancasters with 11,000lbs of bombs in the form of five armour-piercing 2,000 pounders and a single 1,000 pounder and dispatched them between 18.43 and 18.49 with the crews of F/Ls Ainley, Clark, Scutt and Thomas and F/O Southfield on board. They headed towards the south, joining up with the other elements, which included nine Lancasters from 83 Squadron to act as the flare and marker force. The flight out was in daylight, which enabled the Deputy Master Bomber to recognise that the formation had become somewhat disorganised. There were about twenty main force aircraft ahead of the flare force, and the remainder behind it to starboard, but they were catching up, and veering further and further to starboard, until they were some ten to twenty miles off track. Fortunately, the situation rectified itself, and the force arrived in the target area to find clear skies with a little ground haze. As they ran in on the aiming-point, a limited amount of heavy flak began to burst at 16,000 to 18,000 feet, while the considerable light flak fell short, and neither proved to be troublesome. Within thirty seconds of the flares illuminating the ground, the TIs were burning close to the aiming-point and the 57 Squadron crews bombed from 16,000 to 19,000 between 22.32 and 22.45. Returning crews were confident of a successful attack and observed black smoke rising, but, as few explosions were observed, it was difficult to accurately assess the outcome.

On the 11th, while 617 Squadron took care of the U-Boot pens at la Pallice, thirty-nine other Lancasters and two Mosquitos from 5 Group attacked a similar target at Bordeaux under the protection of six Mosquitos of 100 Group, the first time that the "serrate" radar-equipped type had been employed in this role. 57 Squadron made ready five Lancasters and sent them on their way from East Kirkby between 11.59 and 12.04 with S/L Wyness the senior pilot on duty. Each crew was again sitting on five 2,000 pounders and a single 1,000 pounder, all of which reached the target, where excellent conditions prevailed to enable the entire dock complex to be identified from a distance. Up to a dozen flak guns targeted the force as it ran in, but the Lancasters held their course to deliver the contents of their bomb bays accurately across the pens. No enemy fighters were encountered, and Spitfires were on hand off the Brest peninsula to escort the bombers the rest of the way home.

For the evening operation, 5 Group was switched to communications targets at Givors, located about twenty miles to the south of Lyon in south-east-central France. There were to be two aiming-points, the town's marshalling yards to the north and a railway junction to the south, and 57 Squadron's eight-strong element was assigned to the former in an overall force of 175 Lancasters and ten Mosquitos. They departed East Kirkby between 20.31 and 20.37 with F/L Scutt the senior pilot on duty and arrived in the target area to find clear skies and a little haze, favourable conditions, which the seemingly usual organized chaos of contradictory or confusing instruction via VHF and W/T threatened to waste. Unaccountably, the 5 Group ORB described the W/T control as excellent and the VHF R/T as good. The initial marking was accurate, but the backing up erratic, which delayed permission to bomb until 01.12, by which time some crews had been forced to orbit three times while the Master Bomber and his Deputy discussed the accuracy of the markers. At 01.14½ the Master Bomber ordered the bombing of a concentration of red TIs, which most crews were unable to see, but they did spot a rough crescent of isolated reds across the yards which the 57 Squadron crews bombed from 6,150 to 8,800 feet between 01.07 and 01.23 after confirming their positions by Gee and H2S. Despite the wrinkles, both aiming-points were eventually well-illuminated and marked, and the bombing was concentrated in the correct place. They all returned to home airspace critical of some aspects of the raid, but confident that it had been concluded successfully. Photo-reconnaissance revealed heavy damage to both aiming-points, with the ground badly-cratered and many tracks severed, and the middle span of the railway bridge over the river Rhône had received a direct hit.

The main operation on the 12th was an experiment to gauge the ability of main force crews to locate and attack an urban target on the strength of their own H2S equipment in the absence of a Path Finder element. This resulted from the huge volume of operations generated by the four concurrent campaigns, each of which called upon the finite resources of 8 Group, compelling it, in the short term at least, to spread itself more and more thinly. The conclusion of the flying-bomb campaign at the end of the month, together with the end of tactical support for the ground forces, would remove the pressure, and the planned independence of 3 Group through the G-H bombing system from the autumn would solve the problem altogether. In the meantime, however, no one knew what demands might be made of the Command, and it would be useful to see what main force crews could do when left to their own devices. The target was to be Braunschweig, for which a force of 379 aircraft was assembled, seventy-two of the Lancasters provided by 5 Group. 57 Squadron made ready nine Lancasters, which departed East Kirkby between 21.22 and 21.29 with F/Ls Ainley and Thomas the senior pilots on duty.

It was a night of heavy Bomber Command activity at numerous locations involving more than eleven hundred sorties. A second large operation over Germany was directed at the Opel motor factory at Rüsselsheim in the south, and involved 297 aircraft, but this would not weaken the enemy night-fighter defences, and powerful elements of the Nachtjagd were waiting for the Braunschweig force as it crossed the German coast at around 18,000 feet. Night-fighter flares were in evidence from then until the coast was crossed again on the way home, and it would prove to be an expensive night for the Command as a whole. The Braunschweig force made its way eastwards under clear skies, before encountering nine to ten-tenths thin cloud in the target area with tops at 7,000 feet. This was not a problem, as the whole purpose of the operation was to locate and bomb the target blind. The 57 Squadron effort had been reduced by the early return of F/O Cook and crew, whose navigator became unwell, leaving the others to bomb from 18,500 to 22,800 feet between 00.03 and 00.08. They observed the glow of fires beneath the cloud, and some of the bombing did, indeed, hit Braunschweig, but there was no concentration, and many outlying towns also reported bombs falling. Twenty-seven aircraft failed to return from this operation and a further twenty from a disappointing tilt at the Opel factory, and this was despite the fact that the targets were located two hundred miles apart and should have acted as an effective diversion for each other.

While the above was in progress, a "rush job" called upon the services of 144 crews to attack German troop concentrations and a road junction north of Falaise. 5 Group supported the attack with twenty-five Lancasters, five of them representing 57 Squadron, and they took off from East Kirkby between 00.16 and 00.32 led by F/L Scutt. They found a blanket of ten-tenths stratus cloud with tops at 2,000 feet, through which the green TIs were clearly visible, and bombed them from 5,800 to 8,000 feet between 02.18 and 02.23. Post-raid reconnaissance confirmed that the area around the junction was heavily cratered and the roads leading from it were mostly blocked.

The main activity during the afternoon of the 14th was an operation in support of Canadian divisions in the Falaise area, which involved 805 aircraft targeting seven enemy troop positions. 5 Group took part, by sending sixty-one Lancasters to Quesnay Wood, which was concealing a concentration of German tanks. The six 57 Squadron participants departed East Kirkby between 12.12 and 12.19 with S/L Wyness the senior pilot on duty and each carrying eleven 1,000 and four 500 pounders. They all arrived in the target area, where the Master Bomber issued clear instructions to bomb on the yellow TIs, which, because of rising smoke, were not always visible. Crews unable to see the TIs bombed the upwind edge of the smoke, those from 57 Squadron delivering their attacks from 6,000 to 8,700 feet between 14.21 and 14.22½.

Master Bombers were on hand to control the bombing at each of the other aiming-points because of the close proximity of the opposing armies, but, despite the most stringent efforts to avoid friendly fire incidents, some bombs did fall into a quarry occupied by Canadian troops, killing thirteen men. injuring fifty-three others and destroying a large number of vehicles. The group had actually begun the day with an attack by elements of 617 and 9 Squadrons on the derelict French cruiser Gueydon at berth at Brest, which, it was believed, the enemy might sink strategically along with other ships in the harbour, to render it unusable if liberated. In the evening, 128 Lancasters and two Mosquitos were made ready to send back to Brest for another go at the Gueydon, a tanker and a hulk, and among those taking part were eight crews from 57 Squadron, who departed East Kirkby between 17.39 and 17.47 with F/L Thomas the senior pilot on duty. They arrived over the port to find clear skies and excellent visibility, but also a fierce flak defence, and a number of aircraft would return bearing the scars of battle. The squadron bombed from 16,000 to 18,500 feet between 20.23 and 20.33, and a number of direct hits were observed on both vessels, with smoke issuing out of the tanker. Photo-reconnaissance revealed that the tanker had settled on the bottom, and the cruiser had suffered a similar fate with its decks awash.

In preparation for his new night offensive against Germany, Harris called for operations against enemy night fighter airfields in Holland and Belgium. In response, a list of nine such targets was prepared for attention by daylight on the 15th, and they would involve a thousand aircraft. According to the ORB, these were in addition to a massive commitment by the American 8th Air Force to enable the Allies to deploy more than three thousand aircraft. 5 Group was handed Deelen in central Holland and Gilze-Rijen in the south, and prepared forces of ninety-four Lancasters and five Mosquitos for the former and 103 Lancasters, four Mosquitos and the P38 Lightning for the latter. The P38 contained S/L "Count" Ciano flying as navigator to W/C Guy Gibson, who was desperate to get back onto operations. 55 Base was assigned to Deelen, and 57 Squadron dispatched fourteen Lancasters between 09.53 and 10.03 with F/Ls Ainley, Scutt and Thomas the senior pilots on duty. They found the target under clear skies in excellent visibility and were able to identify the aiming point visually as they ran in through the accurate fire from up to twenty flak guns. Each was carrying eleven 1,000 and four 500 pounders, which were delivered onto yellow TIs from 16,000 to 18,000 feet between 12.08 and 12.11½, in accordance with instructions from the Master Bomber. Many bomb bursts were observed on the aerodrome, and post-raid reconnaissance confirmed 230 craters on the runways and damage to hangars and other buildings.

The new offensive began with simultaneous attacks on Stettin and Kiel on the night of the 16/17th, 5 Group contributing 145 aircraft to the overall all-Lancaster force of 461 assigned to the former. At East Kirkby, 57 Squadron's fifteen Lancasters took off between 20.55 and 21.23, nine bound for the main event and six others to sneak in under cover to mine the waters of the Young Geranium garden, which is believed to be in the Stettiner Haff, a body of water linking Stettin with the Baltic at Swinemünde some thirty miles to the north. The senior pilots on duty, S/L Fairbairn and F/Ls Ainley, Scutt and Thomas, were all in the mining element, which was part of a 5 Group force of thirty Lancasters, including one containing a raid controller. Part of his job was to lay a line of flame floats, and two of the 57 Squadron crews dropped their five mines each along it as instructed from 250 to 300 feet between 01.16 and 01.22, while a third crew decided that the flame float line was 30 degrees off track to the east and selected their own course on a timed run from Leitholm Island (untraced). Very active defences were encountered in the form of heavy and light flak from the northern and southern shores and from flak ships, and LL940 was hit as it turned to begin the timed run. In order to maintain control, F/L Thomas ordered the mines to be jettisoned live from 150 feet and they made it home without further incident. The ORB comments relating to ND509 are ambiguous but seem to suggest that F/O Shamback and crew were on the way to an alternative garden when hit by flak, which caused extensive damage to the hydraulics system and persuaded the raid controller to send them home at 01.26. PB384 was abandoned by the crew of F/L Scutt in the target area after the port-outer engine was hit by flak and burst into flames, and two of them landed on the shore to be taken into captivity. The flight engineer also landed in the sea but managed to swim ashore to join his crew mates in enemy hands, but the pilot and two others failed to survive.

Meanwhile, it had taken some three-and-a-half hours for the bombing brigade to reach Stettin, where they were greeted by up to nine-tenths high cloud with a base at 18,000 to 20,000 feet and sufficient breaks to register clear visibility below. Concentrated red and green TIs could be seen marking out the aiming-point, and the 57 Squadron crews bombed these from 17,200 to 21,000 feet between 01.03 and 01.22 and reported fires taking hold. Not all returning crews were confident about the outcome, some suggesting that concentrations of red and green TIs had fallen wide of the aiming point to the north and west and caused the bombing to be scattered. In fact, it had been a highly successful operation, which destroyed fifteen hundred houses, numerous industrial premises and sank five ships in the harbour, while seriously damaging eight more.

Nine 57 Squadron crews were called to briefing early on the 18th to be told of that morning's operation against two flying-bomb dumps in the Forét-de-L'Isle Adam, north of Paris. 158 Lancasters, six Mosquitos and the P38 Lightning were to be involved, with 83 Squadron leading and providing the back-up marking on the heels of the low-level Mosquitos at the two aiming points in the east and west. They departed East Kirkby between 11.49 and 12.12 with S/L Fairbairn the senior pilot on duty and each Lancaster carrying eleven 1,000 and four 500 pounders. They headed south in squadron formation to rendezvous with the rest of the force and pick up the fighter escort, and, when over the mid-point of the Channel at 13.15, sixty or seventy American Liberators passed across the bows of the gaggle heading east a thousand feet higher, persuading the lead Lancaster to change course. This may have been what prompted comments by some crews on return, that not all had observed station keeping as set out at briefing, and that would result in aircraft bombing out of the planned sequence and on wrong headings. On arrival in the target area, they encountered five to seven-tenths cloud with tops at around 8,000 feet, which hampered identification of both aiming-points, and instructions were issued to not bomb unless a clear view of the target had been established. Some were able to pick out the aiming-points assisted by smoke markers, and all of the 57 Squadron crews bombed from 9,500 to 10,000 feet between 14.01 and 14.13, observing a number of bursts. Those unable to pick up the aiming-point jettisoned part of their load and brought the rest home. Photos snapped from main force aircraft suggested that the attack had overshot to the north, and this was confirmed by PRU pictures.

A spell of wet, cloudy and, sometimes, windy weather set in for the next week, and, although crews were alerted daily for operations, little came of it apart from a small mining operation by seven aircraft in the Cinnamon garden off the port of La Pallice during the evening of the 20th. 57 Squadron provided four of the Lancasters, in which the crews of F/Ls Nicklin and Weber and F/Os Lumsden and McKellar departed East Kirkby between 19.56 and 20.00. The Weber and McKellar crews returned within three hours for undisclosed reasons and landed at Predannack in Cornwall, leaving the remaining two to plant their six vegetables each in the briefed locations and land at Woodvale on the Sussex coast shortly after 02.00. W/C Humphreys received the immediate award of a DFC on the 23rd in recognition of his recent encounter with an enemy night-fighter, and S/L Wyness DFC was posted to 617 Squadron on the 25th to assume the role of flight commander. His successor as B Flight commander at 57 Squadron was acting S/L Ward, who arrived with his crew from 50 Squadron at Skellingthorpe.

When major operations resumed that night, more than nine hundred sorties would be launched against three targets, Rüsselsheim and nearby Darmstadt in southern Germany, and Brest, while a further four hundred aircraft would be engaged in a variety of smaller endeavours. The largest operation would be the all-Lancaster affair involving 461 aircraft from 1, 3, 6 and 8 Groups in a return to the Opel tank works, while 334 others attended to eight coastal batteries around Brest. 5 Group was assigned to Darmstadt, a university city and centre of scientific research and development, and one of a few almost virgin targets considered to be worthy of attention. A force of 191 Lancasters and six Mosquitos was assembled, sixteen of the former made ready by 57 Squadron, and they departed East Kirkby between 20.30 and 20.52 with W/C Humphreys and S/L Fairbairn the senior pilots on duty. There were no early returns but the Master Bomber was forced to turn back, leaving his two Deputies from 83 Squadron to step into the breach. The target area was free of cloud and some ground haze was present, but this was not responsible for matters going awry early on. VHF communication proved to be weak, which made it difficult for the Deputy Master Bombers to pass on instructions, and the flares dropped by five aircraft at 01.05 turned out to be too far to the west. The low-level Mosquitos reported at 01.07 that they were unable to locate the aiming point, as a result of which, H-hour was pushed back to 01.22, although bombing actually began at 01.19. Soon afterwards, someone left their VHF on transmit, creating a noise that drowned out all voice communications, at the same time that W/T became jammed. One of the Deputies was heard indistinctly instructing the crews to "bomb on the box" (H2S), and then he and the other Deputy were shot down. The main force crews did their best to comply, among them those from 57 Squadron, who were over the target at 6,000 to 10,000 feet between 01.12 and 01.49 and described a widely scattered attack. LM579 was one of seven missing Lancasters, after being abandoned by the crew of F/O Russell somewhere near the target, and all but the wireless operator survived in enemy hands. The consensus at debriefings was of a widely scattered attack, and many crews admitted to seeking out alternative targets in the face of sparse marking, most choosing to join in the raid on Rüsselsheim just fifteen miles to the north-west and close to the route home and identifiable by red and green TIs.

The German port of Königsberg, now Kaliningrad in Lithuania, is located on the eastern side of the Bay of Danzig and was being used by the enemy to supply its eastern front. It lay some 860 miles in a straight line from the bomber stations surrounding Lincoln, which increased to a round trip of 1,900 miles when routing across Denmark was taken into account. This made it the most distant location ever targeted by Bomber Command and was exceeded only by SOE flights to Poland. Such a distance required sacrificing bombs for fuel, and it was a reduced load of a single

2,000 pounder and twelve 500lb J-cluster bombs that was loaded into each of 57 Squadron's fourteen aircraft, which were part of an overall force of 174 Lancasters. Having been briefed for this target twice before without going, there was some doubt as to whether or not this one would take place, but it did, and the first 57 Squadron Lancaster began to roll at East Kirkby at 20.04 to be followed by the others over the ensuing fourteen minutes with W/C Humphreys and S/L Fairbairn the senior pilots on duty. Accompanying the force to the target area would be ten Lancasters carrying mines for delivery into the sea-lanes in the Tangerine garden off Pillau at the entrance to the estuary serving Königsberg, and among these was the 57 Squadron crew of F/L Clark, who got away at 20.17. Ahead of them lay a ten to eleven-hour marathon, which, it is believed, all from 57 Squadron would complete.

When they arrived in the target area almost five hours later, after flying through electrical storms and icing conditions over Denmark, the skies were clear and the visibility good, and they were greeted by around a hundred searchlights and an intense flak defence. The flare force went in at 14,000 to 15,000 feet between 01.05 and 01.12, to be followed minutes later by the heavy markers at a lower level. The TIs fell in two concentrations, 350 yards to the north-west of the aiming point and 1,200 yards to the north-east, prompting the Master Bomber to add his own between the two and call for his to be backed up. Unfortunately, the backing up focused on the north-eastern TIs and these attracted the main weight of bombs. The 57 Squadron crews bombed on red TIs from around 10,000 feet between 01.10 and 01.30 and, on return, were fairly enthusiastic about the outcome, reporting punctual marking, concentrated bombing and fires that could be seen, according to some, from 250 miles into the return journey. Photo-reconnaissance revealed that the main weight of the attack had, indeed, fallen into the town's north-eastern districts, where fire had ripped through many building blocks at a cost of just four Lancasters. 57 Squadron's LM232 disappeared without trace with the crew of F/O Russell RNZAF, the second Russell crew to go missing on consecutive operations, this one containing three other members of the RNZAF. It was decided that the job was not yet done, and a second operation would have to be mounted. LM278 was brought down by flak during the gardening operation and only the wireless operator escaped with his life from the highly experienced crew of F/L Clark DFC, RCAF, who were on their twenty-ninth sortie.

Later, on the 26th, all ground personnel were posted out of 57 Squadron to become part of 55 Base HQ, a move that alleviated administrative pressures. The final operations in the long-running flying-bomb campaign were conducted by small Oboe-led forces against twelve sites on the 28th, and Allied ground forces took control of the Pas-de-Calais a few days afterwards.

Having established that a decisive blow had not been delivered on Königsberg, a return was posted on the 29th, and thirteen 57 Squadron crews called to briefing at 17.30 to learn that they were to be part of a 5 Group force of 189 Lancasters. They departed East Kirkby between 19.58 and 20.09 with F/L Ainley the senior pilot on duty, and, because of the extreme range, the entire force again carried between them only 480 tons of bombs to deliver onto four aiming-points. F/O McKellar and crew turned back early because of starboard-outer engine failure, while the rest of the bomber stream made its way across the North Sea and Denmark and reached the target to encounter eight to ten-tenths cloud with a base at around 10,000 feet. The Master Bomber, W/C Woodroffe, one of 5 Group's most experienced raid controllers, decided on a visual attack and instructed the first flare force wave to drop below the cloud, a move that kept the spearhead of the main force circling for twenty minutes before the marking began. The later arrivals could see the markers going down as they approached for what was a complex plan of attack that proceeded with the first flares falling at around 01.05 and continuing at regular intervals thereafter. At 01.24, the third flare force wave was instructed to illuminate the red spot fire, and a minute later an instruction was given to overshoot by four hundred yards to the east of the aiming-point. At 01.26 a marker aircraft was told to run over the red marker and overshoot by three hundred yards, while, at 01.27, another was ordered to overshoot by six hundred yards east of the aiming-point, before the visual backers-up were sent to track over the reds and greens and overshoot by three hundred yards. The flare force was invited to go home at 01.30, and, at 01.34, the visual marker crews were instructed first to back up the greens by six hundred yards on a westerly heading, and, two minutes later, the concentrations of reds and greens. The 57 Squadron crews identified the target by the red and green TIs and searchlight concentrations and confirmed their positions by H2S before bombing from 9,000 to 16,000 feet between 01.23 and 01.56.

The Master Bomber called a halt to bombing at 01.52 and sent the force home, at which time some main force crews still had their bombs on board, having circled for up to thirty minutes, often coned and constantly under a flak barrage. Understandably, they and others in the same situation became increasingly agitated at the controller's refusal to let them bomb until further backing up had taken place. Enemy night-fighters were much in evidence over the target and would play their part in bringing down fifteen Lancasters. At debriefings across 5 Group stations, scathing comments about the performance of W/C Woodroffe were rife, and his stubbornness was blamed for the high casualty rate of 7.9%. They maintained that the backers-up had confirmed the marking to be accurate, despite which, he kept some crews orbiting for up to forty minutes. Post-raid reconnaissance confirmed that the operation had been an outstanding success, which destroyed over 40% of the town's residential and 20% of its industrial buildings.

The flying-bomb campaign may now have ended, but a new one against V-2 rocket storage and launching sites began on the 31st with raids on nine suspected locations in northern France. 5 Group sent three forces of forty-nine, forty-six and fifty-two Lancasters with two Mosquitos each to respectively target sites at Auchy-les-Hesdin, Rollancourt and Bergueneuse, all situated some twenty miles inland from the coast at Berck-sur-Mer. Elements of 55 Base were assigned to the last-mentioned, for which 57 Squadron made ready thirteen Lancasters and dispatched them from East Kirkby between 15.50 and 16.00 with S/Ls Fairbairn and Ward the senior pilots on duty. All reached the target area to find five-tenths cloud with a base at 6,000 feet and tops as high as 18,000 feet, out of which issued occasional heavy rain showers. The Master Bomber ordered the force to orbit until the cloud had drifted clear, and once Mosquitos had dropped smoke markers, he descended to beneath the cloud to establish their accuracy. Satisfied, he called in the main force crews, and those from 57 Squadron bombed visually from 5,000 to 14,000 feet between 18.06 and 18.36. F/O Watt and crew suffered the frustration of a complete hang-up over the target and had to bring their eleven 1,000 and four 500 pounders home. The operations appeared to be successful, and this concluded a month of feverish and record activity for most heavy squadrons, during which 57 Squadron took part in twenty-five operations and dispatched 216 sorties for the loss of four Lancasters and their crews.

September 1944

The destructive power of the Command was now almost beyond belief. Each of its heavy bomber groups was capable of laying waste to a German town and city at one go, and, from now until the end of the war, this would be demonstrated in awesome and horrific fashion. Much of the Command's effort during the new month would be directed towards the liberation of the three French Channel ports remaining in enemy hands, Le Havre, Boulogne and Calais. Operations began for 5 Group with an attack on shipping at Brest on the 2nd, for which sixty-seven Lancasters were detailed from 55 Base. A dozen 57 Squadron Lancasters took off from East Kirkby between 11.05 and 11.24 with W/C Humphreys and S/L Ward the senior pilots on duty and flew immediately into cloud as they headed south. LM279 was observed to emerge from the cloud base in a steep dive and crash at 11.45 near the village of Crick, situated some five miles south-east of Rugby on the border between Warwickshire and Northamptonshire. It had a full bomb load on board and there was little left of the Lancaster and nothing at all of the crew of F/O Brain, whose names are recorded on the Runnymede Memorial. The others flew through thunderstorms on the way out, and, on arrival in the target area, initially found a layer of five to seven-tenths cumulus cloud between 2,000 and 9,000 feet affording a range of visibilities between good and poor. However, as the cloud appeared to be drifting away, they were ordered to orbit until the aiming-point could be identified visually. The bombing was carried out unopposed from 10,800 to 12,700 feet between 14.33 and 15.22 and was observed to straddle the quays, although some of it hit the town also. Post-raid reconnaissance revealed damage to a number of the vessels at berth.

Preparations were put in hand on the following morning to launch attacks on six Luftwaffe-occupied aerodromes in southern Holland. A total of 675 aircraft was to be involved, 5 Group detailing 103 Lancasters and two Mosquitos from 55 and 54 Bases for its target at Deelen, seventeen of the Lancasters representing 57 Squadron. They departed East Kirkby between 15.23 and 15.39 with S/Ls Fairbairn and Ward the senior pilots on duty and encountered cloud on the way out that created challenging conditions for formation-keeping. F/O McDonald and crew returned early with a dead starboard-inner engine, while the others pressed on and found varying amounts of cloud up to nine-tenths over the target with tops at 7,000 feet. The Lancasters orbited to allow time for gaps to appear, through which to identify the aiming-point visually, and even then, some had to make a second run to gain a clear sight. The 57 Squadron crews bombed from 13,700 to 16,500 feet between 17.31 and 17.42, and despite a spirited flak defence from the airfield, there were no losses and returning crews were relatively confident that they had fulfilled their brief. It would be the 6th before photo-reconnaissance provided a partial cover of the target area and revealed at least sixty craters around runway intersections and taxiways.

Most of 5 Group remained at home over the ensuing five days, while enemy strong-points in and around Le Havre received daylight visitations from other elements of the Command on the 5th, 6th, 8th and 9th. These operations took place during a spell of unhelpful weather conditions, and the attacks of the 8th and 9th were not fully pressed home. Mönchengladbach was posted as the target for 113 Lancasters and fourteen Mosquitos on the 9th, for which briefings took place at 01.30. The fourteen 57 Squadron crews learned that they were to attack the centre of this town located on the western fringe of the Ruhr, which, with Operation Market Garden looming, was expected soon to be within striking distance of the advancing Allied forces. They would have to wait until the early hours of the 10th before departing East Kirkby between 02.55 and 03.10 with

S/L Ward the senior pilot on duty, and there would be no early returns as they made their way via Ostend to the target. They found clear skies and good visibility as they followed on the heels of the flare forces, which had started a little early at 05.05 and continued until 05.14, at which point they were sent home and the main force was called in to attack. The 57 Squadron crews identified the aiming-point by means of red TIs and bombed from 16,000 to 18,000 feet between 05.17 and 05.30. Large explosions occurred at 05.21 and 05.23 and the glow of fires could be seen from the Dutch coast up to eighty miles away. There were no losses, and photo-reconnaissance confirmed the claims of the crews, that they had participated in a highly successful raid, which had left the town centre in ruins.

A further attack on German positions around Le Havre was carried out on the 10th and involved almost a thousand aircraft. 5 Group supported the effort with 108 Lancasters and two Mosquitos from 53 and 54 Bases, all of which reached the French coast to be greeted by clear skies and just a little ground haze, which enabled the crews to identify the target visually. They released their bombs onto red TIs from around 10,000 to 13,000 feet roughly between 17.15 and 17.30, and observed the area become enveloped in smoke. The 11th brought the final attacks on the environs of the port, and involved 218 aircraft drawn from 4, 5, 6 and 8 Groups. 5 Group contributed ninety-three Lancasters, fourteen of them representing 57 Squadron, and they departed East Kirkby between 05.23 and 05.37 with S/L Fairbairn the senior pilot on duty. They all arrived in the target area under clear skies with slight haze, and located their aiming points, to the north and south of the outer defences just after dawn. Each aiming point had been given the name of a car manufacturer, and the one assigned to 57 Squadron was Cadillac 1. The attack was due to begin at 07.30, but there were no markers on the northern aiming-point, and nothing was heard from the Master Bomber, which left the crews to their own devices. The 57 Squadron crews bombed visually from 10,000 to 13,000 feet from 07.30 until the first red and green TIs were seen to go down at 07.43, and aimed at these, thereafter, until turning for home at 07.50. Photo-reconnaissance confirmed accurate and concentrated bombing, and, within hours of this operation, the German garrison surrendered to British forces.

Eleven of the crews who had participated in the morning operation found themselves back in the briefing room later, along with six others, to learn of their part in 5 Group's return to Darmstadt, which had escaped serious damage at its hands during the last week of August. A force of 221 Lancasters and fourteen Mosquitos was made ready, and the 57 Squadron element took off between 20.53 and 21.08 with S/L Ward the senior pilot on duty. The force arrived in the skies over southern Germany to find them clear of cloud, and, despite some ground haze, the visibility was good as the flare force went in at 17,000 feet at 23.52, homing in on a green Mosquito-laid TI. The Master bomber seemed satisfied with the illumination, and required no further flares, leaving the backers-up to drop their TIs over the ensuing four minutes before being sent home at 23.59. The main force followed up with extreme accuracy and concentration, the 57 Squadron crews bombing on red and green TIs from 12,000 to 13,800 feet between 23.50 and 00.09. The city centre became engulfed in flames, which spread outwards to consume large parts of the built-up area, and the glow, according to some, could be seen from the French coast, 250 miles away. The conditions had been ideal for the 5 Group marking method, and photo-reconnaissance confirmed the main weight of the attack to have fallen in the centre and surrounding districts to the south and east. It was learned after the war, that the attack had resulted in a genuine firestorm, only the third to be recorded after Hamburg and Kassel in 1943. More than twelve thousand people died in the inferno, and a further seventy thousand, 60% of a total population of 120,000, were made homeless. The operation cost the group twelve Lancasters, but all from 57 Squadron returned safely, one unnamed crew to claim the destruction of Ju88 and one to report assisting another Lancaster to bring down an unidentified enemy aircraft.

Orders were received on 5 Group stations on the 12th to prepare for a return to southern Germany that night, this time to target Stuttgart. Fifteen 57 Squadron crews attended the briefing at East Kirkby and learned that they were to be part of a force of 195 Lancasters and fourteen Mosquitos, which would be accompanied by nine ABC Lancasters from 1 Group's 101 Squadron. A simultaneous operation by 378 Lancasters and nine Mosquitos of 1, 3 and 8 Groups would take place at Frankfurt, a hundred miles to the north. The 57 Squadron element took off between 18.40 and 19.16 with F/L Thomas the senior pilot on duty and lost the services of F/O Smith and crew to a broken oil pipe to the port-outer engine. The others mostly enjoyed an uneventful flight across France to Stuttgart, which was found to be under clear skies with moderate visibility and ground haze, and, therefore, ideal conditions for the low-level marker Mosquitos. The marking and backing up were very accurate, and the main force bombing concentrated upon the city centre, with a slight tendency to creep back towards the north-eastern district of Bad Canstatt and beyond into Feuerbach. The 57 Squadron crews bombed on red TIs, many witnessing a huge explosion at 23.25, which lasted for about five seconds and reported the glow from the fires to be visible for a hundred miles into the return flight. At debriefing, one crew claimed to have heard a suspicious voice issuing peculiar instructions while using the main force call sign but not that of the Master Bomber. A PRU aircraft photographed the city on the following morning and found the entire centre to be obscured by the smoke from numerous and widespread fires. Only four Lancasters were missing from this operation, and 57 Squadron again came through unscathed. Local reports from Stuttgart described the central districts as "erased", and it seems that a firestorm erupted in northern and west-central districts, wiping them from the map. Almost twelve hundred people lost their lives, the highest death toll ever in this much-bombed city.

Other than 617 and 9 Squadrons' first of three attacks on the battleship Tirpitz on the 15th, 5 Group undertook no further operations until the morning of the 17th, when contributing to a total of 762 aircraft made ready to attack troop positions at seven locations around the port of Boulogne. The raids would be staggered over a four-hour period and benefit from a 5 Group effort of 195 Lancasters and four Mosquitos, seventeen of the former representing 57 Squadron and departing East Kirkby from 06.30 with S/L Fairbairn the senior pilot on duty. *(The Squadron ORB listed only eleven crews)*. The 55 Base squadrons were in the first wave of aircraft to attack one of two aiming-points assigned to the group, and they found clear skies and good visibility along with red TIs at which to aim their twelve 1,000 and four 500 pounders from around 7,000 feet shortly after 08.30. One 57 Squadron crew did not reach the point of release before the Master Bomber called a halt to proceedings and sent them home. The second 5 Group element went in an hour later to contribute to the three thousand tons of bombs that were dropped, paving the way for Allied ground forces to move in shortly afterwards to accept the surrender of the German garrison. This left only Calais of the major French ports still under enemy occupation.

5 Group stations received orders on the 18th to prepared for an operation that night against the port of Bremerhaven, located on the East Bank at the mouth of the river Weser, some thirty miles north of Bremen. It was to be a classic 5 Group-style attack, employing the low-level visual

marking method and involved 206 Lancasters and seven Mosquitos. At East Kirkby, 57 Squadron loaded its nineteen Lancasters with all-incendiary loads, before sending them on their way between 18.19 and 18.46 with S/L Fairbairn the senior pilot on duty. F/O Shamback became unwell and turned back, leaving the others to arrive in the target area and find favourable weather conditions and good visibility. They ran in on the aiming-point at medium level and released their loads in accordance with the Master Bomber's instructions onto red TIs from around 21.00 onwards. A number of huge explosions were witnessed at 21.02 and 21.07, and, as they headed out of the target area, crews could see many large fires spreading throughout the built-up area, the glow from which remained visible for at least 150 miles. Post-raid reconnaissance revealed that this first major attack on the port, carried out by what, at the time, could be considered to be a modest force, had devasted the built-up areas north and south of the harbour entrance, wiping out installations and warehousing, and only the most northerly and southerly suburbs had escaped complete destruction. Local reports produced a figure of 2,670 buildings reduced to rubble and thirty-thousand people bombed out of their homes, all at the modest cost to 5 Group of a single Lancaster and a Mosquito. Sadly, the Lancaster was 57 Squadron's NG126, which crashed at 22.06 on the eastern outskirts of the town and only the bomb-aimer from the experienced crew of F/O Waugh escaped with his life to spend the final seven months of the war as a guest of the Reich.

Seventeen 57 Squadron crews assembled for briefing at East Kirkby on the 19th and learned that they were to be part of a predominantly 5 Group attack on the twin towns of Mönchengladbach and Rheydt. This represented a shallow penetration into Germany, just ten minutes from the Dutch border, and, therefore, a short round trip of four-and-a-half to five hours followed by a night in bed. 217 Lancasters and ten Mosquitos were made ready, along with ten ABC Lancasters from 101 Squadron. The Master Bomber for the operation was W/C Guy Gibson VC, DSO, DFC, who, as previously mentioned, had been agitating to get back into the war before it was over and didn't want his service to end in a backwater, while others gained the glory by being in at the death. Gibson was a warrior, and the war had brought out of him qualities, which, in peacetime, may have lain dormant. War had also given him a direction, and he revelled in the company of fellow operational types, particularly those of the officer class. Having been torn away from the operational scene following the success of Operation Chastise, his direction had gone, and he had become listless, frustrated and discontented. His time in the operational wilderness had not, however, deprived him of his arrogance and self-belief, and when the opportunity to fly as Master Bomber on the coming raid presented itself, he grabbed it. He was driven the three miles from Coningsby to Woodhall Spa to collect his 627 Squadron Mosquito, which, for whatever reason, he rejected, and swapped with F/L Mallender, causing a degree of resentment. Gibson had already set the tone for the evening by rejecting the advice of W/C Charles Owen, who had been Master Bomber at this target ten nights earlier. Owen had advised him to leave the target by a south-westerly route, and cross north-eastern France to the coast, and also to observe orders to remain above 10,000 feet. Gibson insisted that he would fly home via a direct route across Holland at low level and would not be dissuaded. He took off ahead of the 627 Squadron element at 19.51, to meet up with the main force over the target, where two aiming-points were to be marked.

The 57 Squadron participants took off between 18.54 and 19.08 with W/C Humphreys the senior pilot on duty and each Lancaster carrying a 2,000 pounder and twelve 500lb J-cluster bombs, all of which would reach the target. Some crews reported icing clouds at around 9,000 feet as they made their way to the target over Belgium at around 9,000 feet, and chose to keep below, before climbing fast to 15,000 feet as the cloud dispersed. The marking was complex, with a green marker to be dropped on a factory in a western district of Mönchengladbach, and a yellow marker on railway yards in the north, while a red marker was to be placed on railway yards in Rheydt, two miles to the south. It would have been a demanding plan even for an experienced Master Bomber, which Gibson was not, but, even so, his instructions were heard clearly. All seemed to be going to plan, with accurate and punctual marking for the green and yellow forces, but late, though accurate marking for the red force, and some of the red force crews were diverted to the green aiming-point. The 55 Base squadrons were among those assigned to the green force, and identified it by flares and TIs, before bombing from around 10,000 to 11,500 feet shortly before 22.00. They observed the target to be well ablaze with the glow visible for at least a hundred miles into the return flight, and post-raid reconnaissance confirmed a highly destructive attack on both towns for the loss of four Lancasters and a Mosquito. Gibson had returned low over Holland, just as he said he would, and had crashed on the outskirts of Steenbergen in south-western Holland, with fatal consequences for him, and Coningsby's recently appointed station navigation officer, S/L James Warwick. The likelihood is, that Gibson's lack of familiarity with the Mosquito led to the failure to locate the fuel transfer cocks, and the engines simply became starved of fuel.

It was now time to turn attention upon Calais as the final port still under enemy occupation. Only one 5 Group Lancaster was involved in the first round of attacks on enemy positions on the 20th, after which, the group remained inactive until the 23rd. Orders came through on that morning to prepare 136 Lancasters and five Mosquitos for an attack that night on the aqueduct section of the Dortmund-Ems Canal south of Ladbergen, a target associated with the group since June 1940. It was also the scene of a disaster in September 1943 for 617 Squadron, which would be on scene also on this night to open the attack with Tallboys, to which the raised banks containing the waterway were particularly vulnerable. Germany's canal system was a vital component in the transport network and facilitated the import of raw materials and the export of finished goods to support the war effort. Its wide thoroughfares allowed the passage of large barges, and, as the slack in Germany's war production was taken up during 1944, traffic was being pushed through at increasing levels. While this operation was in progress, a second 5 Group force of 108 Lancasters, four Mosquitos and the P38 Lightning would hit the Handorf night-fighter airfield some ten miles to the south to prevent it from interfering. The main operation on this night, however, would be conducted by 549 aircraft from 1, 3, 4 and 8 Groups seventy miles to the south-west at Neuss, situated across the Rhine opposite Düsseldorf, and this, hopefully, might help to split the enemy defences.

57 Squadron prepared eighteen Lancasters for Handorf, and they departed East Kirkby between 18.29 and 18.48 with S/L Fairbairn the senior pilot on duty and all reached the target area to encounter a layer of ten-tenths cloud between 8,000 and 9,500 feet, but with good visibility beneath. The Master Bomber found himself unable to direct the attack, and experienced great difficulty in communicating that to his Deputy because of intense interference on VHF. Identification and marking of the aiming-point proved to be difficult despite the flare force illuminating a wide area, and only two green TIs and a few isolated yellows could be seen by a few crews. There would be complaints later that there was no control, and some crews orbited and remained in the target area for up to thirty-five minutes before bombing either on green TIs at Handorf or on yellows at the alternative target of Münster. It is difficult to identify which

aiming-points were attacked by the 57 Squadron crews, and an analysis revealed that only twenty-two crews in total bombed Handorf. An assessment of the results was out of the question, but post-raid reconnaissance revealed no new damage at a cost of a single Lancaster. Among eighty-nine Lancaster attacking the canal were some from 617 Squadron, whose Tallboys were probably responsible for breaches in both branches, which left a six-mile stretch drained and unnavigable.

The second of the series of raids on enemy positions around Calais was mounted by 188 aircraft on the 24th, for which 5 Group detailed thirty Lancasters from the 53 Base stations of Skellingthorpe and Waddington. They climbed away into the most adverse weather conditions with a cloud base at 200 feet and as they approached the French coast, many crews picked up a series of signals between 18.20 and 18.26 telling them to "cease bombing". 126 others continued on to find the target concealed beneath ten-tenths cloud with a base hovering at around 2,000 to 2,500 feet and carried out their bombing runs at that height to deliver 1,000 and 500 pounders onto red TIs. It was a similar story on the following day, when only a third of more than eight hundred aircraft were able to deliver their bombs, before the Master Bomber called a halt to proceedings in the face of low cloud. The campaign continued on the 26th, with two separate raids against seven enemy positions around Cap Gris Nez and nearer Calais involving more than seven hundred aircraft. This time the conditions were favourable, and bombing was observed to be concentrated around the aiming points.

On the afternoon of the 26th, nineteen 57 Squadron crews attended briefing, and learned that the night's operation was to be against Karlsruhe in southern Germany, for which 216 Lancasters of 5 Group were made ready, along with ten of the ABC variety from 101 Squadron and eleven Mosquitos. It was to be a two-phase attack with a two-hour gap between and the 53 and 55 Base elements assigned to the second phase. This meant a late take-off, and it was between 00.37 and 00.55 that the 57 Squadron crews departed East Kirkby with W/C Humphreys and S/L Fairbairn the senior pilots on duty but lost the services of F/O Hughes and crew because of the failure of their port-outer engine. The others flew out over France with ten-tenths cloud beneath them, which persisted all the way to the target, but thinned to a narrow band with the base estimated to be between 6,000 and 7,000 feet. The plan was to bomb through the cloud on H2S, guided by Wanganui flares, and some approaching crews observed a red TI cascade above the cloud at 03.54. The 57 Squadron crews focused on the glow of red and green TIs and bombed them from around 12,000 feet in accordance with the instructions of the Master Bomber. All returned safely to East Kirkby to report what appeared to be a city in flames and the glow of fires visible for up to 150 miles into the return journey. There were no plottable bombing photos, but reconnaissance confirmed that the attack had been spread throughout the city and had left a large part of it devastated.

As the crews returned to their stations after 07.00, elements of 1, 3, 4 and 8 Groups were preparing to leave theirs for a further attack on the Calais area. On arrival, the Master Bomber ordered the 340-strong force to come below the cloud base to bomb visually, and another successful operation ensued. Later that day, seventeen 57 Squadron crews attended briefing for an operation that night against Kaiserslautern, an historic city on the edge of the Palatinate Forest, some thirty miles west of Mannheim. It would be the first major attack of the war on this location, for which a force of 217 Lancasters, including ten from 101 Squadron and ten Path Finder Mosquitos, was made ready. Four of the 57 Squadron Lancasters were loaded with a 2,000 pounder and a dozen 500lb J-cluster bombs each for use against railway workshops, while the remainder carried all-incendiary loads to drop on the city. They departed East Kirkby between 21.41 and 22.29 with S/L Ward the senior pilot on duty and climbed into clear skies, which gave way to a build-up of cloud over the Channel. F/O Donkin and crew turned back with a starboard-inner engine issue, leaving the others to continue on over cloud increasing to ten-tenths from the French coast to near the target with a base at a lowly 2,800 feet. The target itself was partially covered by a thin layer of five to eight-tenths cloud with tops at 3,000 feet, with a further layer at 6,000 to 7,000 feet, through which the punctual and accurate red and green TIs were visible. A green TI in the centre of the town became the objective for the main force crews in accordance with the Master Bomber's instructions at 00.58, while red spotfires pointed the way to the railway workshops. The bombing took place from 3,500 to 5,500 feet between 01.00 and 01.15 and was observed to be concentrated. Two yellow explosions were seen at 01.02, and fires were beginning to take hold as the force retreated towards the west. Reconnaissance revealed massive damage within the city, caused by more than nine hundred tons of bombs, and an estimated 36% of the built-up area was reduced to ruins.

The final raids on German positions around Calais were carried out by 490 aircraft of 1, 3, 6 and 8 Groups on the 28th, and the garrison surrendered to Canadian forces shortly thereafter. On the 29th, 57 Squadron dispatched five Lancasters from East Kirkby between 19.00 and 19.04 bound for the Rosemary garden in the Heligoland Bight. F/L Warburton and crew returned early after their H2S let them down, but the crews of F/Ls Ainley, Ottewell and Watt and F/O Southfield carried on to release their six mines each in the briefed locations before returning safely. During the course of the month the squadron participated in thirteen operations and dispatched 201 sorties for the loss of two Lancasters and crews.

October 1944

Now released from the bulk of its obligations to SHAEF, Bomber Command could return with a will to industrial Germany, and from this point until the end of hostilities, it would suffer an unprecedented assault by a force at peak strength. There was nothing to occupy 5 Group for the first two days of the new month, until contributing 128 Lancasters to an operation that was part of a campaign against the island of Walcheren in the Scheldt estuary, where heavy gun emplacements were barring the approaches to the much-needed port of Antwerp some forty miles upstream. Attempts to bomb these positions in September had proved unsuccessful, and it was decided to flood the land, both to inundate the batteries, and to render the terrain difficult to defend when the ground forces moved in. 252 Lancasters were drawn from 1, 5 and 8 Groups and made ready on the 3rd to attack the seawalls at Westkapelle, the most westerly point of the island. 5 Group would occupy four of eight waves of thirty aircraft each, with Tallboy carrying 617 Squadron Lancasters standing off to be deployed only if absolutely necessary. A breach was opened by the fifth wave, which was extended to more than a hundred yards by those following behind, and the flood waters had reached the town by the time the last Lancasters turned for home.

57 Squadron had not been invited to take part in the above and had to wait until 5 Group's first major outing of the month, a daylight attack on the port of Wilhelmshaven, which was posted on the 5th. Once a frequent target for Bomber Command, it had been left to the American 8th Air Force for twenty months by the time that a force of 227 Lancasters, one Mosquito and the P38 Lightning was assembled in its honour. 57 Squadron provided twenty Lancasters, which set out

from East Kirkby between 07.59 and 08.14 with W/C Humphreys the senior pilot on duty. A new tactic had been briefed for this operation to present a broad front at the target rather than a spearhead, and, in order to facilitate the forming-up process, the Master Bomber led the force around the northern side of Heligoland, before heading for Jade Bay on Germany's north-western coast. As forecast, they found the target concealed beneath a layer of ten-tenths cloud at between 3,000 and 5,000 feet with good visibility above and positions were fixed by H2S or by observing others. The tactic proved to be unworkable as the Master Bomber struggled to control such a large force attacking on a broad front and many aircraft were pushed wide and off course. He instructed crews to bomb on instrument at the primary target or seek out any suitable built-up area as an alternative, and, while all of the 57 Squadron crews carried out an attack, three chose the latter option. No results were observed, and there was no possibility of making an assessment, but the impression of a scattered attack was confirmed later when reconnaissance photos were studied.

A second Ruhr campaign opened at Dortmund, for which a 3, 6 and 8 Group force of 523 aircraft was made ready on the 6th. 5 Group, meanwhile, had its own target, and prepared 237 Lancasters and seven Mosquitos for what would prove to be the thirty-second and final raid of the war on the city of Bremen. 57 Squadron loaded each of its eighteen Lancasters with eighteen SBCs of 4lb incendiaries and dispatched them from East Kirkby between 17.22 and 18.02 with S/L Ward the senior pilot on duty. Among them were two additional Lancasters bearing the crews of F/Ls Ottewell and Watt, who were bound for mining duties in the Young Yams garden in the river Weser. Having climbed out and set course, they left the cloud behind and headed into crystal clear skies with a three-quarter moon, which would provide ideal conditions for the 5 Group low-level marking method and hand the hapless city on a plate to the bombers. The crews of F/O Bauch and McCusker returned early because of hydraulics and engine issues respectively, leaving the rest of the 57 Squadron crews to carry out their attacks in the face of many searchlights and the usual flak response. They aimed for the red and green TIs from around 17,000 feet either side of 20.30 and turned away from a city in flames, the glow from which remained visible for a hundred miles and more. The gardeners, meanwhile, planted six vegetables each into the allotted location and returned safely with the others to report an effective night's work. The success of the operation was confirmed by post-raid reconnaissance and local reports, which described a huge area of fire, and catalogued the destruction of more than 4,800 houses and apartment blocks, and severe damage to war industry factories, all achieved at the modest cost of five Lancasters. Earlier in the day it had been announced that the number of sorties to complete a tour had been reduced from thirty-five to thirty-three, and this would be an unexpected bonus to some crews, who could spend the evening celebrating in the mess rather than exposing themselves to risk over Germany. However, this was not the final word on the length of a tour, which would take on the characteristics of elastic.

53 Base's strength increased on the 7th with the reformation at Bardney of 227 Squadron from A Flight of 9 Squadron and B Flight of 619 Squadron. While this process was taking place, forces of 351 and 340 aircraft were being assembled by 3, 4 and 8 Groups and 1, 3 and 8 Groups respectively to attack the German frontier towns of Cleves (Kleve) and Emmerich following the failure of Operation Market Garden. Situated five miles apart and separated by the Rhine, both would suffer massive damage, while 5 Group returned to Walcheren to target the seawalls near Flushing. The task was to be undertaken by 121 Lancasters and three Mosquitos, sixteen of the former representing 57 Squadron, and they departed East Kirkby between 12.01 and 12.26 with

no senior pilots on duty. All reached the target area to identify the two aiming-points visually and by red TIs and delivered their fourteen 1,000 pounders each from around 6,000 to 8,500 feet from 14.00. Despite the fact that the bombs had been fitted with a thirty-minute delay fuse, some detonated on impact and the dyke was already beginning to crumble as they turned for home.

617 Squadron was also in action on this day to attack the heavily defended Kembs barrage, a dam-like structure across the Rhine deep in southern Germany at the point where the frontiers of Germany, France and Switzerland meet. The former 57 Squadron flight commander, S/L Drew "Duke" Wyness, was part of the low-level force briefed to deliver their Tallboys from around 600 feet in broad daylight. His Lancaster was hit by flak and sustained terminal damage but was too low for a bale-out. He was left with few options to save his crew, and according to one unconfirmed report, he headed northwest from the barrage following the course of the river, until he flew into the teeth of another flak position, which forced him to wheel back round to the south. A letter sent by the Air Ministry (New Zealand) to the parents of wireless operator F/O Bruce Hosie RNZAF in 1948 provides us with perhaps the most accurate sequence of events. It described the Lancaster being hit by light flak and hitting a power line over or near the barrage, before coming down on the Rhine about five hundred yards further on. The aircraft must have been close to becoming uncontrollable, and Wyness opted for a ditching with the hope and intention of gaining the sanctuary of the Swiss bank. The Lancaster came to rest intact in shallow water near the village of Rheinweiler and two members of the crew ran along the starboard wing, jumped onto the French bank, and disappeared into woodland, while the remaining five inflated the dinghy and paddled away, presumably in the direction of Switzerland to gain the sanctuary of the neutral bank. The Germans dispatched a boat to intercept them, and this persuaded one crew member to abandon the dinghy and swim to the French shore. The three men now on French soil were never seen alive again, and their bodies have never been recovered. It is believed that they were captured, perhaps by French gendarmerie, and handed over to the Nazi authorities, or simply by the German occupying forces, and following their murder, were buried in unmarked graves.

Wyness and the others were captured by the Wehrmacht and taken to Rheinweiler to be met by the local Burgomeister, along with officials from the gendarmeric station at Schliengen, and the Kreisleiter of Mullheim, Hugo Grüner. They were put in pairs into two cars, one of them belonging to Grüner, accompanied by a guard, and were driven in the direction of Schliengen. At the village of Bellingen, they turned off towards the river and drew to a halt near the river bank at a place known as Steinplatz, where the guard, Rudolf Birlin, was ordered to take the prisoners to the water's edge, while a second guard, Hans Reimer, remained by the car. Shots were fired, and the two airmen fell into the Rhine. Grüner, Birlin and Reimer returned to Rheinweiler to collect the two surviving airmen, and the bloody process was repeated. Grüner ordered the guards to remain silent about the incident, or at least to say that they had been ambushed, and that the prisoners had been taken from them. This kind of atrocity against RAF prisoners of war was a rarity, although there was a slight increase in 1945, as a desperate Germany's defeat loomed ever nearer. Even then, it was the civilian Nazi authorities, those individuals who owed everything to the party and knew their power was slipping from their grasp, that were most likely to commit war crimes.

The body of Wyness was recovered from the Rhine at Markolsheim, some fifty kilometres from where the ditching took place and was initially buried there. After the war, all four murder victims were re-interred in war cemeteries in Germany and France, and Wyness and wireless operator Hosie now rest side-by-side in Choloy. After the war Rudolf Birlin was arrested and a trial convened by a French court in 1946. The case collapsed, however, because the crime had not taken place on French soil, and the victims were not French. The accused remained in custody at Neumunster pending a second trial by an American court. Hugo Grüner was arrested in May 1945, and indicted for the crime, remaining in custody until his trial in April 1946. In his defence he laid the blame on the Gestapo and Birlin, but escaped from custody at Recklinghausen in 1947, after being handed over to the Americans. He was never recaptured but was tried in his absence at Hamburg in 1948, along with Birlin and Reimer. Reimer could not be found, and was assumed to be dead, and Birlin was found not guilty, on the grounds that he had not actually committed the act, nor had he actively condoned or encouraged it. While he had not attempted to prevent the crime, it was accepted by the court, that any move on his part to do so would have resulted in his death also. Grüner was found guilty and was sentenced to death, but he remained at large to cheat the hangman.

Focus remained on the Scheldt defences, and the gun battery at Fort Frederik Hendrik near Breskens on the East Scheldt was targeted by elements of 1 and 8 Groups on the 11th, while 115 Lancasters from 5 Group were assigned to others near Flushing on the North Bank of the West Scheldt. At the same time sixty-one Lancasters and two Mosquitos from 5 Group were to attempt to breach the seawalls at Veere, situated on the eastern side of Walcheren opposite Westkapelle. 57 Squadron contributed nine Lancasters to Veere and five to Flushing, the former loaded with fourteen 1,000 pounders each and the latter with twelve 1,000 and four 500 pounders, and they departed East Kirkby between 12.51 and 13.05 with W/C Humphreys the senior pilot on duty and bound for Veere. On arrival in the target area, they encountered varying amounts of well-broken cloud between two and seven-tenths with tops at 4,000 to 5,000 feet. The 57 Squadron crews carried out their attacks at Veere from 4,000 to 7,500 feet between 14.41 and 15.01 and at Flushing from 4,200 to 7,600 feet between 14.47 and 14.54, and post-raid reconnaissance revealed several breaks in the dyke at Veere, the largest of two hundred yards, and an area of flooding of 800 x 250 yards but no new damage to the gun positions.

The 14th was the day on which were fired the opening salvoes of Operation Hurricane, a terrifying demonstration to the enemy of the overwhelming superiority of the Allied air forces ranged against it. Bomber Command ordered a maximum effort from all but 5 Group to attack Duisburg, for which 1,013 Lancasters, Halifaxes and Mosquitos answered the call. The American 8th Air Force would also be in business on this day, targeting the Cologne area further south with 1,250 bombers escorted by 749 fighters. The RAF force took off at first light, picked up its own fighter escort, and delivered 4,500 tons of high-explosives and incendiaries into Duisburg shortly after breakfast time, causing unimaginable destruction. That night, similar numbers returned to press home the point about superiority, bringing the total weight of bombs over the two raids to 9,000 tons from 2,018 sorties in fewer than twenty-four hours. The only involvement by 5 Group were single sorties by a Lancaster and a Mosquito to conduct a photo-reconnaissance of the operation.

However, 5 Group took advantage of the evening activity over the Ruhr to return to Braunschweig, the scene of quite a number of unsatisfactory previous attempts to land a really telling blow. A force of 232 Lancasters and eight Mosquitos was made ready, of which twenty of the former were provided by 57 Squadron, and they departed East Kirkby between 22.11 and 22.46 with W/C Humphreys and S/L Ward the senior pilots on duty. They flew out over the Lincolnshire coast and made landfall over the Den Helder peninsula, before arriving in the target area to find conditions ideal for the low-level marking by Mosquitos. Approaching the target at 18,000 feet from the south-west over Hallendorf and Salzgitter, the latter the home to the Reichswerke Hermann Göring steelworks, crews had to run the gauntlet of searchlight cones and heavy flak for the three minutes it took to pass through. They were greeted by clear skies and good visibility on the other side, which facilitated accurate marking with red and green TIs by the heavy brigade, and, although the early stages of bombing tended to undershoot, the Master Bomber quickly brought it back on track, calling for crews to overshoot by up to nineteen seconds. The 57 Squadron contingent passed over the aiming-point at 17,000 to 19,500 feet between 02.30 and 02.39 and delivered their loads accurately to contribute to a highly effective raid. The return flight was conducted by the entire force at 3,500 feet to fox the night-fighter controller and was covered by cloud. Passing to the south of the Ruhr, the effects of the attack on Duisburg were clearly visible over to starboard. The tactic proved to be a major success, although 83 Squadron's F/O Price complained that main force crews were jettisoning incendiaries all the way back as far as the Rhine, and thereby illuminating the track for any stalking night-fighters. In the event, only a single Lancaster failed to return from what was, indeed, confirmed to be an outstanding result, which had wiped out the entire centre of this historic city, and visited damage on almost every other district.

Stubborn resistance by the occupiers on Walcheren demanded further operations against the seawalls at Westkapelle, for which a 5 Group force of forty-seven Lancasters and three Mosquitos was made ready on the 17th. Six 57 Squadron Lancasters had fourteen delayed-action 1,000 pounders winched into their bomb bays, and were sent on their way from East Kirkby between 12.45 and 13.03 with S/L Neil the senior pilot on duty for the first time since his recent posting. They arrived at the target to find favourable conditions and bombed on red TIs from 5,000 to 5,250 feet between 14.00 and 14.16, observing most loads to fall between the TIs and the existing breach. Each returned home safely with an aiming-point photo, while a reconnaissance aircraft remained over the target from 14.55 to 15.10 to record the delayed-action bomb blasts. Disappointingly, the photos would reveal no extension to the breach in the dyke.

Following a night off, 57 Squadron called twenty-one crews to the briefing room on the 19th to learn the details of the operation that night against Nuremberg, which was to be a 5 Group affair involving a new record of 263 Lancasters and seven Mosquitos, while 560 aircraft from the other groups plied their trade at Stuttgart, some ninety miles to the south-west. The 57 Squadron element departed East Kirkby between 17.00 and 17.42 with S/L Neil the senior pilot on duty and were to act as Path Finder supporters during their first pass over the aiming point. There were no early returns by 57 Squadron aircraft and the outward flight across France was uneventful, allowing a largely intact bomber stream to arrive in the target area to encounter a wedge of eight to ten-tenths cloud at between 3,000 and 10,000 feet, with poor visibility below. The marker force laid down flares and backed them up with others along with red and green TIs, which were observed to be somewhat scattered, and bombing had to take place on their glow seen through the cloud. The 57 Squadron crews carried out their attacks from 15,500 to 19,250 feet between 20.55 and 21.19 in accordance with the Master Bomber's instructions, before all but one returned home uncertain as to the outcome. F/Sgt Brunton RNZAF and crew failed to return in PB425, on what had been their fifteenth operation. Their Lancaster came down in southern Germany and the pilot lost his life, while his crew all survived to be taken into captivity. The impression given by the glow of fires was of an effective attack, but post-raid reconnaissance revealed the bombing to have fallen not on the intended city centre aiming-point, but predominantly into the more industrial southern districts, where almost four hundred houses were destroyed along with forty-one industrial buildings.

It was back to Walcheren on the 23rd for 112 Lancasters of 5 Group, this time to target the coastal battery at Flushing. 57 Squadron loaded six Lancasters with fourteen 1,000 pounders each and sent them skyward between 15.14 and 15.19 with no senior pilots on duty. They were greeted at the target by eight to ten-tenths cloud with a base at between 3,000 and 5,000 feet, and poor visibility below caused by haze and rain. The force was led in on what appeared to be a decent approach but was ordered to "orbit port" as the lead crews experienced great difficulty in identifying their respective aiming-points. A second run was no more revealing, even for those crews who ventured down as low as 2,000 feet, and twenty would still have their bombs on board when ordered to go home. The 57 Squadron crews were among eighty-eight to deliver their bombs, doing so from 3,800 to 4,800 feet between 16.24 and 17.25. Post-raid reconnaissance revealed evidence of seventy bomb bursts, including four near-misses, and the destruction of a number of buildings on the site.

That evening, a new record force of 1,055 aircraft was sent against Essen as part of the Hurricane "message", and dropped 4,538 tons of bombs, more than 90% of which was high explosive. This number was achieved without 5 Group, which took the night off, and committed only twenty-five Lancasters to gardening duties in northern waters on the following night. 57 Squadron briefed the crews of F/Ls Ottewell and Warburton and F/Os Mallinson and Southfield for the Kraut garden, located in the Lim Fjord running between Ålborg and Hals in northern Jutland. They departed East Kirkby between 17.23 and 17.48 and reached the target area to find ten-tenths very low cloud with tops at between 2,000 and 6,000 feet. They established their positions by H2S-fix and delivered their six mines each into the briefed locations before returning safely from uneventful sorties. Essen was pounded again by more than seven hundred aircraft in daylight on the 25th, after which it ceased to be an important source of war production. Operation Hurricane moved on to Cologne on the 28th, when two districts east of the centre were totally devastated by more than seven hundred aircraft.

5 Group occupied the 28th with the preparation of a force of 237 Lancasters and seven Mosquitos for an operation that night against the U-Boot pens at Bergen in Norway. 57 Squadron made ready twenty Lancasters and dispatched them from East Kirkby between 22.33 and 22.52 with S/L Neil the senior pilot on duty. They reached the target area after a three-and-a-half-hour outward flight, having battled their way through electrical storms. They had been told to expect clear conditions, although some doubts had been expressed about the forecast, and these were confirmed when the force was met by eight to ten-tenths cloud at between 4,000 and 14,000 feet, which obscured the aiming-point. This would not have been a problem over Germany, but the risk to Norwegian civilians was uppermost in the mind of the Master Bomber as he pondered his options before calling for the main force crews to descend. Even then, most were unable to pick out any markers, and the situation was exacerbated by intermittent VHF reception, which persuaded 83 Squadron's F/L Cornish to fly up and down the coast acting as a communications link between the Master Bomber and the main force. The flare force contingent did what they could from between 12,500 and 15,000 feet, and the main force supporters flew as low as 4,500 feet, without being able to identify the target. Forty-seven aircraft bombed, including those containing the 57 Squadron

crews of F/Os Ford and Hughes, who aimed at red TIs from 6,000 feet at 02.07, while the others orbited up to four times until the Master Bomber called a halt and sent them home at 02.10.

The final operations against Walcheren were undertaken by 5 Group on the 30th, when two forces of fifty-one Lancasters and four Mosquitos each were sent against coastal batteries at Westkapelle and Flushing. 57 Squadron contributed nine Lancasters to the Westkapelle attack, and they departed East Kirkby between 10.03 and 10.45 with S/L Ward the senior pilot on duty. They ran into four to seven-tenths cloud at 6,000 feet over the target, despite which, visibility was good, and the aiming-point was identified visually and marked by red TIs. Some of these became buried in the dunes and were partially concealed, leading to a little overshooting, but the 57 Squadron crews were able to deliver their fourteen 1,000 pounders each accurately from 3,000 to 4,000 feet between 12.09 and 12.28. Ground forces went in on the following day, and a week of heavy fighting preceded the island's capture. Even then, the clearing of mines from the approaches to Antwerp would keep the port out of commission for a further three weeks. On the evening of the 30th, nine hundred aircraft returned to Cologne, and almost five hundred went back again twenty-four hours later to complete the destruction of the Rhineland Capital.

During the course of the month the squadron carried out thirteen operations and dispatched 156 sorties for the loss of a single Lancaster and crew. The crews of F/L Ainley DFC and F/O McDonald DFC both completed their first tour of operations on thirty-three sorties.

November 1944

The new month began for 5 Group with a daylight operation on the afternoon of the 1st, against a synthetic oil plant referred to by the raid planners simply as Homberg, a name with an evil reputation among 3 Group squadrons, which had suffered heavy casualties in repeated attacks on the plant during the summer. The Gewerkschaft Rheinpreussen A G production site lay in the Meerbeck district of the town of Moers, which is situated a mile-and-a-half to the west of Homberg on the West Bank of the Rhine opposite Duisburg. Its reputation probably meant less to the likes of 5 Group squadrons, whose hearts were more likely to be set racing by the mention of the Wesseling refinery south of Cologne. 57 Squadron briefed twenty-one crews as part of an overall 5 Group force of 226 Lancasters and two Mosquitos, which were to be joined by fourteen 8 Group Mosquitos to provide the Oboe marking. Some good news before the crews made their way to their aircraft, was that the number of sorties for a tour had been reduced again to thirty, which would be a cause for celebration among a select few who had already reached that milestone. The 57 Squadron element took off from East Kirkby between 13.28 and 13.48 with S/L Neil the senior pilot on duty and all reached the target to find it completely obscured by cloud with tops at between 6,000 and 9,000 feet. The head of the bomber stream arrived either before the Wanganui flares went down or were on top of them before they became evident and faced with an intense and accurate flak response coming up at them through the cloud, some crews simply turned for home with their fourteen 1,000 pounders safely tucked away in their bomb bays. The marking was confused by bad timing and the release point flares were well-scattered over a circle with a ten-mile radius, prompting a backer-up from 83 Squadron to drop a yellow TI over the built-up area in the hope of attracting some bombing. Some crews caught a glimpse of the target area through a chink in the cloud, while others carried out a time-and-distance run from the last visual pinpoint, before aiming at red skymarkers with green stars. F/Sgt Presland and crew returned with the body of the mid-upper gunner, Sgt Cross, and a wounded rear gunner, both victims of flak splinters. At debriefing it was evident that a lack of clear communication with the Master Bomber and the wide spread of the markers were major factors in the failure of the operation, and the repair of flak damage would keep the airframe and engine fitters busy into the night. At debriefing many crews reported that the Master Bomber's VHF transmissions had been jammed by someone in another aircraft leaving the transmit button on. Ultimately, the conditions rendered the whole attack ineffective, and, although 159 crews released their bombs, it is unlikely that any hit the intended target.

Düsseldorf's turn to face a massive force came on the 2nd, when 992 aircraft were made ready for what would prove to be the final major raid of the war on this much-bombed city on the southern edge of the Ruhr. 5 Group put up 187 Lancasters, seventeen provided by 57 Squadron for this rare experience for the "Lincolnshire Poachers" to operate with the rest of the Command. They departed East Kirkby between 16.30 and 16.42 with no senior pilots on duty, and all arrived at the target to find clear skies, moonlight and only ground haze to slightly mar the vertical visibility. The moonlight nullified the searchlights ringing the city, but, of greater concern was the heavy flak bursting at 17,000 to 20,000 feet. The main force crews found the aiming-point to be well illuminated and marked with red and green TIs, which the 57 Squadron participants bombed from 17,000 to 21,000 feet between 19.13 and 19.37. Returning crews reported fires beginning to take hold and smoke rising to 2,000 feet as they turned away and were confident of a successful attack. F/O Vasey and crew landed at Woodbridge with a severely wounded rear gunner on board, who may have been a victim of the night-fighter activity between the target and 04.30° East homebound. The success of the operation was confirmed by post-raid reconnaissance, which revealed that the northern half of the city had received the main weight of bombs, and that five thousand houses had been destroyed or seriously damaged.

The continuing campaign against Ruhr cities would be prosecuted by 749 aircraft at Bochum on the 4th, while 5 Group renewed its acquaintance with the Dortmund-Ems Canal, which had been repaired following the successful breaching of its banks near Münster in September. Now that Germany's railways were being pounded, the Dortmund-Ems and the nearby Mittelland Canal took on a greater significance as vital components in the transportation system, particularly with regard to supplying the front and the movement of raw materials like coal and coke to the steel works of the Ruhr region. A force of 168 Lancasters and two Mosquitos contained thirteen 57 Squadron aircraft, which took off between 17.25 and 17.40 with S/L Neil the senior pilot on duty. They were headed for the familiar aqueduct section of the canal south of Ladbergen and hoped to sneak in under cover of the main operation sixty miles to the south, hopefully, thereby, avoiding the attentions of night-fighters. The first marker aircraft of 83 Squadron arrived at the target at 19.19, after making a GPI run (ground position indicated) by means of H2S from Münster and encountered clear skies with ground haze. A blind-dropped green TI burst on the canal bank four hundred yards short of the aiming-point, which the flare force crews employed as a reference for their runs between 19.20 and 19.28. Red TIs were observed to fall between the two aqueducts, after which, the Master Bomber cancelled the third wave of flares and sent those crews home to leave the way clear for the main force. The first bombs tended to overshoot, but, thereafter, an accurate and concentrated attack was delivered from around 10,000 to 13,000 feet from 19.30 onwards. Photo-reconnaissance confirmed that both branches of the canal had been breached and drained, leaving barges stranded and the waterway unnavigable.

To capitalize on this success, an attack was planned for the 6th against the Mittelland Canal at Gravenhorst, a point about a mile north of Das Nasse Dreieck, the "Wet Triangle" at Bergeshövede. This was a triangular basin, where the two waterways converge about ten miles north of Ladbergen, before the Dortmund-Ems continues to the west, and the Mittelland north and then to the east. It was a 5 Group show involving 239 Lancasters and seven Mosquitos, seventeen of the former representing 57 Squadron. They departed East Kirkby between 16.18 and 16.35 with F/L Warburton the senior pilot on duty, and all reached the target area to find clear skies but haze up to around 4,000 feet that affected the vertical visibility. The Master Bomber called in the flare force, despite which, the low-level Mosquito markers experienced great difficulty in identifying the aiming-point. A single Mosquito piloted by F/L De Vigne eventually did deliver its target indicator accurately onto the aiming-point, where it fell into the water and was extinguished. Only thirty-one aircraft had bombed before the Master Bomber called a halt to proceedings at 19.38, and all from 57 Squadron withheld their loads, jettisoning the delayed-action 1,000 pounders before setting course for home and encountering not only night-fighter activity, but also very challenging weather conditions in the form of electrical storms and low cloud. Ten Lancasters failed to return, a high rate of loss with nothing to show for it, and among them was 57 Squadron's LM624, which disappeared without trace with the crew of P/O Cooper RAAF, who were on their ninth sortie. Three others in the crew were also members of the RAAF.

Earlier on the 6th, a series of raids on Ruhr oil refineries had begun with an area attack by more than seven hundred aircraft at Gelsenkirchen, where the Nordstern plant (Gelsenberg A G) and the city centre were the aiming-points, and this was followed by smaller-scale operations at Homberg on the 8th, Wanne-Eickel on the 9th and Castrop-Rauxel on the morning of the 11th.

Later, on the 11th, nineteen 57 Squadron crews assembled in the briefing room, sixteen to learn that they would shortly be attacking the Rhenania-Ossag synthetic oil plant at Harburg, a town situated on the South Bank of the Elbe opposite Hamburg. 237 Lancasters and eight Mosquitos were to take part in this all-5 Group show, while elements of 1 and 8 Groups targeted a similar plant at Dortmund. At the same time, the crews of F/Ls Ottewell and Warburton and F/O Cook were to carry out mining sorties, and while the ORB does not specify the location, it is believed to have been the Eglantine garden in the Elbe estuary. Each of the 57 Squadron Lancasters for the main event was loaded with a cookie and fourteen 500lb incendiaries and departed East Kirkby together with the gardeners between 16.09 and 17.04 with no senior pilots on duty. They reached the target area to find largely clear conditions, with only a thin layer of stratus at 8,000 feet and another at 17,000 to 18,000 feet between them and the aiming-point. This they identified either by H2S or red and green TIs, before delivering their loads in accordance with instructions from the Master Bomber from around 16,000 to 19,000 feet. The defenders threw up a heavy flak barrage, which reached as high as 23,000 feet, and seven Lancasters failed to return. Absent from debriefing at East Kirkby was the crew of F/O Bowden, who were in LL939 and on their first sortie together. Hit by flak in the target area and terminally damaged, three crew members baled out, leaving F/O Bowden to attempt a crash-landing with the remaining three crew members still on board. The first impact with the ground occurred at Beckdorf, five miles south-south-west of Buxtehude at 19.27, at which point an engine and the rear turret were torn away, while the rest of the Lancaster bounced back into the air to cover a further fifteen hundred yards. None survived the second impact, and after the flight engineer's parachute failed to deploy, only two men lived to be taken into captivity. At debriefing, crews reported a large explosion at 19.28, followed by an oil fire, and local reports would confirm that heavy damage had been inflicted upon the town's residential and industrial districts. Meanwhile, the gardening trio planted eighteen vegetables into the briefed locations during uneventful sorties.

The 16th was devoted to the erasure from the map of the three small towns of Heinsberg, Jülich and Düren, located respectively in an arc from north to east of Aachen, and close to the German lines upon which American ground forces were advancing. A total of 1,188 aircraft was involved, and 1, 5 and 8 Groups provided the heavy bombing and marking force of 485 Lancasters for the last-mentioned. 57 Squadron contributed eighteen of its own to the 5 Group effort of 214, but listed only thirteen in the ORB, which took off from East Kirkby between 12.49 and 13.02 with W/C Humphreys the senior pilot on duty. Each Lancaster lifted eleven 1,000 and four 500 pounders through the ten-tenths cloud which would accompany them most of the way to the target, where all but two of the 57 Squadron contingent would arrive after two unidentified crews had turned back for undisclosed reasons. The cloud thinned to three-tenths stratus above 6,000 feet as they approached the aiming-point in the final wave of the attack, and some heard the Master Bomber calling for them to descend to 1,000 feet. Most failed to pick up the signal in conditions of poor reception, however, and it is believed that all from 57 Squadron carried out their attacks from around 10,000 to 13,000 feet between 15.31 and 15.42 and observed smoke rising through 9,000 feet as they turned for home confident in the success of the operation. Most of the bombing photos were unplottable because of the smoke covering the area, but post-raid reconnaissance revealed that the town had been all-but erased from the map, and local reports gave a death toll in excess of three thousand inhabitants at a cost to 5 Group of four Lancasters. In the event, unfavourable ground conditions prevented the American advance from succeeding.

Twenty 57 Squadron crews were called to briefing on the 21st, to be told, that the 55 Base squadrons were going back to the Gravenhorst section of the Mittelland Canal on a night of multiple operations involving 1,345 sorties. Three operations, each by 270 aircraft, were to be directed at railway yards at Aschaffenburg, situated about twenty miles south-east of Frankfurt, and oil plants at Castrop-Rauxel and Sterkrade in the Ruhr. 5 Group prepared two forces of 137 and 123 Lancasters respectively with Mosquito support for the Mittelland and Dortmund-Ems Canals, while a whole host of minor operations would complete the Order of Battle. The 57 Squadron element departed East Kirkby between 17.09 and 17.35 with every crew captained by a pilot of flying officer rank and each Lancaster carrying either a dozen 1,000 pounders or six American-built 1,900 pounders. They encountered a layer of six to ten-tenths cloud in the target area between 4,000 and 8,000 feet, which did not inhibit the accuracy of the marking, but the instructions of the Master Bomber caused some confusion, a situation exacerbated by a week VHF signal. At first, he ordered the crews to come below the cloud base, to which some responded, before he changed his mind and told them to return to the briefed bombing height. He issued instructions to aim for the more southerly of two red TIs, and most complied to deliver what appeared to be a good concentration of bombs. Post-raid reconnaissance revealed that the canal had been breached over a distance of fifty feet on the western bank, south of the road bridge, and had been drained to leave vessels stranded and damaged by direct hits. The attack on the Dortmund-Ems Canal was better organized and reconnaissance revealed the left-hand channel, which was the only one repaired since the last attack, to have been breached again where it crossed the River Glane. The river had been unable to cope with the volume of water released and extensive flooding occurred on both sides of the canal. In contrast to the criticism of the master Bomber at Gravenhorst, the verdict by main force crews on the performance of the Master Bomber at Ladbergen was unanimously favourable. The two operations were concluded for the loss of just two 49 Squadron Lancasters.

The Germans recognized that repairing the canals was an open invitation to Bomber Command to return, and, so vital were they to the transportation system, that they could not be abandoned. The answer was to complete repairs, but to leave the sections drained and apparently still under repair, until sufficient traffic had built up to push through in one night. They would then be flooded and re-emptied to dupe RAF reconnaissance flights and maintain the deception.

On the following night, 5 Group dispatched 171 Lancasters and seven Mosquitos to attack the U-Boot pens at Trondheim in Norway, a straight-line distance from East Kirkby of some eight hundred miles. 57 Squadron launched thirteen Lancasters into the air between 15.43 and 16.25 with F/L Ottewell the senior pilot on duty, and all arrived in the target area some five-and-a-half hours later to find clear skies and excellent visibility. However, an effective smoke screen prevented the marker force from finding the aiming-point, and the Master Bomber had no option but to send the force home, where they arrived between 01.44 and 03.52 after more than ten hours aloft.

The weather was mainly responsible for curtailing operations over the next few days until the 26th, when briefings took place on 5 Group stations at 20.00. The seventeen attending 57 Squadron crews learned that Munich was to be their target for an all-5 Group affair involving 270 Lancasters and eight Mosquitos, which represented a maximum effort. They departed East Kirkby between 23.00 and 23.52 with S/L Ward the senior pilot on duty and each Lancaster carrying a 1,000 pounder and cluster bombs. Forming up and climbing to operational altitude was a time-consuming business, and it would be five hours before the target was reached, while, in the meantime, isolated aircraft turned back, including those of F/Os Kirton and Palling of 57 Squadron because of an indisposed wireless operator and engine failure respectively. Some crews struggled with icing conditions and tried in vain to find clear lanes in the cloud, before abandoning their sortie because of sluggish controls. The others found the target area under clear skies with good visibility and confirmed their positions by means of H2S. Aside from one errant red TI, the low-level Mosquito marking was accurate, and the Master Bomber ensured that the crews focused upon the reds and greens on and close to the planned aiming-point, calling on some to carry out a twenty-two second overshoot. The bombing was carried out from around 18,000 to 20,000 feet either side of 05.00 and a very large explosion was witnessed near the marshalling yards at 05.07. All from 57 Squadron returned safely to praise the quality of the route, the target marking and the performance of the Master Bomber and reported smoke rising through 18,000 feet as they turned away and fires visible for a hundred miles into the return flight. The confidence in a concentrated and effective attack was justified, when post-raid reconnaissance confirmed it as such, and a local report singled out railway installations as being particularly hard-hit.

During the course of the month, the squadron carried out ten operations and dispatched 155 sorties for the loss of two Lancasters and their crews. W/C Humphreys concluded his tour as did four other crews, but the commanding officer would not immediately depart for pastures new.

December 1944

There were no operations for 5 Group for the first three nights of the new month, largely because of the weather, and, in the meantime, 1, 4, 6 and 8 Groups pounded the Ruhr town of Hagen on the 2/3rd. Worthwhile targets were becoming more and more scarce at a time when the Command was at its most powerful, and this final period of the war would bring the most devastating attacks to date on the German homeland. When 57 Squadron returned to action in the early evening of the 4th, it was to provide twenty Lancasters as part of a 5 Group force of 282 of the type and ten Mosquitos. Their target was the town of Heilbronn, situated thirty miles due north of Stuttgart, which had the river Neckar and a north-south rail link running through it, but, otherwise, was of no obvious strategic importance, and would not have been expecting to be attacked. The main operation on this night was actually by 535 aircraft of 1, 6 and 8 Groups at Karlsruhe, some fifty-six miles west-south-west of Heilbronn, and the concentration of aircraft in this area would be certain to bring out the night-fighters.

The 57 Squadron element departed East Kirkby between 16.17 and 16.31 with S/Ls Neil and Ward the senior pilots on duty, but the latter was forced to return early because of the failure of his port-outer engine. The others made their way across France in good conditions to find three to five-tenths thin stratus over the target at around 12,000 feet and watched the illuminator flares falling ahead of them to light the way for the low-level Mosquitos seeking out the marshalling yards and city centre aiming points. They dropped red TIs for the heavy brigade visual marker crews to back up with yellows at the marshalling yards, but the main force element was unable to distinguish them in the burgeoning fires and turned their attention instead upon the town. The 57 Squadron crews attacked from 7,300 to 15,000 feet between 19.30 and 19.43, adding to the general destruction, and, as the force retreated westwards into electrical storms, 82% of the city's built-up area was in the process of being destroyed by what probably amounted to a firestorm. F/O Braham and crew had been delayed by a fire in their port-outer engine and arrived just in time to hear the Master Bomber call a halt. They headed towards the glow of fires emanating from Karlsruhe and dropped their load there as a last resort target. The post-war British Bombing Survey estimated 351 acres of destruction in Heilbronn, and a death toll of at least seven thousand people. It cost the group twelve aircraft, one of which, 57 Squadron's NG145, crashed ten miles south-south-east of the target killing Lt Becker SAAF and all but his bomb-aimer, who was taken prisoner. This was their first sortie with 57 Squadron after completing twelve with 106 Squadron.

The town of Giessen was 5 Group's objective on a night of heavy Bomber Command activity on the 6/7th. Other operations centred on the oil refinery at Leuna (Merseburg), which was the target for 475 Lancasters of 1, 3 and 8 Groups, while 450 aircraft from predominantly 4 and 6 Groups attacked railway installations at Osnabrück, north of the Ruhr. 57 Squadron briefed fifteen crews as part of an overall 5 Group heavy force of 255 Lancasters, and they set off from East Kirkby between 16.30 and 17.00 with S/L Neil the senior pilot on duty, and each Lancaster carrying a cookie and 1,950 x 4lb incendiaries. F/O Mallinson and crew were back in the circuit within two hours with one dead engine and intercom failure, and they were just six minutes ahead of Capt Evensen and crew, whose W/T had let them down. The others pressed on, their destination lying some eighty-five miles south-east of Cologne in west-central Germany, and thirty-five miles north of Frankfurt. The main force crews had been assigned to two aiming-points, two-thirds of them to the town, and the remainder to the marshalling yards, and, on arrival in the target area, they found predominantly clear skies and good visibility. The flare force began illuminating three minutes early and to the west of the target, but the Mosquito-laid red TIs fell close to the aiming-point and the Master Bomber ensured that they were backed up by greens. The 57 Squadron crews bombed from 9,500 to 12,200 feet between 20.14 and 20.35, and all but one returned safely to report another successful raid, which would be confirmed by reconnaissance photographs. Eight Lancasters failed to return and two of them belonged to 57 Squadron. S/L Neil and crew were on their seventh sortie, presumably of their second tour, and all were killed when NG199 crashed in the Hannover defence zone. S/L Neil was a New Zealander serving in the RAF. PD264 is believed to have come down in the well-defended same general area with fatal consequences for F/O Riddell and four of his crew, who were on their twelfth sortie, and the badly injured bomb-aimer lingered until the 10th before losing his fight for life. The rear gunner was the sole survivor, and he joined the roll call of 57 Squadron airmen in enemy hands.

The Urft Dam was one of a number of similar structures in the beautiful Eifel region of western Germany, close to the Belgian frontier. There was a fear that the enemy might strategically release flood water to hamper the American advance into Germany, and it was decided to attempt to breach the dam, to allow any excess water to drain away. The first of a number of attacks on the region began on the 3rd at Heimbach, the small town nestling against the northern reaches of the reservoir, but the 1 and 8 Group force failed to identify it, and no bombs fell. On the following day, a small 8 Group effort against the dam was unsuccessful, as was a 3 Group attack on the nearby Schwammenauel Dam on the 5th. The job was handed to 5 Group on the 8th, for which a force of 205 Lancasters was made ready, fourteen of them by 57 Squadron and nineteen from 617 Squadron, the latter carrying Tallboys. The 57 Squadron element departed East Kirkby in wintry conditions between 08.38 and 08.58 with F/Ls Mersh and Shaw the senior pilots on duty and each carrying fourteen 1,000 pounders. All reached the target to be greeted by six to nine-tenths cloud at between 6,000 and 8,000 feet and moderate visibility, which partially obscured the aiming-point for some as they ran in to bomb. The instruction at briefing had been to not orbit, and W/C Douglas of 467 Squadron took the decision to lead his squadron away from the target and head for home, as did W/C Tait, who refused to allow the 617 Squadron element to waste their Tallboys in such unfavourable conditions. The 57 Squadron crews carried out their attacks from 9,250 to 10,200 feet between 11.02 and 11.11 and returned home to report bombs around the aiming point and straddling the dam. An analysis of the operation revealed that 129 crews had carried out a scattered attack before the Master Bomber called a halt.

The conditions had prevented any assessment of results, which meant that another attempt on the dam would be necessary, and preparations were put in hand on the 10th to return with a force of 217 Lancasters. 57 Squadron detailed fourteen Lancasters, which departed East Kirkby between 04.08 and 04.47 on a cold and frosty morning with F/L Shaw the senior pilot on duty, but the entire force was recalled before it reached the English coast. The operation was rescheduled for early on the following morning, when 233 Lancasters and a Mosquito were to join five 8 Group Mosquitos at the target, but take-off was postponed until midday. The fifteen 57 Squadron participants got away between 12.10 and 12.33 with F/Ls Hughes and Shaw the senior pilots on duty and joined up with the rest of the force on the flight south to the Channel coast. They encountered icing conditions at the French coast and weather conditions in the target area that were barely an improvement on the previous day. Up to nine-tenths cloud with tops at 8,000 feet made life difficult for the Master Bomber, who tried to bring the crews down below the 4,000-

foot cloud base, some complying, while others were able to identify the aiming-point through a four-mile-long gap. It is believed that all from 57 Squadron carried out an attack from 4,300 to 10,000 feet between 14.46 and 15.15, some after making two or three passes over the aiming point, but a few aircraft from other squadrons had not bombed before the Master Bomber's "Dewdrop" instruction to cease bombing and go home. The operation's only casualty was 57 Squadron's PD263, which crashed in Germany on the way home with fatal consequences for the crew of F/O Searl, who were on their twenty-first sortie. Post-raid reconnaissance revealed a number of hits on the stepped apron of the dam, and cratering all around, but no actual breach had occurred.

W/C Tomes arrived from Strubby on the 13th after undertaking two sorties with 619 Squadron to gain operational experience. He had only recently completed a course at 5LFS and would succeed W/C Humphreys as 57 Squadron's commanding officer early in the New Year. One wonders what operational crews thought of being commanded by an officer who had faced the enemy less than they, when there were so many among their ranks who had earned the right to command but were not rewarded with the opportunity.

A 5 Group contingent of ten Lancasters was sent mining in the Silverthorn III garden in the Kattegat on the 14th, and among them were the 57 Squadron crews of F/L Warburton and F/O Donkin. They departed East Kirkby at 15.23 and 15.26 respectively and reached the drop zone between the east coast of northern Jutland and the north-western tip of Sjaelland Island some three hours later to find ten-tenths cloud between 2,000 and 8,000 feet. Positions were established by H2S and the six vegetables each were delivered into the briefed locations from around 15,000 feet.

The main operation on the night of the 15/16th was directed at Ludwigshafen in southern Germany, home to a number of I G Farben factories, which were among the most blatant exploiters of slave workers in the production of synthetic oil. The attack by 327 Lancasters and fourteen Mosquitos of 1, 6 and 8 Groups landed 450 high explosive bombs and incendiaries in the Ludwigshafen plant, causing massive damage and fires, and was the greatest setback to production during the war. Further north, the Oppau factory ceased production completely for an extended period, and five other industrial concerns also sustained severe damage, as did some residential areas. It was on the 16th that German ground forces began a new offensive in the Ardennes, in an attempt to break through the American lines and reach the port of Antwerp in what would become known as the Battle of the Bulge.

Munich had become something of a 5 Group preserve during the year, and a further operation against it was planned for the night of the 17/18th, which would turn out to be another night of heavy Bomber Command activity. The main raid was to be by more than five hundred aircraft, predominantly of 4 and 6 Groups, on Duisburg, while 1 Group targeted Ulm with over three hundred Lancasters, leaving 5 Group to send 280 Lancasters some seventy miles beyond to the Bavarian Capital City. 57 Squadron briefed eighteen crews, while their Lancasters were being prepared for the 1,300-mile round-trip, and they departed East Kirkby between 16.14 and 16.46 with F/L Shaw the senior pilot on duty. It turned out to be a night of poor serviceability for 55 Base, with six Spilsby crews and two from 57 Squadron among fifteen early returns for a variety of technical issues. The French coast was crossed near Berck-sur-Mer, and it was probably afterwards that the crews of F/Os Appleton and Bennett were prevented by severe icing conditions from climbing sufficiently to warrant them continuing on. The others reached the target to find generally clear skies and good visibility and bombed on red and green TIs from 12,000 to 15,000 feet between 21.17 and 22.13 in accordance with the instructions of the Master Bomber, who declared himself satisfied with the results. Returning crews were confident that they had participated in an effective attack and cited as evidence the glow from the fires to be visible from a hundred miles into the return journey. Absent from debriefing were the crews of Capt Evensen of the Royal Norwegian Air Force and F/O Donkin in SW245 and LM626 respectively, the former having crashed into the sea off Dieppe with just one survivor, the mid-upper gunner, who would succumb to his injuries on the 6th of January. They had been undertaking their ninth sortie. The latter crashed near Rouen while homebound at 23.00, almost certainly having turned back early, and exploded with great force, suggesting that some bombs were still on board. Of the eight occupants, only the remains of the pilot, second pilot and mid-upper gunner were recovered for burial, while their crew mates are commemorated on the Runnymede memorial. They had been on their twenty-sixth sortie. As usual at this target, no local report emerged, but Bomber Command claimed severe and widespread damage to the city.

On the following night, it was the turn of the distant Baltic port of Gdynia to play host to 5 Group, for which 57 Squadron put up ten Lancasters in an overall force of 236 of the type. The intention was to catch elements of the German fleet at anchor, in particular, the Lützow, and also to destroy harbour installations as well as cause damage within the town. *(The original Lützow was actually never completed and had been sold to the Russian navy in 1940 as a hull minus superstructure. The pocket battleship, Deutschland, was renamed Lützow, to avoid humiliation for the nation should she be lost in battle.)* While this operation was in progress, fourteen other Lancasters of the group were to sneak in under cover of the main activity to deliver mines to the Privet and Spinach gardens in Danzig (Gdansk) Bay. 57 Squadron supported this undertaking with the crews of F/L Warburton and F/O Ford, and the two elements departed East Kirkby together between 16.42 and 17.26 with S/L Hodgkinson the senior pilot on duty on his return to the squadron for a second tour. F/O Conner and crew were some distance into the outward flight when their compass let them down, but they were the only 57 Squadron "boomerang" as the others pressed on to reach the target area after an outward flight of almost five hours. They found clear skies and good visibility in which the harbour and town could be picked out visually until a smoke screen was activated, but in keeping with standard practice, the initial identification was by H2S. The crews of F/Os Ledeboer and Ross were among those assigned to the Lützow, which they found to be in the briefed location, but came upon it too late to establish a solid bombing run. Their bombs were delivered from 11,750 and 15,500 feet at 21.56 and 21.59 and were observed to straddle the vessel and the jetty, setting off a large explosion and an oil fire. The smoke screen eventually obscured the Lützow, and crews with bombs still to deliver turned their attention upon the port area and town, where the illumination and marking proceeded according to plan. The 57 Squadron crews delivered their eight 1,000 pounders each on red and green TIs from 11,700 to 13,800 feet between 22.02 and 22.16 in accordance with the Master Bomber's instructions and in the face of intense light flak. It was not possible to make an accurate assessment of results, but bomb bursts were seen across the docks and quaysides. Reconnaissance photos confirmed that damage had been inflicted upon shipping, port installations and residential property in the waterfront districts, at a cost of four Lancasters. Meanwhile, the gardeners were experiencing some difficulties in identifying the drop zone by H2S, but both from 57 Squadron planted their vegetables into the briefed locations from around 15,000 feet, probably after pinpointing on Point Hel.

Thick fog kept the crews on the ground on the 20th, and threatened to do so also on the 21st, but an operation was called on the basis that the weather over Scotland after midnight would be clear for returning aircraft, even if Lincolnshire remained fogbound. Six 57 Squadron Lancasters were detailed for the 5 Group operation that night, and briefings took place while the ground crews did their best to get the aircraft ready in time. In briefing rooms across southern and south-eastern Lincolnshire, crews learned that their target would require them to retrace their recent steps to Germany's eastern Baltic region, although the I G Farben-owned Wintershall oil refinery at Politz, situated less than ten miles north of the port of Stettin, was some two hundred miles short of their trip to Gdynia. *(This location is often wrongly spelled Pölitz, which is a town in Germany's Schleswig-Holstein region at the western end of the Baltic. Politz is now Police in Poland.)* A force of 207 Lancasters and a single Mosquito was assembled, and, unusually, it included an element from 617 Squadron carrying Tallboys. The 57 Squadron element departed East Kirkby between 16.51 and 17.20 with S/L Hodgkinson the senior pilot on duty, each crew sitting on a cookie and twelve 500 pounders. F/O Campbell and crew were heading eastwards across the North Sea when the navigator became unwell and they had to turn back, but the others reached the target, many after cutting corners to keep up with the stream, and found clear skies with ground haze, which may have been a smoke screen. This important war-industry asset was protected by around fifty searchlights, and heavy flak accompanied the Lancasters as they ran in on the aiming-point. The markers fell some two thousand yards north-north-west of the plant, a situation recognized by the Master Bomber, but he was unable to persuade the backers-up to shift the point of aim accordingly, and most of the bombing would miss the mark. The 57 Squadron element bombed on red and green TIs from 14,800 to 19,700 feet between 22.03 and 22.15 and observed most of the bomb bursts to be around the markers. Fires remained visible for almost a hundred miles into the return journey, but the plant had not been destroyed and it would be necessary to mount further raids.

The final wartime Christmas period was celebrated on 5 Group stations in traditional style and undisturbed by operational activity between the 22nd and Boxing Day, which was not the case for some other groups. The peace came to an end on the 26th, when crews from all groups were roused from any resulting stupor to attend briefings for operations against enemy troop positions at St Vith in Belgium. The German advance towards Antwerp had run out of steam after its earlier successes, and starved of fuel and ammunition, it was now attempting to withdraw back into Germany. 5 Group contributed twenty-six Lancasters to the force of 296 aircraft for the first joint operation since October. F/O Palling and crew were the sole 57 Squadron representatives and departed East Kirkby at 13.00 carrying fourteen 1,000 pounders. After the sea crossing, they made landfall between Ostend and Dunkerque and found the target, situated within five miles of the German frontier, to be under clear skies with good visibility, and could identify the aiming-point visually and by a red TI. The Palling crew bombed from 14,000 feet at 15.00, before the aiming point became obscured by smoke, at which point, the Master Bomber ordered the crews to descend to 10,000 feet and bomb the upwind edge of the smoke. A number of crews reported a four-engine bomber going down but not crashing, and five parachutes were observed.

On the 28th, the 57 Squadron crews of F/Ls Hughes and Mersh and F/O Ford were told that they were to fly over to Strubby, from where they would take off as part of a 5 Group force of sixty-seven Lancasters targeting shipping, specifically the cruiser Köln, at Horten in Oslo Fjord. They departed Strubby in company with five Lancasters of 619 Squadron and four of 630 Squadron between 19.38 and 20.17 and reached the target area after an outward flight of four-and-a-half hours. The skies were relatively clear and the visibility good, but a thin layer of alto-cumulus cloud at between 15,000 and 20,000 feet reduced the brightness of the moonlight and cast deceptive shadows on the water to prevent a clear identification of the target. The aiming-point was marked by Wanganui flares, but most crews followed the Master Bomber's instructions after establishing their own reference point. A patch of light flak to the north-east of the harbour mole was thought to be concealing a large naval unit, and this area was marked and bombed. Some crews would claim to have attacked a large vessel moving from this area in a southerly direction, and other shipping in the harbour, all in the face of intense shipboard and shore-based light flak. The 57 Squadron trio bombed from 8,000 feet between 23.44 and 23.57 but claimed no direct hits and the operation produced inconclusive results.

The 29th dawned fine and frosty, and, shortly after lunch, 5 Group sent eleven crews on daylight mining sorties in the Onion garden in Oslo harbour. The 57 Squadron crews of F/Os Palling, Ross and Vasey departed East Kirkby between 15.50 and 16.10 and returned safely six-and-a-half to seven hours later to report successful sorties.

57 Squadron would conduct its final operations of the year on New Year's Eve, beginning with the departure from East Kirkby of ten Lancasters as part of a 5 Group force of 154 assigned to attack an enemy supply line at Houffalize in the Ardennes region of Belgium. They took off between 02.24 and 02.47 with F/L King the senior pilot on duty and found the target area under five to seven-tenths stratus cloud at 5,000 to 6,000 feet, with another layer of eight-tenths with tops at 9,000 feet. This rendered identification something of a challenge, despite which, the marking was punctual and accurate, although the red TIs were observed only by a proportion of the crews who chanced upon a gap in the clouds directly over the aiming-point. While some crews withheld their bombs, those from 57 Squadron delivered theirs from 9,000 to 12,000 feet between 05.01 and 05.13. A number of crews in the force descended to below the cloud base and confirmed that the bombing was concentrated around the markers, but it would be deemed necessary to revisit this objective within a short time.

It was dusk when the crews of F/O Ford and F/L Mersh took off from East Kirkby at 16.15 and 16.19 to head for the Yewtree garden, the channel in the Baltic between Læsø Island and the east coast of North Jutland. They established their positions by H2S and carried out timed runs at around 15,000 feet to deposit their mines into the allotted locations before returning home safely to wrap up a very successful, if, testing year for the squadron.

During the course of the month the squadron conducted fifteen operations, including those recalled, and dispatched 136 sorties for the loss of six Lancasters and their crews. The New Year beckoned with the scent of victory in the air, however, any thoughts that the enemy defences were spent were misplaced, and even though they were unable to protect every corner of the Reich, they would continue to provide stubborn opposition for a further three months.

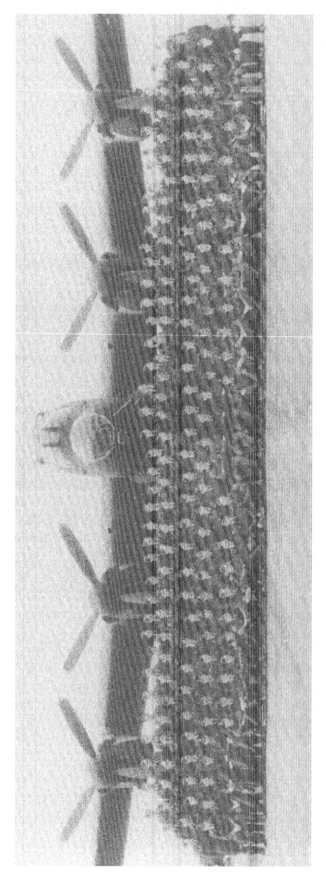

Figure 1 57 Squadron at East Kirkby – 12th April 1944

This photo of 57 Squadron's aircrew was taken on 12th April 1944, at East Kirkby to mark the departure of Wing Commander H W F Fisher DFC. To the left and right of the Boss sit Squadron Leaders P M Wigg DFC and M I Boyle DFC the two Flight Commanders. Within two weeks of the photo being taken, both were dead. Wigg and his crew were killed when they were shot down on 21st April. Boyle and his crew were lost when their aircraft collided mid-air with a 44 Squadron Lancaster on the night of 26/27th April 1944.

F/Sgt Thomas James (Jim) Lightfoot who flew as a navigator with 57 Squadron from East Kirkby. Jim's crew was shot down on 24th February 1944 and along with Sgt Francis Butler lost his life, while the other crew members were taken POW – with the exception of Sergeant Greenwell who evaded; his photo is in the museum at East Kirkby.

F/Sgt Thomas James (Jim) Lightfoot

57 Squadron crew of K- King. November 1944-May 1945
Harry Cowan (FE) RCAF, Phil Illot (RG) RCAF, Fred Moriarty (MUG) RCAF, Bernard Pearson RCAF
Eric Johnson (Nav) RCAF   Harold Ritchie (BA) RCAF   Robert Chisholm (W/Op)

F/Sgt Bridgeman   *F/O A V H Wardle DFC*   *Sgt C J Ludlow*

F/O Robertson   F/Sgt Bridgeman   Sgt Eden
Crew of Lancaster ME864 28/29th July 1944. Sgt Ludlow was murdered on capture.
(Aircrew Remembered)

Avro Lancaster BIII LM517 of 57 Squadron undergoing maintenance at East Kirkby. This aircraft served with 57 Squadron from March 1944 to October 1945. It then went to the Royal Aircraft Establishment until it was broken up in 1946.

Lancaster construction at Woodford 1944

57 Squadron Lancaster JB486 DX-F lost 5th July 1944.   F/L. A E Grubb & crew graves in Poix-De-Picardie Churchyard, France.

F/O Ross and Crew. George Horne second from left.

George (left on middle row)

J Alan Edwards

57 Squadron Lancaster W4232 DX-B landing at East Kirkby

Crew of L-Love 57 Squadron 1943 - May1944.
F/O Sid Bradley (Nav), F/O C Paton DFC, F/L Frank Thomas DFC Pilot, F/Sgt
Wally Adams (FE), W/O Robbie Young (MUG), F/Sgt Buck Buckley (RG), F/L
Mike Kingsley (W/Op)

57 Squadron Crew East Kirkby September 1944 – April 1945.
Back: Doug Kidgell (W.Op), Ted (FE), Ron Hurst (BA), Bob Fidler (Nav),
Front: Jim Whinney (MUG), Phil Keen DFC (Pilot), Dick Vernel (R/G).
Took part on 18th December 1944 on raid after battleships Scharnhorst and
Gneisnau. (Donated by Jim Whinney)

57 Squadron Crew at the side of a 514 Lancaster.
L-R rear – Peter Smith (FE), F/O Norman Browne (BA), F/O Ron Gill (Pilot),
Fred Stogdale (Nav). Front: Roy Pitt (W/Op), Eric Cousins (RG).

Sgt Lorne Todd RCAF

Sgt J Woodrow Air gunner

Ground staff East Kirkby 1944.

W/C Fisher and crew 57 Squadron B Flight DX-K. November 1943.
F/O Joe Simms, P/O Joe Sherriff, W/C Fisher, F/L Nobby Clarke, F/O Harry Ward.
In front: F/Sgt Jimmy McFalls, F/O Johnny Johnson

End of tour – a 57 Squadron crew

57 Squadron Lancaster DX-C 1944
L-R: Frank Carrall, Tommy Thompson, James Major Dunkley

57 Squadron Crew on a 'Cookie'

*AC2 R F 'Frank' Jackson
Armourer, 57 Squadron*

57 and 630 Squadron Ground crew

57 Squadron, East Kirkby
Crew including Sgt James Major Dunkley (far right of lower photo) and
Sgt Alf Thompson (middle of lower photo)

January 1945

The final year of the war began with a flourish, as the Luftwaffe launched its ill-conceived and, ultimately, ill-fated Operation Bodenplatte (Baseplate) at first light on New Year's Day. The intention to destroy the Allied air forces on the ground at the recently liberated airfields in France, Holland and Belgium was only modestly realized, and it cost the German day fighter force around 250 aircraft. Many of the pilots were killed, wounded or fell into Allied hands, and it was a setback from which the Tagjagd would never fully recover, while the Allies could make good their losses within hours from their enormous stockpiles.

5 Group was also active that morning, having roused the crews early from their beds to attend briefings for an attack on the recently repaired Dortmund-Ems Canal near Ladbergen, for which 102 Lancasters and two Mosquitos were made ready. The 57 Squadron element of ten departed East Kirkby between 07.47 and 08.03, each captained by a pilot of flying officer rank and each Lancaster carrying twelve to fourteen 1,000 pounders. After climbing out over their respective stations, the 54 Base squadrons from Coningsby and Metheringham fell in line behind 83 Squadron, with the 55 Base squadrons from East Kirkby and Spilsby about three miles further back, and a third section, made up of 53 Base units from Waddington, Skellingthorpe and Bardney some twenty miles to the rear. The last-mentioned were allowed to catch up, putting the force two minutes behind schedule at point C over the North Sea. It was between points C and D that the fighter escort was expected to join them, and, although it was not immediately apparent, it did eventually put in an appearance. The gaggles held together fairly well, although the controller would complain later that the legs were too short to keep them tight and some aircraft were seen to break formation. When about eight minutes from the target, smoke from a Mosquito-laid red TI could be seen, which was assessed as being on the southern tip of the island between the two branches of the canal. It was clearly visible to all crews, who were able to home in on it without difficulty. A six-gun flak battery greeted their arrival with accurate salvoes, but this did not inhibit the bombing runs, which were carried out by the 57 Squadron crews from 9,200 to 11,000 feet between 11.17 and 11.21. The impression was of an effective operation, but. on return, a number of 55 Base crews complained that the gaggle was too tight and put crews at risk from "friendly" bombs. The use of delay fuses prevented an immediate assessment of the results, but photo-reconnaissance revealed later that the canal had been breached again and the surrounding fields had become flooded.

Operations for the day were not yet done for 5 Group, which now had an appointment with the Mittelland Canal at Gravenhorst, for which 152 Lancasters and five Mosquitos were made ready. 57 Squadron loaded eight Lancasters with twelve or thirteen 1,000 pounders and dispatched them from East Kirkby between 16.54 and 17.09 with F/Ls Hughes, King and Mersh the senior pilots on duty. All reached the target area to find that the clear conditions enjoyed during the morning raid nearby had persisted, and so accurate were the initial TIs and illumination, delivered visually or by H2S, that the third flare force was not required and was sent home. The main force was called in ahead of H-Hour at around 19.10, and the 57 Squadron element bombed on red TIs from around 9,500 to 12,000 feet. One of the perils of operating on New Year's Day was the risk of falling victim to trigger-happy American flak gunners, who had been spooked by the German raids at dawn and now fired at anything that moved. Such "friendly fire" incidents would cost Bomber Command a number of aircraft and their crews. The employment of predominantly delayed-action bombs again prevented an immediate assessment of results, but a highly successful operation was confirmed later by photo-reconnaissance. All but one of the 57 Squadron aircraft landed at Kinloss and would straggle home later on the 2nd.

5 Group remained on the ground when Nuremberg and Ludwigshafen were raided by large forces on the night of the 2/3rd, and both operations were hugely destructive. A controversial attack was planned against the small French town of Royan in the early hours of the 5th, in response to requests from Free French forces, which were laying siege. Situated on the east bank at the mouth of the Gironde Estuary, it was occupied by a German garrison and was in the way of an advance towards the port of Bordeaux. The inhabitants had been offered an opportunity by the German garrison commander to evacuate the area, but around two thousand had declined, and would suffer the consequences. 1, 5 and 8 Groups put together a force of 347 Lancasters and seven Mosquitos, of which eighteen of the former represented 57 Squadron. They departed East Kirkby between 00.30 and 00.57 with W/C Tomes the senior pilot on duty for the first time. According to official records, he would not be appointed commanding officer officially until the 8th of January but clearly had assumed the role already. Each Lancaster was carrying a cookie and sixteen 500 pounders, not all of which was destined to reach its intended destination. Shortly after taking off, PB348 ran into severe icing conditions which caused both starboard engines to shut down. F/O Curran was unable to feather them, and the situation became even more serious when the a.s.i., froze. The bombs were jettisoned, and an attempt made to return to base, but after forty-five minutes of the most challenging flying, the order was given to abandon the Lancaster to its fate. All of the occupants landed safely, and the wreckage of the Lancaster was found on the beach to the north of Mablethorpe. The others continued on as part of the first of two waves heading for the unsuspecting target an hour apart, and it was approaching 04.00 as they lined up for the bombing run in cloudless skies and excellent visibility. The start of the attack was delayed for two minutes to allow misplaced markers to be corrected, but a red TI went down at 04.01 very close to the aiming point, and another fell in the middle of the town, near the beach, at which point, the Master Bomber called in the main force. The 57 Squadron crews carried out their attacks from 8,250 to 10,500 feet on Path Finder markers between 04.01 and 04.15 and witnessed a yellow oil fire at 04.08, which began to emit volumes of black smoke. This was just one of several large explosions created by the first phase of bombing, and the resultant fires would act as a beacon to the 1 Group force following behind. The attack destroyed about 85% of the town, and between five and eight hundred people lost their lives. In the event, the town was not taken, and it would be mid-April before the garrison surrendered. Six 5 Group Lancasters failed to return, two of them as the result of a collision on the way home over Allied territory.

A major attack was carried out by more than 650 aircraft of 1, 4, 6 and 8 Groups on Hannover on the night of the 5/6th, the first large-scale raid on this northern city since the series in the autumn of 1943. Massive damage was inflicted, but twenty-three Halifaxes and eight Lancasters failed to return in a sharp reminder that the Luftwaffe was not entirely spent. 5 Group had not been intended to operate on this night, but a rushed battle order came through to 5 Group stations at 18.30, which would lead to another late briefing and take-off for 131 crews. Eleven 57 Squadron Lancasters departed East Kirkby between 00.15 and 00.53 bound for the German supply column still trapped at Houffalize in the Belgian Ardennes. S/L Hodgkinson was the senior pilot on duty as they made their way south on a clear night above low cloud, which, over the target, formed thin layers of eight to ten-tenths cover between 4,000 and 10,000 feet. The marker force crews were able to identify the aiming-point visually, and the first red Mosquito-laid TIs were seen to go down close together, followed by greens at H-3. They were backed up to leave a compact group of reds and greens visible by their glow through the clouds, at which point, the Master Bomber, who was circling at 10,000 feet, called in the main force to bomb. The 57 Squadron crews complied from 5,250 to 11,000 feet between 03.01 and 03.07, while around a third of the force retained their bombs in accordance with instructions at briefing, if they failed to identify the aiming-point. Afterwards, one of the marker crews descended to 3,500 feet between the cloud layers, where they saw two large columns of smoke, the source of which could not be identified. Post-raid reconnaissance confirmed that the target had been bombed with great accuracy, and the success had been gained for the loss of two Lancasters.

On the following afternoon, 5 Group dispatched thirteen Lancasters for mining duties in the Spinach garden off the port of Gdynia and seven for Privet off Danzig. The 57 Squadron crews of F/Ls Hughes and Mersh and F/O Palling departed East Kirkby between 16.08 and 16.11 and reached the target area to find a layer of ten-tenths cloud with good visibility above. They established their positions by H2S before planting sixteen vegetables between them into the briefed locations from around 15,000 feet and returned safely after more than nine hours aloft to report a successful night's work.

A major operation against Munich was planned for the 7th, for which a two-wave force of 645 aircraft was drawn from all five of the Lancaster-equipped groups. 5 Group, which was unused to sharing this target, would lead the way with 213 Lancasters and three Mosquitos, leaving the second wave to follow on two hours later, the tanks of the heavy brigade containing sufficient fuel for a nine-hour round-trip. The 57 Squadron element of fifteen Lancasters departed East Kirkby as dusk was descending between 16.44 and 17.01 with S/L Hodgkinson the senior pilot on duty, but he and his crew would be forced to abandon their sortie after the hydraulics system failed some two hours into the flight. The others encountered broken medium-level cloud at 14,000 feet above the target, with haze or thin cloud below, by which time, the Master Bomber had made a visual identification of the aiming-point. He sent the first two primary blind markers in to deliver their TIs at the same time thirty seconds ahead of the planned opening of the attack and the flare force immediately afterwards to illuminate the city very effectively and allow ground detail to be identified. Red TIs went down west and east of the river Isar, bracketing the aiming-point, and the Master Bomber ordered the backers up to drop their TIs between the reds, after which, the next batch of flares formed a circle around the aiming-point. The main force was then called in, and the 57 Squadron participants delivered their loads accurately within the specified area from 15,700 to 20,000 feet between 20.31 and 20.44. The city was seen to be burning well as the force withdrew, and the glow of fires was still visible from up to 130 miles away. Two hours after the 5 Group attack, in what would become an established pattern, the 1, 3, 6 and 8 Group force arrived to complete the destruction of the central and some industrial districts, and this proved to be the final large-scale attack of the war on Munich. Fourteen Lancasters failed to return, but 57 Squadron maintained its loss-free start to the year.

With the exception of 617 Squadron, 5 Group remained on the ground for the ensuing six days, with snow-clearing providing exercise for all capable of wielding a shovel. The crews were, therefore, relieved to be called to briefing on the 13th to learn that 5 Group would be operating alone against the Wintershall oil refinery at Politz near Stettin. The plant had sustained damage in the previous attack in December, but production had not been halted, and a force of 218 Lancasters and seven Mosquitos was assembled for the return, of which a dozen of the Lancasters were provided by 57 Squadron. Under cover of the main event, ten Lancasters, including three representing 57 Squadron, were to mine the approaches to the area in the Geranium garden off the port of Swinemünde. Another dusk departure saw the bombing element take off between 16.06 and 16.22 with F/Ls Bennett and Shaw the senior pilots on duty, and they were followed into the air between 16.24 and 16.29 by the gardeners led by S/L Ward. The bomber stream crossed the North Sea at 1,500 feet in accordance with instructions to not climb until approaching the Danish coast at 19.30, and they arrived in the target area on time to find clear skies with slight haze, by which time the blind marker crews had identified the target by means of H2S and delivered their green TIs shortly after 22.00. The illuminators then dropped their flares, which caused ground detail to stand out, highlighted by the snow on the ground. A blind-bombing attack had been planned, but, because of the excellence of the conditions, Mosquitos were able to go in at low level to be followed soon afterwards by the main force. The plant was protected by fifty to eighty searchlights which were not troublesome and were employed largely in co-operation with night-fighters. The 57 Squadron crews bombed from 14,000 to 18,250 feet between 22.14 and 22.29 and a particularly large explosion at 22.17 sent a pall of black smoke into the air. Photographic reconnaissance confirmed that the plant had been severely damaged, while Bomber Command claimed it to be in ruins. Meanwhile, the gardeners had fulfilled their briefs and returned safely to complete a very satisfactory night's work.

Oil targets would continue to dominate during the remainder of the month, and a two-phase attack was planned for the following night against the I G Farbenindustrie A G Merseburg-Leuna refinery, which employed the Bergius process and lay some 250 miles from the Dutch frontier and five hundred miles from the bomber bases of eastern England. This was one of many similar sites situated in an arc on the western side of Leipzig from north to south. The first phase would be carried out by 5 Group, which detailed 210 Lancasters and nine Mosquitos, fifteen of the former contributed by 57 Squadron. They took off from East Kirkby between 16.09 and 16.38 with F/Ls Bennett, Langridge, Shaw and Warburton leading the way and headed for the Sussex coast near Brighton to begin the Channel crossing for the southern approach to eastern Germany. F/O Appleton and crew lost their starboard-inner engine and turned back, leaving the others to reach the target area and find clear skies but poor vertical visibility due to a layer of haze. In the event, this proved to be no hindrance to the primary blind markers, whose job was to establish their position over the aiming-point by means of H2S. They delivered their TIs from 18,000 feet, after which, the first element of the flare force went in. The Master Bomber called for ground marking only, which was carried out by the low-level Mosquito element, and, by 20.50, he was satisfied and sent the marker aircraft home. The main force crews produced what appeared to be concentrated bombing, those from 57 Squadron dropping their loads of a cookie and nine 500 pounders each onto red and green TIs from 13,000 to 16,600 feet between 21.01 and 21.08 with a fourteen-second overshoot in accordance with the Master Bomber's instructions. Returning crews reported explosions and smoke rising upwards as they turned for home, leaving behind them a beacon for the second wave of 363 Lancasters and five Mosquitos of 1, 6 and 8 Groups following three hours behind. They would add to the massive destruction, which effectively put the plant out of action for the remainder of the war.

Three oil plants were selected for attention on the night of the 16/17th, at Zeitz, near Liepzig, Wanne-Eickel in the Ruhr, and Brüx in north-western Czechoslovakia (now Most in the Czech Republic), some 140 miles due south of Berlin. It was for the last-mentioned that nine 57 Squadron crews were briefed as part of a 5 Group force of 224 Lancasters and six Mosquitos, which would be accompanied by seven 101 Squadron ABC Lancasters for RCM duties. They were each carrying a cookie and nine 500 pounders for what would be a nine-hour round-trip and departed East Kirkby between 17.42 and 17.57 with W/C Tomes the senior pilot on duty. There were ten early returns from the force, and among them was the 57 Squadron crew of F/O Campbell, who lost the use of their navigation equipment. The others reached the target area to encounter nine to ten-tenths low cloud with tops at 3,000 feet, which interfered with the low-level marking system. The four primary blind markers identified the target by means of H2S, and dropped green TIs, and they were followed by the first illuminators, who also relied on H2S to deliver their flares. It seems that a number of Mosquitos managed to get below the cloud base to put red TIs onto the aiming-point and reported that the greens were among the oil tanks. However, the reds were not generally visible through the clouds, and the Master Bomber called for skymarking, while informing flare force 3 that it would not be required. The 57 Squadron participants bombed either on the glow of the red TIs or on the cascading greens from 12,500 to 17,750 feet between 22.31 and 22.43, and observed many explosions and large columns of thick, black smoke emerging through the cloud tops. Photo-reconnaissance would confirm that massive damage had been inflicted upon the plant, and a severe setback delivered to the enemy's oil production.

Adverse weather conditions would ensure that there would be no further operations for 5 Group during the month, although a number would be posted before being cancelled. The squadron spent the period inducting new crews, attending lectures, training, and, during the last few days, clearing snow from the runways. During the course of the month, ten operations were undertaken, and 104 sorties dispatched for the loss of a single Lancaster and there were no crew casualties.

February 1945

The weather at the start of February provided difficult conditions for marking and bombing, particularly for 5 Group, and a number of operations would struggle to achieve their aims in the face of thick, low cloud and strong winds. 5 Group was back in harness immediately at the start of the new month following the long lay-off, and 271 Lancaster and eleven Mosquito crews were called to briefings on all 5 Group stations on the 1st to learn that their target was to be the marshalling yards in the town of Siegen, situated some fifty miles east of Cologne. This was a 5 Group show, and was one of three major operations planned for the night, the others, by larger forces, taking place at Ludwigshafen and Mainz further into southern Germany. A high wind during the night had helped to clear some of the snow, and the nineteen 57 Squadron Lancasters took off without incident between 16.00 and 16.30 with W/C Tomes and S/L Hodgkinson the senior pilots on duty. They were carrying a variety of loads with cookies, 2,000, 1,000 and 500 pounders in use along with 4lb incendiaries, all of which reached the target area shortly after 19.00. Ten-tenths cloud was encountered at between 3,000 and 7,000 feet, which caused problems for the flare and marker force, some of which were finding it difficult to obtain a clear H2S image on their screens. Eventually, one of the primary blind markers ran in and dropped green TIs at 19.05 from 15,000 feet, and their glow was visible through the clouds. This prompted the first flares, followed by an attempt to mark at low-level with red TIs, which were not visible through the clouds, and, when the Master Bomber called for skymarking at 19.10, the remaining illuminator aircraft were superfluous to requirements and were sent home. The bombing phase was put back by four minutes until 19.20, forcing crews to either orbit or dogleg to waste time if they were still on approach, and then instructions were issued to aim at the skymarkers, which were being driven by the strong wind across the intended aiming-point and beyond the target. The glow of red target indicators was faintly visible through the clouds, but this was most likely a decoy fire site prepared by the Germans. It attracted many bomb loads, perhaps some from the 57 Squadron participants, who carried out their attacks from 8,000 to 12,000 feet between 19.19 and 19.37, contributing to what became a widely scattered raid. Much of the bombing fell into open and wooded country, and, although the railway station sustained damage, the marshalling yards escaped.

The next briefing revealed the bad news that a tour of operations was to be increased again to thirty-six sorties. Seventeen 57 Squadron crews were in attendance at 15.00 on a drizzly afternoon on the 2nd, to be told further, that the night's operation was to be against Karlsruhe, a city in southern Germany. This was to be another 5 Group effort involving 250 Lancasters and eleven Mosquitos, and was again, one of three major operations taking place. Wiesbaden was to receive its one and only major raid of the war at the hands of almost five hundred aircraft, while a 320-strong predominantly Halifax force dealt with an oil plant at Wanne-Eickel in the Ruhr. The 57 Squadron element departed East Kirkby between 19.38 and 20.11 with S/L Hodgkinson the senior pilot on duty and headed for the assembly point over Reading. F/O Ross and crew returned early for an undisclosed reason, while the remainder pressed on in winds that turned out to be lighter than forecast, and this caused a change in route, which now took the force directly from Reading to the target, straddling the Franco-Belgian frontier all the way to Germany, where they encountered heavy cloud between 3,000 and 15,000 feet. The flare force arrived over the target at 17,500 to 18,500 feet between 23.03 and 23.28 and tried to perform their assigned tasks in difficult conditions, some with malfunctioning H2S boxes. The Mosquito crews attempted to establish an aiming-point, but the illumination was not getting through to the ground, and, even had they dropped red TIs, it is unlikely that they would have been visible. At 23.11 the Master Bomber called for skymarking and sent the Mosquitos and remaining illuminators home. He ordered the main force crews to bomb on the southern edge of the glow from the descending green Wanganui flares and the 57 Squadron crews complied from 12,000 to 17,000 feet between 23.16 and 23.31. On return, F/L Hughes and crew claimed one Me410 destroyed and another probably so. This final raid of the war on Karlsruhe was a complete failure, and cost fourteen Lancasters, four of them from 189 Squadron.

While the frontier towns of Goch and Cleves were being pounded by the other groups on the night of the 7/8th, ahead of the advancing British XXX Corps, 5 Group returned to the Dortmund-Ems Canal at Ladbergen with 177 Lancasters and eleven Mosquitos, the heavy brigade carrying delayed action bombs. 57 Squadron made ready a dozen Lancasters for the main operation and three others to be occupied by the crews of F/L Hughes and F/Os Palling and Ross for mining duties in the Forget-me-not garden in Kiel harbour. The latter element departed East Kirkby first at 19.20, leaving the bombing brigade to follow them into the air between 20.42 and 21.08 led by W/C Tomes and S/L Ward. The bombing element all reached the target area to find seven to ten-tenths cloud at between 6,000 and 9,000 feet and quite widely scattered red TIs, and, in the absence of clear instructions from the Master Bomber, were uncertain which to aim for. Having selected a red TI or at least its glow, nine of the 57 Squadron crews released their twelve or fourteen 1,000 pounders each from 9,200 to 11,500 feet between 23.59 and 00.14 and returned unconvinced of the effectiveness of the operation. It turned out to be a rare unsuccessful attack on this target, photographic reconnaissance revealing that the bombs had fallen into fields and had failed to cause any breach. Meanwhile, the gardeners had established their positions by H2S and had delivered their mines into the briefed locations through a layer of thin cloud at 8,000 feet.

Nineteen 57 Squadron crews found themselves at briefing on the following day to learn of another long round-trip to the Wintershall oil refinery at Politz as part of a 5 Group force of 227 Lancasters and seven Mosquitos. They were to act as the first wave in a two-phase attack, which would be completed two hours later by 248 Lancasters from 1 and 8 Groups. They departed East Kirkby between 16.34 and 17.25 with S/L Hodgkinson the senior pilot on duty, and all made it across northern Jutland to enter Swedish air space near Helsingborg before turning south on a direct heading for the target. It was not unusual to violate Swedish air space intentionally, and the Swedes would normally respond with inaccurate warning flak, but, on this night, it brought down PB382 to crash on farmland at Hjortshög, killing all but the pilot, F/O Clifton RAAF, who was interned. The blind marker and flare force crews went in at 13,000 to 14,500 feet between 21.03 and 21.15 to carry out their assigned tasks in the face of an ineffective smoke screen, which covered all ground detail but the tops of the tall chimneys. Fierce night-fighter activity was evident to the main force crews as they reached the target area to find clear skies and excellent visibility and those from 57 Squadron identified the aiming point in the light of the illuminating flares before delivering their loads onto red TIs in accordance with the Master Bomber's instructions. A series of up to six violent explosions was witnessed including two of particular note at 21.18 and 21.23 and smoke was rising through 3,000 feet as they turned away to the west, confident in the quality of their work. 1 and 8 Groups completed the destruction of the plant, and no more synthetic oil would be produced before war's end.

Briefings took place on the 13th for the first round of Operation Thunderclap, the Churchill inspired offensive against Germany's eastern cities, which was devised partly to act in support of the advancing Russians, and also as a demonstration to Stalin of RAF air power, should he turn against the Allies after the war. The historic and culturally significant city of Dresden was selected to open the offensive in another two-phase affair, with a 5 Group force of 246 Lancasters and nine Mosquitos leading the way, to be followed three hours later by 529 Lancasters of 1, 3, 6 and 8 Groups. It had proved to be a successful policy thus far, with the 5 Group low-level marking system and main force attacks providing a beacon for the second force, and should it be required on this night, 8 Group would provide any necessary marking for phase two from high level. The 57 Squadron contingent of eighteen Lancasters took off between 17.50 and 18.08 with S/L Ward the senior pilot on duty, and the crews had absolutely no concept of the ramifications of the operation, both in terms of its outcome on the ground, and its hysterical aftermath. Dresden was Germany's seventh largest city, and its largest remaining largely un-bombed built-up area, which, according to American sources, contained more than a hundred factories and fifty thousand workers contributing to the war effort. It was also an important railway hub, to the extent that the marshalling yards had been attacked twice in late 1944 by the USAAF.

The heavy force was two hours out when W/C Maurice Smith of 54 Base, the Master Bomber for the 5 Group attack, lifted off the Woodhall Spa runway at a few minutes before 20.00 hours in Mosquito KB401 AZ-E, a 627 Squadron aircraft, and he was followed away by eight others from 627 Squadron. The heavy brigade and the Mosquitos arrived in the target area at the same time to encounter three layers of cloud, between 3,000 and 5,000 feet, 6,000 to 8,000 feet and 15,000 to 16,000 feet, but otherwise good visibility. The first primary blind marker delivered green TIs from 15,000 feet at 22.03, and was followed in by the flare force, which lit the way for the low-level Mosquitos. The main force Lancasters were carrying eight hundred tons of bombs, those representing 57 Squadron in the form either of a cookie and twelve 500 pounders or one 2,000 pounder and fourteen cluster bombs, and these were delivered from around 13,000 to 15,000 feet onto the glow of red TIs in accordance with the Master Bomber's instructions. As far as the crews were concerned this was no different from any other attack, and the fires visible for more than a hundred and fifty miles into the return journey nothing out of the ordinary.

By the time the second force of 1, 3, 6 and 8 Group Lancasters arrived over Dresden three hours after 5 Group, the skies had cleared, and the fires created by the earlier attack provided the expected reference point. A further eighteen hundred tons of bombs rained down onto the historic and beautiful old city, setting off the same chain of events that had devastated parts of Hamburg in July 1943 and a number of other cities since. Dresden's population had been swelled by masses of refugees fleeing from the eastern front, and many were engulfed in the ensuing firestorm. On the following morning, three hundred American bombers carried out a separate attack under the umbrella of a fighter escort and completed the destruction. There were claims that RAF aircraft had strafed the streets and open spaces to increase the level of terror, and such accusations abound in the city to this day. In fact, American fighters were responsible, and were trying to add to the general confusion and chaos. Initial propaganda-inspired reports from the Office of the Propaganda Minister, Joseph Goebbels, falsely claimed a death toll of 250,000 people, but an accurate figure of twenty-five thousand has been settled upon since.

The destruction of Dresden has been used even by some in this country as a weapon with which to denigrate Bomber Command and Harris, and label them as war criminals. Curiously, no accusations have been levelled at the Americans. It should also be understood that Harris had no interest in attacking Dresden and had to be nagged by Chief-of-the-Air-Staff Portal to fulfil Churchill's wishes. The aircrew simply did the job asked of them, and the Dresden raid was no different from any other attack on a city. The death toll at Hamburg was much higher, and yet, there has been no similar outcry. The legacy of this operation served to deny Harris and the men under his Command their due recognition for the massive part they played in the ultimate victory, and only in recent times has a monument been erected in Green Park in London and a campaign clasp awarded, sadly, far too late for the majority. Churchill, with his eyes set on a peacetime election, betrayed Harris and the Command in a typical politically motivated U-turn, in which he accused Harris of bombing solely for the purpose of inflicting terror. In the post-war honours, Harris was the only commander in the field to be denied recognition.

Round two of Thunderclap was planned for the following night, when Chemnitz was posted as the target for 717 aircraft drawn from 1, 3, 4, 6 and 8 Groups, while 224 Lancasters and eight Mosquitos of 5 Group targeted an oil refinery in the small town of Rositz, situated twenty-five miles due south of Leipzig and thirty miles north-west of Chemnitz. Sixteen 57 Squadron Lancasters were made ready, and they all departed East Kirkby safely between 16.29 and 17.15

with S/L Hodgkinson the senior pilot on duty. They pushed on across Germany to be greeted by six to ten-tenths thin cloud in the target area in two layers, one at 6,000 to 8,000 feet, and the other at 10,000 to 12,000 feet, but the primary blind marker made a good run on H2S at 15,000 feet at 20.48 to drop green TIs, and the illuminators followed up between 20.51 and 20.58 from a similar height. The main force crews arriving on time carried out support runs with the marker element, before being called in to bomb at 21.07, those from 57 Squadron carrying out their attacks on red and green TIs, or on their glow, from 7,200 to 11,500 feet between 21.01 and 21.15. Three or four large fires were evident in the oil plant, and black smoke was rising through 5,000 feet as the force turned away. It was established afterwards, that the southern part of the site had been damaged, but it would be necessary to return to finish the job. The Chemnitz raid had been compromised by adverse weather conditions, and it would be March before success was achieved against this target.

On the 15th, 5 Group dispatched eight Lancasters on mining duties in one of the Silverthorn gardens in the Kattegat and among them were those carrying the 57 Squadron crews of S/L Ward and F/O Palling. They departed East Kirkby at 17.15 and employed H2S to establish their positions over the cloud-covered drop zone, before delivering six mines each and landing at Kinloss after a round trip of more than six hours.

An oil refinery at Böhlen was posted as the target on the 19th for a 5 Group force of 264 Lancasters and six Mosquitos. It was another of the collection of similar plants in the Leipzig area and some ten miles north of Rositz, for which 57 Squadron dispatched sixteen Lancasters in a late take-off between 23.43 and 00.02 with S/L Hodgkinson the senior pilot on duty. They all completed the three-and-a-half-hour flight out and would meet up with the later-departing Mosquito element at the target, among them the Master Bomber for the occasion, 54 Base's W/C Benjamin, who was flying the same Mosquito used by W/C Smith at Dresden six nights earlier. They encountered ten-tenths cloud over the target in two layers at 5,000 to 8,000 feet and 10,000 to 14,000 feet, and this would introduce a challenging element to the operation. The illuminators went in at around 15,000 feet between 04.05 and 04.13, and the VHF chatter suggested that a Mosquito had been able to mark a factory building with a red TI, which had been backed up. The main force was called in, before W/C Benjamin's VHF was suddenly cut off, and his Deputy took over. It would be established later, that the Master Bomber's Mosquito had been shot down by flak, and that W/C Benjamin DFC & Bar had died alongside his navigator. The 57 Squadron crews carried out their attacks in accordance with confusing instructions from 9,000 to 13,000 feet between 04.16 and 04.35, aiming mostly at the glow in the cloud of red and green TIs. Post-raid reconnaissance revealed only superficial damage to the site, which would have to be attacked again.

The following night, the 20th, proved to be a busy one, with more than five hundred Lancasters targeting Dortmund, while 268 Halifaxes from 4 and 6 Groups provided the heavy elements for raids on Rhenania-Ossag oil refineries in Düsseldorf and Monheim. 5 Group, meanwhile, prepared itself for a further attempt on the Mittelland Canal at Gravenhorst, for which eleven 57 Squadron crews were briefed as part of an overall force of 154 Lancasters and eleven Mosquitos. They departed East Kirkby between 21.35 and 21.47 with S/L Ward the senior pilot on duty, and all reached the target area to find ten-tenths cloud between them and the aiming-point. The primary blind marker succeeded in delivering two green TIs by H2S from 12,000 feet at 00.53, and they fell on the starboard side of the canal. After the flare force went in, the Mosquito element descended to 400 feet, but could not identify the aiming-point, and, just before H-Hour, the Master Bomber sent the markers home, to be followed almost immediately by the main force as he abandoned the operation.

The operation was rescheduled for twenty-four hours later, when Duisburg and Worms were also to be attacked by heavy forces of 362 and 349 aircraft respectively. 5 Group detailed 165 Lancasters and twelve Mosquitos, and, among those attending the briefing at Coningsby was G/C Evans-Evans, the station commander, who would be taking the bulk of the 83 Squadron commanding officer's highly experienced crew with him. Evans-Evans was 43 years old and a larger-than-life character, who had commanded 115 Squadron for a spell earlier in the war during its Wellington era and had never lost the enthusiasm to be "one of the boys" and take part in operations. A number of years of good living had widened his girth, and it must have been a struggle to fit into the cramped confines of a Lancaster cockpit. The thirteen 57 Squadron participants took off between 17.16 and 17.25 with S/L Ward the senior pilot on duty and reached the target area to find moonlight beaming down from clear skies with some ground haze. One of the primary blind markers was able to deliver his green TIs, but two minutes late because of a change in the wind, and they fell about a mile south of the aiming-point, quite close to the Wet Triangle meeting point of the Mittelland and Dortmund-Ems Canals. After the flare force had done its job, the Mosquitos delivered their red TIs, which were backed up successfully, before the main force was called in at 20.25. The 57 Squadron crews released their loads of eleven to thirteen 1,000 pounders each from 8,000 to 11,000 feet between 20.31 and 20.43 but could not assess the outcome because of the use of long-delay fuses. The presence of night-fighters was clearly evident by the number of combats taking place, and among nine missing Lancasters was the one belonging to 83 Squadron containing G/C Evans-Evans and seven others. Only the rear gunner survived, and particularly tragic was the loss of the twenty-two-year-old navigator, S/L Wishart DSO, DFC & Bar, who had completed sixty-one operations in Lancasters with 97 Squadron and eighteen in Mosquitos as navigator to Master Bombers. G/C Ingham was left deeply saddened by the loss of his crew.

55 Base did not take part in the 5 Group operation by seventy-four Lancasters to bomb what was believed to be a U-Boot base at Horten in Oslo Fjord on the night of the 23/24th. Whether or not a U-Boot base existed is uncertain, but no shipping was seen by the crews, and a local report described heavy damage in the port area and a shipyard, and the sinking of a tanker and floating crane. While this operation was in progress, seven others from the group sneaked in under cover of the main event to mine the waters of the Onion garden in Oslo harbour, a little further north. F/O Palling and crew took off at 17.25 as the sole 57 Squadron representative but were thwarted by H2S failure and were unable to fulfil their brief.

Meanwhile, some 770 miles to the south, a force of 366 Lancasters, plus one from the Film Unit, and thirteen Mosquitos drawn from 1, 6 and 8 Groups had been sent against the city of Pforzheim, situated in southern Germany between Karlsruhe to the north-west and Stuttgart to the south-east. This would be the first area raid on the city, which was known as a centre for jewellery and watch manufacture but was believed by the Allies to be involved in the production of precision instruments in support of Germany's war effort. They were greeted by clear skies and bright moonlight in the target area, and the thin veil of ground haze proved to be no impediment as the first red Oboe TIs went down at 19.52, to be followed quickly by illuminator flares and salvoes of concentrated reds and greens. Fires rapidly took hold until the whole town north of the river looked like a sea of flames, and, by 20.06, the fires were too dazzling for the TIs to be visible, after which, the Master Bomber ordered the smoke to be bombed. The raid lasted twenty-two minutes, during which 1,825 tons of bombs fell into the built-up area, reducing 83% of it to ruins and setting off a firestorm in which 17,600 people lost their lives. This was the highest death toll to result from a single attack on a German city after Hamburg (40,000) and Dresden (25,000). It was during this operation that the final Victoria Cross was earned by a member of RAF Bomber Command. It went posthumously to the Master Bomber from 582 Squadron, Captain Ed Swales of the South African Air Force, who continued to control the attack in a Lancaster severely damaged by a night-fighter, before sacrificing his life to allow his crew to abandon the stricken aircraft.

A daylight attack on the Dortmund-Ems Canal at Ladbergen was planned for the afternoon of the 24th, and would involve 166 Lancasters and five Mosquitos, eighteen of the former provided by 617 Squadron with Tallboys on board, while 57 Squadron contributed thirteen, each loaded with 1,000 pounders. They departed East Kirkby between 13.54 and 14.02 led by five pilots of flight lieutenant rank and reached the target accompanied by an 11 Group fighter escort to encounter ten-tenths cloud with tops at between 4,000 and 9,000 feet, at which point, the Master Bomber abandoned the operation and sent the force home with its bombs. Once back home at their respective stations, crews complained about the unsatisfactory forming up of Base gaggles, which had been generally chaotic.

During the course of the month the squadron carried out eleven operations, including those aborted, and dispatched 157 sorties for the loss of a single Lancaster and crew, whose pilot was enjoying the legendary hospitality of his Swedish hosts.

March 1945

The new month would see the Command bludgeon its way across Germany, concentrating on oil, rail and road targets, along with the few towns still boasting a built-up area. The new 5 Group A-O-C, AVM Constantine, visited 55 Base stations on the 1st, having succeeded AVM Cochrane on his departure to head Transport Command. Mannheim was raided for the last time in numbers by a large force from 1, 6 and 8 Groups on that day, while 5 Group remained at home. The month began for 57 Squadron with a tragic collision between F/O Anscomb's ND572 and ME473 of 207 Squadron, during a night fighter affiliation exercise. Both Lancasters crashed on Fen Farm, Ruskington, some four miles north-north-east of Sleaford at 01.18 on the 2nd, killing all sixteen men on board, including an ATC cadet in the 57 Squadron aircraft, who was gaining air experience. Later, on the 2nd, Cologne was pounded for the final time, first by a force of seven hundred aircraft, which inflicted huge destruction across the city, particularly west of the Rhine, and, later, by a 3 Group force, of which only fifteen bombed because of a faulty G-H station in England. The city ceased to function, thereafter, and was still paralyzed when American forces marched in four days later. Just when it seemed that German resistance to air attack might end, March would prove that the defenders were still capable of mounting a challenge, even though they were stretched beyond their capacity to protect every corner of the Reich.

5 Group opened its March account with a return to the Ladbergen aqueduct section of the Dortmund-Ems Canal on the evening of the 3rd, for which 212 Lancasters and ten Mosquitos were made ready. Fifteen 57 Squadron crews attended briefing, thirteen to learn of their part in the main event, while those of F/Ls Hughes and Mersh were assigned to mining duties in the Tomato garden at the southern end of Oslo Fjord. The latter pair departed East Kirkby first at 17.21 and 17.30, to be followed into the air between 18.42 and 18.57 by the bombing brigade led by four pilots of flight lieutenant rank, each crew sitting on twelve or thirteen 1,000 pounders with long delay fuses. They encountered eight to ten-tenths cloud in the target area at between 3,500 and 6,000 feet, and it was noted that the defences had been strengthened since the last attack and were throwing up a curtain of intense light flak as high as 15,000 feet. H2S allowed the two 83 Squadron primary blind markers to locate the canal and deliver their green TIs from 14,000 feet at 21.47 and 21.49, and the first illuminators went in a minute later to light the way for the Mosquitos, after which, a large red glow could be seen through the clouds. At 21.59, the Master Bomber called in the main force to bomb on the glow or on sight of the TIs through gaps in the thin cloud, and the 57 Squadron crews complied from around 8,000 to 10,000 feet between 21.45 and 22.12. They contributed to the breaching of both branches, which rendered the waterway unnavigable and out of action for the remainder of the war.

Meanwhile, the gardeners had found clear skies and good visibility over Oslo Fjord and had delivered their mines unopposed into the briefed locations. The Luftwaffe launched Operation Gisella on this night, sending two hundred fighters to stalk the bombers as they returned to their stations. East Kirkby came under attack after four 57 Squadron Lancasters had landed safely, and the remaining nine were diverted to other airfields, seven to Bruntingthorpe and one to Bitteswell, both in Leicestershire and one to Lichfield. Squadron offices and buildings were damaged by cannon shells and a squadron signals analysis officer killed, while the WAAF commanding officer, the squadron gunnery leader and two others sustained wounds that required hospital treatment. Twenty bombers were shot down, and this demonstrated the possible impact on Bomber Command operations had Hitler not restricted this type of operation on the basis that it made better propaganda to show downed bombers on German rather than English soil.

Twenty-one 57 Squadron crews attended briefing on the 5th, to learn that 5 Group would be sending 248 Lancasters and ten Mosquitos back to Böhlen, for another crack at the synthetic oil refinery. A simultaneous operation by a Thunderclap force of 760 aircraft would attempt to redress the recent failure at Chemnitz, some thirty-five miles to the south. Take-off from East Kirkby was accomplished without incident between 16.51 and 17.21 with a whole host of flight lieutenants representing the senior pilots on duty, and with the exception of F/O Kirton and crew, whose intercom failed, all reached the target area, some after climbing above 15,000 feet to escape icing conditions. Ten-tenths cloud lay over the target in layers between 2,000 and 11,000 feet, but uncertainty concerning the prevailing conditions on arrival had been anticipated and two marking plans prepared, low-level and skymarking, and the lead primary blind marker made his first run at 14,000 feet to drop green TIs at 21.40. He did not see them burst because of the cloud but thought that the illuminator flares were well-placed. Some of the Coningsby crews experienced H2S difficulties, and not all were able to pinpoint on Leipzig for the run-in. This meant that they were unsure of their position, and, when the Master Bomber called for Wanganui flares at 21.45, they withheld them, rather than risk dropping them inaccurately and attracting some of the bombing. A large explosion was witnessed at 21.50, and, three minutes later, Wanganui flares were observed by the approaching main force element. The 57 Squadron crews delivered their cookie and twelve 500 pounders each from 9,500 to 14,000 feet between 21.51 and 22.03, observing another large explosion at 21.57, before the Master Bomber called a halt at 22.01 and sent everyone home, leaving evidence of fires and smoke behind them. F/O Dimond RAAF and crew were low on fuel and attempted a landing at Bramcote, near Nuneaton in Warwickshire, writing off NG410 in the process. Post-raid reconnaissance revealed extensive damage to the coal-drying plant, and some hits in other areas of the site, but it was still not a knockout blow. Meanwhile, the Thunderclap force had succeeded in inflicting severe fire damage in central and southern districts of Chemnitz.

The target posted on 5 Group stations on the 6th was the town and port area of Sassnitz, located on the Baltic Island of Rügen, about thirty miles north of Peenemünde, a region with memories of heavy casualties sustained by 5 Group in August 1943. The two-fold purpose of the operation was to destroy the port installations and facilities and sink shipping to render it unusable as a refuge for escaping Kriegsmarine units. 150 Lancasters and seven Mosquitos were made ready, eleven of the former by 57 Squadron, which also loaded five others with mines destined for the Willow garden on the approaches to Sassnitz. The two elements departed East Kirkby together between 18.12 and 18.25 with no senior pilots leading the bombing brigade and four of flight lieutenant rank among the gardeners. They reached the target area to find five to nine-tenths drifting cloud with tops in places at 8,000 feet. An 83 Squadron blind marker made a run at 22.50 to drop green TIs over the port from 12,000 feet, and the flare force maintained illumination of the town and outer harbour for the next twenty-five minutes. Apart from a short break, when cloud slid across the aiming-point, the markers remained visible to the main force crews, and those from 57 Squadron bombed on red TIs from 8,200 to 10,000 feet between 23.00 and 23.16, some after orbiting to await a clear view of the ground. Bombing activity ceased at H+18, and those with bombs still aboard took them home. A destroyer was observed to blow up after receiving a direct hit by a large bomb and may have been one of three large ships identified and attacked in the harbour, and, according to post-raid reconnaissance, sunk, and there was also extensive damage in the northern part of the town. Meanwhile, the gardeners had encountered five to seven-tenths cloud with tops at 9,000 feet and dropped their six mines each into the allotted location before returning safely.

It was back to the oil campaign for 5 Group on the following night, for an attack on the Rhenania-Ossag synthetic oil plant at Harburg, south of Hamburg, for which a force of 234 Lancasters and seven Mosquitos was made ready. They would not be alone over Germany, however, as more than a thousand other aircraft would be engaged against similar targets at Dessau and Hemmingstedt and in minor and support operations. 57 Squadron provided sixteen Lancasters, which took off between 17.59 and 18.25 with S/L Hodgkinson the senior pilot on duty. The force arrived over the target to find eight-tenths thin cloud and red and yellow target indicators clearly visible, which they bombed in accordance with the Master Bomber's instructions with a seven-second overshoot from 10,000 to 13,000 feet between 21.56 and 22.13. Bomb bursts were clearly seen, along with explosions and black smoke rising through 10,000 feet, and all but one from 57 Squadron returned safely to East Kirkby, confident in the success of the operation. PB852 disappeared without trace with the crew of F/O Baush, who were on their twenty-sixth sortie. 5 Group distinguished itself on this night by claiming the destruction of seven enemy fighters, one of them, a FW190 shot down over the target by the crew of F/O Meeking. Post-raid reconnaissance confirmed further damage to this previously attacked target, with oil storage tanks taking the most hits, and revealed that a rubber factory had also been severely damaged.

An all-time record was set on the 11th, when 1,079 aircraft, the largest Bomber Command force ever for a single target, was assembled to attack Essen for the last time. 5 Group contributed 199 Lancasters and a single Mosquito, 57 Squadron loading fifteen Lancasters with a cookie and sixteen 500 pounders each and dispatching them between 11.57 and 12.08 with W/C Tomes the senior pilot on duty. They found the target city covered by ten-tenths cloud with tops at 6,000 feet, which required the Path Finder element to employ skymarkers in the form of red and blue smoke puffs, and these were bombed by the 57 Squadron crews from around 16,000 to 19,000 feet between 15.17 and 15.24. More than 4,600 tons of bombs were dropped into the already ravaged city and former industrial powerhouse and left it with smoke rising through 10,000 feet as the force turned away. It would still be in a state of paralysis when the American ground forces captured it unopposed on the 10th of April. Operations were not yet over for the 11th, as 5 Group sent eleven Lancasters that night to mine the approaches to Oslo harbour in the Onion III garden. The crews of F/L Langridge and F/O Keen departed East Kirkby at 17.40 and found the target area to be under clear skies with good visibility. They identified the drop zone by H2S, before making timed runs to deliver their stores and return safely.

A little over twenty-four hours after the launching of the Essen raid, the short-lived record was surpassed by the departure from their stations in the early afternoon of 1,108 aircraft, which had Dortmund as their destination. This time 5 Group provided 211 Lancasters, seventeen of them from 57 Squadron, which departed East Kirkby between 13.18 and 13.41 with W/C Tomes the senior pilot on duty. Each was carrying a cookie and sixteen 500 pounders, which arrived over the eastern Ruhr to find it still under a blanket of ten-tenths cloud, this time with tops at 6,000 feet. The Path Finders marked the target with green and blue smoke puffs, and the main force was directed by the Master Bomber to aim for the blues, which the 57 Squadron crews strived to do from 13,000 to 17,000 feet between 16.45 and 16.48. Returning crews spoke of brown smoke climbing through the clouds to 8,000 feet from the northern end of the city, and also a ring of smoke encircling the area. In fact, the smoke was so dense, that it remained visible for 120 miles into the return flight. A new record of 4,800 tons of bombs had been delivered, and photo-reconnaissance revealed that the central and southern districts of the city had received the greatest weight and had been left in chaos with all industry silenced permanently and railway tracks torn up.

The Group's next objective was the Wintershall oil refinery at Lützkendorf, another site to the west of Leipzig and south-west of Leuna in the Geiseltal. *(Lützkendorf no longer exists on a map of Germany and is now known as either Mücheln or Krumpa)*. The briefing of 244 Lancaster and eleven Mosquito crews took place on the 14th, seventeen of the former representing 57 Squadron, and they departed East Kirkby between 16.58 and 17.11 led by pilots of flight lieutenant rank. They headed out over the Wash and the bulge of East Anglia en-route to the Scheldt Estuary and crossed Belgium to swing south of Cologne, before pointing their snouts to the east for the long leg to the target. They were met on arrival by conditions described variously as ten-tenths cloud, no cloud, thin layer of cloud, thin banks of stratus with tops at 12,000 feet, a little medium cloud, poor visibility and good visibility, but there was unanimity with regard to the haze. Ahead, the primary blind markers could be seen delivering their green TIs at 21.49, followed by the illuminators immediately afterwards between 21.51 and 22.00 to drop flares and bombs. Finally, the low-level Mosquitos did their job to accurately mark the aiming-point before the main force crews were called in, and the 57 Squadron participants bombed on red and green TIs in accordance with the Master Bomber's instructions from 8,000 to 11,000 feet between 22.03 and 22.11. Returning crews claimed an accurate attack, reporting explosions and fires and thick black smoke drifting across the plant and ascending through 7,000 feet, which rendered impossible a detailed assessment. Night-fighters were very much in evidence over the target and during the return flight, and a hefty eighteen Lancasters failed to return, 7.4% of those dispatched. Among them was 57 Squadron's NG398, which crashed in southern Germany with no survivors from the crew of F/O Pauline RAAF. Post-raid reconnaissance revealed a partially successful operation, which meant that a further visit would be required.

Fourteen 57 Squadron crews assembled in the briefing room at 14.00 on the 16th, to learn that they were to attack the virgin target of Würzburg, a small city on the river Main, situated some sixty miles south-east of Frankfurt in southern Germany. While this operation was in progress, a similar-sized force, drawn from 1 and 8 Groups, would be delivering the final attack of the war on Nuremberg, fifty miles to the south-east. A 5 Group force of 225 Lancasters and eleven Mosquitos was made ready for an early-evening take-off, and the 57 Squadron element got away between 17.26 and 17.35 with W/C Tomes the senior pilot on duty. They reached the target area to find clear skies with ground haze and the marking and flare forces ahead of them carrying out their assigned tasks between 21.25 and 21.34 to leave the way clear for the main force crews to exploit the favourable bombing conditions. They found red and yellow target indicators marking the aiming-point and complied with the Master Bomber's call for a sixteen-second overshoot for their cookies and incendiaries. All but a single 630 Squadron Lancaster returned to East Kirkby apparently without incident to report a successful operation but had to wait for the reconnaissance reports to discover the extent of the destruction. The bombing had lasted just seventeen minutes, during which period 1,127 tons of bombs had fallen into the historic old cathedral city, destroying an estimated 89% of the built-up area and killing four to five thousand people. The Nuremberg operation had also been highly destructive, but had cost 1 Group twenty-four Lancasters, thus proving, that the enemy defences were still capable of giving the Command a bloody nose. There was still business to attend to at the Böhlen oil refinery, and 5 Group prepared a force of 236 Lancasters and eleven Mosquitos on the 20th, to deal what was hoped to be the knockout blow. Briefings began at 20.00, and at East Kirkby was attended by fifteen 57 Squadron crews, a dozen of which would participate in the main event and three in a small-scale diversionary raid on Halle, situated some twenty miles to the north-west of Leipzig. They took off together between 23.31 and 23.49 with S/L Hodgkinson the senior pilot on duty and each Lancaster carrying a cookie and up to fourteen 500 pounders. A few minutes after leaving the ground, RA530 returned to it and crashed into a house in the village of Stickney some four miles south of the airfield, killing the pilot, F/O Cobern RAAF, and three of his crew and injuring three others, one of whom would succumb on the 1st of April. The others set out on the now familiar path to eastern Germany and arrived in the target area to encounter reasonably favourable conditions with three to six-tenths cloud topping out at 6,000 to 8,000 feet. The bomber stream arrived early because of stronger-than-forecast winds, and the main force had to orbit while the first primary blind marker crew delivered green TIs at 03.33. They fell 750 yards south of the plant, to be followed at H-16 by a yellow TI bursting two miles short of the target. A cluster of illuminator flares ignited ahead, revealing that a smoke screen had been activated and was generating much smoke to create difficulties for the Mosquito low-level markers, despite which, they deposited red TIs on the button, and the main force was called in. A few dummy TIs attracted a number of bomb loads, but the 57 Squadron crews complied with the instructions of the Master Bomber to bomb on specific reds and yellows from 10,500 to 15,500 feet between 03.44 and 03.55. The main weight of the attack was concentrated around the target, and numerous explosions were witnessed, as was smoke rising through 5,000 feet as they turned away. LM653 failed to return from the diversionary raid having come down in the Hannover defence zone with fatal consequences for the predominantly Australian crew of F/L Palling RAAF, who were on their thirty-third operation and tantalizingly close to going home. The operation put the oil plant out of action, and it was still idle when American forces moved in a few weeks later.

It was after 22.00 on the 21st that 151 Lancaster and eight Mosquito crews of 5 Group were informed that the Deutsche Erdölwerke synthetic oil refinery at Hamburg was to be their target that night. 57 Squadron loaded a eleven of its Lancasters with a cookie and sixteen 500 pounders each, and sent them into the air between 01.06 and 01.46 with W/C Tomes the senior pilot on duty. They pinpointed on the Danish coast to approach the target from the north, and found thin stratus cloud at around 2,000 feet, through which the primary blind marker aircraft dropped green TIs on H2S from 14,000 feet at 03.55. The first illuminator Lancasters went in thirty seconds later and continued to light up the aiming-point until 04.01, by which time the Mosquitos had marked, allowing the main force to be called in at 04.05. The 57 Squadron crews bombed from 15,500 to 18,000 feet between 04.06 and 04.15, observing many fires and a large explosion at 04.11 that produced red flame and black smoke. Another was reported at 04.16, and it was clear to the homebound crews that the attack had been successful, a fact confirmed by post-raid reconnaissance, which revealed that twenty storage tanks had been destroyed in exchange for the loss of just four Lancasters.

The 55 Base squadrons were not involved in 5 Group's operations against railway bridges at Nienburg and Bremen on the 22nd and 23rd, but they were called to briefing on the afternoon of the 23rd to learn of their part in a raid that night on the town of Wesel. This had the misfortune to lie close to the Rhine and in the path of the advancing British 21st Army Group, which, since the 16th of February, had caused it to be systematically reduced to rubble by repeated air attacks, and now had one final onslaught to face, having already endured one by 3 Group earlier in the day. 195 Lancasters and eleven Mosquitos were made ready, the thirteen representing 57 Squadron departing East Kirkby between 19.15 and 19.43 with S/L Ward the senior pilot on duty. They found the target under clear skies with slight ground haze and were able to identify it visually, observing the aiming point to be well-marked by red and green TIs, which were bombed from 8,000 to 12,000 feet between 22.33 and 22.42 in accordance with the Master Bomber's instructions. It was noticed, that, despite the Master Bomber ending the attack at H+8, bombing had continued. Post-raid reconnaissance confirmed the effectiveness of the raid, which left only 3% of Wesel's buildings standing, and, after the war, it would claim justifiably to be the most completely destroyed town in Germany.

During the course of the month the squadron undertook fifteen operations and dispatched 172 sorties for the loss of five Lancasters, three complete crews and five members of another. Fewer than four weeks of operations remained ahead of the crews before the bombing war finally came to an end.

April 1945

There would be a gentle introduction to April for 5 Group, with no operations posted until the evening of the 3rd, when briefings were held for an attack on what was believed to be a military barracks at Nordhausen, situated in the Harz Mountains between Hannover to the north-west and Leipzig to the south-east. The site was actually a pair of enormous parallel tunnels under the Kohnstein Hill, which had been developed originally by the BASF Company to mine gypsum between 1917 and 1934. Following the destruction of Peenemünde, smaller tunnels had been created as a link between them to form a horizontal ladder effect, and the site turned over to the Mittelwerk GmbH (Gesellschaft mit beschrenkter Haftung, or Limited Company) for the manufacture of V-2 rockets and other secret projects. The "barracks" were part of the Mittelwerk-Dora forced workers camp, where inmates existed under the most horrendous conditions and brutal treatment, while they were starved, worked to death or simply executed by an increasingly desperate regime seeking to change the course of the war. The site had been attacked by 1 Group on the previous day and heavy damage inflicted but it was decided to send 5 Group in to hit the barracks again and the nearby town.

There was an early start on the 4th for the 243 Lancasters, which were to be divided between the two aiming points, ninety-three to the barracks and 150 to the town, with the 55 Base squadrons assigned to the former and each of their Lancasters carrying a cookie and sixteen 500 pounders. The 57 Squadron element of eighteen departed East Kirkby between 05.58 and 06.37 with S/L Hodgkinson the senior pilot on duty and arrived at the target to encounter five-to-seven-tenths cloud with tops as high as 9,000 feet, through which they were able to establish a visual reference until smoke began to obscure the barracks. Thirteen of the 57 Squadron participants bombed the barracks from 12,500 to 16,000 feet between 09.13½ and 09.20, while five attacked the town as the designated alternative from 11,500 to 16,000 feet between 09.14 and 09.22. Some of the early bombing of the town was seen to undershoot, but the Master Bomber corrected this by calling for a five-second overshoot, and, thereafter, the markers were soon obscured also by smoke. At debriefing, the crews were able to report a concentrated attack on both aiming-points, claiming severe damage, but, tragically and inevitably, heavy casualties were suffered by the unfortunate slave workers.

The only sizeable effort on the night of the 7/8th was by 175 Lancasters and eleven Mosquitos of 5 Group, which had a benzol plant at Molbis, near Leipzig, as their target. Situated south of the city, and fewer than two miles east of Böhlen, it was becoming a familiar destination for 5 Group via a well-trodden route across Belgium to pass south of Cologne. 57 Squadron made ready fifteen Lancasters, which departed East Kirkby between 18.22 and 18.34 with pilots of flight lieutenant rank leading the way. They found themselves delayed by wrongly forecast head winds, and, although they would reach the target area, not all would do so in time to participate in the attack. Two 83 Squadron primary blind markers formed the tip of the spear, and identified Zeitz on H2S, before making the ten-mile north-easterly run from there to the target. Green TIs were released from 15,000 feet at 22.48, and the flare force followed up between 22.50 and 22.57 to enable the low-level Mosquitos to drop red and green TIs among the chimneys of the plant. The approaching main force crews were greeted by clear skies with ground haze, or, perhaps, a smoke screen in operation, but the highly accurate and visible marking was an invitation for them to plaster the aiming-point with high explosives. Eleven 57 Squadron crews bombed on red and green TIs from 10,000 to 15,000 feet between 23.03 and 23.10, at which point the Master Bomber called a halt, leaving four with bombs still on board. Photo-reconnaissance confirmed the operation to have been a complete success, which ended all production at the plant. Later in the day, the length of a tour would be reduced from thirty-six to thirty-three sorties.

Two major operations were scheduled for the 8th, the larger one involving 440 aircraft from 4, 6 and 8 Groups to be directed against Hamburg's shipyards, where the new Type XXI U-Boots were under construction. 5 Group, meanwhile, would take on the Lützkendorf refinery, following a failed attempt on the 4th by 1 and 8 Groups to conclusively end production at the site. A force of 231 Lancasters and eleven Mosquitos was put together, of which the eighteen 57 Squadron participants departed East Kirkby between 17.50 and 18.06 with S/L Hodgkinson the senior pilot on duty. They all reached the target area, where conditions were as they had been twenty-four hours earlier, with clear skies and either ground haze or generated smoke. The primary blind markers ran in at 14,000 feet at 22.33 to deliver green TIs, and the illuminators followed between 22.35 and 22.42, after which, the main force was called in. The 57 Squadron crews attacked in accordance with the Master Bomber's instructions to bomb the southerly red and yellow TIs after an eleven second overshoot. They ran in at 11,000 to 14,000 feet between 22.45 and 22.52, and all returned safely to diversion airfields, confident that it would not be necessary to return to that particular target. They described their experiences to the intelligence section at debriefing, reporting many explosions, including a large one at 22.47, which was surpassed in size by another one two minutes later, and flames were said to have reached up to 3,000 feet. The complete destruction of the site was confirmed by photo-reconnaissance, and the plant would remain out of action for what remained of the war.

55 Base sat out a modest 5 Group raid on oil storage tanks and U-Boot pens at Hamburg in daylight on the 9th, and, when its crews were called to briefing on the 10th, it was to discover that they would be going back to the Leipzig area for the third successive operation, this time to hit a stretch of railway track linked to the Wahren marshalling yards, situated to the north-west of the city. A larger operation on this night, involving more than three hundred aircraft from 1 and 8 Groups, was to be directed at the Plauen marshalling yards to the south-west of Dresden, and the two forces would adopt a similar route until shortly before reaching Leipzig. 5 Group contributed all seventy-six Lancasters for Leipzig and eleven Mosquitos, with 8 Group providing the other eight Oboe Mosquitos, which, now that mobile Oboe stations had been set up on the Continent, could operate over the whole of Germany. The 57 Squadron element of eleven took off between 18.21 and 18.40 with F/Ls Langridge and Sims the senior pilots on duty and each Lancaster carrying ten or eleven 1,000 pounders. They reached the target area to find clear skies and excellent conditions for bombing, noting many ineffective searchlights and modest flak, probably because of a heavy night-fighter presence. The Oboe Mosquitos dropped green TIs as a reference for the 83 Squadron crews, which provided the illumination between 22.51 and 22.57 for the low-level Mosquito element. They placed their red TIs accurately onto the aiming-point, before the main force bombed the southernmost red TI in accordance with the Master Bomber's instructions, those from 57 Squadron from 11,700 to 14,000 feet between 22.57 and 23.05. Photographic-reconnaissance would confirm serious damage to the eastern half of the targeted stretch of track.

A major attack on Kiel by elements of 3, 6 and 8 Groups was planned for the night of the 13/14th, while 5 Group took advantage of that activity to send eighteen Lancasters to lay mines in the Forget-me-not garden in Kiel harbour. The crews of F/L Langridge and F/O Keen departed East Kirkby at 20.30 and reached the target area to encounter six to ten-tenths stratus with tops up to 7,000 feet, through which the Keen crew delivered their vegetables by H2S from an undisclosed altitude at some time around 23.30. F/L Langridge and crew were thwarted by the failure of their H2S and were unable to deliver their stores.

5 Group was used to being handed the most distant targets, and, as the final days of the bombing war approached, it found itself facing three long-range trips on consecutive nights, all to railway targets. The first of these was at Pilsen in Czechoslovakia, for which a force of 222 Lancasters and eleven Mosquitos was made ready. The fourteen 57 Squadron element took off between 23.21 and 23.53 and found clear skies in the target area with only slight haze. Ahead, they watched the first primary blind marker deliver green TIs at 03.38, before the flare forces followed between 03.51 and 03.56. The main force was called in at 03.58, and all but one of the 57 Squadron participants bombed from around 13,000 to 16,000 feet either side of 04.00, aiming at the north-westerly red and yellow TIs with an eight-second overshoot in accordance with the Master Bomber's instructions. F/O Saunders and crew did not bomb, and it must be concluded that they arrived too late. Returning crews reported a large explosion at 04.00, followed by oily smoke, and it was concluded that the raid had been successful.

There was good news to celebrate on the 17th, when the length of a tour was reduced yet again to thirty sorties, releasing many crews to contemplate a long future. The target posted for 5 Group that night was the marshalling yards at Cham, on Germany's border with Czechoslovakia, for which 55 Base crews were among those briefed. Out on the 57 Squadron dispersals, a fire broke out beneath PB360 causing the bomb load to explode at 17.45 and fling debris in all directions, destroying LM673, ND472, NN765, PD347 and RF195 and damaging fourteen other Lancasters to some extent. Four ground personnel were killed and five injured and Nº3 hangar and Hagnaby Grange farm were seriously damaged. Fire appliances were called in from Spilsby and Coningsby to help deal with the incident as aircraft burned throughout the night and bombs exploded, and by the following morning onlookers were faced with a scene resembling a battlefield. Many acts of courage were witnessed, and they would result in the awards of an MBE, two George Medals and three BEMs. The incident removed East Kirkby from the Order of Battle leaving ninety Lancasters to set off for the more-than four-hour flight to the target area, where they would be joined by eleven Mosquitos and greeted by clear skies with slight ground haze. The primary blind marker dropped the first green TIs on H2S from 14,000 feet at 03.47, and the flare forces went in between 03.51 and 03.54 to light the way for the Mosquito low-level markers. Their efforts were seen to be very concentrated, but the use of delay-fused bombs meant that no immediate assessment would be possible. Photo-reconnaissance later confirmed that tracks had been torn up and rolling stock damaged, and it was another success for the group.

5 Group was not involved when a force of over nine hundred aircraft reduced the island of Heligoland to the appearance of a cratered moonscape on the 18th, and the 55 Base squadrons also sat out a raid that night by 113 Lancasters and ten Mosquitos of 5 Group that put out of action the railway yards at Komotau (now Chomutov), also in Czechoslovakia. This proved to be the last raid in the communications offensive, which had begun more than a year earlier in preparation

for D-Day. East Kirkby was not called into action again until the 23rd, when 5 Group sent 148 Lancasters to attack the railway yards and port area of Flensburg on the eastern coast of the Schleswig-Holstein peninsula. The twelve-strong 57 Squadron element took off between 15.15 and 15.24 with W/C Tomes the senior pilot on duty, and after climbing out, formed up with the other 55 Base squadrons to fall in behind the 53 Base formation. They reached the target area to encounter ten-tenths cloud with tops at 4,500 feet, which persuaded the Master Bomber to send the force home with their bomb loads intact.

5 Group operated for the final time on the 25th, with an operation in the morning against the SS barracks at Hitler's Eaglesnest retreat at Berchtesgaden in the Bavarian mountains, and later that night on an oil refinery at Tonsberg in Norway. 5 Group supported the former with eighty-eight Lancasters and a single Mosquito in an overall 1, 5 and 8 Group force of 359 Lancasters and sixteen Mosquitos. The five 57 Squadron participants departed East Kirkby between 04.17 and 04.38 with the newly promoted S/L Shaw the senior pilot on duty, and all arrived in the target area to find clear skies. Despite the favourable conditions, the Master Bomber's instructions were not getting through and high mountains on the run-in hid the target almost until it was too late, and S/L Shaw and crew did not bomb. It proved difficult to identify the barracks in the absence of visible markers, however, a nearby lake and the town stood out clearly, and the 57 Squadron crews were able to establish their position before carrying out their attacks from around 15,000 to 16,000 feet either side of 09.00. It was difficult to assess the accuracy of this operation, but it appeared to be effective, and no local report emerged to provide clarity.

That night, 5 Group conducted its and Bomber Command's final offensive operation of the war involving heavy bombers, when sending 107 Lancasters and seven Mosquitos to attack a target, believed to be oil-related, at Tonsberg, situated close to the western shore of Oslo Fjord, a dozen or so miles south of the recently attacked Horten. At the same time, fourteen 5 Group Lancasters carried out the final gardening sorties of the war nearby in Oslo Fjord, and it was for the latter that 57 Squadron dispatched the crews of F/L Mersh and F/Os Howard, Meeking and Pearson from East Kirkby between 20.06 and 20.13. They all reached the target area to find a layer of eight to ten-tenths cloud and established their positions by H2S before delivering their mines as briefed. When F/O Meeking and crew touched down in LM231 at 02.59, they had the honour of bringing to a close the offensive operational career of 57 Squadron.

Operations were posted over the ensuing days, but cancelled, and, meanwhile, the humanitarian Operations Manna and Exodus were under way to feed the starving Dutch people still under German occupation and to repatriate prisoners of war. 57 Squadron was not involved in Operation Manna but sent seven Lancasters to Belgium on the 2nd of May to collect 158 former PoWs from Brussels and Juvincourt. They collected 208 more in twelve Lancasters on the 4th and a further 192 in thirteen repatriation flights on the 8th, the day on which the war in Europe ended officially. Operation Manna ended on this day, but Exodus would continue on into the summer.

During its long wartime service, 57 Squadron served with distinction in the front line of 2, 3 and 5 Groups and contributed to the success of each of Bomber Command's campaigns. It suffered the highest percentage loss rate in each group and the highest combined in Bomber Command. The memory of this fine squadron, and that of 630 Squadron, is perpetuated at the Lincolnshire Aviation Heritage Centre on the site of the wartime East Kirkby airfield, where the Panton family have restored Lancaster NX611 to taxying status. The museum stands as a tribute to Bomber Command and to the thousands of airmen and support staff who served at East Kirkby, particularly those who lost their lives in the air and on the ground.

57 Squadron ground crew 1945 in front of a Lincoln
J W Jones, J Dobie, R Coupe, A W Cairns, Paddy Peacock, Cpl Hares, V C Britten,
Taff Williams, Cpl. Johnson, R Wake, R Wright, Cpl. Goodyer, L J Fox, A Bryant,
Sgt Watkins, R Foxon, Sgt Jones, Sgt English, Sgt Hunt

57 Squadron Lancaster RA530 DX-Y. Crashed on take-off 20th March 1945. Crew killed:
Pilot – F/O Charles Cobern R.A.A.F, F/O William Calderbank, Sgt Alan Ramsbottom, Sgt
K C Ashun, F/Sgt William Searby (succumbed to his wounds and died on the 1st April 1945).
The injured crew were Sgt R. Bates and Sgt E. Lawrence.

*L – R – Standing: unknown, F/O Watkinson, F/Sgt Campbell, F/L Jones, Sgt Baker.
Kneeling: F/Sgt Harmer, unknown.*

*57 Squadron Crew. L-R: F/Sgt Campbell, Sgt Baker, F/Sgt West, F/Sgt
Harmer, F/L Jones, F/O Watkinson, Sgt Lambell.*

57 Squadron Target Photo. Berchtesgaden 25ᵗʰ April 1945.

F/L Appleton and crew

Lancaster LL940 S-Sugar
F/O Blank (Pilot), W/O Spencer (Nav), F/Sgt Carter (BA), Sgt Dean (W/Op),
F/Sgt Henderson (FE), F/Sgt Passingham (RG), W/O Woodrow (MUG)

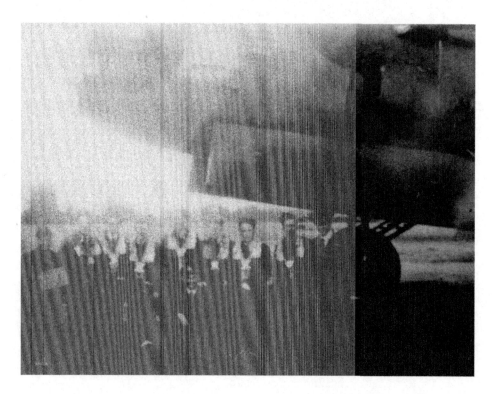

Lancaster R-Rodger and crew at dispersal, East Kirkby 1944

57 Squadron Lancaster DX-E Peter Bennett's crew. January 1945

Memorial to 57 Squadron and 630 Squadron. East Kirkby

Unknown 57 Squadron Crewmen

Roll of Honour

F/Sgt	Ronald Ross	ABERCROMBIE	11.11.42.
Sgt	Arthur Leslie	ABRAHAM	21.12.42.
F/Sgt	George William	ACKERMAN	21.03.45.
F/O	William Ward	ADAM	15.03.40.
P/O	Henry Harris	ADAMS	19.04.44.
Sgt	John McLean	ADAMSON	24.12.43.
F/Sgt	Thomas James	ADKISON	24.03.44.
AC2	Hunter Mason	AITKEN	02.03.45
Sgt	Henry	ALEXANDER	22.06.43.
P/O	Kivell Harold William	ALDERTON	18.08.42.
Sgt	Robert Frederick	ALDOUS	28.12.41.
F/Sgt	Arthur Hayes	ALLISON	30.07.44.
P/O	Ernest Frank	ALLWRIGHT	30.07.43.
Sgt	Edmund Dawson	ANDERSON	31.07.44.
Sgt	Frank Iron	ANDERSON	27.04.44.
Sgt	Richard	ANDERSON	27.01.44.
Sgt	John Gordon	ANDREW	09.07.40
Sgt	George Edward	ANDREWS	09.11.42.
F/Sgt	Harold Clifford	ANDREWS	03.06.42.
Sgt	Rodney Sydney	ANDREWS	18.04.42.
P/O	Walter Harold	ANDREWS	29.01.44.
F/O	Robert Joseph	ANSCOMB	02.03.45.
F/Sgt	Geoffrey Ronald	ANSDELL	22.06.44.
Sgt	Albert Victor	ANSELL	01.05.43.
F/O	Thomas Henry	ANTHONY	27.01.43.
Sgt	Donald Percy	APLIN	08.02.45.
Sgt	William Frederick	ARCHER	16.07.41.
Sgt	Arthur Meakin	ARMIN	23.05.44.
P/O	Thomas	ARMSTRONG	05.05.43.
W/OII	William Henry	ARNOLD	24.09.43.
Sgt	Colin Dingwall	ASHER	27.06.41.
Sgt	Kenneth Cromwell	ASHUN	20.03.45
Sgt	Donald William	ASHWORTH	20.06.42.
Sgt	Jack Glyn	ASHTON	22.11.42.
P/O	Samuel Cunningham	ATCHESON	16.03.44.
Sgt	Eric	ATKINS	04.01.43.
F/Sgt	Frank John	AUSTEN	23.09.43.
Sgt	George Alfred	AYRES	13.06.43.
Sgt	Edward Ronald	BACKHOUSE	11.10.41.
Sgt	Alan Frederick	BADCOCK	09.11.42.
Sgt	Arthur Eddie	BAGLEY	02.04.43.

Sgt	John Watts	BAGLEY	21.04.43.
F/Sgt	Harold Roy	BAILEY	23.05.44.
Sgt	Arthur Charles Henry	BAKER	08.07.44.
Sgt	Frank Edwin Fricker	BALE	06.09.44.
Sgt	Alex William Charles	BALL	03.01.44.
F/Sgt	Donald Leslie	BALLINGALL	27.03.42.
P/O	Myron Edward	BARKER	14.03.43.
Sgt	William Geoffrey	BARNES	02.04.43.
F/Sgt	William James	BARNES	05.06.42.
F/Sgt	Harold Lawrence	BARRON	22.06.44.
Sgt	James Harold	BARRY	11.11.42.
F/O	Charles William	BAUSH	08.03.45.
Sgt	Cyril	BAYFORD	11.11.44.
Sgt	Thomas Richard	BAYLES	23.05.43.
F/L	Henry Roy	BAILEY	23.05.44.
Sgt	Frank Alexander	BANDEEN	30.03.43.
F/L	Anthony Louis Henry	BARBER	22.03.41.
Sgt	James Harold	BARRY	11.11.42.
Sgt	Albert James Alfred	BARTLE	09.11.42.
F/L	Alan Frederick	BAYLEY	22.06.44.
Sgt	Alfred Kenneth	BEACH	06.11.44.
P/O	Harold	BEANE	26.11.43.
F/Sgt	John George	BEARDSHAW	17.12.44.
AC2	Owen Ralph	BEAUMONT	14.05.40.
F/L	Ronald Alfred William	BEAUMONT	22.06.44.
Lt.	Philip August	BECKER	04.12.44.
Sgt	Leslie Joseph	BEECH	14.05.43.
W/O	Thomas Francis	BEECHER	22.06.44.
Sgt	Ernest	BELL	30.07.43.
Sgt	William James	BELLINGER	17.12.43.
Sgt	Douglas James	BENDALL	25.01.40.
Sgt	Walter James	BENNETT	23.05.43.
Sgt	George Leslie	BENTLEY	24.06.41.
Sgt	Logan Carmon	BENTLEY	26.01.41.
Sgt	William Henry	BESTWICK	23.05.43.
Sgt	Peter	BIGG	21.04.43.
Sgt	Robert	BISHOP	02.10.43.
Sgt	Hakon Granly	BJOROY	17.12.44.
F/O	Angus John	BLACK	22.06.44.
F/Sgt	Frank Alexander	BLACK	06.12.44.
Sgt	Clement Peter	BLACKBURN	16.07.41.
Sgt	Sidney Frederick Ogeley	BLACKMORE	24.07.42.
Sgt	Frank Sidney	BODKIN	24.03.44.
Sgt	David Watson	BOND	26.03.42.

P/O	Gregory Ross	BOURDON	23.09.43.
F/Sgt	Frederick Samuel	BOWDEN	15.11.39.
F/O	Samuel	BOWDEN	11.11.44.
F/O	Ronald Alfred	BOWLES	21.12.42.
W/OII	Bruce Allan	BOYD	09.11.42.
S/L	Michael Innes	BOYLE	27.04.44.
Sgt	Edward	BRACKEN	30.07.43.
Sgt	Snowdon Cawood	BRADLEY	27.01.43.
Sgt	Ronald Vincent	BRAGG	02.08.43.
F/O	Dennis Ingham	BRAIN	02.09.44.
Sgt	Leonard Charles	BRAY	12.08.42.
W/OII	Lloyd Willis	BRAYFORD	11.02.43.
Sgt	Arthur C	BRETT	11.11.44.
F/O	Thomas Watt	BRIGGS	15.02.44.
Sgt	Arthur James	BRITTON	20.04.43.
P/O	John Frank	BROADBENT	11.08.43.
F/Sgt	John Alexander	BROOKS	07.09.41.
F/Sgt	Bruce Harold	BROWN	06.11.44.
Sgt	Daniel Frank	BROWN	02.09.44.
P/O	Eric Ernest	BROWN	07.11.41.
F/Sgt	Kenneth Charles	BROWN	29.08.42.
Sgt	Leonard Charles	BROWN	02.12.43.
F/Sgt	Anthony Charles	BROWNING	02.08.43.
F/Sgt	William Edward	BRUNTON	19.10.44.
Sgt	Edward Oscar	BRYANT	24.09.43.
Sgt	James	BRYANT	20.04.43.
F/Sgt	Stanley Lloyd George	BUCHANAN	12.08.42.
P/O	Arthur Wilbert Chesley	BUGDEN	22.05.44.
F/L	John Alec	BULCRAIG	19.07.44.
W/O	Edward Trezise	BUNT	18.02.43.
Sgt	Thomas Mountford Adie	BURGESS	13.06.43.
P/O	Aaron	BURNS	11.08.43.
Sgt	Maynard Hargrave	BURSTON	22.06.43.
F/O	Robert Edward Halliburton	BURTON	02.10.43.
P/O	John William Arthur	BUSTIN	30.06.43.
F/Sgt	Maurice Percival	BUTLER	27.04.44.
Sgt	Donald Frederick	BUTLER	17.12.43.
Sgt	Francis Charles	BUTLER	24.02.44.
Sgt	Frank	BUTTERFIELD	14.05.43.
Sgt	Frederick Oswald	BUTTON	11.11.42.
F/Sgt	William Harold Stanley	BYERS	12.10.41.
Sgt	John Edward	CADDICK	09.04.41.
F/O	James Gordon	CAHIR	27.08.44.

F/O	William Frederick	CALDERBANK	20.03.45.
P/O	Phillipe Emmanuel	CAMILLE	22.10.43.
Sgt	Eric William	CAMPBELL	27.01.43.
F/O	Victor Robert	CAMPBELL	21.03.45.
Sgt	Dennis Mark	CARMAN	02.09.44.
F/Sgt	Charles Louis	CARPENTER	08.07.44.
Sgt	James Clement	CARPENTER	30.07.43.
Sgt	John Alexander	CARPENTER	13.07.43.
F/Sgt	James Thomson	CARRUTHERS	04.09.43.
Sgt	Douglas	CARTER	08.07.44.
Sgt	Edwin Rowland	CARTER	11.12.41.
S/L	John Noel Graydon	CARTER	09.11.42.
F/Sgt	Gordon	CARTWRIGHT	14.03.45.
F/L	Michael James	CASEY	31.03.44.
F/Sgt	Theadore Edgar James	CASEY	11.02.43.
Sgt	Andrew Stanley	CASSELLS	04.08.41.
Sgt	Gerald Coodon	CEASAR	16.07.41.
F/Sgt	Thomas Patrick	CHADWICK	24.09.43.
P/O	Clifford James	CHALLENGER	13.06.43.
Sgt	Jack Harvey	CHAMBERS	02.12.43.
Sgt	Richard	CHAMBERS	22.10.43.
F/Sgt	Robert Alfred	CHAPMAN	27.01.43.
Sgt	Gordon Lindsay	CHAPMAN	29.09.41.
F/Sgt	William Michael	CHING	04.12.44.
Sgt	Gordon Thomas Lister	CHISHOLM	22.11.42.
F/O	Gavin Keith Henry	CHRISTENSEN	27.08.44.
Sgt	Ernest Tastard	CHRISTIE	15.10.41.
Sgt	Robert Alfred	CHUMBLEY	20.10.43.
F/O	Ernest Keele	CHIVERS	23.05.43.
F/L	Austin Thomas	CLARK	27.08.44.
Sgt	Bernard Allison	CLARK	07.09.41.
F/O	Harry	CLARK	17.12.43.
Sgt	John Calder	CLARK	29.04.42.
Sgt	Kenneth William Charlton	CLARK	16.09.41
F/Sgt	Maurice Arthur	CLARK	22.06.44.
Sgt	Wilfred	CLARK	08.07.44.
F/L	Richard Towers	CLARKE	31.07.44.
Sgt	Claude Venables	CLARKE	20.02.44.
Sgt	James Clifford	CLARKE	15.10.42.
P/O	John Clifford Alfred	CLARKE	31.01.43.
Sgt	William	CLARKE	21.04.44.
F/Sgt	Thomas Roy	CLAYTON	04.05.44.
P/O	Robert Kelly	CLEMENTS	02.10.43.
P/O	Eric Percy	CLIBURN	25.03.44.

Sgt	Charles Frederick	CLOUT	11.02.43.
F/O	Charles Alan	COBERN	20.03.45.
Sgt	Ronald Cust	COCKAYNE	12.08.42.
F/O	William Glen	COCKWILL	03.01.44.
F/Sgt	Raphael Michael	COCOZZA	14.03.45.
Sgt	Abraham	COHEN	03.01.44.
Sgt	John	COLLIE	08.05.42.
F/O	Roy Frederick	COLLINS	20.04.43.
Sgt	William Edwin	COLLINS	18.08.42.
Sgt	William Edward	COLLIS	20.06.42.
Sgt	Thomas James	COLSTON	22.10.43.
Sgt	Andrew Harry Theodore	COOK	08.11.41.
F/Sgt	Ronald Anthony	COOK	27.01.44.
Sgt	Percy Frederick Meadows	COOKE	12.10.41.
Sgt	Thomas Phillip	COOKSON	02.09.44.
Sgt	Harold James	COOMBES	11.04.43.
Sgt	George	COOPER	20.04.43.
F/O	Joseph Arthur Gordon	COOPER	06.11.44.
F/Sgt	Norman	COOPER	08.03.45.
Sgt	Basil John	COOPER	18.09.44.
Sgt	Frederick William	CORNWELL	23.09.43.
Sgt	Thomas	COSFORD	04.02.43.
Sgt	Norman	COTTRELL	20.01.44.
Sgt	James	COULTER	21.04.44.
Sgt	George Frederick	COUZENS	12.05.40
Sgt	Reginald Sidney William	COWDREY	20.01.44.
Sgt	Robert Hurst	COWLEY	02.09.40
P/O	Alwyn Trevor	COX	27.04.44.
Sgt	David George	CRAILL	29.08.42.
Sgt	Kenneth John	CRESSWELL	21.04.44.
Sgt	Maxwell Joseph	CRONIN	28.12.41.
Sgt	Charles	CROSS	01.11.44.
P/O	Edmund Forbes	CROSSLEY	19.04.44.
Sgt	Francis Kenneth	CROSSLEY	03.09.41.
Sgt	Thomas Raymond	CROWTHER	28.08.43.
Sgt	Henry Eric	CRUZE	02.04.42.
Sgt	Mervyn Wyndham	CULLERNE	07.11.41.
P/O	Ronald Firth	CULLIFORD	19.04.44.
F/O	Noel Somervell	CULPAN	17.12.44.
F/Sgt	Vincent Patrick	CUMMOCK	03.06.42.
Sgt	Claude Francis	CURTIS	01.04.42.
F/Sgt	Calvin Warren	DAHL	02.04.43.
Sgt	Jack	DALBY	11.12.44.

P/O	Jack Proctor	DALTON	02.12.43.
Sgt	Peter	DALY	23.05.43.
Sgt	Gerald Edward	DANDY	02.03.45.
F/Sgt	Arthur	DANIELS	29.07.42.
Sgt	Charles Kenneth	DAVEY	08.02.45.
Sgt	Alfred Henry	DAVIES	24.07.42.
F/O	Donald Leslie	DAVIES	30.07.44.
Sgt	John	DAVIES	14.03.45.
P/O	WG	DAVIES	20.02.44.
Sgt	Eric	DAVIS	02.03.45.
P/O	Sidney Hubert	DAVIS	29.01.44.
P/O	Philip	DAWSON	12.08.42.
Sgt	Donald	DAY	09.04.41.
Sgt	William George Thomas	DAY	25.06.43.
F/Sgt	Norman Tudor	DEACON	04.12.44.
F/L	Josiah Arthur	DEAN	29.07.42.
Sgt	Alick George	DEANE	30.03.43.
F/Sgt	Philip Damon	DEMPSEY	29.07.42.
P/O	Arthur Cecil	DENISON	02.09.40.
Sgt	Edgar Alfred	DICKHART	06.01.44.
Sgt	Raymond	DIGGLE	23.09.43.
Sgt	Robet Edward	DIGNUM	11.02.43.
F/Sgt	Raymond Bernard	DION	10.12.42.
P/O	Harold	DIXON	27.04.44.
Sgt	Derek Arthur	DIXON	03.01.44.
Sgt	John	DIXON	20.02.44.
Sgt	Vincent John Mervyn	DONALDSON	09.01.43.
F/O	Alfred Victor	DONKIN	17.12.44.
Sgt	John Henry	DONOVAN	22.06.44.
Sgt	Robert Sidney	DOORE	17.12.42.
P/O	Kenneth Alfred Reid	DOUGLAS	06.01.44.
F/Sgt	William Henry Charles	DORAN	13.07.43.
P/O	Kenneth Butler	DOWDING	13.06.43.
Sgt	Peter James	DOYE	15.02.44.
Sgt	John Arthur	DRAIN	21.12.43.
Sgt	Richard Ellsworth	DRAKE	25.07.41.
F/O	Lloyd	DRAYSEY	06.11.44.
Sgt	William McFarlane	DRUMMOND	05.42.
Sgt	Adam Thomas	DRYSDALE	27.07.42.
F/O	Gordon Alexander	DUFF	23.09.43.
Sgt	Thomas Norman	DUNLOP	08.03.45.
Sgt	Ruben Joseph	DUNSTER	11.12.44.
Sgt	Frank Victor James	DUNSTONE	08.02.45.
Sgt	Kenneth Trevor	DUTTON	11.02.43.

F/O	Bernard Paul	DUVAL	02.12.43.
F/Sgt	John Henry Patrick	DWYER	09.11.42.
Sgt	Walter	DWYER	26.11.43.
Sgt	Fred	DYSON	09.11.42.
P/O	Cyril William	EAMES	29.07.42.
Sgt	John	EDMUNDS	03.11.43.
Sgt	Thomas Emlyn	EDWARDS	09.11.42.
Sgt	Thomas	EDWARDS	22.05.44.
Sgt	Anthony Graham	ELCOX	30.07.43.
Sgt	Hugh Miller	ELDER	07.09.41.
Sgt	Anthony Edward	ELEY	24.12.43.
P/O	George	ELY	03.01.44.
F/O	Alfred Charles	ELLIOTT	21.04.44.
Sgt	Harold Roy	ELLMER	23.09.43.
Sgt	Richard Vincent	EMERSON	20.04.43.
Sgt	Alfred George	ENNIS	29.04.42.
Sgt	Albert Rowlands	EVANS	05.04.43.
Sgt	Arthur Walford	EVANS	16.07.41.
F/Sgt	Evan David	EVANS	04.07.41.
P/O	John Colin	EVANS	26.06 43.
Sgt	Thomas John	EVANS	25.03.44.
Capt.	Niels Christian	EVENSEN	17.12.44.
F/Sgt	Michael Gerrard	EVERARD	11.11.42.
Sgt	George Walter James	EVERETT	09.11.42.
P/O	Samuel	EWART	22.06.44.
Sgt	Warren Morgan	EWING	14.05.43.
Sgt	Eric	EWINGS	06.01.42.
Sgt	Stanley	FALLOWS	25.06.43.
Sgt	Stanley John	FARMER	15.11.39.
P/O	Victor Douglas	FARMER	05.05.43.
F/O	Jack	FARNHILL	17.08.44.
Sgt	Donald Frederick	FAULKNER	17.12.43.
Sgt	Horace Cyril	FAZAKERLEY	20.04.43.
F/Sgt	Sidney	FELMAN	10.04.41.
F/O	George	FERGUSON	22.05.44.
P/O	Jack	FINCH	10.04.44.
P/O	Stanley	FINDLEY	08.07.44.
P/O	Alfred Ernest	FISHER	30.03.43.
Sgt	Denis Alexander John	FISHER	24.12.43.
Sgt	Donald Sutherland	FISK	26.01.41.
Sgt	James Charles	FLELLO	06.12.44.
Sgt	Alan St.John	FLOYD	11.08.43.

F/O	Kenneth Albert	FOLEY	06.12.44.
W/O	Donald	FORBES	08.03.45.
S/L	John Henry	FRANKS	29.06.42.
Sgt	Andrew Taylor	FRASER	05.06.42.
Sgt	Gilbert Gordon	FRASER	24.10.42.
Sgt	Christopher Grant	FREEMAN	27.03.42.
Sgt	Anthony Cecil	FROST	24.06.41.
F/Sgt	Harry Theodore Franklin	FREYSTEINSON	29.07.42.
Sgt	Alfred William	FRICKER	29.07.42.
Sgt	Reginald Roy	FROST	23.05.44.
Sgt	Robert Edwin	FURNELL	01.08.42.
Sgt	William	FYFE	21.04.44.
F/Sgt	Norman Leslie Ernest	GALE	19.07.44.
Sgt	Denis Charles	GALLAGHER	23.05.44.
Sgt	Michael Montague	GALLEWSKI	04.09.41.
Sgt	Kenneth Frederick	GARDINER	09.11.42.
F/O	Alfred Edward Walter	GARDNER	18.11.43.
F/O	John Roger	GARLING	17.12.44.
Sgt	Raymond Kenneth	GARMENT	11.08.43.
F/Sgt	Francis Julian Herbert	GARRICK	10.04.44.
Sgt	Peter Edward	GARTELL	29.06.42.
P/O	Alfred Leslie	GASKIN	12.08.42.
F/Sgt	Cecil Louis	GERDING	13.05.43.
Sgt	Alexander	GIBSON	26.08.40.
Sgt	Kenneth Eric	GIBSON	25.07.44.
F/Sgt	Cyril	GIDMAN	29.07.44.
P/O	Denis Charles	GILL	28.08.42.
F/Sgt	William Albert	GILLEN	09.01.43.
Sgt	Alexander John Shields	GILLESPIE	17.04.42.
Sgt	Frederick Leonard Reginald	GILLIVER	13.05.43.
Sgt	Kenneth Eric	GILSON	25.07.44.
F/Sgt	Gerald Grant	GIROUX	02.04.42.
Sgt	William John	GLOTHAM	01.05.43.
Sgt	Jenkin Morgan	GITTOES	29.07.44.
Sgt	Alan Arthur Frank	GODDARD	31.03.44.
W/OII	Edward Henry	GOEHRING	22.06.44.
Sgt	Ernest Edward	GOLDSTRAW	12.07.43.
F/Sgt	Henry	GORDGE	31.07.44.
Sgt	Harry	GORDON	06.01.44.
F/Sgt	John Peter Campbell	GORDON	24.09.43.
Sgt	Leonard	GORMAN	06.01.44.
Sgt	Michael James	GRACE	01.05.43.
F/O	Horace Gaulterus	GRAHAM-HOGG	14.04.40.
P/O	Edward George	GRAVES	23.05.44.

Sgt	Edward William	GRAVES	02.12.43.
Sgt	Sidney Dennis Colley	GRAY	07.11.41.
Sgt	Donald	GREEN	
Sgt	Frederick Louis	GREEN	25.07.41.
F/Sgt	Louis Henry	GREEN	25.03.44.
F/Sgt	Sidney Charles	GREEN	11.11.44.
Sgt	Stirling Lindfield	GREEN	02.04.42.
F/O	John Fergus	GREENAN	02.03.43.
Sgt	Arthur Henry	GREENWOOD	29.09.41.
F/Sgt	Jack	GREENHALGH	16.03.44.
Sgt	Eric Ivor Llewellyn	GREGO	07.11.41.
Sgt	Thomas Joseph	GREGORY	13.05.43.
Sgt	Richard William	GRELLIER	09.11.42.
Sgt	Gordon Charles	GREW	13.07.43.
W/OII	Robert George	GRIFFIN	11.04.43.
P/O	Walter William	GRIFFIN	09.11.42.
Sgt	Harold De Cray	GRIFFITHS	22.05.44.
P/O	William Edward	GRINDLEY	04.09.43.
Sgt	Ivor Francis	GROVES	02.12.43.
F/L	Anthony Edward	GRUBB	05.07.44.
F/Sgt	Walter Hartmann	GULLIKSEN	17.12.44.
Sgt	Philip Leslie	GURD	11.12.41.
AC2	Aubrey Nigel	GURNEY	15.07.44.
P/O	Guilyn Penry	GUY	22.06.44.
Sgt	Alan	HADDOW	05.04.43.
Sgt	David Hastings	HALL	17.11.43.
Sgt	Thomas Joseph	HALL	23.09.43.
Sgt	John Frederick	HALLETT	02.08.43.
Sgt	William	HALLIDAY	11.02.43.
F/Sgt	Archibald	HAMILTON	25.03.44.
F/O	Williiam Caldwell	HAMILTON	24.10.42.
P/O	George Alfred	HAMPTON	24.03.44.
Sgt	Josiah George	HANLIN	11.10.41.
Sgt	Cecil Thornton	HARBOTTLE	11.10.41.
Sgt	George Raymond	HARBOTTLE	05.04.43.
P/O	George Melton (Tim)	HARGRAVE	28.09.43.
Sgt	John Furniss	HARKNESS	17.08.43.
Sgt	Kenneth Horridge	HARPER	03.01.44.
Sgt	Michael Anthony	HARRAN	09.11.42.
Sgt	Clifford Alfred	HARRIS	17.08.44.
Sgt	Ernest Edward James	HARRIS	22.06.44.
Sgt	Cyril Thomas	HARSTON	20.10.43.
S/L	Guy De Laval	HARVIE	02.04.42.

W/C	Walter Ralph	HASKELL	17.08.43.
F/Sgt	Ronald Henry	HASKINS	16.08.43.
Sgt	Max Emmanuel Gerald	HASTINGS	11.10.41.
Sgt	Basil Theodore	HAYLOCK	03.06.42.
Sgt	Reginald Frank	HAYNES	15.06.43.
Sgt	George	HAYWOOD	13.07.43.
Sgt	Jeremiah	HEALY	08.07.44.
Sgt	William Edward	HEARL	11.10.41.
Sgt	Francis Patrick	HEATON	03.11.43.
Sgt	Arthur Francis	HEFFERNAN	24.10.42.
Sgt	Peter	HEMINGWAY	23.05.43.
Sgt	Alexander Keir	HENDERSON	23.05.43.
Sgt	David	HENDERSON	01.04.42.
F/Sgt	James	HENDERSON	21.03.45.
Sgt	Thomas	HENDERSON	12.08.42.
P/O	Francis Norman	HENLEY	23.05.44.
F/Sgt	Philip Richard	HERBERT	29.06.42
F/Sgt	Brian	HESFORD	06.11.44.
Sgt	Eric	HIBBERT	02.12.43.
Sgt	Joseph William	HIGDON	27.04.44.
F/O	Cecil George	HILL	02.08.43.
Sgt	John Valentine	HILL	26.03.42.
F/Sgt	Edward Francis	HILL-COTTINGHAM	21.04.44.
Sgt	Eric Bernard	HILLIER	13.10.39.
P/O	John Walter	HINDE	17.12.43.
Sgt	Charles Cornelius	HOCKLEY	09.11.42.
Sgt	George Samwell	HODGES	26.06.43.
F/O	Jack Paull	HODGES	05.07.44.
Sgt	Joseph	HODGSON	01.05.43.
F/O	Nathaniel Edmund	HODSON	27.07.42.
F/O	Joe Douglas	HOGAN	24.09.43.
F/Sgt	Clifford Frederick John	HOLE	14.03.45.
W/O	George Russel	HOLM	11.04.43.
P/O	George Royal	HOLYOKE	04.09.40.
Sgt	William Ernest	HOLLOWELL	30.06.42.
W/O	Allan Lockwood	HOME	13.05.43.
F/Sgt	Ronald William	HOMEWOOD	03.01.44.
P/O	Frederick William	HOOD	05.07.44.
F/O	Alan Thomas	HOOK	02.12.43.
Sgt	Ernest Henry	HOOPER	15.10.42.
F/Sgt	Eric George	HOPKINS	25.07.44.
F/O	Richard Adrian	HOPKINSON	09.07.40
Sgt	James	HORTON	08.07.44.
Sgt	William Joseph Harry	HOSKINS	04.07.41.

F/Sgt	Kenneth Turner	HOWARTH	01.08.42.
Sgt	Ronald	HOWARTH	23.09.43.
Sgt	George	HUDSON	29.09.41.
Sgt	Kenneth	HUDSON	27.07.42.
Sgt	Eryl Rowlands	HUGHES	03.01.44.
P/O	Norman Edward	HUGHES-GAME	28.09.44.
Sgt	George	HULL	22.06.43.
P/O	Oliver Carlisle	HUME	23.11.39.
F/Sgt	Francis Ridout	HUMPHREYS	11.10.41.
P/O	Basil Oliver	HUNT	30.07.44.
F/O	Harold Eric	HUNTER	16.03.42.
Sgt	Henry Philip	HUNTER	02.04.43.
AC2	John Raymond	HUNTER	25.01.40.
W/O	Charles Henry Thomas	HURLEY	22.06.44.
Sgt	Lindsay Thomas	HUTCHINSON	03.09.41.
Sgt	Robert Keith	HUTT	07.09.41.
Sgt	Jack Louis	HYAM	13.06.43.
Sgt	Herbert John William	HYNDS	02.10.43.
F/Sgt	Alan	IFE	23.05.44.
Sgt	Eric William	INWOOD	11.02.43.
Sgt	John Oswald	IRVING	17.12.42.
F/Sgt	John Percival	IRWIN	20.01.44
Sgt	John Cecil Brandon	IRWIN	04.07.41.
Sgt	Andrew Bradshaw	JACKSON	11.11.42.
Sgt	George William Turner	JACKSON	15.10.41.
P/O	Rutherford James	JACKSON	29.06.42.
Sgt	Stanley Heelis	JACKSON	11.12.41.
Sgt	Stuart William	JACKSON	16.07.41.
W/O	Thomas	JACKSON	17.12.44.
Sgt	Alexander	JACOBSEN	09.01.43.
Sgt	Albert Maldwyn	JAMES	05.05.43.
W/O	Cyrus	JARDINE	21.03.45.
Sgt	Arthur William	JEFFRIES	12.10.41.
F/L	Ian Shirley	JENKS	20.04.43.
Sgt	David Walter	JENNINGS	15.10.41.
Sgt	Ivor Armstrong	JERVIS	23.05.43.
Sgt	Terence James	JERVIS	09.07.40.
Sgt	John Elwyn	JOHN	17.08.43.
P/O	Leonard Knut	JOHNSON	27.08.44.
Sgt	Brynmor Samuel	JONES	15.10.41.
Sgt	Frederick Albert	JONES	22.11.42.
Sgt	Hugh Ivor	JONES	04.09.43.

F/O	James	JONES	17.08.43.
F/Sgt	Stanley	JONES	02.04.42.
Sgt	Thomas	JONES	24.06.41.
Sgt	Thomas Abel	JONES	22.07.42.
LAC	Leslie Frederick	JORDAN	10.05.40.
Sgt	Thomas	KELLY	11.10.41.
P/O	Thomas Whiteside	KENYON	24.07.42.
Sgt	Cyril Leslie	KINGSNORTH	24.09.43.
Sgt	William Duncan	KINNES	19.04.44.
F/Sgt	Peter Leeton	KIRKPATRICK	08.02.45.
F/Sgt	Stanley Charles	KITCHEN	22.10.43.
Sgt	George Graham	KITSON	22.06.43.
Sgt	Harry	KLEINER	23.05.43.
P/O	Albert John	KNELL	12.08.42.
Sgt	Arthur Cecil Peter	KNOWLES	05.06.42.
Sgt	Noel John	LAKE	07.09.41.
Sgt	Gilbert Owen Hugh	LAKEMAN	08.04.42.
W/OII	Lawrence Joseph	LALONDE	11.04.43.
F/Sgt	James Lawrence	LAMB	18.08.43.
Sgt	Thomas	LANCASTER	30.07.43.
Sgt	Sydney David	LANE	16.07.41.
F/Sgt	Denis Paul	LANGLEY	18.02.43.
F/Sgt	Lloyd Theodore	LAWSON	03.09.41.
Sgt	Ronald	LARGE	02.10.43.
Sgt	James Beattie	LARKINS	23.06.42.
Sgt	Samuel	LAUGHLIN	13.05.43.
Sgt	Ronald William	LEA	02.04.43.
Sgt	Frederick Douglas	LEAHY	02.03.45.
Sgt	Leonard Henry	LEANEY	05.05.43.
Sgt	Frederick Ernest	LEE	14.05.43.
Sgt	Charles Grey	LEES	04.12.44.
P/O	Harry	LEES	05.07.44.
W/OII	John Harold	LEMON	11.04.43.
F/Sgt	Victor Raymond	LENICHEK	27.07.42.
Sgt	Alan Ramsay	LESLIE	23.05.43.
F/Sgt	Milford Glen Thomas	LEVINS	13.05.43.
F/O	Paul Albert	LEVY	28.08.43.
Sgt	Neville John	LEWERY	15.10.41.
P/O	Roy Arthur	LEWIS	02.12.43.
Sgt	Samuel	LEWIS	03.01.44.
Sgt	Harry	LEWIS	15.02.44.
F/Sgt	Thomas James	LIGHTFOOT	24.02.44.

P/O	Gilbert Owen Hugh	LIND	21.03.45.
A/C	George	LINDSAY	11.04.40.
F/Sgt	David	LIVINGSTONE	04.09.43.
Sgt	Richard Leslie	LLOYD	27.07.42.
Sgt	Robert Ernest	LOCKE	31.03.44.
F/O	Abraham Gordon	LODGE	23.05.44.
Sgt	Alan Frederick	LOGAN	02.04.42.
P/O	Frederick Willis	LOGAN	30.07.44.
S/L	Donald George	LONG	31.01.43.
Sgt	Norman	LONG	05.05.43.
Sgt	Thomas	LOUGHLIN	19.07.44.
Sgt	Richard Bruce	LOVERSEED	13.05.43.
F/L	David Septimus Stewart	LOW	27.07.42.
Sgt	William	LOW	23.05.44.
Sgt	Cyril John	LUDLOW	29.07.44.
P/O	Harold William	LUGG	27.08.44.
F/Sgt	Harvey William	LUNDY	02.04.42.
F/Sgt	Phillip	LUNT	18.09.44.
Sgt	Alan George	LUXFORD	16.08.43.
Sgt	Cyril Duncan	LYNCH	25.07.41.
Sgt	Harry Ponsonby	LYNCH	25.07.41.
Sgt	Walter Stanley	LYNN	28.08.43.
Sgt	Donald	MacDONALD	11.10.41.
P/O	John Campbell	MacGILLIVRAY	20.01.44.
Sgt	Peter James	MacINNES	25.03.44.
P/O	Norman Crichton	MacIVER	22.03.41
Sgt	James	MacKAY	26.11.43.
F/Sgt	William	MacKILLOP	28.08.43.
Sgt	Allan	McKINLAY	22.11.42.
F/Sgt	Thomas Norman	MacLEOD	12.12.42.
W/O	John Ferguson	MacMILLAN	29.01.44.
F/O	Hugh Columba	MacNEIL	13.05.43.
P/O	James Forbes	MacPHERSON	13.12.42.
Sgt	Albert Elvin	MACKRILL	09.11.42.
Sgt	James Edward	MADDOCK	02.08.43.
Sgt	George Samuel	MADDOCKS	30.07.43.
Sgt	George	MAHER	11.10.41.
F/L	John Joseph	MAHONEY	23.05.44.
Sgt	Gordon Cecil	MAJOR	11.08.43.
Sgt	John Burns	MALLETT	02.03.43.
F/Sgt	Peter Douglas	MANN	06.12.44.
Sgt	Peter	MANN	23.09.43.
Sgt	John Kenneth	MANSLEY	01.05.43.

Sgt	John	MANSON	23.05.44.
Sgt	Thomas Irvine	MANSON	17.12.42.
Sgt	Charles Lewis	MANUEL	22.10.43.
LAC	Frederick John	MANTLE	15.03.40.
Sgt	Ranulph Paul	MANWARING	11.12.41.
F/O	John Colin	MARLAND	23.05.44.
Sgt	Wilfred	MARLOW	02.08.43.
Sgt	Kenneth Robert	MARRIOTT	31.03.44.
Sgt	Ronald	MARSHALL	01.04.42.
Sgt	James George Louis	MARTIN	18.09.44.
Sgt	George Edward	MARWICK	31.01.43.
F/O	Leonard Eric	MASON	23.05.44.
F/O	Stanley	MASON	27.04.44.
F/O	Gerald	MATHEWS	30.07.43.
P/O	Thomas Henry	MAYNE	22.06.44.
P/O	Antony Patrick	McCALL	16.03.44.
Sgt	William	McCARRON	18.02.43.
P/O	Denis Joseph	McCRUDDEN	22.06.44.
F/Sgt	Reginald Thomas	McCUDDEN	23.09.43.
F/Sgt	Thomas Alexander	McDOWELL	20.04.43.
F/Sgt	Neil Francis Dalloway	McGLADRIGAN	10.12.44.
Sgt	John	McGUIRK	02.10.43.
F/Sgt	Reginald Colin	McINTYRE	21.04.44.
Sgt	John Mortimer	McKENZIE	11.12.41.
Sgt	Harry Francis	McKERNIN	03.11.43.
Sgt	Alan	McKILLOP	08.11.41.
Sgt	Robert Shaw	McKILLOP	06.12.44.
Sgt	Allan	McKINLEY	22.11.42.
P/O	Daryl Owen	McMAHON	11.04.43.
P/O	Robert Perrin	McLAREN	18.08.42.
P/O	Andrew Joseph	McLAUGHLIN	10.12.42.
Sgt	James Aloysius	McLAUGHLIN	11.11.44.
P/O	William Wilson	McMASTER	22.03.41.
P/O	Robert Hudson	McNABB	27.08.44.
Sgt	William James Bryden	McNAUGHT	22.10.43.
Sgt	Douglas	McNEILL	04.02.43.
F/Sgt	Ewen Cameron	McPHEE	17.12.42.
P/O	Keith Cumming	McPHIE	29.01.44.
Sgt	Arthur David	MEDCALF	02.09.44.
Sgt	Joseph Ernest	MEDHURST	11.10.41.
F/O	Henry Noel Trevor	MEDRINGTON	17.12.44.
P/O	George James	MEE	27.04.44.
Sgt	Ernest	MELL	15.02.44.
Sgt	Robert Denhohlm	MERCER	05.07.44.

Sgt	George Alfred	MILES	09.07.40.
P/O	John Thomas Norie	MILES	24.10.42.
F/O	Raymond Norman	MILLAR	24.09.43.
P/O	Bruce Armstrong	MILLER	29.06.42.
P/O	David	MILLER	22.10.43.
Sgt	Francis Henry	MILLER	02.04.42.
Sgt	Frank Cyril Edward	MILLER	02.03.43.
P/O	Keith John	MILLER	15.10.41.
Sgt	Dennis Raymond	MILLS	20.01.44.
Sgt	Frank George	MILLS	09.07.40.
F/Sgt	William Raymond	MINTER	22.10.43.
F/Sgt	Harold Alexander	MOAD	02.12.43.
AC2	Frederick George	MOLLER	13.10.39.
F/Sgt	Allan Davis	MONOGHAN	14.05.43.
Sgt	James Leslie	MONTAGUE	22.03.41.
Sgt	Albert	MOORE	04.09.43.
Sgt	Alan John	MOORE	25.07.44.
Sgt	James Alexander	MOORE	23.05.44.
Sgt	Peter William Lewis	MOORE	27.08.44.
F/Sgt	Walter Raymond	MOORE	05.07.44.
F/Sgt	Bruce Edward	MOREAU	11.12.44.
W/O	Kenneth	MORETON	29.01.44.
F/Sgt	James Kenneth	MOREY	04.05.44.
Sgt	Charles John	MORGAN	20.06.42.
Sgt	John Willoughby	MORGAN	22.07.42.
Sgt	Eric Louis Bowen	MOORE	31.01.43.
F/Sgt	Sydney	MORRIS	23.05.44.
P/O	Noel Percy	MORSE	08.04.42.
P/O	Alexander Donald	MORTON	06.11.39.
P/O	John Robert	MORTON	23.05.43.
Sgt	Raymond Hill	MOSES	27.07.42.
Sgt	Victor Haig	MOUNTSEPHENS	06.01.42.
Sgt	Alexander Rattray	MUIR	27.04.44.
F/O	Alexander Eric	MULHOLLAND	21.12.42.
F/Sgt	Arnold	MUNDAY	15.02.44.
F/Sgt	Thomas Francis	MURPHY	01.08.42.
F/Sgt	Frederick Warren	MUSIC	02.03.43.
Sgt	Rodney Roy	MUTTON	24.12.43.
P/O	Hilyard Lowell	MYERS	12.10.41.
Sgt	Harry	NAIMAN	25.06.43.
Sgt	Norman Joseph	NAYLOR	08.04.42.
Sgt	James Willie	NAYLOR	16.03.44.
S/L	William Alexander Stevenson	NEIL	06.12.44.

Sgt	William Frederick	NEILL	03.11.43.
Sgt	Clyde	NEILSON	22.11.42.
Sgt	Patrick George	NEILSON	10.11.42.
F/Sgt	John Oliver Hugh	NEVILL	02.04.42.
P/O	Richard William	NEWCOMB	18.11.43.
Sgt	Sydney James	NEWCOMBE	09.07.40.
Sgt	Frank Joseph Leslie	NICHOLAS	02.09.40.
P/O	William	NISBET	12.08.42.
F/O	George Franklyn	NIXON	03.01.44.
Sgt	George	NIXON	06.12.44.
Sgt	Joseph Terence	NIXON	05.07.44.
Sgt	Richard Kenneth	NIXON	08.07.44.
Sgt	Keith	NORRIS	20.04.43.
F/Sgt	William Thomas Nichol	NORRIS	23.05.44.
Sgt	Hunter Arthur Aubrey	NORTH	30.09.41.
Sgt	Leslie	NORTH	15.02.44.
Sgt	George Henry	NORTON	04.05.44.
F/L	Alexander	NOVICK	22.10.43.
Sgt	Walter Crone	NUGENT	05.06.42.
Sgt	William	NUGENT	01.05.43.
Sgt	Donald Edwin	NYE	17.08.43.
P/O	Albert Edward	OBERG	19.04.44.
F/Sgt	Poraumati	O'CALLAGHAN	27.08.44.
P/O	Ronald George	ODDEN	22.06.44.
Sgt	Ross	ODGERS	23.05.44.
Sgt	James	O'DONNELL	27.06.41.
Sgt	John	O'LEARY	20.10.43.
Sgt	Dennis	O'LOUCHLIN	20.04.43.
P/O	Patrick Edmund	O'MEARA	29.06.42.
F/Sgt	Mortimer	O'LOUGHLIN	21.03.45.
F/Sgt	Ronald	O'NEIL	09.11.42.
P/O	John Noel	O'REILLY-BLACKWOOD	25.01.40.
F/O	Arthur Joseph	ORGAN	16.08.43.
Sgt	Tom Lawrence	ORMEROD	30.07.43.
Sgt	Albert James	OSBORN	22.06.44.
Sgt	George Thomas	OSBORNE	05.07.44.
Sgt	Gordon David	OSBORNE	16.07.41.
Sgt	Ronald Charles	OSMAN	04.12.44.
Sgt	Orthin Vaughan	OWEN	12.08.42.
Sgt	Peter Reginald	OXLEY	25.03.44.
Sgt	Arthur Douglas	PAIN	22.06.43.
F/Sgt	Peter John	PAINE	26.03.42.

F/L	Aubrey Robert	PALLING	21.03.45.
Sgt	Douglas Gerald	PALMER	04.09.40.
P/O	James Walter	PALMER	26.06.43.
P/O	Douglas	PARK	02.12.43.
P/O	Frank Ernest Saville	PARKER	20.10.43.
P/O	Geoffrey Albert Norris	PARKER	30.07.43.
Sgt	Philip	PARKIN	23.05.43.
F/Sgt	James Douglas	PARKINSON	28.08.42.
Sgt	William Ronald	PARKINSON	22.06.44.
LAC	Ivor Robert William	PARTLOW	15.11.39.
Sgt	William John	PATERSON	02.04.42.
P/O	Ernest Harold	PATRICK	02.12.43.
P/O	Ernest Henry	PATRICK	26.06.43.
Sgt	John William	PAUL	29.09.41.
F/O	Claude Desmond	PAULINE	14.03.45.
W/O	Owen John	PAWSEY	11.12.44.
Sgt	Harry Arthur	PAYNE	20.06.42.
F/Sgt	Donald Maurice	PEARCE	17.12.44.
Sgt	Maurice Charles	PEARMAN	21.12.42.
F/Sgt	Henry Mitchell	PECKETT	04.05.44.
F/Sgt	George Edward	PENNY	28.09.43.
P/O	Dennis	PERCIVAL	08.05.42.
Sgt	Eric Norman	PERKINS	04.02.43.
F/Sgt	John Charles	PERRY	28.08.43.
Sgt	Roy Donald	PETERS	24.07.42
W/C	Murrey Vernon	PETERS-SMITH	27.07.42.
Sgt	George	PETTEFAR	11.08.43.
Sgt	Kenneth William	PHAROAH	10.12.42.
F/O	David Leslie	PICKARD	26.11.43.
F/Sgt	John	PICKETT	13.07.43.
P/O	Robert Leslie	PICKUP	02.04.43.
Sgt	Arthur Walter	PIERARD	27.07.42
Sgt	Anthony Stopher	PILBEAM	03.01.44.
Sgt	Henry William	PIKE	29.08.42.
AC1	George Rosse	PIRIE	22.05.40.
P/O	Herbert Rex	PIZZEY	19.04.44.
Sgt	William John	PHIPPEN	30.06.42.
P/O	Robert Leslie	PICKUP	02.04.43.
Sgt	Herbert Eugene	POLLARD	27.04.44.
F/Sgt	Douglas James	POPPLE	24.07.42.
F/O	Peter Simpson	PORTEOUS	20.10.43.
F/Sgt	Henry Mitchell	PORTEOUS	04.09.43.
F/Sgt	Ronald George	POSTANS	29.09.41.
Sgt	Walter James	POULTON	28.12.41.

Sgt	Arthur Royston	POWELL	06.01.45.
Sgt	Maurice	PRESCOTT	08.05.42.
Sgt	John Rose	PROCTOR	14.04.40.
F/Sgt	William Ronald	PRYDE	23.09.43.
W/O	Thomas	PURDY	28.12.41.
Sgt	John Robert	PYPER	18.02.43.
F/O	Thomas	QUAYLE	07.06.44.
P/O	Harold Edward	QUINN	10.04.44.
Sgt	Charles Quinn	RAFFERTY	14.03.45.
W/OII	Gordon Howard	RAMEY	10.12.42.
Sgt	Alan	RAMSBOTTOM	20.03.45.
Sgt	Basil Lyne	RANDALL	02.04.42.
F/Sgt	Ian Albert	RANDS	10.04.44.
Sgt	Jacky	RATCLIFFE	22.06.44.
P/O	Robert James	RATCLIFFE	11.08.43.
F/Sgt	Edward George	RAWLEY	17.12.44.
Sgt	William Barrymore	RAWNSLEY	23.05.43.
Sgt	Louis John	RAY	22.06.43.
Sgt	Philip Herbert	REAY	04.07.41.
Sgt	Walter George	REDMAN	13.06.43.
F/O	Frederick Charles	REED	31.01.43.
F/Sgt	John Knox	REED	20.10.43.
Sgt	Walter	REES	20.02.44.
Sgt	William	REEVE	28.09.43.
Sgt	Frederick Sydney Gordon	REEVES	29.01.44.
F/L	Dougal Hamish	REID	26.06 43.
F/Sgt	George	RICHARD	08.05.42.
F/L	Arthur Thomas	RICHARDS	22.05.44.
Sgt	Joseph Stewart	RICHARDS	19.04.44.
F/Sgt	Douglas Roy	RICHARDSON	06.01.42.
Sgt	GW	RICHARDSON	07.09.41.
Sgt	Harry	RICHARDSON	30.03.43.
Sgt	Harold William	RICKETTS	02.03.43.
F/Sgt	Robert	RIDDELL	12.08.42.
F/O	William	RIDDELL	06.12.44.
Sgt	Eddie Andreas Hals	RILEY	26.08.42.
Sgt	Sidney Richard	RISHWORTH	16.07.41.
F/O	Alister Frank Gray	RITCH	04.02.43.
Sgt	David Arthur	ROBB	23.05.43.
Sgt	Kenneth Thomas	ROBBINS	22.06.44.
Sgt	Richard Hywel	ROBERTS	11.04.43.
Sgt	Robert Cecil	ROBERTS	02.04.42.

Sgt	Robert Elwyn	ROBERTS	09.01.43.
Sgt	Ronald Harold Percival	ROBERTS	02.03.43.
Sgt	William Arthur	ROBERTS	05.07.44.
Sgt	George Albert	ROBINSON	22.06.43.
Sgt	Henry Edmund	ROBINSON	16.07.41.
F/O	Edward Chatterton	ROBSON	19.07.44.
Sgt	John George	ROBSON	10.04.44.
Sgt	George	ROE	09.01.43.
Sgt	Lawrence Joseph	ROE	06.01.42.
Sgt	Allan Thomas	ROGERS	18.09.44.
F/O	Phillip Neville	ROLFE	23.09.43.
F/O	Edward William George	ROSAM	31.01.43.
Sgt	Derrick John	ROSE	16.08.43.
P/O	Herbert Percy	ROSE	03.06.42.
F/O	Max	ROSE	08.07.44.
Sgt	Adrian Ruyseh	ROSELT	04.12.44.
Sgt	Hamish	ROSS	22.07.42.
F/Sgt	John	ROSS	27.07.42.
Sgt	Maxwell Robert	ROSS	27.06.41.
W/OII	John Hoskin	ROWNEY	29.08.42.
F/O	Alfred Gordon	RUSSELL	27.08.44.
F/Sgt	John De Forest	RUSSELL	15.10.42.
Sgt	Alan McGeogh	SANDARS	26.06.43.
Sgt	Lawrence Anthony Wykeham	SANDERS	05.05.43.
P/O	Roi Leonard	SAUNDERS	22.05.40.
Sgt	Gerald	SAVILLE	06.11.44.
F/O	Ronald Cave	SCARLETT	27.12.41.
Sgt	John	SCOTT	06.12.44.
Sgt	Donald Charles	SCOTT	17.12.44.
F/O	Rendal Anthony Fenwick	SCRIVENER	04.05.44.
P/O	Gordon John	SCUFFINS	30.07.44.
F/Sgt	Stanley Leslie	SCUTT	17.08.44.
F/Sgt	William Stacey	SEARBY	01.04.45.
F/O	Jack Laidlaw	SEARL	11.12.44.
Sgt	Frederick Charles	SEARLE	04.05.44.
Sgt	William Francis Philip	SELLERS	07.11.41.
F/Sgt	Wilfred Alderic	SENEZ	09.11.42.
Sgt	Howard	SHAKESPEARE	18.09.44.
Sgt	Douglas Malcolm	SHARP	03.06.42.
Sgt	John Kay	SHARP	02.04.42.
Sgt	James Frederick	SHEARON	14.03.45.
F/Sgt	Ronald	SHEARS	04.02.43.
W/O	Henry Augustine	SHEEHAN	13.05.43.

F/O	Francis George	SHELL	17.12.42.
F/Sgt	William Charles	SHEPHERD	27.06.41.
Sgt	John Hillhouse	SHERRIFF	21.09.41.
F/O	David Allan	SHEWAN	03.01.44.
AC1	James	SHUTTLEWORTH	14.04.40.
Sgt	Donald John	SIMMONS	30.03.43.
Sgt	Robert Louis Nathaniel	SIMMONS	06.01.42.
Sgt	Samuel Frank	SIMMONS	22.05.40.
Sgt	Herbert Munro	SIMS	17.12.42.
P/O	Arnold Galloway	SIMPSON	17.11.43.
Sgt	Raymond Brindley	SIMPSON	25.06.43.
F/O	Royston Hubert	SIMSON	25.07.44.
Sgt	Donald James	SKEITES	27.04.44.
S/L	Leslie Harold	SKINNER	02.02.45.
Sgt	Edwin Douglas	SLADE	30.07.43.
F/Sgt	Edward Crone	SLAUGHTER	08.02.45.
P/O	John Adam	SLIGO	08.05.42.
Sgt	Frederick John	SLOANE	06.11.44.
F/O	Reginald Hannam	SMART	31.03.44.
Sgt	Robert	SMEDLEY	10.04.44.
F/Sgt	Bert	SMITH	11.12.44.
Sgt	Frederick Charles	SMITH	18.02.43.
Sgt	Francis John	SMITH	01.08.42.
P/O	Gordon John Leslie	SMITH	27.04.44.
Sgt	Henry Toomer	SMITH	11.10.41.
Sgt	Herbert Blatch	SMITH	24.10.42.
Sgt	Herbert Walter Lawrence	SMITH	21.04.44.
Sgt	James Murray	SMITH	16.07.41.
F/Sgt	James Edgar	SMITH	29.07.42.
Sgt	Joseph	SMITH	02.08.43.
Sgt	Kenneth	SMITH	26.08.44.
F/O	Norman Alfred	SMITH	04.05.44.
F/Sgt	Raymond Purser	SMITH	23.09.43.
F/O	Ronald Richard	SMITH	05.07.44.
Sgt	Alan	SMITHDALE	20.04.43.
P/O	Jack	SMITHERS	16.08.43.
Sgt	John Clayton	SMITHSON	31.01.43.
P/O	Wallace Robert	SMYTH	30.07.43.
F/Sgt	Richard Vernon	SNOOK	27.03.42.
Sgt	Donald Enright	SOLES	03.09.41.
Sgt	Robert Simeon	SPARKES	04.07.41.
F/Sgt	George Wilson	SPEICHER	23.09.43.
F/Sgt	Charles Frederick	SPENCER	05.07.44
Sgt	Harold Arthur	SPENCER	25.03.44.

F/L	James Basil Percy	SPENCER	31.07.44.
Sgt	Thomas	SPENCER	08.07.44.
Sgt	Benjamin Ernest	SPICER	05.04.43.
Sgt	Clifford Neil	STALKER	05.07.44.
Sgt	Gibbard Selkirk	STANDRING	23.06.42.
Sgt	Robert Horace	STANGHAM	23.06.42.
Sgt	Alfred	STANSFIELD	22.11.42.
Sgt	Alexander	STEEL	13.05.43.
Sgt	Francis John Maddock	STEER	25.06.43.
Sgt	John Brynmor	STEPHENS	15.10.42.
F/Sgt	Ronald	STEVENSON	03.01.44
F/O	Arthur	STIENSTRA	17.08.44.
Sgt	Royston Charles Edward	STILES	26.08.40.
Sgt	Cecil Edgar Pollard	STILL	13.07.43.
F/Sgt	John Leslie	STONE	08.03.45.
Sgt	William Connor	STONE	22.03.41.
Sgt	Geoffrey	STORR	06.11.39.
Sgt	Robert	STRAUGHAN	24.06.41.
Sgt	Ronald Amos Charles Martin	STRINGER	18.08.43.
P/O	Carl Walter	STROM	24.03.44.
F/Sgt	William James	STRUTHERS	20.04.44.
Sgt	Cecil Raymond	STUBBS	21.12.42.
Sgt	Arthur	SUTCLIFFE	04.09.43.
Sgt	William Robertson	SUTHERLAND	24.06.41.
Sgt	Leslie Seton Dewar	SWANSTON	15.02.44.
Sgt	John Walter	SYKES	25.06.43.
F/O	Chester	SZYMANSKI	22.06.44.
Sgt	William John	TANNER	01.08.42.
P/O	Ernest Henry	TANSLEY	02.12.43.
F/O	Francis Richard Harry	TATE	20.04.43.
F/Sgt	Edgar Francis	TAYLOR	22.10.43.
Sgt	Herbert George	TAYLOR	30.03.43.
Sgt	Joseph Gordon	TAYLOR	24.10.42.
F/Sgt	John Thomas	TAYLOR	05.05.43.
Sgt	Vincent Nelson	TAYLOR	11.12.44.
Sgt	William Henry	TAYLOR	17.12.42.
F/Sgt	William Valentine	TAYLOR	02.09.44.
Sgt	Douglas	TELFER	26.06.43.
Sgt	Solomon	TERRY	10.04.41.
Sgt	Kenneth Arthur	TESTER	02.04.43.
Sgt	George Hazen	TETT	27.06.41.
P/O	Alban	THOMAS	10.05.40.
Sgt	Penry Llewellyn	THOMAS	10.05.40

Sgt	Brian Henry Maude	THOMAS	16.03.44
Sgt	William Charles Marcus	THOMAS	28.08.43.
F/Sgt	Balder	THOMASBERG	02.12.43.
W/O	Albert	THOMASON	17.12.44.
Sgt	Arthur Anthony	THOMSON	08.11.41.
F/O	Duncan Gordon	THOMPSON	15.10.42.
F/Sgt	John Ernest	THOMPSON	08.03.45.
Sgt	Wilfred	THORPE	02.04.42.
Sgt	Cyril Douglas	TODD	01.05.43.
F/Sgt	William Frederick	TOWLSON	27.06.41.
F/Sgt	Donald George	TOWNSEND	22.06.44.
F/L	Thomas Henry	TOZER	02.04.42.
F/O	Kenneth John	TUBBS	20.02.44.
Sgt	Stanley Ernest	TUCK	13.06.43.
F/Sgt	Augustin Charles	TURGEON	03.09.41.
Sgt	Herbert Henry	TURKENTINE	02.03.43.
Sgt	Raymond Burn	TURNER	07.07.41
Sgt	Leonard	TURVEY	20.04.43.
AC1	Frederick Albert	TWINNING	06.11.39.
F/Sgt	George Hillary	VOGAN	08.04.42.
P/O	Frank William	WADE	26.10.41.
F/Sgt	Thomas	WAKEFIELD	22.07.42.
Sgt	Walter John	WAKELIN	24.10.42.
Sgt	Hector John	WAKEMAN	18.08.42.
P/O	John Douglas	WALLACE	13.05.43.
S/L	Stanley Norman Tuttell	WALLAGE	05.04.43.
Sgt	Peter Anthony	WALLER	18.02.43.
F/O	Frank Antony Stanley	WALLIS	15.10.42.
P/O	Maurice Edward	WALSH	09.11.42.
Sgt	Louis Edward	WALTERS	30.07.43.
Sgt	Hartley	WARD	24.06.41.
F/O	Anthony Valentine Hutchinson	WARDLE	29.07.44.
Sgt	David Stanley	WARLOW	09.01.43.
Sgt	William Howard	WARREN	10.11.42.
]	Cyril John	WATERS	02.03.45.
Sgt	George Lawrence	WATERS	06.01.44.
F/Sgt	Eric Howard Pitt	WATKINS	06.12.44.
Sgt	Arthur William	WATSON	17.12.43.
Sgt	Donald Austin	WATSON	11.12.41.
P/O	John Archibald	WATSON	27.10.41.
Sgt	Samuel Frederick	WATT	18.02.43.
Sgt	Arthur	WATTON	27.08.44.

Sgt	Cyril William	WATTS	02.03.45.
F/O	Robert John	WAUGH	18.09.44.
Sgt	Frank Slater	WEAVER	16.03.44.
Sgt	Maurice	WEBB	27.04.44.
Sgt	Jack	WEBBER	09.01.43.
Sgt	Leonard Edwin	WEBBER	22.11.42.
P/O	Faber Ernest Frederick	WELDON	05.04.43.
P/O	Albert Edward	WEST	29.07.44.
1/Lt	Donald	WEST	03.11.43.
Sgt	Harry Bateman	WEST	10.04.44.
Sgt	William George Edwin	WEST	31.07.44.
Sgt	Jack	WESTERDALE	30.03.43.
Sgt	William Roy	WESTON	29.01.44.
Sgt	Ronald Bainbridge	WETHERELL	27.01.43.
P/O	James William	WEYERS	05.07.44.
Sgt	Leslie Frank	WHALE	06.12.44.
Sgt	Charles James	WHALLEY	29.08.42.
Sgt	Charles	WHARTON	20.10.43.
F/Sgt	James Frederick	WHEATLEY	02.10.43.
W/OII	James Arnold	WHEELER	20.02.44.
F/O	Walter John	WHEELER	26.06.43.
Sgt	Keith Robert Arthur	WHITCOMBE	20.04.43.
Sgt	Derrick	WHITEFOOT	02.03.45.
F/Sgt	Donald Stuart	WHITEHOUSE	08.03.45.
P/O	Peter Percy	WHITLEY	15.10.42.
Sgt	James	WHITFIELD	25.07.44.
Sgt	Richard Frank	WHITTON	07.11.41.
S/L	Philip Mervyn	WIGG	21.04.44.
F/Sgt	Charles John Geoffrey	WILCE	06.01.44.
Sgt	Cyril James	WILDE	20.11.43.
Sgt	Norman Seymour	WILDING	28.08.42.
Sgt	Stanley Albert	WILKINS	22.03.41.
F/O	John Alfred	WILLIAMS	02.12.43.
Sgt	John Charles	WILLIAMS	18.08.42.
F/Sgt	Ronald Franklin	WILLIAMS	13.05.43.
W/O	Sidney Buxton	WILLIAMS	02.09.44.
Sgt	Lawrence Arthur	WILLIAMSON	26.11.43.
Sgt	John Frederick	WILLIS	19.04.44.
Sgt	Francis	WILSON	20.01.44.
Sgt	Francis James	WILSON	27.08.44.
F/Sgt	John Kevin	WILSON	08.02.45.
Sgt	Peter	WILSON	16.07.41.
F/L	Robert Hay	WILSON	11.08.43.
Sgt	Sidney	WILSON	09.11.42.

Sgt	Stanley	WILSON	09.11.42
F/O	Victor Albert	WILSON	13.05.43.
F/Sgt	Warwick St George Ruxton	WILSON	18.04.42.
Sgt	Norman	WINDLE	29.06.42.
P/O	Leslie Harold	WINNEKE	23.05.44
Sgt	Hebry Charles James	WINSLADE	27.08.44.
Sgt	Arthur John	WITHERINGTON	16.09.41
Sgt	Alan Richard	WOOD	05.04.43.
Sgt	Ernest Albert	WOOD	05.07.44.
Sgt	William Christopher	WOOD	12.10.41.
Sgt	William Haseltine	WOOD	27.01.43.
F/O	William Thomas	WOODALL	22.05.44.
Sgt	Cyril James	WOODMASS	22.05.44.
Sgt	Albert Victor	WOOLGAR	09.11.42.
Sgt	Charles William	WOODS	25.07.44.
P/O	Antony Oliver	WRIGHT	27.01.44.
F/O	Brian Edward	WRIGHT	17.12.44.
F/Sgt	Dennis William	WRIGHT	25.07.44.
Sgt	John Alfred	WRIGHT	22.07.42.
Sgt	Raymond Hedley	WRIGHT	23.05.44.
Sgt	William Edward	WRIGHT	06.12.44.
F/Sgt	John Francis	YABSLEY	06.01.44.
Sgt	Henry William John	YARDLEY	22.06.44.
Sgt	David	YOUNG	27.08.44.
F/O	Harold James	YOUNG	21.04.44.
Sgt	John Ernest	YOUNG	11.11.42.
Sgt	Michael Clive	YOUNG	11.10.41.
Sgt	Desmond Claude	YOUNGS	24.03.44.

STATIONS

UPPER HEYFORD	05.09.32. to 24.09.39.
ROYE/AMY	24.09.39. to 18.10.40.
ROSIERES-EN-SANTERRE	18.10.39. to 17.05.40.
POIX	17.05.40. to 19.05.40.
CRECY-EN-PONTHIEU	19.05.40. to 21.05.40.
WYTON	21.05.40. to 27.05.40.
HAWKINGE/GATWICK	27.05.40. to 11.06.40.
WYTON	11.06.40. to 24.06.40.
LOSSIEMOUTH	24.06.40. to 13.08.40.
ELGIN	13.08.40. to 01.11.40.
WYTON	01.11.40. to 20.11.40.
FELTWELL	20.11.40. to 04.09.42.
METHWOLD Squadron HQ only	05.01.42. to 04.09.42.
SCAMPTON	04.09.42. to 28.08.43.
EAST KIRKBY	28.08.43. to 25.11.45.

COMMANDING OFFICERS

WING COMMANDER H M A DAY	21.08.39. to 13.10.39.
WING COMMANDER A H GARLAND	14.10.39. to 05.12.39.
WING COMMANDER R H HAWORTH-BOOTH	05.12.39. to 10.03.40.
WING COMMANDER A H GARLAND	10.03.40. to 24.02.41.
WING COMMANDER S S BERTRAM DFC	24.02.41. to 08.05.41.
WING COMMANDER J M SOUTHWELL	08.05.41. to 19.03.42.
WING COMMANDER M V PETERS-SMITH DFC	19.03.42. to 27.07.42.
WING COMMANDER E J LAINE DFC	30.07.42. to 23.09.42.
WING COMMANDER F C HOPCROFT	23.09.42. to 28.07.43.
WING COMMANDER W R HASKELL	28.07.43. to 18.08.43.
WING COMMANDER H W H FISHER DFC	19.08.43. to 15.04.44.
WING COMMANDER H Y HUMPHREYS DFC	15.04.44. to 08.01.45.
WING COMMANDER J N TOMES	08.01.45. to 12.06.45.

AIRCRAFT

BLENHEIM I	03.38. to	03.40.
BLENHEIM IV	03.40. to	11.40.
WELLINGTON IC	11.40. to	02.42.
WELLINGTON II	07.41. to	02.42.
WELLINGTON III	02.42. to	09.42.
LANCASTER I/III	09.42. to	05.46.

OPERATIONAL RECORD

OPERATIONS	SORTIES	AIRCRAFT LOSSES	% LOSSES
558	5151	172	3.3

CATEGORY OF OPERATIONS

BOMBING	MINING	OTHER
482	42	34

BLENHEIM

OPERATIONS	SORTIES	AIRCRAFT LOSSES	% LOSSES
37	58	10	17.2

CATEGORY OF OPERATIONS

BOMBING	SWEEPS
3	34

WELLINGTON

OPERATIONS	SORTIES	AIRCRAFT LOSSES	% LOSSES
173	1056	54	5.1

CATEGORY OF OPERATIONS

BOMBING	MINING
166	7

LANCASTER

OPERATIONS	SORTIES	AIRCRAFT LOSSES	% LOSSES
348	4037	108	2.7

CATEGORY OF OPERATIONS

BOMBING	MINING

Aircraft Histories

L1105	From 82 Squadron. To 219 Squadron.
L1113	From 82 Squadron. To 229 Squadron.
L1117	From 82 Squadron. To 219 Squadron.
L1128	To 229 Squadron.
L1129	Crashed in France while training 23.11.39.
L1136	To 229 Squadron.
L1137	To 218 Squadron.
L1138	FTR from reconnaissance sortie to central Germany 13.10.39.
L1139	To 1AAS.
L1140	To 17 Operational Training Unit.
L1141	FTR from reconnaissance sortie 16.10.39.
L1142	To 17 Operational Training Unit.
L1145	FTR from reconnaissance sortie over Germany 6.11.39.
L1146 DX-G	To Royal Aircraft Establishment.
L1147	Crashed in Hertfordshire on return from reconnaissance sortie 13.10.39.
L1148	Force-landed in Belgium during reconnaissance sortie 16.11.39 and interned.
L1149	To 1 Operational Training Unit.
L1171 DX-K	From 18 Squadron. To 5 AOS.
L1240	From 34 Squadron. To 219 Squadron.
L1246	From 34 Squadron. Crashed near Paris during ferry flight 15.11.39.
L1266	Became ground instruction machine.
L1280	From 21 Squadron. FTR from reconnaissance sortie 25.1.40.
L1319	From 21 Squadron. To Upper Heyford.
L1325	From 61 Squadron. FTR from reconnaissance sortie over Germany 7.11.39.
L1331	From 82 Squadron. To 105 Squadron.
L1333	From 82 Squadron. Struck Off Charge 31.3.42.
L1360	To 34 Squadron.
L1361	To 34 Squadron.
L6775	To 1 Operational Training Unit.
L6786	To 600 Squadron.
L6793	To 13 Operational Training Unit.
L6795	To ATA.
L6796	To 139 Squadron.
L6811	To 114 Squadron.
L8597 DX-T	From 18 Squadron. To 5 Bombing and Gunnery School.
L9027	To 34 Squadron.
L9180	FTR from reconnaissance sortie 14.5.40.
L9181	Crashed in France while training 11.4.40.
L9182	Lost in France May 40. Details uncertain.
L9183	To 139 Squadron.
L9184	FTR from reconnaissance sortie to France 22.5.40.
L9188	To 18 Squadron.
L9243	Lost 23.5.40. Details uncertain.

L9244	To 105 Squadron.
L9245	FTR from reconnaissance sortie to France 10.5.40.
L9246	Damaged during reconnaissance sortie 10.5.40. and abandoned on withdrawal 17.5.40.
L9247	To 53 Squadron.
L9248	Lost in France May 40. Details uncertain.
L9249	FTR from reconnaissance sortie to France 15.3.40.
L9266	To 59 Squadron.
L9268	To 101 Squadron.
L9272	To 107 Squadron.
L9325	From 53 Squadron. To 18 Squadron.
L9462	Crashed in Scotland during training 23.8.40.
L9465	FTR from reconnaissance sortie 14.4.40.
N3583	From 21 Squadron. Crashed in Moray Firth while training 2.9.40.
N3598	From 15 Squadron. To 71 Wing.
N3614	To 59 Squadron.
P4856	From 107 Squadron. To 13 Operational Training Unit.
P6928	From 53 Squadron. FTR from attacks on airfields in France 25/26.8.40.
P6930	FTR from reconnaissance sortie 12.5.40.
P6931	To 53 Squadron.
P6932	Lost in France May 1940. Details uncertain.
P6933	To 53 Squadron.
R3591	To 17 Operational Training Unit.
R3592	To 5 BGS.
R3594	To 15 Squadron.
R3595	Lost in France May 1940. Details uncertain.
R3598	To 18 Squadron.
R3607	From 59 Squadron. To 40 Squadron.
R3608	To 11 Squadron.
R3638	From 53 Squadron. To 59 Squadron.
R3666	To 218 Squadron.
R3667	SOC 14.10.40.
R3680	Crashed on landing at Dyce while training 4.7.40.
R3682	From 40 Squadron. To 105 Squadron.
R3708	21 Squadron. To 13 Squadron.
R3750	FTR Stavanger 9.7.40.
R3751	To 13 Operational Training Unit.
R3752	To 18 Squadron.
R3806	From 114 Squadron. To 107 Squadron.
R3825	To 107 Squadron.
R3830	To 101 Squadron.
R3832	To 110 Squadron.
R3847	From 59 Squadron. FTR Stavanger 9.7.40.
R3848	To 13 Operational Training Unit.
R3882	From 59 Squadron. Crashed in Scotland while training 4.9.40.
R3883	From 59 Squadron. To 8 Squadron.
R3889	To 59 Squadron.

R3890	To 59 Squadron.
T1824	To 107 Squadron.
T2176	Crashed during ferry flight to Middle East.
T2223	To 21 Squadron.

WELLINGTON.   **From November 1940 to September 1942.**

L4343	From 40 Squadron. To 15 Squadron.
N2783	To 149 Squadron.
N2784 DX-N	Crashed on approach to Feltwell on return from Duisburg 16.7.41.
N2810	To 9 FPP.
N2841 DX-C	To 27 Operational Training Unit.
N2853	To 149 Squadron.
N2938	From 37 Squadron. To 311 Squadron.
P9209	From 311 Squadron. To Central Gunnery School.
R1040	To 9 Squadron.
R1240 DX-W	From 40 Squadron. Returned to 40 Squadron.
R1271 DX-P	Ditched during operation to Berlin 20/21.9.41.
R1281	To 9 Squadron.
R1369	FTR Kiel 24/25.7.41.
R1437 DX-X	FTR Vegesack 9/10.4.41.
R1441	From 311 Squadron. Crashed on approach to East Wretham on return from Cologne 28.3.41.
R1462	To 214 Squadron.
R1508	To 20 Operational Training Unit.
R1589 DX-M	From 75(NZ) Squadron. Crashed near Feltwell when bound for Essen 4.7.41.
R1592 DX-J	From 150 Squadron. To 22 Operational Training Unit.
R1605 DX-A/R	To 1503 BAT Flt.
R1608	FTR Kiel 24/25.6.41.
R1624 DX-U	FTR Duisburg 15/16.7.41.
R1706 DX-W	Damaged beyond repair following operation to Frankfurt 20/21.9.41.
R1707 DX-M	From 9 Squadron. To 156 Squadron.
R1722 DX-K	From 9 Squadron. Crash-landed in Suffolk on return from Hamburg 27.10.41.
R1757 DX-X	From 9 Squadron. FTR Nuremberg 12/13.10.41.
R1763 DX-H/D	From 9 Squadron. To 18 Operational Training Unit.
R1792	From 75(NZ) Squadron. Crashed on take-off from Feltwell when bound for Brest 13.9.41.
R1794 DX-R	FTR Bremen 27/28.6.41.
R1799 DX-F	To 1503 BAT Flt.
R3169	From 75(NZ) Squadron. Returned to 75(NZ) Squadron.
R3195 DX-O	From 75(NZ) Squadron. To 20 Operational Training Unit.
R3231	From 75(NZ) Squadron. To 11 Operational Training Unit.
R3275	From 75(NZ) Squadron. To 12 Operational Training Unit.
R3297	From 75(NZ) Squadron. To 25 Operational Training Unit.

T2504	From 75(NZ) Squadron. Destroyed by enemy action at Feltwell 7.5.41.
T2713 DX-Q	To 149 Squadron.
T2715 DX-S	From 15 Squadron. To 16 Operational Training Unit.
T2721 DX-S	To 99 Squadron.
T2804	FTR Berlin 9/10.4.41.
T2957	To 99 Squadron.
T2959 DX-D	Crashed near East Wretham on return from Le Havre 11.12.41.
T2961 DX-Q	From 15 Squadron. To 18 Operational Training Unit.
T2962 DX-L	To 311 Squadron.
T2970	FTR Hamburg 13/14.3.41.
W5434	From 218 Squadron. Crashed in Cambridgeshire on return from Frankfurt 3.9.41.
W5445 DX-X	From 9 Squadron. FTR Hamburg 30.9/1.10.41.
W5616 DX-K	Crashed on approach to Methwold during air-test 7.7.41.
W5704 DX-G	From 40 Squadron. To AFDU.
X3162	FTR Ostend 21/22.3.41.
X3221 DX-Z	From 311 Squadron. To 103 Squadron.
X3278	To 3 Operational Training Unit.
X3284	To 424 (Tiger) Squadron.
X3285 DX-U	From 101 Squadron. To 75(NZ) Squadron and back. To 23 Operational Training Unit.
X3305 DX-Q	From 9 Squadron. To 150 Squadron.
X3331 DX-F	FTR Kassel 27/28.8.42.
X3332	From 9 Squadron. To 25 Operational Training Unit.
X3333	To 156 Squadron.
X3346	From 9 Squadron. To 23 Operational Training Unit.
X3353 DX-J	From 9 Squadron. To 25 Operational Training Unit.
X3371 DX-G	FTR Flensburg 18/19.8.42.
X3387 DX-H	Force-landed near Lakenheath when bound for Cologne 31.5.42.
X3389	To 9 Squadron.
X3390	From 419 (Moose) Squadron. Returned to 419 (Moose) Squadron.
X3402 DX-M	From 115 Squadron. To 75(NZ) Squadron and back. To 1483 Flight.
X3410 DX-A	FTR Hanau 1/2.4.42.
X3425 DX-L	FTR Hanau 1/2.4.42.
X3448	To 115 Squadron.
X3450	To 115 Squadron.
X3460 DX-E	To 424 (Tiger) Squadron.
X3470 DX-R	From 9 Squadron. To 419 (Moose) Squadron via 8 MU.
X3474	To 9 Squadron.
X3478 DX-O	FTR Hamburg 17/18.4.42.
X3542 DX-Y	FTR Hamburg 17/18.4.42.
X3558	To 75(NZ) Squadron.
X3584 DX-B	From 115 Squadron. To 75(NZ) Squadron and back. FTR Duisburg 21/22.7.42.
X3599 DX-V	Crashed in Ireland during training 16.3.42.
X3600 DX-J	To 426 (Thunderbird) Squadron.

X3607 DX-N	FTR Hanau 1/2.4.42.
X3608 DX-M	To 23 Operational Training Unit.
X3640 DX-W	FTR Gennevilliers 29/30.4.42.
X3653 DX-P	FTR Bremen 27.7.42.
X3658 DX-P/C	To 12 Operational Training Unit.
X3665 DX-U	FTR Essen 26/27.3.42.
X3696 DX-X	To 426 (Thunderbird) Squadron.
X3698 DX-M	
X3726	From 419 (Moose) Squadron. To 115 Squadron.
X3745	From 150 Squadron. Returned to 150 Squadron.
X3746 DX-Q	Force-landed at Feltwell during training 17.6.42.
X3747 DX-K	To 75(NZ) Squadron.
X3748 DX-D	FTR Hanau 1/2.4.42.
X3755	From 150 Squadron. To 75(NZ) Squadron.
X3756 DX-N	Abandoned near Weston-Super-Mare on return from a mining sortie to St-Nazaire 3.5.42.
X3757 DX-	FTR Hamburg 8/9.4.42.
X3758 DX-C	FTR Emden 22/23.6.42.
X3946 DX-D	To 75(NZ) Squadron.
X9642 DX-A	To 18 Operational Training Unit.
X9744	From 214 Squadron. To 99 Squadron.
X9745 DX-N	To 218 Squadron.
X9748 DX-B	To 419 (Moose) Squadron.
X9756 DX-U	FTR Cologne 10/11.10.41.
X9760 DX-U	From 75(NZ) Squadron. To 311 Squadron.
X9786 DX-T	From 9 Squadron. To 26 Operational Training Unit.
X9787 DX-X	From 311 Squadron. FTR Essen 2/3.6.42.
X9874 DX-K/V	To 419 (Moose) Squadron.
X9923	From 9 Squadron. Crashed on landing at Marham on return from Hamburg 16.9.41
X9924 DX-O	From 9 Squadron. To 99 Squadron.
X9978 DX-O	FTR Cologne 15/16.10.41.
X9982 DX-P	To 16 Operational Training Unit.
Z1053 DX-M	From 75(NZ) Squadron. To 419 (Moose) Squadron.
Z1067	To 419 (Moose) Squadron.
Z1073 DX-O	From 40 Squadron. Damaged Cat B during landing on return from Dunkerque 23/24.11.41.
Z1085 DX-E	To 1503 BAT Flt.
Z1087 DX-Q/V	From 75(NZ) Squadron. To 20 Operational Training Unit.
Z1091 DX-W	From 75(NZ) Squadron. To 419 (Moose) Squadron.
Z1093 DX-Y	From 75(NZ) Squadron. To 1506 BAT Flt.
Z1096 DX-S	From 75(NZ) Squadron. Crashed soon after take-off from Feltwell when bound for Cherbourg 6.1.42.
Z1097 DX-T	FTR Düsseldorf 27/28.12.41.
Z1145 DX-H	From 75(NZ) Squadron. To 419 (Moose) Squadron.
Z1147 DX-F	To 311 (Czech) Squadron.
Z1564 DX-S	FTR from mining sortie 7/8.5.42.
Z1565 DX-T	FTR Hanau 1/2.4.42.

Z1567 DX-R	To 25 Operational Training Unit.
Z1568 DX-K	To TFU.
Z1569	To 101 Squadron.
Z1578 DX-R	FTR Bremen 29/30.6.42.
Z1611 DX-V	FTR Emden 19/20.6.42.
Z1618 DX-N	FTR Bremen 29/30.6.42.
Z1650 DX-J	FTR Hamburg 28/29.7.42.
Z1652 DX-C	To 75(NZ) Squadron.
Z1653 DX-E	To 115 Squadron.
Z1654 DX-V	FTR Hamburg 26/27.7.42.
Z1656 DX-D	FTR Mainz 11/12.8.42.
Z1657 DX-A	To 115 Squadron.
Z1663 DX-I	From 9 Squadron. To 115 Squadron.
Z1747 DX-B	To 75(NZ) Squadron.
Z8403 DX-C	To 12 Squadron.
Z8429 DX-Q	To 75(NZ) Squadron.
Z8704 DX-V	FTR Mannheim 6/7.8.41.
Z8789 DX-K	Crashed on landing at Feltwell on return from Genoa 29.9.41.
Z8792 DX-J	Force-landed in Suffolk on return from Mannheim 23.10.41.
Z8794 DX-H	FTR Hüls 6/7.9.41.
Z8800 DX-U	To 419 (Moose) Squadron.
Z8868	From 75(NZ) Squadron. FTR Genoa 28/29.9.41.
Z8893 DX-A	To 23 Operational Training Unit.
Z8897 DX-S	FTR Cologne 10/11.10.41.
Z8903 DX-T	FTR from Rover patrol to Münster 7/8.11.41.
Z8904 DX-U	To 75(NZ) Squadron.
Z8946 DX-S	FTR Hamburg 26/27.10.41.
Z8951 DX-C	To 214 Squadron.
Z8961	To 75(NZ) Squadron.
Z8965	To 218 Squadron.
Z8968 DX-Y	To 75(NZ) Squadron.
Z8972	To 15 Operational Training Unit.
Z8977	To 75(NZ) Squadron.
Z8978 DX-S	To 75(NZ) Squadron.
Z8980	To 99 Squadron.
Z8981 DX-J	From 40 Squadron. To 419 (Moose) Squadron.
Z8985 DX-V	FTR from Rover patrol to Münster 7/8.11.41.
BJ581 DX-Q	To 101 Squadron.
BJ582 DX-Y	To 199 Squadron via 11 Operational Training Unit.
BJ593 DX-O	Crashed on approach to Methwold while training 11.8.42.
BJ596 DX-H	To 75(NZ) Squadron.
BJ607 DX-T	FTR Düsseldorf 31.7/1.8.42.
BJ612 DX-C	To 16 Operational Training Unit.
BJ619 DX-G	FTR Nuremberg 28/29.8.42.
BJ667 DX-R	To 23 Operational Training Unit.
BJ673 DX-R	FTR Duisburg 23/24.7.42.
BJ701 DX-N	FTR Nuremberg 28/29.8.42.
BJ705 DX-X	To 101 Squadron.

BJ707 DX-M	To 75(NZ) Squadron.
BJ711 DX-O	To 101 Squadron.
BJ770 DX-W	To 115 Squadron.
BJ771 DX-Z	To 115 Squadron.
BJ830	FTR Mainz 11/12.8.42.
BJ833	To 115 Squadron.
DV759 DX-Y	To 304 Squadron via 18 Operational Training Unit.
DV806 DX-A	Ditched off Kent coast during operation to Boulogne 17/18.5.42.
DV809 DX-D	To 1483 Flight.
DV816 DX-T	FTR Essen 1/2.6.42.
DV819 DX-V	To 109 Squadron.
DV845	To 109 Squadron.
DV865	To 1429 Flight.
DV870 DX-A	To 109 Squadron.
DV883 DX-V	To 1429 Flight.
DV884	To 1429 Flight.
HF915 DX-O	FTR Essen 5/6.6.42.
HF921	To 311 Squadron.

LANCASTER. **From September 1942.**

R5751 DX-M	From 49 Squadron. To 1661 Conversion Unit.
R5865 DX-D	From 207 Squadron. To 1661 Conversion Unit.
R5894 DX-T	From 9 Squadron. Crashed near Scampton on return from Berlin 2.3.43.
W4130 DX-B	From 207Squadron. FTR Cologne 15/16.10.42. Squadron's first Lancaster loss.
W4132	To 9 Squadron.
W4165 DX-R	From 207 Squadron. FTR Hamburg 9/10.11.42.
W4189 DX-A	First off on Squadron's first Lancaster operation. FTR Hamburg 30/31.1.43.
W4190 DX-N	To 1661 Conversion Unit.
W4201 DX-F	Crashed at Scampton on return from mining sortie 14.3.43.
W4232 DX-G/C/B	To 50 Squadron via 1660 Conversion Unit.
W4234 DX-P	FTR Munich 21/22.12.42.
W4240 DX-Q	To 467 Squadron.
W4246 DX-L	Abandoned over Kent on return from mining sortie 7.11.42.
W4247 DX-S/X	FTR Hamburg 9/10.11.42.
W4250 DX-K	Crashed in Lincolnshire during operation to Turin 9/10.12.42.
W4251 DX-T	FTR Milan 24.10.42.
W4252 DX-X	FTR Kiel 4/5.4.43.
W4254 DX-S	From 9 Squadron. FTR Stettin 20/21.4.43.
W4257 DX-V/O	FTR St Nazaire 2/3.4.43.
W4262	Crashed near Binbrook on return from mining sortie 10.11.42.
W4267	From 44 (Rhodesia) Squadron. Crashed in Lincolnshire while training 27.1.43.
W4307 DX-O	FTR Hamburg 9/10.11.42.
W4358 DX-O/L	To 9 Squadron via 1661 Conversion Unit.

W4359	Crashed in Cornwall while training 17.12.42.
W4360	FTR Stuttgart 22/23.11.42.
W4375 DX-X	From 467 Squadron. FTR Wilhelmshaven 18/19.2.43.
W4376	From 467 Squadron. To 103 Squadron.
W4377 DX-L	From 467 Squadron. FTR Krefeld 21/22.6.43.
W4384 DX-D	From 467 Squadron. FTR Wilhelmshaven 11/12.2.43.
W4766	To 61 Squadron.
W4772 DX-G	To 50 Squadron Conversion Flight.
W4775 DX-J	To 1661 Conversion Unit.
W4797 DX-S/U-	From 467 Squadron. To 1668 Conversion Unit.
W4822 DX-P	From 49 Squadron. FTR Düsseldorf 3/4.11.43.
W4824 DX-H	From 467 Squadron and back via 1660 Conversion Unit.
W4834	From 1656 Conversion Unit. Destroyed at Scampton when bomb load exploded 15.3.43.
W4940	To 617 Squadron.
W4944 DX-X/X-	FTR Pilsen 13/14.5.43.
W4948 DX-J/S	Shot down by intruder over Lincolnshire on return from Hannover 23.9.43.
W5008 DX-B	To 617 Squadron on loan. Returned to 57 Squadron. FTR Nuremberg 27/28.8.43.
DV161	From 460 Squadron. To 9 Squadron.
DV201 DX-M	FTR Mannheim 23/24.9.43.
DV235 DX-C	FTR Munich 2/3.10.43.
ED306 DX-W	Destroyed at Scampton when W4834's bomb load blew up 15.3.43.
ED308 DX-D	From 9 Squadron. To 630 Squadron.
ED319 DX-H	FTR Essen 9/10.1.43.
ED320	To 101 Squadron.
ED329	From 617 Squadron. FTR Duisburg 12/13.5.43.
ED348 DX-U	From 49 Squadron. To 44 (Rhodesia) Squadron.
ED352 DX-Q	From 49 Squadron. FTR Turin 4/5.2.43.
ED371 DX-Q	From 207 Squadron. No operations.
ED385	To 106 Squadron.
ED390 DX-V	FTR Dortmund 4/5.5.43.
ED392	To 12 Squadron.
ED411	To 166 Squadron.
ED412 DX-O	To 207 Squadron.
ED413 DX-C	To 630 Squadron.
ED594	From 83 Squadron. Destroyed at Scampton when W4834 blew up 15.3.43.
ED616 DX-B	FTR Hamburg 29/30.7.43.
ED617	FTR Gelsenkirchen 9/10.7.43.
ED655 DX-X/X-	To 630 Squadron.
ED667 DX-W	FTR Pilsen 13/14.5.43.
ED668 DX-B	FTR Bochum 12/13.6.43.
ED698 DX-R	To 630 Squadron.
ED706 DX-F/A	FTR Essen 30.4/1.5.43.
ED707 DX-X/J/F	FTR Dortmund 23/24.5.43.
ED757 DX-K	Crashed while landing at Scampton following air-test 10.7.43.

ED758 DX-N	To 630 Squadron.	
ED761 DX-Z	FTR Berlin 29/30.3.43.	
ED762 DX-Y	Crash-landed while trying to land at Scampton during training 3.5.43.	
ED766 DX-P	FTR Frankfurt 10/11.4.43.	
ED770 DX-E	FTR Stettin 20/21.4.43.	
ED777 DX-Q	To 630 Squadron.	
ED778 DX-I	FTR Duisburg 12/13.5.43.	
ED779 DX-U	To 300 Squadron.	
ED781 DX-E/J	From 97 Squadron. FTR Wuppertal 24/25.6.43.	
ED827 DX-Z	Crashed at Scampton on return from Nuremberg 28.8.43.	
ED861 DX-D	FTR Turin 12/13.7.43.	
ED920 DX-A	To 630 Squadron.	
ED931 DX-C	To 617 Squadron on loan and back. FTR Hamburg 29/30.7.43.	
ED941 DX-V	Crashed on approach to East Kirkby during transit flight from Waterbeach 28.9.43.	
ED943 DX-T	FTR Gelsenkirchen 25/26.6.43.	
ED944 DX-I	To 630 Squadron.	
ED946 DX-E	Crashed soon after take-off from Swinderby while training 28.8.43.	
ED947 DX-G	FTR Cologne 8/9.7.43.	
ED970 DX-H	FTR Dortmund 23/24.5.43.	
ED989 DX-F	From 83 Squadron. FTR Peenemünde 17/18.8.43.	
ED992 DX-O	FTR Nuremberg 10/11.8.43.	
ED994 DX-W	To 576 Squadron.	
EE193 DX-S	To 166 Squadron.	
EE197 DX-Y	To 617 Squadron on loan. Returned to 57 Squadron. To 207 Squadron.	
JA695	To 61 Squadron via 5 Maintenance Unit.	
JA696 DX-J	FTR Hamburg 2/3.8.43.	
JA872 DX-U	To 630 Squadron.	
JA875 DX-K	FTR Mannheim 23/24.9.43.	
JA896 DX-D	Crashed on landing at Scampton on return from Milan 16.8.43.	
JA910 DX-H/O-	FTR Bochum 29/30.9.43.	
JA914 DX-O-	FTR Berlin 3/4.9.43.	
JB135	To 630 Squadron.	
JB233 DX-F	FTR Berlin 23/24.12.43.	
JB234 DX-E	FTR Leipzig 20/21.10.43.	
JB236	To 630 Squadron.	
JB237 DX-Z	FTR Kassel 22/23.10.43.	
JB311 DX-B	FTR Berlin 28/29.1.44.	
JB315	Crashed in Leicestershire during training 17.11.43.	
JB318 DX-O/Q/L	FTR Revigny 18/19.7.44.	
JB320 DX-X	FTR Kassel 22/23.10.43.	
JB364 DX-M	FTR Berlin 2/3.1.44.	
JB366 DX-S/N	FTR Berlin 27/28.1.44.	
JB370 DX-O	To 617 Squadron on loan. Returned to 57 Squadron. FTR St Leu-d'Esserent 7/8.7.44.	

JB372 DX-R	FTR Berlin 2/3.12.43.	
JB373 DX-N	FTR Berlin 16/17.12.43.	
JB418 DX-I	FTR Berlin 18/19.11.43.	
JB419 DX-E	FTR Berlin 20/21.1.44.	
JB420 DX-S	FTR Berlin 15/16.2.44.	
JB474 DX-F	FTR Stuttgart 15/16.3.44.	
JB485 DX-L	FTR Berlin 26/27.11.43.	
JB486 DX-F	FTR St Leu-d'Esserent 4/5.7.44.	
JB526 DX-D	FTR Wesseling 21/22.6.44.	
JB529 DX-P	FTR Berlin 2/3.12.43.	
JB539 DX-S/X	FTR Berlin 24/25.3.44.	
JB541 DX-A	FTR Stettin 5/6.1.44.	
JB546	To 630 Squadron.	
JB548 DX-O/Q	FTR Berlin 1/2.1.44.	
JB565 DX-I	From 61 Squadron. FTR Schweinfurt 24/25.2.44.	
JB681 DX-J	FTR Berlin 2/3.1.44.	
JB723 DX-L/P	FTR St Leu-d'Esserent 4/5.7.44.	
JB725 DX-M	FTR from mining sortie 9/10.4.44.	
LL893 DX-J	FTR La Chappelle 20/21.4.44.	
LL935 DX-A	To 115 Squadron.	
LL939 DX-B/H	FTR Harburg 11/12.11.44.	
LL940 DX-S	Damaged in accident 15.1.45.	
LL967	To 1651 Conversion Unit.	
LM114 DX-O	To 38 Maintenance Unit.	
LM115 DX-M	FTR Wesseling 21/22.6.44.	
LM132	From 103 Squadron.	
LM186 DX-D		
LM214 DX-U	To 1653 Conversion Unit.	
LM231 DX-T		
LM232 DX-G/F/P	FTR Königsberg 26/27.8.44.	
LM278 DX-L	FTR From mining sortie 26/27.8.44.	
LM279 DX-T	Crashed in Northamptonshire when bound for Brest 2.9.44.	
LM284	FTR from air test 30.7.44.	
LM322 DX-X	Crashed on take-off from Scampton when bound for Hamburg 3.8.43.	
LM336 DX-G	FTR Mannheim 23/24.9.43.	
LM340	From 405 (Vancouver) Squadron. To 1668 Conversion Unit.	
LM517 DX-B/C		
LM522 DX-G	FTR St Leu-d'Esserent 7/8.7.44.	
LM573 DX-U	FTR Wesseling 21/22.6.44.	
LM579 DX-O	FTR Darmstadt 25/26.8.44.	
LM580 DX-L	FTR Wesseling 21/22.6.44.	
LM582 DX-B/F		
LM624 DX-A	FTR Gravenhorst 6/7.11.44.	
LM626 DX-M	FTR Munich 17/18.12.44.	
LM653 DX-Q	From 49 Squadron. FTR Halle 20/21.3.45.	
LM673 DX-U	To 630 Squadron and back. Destroyed when PB360 blew up at East Kirkby 17.4.45.	

LM678 DX-V	To 227 Squadron.
ME626 DX-J	To 1653 Conversion Unit.
ME679 DX-K	FTR Munich 24/25.4.44.
ME845 DX-F	From 630 Squadron.
ME864 DX-E	FTR Stuttgart 28/29.7.44.
ME868 DX-K	FTR St Leu-d'Esserent 7/8.7.44.
ND405	To 550 Squadron.
ND406 DX-T	To 156 Squadron.
ND468 DX-M	FTR Mailly-le-Camp 3/4.5.44.
ND471 DX-A	Ditched in North Sea on return from Wesseling 22.6.44.
ND472 DX-G/I	To 617 Squadron on loan. Returned to 57 Squadron. Destroyed when PB360 blew up at East Kirkby 17.4.45.
ND475	Crashed in Cambridgeshire on return from Juvisy 18/19.4.44.
ND503 DX-E	FTR Leipzig 19/20.2.44.
ND506 DX-C	To 166 Squadron.
ND509 DX-C/I/P	To 61 Squadron.
ND560 DX-N/M	FTR Stuttgart 24/25.7.44.
ND572 DX-F	From 103 Squadron. Collided with ME473 of 207 Squadron over Lincolnshire during fighter affiliation exercise 2.3.45.
ND582 DX-S	Crashed on return from La Chapelle 21.4.44.
ND622 DX-E	FTR Nuremberg 30/31.3.44.
ND671 DX-I	FTR Berlin 24/25.3.44.
ND786 DX-I	FTR Munich 24/25.4.44.
ND878 DX-B	FTR Braunschweig 22/23.5.44.
ND879 DX-H	FTR Braunschweig 22/23.5.44.
ND954 DX-Q	FTR Joigny la Roche 31.7.44.
ND960 DX-I	FTR from mining sortie 21/22.5.44.
ND977 DX-R	
NE127 DX-J	FTR Dortmund 22/23.5.44.
NG126 DX-L	FTR Bremerhaven 18/19.9.44.
NG145 DX-J	From 630 Squadron. FTR Heilbronn 4/5.12.44.
NG199 DX/L	FTR Giessen 5/6.12.44.
NG225 DX-K	
NG395 DX-J/L	
NG398 DX-N	FTR Lützkendorf 14/15.3.45.
NG410 DX-D/G	Force-landed in Warwickshire on return from Böhlen 6.3.45.
NN696 DX-H	FTR Wesseling 21/22.6.44.
NN701 DX-K	
NN723	To 619 Squadron.
NN765 DX-X	From 44 (Rhodesia) Squadron. Destroyed when PB360 blew up at East Kirkby 17.4.45.
NN769 DX-L	
NX580 DX-V	
PA332	
PB261 DX-L	From 619 Squadron.
PB280 DX-W/P	
PB297 DX-H	From 619 Squadron.

PB348 DX-T	From 227Squadron. Abandoned over Lincolnshire when bound for Royan 5.1.45.
PB360 DX-U/N	From 44 (Rhodesia) Squadron. Blew up at East Kirkby while being prepared for operation to Cham 17.4.45.
PB382 DX-I/N	FTR Politz 8/9.2.45.
PB384 DX-F	FTR from mining sortie 16/17.8.44.
PB425 DX-G	FTR Nuremberg 19/20.10.44.
PB744	To 189 Squadron.
PB784 DX-H	
PB844 DX-N	From 49 Squadron.
PB852 DX-V	From 619 Squadron. FTR Harburg 7/8.3.45.
PB894	To 630 Squadron.
PD212 DX-F	FTR Stuttgart 28/29.7.44.
PD236	From 103 Squadron.
PD263 DX-T/G	FTR Heimbach 11.12.44.
PD264 DX-K	FTR Giessen 6/7.12.44.
PD282 DX-E	
PD347 DX-P	Destroyed when PB360 blew up at East Kirkby 17.4.45.
PD348 DX-W	To 227 Squadron.
PD427	
RA530 DX-Y	Crashed in Lincolnshire soon after take-off from East Kirkby when bound for Böhlen 20.3.45.
RA596	
RF124 DX-M	To 630 Squadron
RF193 DX-G	From 103 Squadron.
RF195 DX-F	From 207 Squadron. Destroyed when PB360 blew up at East Kirkby 17.4.45.
RF202 DX-G	
SW245 DX-L	FTR Munich 16/17.12.44.
SW256 DX-I/L	From 49 Squadron.

HEAVIEST SINGLE LOSS. 21/22.6.44. Wesseling. 6 Lancasters FTR. (1 ditched, crew rescued).

Key to Abbreviations

A&AEE	Aeroplane and Armaments Experimental Establishment.
AA	Anti-Aircraft fire.
AACU	Anti-Aircraft Cooperation Unit.
AAS	Air Armament School.
AASF	Advance Air Striking Force.
AAU	Aircraft Assembly Unit.
ACM	Air Chief Marshal.
ACSEA	Air Command South-East Asia.
AFDU	Air Fighting Development Unit.
AFEE	Airborne Forces Experimental Unit.
AFTDU	Airborne Forces Tactical Development Unit.
AGS	Air Gunners School.
AMDP	Air Members for Development and Production.
AOC	Air Officer Commanding.
AOS	Air Observers School.
ASRTU	Air-Sea Rescue Training Unit.
ATTDU	Air Transport Tactical Development Unit.
AVM	Air Vice-Marshal.
BAT	Beam Approach Training.
BCBS	Bomber Command Bombing School.
BCDU	Bomber Command Development Unit.
BCFU	Bomber Command Film Unit.
BCIS	Bomber Command Instructors School.
BDU	Bombing Development Unit.
BSTU	Bomber Support Training Unit.
CF	Conversion Flight.
CFS	Central Flying School.
CGS	Central Gunnery School.
C-in-C	Commander in Chief.
CNS	Central Navigation School.
CO	Commanding Officer.
CRD	Controller of Research and Development.
CU	Conversion Unit.
DGRD	Director General for Research and Development.
EAAS	Empire Air Armament School.
EANS	Empire Air Navigation School.
ECDU	Electronic Countermeasures Development Unit.
ECFS	Empire Central Flying School.
ETPS	Empire Test Pilots School.
F/L	Flight Lieutenant.
Flt	Flight.
F/O	Flying Officer.
FPP	Ferry Pilots School.

F/S	Flight Sergeant.
FTR	Failed to Return.
FTU	Ferry Training Unit.
G/C	Group Captain.
Gp	Group.
HCU	Heavy Conversion Unit.
HGCU	Heavy Glider Conversion Unit.
LFS	Lancaster Finishing School.
MAC	Mediterranean Air Command.
MTU	Mosquito Training Unit.
MU	Maintenance Unit.
NTU	Navigation Training Unit.
OADU	Overseas Aircraft Delivery Unit.
OAPU	Overseas Aircraft Preparation Unit.
OTU	Operational Training Unit.
P/O	Pilot Officer.
PTS	Parachute Training School.
RAE	Royal Aircraft Establishment.
SGR	School of General Reconnaissance.
Sgt	Sergeant.
SHAEF	Supreme Headquarters Allied Expeditionary Force.
SIU	Signals Intelligence Unit.
S/L	Squadron Leader.
SOC	Struck off Charge.
SOE	Special Operations Executive.
Sqn	Squadron.
TF	Training Flight.
TFU	Telecommunications Flying Unit.
W/C	Wing Commander.
Wg	Wing.
WIDU	Wireless Intelligence Development Unit.
W/O	Warrant Officer.

Printed in Great Britain
by Amazon

21485405R00228